THE REGULATORY AFTERMATH OF THE GLOBAL FINANCIAL CRISIS

The EU and the US responded to the global financial crisis by changing the rules for the functioning of financial services and markets and by establishing new oversight bodies. With the US Dodd-Frank Act and numerous EU regulations and directives now in place, this book provides a timely and thoughtful explanation of the key elements of the new regimes in both regions, of the political processes which shaped their content, and of their practical impact. Insights from areas such as economics, political science and financial history elucidate the significance of the reforms. Australia's resilience during the financial crisis, which contrasted sharply with the severe problems that were experienced in the EU and the US, is also examined. The comparison between the performances of these major economies in a period of such extreme stress tells us much about the complex regulatory and economic ecosystems of which financial markets are a part.

EILÍS FERRAN is Professor of Company and Securities Law at the University of Cambridge and a University JM Keynes Fellow in Financial Economics.

NIAMH MOLONEY is Professor of Financial Markets Law at the London School of Economics and Political Science and a Fellow (Household Finance) of the Centre for Financial Studies, Frankfurt.

JENNIFER G. HILL is Professor of Corporate Law and a Director of the Ross Parsons Centre of Commercial, Corporate and Taxation Law at Sydney Law School, Australia.

JOHN C. COFFEE, JR. is the Adolf A. Berle Professor of Law at Columbia University Law School and Director of its Center on Corporate Governance.

INTERNATIONAL CORPORATE LAW AND FINANCIAL MARKET REGULATION

Corporate law and financial market regulation matter. The global financial crisis has challenged many of the fundamental concepts underlying corporate law and financial regulation; but crisis and reform has long been a feature of these fields. A burgeoning and sophisticated scholarship now challenges and contextualizes the contested relationship between law, markets and companies, domestically and internationally. This Series informs and leads the scholarly and policy debate by publishing cutting-edge, timely and critical examinations of the most pressing and important questions in the field.

THE REGULATORY AFTERMATH OF THE GLOBAL FINANCIAL CRISIS

EILÍS FERRAN, NIAMH MOLONEY,
JENNIFER G. HILL
and
JOHN C. COFFEE, Jr.

with a foreword by
ETHIOPIS TAFARA

CAMBRIDGE
UNIVERSITY PRESS

CAMBRIDGE UNIVERSITY PRESS
Cambridge, New York, Melbourne, Madrid, Cape Town,
Singapore, São Paulo, Delhi, Mexico City

Cambridge University Press
The Edinburgh Building, Cambridge CB2 8RU, UK

Published in the United States of America by Cambridge University Press, New York

www.cambridge.org
Information on this title: www.cambridge.org/9781107024595

First published 2012

Printed and bound in Great Britain by the MPG Books Group

A catalogue record for this publication is available from the British Library

Library of Congress Cataloging-in-Publication Data

The regulatory aftermath of the global financial crisis / Eilís Ferran, Niamh Moloney,
Jennifer G. Hill and John C. Coffee, Jr.
p. cm.
ISBN 978-1-107-02459-5 (Hardback)
1. Financial institutions–Law and legislation–United States.
2. Financial institutions–Law and legislation–European Union countries.
3. Financial institutions–Law and legislation–Australia.
4. Financial services industry–Law and legislation–United States.
5. Financial services industry–Law and legislation–European Union countries.
6. Financial services industry–Law and legislation–Australia. I. Ferran, Eilís.
K1066.R435 2012
346′.08–dc23
2012018824

ISBN 978-1-107-02459-5 Hardback

CONTENTS

FOREWORD

Observations about the crisis and reform

ETHIOPIS TAFARA*,**

I: Overview

The most recent financial crisis is of paramount concern. But in the long run, what it reveals may be of greater concern. It is said that this crisis is a once-in-a-century event. If viewed narrowly in terms of the proximate causes, this may be true. But closer examination of the crisis reveals a fertile ground for additional crises, albeit with each one perhaps displaying unique features. So in devising reforms, regulators must not only address the most immediate causes of this crisis, they must also tackle the fertile ground from which they spring.

In essence, this crisis is the result of an evolution in markets and financial services. Over the past fifteen years, the structure and principal characteristics of the world's financial system have dramatically changed. The current turmoil is likely the result of the system having failed to adapt to these fundamental changes.

The modern market:

- is global in nature, featuring highly mobile capital;
- is characterized by fierce competition among financial service providers;
- no longer features barriers between historically separate financial products, sectors and actors;
- features increasing cost to investors, financial entities and regulators of monitoring conduct and risk due to increasing use of complex products; and

* Director, Office of International Affairs, Securities and Exchange Commission. The Securities and Exchange Commission, as a matter of policy, disclaims responsibility for any private publication or statement of any SEC employee. This article expresses the author's views and does not necessarily reflect those of the Commission or other members of the staff.

** This note is the fruit of many hours of reflection and intense debate with my SEC colleagues and friends, Robert M. Fisher and Robert Peterson. As such, it is as much theirs as it is mine.

- features large and relatively liquid unregulated institutional financial markets paralleling the regulated markets.

A sixth pertinent characteristic of modern markets is the rapid incorporation of advanced technologies. But as described in more detail below, technology has tended to act as an amplifier or enabler of the other five market factors.

Taken together, these changes constitute a profound alteration of capital markets, which calls for an equivalent shift in regulatory approach. As capital markets transition, we should expect significant adjustments in industry business models and changes in the nature and degree of risk to investors. The optimal blend of regulatory tools is also bound to follow suit. In 1996, two McKinsey consultants – Lowell Bryan and Diana Farrell – made a rather prescient (but hopefully not too prescient) statement in a book entitled *Market Unbound: Unleashing Global Capitalism*:[1]

> As the market becomes unbound from the constraints of national governments, it is creating the potential for a tidal wave of global capitalism that could drive rapid growth and highly beneficial integration of the world's real economy well into the next century. There is also a somewhat less probable, but nonetheless significant, chance that the power of this market could turn destructive and unleash financial instability and social turmoil such as the world has not seen since the 1920s and 1930s.

In order to define a new strategy or framework, regulators around the world must explore and understand the manner in which the market has been altered, and the ramifications of this shift. I would suggest five changes to the current regulatory framework, and insist upon one constant.

First, of course, the new regulatory framework must address the issue of increased systemic risk. But it must do so without suppressing risk-taking per se. This is crucial if we are to address the challenges inherent in this new environment, yet not undermine economic innovation. To sustain the economic innovation needed to drive the economy, financial capital must be able to take risks.

As a corollary, we need a regulatory framework that provides prudential regulation for those intermediaries that are too big to fail. Surely, the essence of our capital system is to let people and firms take chances

[1] New York: John Wiley & Sons, 1996.

with their money, and to enjoy most of the benefits and to endure most of the pain associated with risk-taking. However, if we are in a world where financial entities are too big, too indebted and too interconnected to fail, we know they will have an incentive to take excessive risk at the ultimate expense of the public. From a policy perspective, we want to end up in a world where we can afford to let firms fail if they make bad decisions.

Second, we need the regulatory framework to address the misaligned incentives that lead to excessive risk-taking. In a world where one can slice and dice risk any way that is desired by trading highly opaque, difficult-to-value instruments, it is challenging to monitor money managers well. Part of the answer will lie in finding different compensation schemes for money managers and financial executives. Part of the answer will lie in fuller disclosure about market actors and the source of their returns. Part of the answer will lie in extending the framework to cover historically unregulated market actors such as hedge fund advisers and credit rating agencies.

Third, we need a regulatory framework that mandates enhanced disclosure so that capital providers can better determine counterparty risk. Capital markets dried up when this crisis hit, because nobody was able to assess anyone else's exposure. A major step in this direction would be the introduction of clearing houses and exchanges in any market (including derivative markets) above a certain scale, and to impose basic disclosure requirements with respect to any type of financial product that achieves a certain prevalence.

Fourth, the regulatory framework needs to account for the fungibility of financial products, actors and markets. Many products, actors and markets have the same underlying economic characteristics, motivations or clientele, yet are regulated based on connection to an institution that can be described as having either a securities, banking or insurance function. This leads to market participants searching for the path of least regulatory resistance and pursuing regulatory arbitrage. Although this is sometimes in the interest of the regulated community, it is frequently to the detriment of consumers and investors. Of course, we need to be vigilant not to pursue uniform regulation for the sake of simplicity or ease given that there are instances where differences in the regulation of securities, banking and insurance are legitimate and, indeed, important.

Fifth, the regulatory framework of the future must be responsive to the fact that capital is mobile, markets are interconnected, and technology makes the movement of capital irrepressible. Capital travels in search of investment opportunities, which means companies, intermediaries and markets can choose their preferred location. Preference is frequently a matter of regulatory comfort. As a consequence, we need to ensure that our regulation is optimal in providing the best cost-justified protection for investors and at the same time comparable across developed markets. Otherwise we will create opportunities for jurisdictional regulatory arbitrage in contrast to functional arbitrage.

Finally, we need a regulatory framework that is ruthless in pursuing the protection of investors. Securities regulators must remain focused on generating well-founded market confidence. Trust is the lubrication that keeps the wheels of a market from grinding to a halt. It is the faith that a buyer is buying what he or she expects, and the faith that the seller will receive the payment promised at the time promised. And this faith has never been blind. Without this basic trust, no market in the world will succeed. In the diamond markets of New York and Amsterdam, trust is based on ethnicity, religion and the personal interaction of a handful of traders. The markets work because of reputation and the small community that makes up these markets. With the anonymous trading that characterizes modern capital markets, this personal trust, perforce, has been replaced by a surrogate – clear, useful and timely information about the products bought and sold, rules on fair dealing between buyers and sellers and their intermediaries, and vigorous enforcement by securities regulators with the powers and resources necessary to do the job.

The chapters by Ferran, Moloney, Hill and Coffee examine in detail how well the ambitious reform programs in the European Union, Australia and the United States respond to these needs. In this foreword, I outline my own personal reflections on some common and quite fundamental challenges that efforts around the world to effect regulatory change must address.

II: Altered terrain

Globalized markets, and capital mobility

Today capital is both widely dispersed and mobile. More investors than ever before invest in domestic capital markets as well as foreign markets. And the mobility of capital allows all actors in securities trading – investors, issuers, brokers, trading facilities and investors – to become entirely mobile as well. Capital raising and financial services are no longer geographically bound. This mobility presents both promises and challenges. The promises include greater competition in the market for financial service providers; an opportunity for investors to diversify their portfolio risk across borders more effectively and at less cost; and the ability of issuers to seek the lowest cost of capital wherever it might be.

The current capital mobility grew out of the collapse of the Bretton Woods system. At the conclusion of the Second World War, the "free-floating" exchange rates of the 1930s were viewed by many as contributing to the Great Depression by discouraging trade and investment and encouraging currency speculation. In light of this, the Bretton Woods system, established in 1944, fixed major world currencies to the value of gold as a mechanism for facilitating international trade. In 1971, the Bretton Woods system collapsed as the United States decoupled the dollar from the price of gold. This collapse has had major and lasting effects on the international financial system.

The most important consequence of Bretton Woods' demise was the elimination of cross-border capital controls in most developed markets. While not mandatory, the Bretton Woods system encouraged capital controls – strict limits on the transfer of capital by investors in or out of a country – to facilitate fixed exchange rates. Ironically, although Bretton Woods was designed to encourage cross-border trade, its collapse greatly expanded cross-border financial services and led to the global financial market that exists today. In short, the collapse of Bretton Woods made capital entirely mobile.

This capital mobility can have a profound effect on financial regulation. While suboptimal financial regulation has always caused both suppliers and users of capital to seek either less costly or less risky alternatives, modern technology greatly accelerates the ability of market participants to search for, and take advantage of, such alternatives. Internationally, this can translate into capital flight, as investors and issuers flee a market for better alternatives overseas. It can also present the financial industry with opportunities for regulatory arbitrage. At the same time, technology can also amplify the types of problems that have historically plagued capital markets by, for example, permitting those who commit financial fraud to transfer assets overseas, or to perpetrate their frauds across borders with greater ease.

Increasing competition and the end of "old boy networks"

The effect competition has had on financial regulation is complicated. Historically, financial markets have been characterized by guild-like organizations, often revolving around exchanges and policed by exchange membership criteria. In some cases, these organizations evolved as an explicit effort by financial service providers to reduce competition.

But since the 1970s there have been a series of regulatory and legislative changes designed to dismantle the guilds and increase competition in the financial services industry. In the United States, these changes include the elimination of fixed commissions and the beginning of efforts at establishing a national market system in the 1970s. Likewise, the Gramm-Leach-Bliley Act of 1999, which substantially repealed the separation of investment and commercial banking, allowed securities, banking and insurance firms to compete against each other within and across financial sectors. While justified partly as a response to globalization (given that European universal banks faced no such prohibition), the end result was increased competition among US financial firms.

Other policy choices have introduced new competitors. For example, while mutual funds in the United States must be registered with the SEC, SEC decisions to offer exemptions to funds with a small number of high net-worth clients led to the creation of the hedge fund industry. This sector competes directly with traditional funds for a particularly lucrative market sector. Likewise, best execution rules led to increased competition among stock exchanges, and Regulation ATS and MiFiD, which fostered the growth of electronic communication networks among broker-dealers, gave rise to alternative trading venues. The competition engendered by these new trading platforms led exchanges both in the United States and abroad to forego their non-profit mutual ownership structure in exchange for a public ownership structure that enables them to access the capital markets directly.

As increased financial market competition proved successful, the trend was emulated in other markets. In many cases, intra-market competition also fueled inter-market coordination, as demutualized stock exchanges and investment firms sought foreign partners and foreign capital to better weather the newly competitive environment. The result is a feedback loop – while globalization increases market competition, competition also increases market globalization.

While greater competition is a boon for investors in terms of cost, choice, and innovation, it also tightens profit margins among many financial service providers. This, in turn, places new pressure on the role of self-policing. Indeed, incentives to commit fraud – or to engage in non-transparent risk taking to enhance returns – at both the individual and firm level are greater since the costs of failure (in terms of foregoing the high bonuses and returns) in a highly competitive environment are more significant. In other cases, where regulated firms face competition from either an unregulated sector (e.g. hedge funds) or foreign competitors facing lower regulatory costs, it leads to pressures on regulators to curtail domestic oversight.

Increased competition in the financial sector has also changed risk management. As is discussed in more detail below, even where intense competition does not lead to fraud, it can distort incentives in such a way as to lead to suboptimal behavior. For example, as competition eroded profit margins for the traditional services offered by broker-dealers, many shifted away from a fee-based business model selling traditional brokerage services to one based on proprietary trading. However, since returns on proprietary trading are limited in a highly competitive market, broker-dealers, hedge funds and other firms used leverage to magnify returns dramatically. In a bull market, the higher returns provided by leverage will draw in new investors, particularly if the degree of leverage is not completely transparent. Investor expectations, in turn, make it impossible for competing firms to avoid a leveraged strategy, regardless of the risks presented to the firm.

Fungibility of financial products, sectors and actors

Since all finance is a measurement of risk, from an economic perspective, banking, securities and insurance products are all variations on a theme. Historically, the users of these different products had different objectives and different risk tolerances, even if banks, investment firms and insurance companies approach risk in a similar fashion. Given these different risk tolerances, the securities, banking and insurance industries are regulated differently.

In the United States, the Gramm-Leach-Bliley Act broke down previously existing barriers between the banking, securities and insurance sectors. Rather than being limited to the United States, this proved to be a global trend. At the same time, the development of financial derivatives markets led to innovative new products with characteristics that clearly cut across the traditional borders erected between banking, insurance and securities sectors. Notwithstanding the current crisis, these new financial derivatives proved better at accomplishing the goals of a particular financial sector than traditional products since the risks inherent in allocating capital can be better spread across different investors with different risk preferences.

The consequences of the Gramm-Leach-Bliley Act, globalization, and increased competition are a new fungibility in financial products and financial service providers. As the recent market turmoil has demonstrated, a hedge fund on one side of a financial derivative contract can be indistinguishable from an insurance firm – except for the manner in which they are regulated. Likewise, money market funds offered by traditional investment banks are used by investors as savings accounts, notwithstanding the differences in regulation and oversight. Many issuers that traditionally sought short-term bridge loans from commercial banks or sold commercial paper through investment banks now seek short-term funds directly from hedge funds or the hedge fund-like proprietary trading arms of consolidated financial firms.

While banking, insurance and securities regulators have fought to build regulatory bridges via working agreements or memoranda of understanding to rationalize the regulation and oversight of financial products that cut across traditional financial sectors, in reality this has proven difficult. Financial regulators in many countries differ not just in their legislative mandates and legal powers, but also in their regulatory cultures. However, even in countries that have adopted consolidated financial regulatory systems (with a single regulator overseeing all sectors of the financial market), the fungibility of financial products and financial actors has proven to be a regulatory challenge. Part of this challenge stems from the rapid evolution of financial products in a global and highly competitive market. But the competition and globalization themselves also present special challenges, since the costs to regulators of getting regulation "wrong" have become higher.

Unregulated institutional markets

In 1990, as sophisticated institutional investors increasingly sought to invest in foreign markets, the SEC adopted Rule 144A, which permitted certain types of issuers to sell securities in the United States to certain types of institutional investors without registering them with the SEC. The goal of Rule 144A was two-fold – to permit sophisticated institutional investors in the United States to buy and sell amongst themselves certain foreign securities without having to direct those transactions through their foreign affiliates; and to facilitate the provision of venture capital funding from institutional investors to start-up companies in the United States.

Rule 144A has been widely viewed as successful in achieving these goals. Over the past several years, and particularly since the bursting of the "Tech Bubble" in 2001, the Rule 144A "market" has expanded rapidly, with Rule 144A issuances occasionally equaling or exceeding in value public offerings in the US market. The reasons for this growth include:

A decrease in general investor interest in new equity offerings following the collapse of the Tech Bubble;
An increase in regulatory costs for public offerings following passage of the Sarbanes-Oxley Act of 2002; and,
The increasing "institutionalization" of the US market, with retail investors preferring to hold diversified investment portfolios via mutual funds, pension funds, hedge funds and other collective investment schemes.

This last point – the increasing institutionalization of the US investor – has meant that issuers making a restricted Rule 144A offering can often attract nearly as much capital as could only be accessed via a public offering in the past. Issuers of Rule 144A products can also structure complex securities tailored to a particular investor without having to make certain public disclosures which either the issuer or the investor believes might prove problematic from a business confidentiality perspective. And since Rule 144A-exempted securities are not sold on an exchange, the transactions are not made public to the market, permitting institutional investors to take a position in or divest themselves of an issuer's securities without that information having as immediate an impact on the price of that security as might be the case on a large, liquid exchange.

The growing fungibility of financial products in the United States has also added to the popularity of the Rule 144A market. For example, insurance products structured as financial derivatives or securities, securitized banking products such as retail mortgage-backed securities (RMBS), or collateralized debt offerings (CDOs) secured by consumer credit card debt can be sold to large institutional investors via a Rule 144A offering, effectively permitting hedge funds or investment firms to take a position in an entirely unrelated financial sector. Furthermore, these offerings can be concluded in a comparatively short period of time versus a public offering of a similar product.

Rule 144A, when combined with the SEC registration exemption for hedge funds, has created an essentially private, more lightly regulated market for securities in the United States. While fraud in an offering or by a market participant remains prohibited, the degree of disclosure, counterparty risk and market transparency is not overseen by any financial regulator. The justification for such an unregulated market was essentially predicated on sophistication – i.e. that private transactions among sophisticated institutional investors did not merit the type of regulatory oversight and disclosure required of a public market, where individual investors might not be in a position to demand the type of information necessary to allow them to make informed investment choices. As this market was originally small and secondary to the public markets, concerns were not raised. But the opacity of this market serves to hide risk from the overall public and this uncertainty is cause for vigilance.

Increasing agency cost

Today, complex, opaque instruments for slicing and dicing risk any way that may be desired are readily available to parties large and small. Many of these markets involve customized products or transactions that are traded "over-the-counter" (i.e. not on an exchange), and can be extremely difficult to value. No one knows who is holding what basket of risks at any given point in time. An enterprise, or an employee of an enterprise, can bet the "farm" in one instant, and then reverse the bet in another. This presents a challenging world for risk managers, investors and regulators.[2] While the availability of these complex instruments brings many benefits to investors and the marketplace as a whole, they also serve to increase what economists refer to as "agency cost" – that is, the cost due to the misalignment of incentives between the principals, who hire someone to perform a service for them, and the agents performing the services.

[2] While derivative markets are nothing new, technology has dramatically lowered their transaction costs as well as provided a means of valuation. This has led to a scale, complexity and (normal) depth of liquidity that is unprecedented. For example, the credit default swap market, in which "default insurance" on bonds may be purchased from counter-parties, has recently involved nominal aggregate valuation of $55 trillion, which is larger than the annual gross domestic product of all nations combined. Neither regulators, nor investors, nor counter-parties are in a position to know the exposures that are created through these transactions. Even small perturbations in markets of this scale can have significant consequences for the real economy.

The availability of these tools renders it much more difficult to determine the risks faced by the particular enterprise. Because the risks being taken by the enterprise are more difficult to monitor, and intrinsically less transparent, its managers might be tempted to take on more risk than is apparent and attempt to tout any returns from taking that risk as the returns from value-added performance (instead of simply the returns from hidden gambling). In addition, if the managers of the enterprise are paid substantially more for upside performance, they may have an incentive to take on risks that are economically inefficient (i.e. that do not provide expected rewards to the enterprise warranted by such risk). The increased prevalence and use of complex instruments presents much greater complexity to the investing public and to regulators in determining what risks enterprises actually face.

The availability of these instruments has shifted the balance of power away from investors and regulators and toward financial intermediaries and agents. The argument that these instruments make the world a better place relies, at least in part, on the notion that risk would be better dispersed and end up being held – more or less – by those better able to absorb it. But the legitimacy of this argument relies on a certain degree of transparency. The question of what impact these new instruments would have on the incentives (and therefore the behavior) of financial intermediaries and other agents cannot be overlooked. If we do not address this new situation with the right set of regulatory tools designed to enhance investor powers, we may find ourselves thrown into crises such as the ongoing one on a regular basis.

Technology

Over the past 40 years, changes in information-processing and communication technology have also had a significant impact on the shape of the US capital market. While often described in revolutionary terms, in many cases these technological innovations have acted as amplifiers of the change enabled by regulatory and policy decisions, or as a result of financial product innovations, rather than as the impetus for regulatory or policy change itself. In many cases, one of the major effects of modern computing and communications technology has been to make other market characteristics seem inevitable, or significant policy decisions intractable once implemented.

For example, although technology advancements did not enable the creation of a global capital market (a market which has existed for decades and which expanded rapidly as a result of economic and regulatory changes), modern communications technology enables even retail investors to access information about investment opportunities abroad, and permits small US institutional investors to have quasi-direct access to foreign trading screens through larger broker-dealers with overseas affiliates. The effect has been more closely to integrate national markets across borders, even where the integration itself is only possible because of regulatory changes such as the elimination of capital controls (i.e. the collapse of the Bretton Woods system) and the acquiescence of national regulators. At the same time, technology can also amplify the types of problems that have historically plagued capital markets by, for example, permitting those who commit financial fraud to transfer assets overseas more readily.

Modern communication and computing technology also makes capital more mobile, both domestically and internationally. Domestically, technology-enabled capital mobility can mean the creation of entirely new financial products or financial sectors, almost overnight, to either circumvent suboptimal regulation or to take advantage of disparities in how economically fungible financial products are regulated.

Technology has also greatly amplified the degree of competition market participants face, while simultaneously amplifying possible systemic risks. For example, cheap computing technology now enables investors to engage in complex algorithmic trading not possible in the past. This translates into potentially greater market risk analysis and price discovery, as computers can execute trades with the introduction of new information far more quickly than can a human. This can make a market significantly more efficient, to the benefit of investors and issuers alike. However, technology also allows successful trading innovations to be deconstructed, reverse-engineered and copied by competitors. While this, too, can prove a boon to both investors and issuers, it also raises systemic risk concerns if widely used assumptions prove inaccurate or if errors are introduced into an electronic trading system. While not substantively different from the past – inaccurate assumptions and error trades have always been a bugbear of a capital market – automated trading systems can rapidly turn a costly but manageable mistake into a market-shattering systemic problem.

Technology also heightens competition across borders. In the past, trading and clearance and settlement systems were complex affairs, difficult to construct and hard to replicate. Now, the most advanced trading and clearance and settlement technology is commercially available to stock markets everywhere, making it possible for even the youngest exchanges to have the type of systems (assuming they can afford them) necessary to make the technical aspects of their operations competitive with more established institutions.

Finally, technology has accelerated both the cross-sectoral fungibility of financial products, and helped entrench policy decisions that have led to large, private and unregulated markets among the largest, most sophisticated financial institutions. Modern computing technology permits a degree of risk analysis not possible in the past. While financial scandals repeatedly demonstrate that this risk analysis is not infallible and can even magnify market difficulties by creating the illusion of greater confidence than is warranted, it also allows for greater risk segmentation. Greater risk segmentation, in turn, permits financial service providers to craft banking, insurance, derivatives and securities products designed to achieve the types of investor objectives once reserved for products solely the province of an entirely different financial sector. Similarly, in the past, while institutional investors frequently traded securities amongst themselves directly, such markets lacked the liquidity of an exchange. Modern technology, by contrast, can now permit institutional investors to emulate a degree of exchange-like liquidity while conducting purely private transactions with other institutions, bypassing exchanges altogether – although, as recent events have shown, quite possibly at the cost of the transparency and safety that an exchange and its clearance and settlement system offers.

III: A cautionary note

As we consider regulatory reform, we should not lose sight of the differences between market regulation and the supervision of institutions. Insurance, banking and securities regulators all historically have a common interest in maintaining the health and soundness of financial firms by, for example, requiring the firms to maintain capital reserves. And all functional regulators have an interest in enforcing the law.

But there also are differences. For example, the inherent tension between "consumer protection" and systemic stability often means that enforcement activities of insurance and banking regulators are negotiated and conducted more discretely. This happens because banking and insurance regulators are concerned that public enforcement activities will lead depositors or consumers to lose faith in the firm involved, possibly leading to a run on the bank or a dramatic reduction in the insurers' ability to distribute risk as consumers leave. By contrast, securities regulators tend to have aggressive and public enforcement programs – with punishment meted out in the public square, as it were. Indeed, securities regulators believe public enforcement actions are necessary to deter fraud and reassure investors in the integrity of the system.

For bank supervisors, the key objective is to maintain the stability of and confidence in financial institutions. The top nightmare for a bank supervisor is a contagious liquidity crisis, where concerns about one bank lead to a run on the entire banking system. Insurance supervisors, for their part, emphasize consumer protection and the solvency of the insurers – which makes perfect sense, since the worst time to learn that an insurer does not intend to live up to its promises is when an insurance claim is made. In short, traditionally, banking regulators have focused on prudential regulation, while securities regulators have focused on disclosure, transparency and enforcement. In the aftermath of the recent crisis, where should we extend the traditional tools of the banking regulator and where should we extend those of the securities regulator?

There is little denying that the recent financial crisis, while involving all types of market participants, was essentially a banking crisis. Although unusual, perhaps, in the number of non-banks that undertook bank-like activities and certainly unique in that securitized financial products were the instigators, the pattern of the crisis differed from other banking crises only in its depth. Financial firms – closely linked to each other through leverage and counterparty arrangements – exposed themselves to too much risk. And when that risk became apparent, there was a "run" on these financial institutions.

At the heart of the problem is the maturity mismatch that characterizes traditional banking. The dangers of a maturity mismatch were amplified, however, by the potential for increased volatility on the asset side of the balance sheet attributable to the "embedded leverage" inherent in certain securitized products. Potential volatility was further increased through derivative products.

Now, clearly, it is important that we understand why these widely varying financial firms were acting like traditional banks. Moreover, I think most of us would agree that when systemically risky financial firms take on the role of banks, they should face the same kind of prudential regulation as do banks. But we must pause here and ask ourselves: if all major sources of financing today are to be treated as banks – with more or less one-size-fits-all capital requirements and conservative risk measurement mandates – where is the financing to come from for the next wave of high-risk/high-payoff innovations? Who will finance the next great development in transportation, or medicine, or artificial intelligence?

In the wake of the recent financial crisis, our regulatory reform efforts have – quite properly – focused upon the reduction of systemic risk. Among the regulatory challenges here, I believe, is the grave danger that our efforts to reduce systemic risk may result in a reduction of the kind of risk taking that drives real innovation. This could result in substantially reduced economic growth – foregone economic growth that might, in fact, serve to address current economic straits.

If we look back at the many fundamental economic innovations of the 20th century – aircraft, antibiotics, the Internet, the transistor and semiconductor, the mass produced automobile and the plastics that Mr. McGuire recommended for investment in the movie, *The Graduate* – we see relatively little bank financing, at least not at the inception of each innovation's lifecycle. This is unsurprising because, as we know, banks are the archetype of systemically risky financial entities. Consequently, banking regulation, when it is done properly, imposes a certain degree of financial conservatism.

But we must ask: as we reform our markets in light of the recent crisis, where will the financing come from for the truly risky enterprises of the 21st century? This is where the traditional tools of the securities regulator come into play. While banking regulation is designed to control and, to a certain extent, suppress risk taking, securities regulation is, in stark contrast, designed to facilitate it. In the financing of economic pursuits that entail substantial risk, the traditional tools of securities regulators – that is, disclosure, transparency and rigorous enforcement efforts to police fraud and abuse – have a substantial comparative advantage over banking regulatory tools. As mentioned above, failure is an essential part of the innovative process. But that's precisely what the banks should try to avoid.

In our collective efforts to reform our markets in light of the systemic crisis, the danger is that the tools of the banking regulator come to dominate the regulation of capital markets and thereby unintentionally suppress needed real innovation. As regulators, we must look at what capital needs to do to support economic growth. We must be careful to recognize why different avenues for financing exist. We need to recognize why securities regulation has historically differed from banking regulation. As legendary venture capitalist William

Draper recently put it in an interview: "Facebook couldn't go to a bank and get a commercial loan to start up a company."

There is much at stake. If we want to encourage innovation and realize its benefits, financial regulation has to make a space for risk-taking. Only by recognizing the inherent functional differences between capital markets and banking can we succeed in both addressing systemic risk while at the same time spurring economic growth through innovation. Those economies that recognize these differences, and which regulate and supervise accordingly, will grow and prosper and become the leaders in the 21st century.

NOTES ON CONTRIBUTORS

EILÍS FERRAN is Professor of Company and Securities Law at the University of Cambridge and a University JM Keynes Fellow in Financial Economics.

NIAMH MOLONEY is Professor of Financial Markets Law at the London School of Economics and Political Science and a Fellow (Household Finance) of the Centre for Financial Studies, Frankfurt.

JENNIFER G. HILL is Professor of Corporate Law and a Director of the Ross Parsons Centre of Commercial, Corporate and Taxation Law at Sydney Law School, Australia.

JOHN C. COFFEE, JR. is the Adolf A. Berle Professor of Law at Columbia University Law School and Director of its Center on Corporate Governance.

ACKNOWLEDGEMENTS

The authors are grateful to the *Cornell Law Review* for permission to reproduce Chapter 4, which was originally published as John C. Coffee, Jr., "The Political Economy of Dodd-Frank: Why Financial Reform Tends to be Frustrated and Systemic Risk Perpetuated," 97 *Cornell L. Rev.* 1019 (2012).

TABLE OF CASES

TABLE OF LEGISLATION

Directives

1

Crisis-driven regulatory reform: where in the world is the EU going?*

EILÍS FERRAN

I: Introduction

Never waste several good crises . . .

On the surface at least, crises shake the status quo and provide space for new ideas to emerge.[1] Complacent assumptions are overturned, policy learning takes place and there is a sharpened focus on the concerns that demand a robust response. The issues acquire the degree of political salience that is needed to push through a reform agenda.

The international regulatory response to the global financial crisis of 2007–9 appears to support the idea of crisis as a game-changer. The world's leading economies have adopted an apparently ambitious agenda for international financial regulation and have put in place institutional changes designed to bolster implementation of international standards

* I have benefitted immensely from having the opportunity to discuss some of the ideas that are developed in this chapter with David Wright, Ben Smulders and Mario Nava (European Commission), Simon Gleeson (Clifford Chance) and the co-authors of this book, and also from other private conversations. Valia Babis, Toussant Boyce and Jason Robinson provided valuable research assistance. Some initial background research was conducted during a period of study leave at Harvard Law School, which was facilitated by several people, including, in particular, Sara Zucker and Jeanne Tai. The research was financially supported by the Newton Trust and by the JM Keynes Endowment for Research in Finance.

[1] W. Mattli and N. Woods, "In Whose Benefit? Explaining Regulatory Change in Global Politics" in W. Mattli and N. Woods (eds.), *The Politics of Global Regulation* (Princeton University Press, 2009), pp. 1–43, p. 37. Or, perhaps, a resurgence of interest in old ideas that had been marginalized by other ideologies more in tune with prevailing economic conditions, as exemplified by the post-crisis renewed interest in Polanyi's ideas on the inherently destructive nature of free-market capitalism: K. Polanyi, *The Great Transformation (The Political and Economic Origins of Our Time)* (Boston: Beacon Press, 1944/2001).

and to reinforce surveillance. They have also been putting in place far-reaching reforms at national or regional level. The United States has passed a mammoth piece of legislation with a view to reforming Wall Street and reinvigorating financial regulation.[2] The European Union (EU) is being no less determined in the extent of its reform program, although it is proceeding on a measure-by-measure basis rather than attempting to deal with everything in a single instrument. A common feature of the reforms on both sides of the Atlantic is that implementation is dependent on the adoption of a large number of detailed rules, many of which are still under development at the time of writing (Spring 2012). The level of government intervention in markets that is involved in these financial reform packages is far removed from mainstream policy preferences of just a few years ago.[3] On the European side, moreover, the pace of both coordination between Member States and centralization at EU level has accelerated. Spillover effects from the reforms that are eventually put in place to resolve the euro area sovereign debt crisis could lead to a still further concentration of EU regulatory power with respect to the financial markets. Since an effective solution to the euro area crisis remains elusive at the time of writing, the possibility that the reforms that are eventually adopted could reverse the trend by triggering a reining in of EU regulatory authority and perhaps even a "repatriation" of powers to Member States must be acknowledged. However, this appears to be a less likely outcome than an expansion and reinforcement of the existing tendencies.

In contrast to those who view crises as major turning points, others suggest that the view that a crisis leads to radical change does not always hold up when it is subjected to close examination. Instead, the set of ideas most likely to triumph after a crisis may be the one which "represents the smallest step into the unknown."[4] A report published by the Organization for Economic Cooperation and Development (OECD) makes the point in this way: "the process of change is always at the margin. Groupthink implicit in economic and market paradigms, unfortunately, takes a long time to change."[5] The absence of a radical break

[2] Wall Street Reform and Consumer Protection Act of 2010 (also known as the "Dodd-Frank Act"). See further, J.C. Coffee, Jr., Chapter 4 below.

[3] R.C. Altman, "Globalization in Retreat," *Foreign Affairs*, 88 (2009), 2–7; R.D. Cudahy, "The Coming Demise of Deregulation II," *Administrative Law Review*, 61 (2009), 543–56.

[4] Mattli and Woods, "In Whose Benefit?," p. 39.

[5] OECD, *The Financial Crisis: Reform and Exit Strategies* (Paris: OECD, 2009), p. 22.

with the past need not be a bad thing if it means that the ideas that are taken seriously and translated into law are relatively familiar ones that have been seriously and soberly debated over a period of time so that their most obvious flaws have already been identified and addressed, and which are designed to fit well with the existing body of regulation so as to enhance its effectiveness.[6] But a troubling aspect of these views is that they suggest that even public clamor for tough action following a crisis may not be an effective counterweight to more reactionary forces, such as powerful industry interest groups that stand to lose from sweeping public interest-oriented reform. Industry interest groups that are adept at exploiting opportunities in law reform processes, which tend to be complex and time-consuming even in the aftermath of a disaster, may succeed in whittling down bold proposals to something they find more palatable. In spite of harsh, business-unfriendly rhetoric, politicians may be complicit in this process, with their words merely serving as a cloak for "gesture politics."

Yet another line of analysis suggests that crisis situations can, indeed, propel far-reaching changes, but that these reforms are likely to turn out to have adverse longer-term consequences for both the particular field at which they are targeted and for other areas that suffer spillover effects. It is argued that crises can lead lawmakers into error because they act too quickly in circumstances of considerable uncertainty.[7] Knee-jerk overreaction can result in misplaced crude simplification of complex issues and faulty policy choices designed to pander to populist sentiments.[8] The general mood of hysteria and heightened political interest can allow popular but fundamentally flawed ideas, which would have been screened out in calmer times, to take hold. Even the most well-intentioned lawmakers can go astray when, in their eagerness to be seen to be doing something, they take up from policy entrepreneurs ideas that seem to be responsive to the topical problem but which, in reality, are

[6] Favoring incremental regulatory adjustments over sweeping regulatory revolution: L.A. Cunningham and D.T. Zaring, "The Three or Four Approaches to Financial Regulation: A Cautionary Analysis Against Exuberance in Crisis Response," *George Washington Law Review*, 78 (2009), 39–113.

[7] R. Romano, "The Sarbanes-Oxley Act and the Making of Quack Corporate Governance," *Yale Law Journal*, 114 (2005), 1521–611, 1523–4; S.M. Bainbridge, "Dodd-Frank: Quack Federal Corporate Governance Round II," *Minnesota Law Review*, 95 (2011), 1779–821.

[8] But see B. Thirkell-White, "Dealing with the Banks: Populism and the Public Interest in the Global Financial Crisis," *International Affairs*, 85 (2009), 689–711 (identifying some benefits in populism).

simply repackaged versions of existing proposals that were formulated long before the crisis to treat a different mischief. If not operating within a system containing appropriate checks and balances, some officials may seek to pursue their own personal agenda rather than to aim at making unbiased choices in the public interest. Decisions about the content of regulation are always at risk of being distorted so as to fit the short-term political goals of those who control the lawmaking process.[9]

Taken in the round, these various arguments suggest that the chances for successful crisis-driven regulatory reform are low, and that they are likely to be very slim indeed in an area as complex and as vast as financial regulation. Furthermore, the concept of success in this context is elusive. The post-global financial crisis regulatory goal has been described in quite daunting terms as being to "restore strong, competitive, innovative financial markets to support global economic growth without once again risking a breakdown in market functioning so severe as to put the world economies at risk."[10] However, it asks too much of regulation to expect a permanent cure that eliminates financial crises forever more.

The speculative bubbles that precede crashes occur for many reasons, and not all of them can be controlled through regulation.[11] Andrew Lo has suggested that financial manias and panics may be "an unavoidable aspect of modern capitalism – a consequence of the interactions between hardwired human behavior and the unfettered ability to innovate, compete, and evolve."[12] "Black swan" events can happen.[13] Even the most insightful architects of well thought out regulatory reform cannot

[9] G.J. Stigler, "The Theory of Economic Regulation," *The Bell Journal of Economics and Management Science*, 2 (1971), 3–21.

[10] Group of Thirty, *Financial Reform: A Framework for Financial Stability* (Washington DC: G30, 2009), p. 8.

[11] J.B. Taylor, "The Financial Crisis and the Policy Responses: An Empirical Analysis of What Went Wrong," National Bureau of Economic Research Working Paper 14631 (2009) (excesses in monetary policy); S.B. Wadhwani, "What Mix of Monetary Policy and Regulation is Best for Stabilising the Economy?" in A. Turner, A. Haldane, P. Woolley, S. Wadhwani, C. Goodhart, A. Smithers, A. Large, J. Kay, M. Wolf, P. Boone, S. Johnson and R. Layard, *The Future of Finance* (London: LSE, 2010), pp. 145–63 (monetary policy mistakes); R.J. Shiller, *The Subprime Solution: How Today's Global Financial Crisis Happened, and What to Do About It* (Princeton University Press, 2008) (irrational exuberance).

[12] A.W. Lo, "Regulatory Reform in the Wake of the Financial Crisis of 2007–2008," *Journal of Financial Economic Policy*, 1 (2009), 4–43, 5. That financial markets tend towards excess is not a new insight: Polanyi, *The Great Transformation*; H.P. Minsky, *Stabilizing an Unstable Economy* (New Haven: Yale University Press, 1986).

[13] N.N. Taleb, *The Black Swan: The Impact of the Highly Improbable* (New York: Random House, 2nd edn., 2010).

guarantee that regulatory shortcomings will not play a significant part in a future crisis. To imagine that regulatory change today could have such a rock-solid effect far into the future would be to conjure up a model that rests on dangerously naïve presuppositions about regulatory foresight.[14] Franklin Allen and Douglas Gale have noted that financial regulation has always involved an element of trial and error.[15] Charles Goodhart has also stressed its pragmatic character.[16]

In the face of inevitable crises and regulatory fallibility, perhaps the best we can hope for is that post-crisis regulatory changes will do as much as is feasible, based on the best current technical knowledge, to reduce the risks of new crises emerging and to anticipate and seek to mitigate at least some of the consequences of future failure, all the while doing as much as possible to avoid handicapping legitimate, economically worthwhile businesses with unnecessary additional costs. Even these are still quite lofty aspirations, and the reality is likely to fall short.

That expectations as to likely effectiveness are best managed downwards, first because of our inability to predict the future and second because of distortions arising from the particularly messy way in which law reform processes tend to operate in the aftermath of a crisis, is a sobering thought with which to begin the task that this chapter undertakes: an examination of the EU's regulatory response to the global financial crisis, also taking account of the way in which that response has been influenced by the euro area sovereign debt crisis. At the same time, being clear-sighted about the inevitability of imperfections and shortcomings in post-crisis law reform also underscores the importance of starting to conduct careful appraisals of policy processes and outcomes while memories of the problems that the changes were supposed

[14] Leading texts giving the historical perspective on financial crises are: C.P. Kindleberger and R.Z. Aliber, *Manias, Panics and Crashes: A History of Financial Crises* (Hoboken, NJ: 5th edn., Wiley, 2005); C.M. Reinhart and K.S. Rogoff, *This Time Is Different: Eight Centuries of Financial Folly* (Princeton University Press, 2009). Reinhart and Rogoff emphasize the dangers of assuming omniscience: "one would be wise not to push too far the conceit that we are smarter than our predecessors. A few years back many people would have said that improvements in financial engineering had done much to tame the business cycle and limit the risk of financial contagion": C.M. Reinhart and K.S. Rogoff, "The Aftermath of Financial Crises," *American Economic Review*, 99 (2009), 466–72, 472.

[15] F. Allen and D. Gale, *Understanding Financial Crises* (Oxford University Press, 2007), p. 190.

[16] C. Goodhart, "How Should We Regulate Bank Capital and Financial Products? What Role For 'Living Wills'?" in Turner *et al.*, *The Future of Finance*, pp. 165–86, p. 165.

to address are still relatively fresh. As time goes on, there will be opportunities to reconsider and make improvements to the post-crisis EU financial services regulatory system. To help ensure that those opportunities are fully exploited, the development of a deeper contextual understanding of the policy choices that were made in the immediate aftermath of turmoil is essential preparatory work. Even though the full impact of some of those policy choices may not be felt for many years, it is not premature to start the process of critical evaluation and audit.

Defining the scope of the chapter and explaining the approach

In 2005, having completed the Financial Services Action Plan (FSAP), a five-year plan launched in 1999 to accelerate progress towards a single EU financial market which had triggered an ambitiously far-reaching revamp of European financial services regulation, the European Commission envisaged a period of relative calm. The Commission thought that the main priorities for the next five years would be consolidating progress, completing unfinished business, enhancing supervisory cooperation and convergence, and removing the remaining economically significant barriers.[17] This was not to be. As a consequence of the global financial crisis, regulatory repair aimed at bolstering the safety, soundness and responsibility of the markets, rather than dismantling remaining barriers and tidying up loose ends, has become the new number one priority.[18] It has also been deemed necessary urgently to look again at the institutional architecture of supervision because existing arrangements – based on a home/host State distribution of responsibilities, pan-EU coordinating committees of national supervisors, and a reliance on gradual, incremental enhancements to promote convergence in national supervisory practices – have proved to be inadequate to prevent disorderly cross-border contagion.[19]

EU regulatory policy has now begun to stray into previously "no-go" zones that were jealously guarded by Member States – albeit rather

[17] European Commission, *White Paper on Financial Services Policy 2005–2010* (COM(2005) 629), p. 4.

[18] European Commission, *Driving European Recovery* (COM(2009) 114); European Commission, *Regulating Financial Services for Sustainable Growth* (COM(2010) 301).

[19] J. Faull, *Some Legal Challenges of Financial Regulation in the EU* (Slynn Foundation, 2011, online: www.slynn-foundation.org/UserFiles/File/Slynn%20Lecture.pdf).

cautiously in some areas – such as national sanctioning regimes[20] and financial sector crisis management arrangements,[21] but more boldly in others, such as the first steps towards direct supervision by EU bodies of financial market actors which have been taken with respect to the European Securities and Markets Authority (ESMA)[22] in relation to credit rating agencies (CRAs)[23] and trade repositories.[24] Furthermore, with the euro area sovereign debt crisis both intensifying some existing problems and adding new issues as well, there has been little sign of the tap of new regulatory reform proposals being closed off.

Early assessments of this response by some political scientists have recorded a sense of underachievement: much activity but relatively weak policy impact,[25] and not as far-reaching as might have been expected given the magnitude of the crisis.[26] From a legal perspective, however, it has been claimed that "[i]n the wake of the crisis, the EU's ascendancy over financial market regulation seems almost complete."[27] The space

[20] European Commission, *Reinforcing Sanctioning Regimes in the Financial Services Sector* (COM(2010) 716). The proposal for the introduction of a Directive on criminal sanctions for market abuse violations marks a significant step forward in this regard: European Commission, *Proposal for a Directive on Criminal Sanctions for Insider Dealing and Market Manipulation* (COM(2011) 654).

[21] European Commission, *An EU Framework for Crisis Management in the Financial Sector* (COM(2010) 579); European Commission, *Proposal for a Directive Establishing a framework for the Recovery and Resolution of Credit Institutions and Financial Firms* (COM (2012) 280) (Recovery and Resolution Directive (proposed)). Crisis management proposals are discussed further in Parts II–IV below.

[22] Regulation (EU) No. 1095/2010 establishing a European Supervisory Authority (European Securities and Markets Authority) (ESMA Regulation), [2010] OJ L331/84. (Note, for convenience this chapter refers to specific provisions of the ESMA Regulation, but the same core content is also contained in the founding Regulations of the European Banking Authority (EBA) (Regulation (EU) No. 1093/2010, [2010] OJ L331/12) and European Insurance and Occupation Pensions Authority (EIOPA) (Regulation (EU) No. 1094/2010, [2010] OJ L331/48)).

[23] Regulation (EC) No. 1060/2009 on Credit Rating Agencies, [2009] OJ L302/1 (CRA Regulation) (amended by Regulation (EU) No. 513/2011, [2011] OJ L145/30).

[24] Regulation (EU) No. 648/2012 on OTC Derivative Transactions, Central Counterparties and Trade Repositories [2012] OJ L201/1 (EMIR).

[25] J. Buckley and D. Howarth, "Internal Market: Gesture Politics? Explaining the EU's Response to the Financial Crisis," *Journal of Common Market Studies*, 48 (Special Issue Supplement), (2010), 119–41.

[26] L. Quaglia, "'The 'Old' and 'New' Politics of Financial Services Regulation in the EU," (online: www.ose.be/files/publication/OSEPaperSeries/Quaglia_2010_OSEResearchPaper2_0410.pdf).

[27] N. Moloney, "EU Financial Market Regulation After the Global Financial Crisis: 'More Europe' or More Risks?" *Common Market Law Review*, 47 (2010), 1317–84, 1381.

between these views serves as a jumping-off point for more detailed inquiry. However, to conduct a comprehensive review of the entire field of EU post-crisis financial services law reform and to assess its effectiveness would require a large team of researchers and a publisher willing to commit to what in all likelihood would turn out to be a multi-volume work written over an extended period in which it has been possible to monitor the resolution of considerable implementation challenges and to discern the practical impact of the intended and unintended consequences of the changes. A chapter such as this necessarily has to be more selective.

When detailed research into the impact of the new laws adopted by the EU in response to the global financial crisis and the euro area sovereign debt crisis eventually comes to be done, the scorecard is bound to be less than perfect for the reasons outlined above. The search for explanations as to why the EU has, or has not, managed to adopt effective reforms can be expected to lead back to the preferences and aims of the main actors and institutions that were involved in the lawmaking process. In anticipation of this, this chapter focuses on the factors driving the Member States and the EU institutions in drawing up the post-crisis regulatory agenda and in transforming policy ideas into legislation. Recognizing that EU financial services regulatory policymaking is a multi-level complex process involving both intergovernmental and supranational components and also that the crises have given rise to new tensions in the interaction between these various components, the chapter seeks to establish the location of significant sources of influence with respect to agenda-setting, to identify the preferences of the key opinion-formers, and to determine the extent to which such preferences have made it into law rather than being filtered out during the many rounds of negotiation and compromise that are part of the EU lawmaking process.

The focus is on public actors, but the extent to which industry preferences can play a part in shaping their views is not ignored. The evolution of EU financial services regulation up to the global financial crisis has been described as having been geared mostly towards serving the needs of large internationally active financial firms.[28] One of the

[28] "The creation of an integrated European financial market" has been "primarily to the benefit of a new European 'champions league' of financial services providers": D. Mügge, "Reordering the Marketplace: Competition Politics in European Finance," *Journal of Common Market Studies*, 44 (2006), 991–1022, 992. On how to lobby effectively in the EU: M Levitt, *Getting Brussels Right: "Best Practice" for City Firms in Handling EU Institutions* (London: Centre for the Study of Financial Innovation, 2011).

major consequences of the financial crisis and subsequent events is that relations between the official sector and the finance industry have seemingly become much more antagonistic. Politicians and public officials have learnt that being home to vibrant financial markets can be very risky business, and that the potential for competitive gain has to be set against the threat that large financial firms, especially those that have become, in effect, "too-big-to-save," may pose to the public interest.[29] The re-setting of public policy to adapt to this new learning may make it less easy in future to characterize EU financial services regulation as a system built largely around the needs and preferences of international financial firms. However, given how pervasive such influences have been in the past and also the strong imperative to bolster financial competitiveness that remains entrenched in the public policies of developed economies, it seems prudent to have low expectations with respect to the likely extent of this recalibration. This chapter is therefore predicated on an assumption that European (EU and Member States') economic prosperity is too intricately tied up with, and dependent on, the prosperity of major actors within the financial system for industry views, and especially those advocated by the biggest internationally-oriented firms, not still to exert considerable influence in policy circles.

Whilst the exercise conducted in this chapter involves some selective examination of the content of new laws, the emphasis is more on the process of institutional decision-making within the legislative bodies and on the use of EU law as a policy instrument than on its substantive doctrinal content. As to what this policy is, in broad terms post-crisis EU financial regulation has been said to be all about producing "a safer, sounder, more transparent and more responsible financial system, working for the economy and society as a whole and able to finance the real economy."[30] The purpose of financial regulation has been said to be to ensure that the financial system provides the "backbone" for the real economy to flourish.[31] These quotations are from a European Commission publication but phrased at such a high level of generality that there is nothing in them to

[29] A. Demirgüç-Kunt and H. Huizinga, "Are Banks Too Big to Fail or Too Big to Save? International Evidence from Equity Prices and CDs Spreads," Centre for Economic Policy Research Discussion Paper No. DP7903 (2010); E.H.G. Hüpkes, "'Too Big to Save' – Towards a Functional Approach to Resolving Crises in Global Financial Institutions," in D.D. Evanoff and G.G. Kaufman (eds.), *Systemic Financial Crisis: Resolving Large Bank Insolvencies* (Hackensack, NJ: World Scientific Publishing, 2005), pp. 193–215.

[30] European Commission, *Regulating Financial Services for Sustainable Growth*, p. 2.

[31] Ibid., p. 3.

which any of the main European actors and institutions (which are, in any case, committed to the overall Europe 2020 strategy, which is aimed at making the EU a smart, sustainable and inclusive economy) would be likely to object. They reflect, moreover, current international policy aspirations, as reiterated by the political leaders of the leading economies at successive G20 meetings.[32] Mainstream policymaking is no longer to be built around the notion that the unrestrained growth of immense, interconnected financial markets and hyper-intense constant financial innovation are inherently desirable from a social perspective. Public policy has gone back to basics in recalling that the core functions of financial institutions are to provide payment mechanisms and deposit-taking facilities, and to channel resources to where they are most needed: financial services should support the real economy.[33]

As well as its explanatory force with respect to the reforms adopted in the immediate aftermath of recent turmoil, there is also a forward-looking dimension to the exercise conducted in this chapter. The Commission has said that the new approach involves putting in place "stringent, efficient and harmonized rules for all operators, coupled with an effective supervisory framework, strong, dissuasive sanctions and clear enforcement mechanisms."[34] But when and where does harmonized EU financial regulation reach its limits? Is the supranational approach now becoming all-embracing? With respect to the content of new laws, will considerations of "stringency" prevail over those of "efficiency" in the drafting of an ever-more prescriptive and lengthy harmonized rulebook? Will the urge to dissuade and deter leave no room to entertain the possibility that providing incentives to comply could produce better results? Will the emphasis on achieving pan-European uniformity in supervision mean that calls for rigid rules trump arguments that favor leaving room for the operation of a judgment-based approach?[35] Where

[32] e.g. G20, *Framework for Strong, Sustainable, and Balanced Growth* (Pittsburgh: G20, September 2009).

[33] M. Barnier, "Mettre les Marchés Financiers au Service de l'économie Réelle" (speech, June 11, 2011, online: http://europa.eu/rapid/pressReleasesAction.do?reference=SPEECH/11/449&format=HTML&aged=0&language=FR&guiLanguage=fr). A. Turner, "What Do Banks Do? Why Do Credit Booms and Busts Occur and What Can Public Policy Do About It?" in Turner *et al.*, *The Future of Finance*, pp. 5–86.

[34] European Commission, *Regulating Financial Services for Sustainable Growth*, p. 3.

[35] Flagging up the need for the EU policy framework to leave scope for supervisors to make informed judgments: Bank of England and FSA, *The Bank of England, Prudential Regulation Authority: Our Approach to Banking Supervision* (London: Bank of England & FSA, 2011), p. 20.

will moderating influences come from? To what extent will these influences include the EU's desire to be an important player on the global regulatory stage, and what impact is this likely to have as a mechanism for curbing regulatory excess? Expectations as to the likely success of process-driven constraints – such as pre-legislative consultations and cost/benefit and impact analyses – in curbing regulatory overkill are best kept low.[36] Moreover, as will become evident from the discussion later in this chapter, EU constitutional legal principles, such as the need for a treaty competence and the notions of subsidiarity and proportionality, are seemingly becoming increasingly weak mechanisms for containing the expansion of EU financial regulation – for instance, if a comprehensive single EU "rulebook" is needed, by definition this must be adopted at EU level (subsidiarity) and its form and content can be highly prescriptive (proportionality)[37] – and therefore a narrow, legalistic approach cannot hope to provide complete answers to these questions. The attenuation of legal constraints also reinforces the crucial importance of paying close attention to the potency of the political safeguards in the legislative process. This chapter therefore draws upon political economy understandings of EU financial market integration and on valuable evaluations of the impact of the global financial crisis that political scientists have already put forward. Some issues take on a different complexion when viewed from a lawyer's perspective.

A note on the chronology of the global financial crisis

The global financial crisis began in earnest in August 2007 with a liquidity freeze resulting from the collapse of the mortgage-backed securities market. The run on Northern Rock in September 2007, the bailout of Bear Stearns in March 2008 and the September 2008 collapse of Lehman Brothers were watershed moments. Lehman Brothers collapsed at a time when financial conditions had so badly deteriorated that the International Monetary Fund (IMF) pointed to "serious doubts about the viability of a widening swath of the financial system."[38]

[36] H. McVea, "The EU Financial Services Action Plan and Its Impact on Corporate Finance," in D. Prentice and A. Reisberg (eds.), *Corporate Finance Law in the UK and EU* (Oxford University Press, 2011), pp. 393–428, p. 426.

[37] Faull, *Some Legal Challenges.*

[38] IMF, *Global Financial Stability Report: Financial Stress and Deleveraging – Macrofinancial Implications and Policy* (Washington DC: IMF, October 2008), p. xi.

A liquidity crisis had morphed into a much more serious state of affairs in which there were widespread fears about significant undercapitalization within the banking sector and rising perceptions of counterparty credit risk. Emergency interventions by governments and central banks to provide liquidity and to recapitalize ailing banks were required. These efforts were successful insofar as they averted outright disaster, although harmful macroeconomic repercussions, not least the sovereign debt crisis in the euro area, are still being felt years later. Whilst policy is constantly being fine-tuned in response to emerging new concerns, the fast-moving events in and around September 2008 can now be viewed as constituting the apex of the global financial crisis. For the purposes of tracking the overall development of EU financial services regulatory policy, this chapter draws a distinction between early Fall 2008–mid-2009, which was a period of emergency and rapid responses to near-to-cataclysmic events, and mid-2009 onwards, which is when the longer-term reform agenda started to become more defined. References in this chapter to "pre" and "post" the global financial crisis should be understood accordingly.

A note on the euro area sovereign debt crisis

The slump that resulted from the global financial crisis of 2007–9 was a proximate cause of the euro area sovereign debt crisis that is not yet resolved at the time of writing.[39] In addition to the costs of using the public balance sheet to shore up the banks, many countries, in Europe and beyond, have also had to contend with a reduction in tax revenues resulting from business slowdowns, and a greater demand on public funds to provide unemployment and other social welfare benefits. Public sector debt has escalated significantly while market confidence in the

[39] This paragraph draws upon various accounts of the euro area sovereign debt crisis: C. Lapavitsas, A. Kaltenbrunner, D. Lindo, J. Michell, J.P. Painceira, E. Pires, J. Powell, A. Stenfors and N. Teles, "Eurozone Crisis: Beggar Thyself and Thy Neighbour," *Journal of Balkan and Near Eastern Studies*, 12 (2010), 321–73; P. de Grauwe, "The Governance of a Fragile Eurozone" (University of Leuven and CEPS, 2011, online: www.econ.kuleuven.be/ew/academic/intecon/Degrauwe/PDG-papers/Discussion_papers/Governance-fragile-eurozone_s.pdf); C. Kopf, *Restoring Financial Stability in the Euro Area* (Brussels: CEPS Policy Brief No. 237, March 15, 2011); P. Krugman, "Can Europe Be Saved?," *New York Times*, January 16, 2011, MM 26 (Sunday magazine); House of Lords European Union Committee, *The Future of Economic Governance in the EU* (London: The Stationery Office, Report of Session 2010–2011, HL Paper No. 124-I).

financial health of a growing number of countries has waned. The impact of these problems on some euro area Member States has been especially severe. Beginning with smaller economies such as Greece and Ireland, but eventually spreading to larger Member States including Spain, Italy and even France, the financial crisis has triggered economic turmoil in the euro area of such magnitude as to put the very viability of the single currency in doubt. The shortcomings of the combination of unitary monetary policy and fragmented fiscal policy have been brutally exposed. A serious "vicious circle" (or even potentially the "death spiral") risk of the collapse of the euro leading to a new and even more severe crisis in the financial markets and related social turmoil has emerged.

The primary focus of this chapter is the development of EU financial services regulation rather than the fate of the euro as such, but given the mutually reinforcing nature of interlinked vulnerabilities, it is impossible to discuss the EU's agenda for financial market regulation without also paying some attention to the crisis in the euro area. Numerous ways in which the euro area crisis has shaped the EU financial services regulatory policy agenda can be easily identified and only a few need be mentioned here. First, negative feedback loops stemming from the symbiotic relationship between banks and sovereigns – i.e., the way in which using public balance sheets to refinance financial institutions has negatively impacted sovereigns' own creditworthiness and, in turn, undermined the quality of existing government and sovereign bonds in which banks tend to be major investors[40] – have given especial urgency to regulatory reforms aimed at improving bank safety and soundness, and at providing for orderly, non-taxpayer-funded resolution of failing institutions – the "never again" sentiment. Second, whilst rating agencies, short selling practices and the aggressive investment strategies associated with hedge funds were propelled to the foreground of regulatory policy as a result of the global financial crisis, that they have remained so firmly in the spotlight can be linked to their perceived role in exacerbating the euro's travails. Some within the European Commission have even gone as far as to suggest the possible introduction of powers to suspend sovereign ratings in exceptional circumstances to ensure the stability of financial markets, and the Commission has indicated that it is a matter that merits further

[40] V.V. Acharya, I. Drechsler and P. Schnabl, "A Pyrrhic Victory? Bank Bailouts and Sovereign Credit Risk" (August 2011, online: http://ssrn.com/abstract=1865465).

consideration. Under proposals now in the pipeline, CRAs will be required to assess sovereign ratings more frequently (every six months rather than annually) and associated disclosure and transparency requirements will be enhanced.[41]

Beyond the immediate regulatory policy concerns, the potential longer term significance of euro-related reforms for the overall design of EU financial services regulation must also be noted. After a series of faltering steps with respect both to euro area crisis management[42] and future crisis prevention,[43] the political leaders of the Member States, faced with the prospect of a catastrophic worldwide economic downturn as a result of the disorderly collapse of the euro, have been forced to consider more radical interventions, involving greater constraints on national budgets and economic policies. The main initiatives enshrined in a new Intergovernmental Treaty on Stability, Coordination and Governance in the Economic and Monetary Union signed in March 2012 by 25 of the 27 Member States (excluding the UK and the Czech Republic, which declined to participate) include a new "fiscal compact," with Commission oversight of national budgets and automatic consequences for breaches of agreed limits, EU Court of Justice verification of national

[41] European Commission, *Proposal for a Regulation Amending Regulation (EC) No 1060/2009 on Credit Rating Agencies* (COM(2011) 747); *European Commission, Proposal for a Directive amending Directive 2009/65/EC and Directive 2011/61/EU on Alternative Investment Funds Managers in respect of the excessive reliance on credit ratings* (COM(2011) 746)).

[42] A temporary European Financial Stabilization Mechanism (EFSM) and European Financial Stability Facility (EFSF) were established in May 2010. A new permanent crisis mechanism, the European Stability Mechanism (ESM) was established by treaty to commence originally in mid-2013, but subsequently brought forward to mid-2012: Treaty Establishing the European Stability Mechanism (July 2011, modified February 2012. The initial lending capacity of the ESM was set at €500 bn. Its powers include capacity to make loans to Member States for bank recapitalizations, and to purchase sovereign bonds on primary and secondary markets.

[43] During 2011, a package of measures aimed at strengthening economic governance in the EU – and more specifically in the euro area – was adopted. This "six pack" of measures comprises a Regulation on the surveillance of Member States' budgetary and economic policies (Regulation (EU) No. 1175/20111, [2011] OJ L306/12); a Regulation on the EU's excessive deficit procedure (Council Regulation (EU) No. 1177/2011, [2011] OJ L306/33); a Regulation on the enforcement of budgetary surveillance in the euro area (Regulation (EU) No. 1173/201, [2011] OJ L306/1); a Regulation on enforcement measures to correct excessive macroeconomic imbalances in the euro area (Regulation (EU) No. 1174/2011, [2011] OJ L306/8); and a Directive on requirements for the Member States' budgetary frameworks (Council Directive 2011/85/EU, [2011] OJ L306/41).

transposition of the balanced budget rule and penalties, and also significantly stronger coordination of economic policies in areas of common interest.[44] These developments in essence point towards greater fiscal consolidation, at least within the euro area. Other, more controversial ideas still under discussion include "eurobonds" or "stability bonds" – that is, centrally-issued, jointly-guaranteed bonds to provide financing for all of the euro area Member States' public debt, which have some strong supporters,[45] but also raise concerns about increasing moral hazard – and the establishment of new euro area institutions, including perhaps a full-blown ministry of finance with power to veto national fiscal policies.[46] Momentum is also building behind the idea of a euro area banking union in which the ECB could become the prudential supervisor of at least the major cross-border banks. Whether any of the proposals on the table at the time of writing will prove to be first, viable, and then any more robust and effective than others that have already been tried is the great unknown. The risk of an implosion of the euro area can no longer be ruled out as being too far-fetched to merit attention, but in view of the disastrous economic, political and social

[44] Treaty on Stability, Coordination and Governance in the Economic and Monetary Union, 2 March 2012. The policy agenda was developed in a series of important publications published between October and December 2011: European Commission, *A Roadmap to Stability and Growth* (COM(2011) 669); European Commission, *Proposal for a Regulation on Common Provisions for Monitoring and Assessing Draft Budgetary Plans and Ensuring the Correction of Excessive Deficit of the Member States in the Euro Area* (COM(2011) 821); European Commission, *Proposal for a Regulation on the Strengthening of Economic and Budgetary Surveillance of Member States Experiencing or Threatened with Serious Difficulties with Respect to their Financial Stability in the Euro Area* (COM/2011/819); European Council Statement of EU Heads of State or Government (October 26, 2011); European Commission, *Green Paper on the Feasibility of Introducing Stability Bonds* (COM/2011/818); A. Merkel and N. Sarkozy, "Letter to President van Rompuy," (December 7, 2011, online: www.elysee.fr/president/root/bank_objects/111207Lettre_adressee_a_M_Herman_Van_Rompuy.pdf); European Council, *Statement by the Euro Area Heads of State or Government* (December 9, 2011).

[45] J.-C. Juncker and G. Tremonti, "Euro-wide Bonds Would Help to End the Crisis," *Financial Times*, December 6, 2010, 13. This idea has attracted support from MEPs: European Parliament, *Resolution on the Financial, Economic and Social Crisis* (T7–0331/2011); European Parliament, *Resolution on Establishing a Permanent Crisis Mechanism to Safeguard the Financial Stability of the Euro Area* (T7–0491/2010). Bonds issued by the EFSF are backed by guarantees from Member States in proportion to their ECB capital subscription, but they do not benefit from a joint guarantee from Member States.

[46] As suggested by Jean-Claude Trichet, then ECB President: J.-C. Trichet, "Building Europe, Building Institutions" (speech, June 2, 2011, online: www.ecb.int/press/key/date/2011/html/sp110602.en.html). See also: European Parliament, *Resolution on the Financial, Economic and Social Crisis* (T7–0331/2011), para. 12.

consequences that could follow from disorderly collapse, extraordinary efforts not to allow this to happen can be expected.[47]

Whilst this chapter steers away from too much speculation about an uncertain future, if the euro survives by being bolstered through increasingly close fiscal arrangements, one plausible prospect deserves to be mentioned. To anticipate briefly, the next Part of this chapter examines in detail how the preferences of the major Member States, whose actions at EU level are driven by the particularities of their national economies, shape EU financial services regulatory policy. The existence of a strong link between domestic economic interests and EU policy design implies that the deepening of common economic interests that could be expected to result from some Member States moving towards greater fiscal consolidation to mirror their monetary union would inevitably create a powerful new dynamic within the EU financial services regulatory policy space. Such convergence of interests could lead eventually to the emergence of a caucus that (in a system where most decisions are made by qualified majority vote) has an effectively decisive say with respect to financial market regulatory policy choices and to the marginalization of those outside the group. This is a disturbing prospect for the outsiders, especially the UK, which has a particular interest because of the size and global significance of its financial services sector.[48] The UK's decision to step out of the arrangements to stabilize the euro that were agreed at the political level by the other Member States in December 2011[49] and thereafter enshrined in the March 2012 Intergovernmental Treaty, may have made sense in domestic political terms as a way of containing growing UK euroskepticism, but the political claims that this was a step that needed to be taken in order to "safeguard" the position of the City of London are misleading. In fact, not being a direct participant in euro rescue efforts does nothing to address the risk of the UK's

[47] B. Eichengreen, "The Breakup of the Euro Area" in A. Alesina and F. Giavazzi (eds.), *Europe and the Euro* (University of Chicago Press, 2010) pp. 11–51.

[48] The UK government initially accepted the desirability of a euro area fiscal union as the way out of crisis and positively advocated it: C. Giles and G. Parker, "Osborne Warns Eurozone Leaders To 'Get A Grip' On Crisis," *Financial Times*, July 21, 2011, 4. Only later, and under pressure from the Euroskeptic wing of the Conservative Party (the main partner in the coalition government), did it begin to press explicitly for "safeguards" to protect the UK's influence over financial services regulatory policy: J. Kirkup and B. Waterfield, "Safeguard the City or I'll Veto EU Treaty, Warns PM," *The Daily Telegraph*, December 7, 2011, 1.

[49] European Council, *Statement by the Euro Area Heads of State or Government* (December 9, 2011).

influence over the critical decisions about EU financial services regulation being increasingly eroded in the longer term. By taking such an antagonistic stance the UK could even have hastened its relegation to the second division, a fate that it has successfully avoided in the past in spite of being outside the euro area.

The next part of the chapter puts the current position in context by examining the recent evolution of relations between Member States with respect to financial services regulation.

II: Intergovernmentalism – the crises and the Member States

Insights from theory

The liberal intergovernmentalism theory of European integration characterizes the EU as an intergovernmental regime designed to manage economic interdependence through a process of bargaining between Member States, in which States are motivated by preferences that have been formed at national level under the influence of dominant, usually economic, groups.[50] It assumes that Member States come together to solve common problems when rational, pragmatic calculations of gains and losses indicate that cooperation will serve their national interest.[51] Since the modern EU has evolved into being a multi-tiered system that involves both national governments and supranational actors in dense, pluralistic policymaking processes, intergovernmentalism is now manifestly inadequate as a comprehensive theory of EU integration.[52] Nevertheless, it can still function as a valuable way of looking at the contribution of Member States to this complex, multi-level system of governance, especially in the aftermath of extreme events that have led the big economic powers among the Member States on occasion to seize the initiative in order to protect their national interests.

[50] A. Moravcsik, "Preferences and Power in the European Community: A Liberal Intergovernmentalist Approach," *Journal of Common Market Studies*, 34 (1993), 473–524; A. Moravcsik, *The Choice for Europe. Social Purpose and State Power from Messina to Maastricht* (London: UCL Press, 1998).

[51] M. Cini, "Intergovernmentalism" in M. Cini and N. Pérez-Solórzano Borragán (eds.), *European Union Politics* (Oxford University Press, 3rd edn., 2010) pp. 86–103.

[52] A. Wiener and T. Diez (eds.), *European Integration Theory* (Oxford University Press, 2nd edn. 2009).

Varieties of capitalism theory interacts with liberal intergovernmentalism by providing a framework for understanding the institutional similarities and differences in developed economies.[53] It characterizes the political economy as a terrain populated with entrepreneurial actors, with firms as key players, all seeking to advance their interests within existing rules and institutions that complement and reinforce each other. Institutional complementarities and interdependencies are found to exist between corporate labor, product and financial market structures and governing frameworks. Varieties of capitalism theory claims that in spite of the forces of convergence and globalization, considerable national diversity will persist in order to reinforce comparative institutional advantages: that is, "nations will specialize according to their comparative advantages."[54]

One of the leading papers on varieties of capitalism, published in 2001, found that two main variant forms of capitalism were present in the EU.[55] The first was the liberal market economy, characterized by arm's-length market transactions, and the second was the coordinated market economy, characterized by the prevalence of non-market long-term relations. The UK was in the first category, Germany the second. France was viewed as occupying a more ambiguous position, representing a type of capitalism, sometimes dubbed "Mediterranean," marked by a large agricultural sector and a history of State intervention.[56]

In the intervening years, some of the differences between the economies of the major EU Member States have become less pronounced, especially with respect to financial markets.[57] The recent growth in

[53] P.A. Hall and D. Soskice, "An Introduction to Varieties of Capitalism" in P.A. Hall and D. Soskice (eds.), *Varieties of Capitalism: The Institutional Foundations of Comparative Advantage* (Oxford University Press, 2001), pp. 1–68. For an overview of earlier literature leading in this direction: H. Macartney, "Variegated Neo-Liberalism: Transnationally Oriented Fractions of Capital in EU Financial Market Integration," *Review of International Studies*, 35 (2009), 451–80, 452–6. Other important contributions to the literature include B. Amable, *The Diversity of Modern Capitalism* (Oxford University Press, 2003); M. Aoki, *Towards a Comparative Institutional Analysis* (Cambridge, MA: MIT Press, 2001).

[54] B. Hancké, "Introducing the Debate" in B. Hancké (ed.), *Debating Varieties of Capitalism: A Reader* (Oxford University Press, 2009), pp. 1–20, p. 5.

[55] Hall and Soskice, "An Introduction."

[56] See also J. Zysman, *Governments, Markets and Growth: Finance and the Politics of Industrial Change* (Oxford: Martin Robertson, 1983); F. Allen and D. Gale, *Comparing Financial Systems* (Cambridge, MA: MIT Press, 2000).

[57] I. Hardie and D. Howarth, "What Varieties of Financial Capitalism? The Financial Crisis and the Move to 'Market-Based Banking' in the UK, Germany and France" (PSI, 2010); H. Macartney, *Variegated Neoliberalism: EU Varieties of Capitalism and International Political Economy* (London: Routledge, 2011), pp. 6–9.

Continental European capital markets,[58] the increasing reliance by banks on securitization and other market-based financing techniques[59] and the emergence of new types of financial intermediaries and institutional investors[60] indicate that at least in wholesale markets there has been a trend towards the liberal market economy model in response to the internationalization of finance.[61] This trend towards financialization has been said to demonstrate a willingness on the part of national governments to liberalize their markets where this has been in the interests of their major internationally-oriented firms.[62]

Proponents of varieties of capitalism contend that such developments do not mean that the approach has become obsolete.[63] Accepting that economies are constantly changing, as market actors respond to pressures coming from the forces of globalization, internationally mobile capital, changing consumer preferences, demographic trends and other quarters, varieties of capitalism theory accommodates change by positing that, conditioned by their diverse existing institutional arrangements, firms in different countries, and in turn their governments, will respond differently to external stimuli.[64] These responses may involve some loosening of existing practices and patterns of behavior but, because

[58] European Commission, *European Financial Integration Report 2007* (SEC(2007) 1696) and London Economics, *The Importance of Wholesale Financial Services to the EU Economy 2008* (City of London, July 2008). See also R. Ayadi, *Integrating Retail Financial Markets in Europe: Between Uncertainties and Challenges* (Brussels: Centre for European Policy Studies (CEPS) Paperbacks, 2011).

[59] I. Hardie and D. Howarth, "Die Krise but not La Crise? The Financial Crisis and the Transformation of German and French Banking System," *Journal of Common Market Studies*, 47 (2009), 1017–39; Hardie and Howarth, "What Varieties of Financial Capitalism?"

[60] On the growth of investment funds, especially in France: Association Française de la Gestion Financière, *The French Asset Management Industry* (online: July 2010, www.afg.asso.fr/index.php?option=com_docman&task=doc). On hedge funds: HedgeFund Intelligence, *Global Review Update 2007* (Online) www.hedgefundintelligence.com/Issue/64282/Global-Review-update-Autumn-2007.html; S. Gray (ed.), *Hedge Funds in Germany 2006 Special Report August 2006* (www.hedgeweek.com), www.hedgeweek.com/sites/default/files/import_attachments/Hedgeweek%20Special%20Report%20-%20Hedge%20Funds%20in%20Germany%202006.pdf.

[61] Mügge, "Reordering the Marketplace." [62] Ibid.

[63] P.A. Hall, "The Evolution of Varieties of Capitalism in Europe" in B. Hancké, M. Rhodes and M. Thatcher (eds.), *Beyond Varieties of Capitalism – Conflict, Contractions and Complementarities in the European Economy* (Oxford University Press, 2007), pp. 39–85.

[64] Ibid. And see also P.A. Hall and K. Thelen, "Institutional Change in Varieties of Capitalism," *Socio-Economic Review*, 7(1) (2009), 7–34.

Member States are on different adjustment trajectories, not a complete break from deeply-embedded national systems.[65] The durability of quite different corporate governance systems has been cited as an example of an observable variation which has persisted in spite of the internationalization of finance, the development of Continental European capital markets, the increasing prominence of institutional investors and alternative investment funds, and interventions at EU level, such as the Takeover Directive, aimed at fostering a more liberalized market-based approach.[66] National corporate governance is not immutable – as evidenced by the transformation of French corporate practices consequential upon the privatization of public enterprises during the 1980s and 1990s[67] – but is said to follow a distinctive national trajectory.[68] Huw Macartney has suggested the term "variegated capitalism" to describe the way in which market liberalization has spread across Europe, but in a divergent fashion from country to country because of important linkages between transnational financial markets and domestic national contexts.[69]

Varieties of capitalism and related theories provide a way of understanding how countries approach international economic and regulatory negotiations.[70] Starting from the rational assumption that countries will

[65] Hall, "The Evolution."

[66] Ibid. See also E. Grossman and P. Leblond, "European Financial Integration: Finally the Great Leap Forward?," *Journal of Common Market Studies*, 49 (2011), 413–35 (referring to corporate governance and also to retail financial services as areas of persistent divergence). Compare A. Dignam and M. Galanis, "Corporate Governance and the Importance of Macroeconomic Context," *Oxford Journal of Legal Studies*, 28 (2008), 201–43 (arguing that macroeconomic institutions (trade and finance) were making it increasingly hard to sustain insider systems of corporate governance). That the Takeover Directive has not achieved its intended market-opening effect (indeed, that it has been counterproductive in certain respects) is clear: European Commission, *Report on the Implementation of the Directive on Takeover Bids* (SEC(2007) 268); P.L. Davies, E.P. Schuster and E. van de Walle de Ghelcke, "The Takeover Directive as a Protectionist Tool?" in U. Bernitz and W.G. Ringe (eds.), *Company Law and Economic Protectionism: New Challenges to European Integration* (Oxford University Press, 2010), pp. 105–60.

[67] P.D. Culpepper, "Institutional Change in Contemporary Capitalism: Co-ordinated Financial Systems Since 1990," *World Politics*, 57 (2005), 173–99.

[68] B. Hancké, "Revisiting the French Model: Coordination and Restructuring in French Industry" in Hall and Soskice (eds.), *Varieties of Capitalism*, pp. 307–37; M. Goyer, "Capital Mobility, Varieties of Institutional Investors, and the Transforming Stability of Corporate Governance in France and Germany" in Hancké, Rhodes and Thatcher (eds.), *Beyond Varieties of Capitalism*, pp. 195–219.

[69] Macartney, "Variegated Neo-liberalism: Transnationally Oriented Fractions of Capital."

[70] Hall and Soskice, "An Introduction," p. 52.

act so as to protect and promote their national interest, theory postulates that the stance that countries adopt with respect to new regulatory initiatives will be influenced by their determination of whether those initiatives are likely to sustain or undermine the comparative institutional advantages of their nation's economy. It predicts that governments should be inclined to support such initiatives only when they are no threat to its firms' most crucial national interests. With reference specifically to the EU, it suggests that when Member States fail to agree on detailed harmonization, this may be attributable to crucial differences in their political economies.

Theories that emphasize the persistence of differences between countries slant expectations with respect to the breadth and depth of regulatory harmonization downwards. They imply that we should expect to find considerable Member State resistance to new layers of prescriptive top-down reforms that could undermine comparative competitive advantages, with such resistance being rooted in the still profoundly distinctive and different characteristics of national political economies. At first blush, financial market regulation in the EU appears not to conform to these expectations, in that the harmonizing effect of the FSAP was very considerable and the reforms being adopted in the wake of the global financial crisis are making this trend even more emphatic. However, theory grounded in differences provides a useful discipline against being too easily taken in by these first impressions. EU financial market integration up to the late 1990s was dubbed a "battle of the systems."[71] One study of EU regulatory and market integration in the period up to just before the crisis felt able to conclude that whilst this battle had not finished, it had become more subtle.[72] In examining post-crisis reforms, it is pertinent to ask whether the battle is becoming so subtle as to be virtually imperceptible but, drawing on the theoretical insights outlined here, to begin the inquiry by noting that it would be a surprising outcome if an unqualified positive answer to this question were to emerge.

Yet with the need not to jump to conclusions based on superficialities duly noted, it is safe to say that much standardization of EU financial market regulation has indeed happened. Since theories that emphasize differences are not apt to explain why and when Member States come together, other perspectives are also called for. The incentives for countries

[71] J. Story and I. Walter, *Political Economy of Financial Integration in Europe: The Battle of the Systems* (Manchester University Press, 1997).

[72] Grossman and Leblond, "European Financial Integration."

to cooperate with each other to tackle collective action problems are much discussed in economic literature: setting standard governing rules narrows the scope for actors from countries that have lax domestic standards to cause cross-border harm, and the opportunities for such actors to exploit domestic laxity to gain a competitive edge are curtailed.[73] The insight that "international financial integration erodes the viability of autarky"[74] is very relevant to the development of international financial regulation in general, and to EU financial regulation in particular.

Public choice theory is also relevant. It links international regulatory cooperation to the private choices of regulators, bureaucrats and politicians rather than an abstract sense of the "public interest":

> specifically, when technological change, market processes or other exogenous variables threaten either to remove power from a nation's regulatory structure or cause it to become irrelevant, then the regulators in that nation will have strong incentives to engage in activities such as international coordination in order to protect their autonomy.[75]

A public choice perspective has been used, for example, to explain the emergence of the Basel Capital Accords and European economic and monetary union.[76]

Historical institutionalism scholarship also offers valuable insights. This approach, applied to the EU, explains current institutions by reference to their location in a historical process and stresses the extent to which Member States have become locked into path-dependent processes that constrain their options.[77] Emphasizing the temporal aspect of politics, it explains how decisions that were made by rational, strong actors who acted in their national interest, but whose ability to predict the future was inevitably imperfect and whose personal time horizons may have been quite short-termist, can often turn out to have unintended and undesired

[73] C. Goodhart, P. Hartmann, D. Llewellyn, L. Rojas-Suárez and S. Weisbrod, *Financial Regulation: Why, How and Where Now?* (London: Routledge, 1998), pp. 173–81.

[74] Ibid., p. 177.

[75] J.R. Macey, "The 'Demand' for International Regulatory Cooperation: A Public-Choice Perspective" in G.A. Bermann, M. Herdegen and P.L. Lindseth, *Transatlantic Regulatory Cooperation: Legal Problems and Political Prospects* (Oxford University Press, 2000), pp. 147–65, p. 152.

[76] Ibid.

[77] P. Pierson, "The Path to European Integration: A Historical Institutionalist Analysis," *Comparative Political Studies*, 29 (1996), 123–63. For a general overview of literature on historical institutionalism in relation to the EU: M.A. Pollack, "Rational Choices and EU Politics" in K.E. Jørgensen, M.A. Pollack and B. Rosamond (eds.), *Handbook of European Union Politics* (London: Sage Publications, 2006), pp. 31–55.

consequences in the longer term; furthermore, it suggests that unless those actors (or, likely, their successors) are willing to contemplate a dramatic break with the past, those consequences will have to be dealt with in a way that fits within the existing institutions and processes.[78] Putting it another way, institutions "leave their own imprint on political outcomes."[79]

Historical institutionalism leads us to expect that institutions will not change easily, but scholars of this school do not deny that there can be critical junctures in which dramatic shocks can lead to massive changes, contending only that such events must be understood as a convergence of a number of factors, each of which must be carefully examined.[80] That the existing institutions and policies may produce "negative feedbacks" that become self-undermining over time is well recognized. Indeed, the potential for EU integration to become self-undermining was already being canvassed in the literature before recent difficulties in the euro area made a major policy reversal a real threat.[81]

From theory to practice: Member States' views on EU financial regulation in the years leading up to the global financial crisis

The stylized portrait of the politics of pre-crisis financial services regulation at the level of the Member States is that, among the major States, France and Germany tended to push for tighter EU regulation and the UK, whilst favorably disposed to negative integration, tended to resist positive integration in the form of ever-more comprehensive common EU rules.

[78] i.e. the determination of what is in the national interest must take account of the EU dimension: W. Sandholtz, "Choosing Union: Monetary Policies and Maastricht," *International Organisation*, 43 (1993), 1–39.

[79] K. Thelen and S. Steinmo, "Historical Institutionalism in Comparative Polities" in S. Steinmo, K. Thelen and F. Longstreth (eds.), *Structuring Politics: Historical Institutionalism in Comparative Analysis* (Cambridge University Press, 1992), pp. 1–32, p. 2. Generally: F. Scharpf, "The Joint-Decision Trap: Lessons from German Federalism and European Integration," *Public Administration*, 66 (1988), 239–78; J. March and J. Olsen, *Rediscovering Institutions* (New York: Free Press, 1989); P. Pierson, *Politics in Time: History, Institutions, and Social Analysis* (Princeton University Press, 2004); K. Thelen, *How Institutions Evolve: The Political Economy of Skills in Germany, Britain, the United States and Japan* (New York: Cambridge University Press, 2004).

[80] S. Steinmo, "The New Institutionalism" in P.B. Clark and J. Foweraker (eds.), *The Encyclopedia of Democratic Thought* (London: Routledge, 2001).

[81] M.A. Pollack, "The New Institutionalisms and European Integration" in Wiener and Diez (eds.), *European Integration Theory*, pp. 125–44, pp. 128–9 and pp. 137–8.

Generalized views can be helpful in setting the scene and in capturing something of the essence of deep-rooted fundamental preferences. Evidence that stylized assumptions about pre-crisis UK antipathy towards the expansion of EU law governing financial markets were not wholly wide of the mark can be found in a joint paper published in 2005 by the UK Treasury, the Financial Services Authority (FSA) and the Bank of England. This paper unambiguously declared one of the UK's priorities for financial services regulation to be that:

> In general, EU legislation should be a last resort and alternative approaches to policy making, such as more use of EU competition policy, market-based solutions and initiatives at national level, should be considered first.[82]

Looking back from a post-crisis vantage point, Adair Turner, chair of the FSA, summarized the UK's old philosophy as being that the European single financial market could operate with little more coordination than applied to the manufacturing or retail sectors of the economy.[83]

However, generalized views can also over-simplify. The passage quoted in the paragraph above loses much of its apparent hostility to Europe when it is viewed as a product of the general "better regulation" thinking that was much in vogue at that time, with "better" often regarded as being synonymous with "less." Moreover, in indicating a preference for national to supranational regulation in circumstances in which intervention was required, the UK authorities were adhering to the EU subsidiarity principle and not expressing a peculiarly UK predilection.

In more concrete terms, whilst it is true that on completion of the FSAP there was a regulatory pause,[84] during which time the EU, influenced by "better regulation" concepts, briefly embraced forms of industry-led self-regulation or non-legally binding soft regulation for alternative investments,[85] rating agencies[86] and clearing and settlement

[82] HM Treasury, FSA and Bank of England, *Supervising Financial Services in an Integrated European Single Market: A Discussion Paper* (London: HM Treasury, FSA and Bank of England, January 2005), p. 6.

[83] A. Turner, *The Turner Review: A Regulatory Response to the Global Banking Crisis* (London: FSA, March 2009), p. 102.

[84] European Commission, *White Paper on Financial Services Policy 2005–2010*, p. 14.

[85] European Commission, *Green Paper on the Enhancement of the EU Framework for Investment Funds* (COM(2005) 314); European Commission, *White Paper on Enhancing the Single Market Framework for Investment Funds* (COM(2006) 686).

[86] European Commission, *Communication on Credit Rating Agencies* (2006/C59/02), [2006] OJ C59/2.

mechanisms,[87] that fitted well with the so-called "light touch" style of regulation that was then associated with the UK's FSA,[88] overall these regulatory innovations, which could have been as much a product of regulatory fatigue as positive ideological preferences, were minor exceptions to the rule. The "rule" was the FSAP. The massive upgrade of the EU's financial services regulatory framework that occurred between 1999 and 2005 under the FSAP, which removed barriers to cross-border trading, but also imposed a significantly expanded core of harmonized requirements on Member States and set in place the foundations of a pan-European supervisory architecture, gives the lie to any suggestion that the UK somehow held an effective block on the imposition of important regulatory controls at EU level. Indeed, it would not have been in the UK national interest to have been obstinately obstructive to the FSAP's imposition of pan-EU regulation as the price for the dismantling of national barriers, since that would have been unwelcome to the many major UK, US and other international firms conducting significant cross-border operations out of the City of London and thus in a position to benefit from efficiency gains flowing from having to comply with only one set of rules while conducting business in several jurisdictions.[89] The FSAP was "deregulatory" insofar as it was designed to remove barriers to a single market in financial services across the EU, but this description never told the full story, because whilst many divergent national rules were indeed swept away, they were replaced by common rules set at EU level instead. As is often the way, negative and positive integration thus proceeded hand in hand.[90]

[87] Federation of European Securities Exchanges (FESE), European Association of Central Counterparty Clearing Houses (EACH) and European Central Securities Depositories Association (ECSDA), *European Code of Conduct for Clearing and Settlement* (Brussels: European Commission, November 2006).

[88] The UK's supposedly "light-touch" approach was itself a somewhat exaggerated simplification: E. Ferran, "The Break-up of the Financial Services Authority," *Oxford Journal of Legal Studies*, 31 (2011), 455–80.

[89] Although it has been claimed that during the 2000s the EU aligned itself with an international deregulatory agenda (E. Posner and N. Véron, "The EU and Financial Regulation: Power Without Purpose?," *Journal of European Public Policy*, 17 (2010), 400–15) this does not sit entirely easily with the emergence during this period of "a full-blown regulatory regime of considerable sophistication and dramatic scale": N. Moloney, *EC Securities Regulation* (Oxford University Press, 2nd edn., 2008), p. 4.

[90] S. Vogel, *Freer Markets, More Rules: Regulatory Reform in Advanced Industrial Countries* (Ithaca: Cornell University Press, 1996).

It helped, of course, that many of the changes adopted at EU level under the FSAP were ones that the UK felt comfortable with. As the EU's only large market-based economy, and with London being the location of one of the world's most significant capital markets, during this period the UK enjoyed a position of considerable influence over EU financial services regulatory policy design.[91] In the boom market conditions before the global financial crisis, the success of the City of London was used in at least two ways in EU regulatory debate – to promote the UK view as being the one to emulate in order to achieve similar triumphs, and to resist alternative proposals that, by not being informed by such extensive practical experience of shaping regulation to fit vibrant capital markets, risked causing wanton damage to a prized economic asset that benefitted Europe as a whole. A strong emphasis in EU policy in the early 2000s on facilitating the development of US–EU financial markets further strengthened the UK position because UK regulation, a system familiar to the large US banks that had major European operations based in London, seemed to offer the approach most easily adaptable to a transatlantic environment.

Notwithstanding that it was very likely based on an over-optimistic miscalculation of the long-term sustainability of its ability to influence the European rules of the game for financial markets, it is clear that the UK's policy in this era moved a long way towards positively embracing an EU-level approach to financial services regulation. Europeanization of domestic regulatory policy also took place,[92] as it was during this period that the UK government and regulatory authorities began to operate a practice dubbed "intelligent copy-out," that is, as far as practicable using the language of the EU instrument as the basis for national implementation and not adding additional requirements, so as to avoid placing any unintended additional obligations on firms.[93] Whilst this

[91] L. Quaglia, "Completing the Single Market in Financial Services: The Politics of Competing Advocacy Coalitions," *Journal of European Public Policy*, 17 (2010), 1007–22.

[92] "Europeanization" is a term that can be understood in a variety of ways, but the interpretation adopted here is that it means "the various ways in which institutions, processes and policies emanating from the European level influence policies, politics and polities at the domestic level": T.A. Börzel and T. Risse, "Europeanization: The Domestic Impact of European Union Politics" in Jørgensen, Pollack and Rosamond (eds.), *Handbook of European Union Politics*, pp. 483–504, p. 485.

[93] Bank of England and FSA, *Joint Implementation Plan for MiFID* (London: Bank of England & FSA, 2006) p. 6. Ending gold-plating now represents general UK government policy: Department for Business, Innovation and Skills, *Guiding Principles for EU Legislation* (London: BIS, 2010).

approach was influenced by a combination of factors, including "better regulation" thinking, pressure from globally-active businesses for reduction of regulatory frictions, and the increasingly prescriptive nature of EU law itself, in essence it amounted to domestic adaptation to the looming prospect of the EU becoming, as Niamh Moloney has said, the "monopoly supplier" of the main rules governing financial market activity.[94] This relocation of regulatory power was something that was to become more explicitly recognized after the global financial crisis, but it was already well underway before it.

Just as it is not entirely consistent with the evolution of EU financial markets and the regulatory response in the years leading up to the financial crisis to view the UK as having been temperamentally predisposed always to resist EU regulation, it also does not ring true to see the UK as having been predestined always to be pitted against an alliance of France and Germany. There are a number of reasons why this polarized view, whilst helpful for some purposes, can also be considered too stark.

First, it risks failing to give due attention to changes that were taking place in Continental European financial markets, including the shift towards more market-based financing, the emergence of securitization, and the growth in investment banking, hedge funds, private equity funds and other capital market activities in a number of European financial centers. Such trends were leading to the emergence of new finance industry groups in Continental Europe whose interests were becoming more similar to those of UK-based firms, a highly significant development given the finance industry's considerable influence over the shaping of official policy positions.[95] Moreover, with US-based firms becoming increasingly active in Europe, arguments for major EU Member States to work together in developing a regulatory framework that would enable all of their firms to compete more effectively for internationally mobile capital and business, rather than focusing unduly on competing with each other, were gathering strength.[96] Though national interests were not fusing into a homogenized European interest, changes in national political economies in response to

[94] Moloney, *EC Securities Regulation*, p. 1014.

[95] Buckley and Howarth, "Internal Market: Gesture Politics?"; Macartney, "Variegated Neoliberalism: Transnationally Oriented Fractions of Capital in EU Financial Market Integration." Generally on the role of private actors in shaping financial regulation: G.R.D. Underhill and X. Zhang, "Setting the Rules: Private Power, Political Underpinnings, and Legitimacy in Global Monetary and Financial Governance," *International Affairs*, 84 (2008), 535–54.

[96] Grossman and Leblond, "European Financial Integration."

globalization and market-liberalization developments were opening up more room for Member States to agree on when a standard European approach would serve each of their distinctive national interests.

Second, the polarized view is faulty in presupposing a commonality of interests between France and Germany, two still quite distinctively different major economies despite market developments that have brought some aspects of their financial systems closer together. Consistent with the expectations of varieties of capitalism theory, during this era there continued to be many disagreements between Member States with respect to financial services legislative policy choices, and these included plenty of occasions when France and Germany were on different sides. In particular, intensely contentious negotiations over the Markets in Financial Instruments Directive (MiFID),[97] the centerpiece of the FSAP, revealed much continuing divergence between French and German positions on key matters, reflecting differences in their national set-ups.[98] These countries also disagreed over the design of the fledgling pan-European regulatory and supervisory architecture, with France apparently tending to support more integrated EU supervision[99] and Germany, although somewhat ambivalent in its stance, eventually aligning more with the UK in preferring the network of national supervisors model that was actually adopted.[100]

It has been argued above that to describe the UK attitude towards EU financial services regulation in the era before the financial crisis as anti-regulation and anti-European would be, for many purposes, an inaccurate over-simplification. Unsurprisingly, the notion that simple, one-dimensional generalizations are often inadequate to capture the many subtle and variegated influences that affect national responses across a range of different matters holds good for other Member States as well.[101] Lucia Quaglia has pertinently remarked that "the" German position on the MiFID was actually hard to pinpoint, because competing different domestic preferences meant that its position in negotiations fluctuated.[102] The insight that national

[97] 2004/39/EC, [2004] OJ L145/1.

[98] N. Aubry and M. McKee, "MiFID: Where Did It Come From, Where Is It Taking Us?," *Journal of International Banking Law and Regulation*, 22 (2007), 177–86 (Germany tended to be somewhere in the middle with its own specific issues, which meant that it tended to be a "swing vote" within the Council on some issues).

[99] Buckley and Howarth, "Internal Market: Gesture Politics?," 127.

[100] E. Ferran, *Building an EU Securities Market* (Cambridge University Press, 2004), pp. 120–1; L. Quaglia, *Governing Financial Services in the European Union* (London: Routledge, 2010), pp. 41–2.

[101] Ibid., p. 90. [102] Ibid.

interests are too multi-faceted, influenced by too many interconnected groups, and too contingent on the nature of the particular matter in question to follow a rigid, clearly-defined straight path is intuitively compelling. Highly important strategic issues may see one set of alliances, whilst less important ones may see other views taken, reflecting a varying range of perceptions of the "national interest" held by individuals who are at different levels in the hierarchy. Recognition of the complex mix of factors that impinge upon the "national interest" makes it possible to understand why coalitions on particular matters that formed during the FSAP period were often quite limited in scope and also quite fragile.[103]

Member States and post-crisis reforms: meeting in the middle?

It is helpful to continue to employ both a stylized view and a more nuanced perspective in seeking to understand the stance taken by Member States in relation to the EU's financial services regulatory response to the global financial crisis and subsequent events.

From the conventional viewpoint, the global financial crisis dealt a blow to "Anglo-American" capitalism, characterized by rampant deregulated markets. As such, it put the UK, the EU's leading proponent of supposedly "light touch" regulation, onto the back foot because that approach had been "discredited." The crisis thus paved the way for a less market-friendly, more stability-oriented approach, associated with France, Italy and, to some extent Germany and Spain, to gain ground.

Early analyses of the EU post-global financial crisis reforms in the political science literature have indeed found evidence of a more intrusive regulatory style, said to reflect Franco-German choices, moving into the ascendancy.[104] From a legal perspective, the array of new measures

[103] Macartney, "Variegated Neo-Liberalism: Transnationally Oriented Fractions of Capital in EU Financial Market Integration."

[104] L. Quaglia, "The 'Old' and 'New' Politics of Financial Services Regulation in the EU"; E. Posner, "Is a European Approach to Financial Regulation Emerging from the Crisis?" in E. Helleiner, S. Pagliari and H. Zimmermann (eds.), *Global Finance in Crisis: The Politics of International Regulatory Change* (London: Routledge, 2010), pp. 108–20; D. Dinan, "Institutions and Governance: A New Treaty, a Newly Elected Parliament and a New Commission," *Journal of Common Market Studies*, 48 (2010), 95–118, 115; J. Schild, "Mission Impossible? The Potential for Franco–German Leadership in the Enlarged EU," *Journal of Common Market Studies*, 48 (2010), 1367–90, 1381–2.

proposed or adopted between 2008 and Spring 2012 certainly confirms a regulatory surge, including a shift away from short-lived experiments with industry-led or other alternative approaches in areas such as rating agencies and market infrastructure.[105] Moreover, Chancellor Merkel and (former) President Sarkozy's practice of sending numerous joint communications setting out shared priorities makes it easy to identify a strong coincidence between Franco-German preferences and key elements of the post-crisis regulatory agenda.[106]

The Alternative Investment Fund Managers Directive (AIFMD) appears to provide particular support for the claim that the financial crisis changed the balance of Member States' power and influence over the financial services regulatory agenda and swung it in a more interventionist direction.[107] France and Germany, working jointly, played a pivotal role in pushing for the EU to regulate hedge funds, private equity funds and other so-called "unregulated" alternative investment funds (a misnomer, because fund managers in Europe were already subject to a patchwork of regulatory requirements although there was no dedicated, sector-specific regime). The UK view that the regulation of alternative investments was a global issue that required a global response did not prevail. There was also noticeable cooperation between France and Germany over the need for new controls on financial sector remuneration.[108] However, politicians around the world, including in the UK, were generally keen to be seen to be cracking down on perceived excesses in financial sector pay arrangements, meaning that views on this matter

[105] CRA Regulation (as amended); EMIR (market infrastructure).

[106] e.g., Sarkozy–Merkel letter to Barroso of June 8, 2010 urging the Commission to bring forward a legislative initiative on short selling and sovereign credit default swaps: B. Hall, Q. Peel and N. Tait, "Paris and Berlin Press EU to Speed Regulation," *Financial Times*, June 10, 2010, 7; joint Sarkozy–Merkel letter to Barroso of May 6, 2010 calling for review of use of ratings in regulation: T. Barber, "US, Germany and France Turn on Rating Agencies," *Financial Times*, May 7, 2010, 8.

[107] Directive 2011/61/EU on Alternative Investment Fund Managers [2011] OJ L174/1 (AIFMD). Analysed in detail in E. Ferran, "After the Crisis: The Regulation of Hedge Funds and Private Equity in the EU," *European Business Organization Law Review*, 12 (2011), 379–414. The account of the disputes over passports that follows in the text is drawn from this article. For further background on the German position, see H. Zimmermann, "Varieties of Global Financial Governance? British and German Approaches to Financial Market Regulation" in Helleiner, Pagliari and Zimmermann, *Global Finance in Crisis*, pp. 121–36.

[108] Analyzed in detail in E. Ferran, "New Regulation of Remuneration in the Financial Sector in the EU," *European Company and Financial Law Review*, (2012), 1–34.

were less polarized than in some other areas, and differences were more ones of degree than fundamental principle.[109]

Yet, whilst it is undeniably right to say that the global financial crisis propelled EU financial services regulatory policy into a more interventionist phase, once the focus is sharpened and individual measures are examined more closely, a more nuanced picture of Member States' preferences starts to emerge. Take again the example of the AIFMD. On the surface, it is easy to understand why hedge funds and private equity funds were prime targets for a Franco-German-led crackdown, because in the pre-crisis years their exploitation of shareholder rights as an investment strategy had disturbed so-called "patient" capital corporate governance systems that are found in Continental Europe and, as such, had attracted much political hostility. However, a tentative overall assessment of the Directive is that as finally adopted it appears to pose less of a threat to the industry than seemed likely given the intense controversy provoked by early drafts.[110] The changes that were made during the passage of the legislation could thus be described in pejorative terms as "watering down" and the process could be viewed as demonstrating that the crisis has done rather less to undermine UK influence (identifying the UK view in stereotypical fashion as being strongly associated with a preference for light regulation) over EU regulatory policy design than has been supposed.[111] However, that view ignores two important considerations.

First, there were serious flaws with the original legislative proposals (which, in an unfortunate departure from established Commission practice, were rushed out without the benefit of full pre-legislative consultation),[112] which from a technical perspective needed to be addressed. Whilst principled concerns about the quality of legislation can be hard to disentangle from more self-interested arguments, it is essential to acknowledge the distinction and therefore not to assume that redrafts of proposed legislation can only ever have a weakening effect. Even in its final form the Directive is still a very detailed and highly complex legal instrument that will impose burdensome new requirements and significantly increased compliance costs. The outcome may be less bad for the industry than it threatened to be, but

109 Ibid. 110 Ferran, "After the Crisis".

111 Ibid.; H. Plumridge, "Hedge Funds Win Big in Brussels," *The Wall Street Journal Online*, October 20, 2010.

112 European Commission, *Impact Assessment* (SEC(2009) 576), pp. 12–13.

it would go too far to dismiss the Directive as a marginal change that will have little meaningful impact.

Second, recalling that elements of the alternative investment fund industry have become established in France and Germany, developments that the national governments have not discouraged and, on occasions, have even sought to foster,[113] there is no reason to suppose that the French or German government would really have wanted to see the imposition of over-stringent new requirements that could have driven hedge funds and private equity funds out of Europe altogether. Beneath the rhetoric, it is possible to discern many powerful factors that would have encouraged the governments of all of the leading EU Member States to work constructively with each other in finding a workable compromise legal text. This view of the true underlying motivations finds support in political science literature. Hubert Zimmermann has written of German ambivalence towards new financial phenomena and actors, an incoherence which, he suggests, can be explained by the bifurcation of the German economy into a competitive international sector and a host of small firms.[114] He has argued, compellingly, that German motivations with respect to the regulation of hedge funds, private equity and other actors, were ones of political legitimacy rather than principled disapproval of their activities.[115] James Buckley and David Howarth have suggested that similar reasoning can be applied to France.[116]

As for the UK, its stance with respect to the AIFMD was also not as clear-cut as could be implied by stereotypical assumptions. The global financial crisis undoubtedly shook the faith of key UK opinion formers in the disciplining effects of self-regulating markets, with consequential effects on its stance towards regulatory policy in general. Adair Turner has described its effect as a "wake-up call."[117] With respect to the alternative investment sector, the UK's government was not adamantly opposed to the post-crisis imposition of regulatory controls as such, and its concerns were more about ensuring proper alignment of EU policy with related initiatives in other countries and at the international

[113] See text accompanying nn. 94–5 above.

[114] Zimmermann, "Varieties of Global Financial Governance," pp. 129–31.

[115] Ibid.

[116] Buckley and Howarth, "Internal Market: Gesture Politics?"

[117] A. Turner, "Speech at the City of London Corporation's Annual Reception for the City Office" (October 6, 2009, online: www.fsa.gov.uk/pages/Library/Communication/Speeches/2009/1006_at.shtml).

level.[118] Indeed, in its efforts to prevent the adoption of an EU framework that could effectively have closed its markets to funds and fund managers from outside the EU, the UK was eventually supported by Germany, leaving France in a somewhat isolated position among the major Member States and under fire for suspected covert protectionism. France eventually withdrew its objections and the text, incorporating a dizzyingly complicated set of provisions on third country access via Member State-administered passport schemes, was unanimously adopted in the Council.

In many areas, the UK's attitude to EU regulation in the immediate aftermath of the global financial crisis was quite strikingly at odds with the ambivalence that is often assumed to characterize its approach. It was openly acknowledged that a minimalist approach had become unsustainable because of cross-border contagion effects, and that more pan-European standardization was thus inevitable if a retreat from single market freedoms was to be avoided, a reorientation dubbed "more Europe."[119] More Europe thinking was prominent in reflections on lessons learnt from the handling of the Icelandic banking crisis.[120] Of course, any serious attempt to pursue a "less Europe" strategy with respect to the operation of cross-border banking would have encountered formidable legal obstacles, given the supremacy of EU law and treaty restrictions pre-empting Member States from taking action in areas where the Union has exercised competence.[121] Specifically, for a host Member State to have sought to impose "less Europe" in the form of mandatory subsidiarization for the conduct of activities within their territory would have required reconsideration at EU level of hallowed, legally-protected rights for financial firms to operate via branches and/or through the provision of services from elsewhere in the Union.[122] In addition to the legal obstacles, pursuit of a "less Europe" strategy would also have had to contend with strong economic arguments against renunciation of the full benefits of the single market and, as such, would have met with deep political opposition. The legacy effects of

[118] FSA and HM Treasury, *European Commission Consultation on Hedge Funds: Response* (London: FSA and HM Treasury, January 2009). In opposition, the Conservative Party had been opposed to the (draft) Directive, but recognized the need to look again at the sector and to consider reform: Conservative Party, *From Crisis to Confidence: Plan for Sound Banking* (London: Conservative Party, 2009), p. 39. The EU-level legislative process had advanced too far by May 2010 for the incoming new coalition government to reverse it.

[119] Turner, *The Turner Review*, pp. 96–102. [120] Ibid., pp. 100–4.

[121] TFEU, art. 2(2); Lisbon Treaty, Annexed Declarations, Declaration 17.

[122] Turner, *The Turner Review*, pp. 100–2.

past decisions can thus be seen to have been highly significant in providing a frame for practical decision-making. The UK's stance in this regard is consistent with Louis Pauly's suggestions that responses to the global financial crisis indicated that "Leading states are behaving as if they have resigned themselves collectively to mitigating and resolving future cross-border emergencies" and yielded scant signs of Member States ever contemplating "serious measures to disentangle themselves from financial networks they themselves spent half a century constructing."[123]

Although its views became more nuanced as crises deepened, the UK was initially unequivocal in its acceptance of the need for a single rulebook in banking and was especially vocal in pressing for strict EU implementation of the Basel III capital requirements.[124] (Indeed, reports indicated that in the international deliberations leading up to the adoption of the Basel III tighter capital requirements it was the UK, along with the United States, that pressed for tough standards, and some Continental European countries that urged compromise.)[125] The UK's top regulator also began to speak openly of being merely an arm of an EU regulatory regime, and of the FSA's role as being to deliver EU rules.[126] Even government ministers from the Conservative Party (which is generally viewed as being the most Euroskeptic of the large political parties) were prepared to acknowledge that agenda-setting for financial services regulation was increasingly done at the EU level.[127]

[123] L.W. Pauly, "The Old and the New Politics of International Financial Stability," *Journal of Common Market Studies*, 47 (2009), 955–75, 970.

[124] G. Osborne, "Speech at the Lord Mayor's Dinner for Bankers and Merchants of the City of London" (June 15, 2011, online: www.hm-treasury.gov.uk/press_58_11.htm); M. King, "Speech at the Lord Mayor's Dinner for Bankers and Merchants of the City of London" (June 15, 2011, online: www.bankofengland.co.uk/publications/speeches/2011/speech504.pdf).

[125] Editorial, "A Better Basel; International Bank Regulators Reach a Compromise," *The Washington Post*, September 17, 2010, A18. Germany's track record of raising significant objections in the negotiations over Basel Accords has been attributed to special features in its bank-centered economic structure: P.-H. Verdier, "Transnational Regulatory Networks and Their Limits," *Yale Journal of International Law*, 34 (2009), 113–72. Switzerland, which, like the UK, has a small number of banks that are outsize relative to its economy, was also a proponent of higher capital standards.

[126] H. Sants, "UK Financial Regulation: After the Crisis" (speech, March 12, 2010, online: www.fsa.gov.uk/pages/Library/Communication/Speeches/2010/0312_hs.shtml); H. Sants, "Speech at FSA PRA Banking Conference" (May 19, 2011, online: www.fsa.gov.uk/pages/Library/Communication/Speeches/2011/1905_hs.shtml).

[127] M. Hoban, "Speech at Reform" (December 1, 2010, online: www.hm-treasury.gov.uk/speech_fst_011210.htm).

The analysis thus far points towards more of a meeting in the middle by Member States than a stark triumph of one view over another. The language of historical institutionalism is quite apt to describe this process of convergence. On the one hand, the UK embraced the need for more public intervention in markets and accepted that its legal obligations as an EU Member State, economic interdependencies, collective action problems and the path-dependencies of EU financial integration made it inevitable for more of this intervention to be organized at EU level. On the other, the urging of France and Germany to impose controls was tempered by considerations arising from each of their own domestic political economies and, unsurprisingly, they did not always agree even between themselves on the path to take. In overall terms, however, all three key Member States found themselves in a situation in which their national interests appeared to depend crucially on their working together across a wide range of matters to find common solutions to shared problems.

Member States were given a particularly sharp reminder of the value of a centrally-managed, co-coordinated approach by events surrounding deposit guarantee schemes. At the height of the global financial crisis, many Member States took urgent unilateral action to improve their domestic deposit guarantee schemes, which were harmonized only on a minimum basis, in order to maintain consumer confidence and prevent bank runs.[128] These disparate steps revealed a striking disconnect between the political rhetoric of Member States' calls for "a comprehensive and coordinated response to the current situation"[129] and the action that national governments felt they had to take domestically in response to domestic circumstances. However, Member States soon discovered that the actions they had taken unilaterally had unintended and unfortunate side-effects. Differences between national schemes produced incentives for depositors to move their funds into accounts with banks covered by the most comprehensive scheme, thereby threatening the stability of the financial institutions in the States from which funds were being withdrawn (although in the longer term, backfiring badly on the overly generous guarantor country, as illustrated by Ireland's economic plight). Lessons were also learnt from the temporary short-selling bans which many Member States imposed at the height of the crisis. These national bans shared a common purpose, but

[128] European Commission, *State Aid: Overview of National Rescue Measures and Deposit Guarantee Schemes* (MEMO/08/619, October 14, 2008).

[129] ECOFIN, *Council Conclusions on Immediate Responses to Financial Turmoil* (13930/08, October 7, 2008).

differed considerably in their details. It later came to be realized that this fragmented approach had limited the effectiveness of supervision, provided scope for regulatory arbitrage, been a source of confusion in markets, and had generated costs and difficulties for market participants.[130]

Still battling . . . and even starting to move further apart?

However, it would go too far to suggest that the global financial crisis has caused Member States' national interests to fuse into a completely homogenized European interest. The outcome of efforts to resolve the euro area sovereign debt crisis could result in declining economic diversity among Member States that choose to move to a close, economically interdependent fiscal union, but for now at least, the individual economies of each Member State remain quite distinctive.

The tenacity of distinctive features in national economies suggests that we should expect still to find many examples of disagreements between Member States over the design of financial services regulation (especially with regard to supervisory structures, with the position with respect to the content of rules varying on a case-by-case basis) notwithstanding the general consensus on the inevitability of "more Europe." The persistence of diverse national preferences may be a key to understanding the sense of "underachievement" that some commentators have identified in the EU's response.[131] This section therefore examines the nature of some of the issues on the post-crisis financial services regulatory agenda that have divided Member States. If EU financial regulation has evolved to the point where all that remains for Member States to fight over are matters of detail, with such disputes playing out around an increasingly solid core of regulation crafted at EU level, it would be stretching things to continue to refer to "battles" between systems to describe EU financial market regulatory integration, and a stress on important differences in capitalist systems that countries will strive to protect would feel increasingly out of place. The decision of the UK government in December 2011 to link its refusal to agree EU Treaty revisions with respect to the euro to the need to "safeguard" the City of London from EU financial regulation

[130] European Commission, *Proposal for a Regulation on Short Selling and Certain Aspects of Credit Default Swaps* (COM(2010) 482), p. 2. Post-crisis reforms have given ESMA a role in coordinating national short selling bans, which has already been tested: ESMA, "ESMA Promotes Harmonised Regulatory Action on Short-selling in the EU" (ESMA/2011/266). This matter is discussed further by Niamh Moloney in Chapter 2 below.

[131] cf. Buckley and Howarth, "Internal Market: Gesture Politics?."

gives a strong hint that the language of "battles" is still apt and suggests that the "more Europe" accord may have been a transient phase that is already breaking down. But closer inquiry is called for.

Market infrastructure/short selling

Protracted negotiations around aspects of new EU requirements relating to market infrastructure provide a good illustration of disagreements on seemingly arcane technicalities that have assumed particular significance because of their potential ramifications for important elements of Member States' domestic political economies. The UK assumed a prominent role in calling for a harmonized framework for central counterparties,[132] but it took a different view from some other Member States on some of the detailed aspects of proposals for the regulation of market infrastructure and related proposals for regulation of derivatives.[133] The UK pressed, against German-led opposition, for the scope of the mandatory clearing requirements to be extended to exchange-traded as well as standardized over the counter (OTC) derivatives.[134] The economic issue at the core of the disagreement was whether "vertical silo" models for trading and clearing, such as the one operated by the Deutsche Börse, should be preserved and protected or opened up to competition. The European Market Infrastructure Regulation (EMIR) requires authorized clearing houses to accept standardized derivative contracts for clearing, hence the crucial importance of the scope of the contracts that can be considered for subjection to the clearing obligation imposed by the Regulation. The EMIR text, as finally agreed, follows the German approach insofar as the clearing obligation is limited to standardized OTC derivatives, but it moves towards the UK position in the negotiations by stipulating that clearing houses must accept for clearing all such contracts on a non-discriminatory and transparent basis, regardless of the trading venue.[135] In addition, trading venues on request are required to provide trade feeds on a non-discriminatory and

[132] HM Treasury and FSA, *Reforming OTC Derivative Markets: A UK Perspective* (London: HM Treasury and FSA, December 2009).

[133] European Commission, *Proposal for a Regulation of the European Parliament and of the Council on OTC Derivatives, Central Counterparties and Trade Repositories* (COM(2010) 484).

[134] J. Grant, "EC Official Urges OTC Derivatives Reform," *Financial Times*, March 1, 2011 (online: ft.com); J. Grant, "Splits Grow Over Derivatives Reform," *Financial Times*, April 18, 2011, 5 (online: ft.com).

[135] EMIR, art. 7.

transparent basis to any clearing house that has been authorized to clear OTC derivative contracts traded on that venue of execution.[136] The inclusion of these provisions during the negotiations was duly reported as "wins for the British camp."[137] A catalyst for the insertions into the text to address fair and open access between clearing houses and trading platforms and to bar discrimination against any Member State as a venue for clearing services in any currency was a European Central Bank (ECB) initiative in July 2011 on oversight arrangements for payment, clearing and settlement systems, in which the ECB advocated that infrastructures handling a certain volume of euro-denominated transactions should be subject to location, incorporation and control requirements. This policy has been challenged by the UK government, which has opened proceedings alleging the policy infringes EU fundamental freedoms and EU competition law, offends the principle of equality, is not proportional and exceeds the competence of the ECB.

On the other hand, the UK "lost out" to Germany with respect to the appropriate regulatory approach to speculative sovereign credit default swap (CDS) transactions. In its original proposal on short selling, the European Commission proposed standing restrictions on uncovered short sales of shares and of sovereign debt instruments, but not on uncovered sovereign swap CDS transactions.[138] This view was endorsed by the UK, which considered that imposing restrictions on sovereign CDS transactions could harm market liquidity, and ultimately increase borrowing costs for sovereigns. The UK was initially supported in this view by many other Member States.[139] However, Germany, together with the European Parliament,[140] continued to press for a ban on uncovered sovereign CDS transactions, a stance that was indirectly helped by the turmoil in the euro area, since this fomented support for a crackdown on "naked" speculation. The final legislative instrument adopts the "insurable interest" principle, whereby uncovered positions in sovereign CDS transactions are generally not permitted.[141] To address the

[136] EMIR, art. 8.

[137] J. Grant, "Quick View: UK Gets Best of Compromise on EMIR," *Financial Times*, October 4, 2011 (online: ft.com).

[138] European Commission, *Proposal for a Regulation on Short Selling.*

[139] The General Approach text adopted by ECOFIN (May 17, 2011) reflected this view.

[140] ECON, *Report on the Proposal for a Regulation on Short Selling and Certain Aspects of Credit Default Swaps* (A7–0055/2011, Rapporteur: Pascal Canfin).

[141] Regulation (EU) No. 236/2012 on Short Selling and Certain Aspects of Credit Default Swaps [2012] OJ L(86/1), art. 14(1).

concerns voiced by the UK and others, national competent authorities are permitted to lift the restrictions for up to twelve months where their sovereign debt market is not functioning properly and the restrictions may be having a negative impact on the CDS market, but they must notify other authorities and obtain an opinion from ESMA before doing so.[142] In spite of the concession, the outcome has been characterized as a "huge blow" to the UK.[143] (Arguably, however, the battle on the issue may be won in another way, since the International Swaps and Derivatives Association's indications during 2011–12 that a restructuring of Greek government debt may not be regarded as a "credit event" triggering default on relevant CDSs has cast some doubt on the commercial value of those instruments.)[144]

As is clear from Niamh Moloney's analysis in Chapter 2 of this book, EMIR and the Short Selling Regulation are but first steps towards extending the EU regulatory perimeter around derivatives and other complex financial products. The sub-field can thus be expected to continue to be a fertile battleground for competing positions. The outcomes could help to establish whether fears about the UK's declining influence over EU regulatory policy design have real substance.

"Too-big-to-fail"

Significant differences of view between Member States have also emerged in relation to reforms aimed at addressing the "too-big-to-fail" problem. The UK intends to require its banks to ring-fence their retail operations from other activities so as to address the risk of cross-subsidization between government-protected retail deposit-taking business and other activities, and also to oblige retail banks and banking groups to hold more capital than required by Basel III international standards.[145] This

[142] Ibid., art. 14(2).

[143] H. Ebrahimi, "Blow to UK as EU Bans Sovereign CDS," *The Daily Telegraph*, October 19, 2011, 1.

[144] ISDA, *Greek Sovereign Debt Q&A – Update* (July 25, 2011, online: www.mondovisione.com/media-and-resources/news/isda-greek-sovereign-debt-qanda-update/).

[145] Independent Commission on Banking (ICB), *Interim Report: Consultation on Reform Options* (London: ICB, April 2011); ICB, *Final Report: Recommendations* (London: ICB, September 2011). The ICB (also known as the Vickers Commission) proposed that large UK retail banks should hold common equity capital of at least 10 percent of risk-weighted assets. The ICB also proposed that large UK bank groups should be required to hold bail in bonds and other instruments raising their overall primary-loss absorbing capacity to at least 17–20 percent. The Government has accepted these proposals: HM Treasury and Department for Business, *Banking Reform: Delivering Stability and Supporting a Sustainable Economy* (Cm 8356, June 2012).

enthusiasm for ring-fencing and permanent capital surcharges is not prevalent elsewhere in Europe (although as a response to the euro area sovereign debt crisis the European Banking Authority (EBA) has recommended banks to build up a temporary capital buffer against sovereign debt exposures and to establish a buffer such that the Core Tier 1 capital ratio should reach nine percent by June 2012).[146] The "universal" banking model adopted by the big "national champions," such as BNP Paribas, Société Générale and Deutsche Bank, prevails in Continental Europe and, overall, there appears to be little support in Member States for tampering with it. On the contrary, the merits of a diversified universal approach have been stoutly defended.[147] Jacques de Larosière, a former managing director of the IMF and governor of the Banque de France, and one of the most respected senior figures in EU financial services post-crisis policy-making circles, has articulated a widely-held view in contending that "this model is well suited to the way the European economy is financed: almost three-quarters through bank intermediation," that it has demonstrated its value by being "resilient through the crisis," and should not therefore be penalized by post-crisis reforms.[148]

Under Basel III the common equity requirement is 7 percent (4.5 percent Tier 1 common equity and 2.5 percent common equity capital conservation buffer). In addition, under Basel standards, global systemically important banks (G-SIBs) will be required to hold additional common equity Tier 1 capital of 1–2.5 percent depending on their systemic importance: Basel Committee, *Global Systemically Important Banks: Assessment Methodology and the Additional Loss Absorbency Requirements* (Basel: BCBS, November, 2011). There is provision for the G-SIB surcharge to go up to 3.5 percent, but the top bucket is to be left open initially to disincentivize the further growth of the biggest G-SIBs. Thus a large UK retail bank will be required to hold slightly more common equity than even the largest G-SIBs.

146 EBA Recommendation on the Creation and Supervisory Oversight of Temporary Capital Buffers to Restore Market Confidence (EBA/REC/2011/1). The groundwork for this Recommendation was laid at ECOFIN Council and European Council meetings in October–November 2011 that agreed on bank recapitalization and funding, including the possibility of this being funded from EFSF loans if necessary.

147 P. Jenkins, "SocGen Rules Out Basel Rights Issue," *Financial Times*, November 4, 2010, 19 (quoting Frédéric Oudéa, SocGen CEO on the soundness of its universal banking model); J. Wilson, "Deutsche Bank Takes Control of Postbank," *Financial Times*, November 27, 2010, 9 (quoting Anshu Jain, Deutsche's investment bank head, welcoming the acquisition of Postbank as strengthening the universal banking model and demonstrating the likelihood of it prevailing over "pure play" investment banking). For an overview of the scholarly debate: I. Ötker-Robe, A. Narain, A. Ilyina and J. Surti, *The Too-Important-to-Fail Conundrum* (Washington DC: IMF, SDN/11/12), pp. 23–4.

148 J. de Larosière, "Don't Punish the Banks that Performed Best," *Financial Times*, March 4, 2011, 9.

These days, the leading UK banks, such as Barclays and HSBC, are also universal banks. Why, then, is the model under scrutiny in the UK in a way that it is not elsewhere in most of Continental Europe?[149] Institutional interdependencies that are at the heart of the varieties of capitalism approach to understanding comparative capitalism may go some way towards helping to explain this divergence. Historical trajectories have been significantly different, in that universal banking is deeply embedded in Continental European national political economies,[150] but has a much shorter track record in the UK, having flourished only after the financial market "Big Bang" of the 1980s, which ended restrictions on the ownership of stockbroking firms and thus facilitated the merger of commercial and investment banking businesses.[151] Universal banking's relatively shallow roots in the UK could be a factor in understanding political support for alternative models.[152] Moreover, universal banks in the UK operate on a vast scale in a market-based financial system, with London serving as the epicenter of many segments of global activity. As such, they are in a different position from their European counterparts, which, in spite of the growth of capital markets in recent years, are still operating within predominantly bank-based financial systems. Most pertinently of all, the UK is particularly exposed to the problem of gigantism – that is, by international standards UK banking is highly concentrated, with only four large banking groups,[153] which have very large balance sheets relative to national gross domestic product (GDP).[154] The fact that at the time when it had to be bailed out by the UK government the Royal Bank of Scotland's total assets equalled approximately the UK's GDP, whereas Citigroup's total

149 But the merits of structural reform are gaining ground in Switzerland, a country that, like the UK, has a small number of super-size banks. The rogue trading scandal that hit UBS in September 2011 and which could cost it up to $2.3bn has galvanized the Swiss debate.

150 Attributing Continental European mistrust of capital markets to the Mississippi Bubble of the early eighteenth century: Allen and Gale, *Comparing Financial Systems*, p. 310.

151 J. Lynton Jones, "Big Bang and the Stock Exchange," *Company Lawyer*, 7 (1986), 99–103.

152 The complicated political trade-offs that were involved in the setting up of a coalition government are worth noting here. Breaking up the banks (i.e. establishing a clear separation between low-risk retail banking and high-risk investment banking) was included in the manifesto of the Liberal Democrat Party (Lib Dems) for the 2010 election. It is open to question whether there would have been so much of a political tailwind behind proposals for structural reform if the Conservative Party had won an overall majority in 2010 and not been obliged to form a coalition government with the Lib Dems.

153 ICB, *Interim Report*, pp. 27–49.

154 Ibid., p. 22.

assets amounted to sixteen percent of US GDP at the time of its bailout, has become the classic illustration of the concerns about size and concentration in the UK banking sector.[155]

For the purposes of EU financial services regulation, the "battleground" here concerns the proposed imposition of mandatory capital surcharges. Structural separation in itself is not an issue, because EU law does not directly dictate the structure of banking groups. The difficulties arise because the UK also wants to impose capital requirements that will exceed the levels that are to be set at EU level. Historically, national policy choices to go beyond EU standards (often referred to as "gold-plating") used to be hemmed in by commercial considerations about international competitiveness, but they were not problematic from a legal viewpoint because of the "minimum harmonization" character of EU requirements. However, this flexibility is giving way to a more rigid "maximum harmonization" approach that is based, in part, on the recognition at EU level that uncoordinated moves to strengthen stability in one Member State could be at the expense of other Member States. Pertinently, this approach is being adopted with respect to the EU's implementation of Basel III capital requirements.[156]

The UK's demands to be allowed to gold-plate EU standards on capital appear to be something of a volte-face, given its pronounced support for a single rulebook in banking in earlier stages of the post-crisis policy formation process. However, it is fair to say that the concept of a "single rulebook" is one whose meaning has not been precisely delineated in the European discourse, and it is likely that many users of the phrase never intended it to imply the complete ousting of national discretions.[157] Jonathan Faull, Director General, European Commission has helpfully indicated that such a far-reaching effect is not intended:

155 Ibid., pp. 23–4.

156 European Commission, *Proposal for a Regulation on Prudential Requirements for Credit Institutions and Investment Firms* (COM(2011) 452), pp. 10–11. The proposed Regulation is referred to hereinafter as CRD IV Regulation (proposed). But maximum harmonization is not being applied universally – see, e.g., Directive 2009/65/EC (UCITS IV) [2009] OJ L302/32, recital 15 and art. 1(7) (as a general rule Member States can establish stricter rules than those laid down in the Directive).

157 E. Wymeersch, "Europe's New Financial Regulatory Bodies," *Journal of Corporate Law Studies*, 11 (2011) 443–62, 453–4 describes the European rulebook as an "interesting captive slogan," but notes that it does not respond to a precise legal definition.

> A single rule book does not mean full harmonisation of all rules. It entails a harmonised core set of standards, applied in a harmonised manner throughout the EU by all supervisors. It will not replace supervisors' exercise of judgment and force them into a one size fits all approach. It is a key lesson from the crisis that supervisors need to apply judgment, assess each bank's business model and take tailor-made measures.[158]

A good case can be made for the UK to be allowed room for maneuver at the domestic level with respect to capital requirements because of the country-specific particularities of the size and nature of its banking sector. The IMF has been supportive of UK efforts in this regard, arguing that the stability and efficiency of the UK financial sector is a global public good, requiring the highest quality supervision and regulation, and against the constraint of rigid EU rules. However, achieving this in a way that is compatible with the EU maximum harmonization policy agenda has not been straightforward. An inelegant compromise has been thrashed out in Council, whereby Member States can impose, for up to two years (extendable), stricter prudential requirements for domestically authorized financial institutions, subject to being overruled by the Council and may apply systemic risk buffers of up to 3 or 5 percent, without having to seek prior Commission approval, and even higher buffers with prior Commission authorization. However, striking this deal involved a quite contentious process and European Parliament approval has still to be secured.[159] The process of negotiation was probably not smoothed by the inclusion of freedom to impose domestic capital surcharge on the list of matters that the UK presented to other EU Member States in December 2011 as preconditions to its agreement to participate in an EU Treaty revision to resolve the euro area sovereign debt crisis. The tensions between Member States on these issues are considerable. Viewed through a lens of cynicism, opposition to the UK's demands to be allowed the flexibility to impose higher standards could be interpreted as a stance that is intended to shield "domestic champions" from market pressure to meet the higher capital standards that the UK wishes to impose.

[158] Faull, *Some Legal Challenges.*

[159] CRD IV Regulation (proposed); European Commission, *Proposal for a Directive on the Access to the Activity of Credit Institutions and the Prudential Supervision of Credit Institutions and Investment Firms etc* (COM(2011) 453), Title VII, ch. 2, ss. III–IV (supervisory review and supervisory measures); Title VII, ch. 4 (capital buffers). The proposed Directive is referred to hereinafter as CRD IV Directive (proposed). The ECOFIN general approach on CRD IV Regulation (proposed) and CRD IV Directive (proposed) was agreed May 15, 2012.

Corporate governance

An area where important pronounced differences in national political economies look especially likely to impede the EU standardization/centralization juggernaut is in the space where financial market law and corporate law overlap, that is, in the regulation of listed companies. There is now no doubt that regulatory competence for the transparency framework applicable to listed companies has shifted to EU level, but regulatory control of matters relating to the internal management and control of companies is a much more sensitive area. These delicacies can be traced back to the fact that despite much talk of convergence towards the "outsider" Anglo-American model, national corporate governance systems of EU Member States remain heterogeneous.[160] The principal–agent problems that are at the heart of corporate governance still take on a different character from country to country because of differences in corporate ownership patterns. Germany's two-tier board and co-determination system continue to make its approach especially distinctive. The persistence of important variations in systems of capital despite forces of convergence and globalization help to explain why past EU attempts to standardize corporate governance from the top down have faltered (certainly when compared to the strides made with respect to harmonizing banking, securities and insurance market regulation). There are no signs that the financial crisis has eroded these differences or made Member States less keen to preserve them. Indeed, if anything, the example of Italy in the aftermath of the crisis repealing an anti-frustration rule in its domestic takeover law that had been modeled on the Takeover Directive in order to enable Italian companies better to protect themselves against foreign bidders, suggests a trend in the opposite direction.[161] Moreover, the resurgence of state ownership of large stakes in banks has reinvigorated the national dimension of corporate ownership in the financial sector.

[160] The significance of path dependencies in national corporate governance systems is well known: L.A. Bebchuk and M.J. Roe, "A Theory of Path Dependence in Corporate Governance and Ownership," *Stanford Law Review*, 52 (1999), 127–70. Predictions of convergence towards a standard model of the corporation (H. Hansmann and R. Kraakman, "The End of History for Corporate Law," *Georgetown Law Journal*, 89 (2001), 439–68) have yet to come good.

[161] This example is taken from K.J. Hopt, "Comparative Corporate Governance: The State of the Art and International Regulation," *American Journal of Comparative Law*, 59 (2011), 1–73, 18.

Whilst it is apparent from history that crisis and scandal can create opportunities for financial services law to subsume within its ever-expanding boundaries some matters that may traditionally have been regarded as being within the domain of company law – a phenomenon that we have seen again recently in that it has become firmly established as a result of the financial crisis that the ambit of prudential regulation extends far into the internal corporate governance of financial firms[162] – opportunistic attempts to hitch an across-the-board listed company corporate governance harmonization agenda onto financial-sector developments will probably struggle, at least in the immediate future, to overcome very vigorous active opposition from Member States. Unlike previous examples in this section, here there remain very many different interests and it is not a case of a small number of Member States (usually including the UK) being out of line with the rest. The EU Internal Market Commissioner, Michel Barnier, has acknowledged the continuing propensity of Member States to fight tooth and nail to sustain national corporate traditions.[163] Whilst further pan-European standardization of corporate governance is on the policy agenda,[164] and a disturbingly wide range of possible measures has been outlined (including an EU legal limit on the number of mandates held by a non-executive director, more mandatory rules with respect to executive remuneration, a role for EU law in promoting more effective monitoring of asset managers by institutional investors, requirements in EU law with respect to the independence of proxy advisers, more legal protection for minority shareholders and reinforced supervisory oversight of corporate governance comply or explain statements)[165] many constellations of interests can be expected to work hard to resist far-reaching reform that could undermine national traditions.

Financial services supervision

On the surface, the organization of financial market supervision is another potential continuing major "battleground" for the Member

[162] P.O. Mülbert, "Corporate Governance of Banks after the Financial Crisis – Theory, Evidence, Reforms," ECGI Law Working Paper No. 130/2009 (April 2010, online: http://ssrn.com/abstract=1448118).

[163] M. Barnier, "Repenser le Droit des Sociétés" (speech, May 16, 2011, online: http://ec.europa.eu/commission_2010–2014/barnier/docs/speeches/20110516/s11_fr.pdf).

[164] European Commission, *The EU Corporate Governance Framework* (COM(2011) 164).

[165] Ibid.; European Commission, *Corporate Governance in Financial Institutions and Remuneration Policies* (COM(2010) 284); European Commission, *Proposal for a Directive on the access to the activity of credit institutions and the prudential supervision of credit institutions and investment firms* (COM(2011) 453).

States. The EU committees of supervisors that were established during the FSAP phase have been upgraded to EU bodies with legal personality – ESMA for securities, the EBA for banking and the European Insurance and Occupational Pensions Authority (EIOPA) for insurance (collectively the European Supervisory Authorities, or ESAs) – and a new EU systemic risk oversight body – the European Systemic Risk Board (ESRB) – has been put in place as well.[166] The new ESAs have certain enhanced powers, including the right in limited circumstances to override national supervisors in their interpretation of EU law and to impose binding decisions to resolve cross-border supervisory disputes.[167] However, for the most part direct, market-facing supervision remains a Member State responsibility and cross-border issues are managed through a home/host allocation of responsibilities and supervisory colleges, which the ESAs help to coordinate.[168] Obligations on national supervisors to consider the impact of their decisions on the stability of other Member States' financial systems are being spelt out.[169]

The UK and Germany have been and remain particularly strong supporters of the principle of Member State control over direct supervision, and maintained this view throughout the negotiations on the establishment of the ESAs. Their hand in the negotiations was strengthened by the recent experience of having to use taxpayers' money to rescue failing financial institutions because "he who pays the piper calls the tune" logic naturally pointed towards continuing to tie supervision firmly to national regimes. The preservation of sovereignty was also a particularly sensitive issue for those newer Member States that still had the memory of being under Soviet rule. Member States' fiscal autonomy is specifically protected in the legal frameworks governing

[166] Regulation (EU) No. 1092/2010 on European Union Macro-prudential Oversight of the Financial System and Establishing a European Systemic Risk Board, [2010] OJ L331/1 (ESRB Regulation). On the ESAs in general: E. Ferran, "Understanding the New Institutional Architecture of EU Financial Market Supervision" in E. Wymeersch, K.J. Hopt and G. Ferrarini, *Financial Regulation and Supervision: A Post-crisis Analysis* (Oxford University Press, 2012); N. Moloney, "Reform or Revolution? The Financial Crisis, EU Financial Markets Law and the European Securities and Markets Authority," *International and Comparative Law Quarterly*, 60 (2011), 521–33.

[167] e.g., ESMA Regulation, arts. 17–20.

[168] The framework for the operation of cross-border supervision has been reinforced: Directive 2009/111/EC amending Directives 2006/48/EC, 2006/49/EC and 2007/64/EC as regards banks affiliated to central institutions, certain own funds items, large exposures, supervisory arrangements, and crisis management, [2009] L302/97 (CRD II).

[169] CRD IV Directive (proposed), arts. 7–8.

the new ESAs: the new powers at EU level cannot extend to directing Member States as to how to spend public funds.[170]

France, however, has adopted a stance that is more supportive of equipping the ESAs with executive power. The resulting divergence of views was evident, for example, in the controversy over the inclusion of third country passports in the AIFMD, mentioned earlier. There may be more to this apparent cleavage between Member States than meets the eye – Buckley and Howarth have suggested that the best interpretation of ostensible French support for integrated EU supervision of financial services could be that it is a stance that has relied on the knowledge that any radical departure from existing nationally-based supervisory arrangements would be vetoed by the UK and, possibly, Germany[171] – but, to the extent that public pronouncements can be taken at face value, France has been noticeably less reticent than other major Member States about expansion of the ESAs' role. In promoting, at least ostensibly, the assumption of direct supervisory responsibilities by the ESAs, France has taken a position that also commands considerable support in the European Parliament (see Part IV below). It is also, broadly speaking, in line with the preferences of the European Commission (but for a more nuanced assessment of the Commission's stance, see Part III below).

Notwithstanding the coalition of supporters for further centralization, the seemingly obvious conclusion to draw from Germany and the UK continuing to find common ground in being broadly disinclined to favor a large-scale transfer of supervisory power from their national supervisory authorities to the ESAs is that it must be quite unlikely to happen. Moreover, those who object on political grounds can call in formidable reinforcement. As discussed further in Part III below, there are obstacles in European law to equipping the ESAs with full-blown supervisory powers. Therefore this is one area where legal constraints on centralization still matter.[172] The issue is complicated as a matter of law because it touches upon constitutional and institutional-balance sensitivities concerning "downwards" delegation of powers entrusted by EU treaties to the Commission and also upon questions about the mechanism for the "upwards" assignment of

170 ESMA Regulation, art. 38.

171 Buckley and Howarth, "Internal Market: Gesture Politics?," 127.

172 One reason for the ECB figuring prominently in banking union proposals as the potential bank supervisor is that this possibility is already envisaged by TFEU, art. 127(b), putting the ECB outside the constitutional restrictions that apply to the ESAs.

6

supervisory powers held by Member States. The matter is also beset by formidable practical challenges concerning the equipping of EU authorities with sufficient resources to be able to perform a wide range of supervisory tasks. There are concerns about ensuring robust mechanisms of accountability. There are also issues of principle about the relative merits of "close to the ground," i.e. locally-based, supervision and a centralized approach. Taking all of these factors together, national supervisors look relatively secure, although the recent focus on the ECB's potential to act as a prudential supervisor in a banking union shows that nothing can be ruled out.

There are already tangible signs that the power of the ESAs to intervene directly in markets is growing in spite of the various constraints. ESMA, in particular, is starting to accumulate direct supervisory powers. Making ESMA directly responsible for the oversight of rating agencies was a breakthrough decision[173] and although this was not meant to set a precedent,[174] experience has quickly demonstrated that it has opened an important door. Under EMIR, ESMA will assume direct responsibility for the registration and surveillance of trade repositories[175] and it will also become the single entry point for third country clearing houses.[176] EMIR will also give ESMA an important (though not formally decisive) role, in consultation with the ESRB, in determining which derivatives contracts should be subject to mandatory clearing through a central counterparty.[177] It will also have a significant role in decisions by a national competent authority to authorize a clearing house where there is disagreement among the college of supervisors on this issue.[178] Under the Short Selling Regulation, ESMA has been given not only a significant coordinating role concerning measures with respect to short selling by national competent authorities,[179] but also direct power itself to restrict or prohibit short selling in limited

[173] Regulation (EU) No. 513/2011, amending the CRA Regulation.

[174] Regulation (EU) No. 513/2011, rec. 22. [175] EMIR, arts. 55–74.

[176] EMIR, art. 25.

[177] EMIR, art. 5. ESMA will prepare the draft implementing technical standards that determine the classes of derivatives that are subject to the clearing obligation but, in accordance with normal procedures for implementing technical standards (see Part III below), formal adoption is the responsibility of the Commission. Under the Commission's original proposal (COM(2010) 484), ESMA itself would have been responsible for making the decisions concerning eligibility for the clearing obligation. This was resisted by some Member States on *Meroni* grounds (see n. 276 below).

[178] EMIR, arts. 17–21. [179] Short Selling Regulation, art. 27.

circumstances.[180] The possibility of ESMA playing a key role in the future in determining when a derivative would be sufficiently liquid to be traded on organized platforms has been raised.[181] As discussed further in Niamh Moloney's chapter in this book, a potential role for ESMA in an EU-wide regime for the banning of products or their distribution is also under active consideration.[182]

How can all of this be happening given the various political, legal and practical factors that might be expected to operate as a brake? Recent history suggests that we should not be too surprised by this turn of events. The pre-crisis EU supervisory coordinating committees grew significantly from quite modest foundations, an incremental process that sometimes involved finding ingenious solutions to apparent technical and practical problems with respect to the scope of their powers.[183] Their successors appear to be on the same path. In spite of certain Member States maintaining as their default position opposition to the general principle of pan-EU conduct of supervision, there are various reasons why it is not implausible to envisage a step-by-step accretion of considerable supervisory power to ESMA and its sister authorities.

Even Member States that do not want the position of their national authorities to be undermined may nevertheless see certain benefits to themselves in promoting the development of the ESAs. The ESAs are hybrid creatures embodying both intergovernmental (the heads of the national supervisors make up the ESAs' Boards of Supervisors, which are in overall charge of the authorities' decision-making apparatus)[184] and supranational (e.g. with respect to funding arrangements,[185] lines of accountability[186] and review mechanisms,[187] which involve the Commission, the European Parliament and the Court of Auditors) aspects. This hybridism is reflected in their designation as "authorities" rather than as EU "agencies."[188] It is too early to say exactly how they will

[180] Short Selling Regulation, art. 28. The conferral of this power on ESMA raises *Meroni* issues, in that it could be said that its exercise must inevitably involve the exercise of a wide discretionary power involving policy choices. The UK has commenced a test case in the European Court on the point.

[181] European Commission, *Review of the Markets in Financial Instruments Directive (MiFID)* (Public Consultation, December 8, 2010), pp. 12–13; European Commission, *Proposal for a Regulation on Markets in Financial Instruments* (COM(2011) 652) (MiFIR) art. 26.

[182] MiFIR, art. 31. [183] Ferran, "Understanding the Institutional Architecture."

[184] ESMA Regulation, arts. 40–4. [185] ESMA Regulation, arts. 62–6.

[186] ESMA Regulation, art. 3. [187] ESMA Regulation, art. 81.

[188] Wymeersch, "Europe's New Financial Regulatory Bodies."

function in practice – although they are designed to be independent autonomous actors under the leadership of full-time Chairpersons[189] and Executive Directors[190] and within a legal framework that both requires and protects impartiality and independence,[191] – they could descend in effect into operating as either a vehicle for the pan-EU promotion of the views of the most powerful Member States or as little more than a technocratic arm of the European Commission. The potential for key Member States to regard them as useful mechanisms for advancing their own interests is certainly present. Moreover, those interests may often align with those of the Commission itself – for instance, where the credibility of the entire system risks being undermined by poor standards of supervision in particular Member States, shortcomings that the Commission itself was unable to target effectively because of intense pressure on its own thinly-spread enforcement capabilities and resources. It is undoubtedly possible to envisage the ESAs and the competent authorities of the Member States having different and mutually supportive roles. That Member States perceive that being in close touch with the ESAs is something of considerable value to their own interests is one way of interpreting the UK government's failed attempt in the December 2011 euro area rescue discussions to obtain a guarantee that the EBA would remain permanently physically located in London.

In particular circumstances there may be relatively little hostility to a proposed expansion of the ESAs' powers – for instance where, as was the case in relation to rating agencies, there are no major domestic "champions" over which governments want to maintain their own protective control – or such hostility as there is may be insufficiently widely shared for an effective blocking coalition to be formed. Given the nature of EU lawmaking, with bargaining between Member States over unrelated matters being a not uncommon part of the process, an accretion of power to the center could also occur as a result of compromise deals. Efficiencies resulting from dealing with particular matters centrally could also move things in that direction. Overall, the cumulative effects, intended and unintended, of decisions made on specific matters could snowball in such a way as to give centralizing forces an unstoppable momentum.

Whilst Member States can be expected to resist any form of centralization that openly threatens fiscal autonomy, there are many areas

[189] ESMA Regulation, art. 48. [190] ESMA Regulation, art. 51.
[191] ESMA Regulation, arts. 1, 42, 46, 49 and 52.

of financial market activity where a need to call upon public funds to preserve systemic stability may be such a remote possibility that it can be safely discounted. Indeed, an unintended consequence of the stress placed on the fiscal safeguard by certain Member States may be that it could allow proponents of centralization to argue that it is only in areas where there is a real likelihood of a potential need for fiscal support that Member State supervision is necessary. Some seeds to this effect are already being planted.[192] If ongoing EU efforts to establish bank resolution funds and better resolution mechanisms in order to reduce the risk of public funds having to be called upon to shore-up financial institutions succeed (but this is a big "if," as Part III below explains), it is conceivable that over time the "no-go" area policed by the fiscal safeguard provisions could become increasingly narrow, notwithstanding its symbolic importance.

Considerations relating to the style and content of the rulebook could also add to the arguments for further centralization of supervisory responsibilities at the EU level. Without reopening here an extensive and perhaps somewhat exhausted debate about the relative merits of principles and rules in financial regulation,[193] it is relevant to note the possibility of EU policymakers being inhibited from opting for open-textured standards that require the exercise of supervisory judgment for fear that regulation in this form could be applied inconsistently by national supervisors. A strong urge to use the rulebook to stamp out supervisory inconsistency would be structurally neat, but it would be likely to lead to benign outcomes only under certain demanding conditions (if the ESAs are able to draft clear and more economically literate rules than regulation in any country tends to be, and the rules are capable of being amended (including reduced) in the light of experience); this is unlikely. A more likely outcome could be an ever-more prescriptive and unwieldy rulebook that eventually becomes unworkable. In that event, reducing supervisory fragmentation through centralization could become an increasingly appealing solution. It is, after all, imperative to leave room within financial regulatory systems for supervisors to exercise judgment; indeed, many now regard the need for

[192] European Commission, *Proposal for a Regulation on OTC Derivatives*, p. 11.

[193] L. Cunningham, "A Prescription to Retire the Rhetoric of 'Principles-Based Systems' in Corporate Law, Securities Regulation, and Accounting," *Vanderbilt Law Review*, 60 (2007), 1411–93.

judgment-led supervision as one of the most important lessons to be learnt from the events of recent years.[194]

Taken in the round, therefore, there are some difficulties in regarding the architecture of EU financial services supervision as a matter on which active opposition from Member States for the foreseeable future will continue to be an effective bar to meaningful further centralization. To be clear, it is, of course, extremely hard to envisage circumstances in which major Member States such as the UK or Germany would be happy to cede full control over financial services supervision to central EU authorities if confronted by the issue head-on. However, that the decisions made in the aftermath of the crisis could turn out to have opened the door to incremental but still fairly rapid progression towards a level of centralization that is not to their liking is not a wholly fanciful scenario. The new ESAs appear keen to flex their muscles and it looks likely that the European Parliament and, at least to some extent, the Commission, will encourage their expansionist tendencies. Moreover, the big cross-border financial firms can be expected to back moves towards more streamlined supervision, since this would allow them to rationalize the operation and management of their multi-jurisdictional compliance functions (although it is not always clear whether this support is for EU-level supervision as opposed to an enhanced role for the coordinating supervisor among the Member State competent authorities).

Evaluation

It has been seen that the persistence of significant differences in the national economies of the Member States continues to operate as a de facto brake on EU financial services regulation. This brake is still quite powerful in areas such as corporate governance, where Member States' national set-ups are still too disparate for detailed top-down standardization to be a serious threat. However, in some other areas its impact as a restraining device is waning. Battles can end in stalemate or, perhaps less pejoratively, in compromise, which in EU regulatory terms implies

[194] e.g., this view is a central part of the thinking that has underpinned the post-crisis reform of financial regulation in the UK: E. Ferran, "The New Mandate for the Supervision of Financial Services Conduct," *Current Legal Problems*, 64 (2012), (forthcoming). It is a view that is also influential at EU level, as the quotation from Jonathan Faull in this chapter (text adjacent to n. 158) indicates.

relatively modest levels of harmonization that leave plenty of room for Member States to adapt arrangements to suit their local circumstances. But they can also produce clear winners and losers. The EU's regulatory response to the turmoil in the financial markets has provided various examples of battles being won and lost, with the UK, in particular, having to adjust to finding itself more often on the losing side. This could be a harbinger of things to come: if euro area Member State economies move closer together in the coming years, the UK and other peripheral Member States will likely face the prospect of finding it increasingly hard to put their imprint on financial services regulatory policy design.

Moreover, it should not be overlooked that the weapons available to Member States to fight these battles are inevitably affected by the legacy effects of their past decisions. During the 1990s and 2000s pre-crises, deepening economic interdependence fostered by the increasingly transnational nature of the finance industry affected Member States' perceptions of their national interests in ways which resulted in them progressively relaxing their direct grip on the regulation of financial services activity in favor of a centralized approach. From today's perspective we can see that decisions during this era to expand Union competences with respect to financial services regulation relative to Member State competences have had cumulative effects, some of which were probably not anticipated. Many miscalculations were made, for instance in determining national interests with special reference to the interests of big finance, in relying on philosophies that overestimated the disciplining effects of markets, and in failing to anticipate fluctuations over time in the degree of influence over the EU agenda that any individual Member State could hope to exert. When the economic and political weather changed as a result of the global financial crisis, the negative implications of past decisions became manifest, but it was also apparent that the practical options for addressing the problems were framed by the institutions and processes that had evolved from earlier choices. Member States found themselves deeply enmeshed politically, legally and economically in a dense supranational system that was malfunctioning and on which they were, in effect, condemned to work closely together to fix from within.

History is likely to repeat itself. In the immediate aftermath of the global financial crisis, Member States coalesced around more Europe, and collectively agreed upon reforms that give much more emphasis to the need for official protections and safeguards at EU level to counteract the side-effects of integration. Important decisions that were taken on a short-term basis at an extraordinary time, when the established canons of finance theory had been shaken to the core and when political resistance to EU regulatory interference in financial markets had weakened considerably, can be expected to have significant long-term consequences, giving rise to new institutions and processes that take on a life of their own. The rapid development of the ESAs is already an early sign of this phenomenon at work. Past miscalculations that do not accord with shifting preferences among the Member States' political elites can once again be expected to emerge. Evidence of this is also already appearing. The UK – which has experienced a change of government in the period since the beginning of the global financial crisis, has recovered confidence as the morphing of the global financial crisis into the euro area sovereign debt crisis has discredited efforts to pin the blame for all economic woes on the excesses of Anglo-American capitalism, and has come to realize that the detailed ramifications of more Europe may not always be a good fit with its domestic political economy – is evincing clear signs of having second thoughts. However, it is also having to face up to the realization that barring an unraveling of deep political and legal commitments to the single market (a scenario that is no longer completely fanciful but still looks unlikely), it is effectively "trapped" by the legacy of past decisions, and that its options for dealing with any resulting discomfort are quite constrained.

III: Supranationalism – the crises and the Commission

Introduction

EU financial services regulation had acquired a significant supranational component long before the global financial crisis. The Commission was overseeing a rulebook that penetrated far, in terms of both breadth and depth. A rudimentary pan-European supervisory architecture was in place. The financial crisis and later events have accelerated these trends to the point where even though the logical and intellectually pure model – an entirely made-in-Europe rulebook supported by a pan-European system of supervision and enforcement – is still some way off, it is no longer possible to dismiss this scenario as being too far-fetched to deserve serious attention. Part II examined this evolutionary process from an intergovernmental perspective. It looked at the way in which individual Member States can lose out to each other in battles for influence over regulatory design. There is another potential battleground, namely, the position of the Member States collectively vis-à-vis the Commission. This is the focus of this Part of the chapter.

The development of an ever-more dense and complex supranational regulatory system presents a considerable challenge for the Member States collectively, in that they are bound to find it impossible to keep tabs on the system on a day-to-day basis, not least because at national level they will see only part of the overall picture. There is every likelihood that they will find themselves increasingly at a disadvantage in this respect to the European Commission, which as principal overseer of the system and its day-to-day controller, is in a position to be able to exploit informational advantages, access to expert policy networks, and extensive bureaucratic competencies in order to mold the detailed design of the system in an entrepreneurial fashion to its own institutional preferences. Moreover, the Commission, as the engineer of integration and the central co-coordinator of policy initiatives, is ideally located to play the Member States off against each other. On issues that it cares deeply enough about to promote heavily even in spite of significant opposition from certain Member States, with the organization of financial services supervision being the obvious example, the Commission could achieve a great deal by putting forward carefully crafted innovations that are seemingly modest and incremental when looked at in isolation or on a short-term basis but which, in the longer run, turn out to have transformative effect. The relationship between the Commission and the Member States and the balance of power between them is also likely to be affected in subtle but important ways by arrangements for the rescue of the euro, which envisage the Commission playing a strengthened role in the oversight of national budgets and in the imposition of sanctions for excessive budget deficits.[195]

The Commission in the pre-crisis era

British-style liberalism was perceived to be the predominant ideology of the European Commission with respect to financial services regulation in the period leading up to the global financial crisis.[196] In part, this can

[195] Intergovernmental Treaty on Stability, Coordination and Governance in the Economic and Monetary Union, March 2, 2012.

[196] Quaglia, "Completing the Single Market in Financial Services."

be understood as the Commission having been influenced by the views that were in the ascendancy at that time among Member States. The European Council's Lisbon Agenda for a world-leading competitive, dynamic, knowledge-based economy, which was the defining statement of EU priorities of the period, espoused competition, liberalization and innovation, sentiments that were very much in tune with contemporary UK domestic policy.[197] However, the Commission's role was not one of simply acting as a mouthpiece for the then dominant Member States. The pro-market, competitiveness-promoting orientation of the Commission in the mid-2000s also appeared to be closely in line with the personal preferences of the then Internal Market Commissioner, Charlie McCreevy (in office between 2004 and 2009), and Commission President, José Manuel Barroso (in office from 2004, re-elected in 2009 for a further five-year term).

Detailed review of the Commission's track record in financial services regulation in this period, which was, it should be recalled, the lull immediately after the conclusion of a spell of regulatory intensity, does not fully support claims about a strong ideological distaste for the imposition of financial services regulation. For instance, in the areas of deposit guarantees, on which the Commission reported in 2006, although it ultimately opted for self-regulatory improvements only, its Communication indicated that it had serious misgivings about shortcomings in the existing arrangements, and its tone suggested that the urge to go further was being held in check not by rampant ideology, but by the evidence-based, cost–benefit analysis disciplines of "better regulation."[198] The Communication included a prescient warning that failure to keep pace with the increased degree of cross-border financial integration in Europe could ultimately prove very costly in the longer term, as the lack of standardized rules could contribute to the inability of the supervisory safety net to function adequately in a cross-border crisis situation. It noted that "the costs to the economy and the undermining

[197] European Council, *Presidency Conclusions*, March 23/24, 2000.

[198] European Commission. *Communication concerning the review of Directive 94/19/EC on deposit guarantee schemes* (COM(2006) 729). Generally on the operation of deposit guarantee systems in the EU: J. Cariboni, E. Joossens and A. Uboldi, "The Promptness of European Deposit Protection Schemes to Face Banking Failures," *Journal of Banking Regulation*, 11 (2010), 191–209. On the rise of self-regulation and other new modes of governance across Commission and EU policy in general during the 2000s (dubbed integration without law): R. van Gestel and H.W. Mickling, "Revitalizing Doctrinal Legal Research in Europe: What About Methodology?," EUI Working Papers Law 2011/05.

of confidence in the single financial market could ultimately prove far higher than the level of investment needed to ensure satisfactory functioning of the pan-EU safety net."[199]

The European Parliament supported the Commission's recommendation for self-regulatory improvements with respect to deposit insurance.[200] However, high-profile disagreements between the Commission and the Parliament on reliance on industry self-regulation in other areas, such as hedge funds and private equity funds, helped to solidify the impression that the Commission was ideologically predisposed towards market-friendly solutions.

The impact of the global financial crisis: the first phase of the response

Given the background, the Commission could not avoid being badly tainted when the global financial crisis blew up. However, for some observers it compounded its difficulties by appearing to be slow and faltering in its initial response on certain issues, a stance that was linked not only to a loss of confidence resulting from ideological setbacks, but also to President Barroso's reluctance to take bold steps that could impair his chances of re-election for a second term.[201] For instance, even though events proved that it had been right to warn of weaknesses in deposit guarantee arrangements, it was the Member States, acting unilaterally, rather than the Commission, that spearheaded emergency efforts to address the manifest problems that eventually emerged in the latter part of 2008. The dominance of the Member States was also evident in taxpayer-funded rescue measures to shore-up individual financial institutions, although, in fairness to the Commission, with no pan-EU bailout funds at its disposal, there was little on that front that even a super-prepared and proactive Commission could have done anyway.[202]

Yet, whilst there was undoubtedly a period during late 2008 when the Commission was relegated to the back seat,[203] blatant sidelining of coordinated Union method and EU institutional processes proved to

[199] European Commission (COM(2006) 729), p. 3.

[200] European Parliament, *Resolution on Deposit Guarantee Schemes* (T6–0626/2007).

[201] W. Münchau, "Like a Fish, Europe is Rotting from the Head," *Financial Times*, May 11, 2009, 9; T. Barber, "In EU Game of Poker Barroso is Player Others Allow to Stay In," *Financial Times*, May 29, 2009, 2.

[202] Member States' interventions are summarized in European Commission, *State Aid: Overview of National Rescue Measures and Deposit Guarantee Schemes* (MEMO/08/619, October 14, 2008).

[203] Quaglia, *Governing Financial Services in the European Union*, p. 160.

be a relatively short-lived phenomenon. The return to order has been linked in part to State Aid restrictions under EU law, as these provided the Commission with a firm foundation for reasserting EU institutional authority. It has been said of the Commission's performance on this front that it showed "remarkable ability to cope with the sudden surge in massive State Aid support."[204] Also significant in propelling a return to supranational order was the chaos unleashed by the disjointed national moves with respect to deposit protection schemes and the difficulties that were caused by the many different approaches to short selling restrictions. As noted already in Part II of this chapter, this painful experience was part of a learning exercise that brought it home to Member States that "more Europe" was the only option realistically open to them. This realization carried with it the implication that they had to look to the Commission – not only as the formal source of the EU legislative initiatives,[205] but also as the main repository of the expertise, knowledge and organizational resources that are needed to operationalize policy aspirations – for support in achieving that goal.

Strong signals of the Commission being restored to a position of centrality were provided by the publication in March and May 2009 of two important Communications: *Driving European Recovery*, containing an action plan for improving regulation and supervision,[206] and *European Financial Supervision*, setting out proposals for strengthening the institutional architecture of EU-level financial services supervision.[207] These documents marked a turning point from fire-fighting and ad hoc interventions to address what were seen to be the most glaring regulatory shortcomings[208] to more holistic thinking about longer-term institutional and other reforms.

With respect to determining the contents of these Communications, it is manifestly the case that the Commission did not have an entirely free hand. It was hemmed in, first, by the international nature of the market turmoil. The rapidly emerging post-crisis consensus that the problems were global and therefore demanded a globally coordinated response made it inevitable that international, regional and national reform agendas would be the product of complex interactions between many

[204] Editorial Comments, "Weathering Through the Credit Crisis: Is the Community Equipped to Cope with It?," *Common Market Law Review*, 46 (2009), 3–12, 12. Also Editorial Comments, "From Rescue to Restructuring: The Role of State Aid Control for the Financial Sector," *Common Market Law Review*, 47 (2010), 313–18.

[205] TEU, art. 17. [206] COM(2009) 114. [207] COM(2009) 252.

[208] Namely, rating agencies, capital adequacy, deposit guarantees and accounting rules.

different actors at a number of different levels, making it a situation that, aspirations for EU internal efforts to serve as an "ambitious agenda for reforming the international financial governance system"[209] notwithstanding, left little room for the European Commission to engage in bold, innovative policy entrepreneurship in developing the EU's position. It was also constrained by internal institutional dynamics. Given the magnitude and shocking nature of the events unfolding in the markets, it was only to be expected that all the main actors in the EU would want to play (and to be seen to be playing) a role in shaping the reform agenda, and that made for a crowded debate.[210]

European Council meetings in 2008 and early 2009 went beyond high-level calls for reform and expressions of support for, and light steering of, the work of the EU legislative institutions, and identified particular areas as priorities.[211] Since the leaders of the largest EU Member States were closely involved in preparations for the various G20 summits at which the main features of the international post-crisis regulatory agenda were being hammered out, they had particular reason to maintain a high profile in relation to the EU agenda as well.

The ECOFIN Council, helped by the fact that the Economic and Financial Committee had been working for some time on crisis management issues,[212] was also quick off the mark in responding to gathering storms, agreeing in October 2007 a set of common principles for

209 European Commission, *Driving European Recovery*, p. 3. See further Part V below.

210 European Commission, *From Financial Crisis to Recovery: A European Framework for Action* (COM(2008) 706) was the Commission's early contribution to the debate.

211 European Council, *Presidency Conclusions*, March 13/14, 2008 (spelling out specific areas (transparency, valuation standards, in particular for illiquid assets, the prudential framework and risk management in the financial sector, improving market functioning and incentive structures (including the role of CRAs))); European Council, *Presidency Conclusions*, October 15/16, 2008 (stressing the need to strengthen the supervision of the European financial sector, particularly cross-border groups, and identifying remuneration as another priority concern; calling for revisions of deposit guarantee rules; establishing financial crisis 'cell'); European Council, *Presidency Conclusions*, March 19/20, 2009 (setting out a list of ten priorities for better regulation of financial markets (as part of agreed language drawn up in preparation for the London G20 summit)). See further on the role of the European Council in shaping the reform agenda: Editorial Comments, "An Ever Mighty European Council – Some Recent Institutional Developments," *Common Market Law Review*, 46 (2009), 1383–93.

212 J. Pisani-Ferry and A. Sapir, "Banking Crisis Management in the EU: An Interim Assessment," Bruegel Working Paper No. 359 (December 2009, online: www.bruegel.org/download/parent/359-banking-crisis-management-in-the-eu-an-interim-assessment/file/835-banking-crisis-management-in-the-eu-an-interim-assessment-english/).

cross-border financial management and setting out a "roadmap" aimed at strengthening EU arrangements for financial stability, including reviewing prudential rules and examining the role of CRAs.[213] Although Niamh Moloney has made the point that this roadmap took a broad-brush approach that was to be of little practical use as market conditions descended into crisis,[214] and the European Commission has noted that the Memorandum of Understanding (MoU) between EU authorities that was revamped in 2008 to incorporate the ECOFIN common principles "failed to provide a sufficient or useful basis for cooperation between Member States,"[215] ECOFIN interventions nevertheless carried weight in the regulatory policy-setting context. During 2008, financial markets issues and the urgent need to correct regulatory weaknesses became more or less permanent agenda items for ECOFIN meetings, and there was an outpouring of roadmaps and other policy statements that helped to build the layers of the first phase of the EU response.[216]

The European Parliament also weighed in on various matters, including making a formal call in October 2008 for the Commission to come up with legislation across a range of matters to improve the supervisory architecture and regulatory framework for financial services in Europe.[217] This resolution set out in quite considerable detail the reform priorities as viewed from the Parliament's perspective.

Characterizing the Commission's action plan for reform as an overall policy prescription that was a distillation of many different opinions and views from a crowded field of actors all vying to put a stamp on the agenda does not mean jumping to the conclusion that the Commission occupied a subordinate position and played a largely secretariat role. It would be hard to claim that its influence was decisive, but to regard its

[213] ECOFIN, *Main Results of the Council* (13571/07, October 9, 2007).

[214] Moloney, "EU Financial Market Regulation After the Global Financial Crisis," 1336–7.

[215] European Commission, *An EU Framework for Cross-Border Crisis Management in the Banking Sector* (COM(2009) 561), p. 13.

[216] Including: *Key Issues Paper* (5267/1/08), endorsed ECOFIN, February 12, 2008; *The EU Supervisory Framework and Financial Stability Arrangements* (8515/3/08), endorsed ECOFIN, May 14, 2008; *Updated Financial Market Stability Roadmaps* (9056/1/08), endorsed ECOFIN, May 14, 2008; *Immediate Responses to Financial Turmoil* (13930/08), adopted ECOFIN, October 7, 2008.

[217] European Parliament, *Resolution with Recommendations to the Commission on Lamfalussy Follow-up: Future Structure of Supervision* (T6–0476/2008).

contribution as being more or less that of a passive recipient of instructions and invitations to act would also seem wide of the mark. The Commission never acts in a vacuum in taking the steps leading up to formal legislative proposals and, for reasons of efficiency as well as constitutionality, must take account of any early indications of what will (or will not) be acceptable to the political leaders and legislative institutions, but this still leaves some room for maneuver.[218] The Commission may say that its approach "echoes the discussion of the Heads of State and Government"[219] or suggest that its proposals are "in the main, a direct follow-up to the roadmap for the current financial turmoil agreed by EU Finance Ministers,"[220] but statements suggesting inter-institutional policy seamlessness serve a range of purposes, including reinforcing the legitimacy of the Commission's own actions, and thus cannot be taken simply at face value.[221] Moreover, the Commission has considerable opportunities to guide the thinking of the other institutions at an early stage, for instance through its involvement in preparatory work for ECOFIN meetings as a participant in, and provision of secretariat functions to, the Economic and Financial Committee,[222] and the impact of these behind-the-scenes activities is hard to measure.

The development of the framework for the architecture of EU financial supervision can be singled out as an issue where, even from the earliest stages of the post-crisis response, the Commission can plausibly claim to have led the way by demonstrating considerable intellectual leadership. A crucial part of the background to the May 2009 Communication on this issue was the Commission's decision, announced in October 2008, to establish an expert group under the chairmanship of Jacques de Larosière, a distinguished French central banker, to advise on

218 Generally on the constraints affecting the Commission's power to make legislative proposals: N. Nugent, *The European Commission* (London: Palgrave, 2001), pp. 236–41. On the interrelationship between formal agenda-setting power and the power more informally to influence the list of matters which are becoming salient at any particular point in time: J.W. Kingdon, *Agendas, Alternatives, and Public Policies* (Boston, MA: Little, Brown, 2nd edn., 1995), p. 3.

219 European Commission, *Driving European Recovery*, p. 19.

220 European Commission, "Commission Proposes Revision of Bank Capital Requirements Rules to Reinforce Financial Stability" (Press Release, October 1, 2008).

221 Nugent, *The European Commission*, p. 214.

222 TFEU, art. 134. The Economic and Financial Committee's webpage explains its role: http://europa.eu/efc/index_en.htm.

supervision.[223] The *de Larosière Report*, published in February 2009, was a pivotal contribution to the evolving EU debate on responding to the crisis.[224] By setting out a clear blueprint for a new EU institutional architecture of supervision that successfully balanced ambition – going beyond mere tinkering with existing arrangements – and pragmatism – being realistic about what was achievable given the existence of numerous sensitivities about the location of supervisory responsibilities, the *de Larosière Report* was instrumental in effecting a step change in thinking. Whereas the ECOFIN Council at its December 2008 meeting had concluded that "work on improving EU-wide supervision of financial undertakings has largely been completed,"[225] the *de Larosière Report* convincingly demonstrated that there was still much to be done, and that advances were possible. It "set the way forward," as the European Council acknowledged.[226]

In the eventual judgment of history, the upgrading of the institutional architecture of EU supervision that resulted from the *de Larosière Report*'s blueprint could come to be seen as *the* key change in EU financial services regulation that is attributable to the global financial crisis. If so, its role in instigating the process that led to those reforms and in supporting the work of the de Larosière group will weigh heavily in its favor in any overall assessment of the Commission's success in putting its imprint on the EU's response to the crisis. However, to qualify that assessment, it is, of course, the case that ingenious institutional design within the boundaries of the EU treaties framework is something that plays to the Commission's established areas of strength; tellingly, there is no major innovation in the global regulatory repair agenda that can be attributed to the Commission with quite the same degree of confidence.[227]

[223] European Commission, *From Financial Crisis to Recovery*, p. 4.

[224] The High Level Group on Financial Supervision in the EU, *Report* (Brussels: February 2009) (*de Larosière Report*).

[225] ECOFIN, *Main Results of the Council* (16231/1/08, December 2, 2008).

[226] European Council, *Presidency Conclusions*, June 18/19 2009 (11225/2/09), p. 7. This statement also credited the conclusions of an ECOFIN meeting with an agenda-setting role in this matter, but that meeting (June 9, 2009, 10737/09) in effect had proceeded on the basis of accepting the broad thrust of the Commission's proposals and starting to refine the detailed features.

[227] It is possible to say that the EU "led the way" with respect to reforms on remuneration, but even there the Commission's policy owed much to the work already done at national level in certain Member States: Ferran, "New Regulation."

Phase two of the response: the Commission's role in concretizing the financial services reform agenda

As the regulatory agenda acquired more substance from mid-2009 onwards, the Commission's formal agenda-setting role – that is, its monopoly power to put forward legislative proposals – became more prominent. In principle, this power gives the Commission the opportunity to prove its indispensability, perhaps not so much as a generator of "big" ideas, but as the institution within the EU that has, or has access to, the technical competence, expertise, experience and judgment needed to sift through broad policy prescriptions and select the most useful, to distil immensely complicated and potentially controversial concepts into workable proposals, and to shepherd them through the lawmaking machinery. Less benignly, writing the first draft of proposals also gives the Commission the chance to fine-tune ideas so that they work to its own advantage; the potential "first mover" advantages may be considerable.[228] Has the Commission exploited these opportunities in generating recent developments in EU financial services regulation and, if so, with what effect? This section explores these issues by examining the Commission's management of the legislative program for financial services regulatory reform, first with respect to overall process management, and then in two substantive areas.

Overall process management of the legislative program

The EU financial services lawmaking machinery came of age during the FSAP and the outcomes, in terms both of the quantity of legislation adopted and its importance, were indisputably significant. However, to put the more recent and ongoing program of far-reaching reform into context, it is worthwhile to recall that many of the legislative initiatives that were brought under the FSAP umbrella had already been under development for some years before the formal adoption of the FSAP. Moreover, the EU legislators and Commission officials then had the luxury of acting in an environment of relatively stable and rising markets (especially as Europe escaped the worst of the fallout from Enron and other corporate collapses) and could claim, without being challenged too hard, that their regulatory policy choices had facilitated Europe's growing international competitiveness. The response to the global financial crisis and subsequent events, by contrast, has had to be

[228] Generally on the proportion of Commission proposals that are amended before adoption: Nugent, *The European Commission*, pp. 259–60.

put together under intense pressure, against a background of extreme, persistent market instability and with constant reminders of past failures in regulatory foresight.[229]

Given the pressures, a qualified assessment of the Commission's performance in holding the administrative and organizational side of the lawmaking process together is unremarkable. Whilst there was only one formal lapse from the now-standard pre-legislative disciplines of in-depth impact assessment and public consultation,[230] the quality of some of the impact assessments conducted during this period was uneven.[231] In many instances, outline timetables for the introduction and passage of legislation proved to be over-optimistic, although market instabilities played a significant part in some delays. For instance, given the problems in the euro area throughout 2011 and the accompanying threat of another round of crisis in the banking sector, it is not surprising that the Commission failed to deliver on promises to publish a formal legislative proposal on bank crisis management by Spring/Summer 2011, and that it was not actually published until June 2012. The euro area crisis was also a factor in the slippage of the timetable for EU regulatory intervention on derivatives and market infrastructure, but this process was also dogged by the disagreements between Member States over the treatment of naked sovereign CDS mentioned in Part II above. Of course, detailed preparatory work can never guarantee a smooth passage for legislation, as the real magnitude of political sensitivities and commercial concerns may only surface some way into the process.

One measure of relative success with respect to process is that it has proved possible to rely on the "fast-track" ordinary legislative procedure,[232] although achieving this has required a degree of maneuvering of the timing of formal parliamentary votes on some matters.[233] Whilst the Commission deserves to be given credit for keeping the agenda moving forward, it should also be acknowledged that it has not had to do all of the heavy lifting with

[229] The Commission has summarized progress: European Commission, *Regulating Financial Services for Sustainable Growth*; European Commission, *Regulating Financial Services for Sustainable Growth – Progress Report* (February 2011).

[230] Directive 2009/14/EC, [2009] OJ L68/3, making emergency repairs to the deposit guarantee framework.

[231] Most notably that for the AIFMD. See also Moloney, "EU Financial Market Regulation After the Financial Crisis," 1339–40 (highlighting short consultation periods).

[232] Ibid., 1338–9.

[233] Utilising European Parliament Rules of Procedure for the postponement of votes (Rule 57.2).

respect to maintaining momentum in the legislative process. Under the rotating Council Presidency system, successive national governments have been deeply involved across a range of measures in brokering agreement on ECOFIN general approaches through the production of (sometimes many) "Presidency Compromise" drafts of legislation and in representing the Council in trilogue deliberations. The European Parliament's Economic and Monetary Affairs Committee (ECON) and its Rapporteurs have played a similarly significant role, as Commissioner Barnier has acknowledged.[234]

"Too-big-to-fail"

Turning now to a substantive policy area, efforts to address the "too-big-/too-important-/too-interconnected-to-fail" problem – that is, working out how banks and other institutions can fail without causing significant systemic disruption, preventing them from becoming too big etc. in the first place and/or imposing capital surcharges, structural changes or activity restrictions on ones that have already become systemically important – provide a good context in which to consider further whether the Commission's handling of issues in the wake of the global financial crisis has enhanced or detracted from its reputation for sound decision-making in determining regulatory priorities and for technical competence in drawing up and shepherding specific proposals through to adoption. The selection of this topic can be justified by reference to the intrinsic importance of the issues. It is also apposite because the Commission's performance in this area has attracted particular criticism.

Morris Goldstein and Nicolas Véron have drawn attention to the "remarkable" fact that, compared to the United States, the too-big-to-fail problem is "barely present in substantial financial policy debates and initiatives in most Continental European countries and at EU level, including the European Commission."[235] Peter Mülbert and Alexander Wilhelm have also noted the lack of a major contribution to this debate from the EU and have suggested that the divergence between the EU and the United States in this respect may be attributable largely to the EU being a treaty-based supranational institution, not a federal state.[236]

[234] M. Barnier, "Rapport d'Étape sur la Mise en Oeuvre de la Réglementation Financière" (speech, November 22, 2011, online: http://ec.europa.eu/commission_2010–2014/barnier/docs/speeches/20111122/speech_fr.pdf).

[235] N. Véron and M. Goldstein, "The European Union Should Start a Debate on Too-big-to-fail," VOX, April 14, 2011 (online: www.voxeu.org/index.php?q=node/6346).

[236] P.O. Mülbert and A. Wilhelm, "Reforms of EU Banking and Securities Regulation after the Financial Crisis," *Banking & Finance Law Review*, 26 (2011), 187–232, 230.

Goldstein and Véron have also accepted that differences in financial and political structures resulting from contrasting historical paths of the United States and the EU have been influential in shaping the policy arguments on these issues, but they contend that European circumstances do not provide an excuse for not conducting a proper in-depth, wide-ranging debate. In a related working paper, the same authors have touched specifically on the European Commission's unwillingness to lead a debate on special requirements tailored specifically to systemically important financial institutions, which they interpret as reflecting the fact that the Commission has yet to establish a new post-crisis "strategic orientation that is compatible with the beguiling diversity of national positions and regulatory cultures within the European Union."[237]

It is certainly true that the Commission has not sought to take a lead with respect to permanent capital surcharges for systemically important financial institutions. This does not seem quite so remarkable when the long-established tradition of EU deferral to international capital adequacy standards is considered.[238] The Commission (for reasons that need not be explored in detail here)[239] has always tended to emphasize the importance of international standardization in this field and has prioritized working within the Basel processes to ensure that what is agreed there will fit into an EU setting,[240] and then implementing those standards with the addition of an EU finish.[241] The Commission, which is not a mere passive consumer of international standards, could, if it wished, work within the Basel processes to promote a "too big" agenda.

[237] M. Goldstein and N. Véron, "Too Big to Fail: The Transatlantic Debate," Peterson Institute for International Economics, Working Paper 11–2, January 2011.

[238] M.S. Barr and G.P. Miller, "Global Administrative Law: The View from Basel," *European Journal of International Law*, 15 (2006), 15–46.

[239] One factor is that nine EU Member States (Belgium, France, Germany, Italy, Luxembourg, Netherlands, Spain, Sweden, United Kingdom) are members of the Basel Committee, giving rise to a particularly strong need for EU obligations to dovetail with international commitments.

[240] G. Bertezzolo, "The European Union Facing the Global Arena: Standard-setting Bodies and Financial Regulation," *European Law Review*, 34 (2009), 257–80; Quaglia, *Governing Financial Services in the European Union*, p. 54.

[241] One example of an EU addition is the 5 percent originator risk-retention requirement in capital requirements for securitization in Directive 2009/111/EC, CRD II: L. Ng, "Changes to Basel II and the EU Capital Requirements Directive: Implications for Securitisation," *Journal of International Banking Law and Regulation*, 25 (2010), 265–74. For a general review of EU capital changes in CRD II and CRD III, see Mülbert and Wilhelm, "Reforms of EU Banking and Securities Regulation after the Financial Crisis."

However, as discussed in Part V below, there are questions about how much real influence the Commission has in that setting. It could also change its attitude and treat international standards as less of a strait-jacket, but any move in that direction (as the IMF[242] and others discerned in the Commission's proposals to implement Basel III,[243] but which the Commission denied)[244] would be a retrograde step from an international consistency perspective.

It is also the case that the Commission, in spite of some urging from the European Parliament,[245] has been slow to come forward with proposals to interfere in the activities of big banks by imposing binding prohibitions or separations of business along the lines of the US Volcker rule (which bans banks from engaging in proprietary trading and restricts them from investing in or sponsoring hedge funds and private equity),[246] the swaps "push out" rule (which, in effect, requires banks to spin off derivatives activities into separate subsidiaries), or limits on size or market share (which, albeit only to a modest extent, have also been part of the US response to the crisis). Commissioner Barnier has specifically indicated that he does not consider caps on size and scope to be the right solution in the European context,[247] although his establishment of a high-level group to look at bank structures is a sign that nothing has been formally ruled out.[248] Since caps and bans are blunt instruments that do not always achieve their desired effect,[249] the European

242 IMF, *United Kingdom: 2011 Article IV Consultation* (IMF Country Report No. 11/225, July 2011), supplementary information, p. 3.

243 CRD IV Regulation (proposed); CRD IV Directive (proposed).

244 Remarks by Jonathan Faull, Director General, Internal Markets and Services, European Commission, reported in M. Cameron, "CRD IV Proposals Do Not Deviate Markedly From Basel III," *Risk Magazine*, September 15, 2011 (online: www.risk.net/risk-magazine/news/2109521/crd-iv-proposals-deviate-markedly-basel-iii-ecs-faull).

245 European Parliament, *Resolution on the Financial, Economic and Social Crisis* (T7–0331/2011).

246 See further, Coffee Jr., Chapter 4 below.

247 M. Barnier, "Informal Remarks – Restoring Confidence in Financial Markets" (speech, March 1, 2010, online: http://europa.eu/rapid/pressReleasesAction.do?reference=SPEECH/10/52&format=HTML&aged=0&language=EN&guiLanguage=en).

248 European Commission, "Commissioner Barnier Appoints Members of a High-level Expert Group on Possible Reforms to the Structure of the EU Banking Sector" (MEMO/12/129, February 22, 2012). The Lii Kanen Group is expected to report in Summer 2012.

249 D.A. Skeel, *The New Financial Deal: Understanding the Dodd-Frank Act and its (Unintended) Consequences* (Hoboken, NJ: Wiley, 2010), pp. 10–11; A.E. Wilmarth, Jr., "The Dodd-Frank Act: A Flawed and Inadequate Response to the Too-Big-to-Fail Problem," *Oregon Law Review*, 89 (2011), 951–1057.

Commission does not deserve to be castigated merely because it has refused to rush to mimic the United States on these points. Of course, it could have tried to have come up with bigger, bolder and better structural rules – but given the tendency of bold reform undertaken in the immediate aftermath of a crisis to backfire, the Commission's reticence on this matter is not necessarily a matter for regret. National political considerations are also in play, as is evident from the discussion in Part II above. In view of the deep-seated tradition of universal banking in many Continental Europe national political economies, the Commission can hardly be blamed for treading warily in the absence of convincing evidence of fundamental flaws in the model.[250]

Moreover, it is not convincing to claim that "too-big" issues have hardly featured in the European debate. The Commission's main regulatory reform priority with respect to too-big-to-fail issues has been the treatment of cross-border distressed banks and banking groups – requirements for financial institutions to maintain recovery and resolution plans (living wills), standardization of early intervention powers to enable supervisors to deal efficiently and effectively with institutions that are in difficulties but not yet insolvent, and the development of an EU crisis framework containing powers (resolution and insolvency) to enable institutions to fail without causing unacceptable harm to society at large. It has been working assiduously on these issues.[251] According to the Financial Stability Board, "any effective approach to addressing the 'too big to fail' problem needs to have effective resolution at its

[250] H.-J. Kim, "Toward Transatlantic Convergence in Financial Regulation," University of Michigan Law & Econ, Empirical Legal Studies Center Paper No. 11–004 (April 18, 2011, online: http://ssrn.com/abstract=1814122) (pointing to Canada as a country that survived the crisis relatively unscathed in spite of having a universal banking system dominated by just five large banks). See also P.K. Staikouras, "Universal Banks, Universal Crises? Disentangling Myths from Realities in Quest of a New Regulatory and Supervisory Landscape," *Journal of Corporate Law Studies*, 11 (2011), 139–75.

[251] European Commission, *An EU Framework for Cross-Border Crisis Management in the Banking Sector* (COM(2009) 561); European Commission, *Innovative Financing at a Global Level* (SEC(2010) 409); European Commission, *Bank Resolution Funds* (COM(2010) 254); European Commission, *An EU Framework for Crisis Management in the Financial Sector* (COM(2010) 579); DG Internal Market and Services Working Document, *Technical Details of a Possible EU Framework for Bank Recovery and Resolution* (January 2011); Demolin Brulard Barthelemy, *Pre-insolvency – Early intervention – Reorganization – Liquidation* (April 2010); Recovery and Resolution Directive (proposed).

base."[252] One of the main lessons from the crisis for the EU and most of its Member States (felt more acutely than in the United States)[253] was that adequate resolvability foundations were missing.[254] The foundational nature of these requirements provides strong justification for making improving resolvability and related matters *the* EU priority, even if this has led to the sidelining of some other strategies for tackling the too-big-to-fail problem.

Many of the potentially desirable elements of a crisis management and insolvency framework involve making inroads on important existing legal principles (for example, to permit the transfer of assets around a banking group by reference to group rather than entity interests, to override the rights that shareholders ordinarily enjoy under company law, and to interfere in the contractual rights of creditors and counterparties) and are thus profoundly complicated from a single-jurisdiction legal perspective, never mind the many differences in the operation of these principles in Member States' divergent national laws.[255] Commercial sensitivities are stirred up by the prospect of the introduction of draconian powers to write down all equity and to force the conversion of debt into equity ("bail-ins"). There are also some politically explosive

[252] FSB, *Reducing the Moral Hazard Posed by Systemically Important Financial Institutions: FSB Recommendations and Time Lines* (Basel: October 2010), p. 3; FSB, *Key Attributes of Effective Resolution Regimes for Financial Institutions* (Basel: October 2011).

[253] Pre-crisis, the United States had already established special resolution regimes for banks insured by the Federal Insurance Corporation and for registered broker-dealers and thus started in a different place. The more flexible dedicated procedures were deemed not to apply to Lehmans, and it was dealt with under the general US Bankruptcy Code, which led to certain difficulties: H. Scott, *The Global Financial Crisis* (New York: Foundation Press, 2009), pp. 58–61. The Dodd-Frank Act reforms include (Title II) a new Orderly Liquidation Authority, which expands the scope of the special regimes by creating a new insolvency regime for large, interconnected financial firms. See further on Dodd-Frank, Coffee, Chapter 4 below.

[254] European Commission, *European Financial Stability and Integration Report*, p. 18; European Commission, *An EU Framework for Cross-Border Crisis Management in the Banking Sector*, p. 7. On the variety of approaches at Member State level before the crisis: M. Čihák and E. Nier, "The Need for Special Resolution Regimes for Financial Institutions – The Case of the European Union," IMF Working Paper WP/09/200; E.H. Hüpkes, *The Legal Aspects of Bank Insolvency: A Comparative Analysis of Western Europe, the United States and Canada* (The Hague: Kluwer, 2000); A. Campbell and P. Cartwright, *Banks in Crisis: The Legal Response* (Aldershot: Ashgate, 2002). Post-crisis, various Member States (including the UK, Denmark, Germany and Ireland) have embarked on reforms to enact special bank resolution regimes.

[255] European Commission, *An EU Framework for Cross-Border Crisis Management in the Banking Sector*, p. 16.

issues, which center on fiscal sovereignty. However much is done to ensure that the private sector absorbs the costs of failure, the possibility of a need to call upon public funds to deal with distressed institutions can never be completely ruled out.[256]

There is much to be said in principle for a pan-EU, or at least a pan-euro area fiscal backstop for failing institutions,[257] but the idea of *ex ante* burden-sharing is inherently unappealing to many Member States. Even the idea of EU-wide coordination of national resolution funds financed by levies on banks, which has been approved in principle by the European Council[258] and which the Commission is working towards as a "first stage" option, with a single pan-EU scheme being its preferred long-term goal,[259] is not entirely straightforward from a political angle, because there is a significant divergence of views among Member States about many aspects of bank levy schemes and even as to the desirability of their introduction during difficult economic conditions.[260] Echoing the debate about the institutional architecture of supervision, concerns about the erosion of the powers of national authorities are an obstacle to the establishment of a single EU resolution authority even though, in the abstract, that would be the logical way of addressing insolvency in a cross-border banking group that has subsidiaries located in a number of different jurisdictions.[261] The Commission has ruled out a single EU resolution authority for now and has begun to put flesh on alternative approaches, which are taking the shape of "resolution colleges" and "group resolution schemes."[262] But the picture could change rapidly: robust cross-border institutional arrangements for resolution are a vital element of the "banking union" proposals that have surfaced in late Spring 2012 as a solution to the euro area crisis.

That this is an area where the technical complexities and the commercial and political sensitivities are exceptional. The global financial crisis confirmed what many already knew – that merely improving the coordination

256 Ibid., p. 15.

257 The IMF has called for this: IMF, *Global Financial Stability Report: Durable Financial Stability – Getting There From Here*, p. 51.

258 European Council, *Presidency Conclusions*, June 17, 2010 (EUCO 13/10), p. 6.

259 European Commission, *An EU Framework for Cross-Border Crisis Management in the Banking Sector*, p. 15; Recovery and Resolution Directive (proposed), arts. 90–99.

260 EFC, *Report to the Ecofin on Financial Levies and Taxes – State of Play* (9918/11).

261 G.A. Ferrarini and F. Chiodini, "Nationally Fragmented Supervision over Multinational Banks as a Source of Global Systemic Risk: A Critical Analysis of Recent EU Reforms" (September 2011, online: http://ssrn.com/abstract=1923756).

262 European Commission, *An EU Framework for Crisis Management in the Financial Sector*, p. 12; Recovery and Resolution Directive (proposed), arts. 11–12 and arts. 80–83.

of national arrangements and bolstering voluntary cooperation between national authorities through memoranda of understanding is an inadequate response to the problems that can arise when banks with cross-border operations get into difficulties[263] – but it did not sweep away all of the barriers to meaningful change. With problems in the euro area further sapping time and attention, the Commission's failure to meet its original timetable for formal crisis management proposals is therefore quite understandable. The resurgent threat of bank failures resulting from exposure to euro area sovereign debt has reinforced the need for effective bank resolution arrangements and has also demonstrated that political objections to using pooled funds to finance the recapitalization of financial institutions are not necessarily immutable, in that as well as the massive levels of support for EU banks' balance sheets that the ECB has made available,[264] there is now provision in the European Financial Stability Mechanism for loans that are provided to Member States to be used to strengthen their banks.[265] However, notwithstanding these developments, the challenges involved in devising a set of proposals on bank crisis management that is both technically feasible and likely to be politically acceptable remain formidable.

Looking ahead to the future, the bank crisis management framework that is eventually adopted by the EU could, as a product of intense, difficult negotiations, contain compromises that make it "under-ambitious" in its overall effect. Yet this charge against the crisis management arrangements may not stick if they are accompanied by a banking union framework. Even if, or to the extent that, it does, more optimistic observers may regard the securing of even relatively low-level agreement in this sub-field as a major achievement, particularly bearing in mind the strong tendency of EU financial services law to accrete once important "first steps" have been taken.

Supervision

The new supervisory arrangements, which became operational at the start of 2011 (slightly later than originally intended),[266] provide an apt

[263] Pisani-Ferry and Sapir, "Banking Crisis Management in the EU"; *de Larosière Report*, pp. 12, 33–4, 76; European Commission, *An EU Framework for Cross-Border Crisis Management in the Banking Sector*, p. 13.

[264] P. Jenkins, "Super Mario's Bank Funding Scheme is no Panacea," *Financial Times*, January 31, 2012, 20 (reporting the provision by the ECB at the end of 2011 of €489bn of new three-year money).

[265] And the ambitious banking union plans emerging in Spring 2012 envisage the possibility of the ESM being used for direct bank recapitalization.

[266] European Commission, *European Financial Supervision*, p. 16.

context in which to consider the Commission's use of "first mover" advantages, not least because Commissioner Barnier has specifically claimed that the most important aspects of the Commission's original proposals on supervision were retained in the final versions of the legislation.[267] The supervisory arrangements mostly follow the blueprint in the Commission-backed *de Larosière Report*, but the Commission did not get its own way on all important features.

The most striking example of a significant departure from the model originally proposed by the Commission is with respect to the location of the power to declare an "emergency situation." In its version of the founding legislative texts, the Commission had proposed to reserve this power to itself[268] but the legal framework, as finally adopted, puts the Council formally in charge.[269] Given the highly sensitive consequences of such a declaration, which include that the ESAs become empowered to require national competent authorities to take action and to impose decisions directly on financial market participants on an accelerated basis, it cannot be considered surprising that Member States insisted on being in control. In spite of support among Members of the European Parliament (MEPs) for the European Systemic Risk Board to be the custodian of the power,[270] its location was a fundamentally non-negotiable point on which intergovernmental preferences prevailed. Member States' concerns about possible ESA encroachment on their national supervisors' authority also explain the fiscal safeguard clause, mentioned in Part II of this chapter, which was introduced into the legal texts for the ESAs some way into the legislative process.[271] Whilst the principle of not impinging on fiscal autonomy had been mentioned briefly in the Commission's pre-legislative communication on the supervisory package,[272] ECOFIN and the European Council made it clear that Member States required this safeguard to be clearly enshrined in the legislation.[273]

[267] M. Barnier, "L'avenir de la Régulation et de la Supervision Financières" (speech May 2, 2011, online: http://europa.eu/rapid/pressReleasesAction.do?reference=SPEECH/11/297&format=HTML&aged=0&language=FR&guiLanguage=en).

[268] European Commission, *Proposal for a Regulation of the European Parliament and of the Council establishing a European Securities and Market Authority* (ESMA) (COM(2009) 506), p. 6.

[269] ESMA Regulation, art. 18.

[270] ECON, *Report on Proposal for a Regulation on ESMA* (A7–0169/2010, Rapporteur: Sven Giegold).

[271] ESMA Regulation, rec. 5 and art. 38.

[272] European Commission, *European Financial Supervision*, p. 12.

[273] European Council, *Presidency Conclusions*, June 18/19, 2009 (11225/2/09), p. 8. ECOFIN, *Main Results of the Council* (10737/09, June 9, 2009).

It is also possible to see the influence of the European Parliament in differences between the Commission's original drafts and the final legislative texts.[274] The Parliament was especially prominent in discussions around tightening the framework governing the making of binding technical standards.[275] Binding technical standards (which take the form of regulatory technical standards under the Treaty on the Functioning of the European Union (TFEU), article 290 and implementing technical standards under TFEU, article 291) constitute a new post-crisis level of detailed EU rulemaking that looks set to become increasingly prevalent unless or until a brake is applied to the pursuit of a standardized EU rulebook. It is not considered possible, for reasons of EU constitutional law, to delegate binding rulemaking powers to the ESAs directly,[276] but the ESA frameworks work creatively around this restriction by having the Commission endorse draft standards developed by the ESAs.[277] The final version of the procedure for making binding technical standards is considerably more sophisticated than the model originally set out by the Commission, and the Commission's powers have been hemmed in by more constraints. Although the Commission has the final say, it may not change the content of a standard without prior coordination with the ESA that prepared it, and can do so only where Union interests require.[278] The final version of the legal text (but not the original Commission draft) expressly includes a statement in the recitals that amendments should happen only in "very restricted and extraordinary circumstances, since the Authority is the actor in close contact with and knowing best the daily functioning of financial markets."[279] It also spells out the coordination between the Commission and the ESA that must occur if the Commission is minded not to endorse or to amend a draft standard and provides for the Council and the Parliament to have a role in such disagreements.[280]

How much it matters that the Commission has been put under more explicit constraints than it outlined in its original proposals remains to

[274] ECON, *Report on Proposal for a Regulation on ESMA*; European Parliament, *Resolution on the Establishment of ESMA* (T7–0270/2010) (partial vote).

[275] ESMA Regulation, arts. 10–15. Some of the refinements introduced during the legislative process reflected the coming into force of the Treaty of Lisbon and were not driven by considerations pertaining exclusively to financial services regulation.

[276] Case 9/56 *Meroni* v. *High Authority* [1958] ECR 11.

[277] With a back-up power for the Commission to step in should an ESA fail to deliver.

[278] ESMA Regulation, arts. 10, 15. [279] ESMA Regulation, rec. 23.

[280] ESMA Regulation, arts. 10, 14, 15.

be seen as experience in the making of technical standards accumulates. It is debatable whether the Commission will see much advantage in making much use of its override powers. Since the Commission maintained from the outset that it would depart from ESA drafts only in exceptional circumstances, having this expressly recorded in the legislation could be regarded as adding little more than a formal gloss.[281] There is evidence from other contexts of the Commission being content in practice to play a more-or-less rubber-stamping role in relation to the operational activities of EU agencies.[282] Technical standards are, after all, low-level requirements that can be written only in prescribed circumstances, involving no strategic or policy choices. The Commission will already have a heavy rule-drafting workload to meet the demands for higher-level delegated acts that are also proliferating in pursuit of the single rulebook goal and in the vast majority of cases may be prepared simply to let the ESAs get on with the job of producing technical standards with minimal interference.[283] Another relevant factor is that as the initiator of legislative proposals, the Commission is in a position to influence the choice of matters that get pushed down to the technical standards level of rulemaking; this provides a mechanism for heading off controversy before it has a chance to arise.

However, the possibility of tensions cannot be completely ruled out.[284] The fact that there were certain difficulties in the early days of relations between the Commission and the ESAs' predecessors, the Lamfalussy supervisory committees, lends credence to these concerns as does the more recent example of the Commission departing from ESMA advice on the content of prospectus disclosure requirements also mentioned by Niamh Moloney in Chapter 2. The Commission's formal attachment to the restrictions in EU law on delegation to agencies[285] and its strict interpretation of

[281] European Commission, *Proposal for a Regulation Establishing ESMA*, p. 5.

[282] E. Chiti, "An Important Part of the EU's Institutional Machinery: Features, Problems and Perspectives of European Agencies," *Common Market Law Review*, 46 (2009), 1395–442, 1405, n. 31.

[283] European Union Select Committee, *The EU Financial Supervisory Framework: an update* (online: www.publications.parliament.uk/pa/ld201012/ldselect/ldeucom/181/18104.htm#n6), para. 6.

[284] Moloney, "EU Financial Market Regulation After the Financial Crisis," 1351–2; N. Moloney, "The European Securities and Markets Authority and Institutional Design for the EU Financial Market – A Tale of Two Competences: Part (1) Rule-Making," *European Business Organization Law Review*, 12 (2011), 41–86, 73–8; Wymeersch, "Europe's New Financial Regulatory Bodies," 456.

[285] European Commission, *European Agencies – The Way Forward* (COM(2008) 135), p. 5.

the limits on delegation is questioned by some as being "more a political preference than a full acceptable legal interpretation of the ECJ's case law."[286] It is possible to interpret the development of the framework to equip ESMA to supervise rating agencies, where a pragmatic interpretation driven by growing political realism about the need for the ESAs to perform an expanding range of functions eventually prevailed over a less ambitions model put forward by the Commission, as an illustration of the Commission seeking to use a strict interpretation opportunistically (but ultimately unsuccessfully) so as to avoid any encroachment on its own power.[287] To the extent that suspicions of this sort have any validity,[288] there is a risk that similar thinking could color the Commission's attitude towards the operation of the technical standard-setting procedure and that this could therefore become a context[289] in which opportunities are taken to

286 Chiti, "An Important Part," 1426. There is much scholarly debate about whether the *Meroni* doctrine is even still valid, about its scope and about how significant an obstacle it is to the evolution of EU agencies: e.g., Chiti; S. Griller and A. Orator, "Everything Under Control? The 'Way Forward' for European Agencies in the Footsteps of the *Meroni* Doctrine," *European Law Review*, 35 (2010), 3–35. For detailed analysis of the issues in the EU financial services context: Moloney, "The European Securities and Markets Authority and Institutional Design for the EU Financial Market – A Tale of Two Competences: Part (1) Rule-Making," 73–8; N. Moloney, "The European Securities and Markets Authority and Institutional Design for the EU Financial Market – A Tale of Two Competences: Part (2) Rules in Action," *European Business Organization Law Review*, 12 (2011), 177–225, 220–5; P. Schammo, *EU Prospectus Law* (Cambridge University Press, 2011) pp. 30–6; P. Schammo, "EU Day-to-Day Supervision or Intervention-Based Supervision: Which Way Forward for the European System of Financial Supervision?," *Oxford Journal of Legal Studies*, 2012 (forthcoming).

287 The Commission suggested that ESMA's enforcement role should be confined to making proposals to the Commission for the imposition of sanctions. In accompanying FAQ commentary, the Commission suggested that the *Meroni* doctrine lay behind this proposed arrangement. The CRA Regulation (as amended by Regulation (EU) No. 513/2011), art. 36a–e and annex III, actually gives ESMA itself direct power to impose penalties and fines, albeit within tightly prescribed limits. The legal framework with respect to ESMA's powers directly to impose fines and penalties on trade repositories has followed the same trajectory: EMIR, arts. 64–70, not following the Commission's initial draft (COM(2010) 484).

288 The evidence on the Commission's stance is mixed. Whereas its position on ESMA's direct powers to impose fines and penalties was, arguably, too strict, in other areas the Commission has arguably swung too far in the opposite direction. With respect to mandatory clearing of OTC derivatives contracts, the original Commission draft (COM(2010) 484) empowered ESMA to determine eligibility for clearing, but this was modified during the legislative process under *Meroni*-related pressure from the Council to give the Commission the decisive role (EMIR, rec. 16 and art. 5). See also the discussion with respect to ESMA's short selling banning powers discussed in n. 180 above.

289 External relations is another area where similar tensions could arise. See Part V below.

remind the ESAs of their (lowly) place in the hierarchy. However, given the damage to the EU system of financial market supervision as a whole that could be caused by needless confrontation, the incentives to maintain a more measured approach will be considerable.

The provisions of the ESAs' legal frameworks relating to organizational set-up, governance and accountability were the focus of much attention during the legislative process. This was only to be expected given the self-interest of each of the Commission, Council and Parliament of embedding itself securely in those arrangements and in maintaining an appropriate inter-institutional balance with respect to the location of power to oversee the new authorities.[290] There was particular inter-institutional tension over control of the process for appointing the ESA chairpersons, with the European Parliament at one stage suggesting that it should select the candidate from a shortlist drawn up by the Commission.[291] Under the final framework, in effect, the Member States win out, because it is for each ESA's Board of Supervisors to appoint its own chair, although this is subject to a right for the European Parliament to object.[292] The Commission was allowed to draw up the shortlists for the first round of appointments, but the matter has been left open for subsequent designations.[293] One particular area where the Commission failed to get its way was with respect to its own formal status in the ESAs' decision-making apparatus. In the original legislative proposal, the Commission had made itself a full member of the Management Board of each ESA[294] but, as finally enacted, its role is that of a non-voting (except on budgetary matters) participant.[295] The Commission is also a non-voting member of each ESA's Board of Supervisors[296] and it is entitled to be an observer on the Joint Committee of the ESAs and the Financial Conglomerates Sub-committee.[297] In spite of not getting exactly what it wanted, the subtle influence that the Commission may be able to exert through its participation rights (which will likely be hard for outsiders to track) may well be considerable.

290 Moloney, "EU Financial Market Regulation After the Global Financial Crisis," 1338, 1351.
291 European Parliament, *Resolution on the Establishment of ESMA* (T7–0270/2010) (partial vote).
292 ESMA Regulation, art. 48. 293 ESMA Regulation, art. 55.
294 European Commission, *Proposal for a Regulation Establishing ESMA*, p. 9.
295 ESMA Regulation, art. 45. 296 ESMA Regulation, art. 40.
297 ESMA Regulation, art. 55 and art. 57.

The crucial importance of a *cordon sanitaire* around the ESAs' operational independence, impartiality and objectivity is reflected in their legal framework.[298] Whilst certain refinements were added during the legislative process, it was never in doubt that "the ESAs should enjoy maximum independence to objectively fulfill their mission."[299] The strong emphasis on independence within the ESAs is a significant advance in terms of the position of agencies within the EU in general as, in the past, these have tended to be more firmly under Commission control, and independence has had a rather limited meaning.[300] In part, this can be viewed as a reflection of the hybrid intergovernmental/supranational character of the ESAs, discussed above in Part II, but it is more than a feature forced upon the Commission by circumstance. Commissioner Barnier has referred explicitly to independence as a determinant of the ESAs' credibility.[301] Whilst the Commission's firm support for ESA independence could be thought surprising given the potential for the ESAs to grow their own power bases, it is possible to explain it by reference to the Commission's own self-interest.

In advancing the supranationalization of administrative functions, the ESAs provide an excellent example of the particular value of agencies in a field of shared competences, when the implementation of new EU policies requires close cooperation between Member States and the EU institutions.[302] As the Commission has explained, the establishment of agencies in this context "can make possible a pooling of powers at EU level which would be resisted if centered on the institutions themselves."[303] At the operational level, the ESAs will perform many tasks that could otherwise have burdened the Commission, or not been done at all at the EU level because of resource constraints.[304] The ESAs take EU "outsourcing" to a new level.[305] They break new ground in the EU

[298] ESMA Regulation, art. 1 (Authority independence); art. 42 (Board of Supervisors independence); art. 46 (Management Board independence); art. 49 (Chair independence); art. 52 (Executive director independence); art. 59 (Board of Appeal independence).

[299] European Commission, *Proposal for a Regulation Establishing ESMA*, p. 4.

[300] Chiti, "An Important Part," 1399–400.

[301] M. Barnier, "The New European Securities and Markets Authority: Helping Enhance the Resilience of Financial Markets" (speech at ESMA, July 11, 2011, online: http://europa.eu/rapid/pressReleasesAction.do?reference=SPEECH/11/514&format=HTML&aged=0&language=EN&guiLanguage=en).

[302] European Commission, *European Agencies – The Way Forward* (COM(2008) 135), p. 5.

[303] Ibid.

[304] Generally on Commission resource constraints with respect to supervising front-line implementation: Nugent, *The European Commission*, pp. 276–80.

[305] Chiti, "An Important Part," 1428.

agencies-related field in their range of responsibilities, their powers, and their potential to expand into the role of direct pan-EU supervisors. An incidental benefit for the Commission is that if the ESAs perform their tasks badly, the Commission will have someone else to blame and can distance itself from failure. The Commission thus needs the ESAs to be, and to be seen to be, independent. If they were to come to be seen as little more than puppets of the Commission, the ESAs would not be able to function effectively vis-à-vis the Member State, and their capacity gradually to assume more direct supervisory responsibilities would be compromised. If the Commission were to be perceived to be putting pressure on the ESAs, its moral authority to stop Member States from doing the same would evaporate.

The ESAs are funded through a combination of a subsidy from the EU budget, contributions from national supervisors and fees paid by market participants that are subject to direct ESA supervision.[306] This raises the prospect of the Commission being able to shape the development of the ESAs through control of the purse strings.[307] MEPs have already raised concerns about the budgetary constraints in relation to the ESAs, and the European Parliament can be expected to play a key role in ensuring that the Commission (and also the Member States) does not inappropriately rein in the ESAs by starving them of adequate resources.[308] The Commission's willingness to augment the EBA's resources in order to equip it to cope with the heavy workload involved in giving effect to Basel III capital standards is a good omen, but this is an issue that will require continuous close monitoring.[309]

Evaluation

In summary, then, what can be said of the European Commission's role in relation to financial services regulation in the aftermath of the global financial crisis? Desmond Dinan's general conclusion about the Barroso Commission that "[i]f not resurgent, arguably the Commission under Barroso is as influential as it could possibly be under extremely difficult

306 ESMA Regulation, art. 62.

307 Moloney, "EU Financial Market Regulation After the Global Financial Crisis," 1353–4.

308 European Parliament, *Resolution on the Financial, Economic and Social Crisis* (T7–0331/2011).

309 European Commission, *Proposal for a Regulation on Prudential Requirements for Credit Institutions and Investment Firms* (COM(2011) 452), p. 15 (Part I) and pp. 211–29 (Part III).

circumstances" fits well when applied in the specific context of its handling of the program of financial services regulatory reforms in this period.[310] In the confusion at the height of the crisis in late 2008, the Commission was undoubtedly overshadowed by Member States. But with taxpayers' money having to be called upon, realpolitik considerations made this inevitable. With respect to the broad contours of the EU's post-crisis regulatory policy agenda that have emerged from 2009 onwards, bear the imprint of many influences and it is impossible to claim that the Commission had a decisive say. Nevertheless, the pro-regulation, pro-integration thrust of the agenda, which reflects the acceptance by Member States of the appropriateness of the expansion of the EU's involvement in financial market matters, has both boosted the Commission's deeply-held long-standing aspirations and confirmed the pivotal nature of the Commission's own role. In particular, notwithstanding that it is possible to identify traces of ambivalence in the Commission's stance towards the new EU supervisory authorities and also to envisage ways in which the relationship between them could become confrontational, these ambiguities do not detract seriously from the core assessment that the EU institutional upgrade, which the Commission played a central role in bringing about, is a major boost for the supranational component of financial regulation. The Commission is also a major beneficiary of these developments in practical terms, because the new arrangements reinforce its access to technical assistance in regulation and relieve it of some of the burden of supervising the front-line implementation of EU law (a function that the Commission has struggled to perform effectively because of its own resource constraints).

The response to the euro area sovereign debt crisis can be viewed in similar terms. By definition, this is a matter on which the Member States, the sovereign entities, were bound to take the lead, thereby making the Commission sometimes appear marginalized, but the search for solutions has made manifest the dependency of Member States on the EU institutions, especially the Commission, for the strengthened budgetary oversight and more draconian deficit disciplines that have come to be regarded as pivotal to the euro's survival. The arrangements now enshrined in the Intergovernmental Treaty thus have the potential to cement the ascendancy of the Commission in the longer term. The faltering nature of the

[310] Dinan, "Institutions and Governance," 109.

intergovernmental political response to the crisis and the fears about policy being dictated by a Franco-German axis that it has stoked among smaller Member States, could also eventually redound in the Commission's favor.[311] If the EU of the future is comprised of "insiders" (euro area Member States that are moving towards a banking and fiscal union) and "outsiders" (other Member States), the Commission's "honest broker" role could become ever-more important because of the ever-present danger that sensitive relations between Member States could be blighted by a dysfunctional lack of cohesion. The Commission's deep concern to ensure that intergovernmental agreements on the euro do not undermine Community methods and EU institutions, and also to be in the forefront of debate on a banking union, is already much in evidence.[312]

The Commission's performance, after a hesitant beginning, with respect to the application of State Aid controls to the financial sector and, latterly, its professional and intellectually robust management of the processes relating to the adoption of legislative proposals for regulatory reform in some key areas, have gone some way towards restoring its reputation for technical competence. Whilst the Commission has been dogged by criticism of the speed of some of its responses, speed is not a reliable proxy for quality, as the hastily-produced notorious first draft of the AIFMD demonstrated. Since the Commission has also been attacked for going too fast, trying to do too much, and risking compromising the quality of its proposals,[313] at least to some extent complaints about the quality of individual measures coming out of the flurry of post-crisis regulatory activity may cancel each other out.

Nevertheless, stepping back from the detail, there are some grounds for concern about the overall direction of the Commission's thinking. Pre-crisis, the primary aim of EU financial services policy was to "consolidate dynamically towards an integrated, open, inclusive, competitive, and economically efficient EU financial market."[314] The need to address at EU level the negative side-effects of removing internal barriers was not ignored, but nor was it the number one priority. Now,

311 J. Chaffin, "Fighting Talk: Barroso Demands Bigger Role for Commission," *Financial Times*, September 29, 2011, 3.

312 European Commission *A Banking Union for Europe* (June 26, 2012).

313 Jean-Baptiste de Franssu of EFAMA, quoted in R. Milne, "Investors Alarmed Over EU Reform Process," ft.com, March 21, 2011.

314 European Commission, *Financial Services Policy 2005–2010*, p. 3.

EU financial services regulation is all about improving safety and soundness. Much has already been achieved in pursuit of this goal, and there are many more new regulatory initiatives in the pipeline.[315] In addition, reviews of existing legislation will provide further opportunities for regulatory tightening, as evidenced by the many ideas for additional regulation that are emerging from the review of the Markets in Financial Instruments Directive, which is discussed further by Niamh Moloney in her chapter. Commissioner Barnier's rhetoric, including warnings of the dangers of the regulatory agenda losing its sense of urgency, suggests considerable keenness to maintain regulatory momentum.[316]

To be fair, there are some signals emanating from within the Commission of the virtues of regulatory restraint not being wholly ignored. The Commission has acknowledged that its financial services regulatory agenda is not "open-ended," that it should be completed by the end of 2012, and that it will then be appropriate to take stock of what has been achieved, using as the benchmark whether the financial sector is fulfilling the function of supporting long-term job creation and the real economy.[317] In spite of the stress on a common or single rulebook, it has demonstrated a willingness to embrace a constructive approach towards giving Member States adequate room to address legitimate domestic concerns in an appropriately differentiated fashion, particularly in the highly contentious area of capital charges.[318]

The Commission will not, of course, ever have a completely free hand in regulatory policy design. The brake that may be applied by the Member States has been examined already. Yet it has been suggested in Part II above that the cumulative long-term effects of short-term decisions could well mean that in some areas this brake will prove to have relatively little force. The Commission could also be restrained by the European Parliament, but as discussed in more detail in Part IV below, the general prospects for the European Parliament to be a moderating influence on Commission regulatory over-zealousness are

[315] European Commission, *Regulating Financial Services for Sustainable Growth – Progress Report*, p. 11.

[316] N. Tait, "Barnier Warns of Complacency as Reform Fatigue Starts to Loom," *Financial Times*, March 21, 2011, 18.

[317] European Commission, *Regulating Financial Services for Sustainable Growth – Progress Report*, p. 8; European Commission, *European Financial Stability and Integration Report 2010*, p. 53.

[318] See text accompanying nn. 158–9 above.

not encouraging. International obligations will also impose some boundaries. As discussed in Part V below, considerations relating to the EU's position in the world have the potential to rein in regulatory excess but much depends on how effectively the Commission, as a participant in international standard-setting processes, exploits opportunities to influence international regulatory design in accordance with its own preferences.

Thus, unease remains. At least some of this disquiet can also be traced back to the crisis-induced shattering of old ideologies that were based on theories of finance that have now fallen out of favor. Universally supported powerful new theories have not emerged to take the place of approaches based on assumptions about the efficiency of markets populated by rational actors, which hitherto dominated modern finance and provided a neat rationale for limiting regulatory intervention to specific market failures such as externalities, information asymmetries and poor incentives. Although pragmatism and incremental responses to changing circumstances have always featured heavily in the Commission's handling of EU financial services regulation, and whilst a degree of skepticism about the wisdom of placing too much faith in theoretical models is warranted by recent experience, the implications of the current gaps in the theoretical underpinning of policy choices are nevertheless still troubling. Regulatory policy choices that have been made in this exceptional period can be expected to put down roots and to have enduring effects that may not look so attractive in a future era, when clearer thinking on the fundamental aims and objectives of financial regulation has emerged, but which cannot easily be reversed. There is a danger that the establishment of an ever-expanding single rulebook could be treated in effect as the overarching policy aim – but rulebooks need to serve a purpose beyond standardization, as uniformity in itself is no guide to substantive contents. Alternatively, "safety" and "soundness" could be treated as the ultimate aims, embracing traditional consumer protection and market integrity objectives – but they, too, are not adequate stand-alone policy goals, since trade-offs need to be made between these considerations and allowing the finance industry enough room to perform economically worthwhile functions that are of benefit to society as a whole.

Having begun this Part by defending the Commission from charges of having been driven by rampant free-market ideology in the pre-crisis period, the ending strikes a less positive note. Niamh Moloney's detailed analysis in her chapter of the implications of the injection of a policy suspicion of market innovation and market intensity and of the growing interest in consumer protection issues at EU level reinforces this sense of foreboding. In the coming years, the Commission is likely to face charges of having swung too far in the opposite direction from the caricature of its pre-crises stance. Mounting a defense may not be easy. John Coffee's chapter in this book powerfully makes the point that regulatory intensity wanes as a crisis subsides, but the EU's market integration ideology makes it a special case in which the dynamics could be significantly different and which could mean that the normal fading of ardor does not occur.

IV: Supranationalism – the crises and the European Parliament

Introduction

The European Parliament tends to be regarded as being strongly pro-integration. It is also generally considered to be skeptical of market- or self-regulation in financial services and to favor formal regulation as the instrument through which to achieve integrationist goals.[319] Of course, it is implausible to regard an institution that is made up of elected individuals representing a constellation of political interests, ranging from the far right to the far left and a spectrum of different national viewpoints, as a monolithic actor with uniform policy preferences, but broadly speaking the main political families represented in the Parliament – i.e. the Christian-Democrats, the Socialists and the Liberals – do adhere to these preferences.[320] A European Parliament resolution of July 6, 2011 on the financial, economic and social crisis provides a valuable snapshot of the Parliament's current stance with respect to financial services regulation. This resolution included calls for stricter regulation and supervision of financial markets, a suitable mechanism for resolving the financial crisis, the development of the concept of a European Treasury, stronger coordination of national tax policies, structural reform of the finance industry, and further institutional progress in order to ensure direct EU-level supervision of systemic institutions and enforcement of a single set of rules.[321]

[319] Posner, "Is a European Approach to Financial Regulation Emerging from the Crisis?," 111.

[320] B. Hörl, A. Warntjen and A. Wonka, "Built On Quicksand? A Decade of Procedural Spatial Models on EU Legislative Decision-Making," *Journal of European Public Policy*, 12 (2005), 592–606; S. Hix, "Parliamentary Behavior with Two Principals: Preferences, Parties, and Voting in the European Parliament," *American Journal of Political Science*, 46 (2002), 688–98.

[321] European Parliament, *Resolution on the Financial, Economic and Social Crisis* (T7–0331/2011).

Finding the Parliament's imprint on crises-related reforms

With confidence in alternative forms of regulation so badly dented and the urgent need for public intervention to strengthen the safety of the cross-border EU market so unequivocally demonstrated, the financial crisis provided a rich opportunity for the European Parliament to further long-cherished aims. Furthermore, the fact that market turmoil coincided broadly with the Parliament acquiring new powers under the Lisbon Treaty has reinforced its position. Numerous parts of the EU post-financial crisis reforms can be seen to bear the imprint of the Parliament. One measure that stands out is the AIFMD. The activities of hedge funds and private equity funds had been a long-standing bugbear for the Parliament, especially MEPs in the socialist grouping (formerly the Party of European Socialists, or PES, but now relabeled as Group of the Progressive Alliance of Socialists & Democrats), and the turmoil unleashed from 2007 onwards provided an opening for a crack-down. This background of long-standing hostility holds the key to understanding why some parts of the Directive, such as the controls that have been applied in respect of companies acquired by private equity funds are, in reality, aiming at a target other than fixing a problem exposed by the crises.[322] In the area of supervision, the Parliament, a long-time strong supporter of the establishment of "real" financial market supervisors at the EU level, successfully championed some quite bold expansions of the ESAs' role. For instance, it was against the rather complicated college of supervisors-based approach to the oversight of CRAs that was originally put in place, and favored vesting this responsibility in ESMA, the model that has since been adopted.[323] It favored giving the ESAs the temporary banning powers in respect of market-threatening activities that is now provided for in their founding instruments[324] and which are being activated by substantive measures in particular areas.[325] It played an important role in securing the general ban on naked sovereign CDS transactions adopted in the Short Selling Regulation.[326] As noted in Part III above, the Parliament was also rather successful in securing for itself

[322] Ferran, "After the Crisis."

[323] Regulation (EU) No. 513/2011, amending the CRA Regulation. For background on the MEPs' view: ECON, *Report on Credit Rating Agencies* (A6–0191/2009, Rapporteur: Jean-Paul Gauzès).

[324] ESMA Regulation, art. 9.

[325] e.g., Short Selling Regulation, art. 28. See also Moloney, Chapter 2 below.

[326] Art. 14.

an important role in relation to the oversight, governance and accountability mechanisms in respect of the new supervisory institutional arrangements, and in refining the procedure for making binding technical standards.

Playing a waiting game?

On the other hand, examples of the views of the Parliament not (yet) prevailing can also be found. In particular, some aspects of its vision for the ESAs, for instance the idea that the EBA should be directly responsible for the prudential supervision of systemically important cross-border institutions, have proved to be overly ambitious at this juncture.[327] The same is true in respect of pan-European institutional arrangements for cross-border bank resolution: whilst MEPs have been quite keen to see the establishment of a pan-European resolution authority, either independently or as a unit of the EBA, this has encountered considerable opposition from Member States and, for now, remains on the drawing board.[328]

In general, it would go too far to label all examples of proposals from the Parliament that have not been adopted as "failures," as that would give insufficient weight to the organic, incremental nature of the evolution of EU regulatory policy: an idea that is deemed to be too radical to be adopted today may nevertheless gain credibility from having been seriously considered and this may help to pave the way for future policy decisions. Examples of "success" mentioned earlier in this Part, which built on foundations laid long before the onset of crisis, demonstrate this process in operation. Ongoing developments with respect to CRAs demonstrate its continuing vitality: MEPs had been pressing for the creation of a new independent, preferably European, CRAs long before the euro area sovereign debt crisis caused it to move into the center of EU policy discourse;[329] although a publicly funded European rating

327 ECON, *Report on Proposal for a Regulation Establishing a European Banking Authority* (A7–0166/2010, Rapporteur: José Manuel García-Margallo y Marfil); European Parliament, *Proposal for a Regulation Establishing a European Banking Authority* (T7–0272/2010, (partial vote)).

328 ECON, *Report on Proposal for a Regulation Establishing a European Banking Authority*; European Parliament, *Resolution with Recommendations to the Commission on Cross-Border Crisis Management in the Banking Sector.*

329 European Commission, *Public Consultation on Credit Rating Agencies* (November 2010), p. 19; ECON, *Report on Credit Rating Agencies: Future Perspectives* (A7–0081/2011, Rapporteur: Wolf Klinz); European Parliament, *Resolution on Credit Rating Agencies: Future Perspectives* (T7–0258/2011); ECON, *Draft Report on Credit Rating Agencies* (A7–0221/2012, Rapporteur: Leonardo Domenici).

agency may still be a step too far, there is certainly growing receptiveness to tailoring regulation so as to foster more competition and choice in the industry.[330] The review clauses that are now standard in EU financial market legislation in effect institutionalize incremental regulatory development because they guarantee opportunities to revive old proposals in potentially more opportune circumstances. For example, largely thanks to the Parliament, the ESAs' founding instruments contain provisions specifically requiring the Commission, as part of scheduled triennial reviews, to assess whether the ESAs should have additional supervisory powers, whether the supervision of banking, securities, pensions and insurance should be integrated, and whether the ESAs should be headquartered in the same city.[331] These are issues that will also be deliberated in the context of banking union proposals, which also include the possible establishment of a cross-border resolution authority.

Financial transactions tax

One particular issue on which it is doubtful whether the long-standing views of the European Parliament will prevail is with respect to the imposition of a financial transactions tax (FTT, also known as a Tobin tax). The considerable popular appeal of a financial transactions tax has, historically, tended to focus on the potential to use the funds raised to address problems outside the financial sector, notably global poverty and climate change. Recent events have heightened interest in an FTT because in an environment of massive public sector debt caused, in part, by publicly funded bailouts of financial institutions and continuing market difficulties, it appears to offer both a "polluter pays" mechanism and a way of striking back directly at the high-frequency trading strategies that, as discussed in Niamh Moloney's chapter below, are coming under close scrutiny for fear that they are irresponsible, socially wasteful activities that may contribute significantly to market destabilization.[332] However, one major drawback is that if an FTT is not introduced on a worldwide basis, mobile capital will likely react by moving to tax-free jurisdictions, leaving markets in jurisdictions where the tax is in place at a significant

330 European Commission, *Proposal for a Regulation amending Regulation (EC) No 1060/2009 on Credit Rating Agencies* (COM(2011) 747), pp. 11–12.

331 ESMA Regulation, art. 81.

332 However, the IMF has doubted whether it is well suited to these aims: IMF, *A Fair And Substantial Contribution by the Financial Sector: Final Report for the G-20* (June 2010), pp. 19–21.

competitive disadvantage. Initially the EU's stance emphasized working towards an international agreement on an FTT,[333] but during 2011 (as the prospects for agreement at the international level appeared to fade and as political concerns about the trauma being inflicted on the euro by the markets deepened) momentum began to build behind the idea of being prepared, if necessary, to implement an FTT at the European level as a first step. The European Parliament was an early promoter of this view,[334] and after some hesitation the European Commission came round to its merits, and included an EU FTT first in EU budget proposals,[335] and then in a formal proposal for an EU Council Directive on the matter.[336]

An EU-only FTT still has many powerful opponents among the Member States, led by the UK which, as the location of the world's largest capital market, would be especially affected by it.[337] There have been serious warnings about the damage it could cause to EU competitiveness, not only from self-interested industry quarters, but also from senior independent voices including the former ECB president,[338] and there is always the possibility that alliances based on support in principle for the tax could fall apart when attention turns to matters of detailed design, such as the contentious question of what funds raised by the tax should be used for.[339] Since the

333 European Commission, *Innovative Financing at a Global Level* (SEC (2010) 409) was the Commission's response to a call from the European Council in October 2009 for the Commission to examine innovative financing at a global level; European Commission, *Taxation of the Financial Sector* (COM(2010) 549) left open the possibility of an EU-only FTT, but noted that "an FTT appears less suitable for unilateral introduction at EU-level since the risks of relocation are high and would undermine the ability to generate revenue" (p. 8).

334 European Parliament, *Resolution on Innovative Financing at Global and European Level* (T7–0080/2011); European Parliament, *Resolution on Financial Transaction Taxes – Making Them Work* (T7–0056/2010). Compare European Council, *Presidency Conclusions*, March 24/25, 2011 (EUCO 10/1/11), p. 6, in which the political leaders of the EU Member States did not go beyond affirming their commitment to seeking a global agreement.

335 European Commission, *A Budget for Europe 2020* (COM(2011) 500), p. 7.

336 European Commission, *Proposal for a Council Directive on a Common System of Financial Transaction Tax and amending Directive 2008/7/EC* (COM(2011) 594).

337 Chancellor of Exchequer, *Written Ministerial Statement*, June 22, 2012.

338 S. Pignal, "Trichet Urges EU to Drop Tobin Tax Plan," *Financial Times*, July 1, 2011, 3.

339 The Commission's early suggestion that an EU FTT tax could be used to raise funds for the EU budget raised hackles. A refinement of this in the Commission's draft Directive proposal, namely that the tax will aim at creating a new revenue stream to gradually displace national contributions to the EU budget, leaving a lesser burden on national treasuries, may have been crafted to respond to this line of criticism. However, presenting it in this way feeds UK suspicions about underlying motivations, in that it assumes the character of a roundabout way of nullifying the notorious rebate on the UK's contribution to the EU budget.

adoption of an EU law on this matter requires unanimity among the Member States (and it is, moreover, not an area in which the Parliament has direct legislative competence (although it must be consulted)), particular skepticism about the likelihood of its adoption is warranted.[340] But even if the proposal is blocked, MEPs may still be able to make a lot of political capital from having given it strong backing.

Implications for the future

Niamh Moloney has convincingly argued that the effect of crisis has been to entrench the Parliament as a key actor in financial regulation and that its pro-regulation stance is likely to have significant enduring influence over EU financial market law.[341] Should the Commission become increasingly zealous in its pursuit of regulatory solutions notwithstanding its professed desire to avoid the imposition of disproportionate burdens, it is unlikely to be the Parliament that will seek to rein this in. Indeed, in some areas, such as supervision, where it may be called upon from time to time to play a role in mediating turf wars between the Commission and the ESAs, the Parliament may be more ambitious than even the Commission about expanding the scope and depth of EU intervention.

The prospect of a progressively influential Parliament makes it increasingly important to ask probing questions about MEPs' technical competence in this sphere, the processes that the Parliament and, in particular, ECON, follow in policy formation and the influences to which they are susceptible, and the mechanisms of accountability. With respect to technical expertise, ECON had already established a good track record before the financial crisis, and its constructive role in relation to some of the more contentious matters that have arisen in the post-crisis regulatory surge, such as its support for the inclusion of third country passports in the AIFMD to alleviate protectionism fears, has enhanced its reputation for competence and judgment. However, the Parliament's responses in other areas, such as financial sector remuneration, have shown at least tinges of populism.

The natural expectation that MEPs would be held accountable for their performance with respect to the shaping of financial services legislation via the ballot box is put in doubt by studies of legislative politics in the European Parliament indicating very weak connections between MEPs and their voters, since these suggest that assumptions

[340] The legal basis would be TFEU, art. 113 (indirect taxation).
[341] Moloney, "EU Financial Market Regulation After the Global Financial Crisis," 1338.

about election-centered legislative behavior may not hold good in this context.[342] The last round of elections to the European Parliament certainly did not suggest that being closely associated with key contributions to the shape of the EU's post-crisis response was a direct route to political gains. In spite of the prominence of the left-leaning PES group in castigating financial market regulatory laxity in the pre-crisis period, its parties fared badly in those elections.[343] At the level of individuals, even though Poul-Nyrup Rasmussen, the President of the PES group and former Danish prime minister, had been one of the most high-profile MEPs on issues of financial services regulation in the period up to and around the crisis, and some of the views that he had championed (particularly with respect to hedge funds and private equity funds) made their way into the new legislation, tentative efforts to put him forward as a rival candidate to the incumbent President Barroso for the position of President of the Commission failed to gain traction.[344] To have done so badly against a background of financial crisis, recession, rising unemployment, preconditions that "seemed to be perfect for socialists and social democrats,"[345] has provoked much general soul-searching on the left.[346] Since the European Parliament's overall stance towards financial services regulation has long been characterized by a strong preference for regulation that, in conventional terms, would likely be regarded as left-leaning and the effect of crisis has, in substance, been only to further the encroachment of the right into traditionally left-wing ideological territory, it could well be that voters struggle to see a clear difference between left and right on these matters.[347]

V: External relations

Introduction

The final piece of the jigsaw is the external aspect of EU post-crisis financial regulation. One reason why this matters so much emerges from a vision of the world of the future that can be drawn from the preceding

[342] G. McElroy, "Legislative Politics" in Jørgensen, Pollack and Rosamond (eds.), *Handbook of European Union Politics*, pp. 175–94, p. 177.

[343] Dinan, "Institutions and Governance," 104.

[344] S. Hix, "The 2009 European Parliament Elections: A Disaster for Social Democrats," *EUSA Review*, 22 (2009), 2–5.

[345] E. Sundström, "The Next Left: Thoughts on the European Elections 2009" in E. Stetter, K. Duffek and A. Skrzypek (eds.), *Renewing Social Democracy: Contributions to a European-wide Debate* (Belgium: The Foundation of European Progressive Studies, 2009), pp. 123–8.

[346] Ibid. [347] Hix, "The 2009 European Parliament Elections."

discussion in this chapter. A plausible picture has emerged of a highly interventionist Commission that is broadly supported by an increasingly powerful Parliament and of an ever-more dense and self-reinforcing system of EU-wide regulation and supervision over which Member States find it increasingly hard to keep tabs, except in a diminishing number of high-profile areas in which their national economies remain too divergent for agreement on detailed harmonization to be forthcoming. In that environment, considerations relating to the EU's position in the world could assume a progressively important role as a moderating influence.

It had become axiomatic long before the recent crises that countries need to pay close attention to the international dimension of financial regulation, both in order to protect themselves from contagion and also to promote their domestic interests abroad and to attract international investment. For major economic powers, the development of domestic and international financial regulation usually involves two-way traffic, with their domestic institutions sometimes acting as the mechanism for the implementation of global standards and at other times assuming a more proactive role in shaping the standards in international fora. Although international engagement is sometimes couched in language that may suggest that it is an altruistic exercise designed to save the world from harm, self-interest is a key motivation.[348] As well as protecting itself from externalities and avoiding putting its nationals at a competitive disadvantage because of an uneven playing field, a major power that successfully "uploads" its domestic standards to the international level minimizes the loss of autonomy that is consequential upon entry into international commitments. Moreover, in effect, its success can amount to a form of regulatory imperialism that enhances its power and prestige. The promotion by the United States and the UK of the original international bank capital accords back in the 1980s is often cited as a classic example of an international initiative that was largely driven by self-interest.[349]

Whilst there is thus nothing intrinsically new about major economic powers striving to exert influence internationally in order to gain and

[348] For a general review of the EU's role as a promoter of its own standards and values abroad: R. Petrov, "Exporting the Acquis Communautaire into the Legal Systems of Third Countries," *European Foreign Affairs Review*, 13 (2008), 33–52.

[349] For a major review of how soft law in international financial regulation really works, see C.J. Brummer, *Soft Law and the Global Financial System: Rule-Making in the Twenty-First Century* (Cambridge University Press, 2012), and in particular ch. 6 for its detailed analysis of clashes between US and European authorities on post-crisis regulatory design issues.

preserve comparative advantages, the financial crisis – a global catastrophe that demanded a concerted global response – provided new opportunities that the EU institutions have undoubtedly sought to exploit.[350] The need to align EU and international developments has proved to be a malleable argument that has been deployed in a variety of ways, sometimes in order to advance an EU project, the idea being that the EU should be the path-breaker that leads the way for others to follow, but on other occasions in order to urge restraint, in case unilateral EU action could lead to regulatory fragmentation or could damage regional competitiveness.[351] Yet another slant has been the use of international commitments as a legitimating device, a tactic employed (with only limited success) by Commissioner Barnier when he declared in evidence before a UK parliamentary committee that had expressed concern about the scale of the post-crisis EU regulatory agenda that "my agenda is essentially the G20 agenda."[352] EU officials and politicians have also sometimes alluded to the EU's good track record in implementing international standards as a means of claiming moral authority in the international arena and to put pressure on other countries that are lagging behind, as in the case of the Basel II Accord, which the United States was slow to implement.[353] The US stance on Basel II has been a long-standing source of frustration for the EU, and there are suspicions that it could be repeated with Basel III.[354] Being a strong backer of international standards has also sometimes been presented as a way for the EU to acquire more influence over the standard-setters, but this is an argument that has to be handled with care in order not to undermine the legitimacy of

[350] European Commission, *Regulating Financial Services for Sustainable Growth*, p. 3.

[351] e.g., in the context of an EU-only FTT discussed in Part IV above, where both versions of the argument have been used.

[352] House of Commons Treasury Committee, *Financial Regulation: A Preliminary Consideration of the Government's Proposals* (HC 430–I), 55. The Committee found that only 14 of the 39 initiatives listed by the Commission were directly related to that agenda.

[353] e.g., European Council, *Presidency Conclusions*, September 16, 2010 (EUCO 21/1/10), p. 4. Generally on Basel II and the United States. R.J. Herring, "The Rocky Road to Implementation of Basel II in the United States," *Atlantic Economic Journal*, 35 (2007), 411–29.

[354] These are hinted at in the European Commission's comment in its introduction to its Basel III implementation proposals that "[t]he Commission is therefore closely monitoring the consistent implementation of Basel III across the globe and would need to draw all the necessary conclusions in due time should other key jurisdictions not follow suit": European Commission, *CRD IV – Frequently Asked Questions* (MEMO/11/527, July 20, 2011). An intention to monitor other countries' performance in meeting international commitments has also been declared in the derivatives context: EMIR, rec. 6.

standard-setting bodies by casting a shadow over their autonomy. Significant tensions in the EU's relationship with the International Accounting Standards Board during the financial crisis have put the spotlight on this concern.[355]

It is evident that references to global and regional alignment and to the exercise of global influence are usually politically loaded. They are also often tinged with considerable amounts of rhetorical flourish to which reality is unlikely to match up.[356] Given the significance of the aspiration to exert influence internationally as a driver of the EU's post-crisis policy choices and also the way in which international considerations can serve as a constraining force, it is crucial to take this inquiry to a deeper level. The stronger the EU's influence in the international sphere, the less attention it will need to pay to moderating its own domestic choices with a view to making them an attractive model for others to follow, and the more space it will have to control its own destiny rather than, in effect, having to play by someone else's rules. The converse also holds.

Exerting influence over international financial regulation as new economic powers challenge the established order – new opportunities for EU regulatory leadership?

One of the striking political consequences of the financial crisis was the emergence of the G20 as a key forum for the development of an

[355] Discussed in Ferran, "Capital Market Openness after Financial Turmoil," in P. Koutrakos and M. Evans (eds), *Beyond the Established Orders* (Oxford: Hart Publishing, 2011), pp. 68–70. On the IASB's success in maintaining its independence: P. Leblond, "EU, US and International Accounting Standards: A Delicate Balancing Act in Governing Global Finance," *Journal of European Public Policy*, 18 (2011), 443–61.

[356] e.g., in spite of Commissioner McCreevy's professed keenness to provide standards for the world on rating agencies (C. McCreevy, Press Conference on Credit Rating Agencies, Brussels, November 12, 2008 (online: http://europa.eu/rapid/pressReleasesAction.do?reference=SPEECH/08/605&format=HTML&aged=0&language=EN&guiLanguage=EN), a considerable amount of the content of the CRA Regulation (as amended by Regulation (EU) No. 513/2011) can be sourced back to the IOSCO, *Code of Conduct Fundamentals for Credit Rating Agencies* (2004, amended 2008). Elsewhere the Commission did acknowledge the IOSCO *Code* as the "global benchmark," but noted that it had "some limitations that need to be overcome to make its rules fully operational": European Commission, *Proposal for a Regulation on Credit Rating Agencies* (COM (2008) 704). In imposing mandatory oversight on CRAs the EU has been part of a post-crisis international trend: IOSCO, *International Cooperation in Oversight of Credit Rating Agencies* (Madrid: IOSCO, March 2009).

internationally-coordinated regulatory response.[357] Allied to this, the Financial Stability Forum, formed after the Asian financial crisis in 1997–8, has been re-established as the Financial Stability Board (FSB), with an expanded membership, including the European Commission, and a stronger mandate for ensuring financial stability within a regulatory system that promotes "strong, sustainable and balanced global growth."[358] The participation of more countries in the key agenda-setting political decisions and international standard-setting processes creates a new dynamic, but the implications are, as yet, unclear.[359] The shifts in the location of economic power that are reflected in the new international groupings[360] could mean that as time goes on, Beth Simmons' convincing explanation of late twentieth-century international capital market regulation as a system shaped mostly by the policy preferences of the United States, the dominant financial center, becomes increasingly less relevant.[361] However, there is much uncertainty about what could replace it.

Another country or regional power could usurp the United States as the de facto global standard-setter. On the other hand, it is also possible that the set of factors that made the United States the hegemon of global financial regulation and sustained it in that position for so long may not

[357] For one account of how this came about, see G. Brown, *Beyond the Crash: Overcoming the First Crisis of Globalisation* (New York; Simon & Schuster, 2010), pp. 117–18.

[358] G20, *Leaders' Statement: The Pittsburgh Summit*, September 24/25, 2009.

[359] L. Mosley and D.A. Singer, "The Global Financial Crisis: Lessons and Opportunities for International Political Economy," *International Interactions*, 35 (2009), 420–9.

[360] As at 2010, relative percentage shares of world GDP were: US (19.7); Euro area (14.6); China (13.6); Japan (5.8); India (5.4); UK (2.9); Brazil (2.9): IMF, *World Economic Outlook: Tensions from the Two-Speed Recovery* (Washington DC: IMF, 2011), p. 171. Projections indicate that the share of world GDP held by E7 countries (China, India, Brazil, Russia, Indonesia, Mexico and Turkey) could overtake the share held by G7 countries (US, Japan, Germany, UK, France, Italy and Canada) by 2020: PwC, *The World in 2050* (2011, online: www.pwc.com/en_GX/gx/world-2050/pdf/world-in-2050-jan-2011.pdf).

[361] B. Simmons, "The International Politics of Harmonization: the Case of Capital Market Regulation," *International Organization*, 55 (2001), 589–620. See also R.D. Germain, "Reforming the International Financial Architecture: The New Political Agenda" in R. Wilkinson and S. Hughes (eds.), *Global Governance: Critical Perspectives* (London: Routledge, 2002), pp. 17–35; C. Brummer, "Post-American Securities Regulation," *California Law Review*, 98 (2010), 327–84. Generally on the "realist" approach to regulation: D.W. Drezner, "The Realist Tradition in American Public Opinion," *Perspectives on Politics*, 6 (2008), 51–70; S.L. Lamy, "Contemporary Mainstream Approaches: Neo-realism and Neo-Liberalism" in Baylis and Smith (eds.), *The Globalization of World Politics*.

arise again. For instance, although China is expected to become the world's biggest economy within the decade,[362] parts of its financial markets are relatively unsophisticated. To the extent that this underdevelopment continues, China will have limited incentives to develop its own home-grown solutions to problems arising from complex markets and therefore will not be able to draw upon domestic experience to proffer innovative regulatory ideas to the rest of the world. In the negotiations around Basel III, for instance, China maintained a low profile, in part because its banks had not experienced the problems that had made necessary that rewrite of the rules.[363] Furthermore, Chinese financial markets remain largely closed to outsiders, a feature which, if it persists, will mean that one of the important mechanisms whereby a country can export its regulatory approach – i.e. by making adherence to an equivalent version of that approach a precondition for access – will not be available.

Without a clear leader and in the absence of some of the incentives/threats that can encourage convergence around a particular view, securing meaningful agreements between relatively large groups of participants at a global level could become harder. In spite of its successful contribution to the early shaping of the post-crisis financial regulatory agenda, there have been signs of the G20 beginning to falter as its focus has shifted to broader economic concerns.[364] In the multipolar world of the future, the result could be more regulatory fragmentation, with regional approaches and bilateral arrangements between key jurisdictions and regions rather than global accords being the main ways in which frameworks for the operation of international financial markets are established and maintained.[365] This changing world could present the EU with a myriad of new opportunities to set the agenda in external relations. Indeed, it has even been claimed in academic discourse that the way could be open "for an international financial architecture under European leadership."[366]

The EU, together with the Member States, was an early mover in relation to some regulatory issues that came to prominence as a result of

[362] PwC, *The World in 2050.*

[363] D. McMahon, "Global Finance: China Seeks Global Finance Pact," *The Wall Street Journal*, October 11, 2010, C3.

[364] C. Giles, "Sarkozy tells G20 'Dare to Dream' or Else Lose Relevance," *Financial Times*, January 28, 2011, 4.

[365] D.A. Singer, "Uncertain Leadership: The US Regulatory Response to the Global Financial Crisis" in Helleiner, Pagliari and Zimmermann, *Global Finance in Crisis*, pp. 93–107.

[366] Posner, "Is a European Approach?," p. 118.

the financial crisis.[367] Addressing flaws in financial sector remuneration structures and practices is one that stands out.[368] Yet it has been argued with some force that the EU failed to sustain its early lead in setting the international agenda and also that when attention is focused on detailed legislative instruments as opposed to broad policy aspirations, it is in fact "hard to unambiguously identify a European impact over the international agenda or the emergence of an alternative 'European model'."[369] In the key area of capital charges, for instance, the Commission has even been taken to task by the European Parliament for being insufficiently proactive.[370] Reticence in such an important area casts a shadow over the EU's "achievements" with respect to leadership on remuneration reforms because whilst they are not completely beside the point, the remuneration restrictions aim at a side-issue rather than the core concerns revealed by the turmoil in the markets.

For the reality of "global leadership" to fall some way short of the rhetoric is not troubling in itself. "Leading" could mean being first to address a problem or going furthest in imposing a crackdown. Neither is it inevitably desirable, given the risks of ill-thought-through knee-jerk responses and over-reactions that crisis situations can so easily provoke. Nor is it necessarily a cause for regret that the new EU regulatory instruments may be short on radically new or fundamentally different ideas, since idiosyncratic regional novelty would likely be a source of unwelcome international regulatory friction. Generally speaking, being in sync with others is a positive, not a negative. Yet, notwithstanding these considerations, the sense of underachievement that some have identified in relation to the international impact of the EU's response to the financial crisis gives pause for thought.

There are two overarching structural issues that bedevil the EU's efforts to lead at the international level. First, whilst the EU institutions and its Member States profess much interest in enhancing the EU's effectiveness as a global actor, this is not the same thing as having the political will actually to make hard decisions about streamlining European participation in international bodies in order to facilitate this

[367] Ibid. [368] e.g., Ferran, "New Regulation."

[369] S. Pagliari, "Building a Wall Around Europe. The European Regulatory Response to the Global Financial Crisis and the Turn in Transatlantic Relations" (online: www.stefano-pagliari.net/SP/Home.html).

[370] ECON, *Report on Basel II and Revision of the Capital Requirements Directives (CRD IV)* (A7–0251/2010, Rapporteur: Othmar Karas); European Parliament, *Resolution on Basel II and Revision of the Capital Requirements Directives (CRD IV)* (T7–0354/2010).

development. Second, many of the key EU preoccupations are very closely tied to the particularities of the Union's legal and institutional situation, which is bound to limit their international relevance. The following sections elaborate on these structural issues, but there are two further considerations that must also be mentioned. The first, which is directly related to the euro area crisis, is the problem of contamination by association. The organization of the euro and financial services regulation are distinct EU policy areas, but there can be no doubt that the euro area turmoil and the faltering efforts to resolve it have undermined the EU's reputation for being a source of workable and safe policy ideas for the operation of financial markets.[371] The lingering after-effects of the reputational self-harm inflicted by the euro area crisis could be hard to eradicate. The second is also related to the euro area crisis, but goes more to its economic consequences than to flaws in the original design of the currency. To the extent that the theory of regulatory influence following economic success still holds good, forecasts of ongoing weaknesses in the euro area economies and in the wider EU, together with the strong likelihood of an even bleaker future should efforts to save the euro fail, imply that the EU could find itself fighting a progressively steep uphill battle to make its views on regulation count at the international level.[372]

"Speaking with a single voice"

One structural hurdle to the EU's effectiveness as a global actor in financial regulation stems from the way in which competences for financial services are shared between EU institutions and the Member States. Whilst certain steps forward have been taken in the aftermath of the financial crisis, including the upgrading of the Commission's status to full membership of the FSB and the growing practice of EU Member States' leaders agreeing on "common" or "unified" EU positions ahead of key meetings of international groupings,[373] the set-up still falls short of the EU "speaking with a single voice." Multiplicity of representation

[371] "Europe on the Road to Irrelevance; Unless the EU Gets its Act Together, It Will Pay a High Price," *Financial Times*, June 18, 2011, 6 (Leader Column).

[372] e.g., Oxford Economics, *Global Outlook: Will the Eurozone Crisis Sink the Global Economy?* (December 20, 2011, online: www.oxfordeconomics.com/FREE/PDFS/WEP-SAMPLEDEC11.PDF).

[373] Examining the efforts by Member States to coordinate responses ahead of G20 meetings: D. Hodson, "The Paradox of EMU's External Representation: The Case of the G20 and the IMF" (March 2011, online: http://euce.org/eusa/2011/papers/6e_hodson.pdf).

does not always lead to insuperable difficulties, as can be seen from experience in the remuneration context where concerted efforts by various European players helped to put a distinctive stamp on the FSB's work.[374] However, EU efforts are still prone to being undermined by larger Member States continuing to use their direct membership of international bodies to promote their own distinctive national agenda. Particular doubts persist about the extent of the Commission's influence within the Basel processes[375] where the Commission's position is at risk of being compromised not only by its lack of formal membership status, which puts it at a disadvantage to those Member States that are members, but also by the divergence of views between Member States, which can hinder the development of coherent, ambitious EU policy.[376] In the post-crisis negotiations over the Basel III Capital Accord there was much evidence of Member States continuing to put their domestic interests first.[377]

In addition to the problem of lack of policy cohesion resulting from several different European agendas being pursued at any given time, the hybrid arrangements can result in the involvement of an indefensibly large number of people as representatives of the EU and its Member States at international gatherings. For instance, two EU presidents (the President

374 Ferran, "New Regulation."

375 The Commission likes to claim that it is influential: European Commission, *European Financial Stability and Integration Report 2010* (SEC(2011) 489), p. 6. The European Parliament, however, doubts whether the Commission is sufficiently proactive in promoting EU interests and also worries about the consequences of standards being agreed in Basel that then have to be incorporated into EU law without meaningful additional input from the EU's democratic bodies: ECON, *Report on the Proposal for a Directive as Regards Capital Requirements for the Trading Book and for Re-securitisations, and the Supervisory Review of Remuneration Policies (CRD 3)* (A7–0205/2010, Rapporteur: Arlene McCarthy); ECON, *Report on Basel II and revision of the Capital Requirements Directives (CRD IV).*

376 D.L. Mügge, "The European Presence in Global Financial Governance: a Principal–Agent Perspective," *Journal of European Public Policy*, 18 (2011), 383–402.

377 Discussing German efforts in Basel to secure a phased introduction of the new requirements: D. Enrich and D. Cimilluca, "International Finance: Most Banks Seem Set on Basel Rules – For Lenders that Need More Capital, 'Generous' Deadline Works in their Favor," *The Wall Street Journal*, September 14, 2010, C2; B. Blackstone and D. Enrich, "International Finance: Germany Digs In Over Basel Rules," *The Wall Street Journal*, July 28, 2010, C2. Splits within Europe were thought to have played a part in the non-endorsement of Co-cos: M. Louis, "Europeans Lose Out to U.S. With Basel Committee's Contingent Capital Vote," *Bloomberg*, June 27, 2010 (online: www.bloomberg.com/news/2011–06–26/basel-committee-decision-on-contingent-capital-backs-u-s-stance.html).

of the Commission and the President of the European Council) attend G20 summit meetings, in addition to the representatives of the larger Member States, who are also entitled to attend in their own right. The position at the G20 finance minister level is even more lavish because, in addition to the representatives of the national finance ministries of member countries, the EU is represented by the Commission, the ECB and the rotating ECOFIN–Council presidency.[378] The EU's recent internal institutional reforms with respect to financial services supervision could make a bad situation worse, because the ESAs' mandate extends to external relations and, predictably, they have begun to demand a "seat at the table" of international bodies in order to perform this role.[379] The ESAs would arguably be a more appropriate participant than the Commission in international bodies comprised of supervisors, such as the International Organization of Securities Commissions (IOSCO) and the International Association of Insurance Supervisors (IAIS). The European Parliament also wants more direct involvement at the international level, which is understandable in view of its increasingly powerful role in EU financial services policymaking but which, from another perspective, adds yet another layer of difficulty.[380]

The over-representation of Europe in international institutions has been a source of international friction for some time. Indeed, the *de Larosière Report* drew attention to the need for the EU to be proactive in addressing this issue.[381] Recent heated debate about IMF governance reform and also deliberations in international fora on matters other than financial regulation (such as the 2009 Copenhagen climate change conference where European players were effectively sidelined) have

378 The role of the two presidents in external relations has treaty backing: TEU, art. 15.6 (European Council) and art. 17.1 (Commission). However, the Treaty does not refer specifically to the G20. Representation at recent G20 finance ministers' meetings has been organized on a rather ad hoc basis: M. Emerson, R. Balfour, T. Corthaut, J Wouters, P. Maciej Kaczyński and T. Renardeu, *Upgrading the EU's Role as Global Actor: Institutions, Law and the Restructuring of European Diplomacy* (Brussels: CEPS, 2011), pp. 106–8.

379 ESMA Regulation, art. [illegible]; S. Maijoor, "Speech" (July 5, 2011, online: www.astrid-online.it/Regolazion/Studi – ric/ESMA_Speech-Maijoor_05_07_11.pdf), in which the ESMA chair called for ESMA to have a seat on the IASB Monitoring Board along with the European Commission.

380 ECON, *Report on Basel II and Revision of the Capital Requirements Directives (CRD IV)*; European Parliament, *Resolution on Basel II and Revision of the Capital Requirements Directives (CRD IV)*.

381 *de Larosière Report*, p. 67.

demonstrated that the EU and its Member States run the risk of being increasingly marginalized by coalitions and alliances of other countries if they do not do more to put their own house in order.[382] Progress could be slow, however. Although the European Council has recognized the need generally to improve the functioning of the EU's external policy through the adoption of a more integrated approach,[383] and the need for streamlining has also been endorsed by the European Parliament,[384] the persistence of some important differences in national economies and the imperative for national politicians to be seen to be robustly defending those interests in all relevant fora, mean that a formidable array of political and institutional sensitivities hinder progress towards this goal. Closer fiscal arrangements within the euro area could lead to a streamlining of representation arrangements within that group of Member States, but these would not necessarily alleviate, indeed could possibly even exacerbate, the complexity of relations between the EU and international organizations and third countries by creating new tensions between "in" and "out" Member States that spill over into disputes about external representation.

Exporting key EU regulatory ideas: issues of suitability

Another obstacle standing in the way of EU efforts to exert global influence is that some of the main EU ideas on regulatory design may be simply unsuitable for export because they relate to a unique situation and depend on the existence of supranational institutions that do not exist elsewhere.[385] Pursuit of the single market agenda over many years has produced a complex regulatory and institutional system that results in the EU being in a very different position from other countries with respect to the options for dealing with cross-border contagion. Because of where it starts from and the particularly acute nature of the problems it faces, the EU has incentives to come up with the world's most advanced regulatory models for the reinforcement of cross-border supervision, crisis management and bank resolution and insolvency. As is evident from the discussion in Part III above, much intellectual

382 Emerson *et al.*, *Upgrading the EU's Role as Global Actor*, pp. 106–8

383 European Council, *Presidency Conclusions*, September 16, 2010 (EUCO 21/1/10).

384 European Parliament, *Resolution on the Financial, Economic and Social Crisis* (T7–0331/2011), paras. 27–8.

385 P.H. Verdier, "Mutual Recognition in International Finance," *Harvard International Law Journal*, 52 (2011), 55–108.

firepower and effort is now going into repairing the weaknesses of the existing EU system with respect to these matters. Yet the very sophistication of the models that are eventually adopted could substantially limit their international relevance.

More generally, whereas before the crisis there was considerable international interest in the seemingly successful way in which the EU had addressed the problem of markets without borders and regulatory systems with borders through a system of "mutual recognition" (though, in fact, the EU approach had evolved far beyond the relatively low levels of comparability that tend to be associated with mutual recognition), enthusiasm has undoubtedly waned.[386] The stalling of the US–Australia mutual recognition arrangement, discussed by Jennifer G. Hill in her chapter, can be regarded as an example of this cooling-off. Memories of the cross-border fallout from the Icelandic banking collapse and the complications of the Belgian–Dutch Fortis rescue, which vividly demonstrated the harm that far-reaching dismantling of barriers to cross-border activity can cause even where supranational institutions and other safeguards are present, can be expected to linger. With the euro area crisis further compounding the impression that EU grand designs can be based on insecure foundations, international mistrust of ambitious "made in Europe" ideas could take a long time to dissipate. It is not that "mutual recognition" has been completely discredited – indeed the notion of recognizing that regimes are, at some level, comparable to each other is implicit in the "equivalence-based" approaches that are discussed next – but simply that the EU's very advanced version of it now comes with a considerable health warning.

The prospects for building global influence through a more equal transatlantic relationship

Based on the discussion thus far, a lackluster assessment of the EU's capacity to make a significant impression on the global stage in financial services regulation is not unwarranted. The message is that it would be quite unwise for the EU to attempt to try to "go it alone" in its efforts to influence global standards, because to do so would run the risk of ending up on the wrong side of many international deliberations and ultimately becoming more of

[386] Discussed in Ferran, "Capital Market Openness," pp. 47–80. See also E.J. Pan, "A European Solution to the Regulation of Cross-Border Markets," *Brooklyn Journal of Corporate, Financial & Commercial Law*, 2 (2007), 133–66, 138–9.

an importer than an exporter of global standards. A more sensible approach would be to build strength in numbers through alliances with like-minded powers outside the EU. Pursuit of this strategy holds out the prospect of international considerations serving as a quite powerful moderating influence on EU internal regulatory policy choices, because a vital precondition for any effective alliance is that the participants must be working to broadly the same agenda and have compatible approaches.

Working bilaterally with other similarly-minded world powers, directly, to address common problems or to further common interests but also, indirectly, to build alliances that may be able to exert formidable global influence in promoting shared game plans, is a well-established part of the EU financial services regulatory policy agenda, focusing mainly, although not exclusively, on the transatlantic relationship; it is not something that has sprung up simply as a result of recent turmoil.[387] On the European side, this dialogue is led by the European Commission, but the ESAs are also involved. In many respects, it would be more natural for the ESAs actually to lead discussions with US supervisory authorities, but the constitutional sensitivities in the relationship between the Commission and the ESAs that were discussed in Part III above in relation to the power to set binding technical standards are once again relevant, as also are certain legal and political delicacies about the respective roles of the ESAs and the Member States' national officials and regulatory authorities. Pragmatic, if somewhat cumbersome, arrangements are emerging in order to accommodate the various parties that demand a say in these matters.[388]

[387] The development of the transatlantic dialogue in financial crisis in the decade up to the financial crisis is discussed in Ferran, "Capital Market Openness." See also Schammo, *EU Prospectus Law*, pp. 142–90.

[388] e.g., the EMIR framework for trade repositories: the Commission determines the equivalence of a third country regime (art. 75(1)); the Commission makes recommendations to the Council for the negotiation of supporting international agreements on information exchange (art. 75(2)); ESMA then establishes a cooperation arrangement with the third country supervisor (art. 75(3)); and finally ESMA recognizes the third country trade repository (art. 77). The EMIR framework for recognition of third country central counterparties (art. 25) is similarly cumbersome, imposing, among other things, a requirement on ESMA to consult with a range of EU parties, including specified national competent authorities, certain Member States' central banks and members of the ESCB of relevant Member States.

In the AIFMD context, ESMA has proposed to assume a central negotiating role with respect to cooperation agreements to be entered into between EU and non-EU competent authorities: ESMA, *Technical Advice to the European Commission on possible implementing measures of the Alternative Investment Fund Managers Directive* (ESMA/ 2011/379), pp. 240–6.

Historically, the EU had to contend with being the junior partner in the transatlantic relationship, and also with being overshadowed to some extent by the UK–US relationship, which often took center-stage because of London's position as the main European financial center. Nevertheless, in the years leading up to the financial crisis the EU, riding the wave of European market expansion and increasing global competitiveness, achieved a number of notable successes in its efforts to correct the lopsidedness of the transatlantic relationship.[389] It was pressure from Europe that forced the United States to put in place a system of consolidated supervision of investment banks administered by the Securities and Exchange Commission (SEC). The instrument that was used to exert this pressure was the Financial Conglomerates Directive, which imposed consolidated supervision requirements on all financial institutions operating in the EU and which would have had the effect of requiring US investment banks to submit to EU-based supervision but for the establishment of the SEC system, which was deemed to meet an EU "equivalence" standard.[390] (Ironically, this system was later to become notorious when the collapse of major US investment banks exposed shortcomings in the SEC's discharge of prudential responsibilities.)[391] In the area of financial reporting, the EU's decision to adopt international financial reporting standards (IFRS) and to require them to be used by foreign issuers subject to a concession based on the equivalence of foreign standards, gave the EU a bargaining chip that was instrumental in securing a reciprocal relaxation of US requirements for foreign reporting issuers.[392] Indeed, until the financial crisis intervened, the United States seemed to be on the brink of going further down the path already taken by the EU, as it was seriously considering the adoption of IFRS for domestic issuers.[393] This was a situation in which the

[389] As well as the specific examples mentioned in the text, "europeanization" of US policy in a broader sense, i.e. a shift from a retail to an institutional focus in securities regulation, has been identified: D.C. Langevoort, "Steps Toward the Europeanization of US Securities Regulation, with Thoughts on the Evolution and Design of a Multinational Securities Regulator," in M. Tison *et al.* (eds.), *Perspectives in Company Law and Financial Regulation* (Cambridge University Press, 2009), pp. 485–506; D.C. Langevoort, "Global Securities Regulation After the Financial Crisis," *Journal of International Economic Law*, 13 (2010), 799–815.

[390] 2002/87/EC.

[391] H. Davies, *The Financial Crisis: Who is to Blame?* (Cambridge: Polity Press, 2010), pp. 66–70.

[392] R.S. Karmel, "The EU Challenge to the SEC," *Fordham International Law Journal*, 31 (2008), 1692–712; Ferran, "Capital Market Openness."

[393] Ibid.

EU's lack of homegrown standards, which can sometimes count against it in assessments of its global influence,[394] actually worked to its advantage, because its adherence to international standards enhanced the credibility of its commitment to the goal of a single universal set of financial reporting requirements and made US declarations of interest in achieving that goal, while in practice still applying domestic standards, sound hollow by comparison.

Post-global financial crisis developments confirm both that the transatlantic relationship remains an EU priority and also that equivalence-based concessions for third countries, which aim at ensuring that firms from third countries are not treated more favorably than EU firms, are becoming ever-more firmly institutionalized in EU financial services law as a lever with which to exert external pressure. Equivalence-based concessionary access provisions, accompanied by a growing list of other access preconditions (including on occasion an explicit reciprocity of treatment requirement),[395] feature prominently in post-crisis EU regulatory reforms in a range of areas including CRAs and derivatives trading and centralized clearing.[396] It is notable that these areas are ones that the EU did not regulate heavily pre-crisis. Given this inexperience, it is quite a turnaround for the EU to hold up its standards (even taking account of the fact that in some respects they draw on international standards) as

394 e.g., Posner and Véron, "The EU and Financial Regulation."

395 e.g., EMIR, art. 25(6) (equivalence-based system for recognition of third country CCPs, including a requirement that the legal framework of the third country must provide for an effective equivalent recognition of third-country-authorized CCPs).

396 As noted by Moloney, Chapter 2 below, the use of an EU equivalence mechanism is also under consideration in the MiFID Review. In the AIFMD context, there is a reference (Art. 21) to duties in third countries' regulatory frameworks that "have the same effect as those provided for" in EU law. In developing advice to the European Commission on this matter, ESMA initially interpreted this as amounting to an "equivalence" test, but did not maintain this view in its final advice: ESMA, *Technical Advice*. This may be explained by the fact that in the heated debate around AIFMD during the legislative process, there was concern that "equivalence" would be interpreted as "identical." In the abstract, equivalence would be best understood as implying comparable or similar outcomes, but evidence thus far is that a more (or less) rigid interpretation may be adopted depending on the particular context: e.g., ESMA, *Framework for Third Country Prospectuses under Article 20 of the Prospectus Directive* (ESMA/2011/36) (prospectus equivalence based on presumption of a literal basis); European Commission, *Formal Request to ESMA for Technical Advice on Possible Delegated Acts Concerning the Amended Prospectus Directive (2003/71/EC)* (Ares(2011)56961 – 19/01/2011) (stressing "similarity" as the benchmark in what should be a "global and holistic" assessment of third country regulatory and supervisory regime equivalence for an employee share scheme prospectus exemption); EMIR, recs. (7)–(8) (similar in substance equivalence test).

the benchmark in a process in which privileged access to European markets from third countries depends, in effect, on a judgment by the European Commission, advised by ESMA, that a foreign legal and supervisory framework is compatible with the European approach.

This more robust approach, encapsulated in a statement by Commissioner Barnier to a US audience that "Europe cannot be and will not be naïve. Equality and reciprocity are not only justified, they are also necessary,"[397] can be seen to reflect an attempt by the EU to use the global financial crisis to reposition itself in the world, particularly vis-à-vis the United States. By putting a massive dent in the reputation of the US financial regulatory and supervisory system and philosophical approach, the global financial crisis gave the EU at least a temporary opportunity to be bolder in its assertions of transatlantic regulatory equality. With the UK tarred by the same brush, its special position at the forefront of transatlantic relationships with the United States was also vulnerable. Crisis-induced shifts in the balance of power and influence among the Member States ensured that the inclination to take full advantage of these opportunities was strong.

Comparison of pre- and post-crisis policy with respect to CRAs neatly illustrates the impact of changing influences on EU external relations. In the aftermath of Enron and other corporate collapses in the early 2000s, the European Parliament had called unsuccessfully for an EU oversight regime for CRAs; the matter was recognized to be political rather than technical and the call was openly associated with the goal of strengthening the European voice in regulation and correcting imbalances between Europe and the United States.[398] That call was ahead of its time because the Commission at that juncture was in the mode of favoring self-regulation and Member States generally backed that approach. The EU now has its own formal oversight framework that is intended to serve as "an efficient counterbalance to other important jurisdictions, notably the US."[399] This framework includes an equivalence-based regime for non-systemically relevant ratings and a regime for systemically relevant rating based on an EU CRA being able to certify that the CRA that issued the rating is part of its corporate group and

[397] M. Barnier, "The Shape of E.U. Financial Regulation and its Impact on the United States and Europe" (speech, June 3, 2011, online: www.eurunion.org/eu/images/stories/brookingsprog-barnier-6–3–11.doc).

[398] European Parliament, *Role and Methods of Rating Agencies* (A5–0040/2004).

[399] European Commission, *Proposal for a Regulation on Credit Rating Agencies*, p. 5.

has fulfilled requirements in the conduct of credit rating activities that are "at least as stringent" as those applicable to EU CRAs.[400] The European Commission and ESMA have, controversially, interpreted the EU framework in a way that seems determined to maximize the pressure on other countries.[401]

However, there are obvious risks in being more assertive. For the EU, informed by thinking that is less wedded to a broad model of Anglo-American capitalism than was the case in the pre-crisis era, to be increasingly robust in its dealings with the United States over the compatibility of their approaches on common problems and for it to be more demanding about the terms on which it is prepared to allow access to its markets otherwise than on the basis of full compliance with EU regulation and supervision, raises the specter of fragmented markets, protectionism and regulatory arbitrage.[402] Protectionism appeared to be gaining ground as a powerful force shaping EU policy in the context of the legislative process for the AIFMD, the early drafts of which looked set to erect a barrier around the European marketplace. As finally adopted, the Directive is less bad than it threatened to be, but there remains scope for defensive influences to distort the processes for the activation of the third country passports that will be undertaken in the coming years.[403] At a time when US financial regulation is dominated by its own domestic concerns, managing a difficult external relationship may not be its authorities' main priority, and thus relations could easily degenerate. There is also the fact that as the euro area crisis has intensified, the more ill-judged the traces of *Schadenfreude* in European views on the global financial crisis as a crisis of Anglo-American capitalism have been shown to be; to the extent that the EU's negotiating position in transatlantic dialogues was briefly strengthened by the misfortunes of others, that moment has passed.

Careful judgments thus need to be made, but that is the case in any negotiating process. Underneath the rhetorical flourishes that stress its determination to drive a hard bargain, the EU is a sophisticated operator with plenty of accumulated transatlantic dialogue experience to help it

400 CRA Regulation (as amended by Regulation (EU) No. 513/2011), arts. 4–5.

401 ESMA, *Guidelines on the Application of the Endorsement Regime under Article 4(3) of the Credit Rating Regulation 1060/2009* (ESMA/2011/~~97~~, ~~March~~ 2011). ESMA's interpretation, in effect, conflates the two formulations. Compare European Parliament, *Resolution on Credit Rating Agencies: Future Perspectives* (T7–0258/2011), para. 14. 139, May

402 Pagliari, "Building a Wall." 403 Ferran, "After the Crisis."

make shrewd decisions on when to push and when to give way. Sensible pragmatism was in evidence, for example, in the decision by ESMA to extend the deadlines in the CRA equivalence process, which showed a willingness to back down when circumstances demand:[404] had this not been done (an outcome which would have rendered US-based ratings ineligible for EU regulatory bank capital adequacy calculations), the result could have been considerable market destabilization. Signs from the derivatives field are also broadly encouraging. Right from the start of the EU regulatory policy process, the Commission laid particular stress on the consistency of its proposals on derivatives with US legislation,[405] although, unsurprisingly, it was soon to make it clear that the EU was not minded simply to fall quickly into line with the US way of thinking and that some hard bargaining would be required.[406] The need for cross-border cooperation in relation to perhaps the world's most borderless segment of market activity is not hard to pinpoint: without careful alignment, transactions could be caught by multiple sets of mandatory clearing, trading, margin, reporting and other requirements, giving rise to wasteful duplication and even, potentially, incompatible obligations.[407] An overarching sense of common purpose and willingness to work constructively and collaboratively to find mutually acceptable solutions has found a concrete shape in the form of a dedicated transatlantic working group consisting of members of US market regulators and the European Commission and ESMA, which was established to iron out the differences.[408] An important contextual consideration here is that derivatives trading is a segment of market activity in which the EU is indisputably a major player, which gives it the economic power to aim for a particularly powerful say in international regulatory design. It is also an area where the importance of international consistency has been stressed by the G20, and the FSB has been especially active in monitoring

404 ESMA, *Guidelines on the Application of the Endorsement Regime.*

405 European Commission, *Proposal for a Regulation on OTC Derivatives, Central Counterparties and Trade Repositories* (COM 2010) 301), p. 3.

406 J. Grant and T. Braithwaite, "Geithner Urges EU to Fall in Line with Derivatives Rules," *Financial Times*, June 9, 2011, 12; J. Grant, "European Rebuke for US on Derivatives," ft.com, June 17, 2011.

407 EMIR, rec. 6. EMIR art. 13 provides for the Commission and ESMA to monitor international developments, including potential duplicative or conflicting requirements and to recommend possible actions.

408 J. Grant, "Avalanche of Rulemaking Blocks Road to OTC Clarity," *Financial Times*, August 1, 2011, (Surveys), 13.

progress towards that goal. The FSB has noted that other countries are looking to the United States and the EU to establish the "international baseline."[409] This can be viewed as subtle pressure on the key jurisdictions to deliver.

This is not the time to attempt to test whether in overall terms the US–EU relationship is becoming more or less lopsided. One reason for this caution is the great uncertainty in the financial markets, especially in Europe. Predictions of EU ascendancy that were made in the immediate aftermath of the financial crisis have already been overtaken by events; the position looks rather different in the wake of the euro area crisis that EU authorities have struggled to resolve. Another is that the ramifications for regulatory influence of the reordering of the location of global economic power have yet to be properly felt; one possibility is that the United States could find itself needing to rely more and more on its partnership with the EU in order to maintain global influence, but other scenarios can also be envisaged. However, a point that can be made with greater certainty is the one that is of direct relevance to the inquiry in this chapter. A finding that emerges from this inquiry is that the EU is insufficiently strong as a global player to act completely autonomously, and therefore that it cannot afford not to prioritize maintaining a healthy relationship with other major economic powers, especially the United States, in its calculations of how best to position itself to exert effective influence over international financial services regulatory design. Putting the point another way, considerations relating to international aspirations have the capacity to play an important role in curbing tendencies towards EU regulatory excess because of the compromises and negotiations on which that quest for influence has to depend. Given the attenuation of other constraints discussed earlier in this chapter, this is a positive conclusion.

VI: Conclusion

A few final reflections follow. These pick out some of the key points that emerge from this chapter's detailed examination of the actors, institutions and processes involved in shaping the EU's response to the financial crisis, and draw some strands together. They do not attempt to summarize all of the arguments.

[409] FSB, *OTC Derivatives Market Reforms: Progress Report on Implementation* (October 2011), p. 21.

From a market integration perspective, the EU's regulatory response to the recent turmoil must be regarded as still being unfinished business. The logical end point is a pan-European system of regulation and supervision with national supervisors reduced mostly to a branch office role; we remain far from that, especially on the supervisory side, where considerations about national fiscal backstops continue to exert formidable force. Even on the regulatory side, as time has passed, the consensus around "more Europe" that was much in evidence after the collapse of the Icelandic banks has started to break down. However, we can now see that the immediate aftermath of the financial crisis was a critical moment when key decisions on regulation and supervision with potentially profound implications for the future were taken. We can also see that those decisions have now started to take on a life of their own. The growth of an ever-more dense and complex supranational system of regulation and supervision over which Member States will struggle to maintain day-to-day control and which will increasingly crowd out local differences looks almost inevitable, although some battles to preserve certain treasured national particularities may be fierce. Uncertainties surrounding the resolution of the euro area crisis mean that it is not possible to dismiss the risk of a massive shock that shakes the foundations of the single market regulatory and supervisory architecture as something that is too fanciful to merit serious attention, but it still seems rather unlikely. On that basis, insights from political science theory and also the strong incremental tendencies evident in the recent history of EU financial services regulation suggest that ardent integrationists need not be too dismayed by "underachievement" in the current state of development in EU financial services regulation, as they probably just need to be patient. Indeed, they may not have long to wait for more dramatic change, depending on how the euro area crisis is finally resolved.

Contrary to indications at the start of the global financial crisis when it was under severe pressure, the European Commission has emerged in a strengthened position within the EU set-up. However, it is also carrying an immense burden of expectation. The European Parliament has declared that it is looking to the Commission to "lift the EU out of crisis and ensure that it is represented and maintains its respected position in the world."[410] This is a heavily-loaded exhortation by an

[410] European Parliament, *Resolution on the Commission Work Programme 2012* (T7–0327/2011).

increasingly important player in EU financial services regulation that can be expected not to hesitate to speak out if results fall short of its expectations.

But expectations need to be realistic. It is too much to expect the Commission to "lift the EU out of crisis," since a sustainable return to growth in fact depends on many actors, both public and private. With characteristic economy of language, Klaus Hopt has explained what the relationship between the state and the market should be: "the market knows better than the state, provided that the state sets the appropriate rules of the game."[411] Applying the Hopt model, it is for the Commission to propose the "rules of the game" and to seek to shepherd the proposals through into law without too much watering down by the compromises that have to be struck in order to secure agreement among legislative actors who still adhere to a diverse range of views on the optimal way for the state to intervene in the organization of financial market activity, even when they agree broadly on the need for "more Europe." This is hard enough, without setting unattainable goals. It should not be overlooked that one of the few certainties in the search for a regulatory framework that is conducive both to financial stability and economic growth is that merely making everything more standardized is insufficient, and could even be counterproductive. Having everyone play by more of the same rules under an increasingly similar system of oversight are developments that may look good from an integration perspective, but the supposed benefits of standardization will quickly unravel if the substantive content of the rules is wrong or if the philosophies and practices of oversight are misguided.

As for the EU's position in the world, the so-called discrediting of the Anglo-American version of capitalism provided an opportunity at the start of the years of crisis for the EU to promote alternative regulatory models, but progress has faltered since then. The EU's ability to lead the world in financial regulation is hindered by a range of structural factors, and it is in serious danger of being further undermined by a long economic downturn in Europe and by the blows to its reputation for sound policy design generated by the faltering efforts to resolve the euro crisis. Since global influence is increasingly likely to hinge on an ability to form powerful bilateral alliances with

[411] K. Hopt, "European Company and Financial Law: Observations on European Politics, Protectionism, and the Financial Crisis" in U. Bernitz and W.G. Ringe, *Company Law and Economic Protectionism: New Challenges to European Integration* (Oxford University Press, 2010), pp. 13–31, p. 31.

other like-minded powers, the EU cannot afford to put too much distance between its approach and that adopted on the other side of the Atlantic. Pragmatic considerations pertaining to global influence thus have the potential to function as a useful safeguard in an environment in which other brakes on over-ambitious EU financial services regulatory policy design have become less powerful.

2

The legacy effects of the financial crisis on regulatory design in the EU

NIAMH MOLONEY*

I: Examining regulatory change

Introduction

This chapter examines the European Union (EU)'s crisis-era reform program from a regulatory design perspective. In particular, it considers the legacy effects of the financial crisis on financial system regulation.

Financial system regulation is traditionally regarded as concerned with three objectives: financial stability; market efficiency, transparency and integrity; and consumer protection. In order to consider the legacy effects of the crisis on regulatory design, this chapter addresses the impact of the financial crisis on the latter two regulatory spheres: market (or securities) regulation – which addresses market efficiency, transparency and integrity, and the conduct of business regulation of market intermediaries[1] – and consumer protection regulation. The chapter questions whether the initial crisis-era, financial stability-driven reform movement has led to regulatory innovation in these two cognate fields, the extent of the innovations and whether innovations have been productive.

Market regulation and consumer protection regulation were not part of the EU's initial regulatory response to the crisis. Concerned with financial stability, the "first generation" response focused on prudential regulation and so on institutional and systemic stability. Bank capital, bank supervision and bank rescue and resolution proposals were the

* I have benefitted greatly from the opportunity to discuss the ideas presented in the chapter at a number of conferences in the UK and in the EU and from discussions with the co-authors of this book.

[1] e.g., IOSCO, *Mitigating Systemic Risk. A Role for Securities Regulators* (Madrid: IOSCO, 2011), outlining the traditional domain of securities regulators.

centerpieces of the initial EU reform agenda, reflecting the international agenda. But market regulation and consumer protection regulation have recently been caught up in the backwash of the financial stability-led reform agenda as a "second-generation" effect, as the EU has moved from shoring up financial stability to becoming the self-styled "architect [s] of a new financial system."[2] In particular, legacy effects related to the dominant financial stability agenda are reshaping the policy goals and the nature of market and consumer protection regulation more generally.

This introductory Part I considers why the market regulation and consumer protection regulation case studies are useful and how they support a discussion of legacy effects. Part II frames the examination of the legacy effects of the crisis on EU market and consumer protection regulation by identifying the emerging policy concern to address financial market intensity and financial market innovation as the key regulatory innovation which is shaping changes to market and to consumer protection regulation. Parts III and IV examine how market and consumer protection regulation are changing in response and whether productive innovation is following. Part V concludes.

Charting innovation and change

The EU's regulatory response to the financial crisis has been vividly likened to "death by a thousand directives,"[3] by contrast with the behemoth US Dodd-Frank Act 2010, the political economy and quality of which is discussed by John C. Coffee, Jr. in Chapter 4 of this book. Since October 2008, when the Commission's proposal for the first of a series of reforms to the 1994 Deposit Guarantee Directive[4] marked the beginning of the reform program, some forty-five or so measures have been proposed or adopted by the EU institutions. The end is now in sight. By the end of 2011, all proposals for primary legislative texts were to have been adopted by the EU Commission, and thus either enacted or

[2] EU Internal Market Commissioner M. Barnier, "Restoring Trust in the Financial Sector" (speech, April 26, 2010, online: http://europa.eu/rapid/pressReleasesAction.do?reference=SPEECH/10/178&type=HTML).

[3] Clifford Chance, *Sea of Change. Regulatory Change for Financial Institutions. Briefing Note* (London: Clifford Chance, November 2010).

[4] European Commission, *Proposal for Reform of the Deposit Guarantee Directive* (COM (2008) 661).

going through the EU legislative process. A related and massive technical "rule-book" will follow from the additional and extensive delegations to secondary Commission law-making which are a common feature of the new measures. An early assessment of the new banking regime has already been made,[5] and plans are underway for a full review: a "fundamental review" of the crisis-era reforms will be carried out in 2014 to ascertain whether the new regime has fulfilled its aspirations and whether any modifications are necessary.[6]

The new EU regime,[7] which has been described as "far-reaching and radical" by a partisan Commission,[8] provides a rich case study for different avenues of inquiry. This chapter examines the new regime from a regulatory design perspective and, in particular, with respect to the nature of the regulatory change engaged by the second-generation reforms, now that the first generation of reforms, discussed by Eilís Ferran in Chapter 1 of this book, for the most part are in place. EU financial market regulation is, increasingly, being examined from a range of perspectives (including governance,[9] political science[10] and regulatory theory[11] perspectives). This has changed the shape of the main debate which, for some time, has been largely concerned with the essential appropriateness or otherwise of EU intervention and national

[5] European Parliament, Economic and Monetary Affairs Committee, *Assessment of the Cumulative Impact of Various Regulatory Initiatives on the European Banking Sector* (2011).

[6] European Commission, *Regulating Financial Services for Sustainable Growth, A Progress Report – February 2011* (2011).

[7] e.g., P.O. Mülbert and A. Wilhelm, "Reforms of EU Banking and Securities Regulation after the Financial Crisis," *Banking and Finance Law Review*, 26 (2010), 187–232.

[8] European Commission, *European Financial Stability and Integration Report* (2011) (SEC (2011) 489), p. 40.

[9] Particularly with respect to EU institutional reform and related delegation dynamics, e.g., M. Thatcher and D. Coen, "Network Governance and Multi-level Delegations. European Networks of Regulatory Agencies," *Journal of Public Policy*, 28 (2008), 49–71 and M. Thatcher, "The Creation of European Regulatory Agencies and its Limits: a Comparative Analysis of European Delegation," *Journal of European Public Policy*, 18 (2011), 790–809.

[10] Particularly, and as discussed further in E. Ferran, Chapter 1 above, with respect to interest group dynamics, and the extent to which different Member State interests in market shaping or market facilitation can drive regulatory reform, e.g., L. Quaglia, R. Eastwood and P. Holmes, "The Financial Turmoil and EU Policy Co-operation in 2008," *Journal of Common Market Studies*, 47 (2009), 63–87.

[11] The EU regime has, e.g., been examined in terms of system management and the ability of the EU to manage a complex, multi-layered market and regulatory system: J. Black, "Restructuring Global and EU Financial Regulation: Capacities, Coordination and Learning," LSE Legal Studies Working Paper No. 18/2010 (November 2010, online: http://.ssrn.com/abstract=1713632).

regulation; this debate was often framed in terms of the relative merits of regulatory competition or rule harmonization.[12] But questioning whether the EU in principle should intervene in EU financial markets is now a somewhat sterile exercise given the political, fiscal and regulatory realities post-crisis.[13] The question does, however, still have some traction politically at national level, as recent events have underlined. The UK's December 8, 2011 exercise of its national veto to prevent the reform of the current Treaties to address stronger fiscal union, leading to the decision of the Eurozone and other Member States to address fiscal reform intergovernmentally through a separate Treaty,[14] was grounded in Prime Minister Cameron's concern to prevent further intensification of the EU's intervention in financial regulation and supervision.[15] However, the UK's perceived need to wield the veto also underlines the commitment across the remainder of the EU bloc, and particularly of its driving Member States, France and Germany, to organizing financial regulation at EU level. Summit politicking aside, the examination by Eilís Ferran in Chapter 1 of this book of the complex and subtle dynamics which shaped the crisis-era interactions between the EU and its Member States, and of how these dynamics influenced the EU's choice of policy instruments over the crisis, underlines the range of factors which, to borrow a memorable phrase from another context, "condemn Member States to co-operate" on financial system regulation.[16] This chapter therefore takes as a starting

[12] e.g., L. Enriques, "EC Company Law Directives and Regulations: How Trivial Are They?" *University of Pennsylvania Journal of International Economic Law*, 27 (2006), 1–78. For a recent consideration with respect to capital-raising, see P. Schammo, *EU Prospectus Law. New Perspectives on Regulatory Competition in Securities Markets* (Cambridge University Press, 2011).

[13] N. Moloney, "The European Securities and Markets Authority and Institutional Design for the EU Financial Market – A Tale of Two Competences: Part (1) Rule-Making," (ESMA Part I) *European Business Organization Law Review*, 12 (2011), 41–86.

[14] European Council, *Statement by the Euro Heads of State or Government*, December 9, 2011. The subsequent European Stability Treaty was signed by 25 Member States on March 2, 2012.

[15] The UK sought a financial services protocol, to be attached to any new Treaty and containing a series of concessions to the UK on financial services regulation, including controls on the further acquisition of power by the EU's new supervisory authorities: G. Parker and A. Barber, "Cameron's Use of Treaty Veto leaves Britain on Outside in New Union," *Financial Times*, December 10, 2011, 2.

[16] EU Internal Market Commissioner C. McCreevy, "Building the Transatlantic Marketplace" (speech, March 7, 2007, online: http://europa.eu/rapid/pressReleasesAction.do?reference=SPEECH/07/131).

point the reality of EU intervention[17] and considers the nature of the EU's response to the crisis from a regulatory design perspective and, in particular, with respect to the nature of the regulatory change which is being wrought by the financial crisis.

In order to consider how EU financial system regulation is being reshaped, this chapter shifts the frame from the first-generation, stability-driven prudential measures which have received extensive attention in the literature[18] and instead examines the spillover or legacy effects of the crisis and the initial stability agenda on the second-generation reforms. It considers whether the crisis has led to productive regulatory innovation in EU market regulation and in EU consumer protection regulation. In doing so, and to track the scale of change and the implications for policy objectives as well as for detailed regulatory rules, it borrows the notion of "regulatory innovation" from the social science literature on the nature of regulation.

It is clear that the financial crisis has led to massive regulatory change to financial system regulation. The notion of change in the form of "regulatory innovation" which has transformative, "step-changing" effects on the nature of intervention (whether through incremental or major systemic innovation), and which is not simply associated with less impactful regulatory "difference" or "change,"[19] provides a useful mechanism for examining the nature of this change. Pre-crisis, regulatory innovation was a major theme of the rich regulatory theory debate on the expanding nature of the regulatory state. The innovation debate engaged with, for example, the nature of regulatory innovation, domestically, regionally and internationally,[20] in different regulatory

[17] In a recent example then FSA Chief Executive Hector Sants underlined that "the rules will be made by the European Supervisory Authorities and the role of [the UK regulator] will primarily be one of supervision and enforcement": "Delivering 'Twin Peaks' within the FSA" (speech, February 2, 2012, online: www.fsa.gov.uk/library/communication/pr/2012/012.shtml).

[18] On the banking and prudential reforms, see e.g.: G. Ferrarini and F. Chiodini, "Regulating Multinational Banks in Europe. An Assessment of the New Supervisory Framework," ECGI Law Working Paper No. 158/2010 (April 2010, online: http://ssrn.com/abstract=1596890) and W. Fonteyne *et al.*, "Crisis Management and Resolution for a European Banking System," IMF Working Paper No. WP/10/10 (March 2010, online: www.imf.org/external/pubs/ft/wp/2010/wp1070.pdf).

[19] J. Black, "What is Regulatory Innovation?" in J. Black, M. Lodge and M. Thatcher (eds.), *Regulatory Innovation. A Comparative Analysis* (Cheltenham: Elgar, 2005), pp. 1–15, pp. 4–8.

[20] e.g., G. Van Calster, "An Overview of Regulatory Innovation in the EU," *Cambridge Yearbook of European Legal Studies*, 11 (2008–9), 289–321.

spheres[21] and with respect to different types of innovation (for example, the "Better Regulation" and "smart regulation" movements).[22] Usefully for the crisis-era and financial system regulation, the debate also probed the productive or otherwise nature of innovation.[23]

In particular, the debate on regulatory innovation has suggested that different types of regulatory change occur, not all of which lead to transformative innovation. It usefully identifies three forms of change, the increasing intensity of which is useful in probing the spillover effects of the financial crisis on regulation. First-level changes can be made to the settings of regulation – technical changes to rules and practices which do not change the regulatory status quo and which might not be associated with innovation, although the cumulative effect may be innovative. Second-level changes can occur to institutional structures and to the nature of intervention – changes to the mix of hard and soft law deployed by regulators, for example – and these changes may often be associated with transformative innovation. Finally, third-level changes can occur to the cognitive or normative nature of regulation, leading, for example, to a resetting of the policy goals of regulation, and typically involving a paradigm shift in the nature of regulation and related transformative effects.[24] Innovative changes of this nature can also generate related first- and second-level changes.

This chapter focuses in particular on the third dimension of regulatory innovation. It identifies the resetting of the policy goals of market and of consumer regulation in the EU in the wake of the crisis as a transformative influence on EU financial system regulation. In particular, it considers the implications of an injection of a policy suspicion of market innovation and market intensity into regulatory design and the associated first-level technical changes and second-level changes (particularly with respect to decreasing reliance on self regulation).

This analysis could, of course, be applied to the initial resetting of EU financial system regulation in the early stages of the crisis to focus on macro prudential regulation, risk regulation and systemic risk, and the

[21] e.g., telecommunications: M. Thatcher, "Sale of the Century: 3G Mobile Licensing in Europe," in Black *et al.*, *Regulatory Innovation*, pp. 92–113.

[22] R. Baldwin, "Better Regulation: The Search and the Struggle," in R. Baldwin, M. Cave and M. Lodge, *The Oxford Handbook on Regulation* (Oxford University Press, 2010), pp. 258–87.

[23] e.g., M. Moran, *The British Regulatory State: High Modernism and Hyper-Innovation* (Oxford University Press, 2003).

[24] This summary is based on Black, "What is Regulatory Innovation?," pp. 9–11.

related second-level institutional change and first-level technical changes which it wrought. But as discussed in the following Part, the second-generation market regulation and consumer protection regulation case studies together provide a useful, and as yet relatively under-researched, case study.

The market regulation and consumer protection case studies

Why target market regulation and consumer protection regulation for this analysis? One of the recurring themes of the financial crisis debate has been that silo-based regulation, which segments regulation into distinct groupings, fails to capture the cross-sector and dynamic nature of financial market risk.[25] A segmented examination, focused on market and on consumer protection regulation, may therefore appear quixotic. This approach, however, supports an examination of the legacy effects of the crisis on the two regulatory spheres which have traditionally operated distinctly from financial stability regulation, and of whether collateral regulatory risks have been generated by the crisis. It thus brings the wider legacy effects of the crisis on regulatory design into sharper focus.

The current reshaping of EU market regulation and EU consumer protection regulation is not only a function of the crisis. The major EU market regulation measures – the Prospectus, Transparency and Market Abuse Directives, which address disclosure in the primary and secondary markets and the control of abusive practices, and the Markets in Financial Instruments Directive (MiFID), which addresses the intermediation and order execution process, including the distribution of investment products[26] – had already been scheduled for review over 2008–10 before the crisis struck. The consumer protection agenda was also gathering steam pre-crisis.[27] But, as discussed in Part II, the financial crisis has

[25] e.g., C. Whitehead, "Reframing Financial Regulation," *Boston University Law Review*, 90 (2010), 1–50 and R. Kroszner, "Making Markets More Robust," in R. Kroszner and R.J. Shiller (eds.), *Reforming US Financial Markets: Reflections Before and Beyond Dodd Frank* (Cambridge, MA: MIT Press, 2011), pp. 51–83, p. 51.

[26] Respectively, Directives 2003/71/EC, [2003] OJ L 345/64; 2004/109/EC, [2004] OJ L390/38; 2003/6/EC, [2003] OJ L96/16; and 2004/39/EC, [2004] OJ L145/1. Subsequent references are to the Prospectus Directive, Transparency Directive, Market Abuse Directive and MiFID.

[27] N. Moloney, "Regulating the Retail Markets: Law, Policy and the Financial Crisis," in G. Letsas and C. O'Cinnéide (eds.), *Current Legal Problems 2010* (Oxford University Press, 2010), pp. 375–447.

reshaped the context in which reform is taking place and is driving innovation in the form of change to the nature and policy goals of market and consumer protection regulation.

The context within which this innovation is taking place is, however, problematic. The financial stability agenda has dominated regulatory reform since the crisis broke. Generally, the momentum for reform generated by crisis conditions can lead to heightened expectations, over-reaction, and poor legislative outcomes, as is discussed across this book with respect to different regulatory contexts. But away from the searing spotlight placed on the problem and reform "du jour," the more heavily resourced and battle-hardened regulatory community, and the enhanced political interest typically associated with crisis, can lead to a productive refreshing of regulation and to useful innovation more generally – particularly where corrective mechanisms, as discussed by John C. Coffee, Jr. in Chapter 4, are likely to address regulatory over-reach and error. The second-generation EU reforms and the innovation associated with them may, however, generate regulatory effectiveness risks arising from the spillover effects of the governing financial stability agenda. These risks are all the greater as correction may not be easy. Corrective mechanisms for crisis-driven regulatory over-reach are available, whether through the inter-institutional law-making process for primary legislative measures, the European Commission-led process for secondary delegated rules, or through the multiplicity of supervisory and quasi-law-making mechanisms the new European Supervisory Authorities (ESAs) can wield.[28] The European Commission, as noted above, has committed to a general review of the crisis-era agenda, and all the new measures contain a review clause which requires the Commission to review experience with the measure in question. But given the complexities of the inter-institutional law-making process, and the multiplicity of market, institutional and political interests which drive EU intervention,[29] corrective action is not straightforward in the EU context. There is also very limited evidence from the long history of EU financial market regulation to suggest that EU rules, once adopted, are removed or changed radically. The last major suite of reforms, the legislation adopted under the 1999–2005 Financial Services

[28] See further Moloney, "ESMA Part I."

[29] See further E. Ferran, Chapter 1 above and N. Moloney, *EC Securities Regulation* (Oxford University Press, 2nd edn., 2008), ch. 14.

Action Plan (FSAP) era, all contained review clauses, but there was little evidence of any institutional or political appetite to revisit these rules prior to the financial crisis. Nonetheless, a commitment to review is a feature of the crisis-era measures. Identification of potential risks is therefore of central importance.

In particular, risks may follow from the dominance of the financial stability agenda. Prudential regulation (the main concern of stability-related regulation), on the one hand, and market regulation and consumer protection regulation, on the other, serve different, if related, purposes. Prudential regulation is concerned with institutional and systemic stability. It has a particular focus on the management and regulation of risk and on the safety and soundness of institutions and the financial system. Consumer protection and market regulation are largely concerned with the conduct of market actors, whether retail, professional, or market infrastructures, and with the protection of market confidence through the support of market efficiency, transparency and integrity, and investor protection.

The adoption by some regulatory systems of a "twin-peaks" institutional model, based on the separation of prudential supervision and market/conduct/consumer protection supervision (on the Australian experience, see the analysis by Jennifer G. Hill in Chapter 3) reflects this essential split, although the extent to which institutional separation is necessary for effective intervention is not clear.[30] It is clear that styles of regulation, regulatory tools and supervisory approaches can be different. In the UK the 2012 Financial Services Bill is designed to reorganize the current institutional structure of financial services regulation and supervision in the UK to incorporate a (broadly) "twin-peaks" institutional model, reflecting a split of supervision between a prudential and a conduct authority. Among the reforms,[31] the consolidated Financial Services Authority (FSA) will be split into the Prudential Regulation Authority (PRA), within the Bank of England, and a distinct Financial

[30] International experience over the financial crisis did not produce a single "magic bullet" in terms of successful institutional design: A. Turner, *The Turner Review. A Regulatory Response to the Global Banking Crisis* (London: FSA, March 2009), p. 91 and K. Regling and M. Watson, *A Preliminary Report on the Sources of Ireland's Banking Crisis* (Dublin: Government Publications Office, 2010), p. 17.

[31] Which also include a Financial Policy Committee responsible for macro prudential supervision.

Conduct Authority (FCA).[32] While politically driven,[33] it is claimed to support greater regulatory specialization, clearer objective setting and achievement and the development of appropriate organizational cultures and supervisory styles.[34]

In terms of regulatory tools, disclosure and transparency-related tools, for example, are strongly associated with market and consumer protection regulation,[35] as is industry-wide, thematic supervision. Prudential regulation deploys additional and more intrusive tools, in particular capital rules and, certainly since the financial crisis, is typically associated with specialist and resource-intensive firm-specific supervision, particularly of systemically significant firms.[36] Ex-post enforcement, whether through private or public mechanisms, to take another example, is a key tool in the market and consumer protection fields. But it is less central to the prudential field, where the focus is on the setting and ex-ante monitoring of risk management standards.[37]

[32] The 2012 Financial Services Bill was introduced into Parliament on January 27, 2012 (Bill 278 2010–2012) (the "Financial Services Bill"). The key government consultations are: HM Treasury, *A New Approach to Financial Regulation: Securing Stability, Protecting Consumers* (London: HM Treasury, January 2012); HM Treasury, *A New Approach to Financial Regulation: The Blueprint for Reform* (London: HM Treasury, June 2011); HM Treasury, *A New Approach to Financial Regulation: Building a Stronger System* (London: HM Treasury, February 2011); and HM Treasury, *A New Approach to Financial Regulation: Judgment, Focus and Stability* (London: HM Treasury, July 2010).

The new structure is expected to be in place by April 2013. Since 2011, the FSA has operated internally in the form of a shadow PRA and FCA and policies are being produced in the name of the proposed entities. From April 2012, the FSA moved over, as far as practically possible within the constraints posed by the primary legislation not yet being in place, to the new operational "twin peaks" model: Sants, "Twin Peaks." The new institutions will accordingly be referred to where appropriate.

[33] Abolition of the consolidated regulator set up under the previous Labour administration was a manifesto commitment of the Conservative Party in the 2009 General Election, and consolidation has been repeatedly claimed by the Coalition government as contributing to supervisory failure over the crisis.

[34] HM Treasury, *A New Approach – The Blueprint*, p. 39 and HM Treasury, *A New Approach – Judgment, Focus and Stability*, p. 6. Then FSA Chief Executive Sants underlined that each new authority has distinct objectives (set out in the Financial Services Bill) and will pursue different goals: Sants, "Twin Peaks."

[35] IOSCO, *Mitigating Systemic Risk – a Role for Securities Regulation. Discussion Paper* (Madrid: IOSCO, 2011).

[36] Sants, "Twin Peaks."

[37] In the UK, the new PRA is projected to engage in enforcement activity to a much lesser extent than the new FCA, given the PRA's focus on forward-looking and remedial action: HM Treasury, *A New Approach – The Blueprint*, p. 47.

The wider disciplining factors which shape regulation in the prudential and in the market and consumer protection spheres are also different. International political and institutional dynamics, and international competition, for example, are key influences on the development of prudential regulation, but they have a more limited role in consumer protection and in market regulation, given the importance of local cultures and market structures.[38]

The relative importance of competition in the prudential and market/consumer protection fields provides a useful example of difference. Competition is often deployed as a tool to support market efficiency and consumer protection, although not without controversy, given the prevalence of market failures in the financial markets,[39] as well as the technical difficulties which a financial services regulator may face in deploying competition-related tools, by comparison with a dedicated competition authority. In the EU, policy support of competition between order-execution venues, for example, has been the driving philosophy behind the EU's regulation of trading markets. At Member State level in the UK, the 2012 Financial Services Bill gives the FCA a specific operational objective with respect to competition; it must promote effective competition in the interests of consumers.[40] This represents a significant enhancement of earlier government drafts, following stakeholder concern that the centrality of competition to effective consumer markets in particular had not been captured.[41] The political commitment is considerable: the UK government has highlighted that competition must be at the core of the FCA's operational model and underlined the importance of the new competition powers in enhancing the effectiveness of the new FCA.[42] Internationally, the Organization for Economic Cooperation and Development (OECD) has similarly linked competitive markets to stronger consumer outcomes.[43] But competition can be a troublesome tool for prudential regulation. Competitive markets can generate excessive risk-taking.

[38] D.C. Langevoort, "Global Securities Regulation after the Financial Crisis," *Journal of International Economic Law*, 13 (2011), 799–815.

[39] Including with respect to poor exercise of choice and limited information. Competition in the consumer markets, e.g., can lead to a proliferation of complex and poorly differentiated products which serve to confuse consumers.

[40] Financial Services Bill, clauses 1B(3) and 1E.

[41] e.g., House of Commons Joint Committee on the draft Financial Services Bill, *Draft Financial Services Bill*, December 2011, pp. 27–8.

[42] HM Treasury, *A New Approach – Securing Stability*, p. 32.

[43] OECD, *G20 High-Level Principles on Consumer Protection* (Paris: OECD, 2011).

The extent to which Global Systemically Important Financial Institutions (G-SIFIs) engage in profitable but systemically risky derivatives-trading activity, while enjoying competitive advantage through their "too big to fail" subsidy, is currently a concern of policy makers internationally.[44] This is well exemplified by the UK's September 2011 "Vickers Report" proposals for ring-fencing retail/corporate and investment banking operations.[45] The UK institutional reforms have taken a cautious approach. Although some concerns have been expressed that a failure to focus on competition may lead to barriers to entry and exacerbate the "too big to fail" problem,[46] the new PRA, unlike the new FCA, will not be conferred with a specific competition-related objective.[47]

Thus, the injection of regulatory innovation associated with the wider financial stability/prudential regulation agenda into market regulation and consumer regulation may not necessarily generate productive reforms. This is particularly the case where the reform agenda leads to regulatory innovation in the form of a radical and untested resetting of the policy goals of regulation, which might be engaged by the current suspicion of innovation and intensity (Part II).

Some degree of resetting post-crisis is, of course, likely to be productive. In particular, the resetting of the policy goals of market regulation to address the systemic risks which financial markets generate was a necessary response to the failures of market regulation which the crisis exposed. The financial crisis was ultimately a crisis of markets, not institutions,[48] and exposed significant failures in market regulation. Financial markets proved unable to recycle credit risk effectively. Complex securitized products were priced incorrectly. The mechanisms of market efficiency, including the risk management functions provided by derivatives, and the information intermediary functions provided by

[44] OECD, *Bank Competition and Financial Stability* (Paris: OECD, 2011), ch. 2.

[45] Independent Commission on Banking (ICB), *Final Report: Recommendations* (London: ICB, September 2011) (widely known as the "Vickers Report"). The follow-up Government White Paper was published in June 2012: HM Treasury and Department for Business, Innovation and Skills, *Banking Reform: delivering stability and supporting a sustainable economy* (London: HM Treasury, 2012).

[46] House of Lords, House of Commons, Joint Committee. On the Draft Financial Services Bill, *Report: Draft Financial Services Bill 2010–12*, December 2011, pp. 24–5.

[47] The government has argued that a competitive objective is not necessary, as the promotion of financial stability provides a strong platform for sustainable industry growth: HM Treasury, *A New Approach – The Blueprint*, p. 24.

[48] FSA Chairman A. Turner, "Reforming Finance: Are we being Radical Enough?" (speech, February 1, 2011, online: www.fsa.gov.uk/pages/Library/Communication/Speeches/2011/0218_at.shtml).

rating agencies, failed. Market regulation failed to capture the build-up of risk in the financial system.[49]

It is not surprising that market regulation struggled to cope with the financial crisis. Market regulation has traditionally been concerned with capital raising and with the related promotion of market confidence by supporting market efficiency, transparency and integrity, and investor protection.[50] The roots of market regulation are in the public offer of securities or, as Donald Langevoort has suggested, in "truth-telling" and the structures which support "truth-telling."[51] At bedrock, market regulation is concerned with removing "lemons" from the capital markets and with ensuring price efficiency and efficient capital raising through the regulation of the primary and secondary markets.[52] While market regulation relies on a range of tools, disclosure and anti-fraud rules are its stock-in-trade, particularly with respect to issuer-facing market regulation and secondary trading market regulation. This reliance on disclosure and so on self-regulation reflects another prevailing theme of market regulation, the assumption that, as described in the UK FSA's *Turner Review*, "financial markets are capable of being both efficient and rational and that a key goal of financial market regulation is to remove the impediments which may produce inefficient and illiquid markets."[53]

But disclosure failed as a regulatory tool over the crisis. Internationally, regulated disclosures did not extend to the range of markets and securities implicated in the crisis.[54] Market-driven disclosures, particularly in the securitization market and with respect to complex products, did not support market discipline.[55] The assumptions as to market efficiency and rationality

[49] On the failure of securities regulation, see Langevoort, "Global Securities Regulation" and A. Anand, "Is Systemic Risk Relevant to Securities Regulation?," *University of Toronto Law Journal*, 60 (2010), 941–81.

[50] e.g., B. Black, "The Legal and Institutional Preconditions for Strong Securities Markets," *UCLA Law Review*, 48 (2001), 781–856.

[51] Langevoort, "Global Securities Regulation."

[52] S. Choi, "Law, Finance and Path Dependence. Developing Strong Securities Markets," *Texas Law Review*, 80 (2002), 1657–728.

[53] Turner, *Turner Review*, p. 39.

[54] e.g., J. Fisch, "Top Cop or Regulatory Flop – The SEC at 75," *Virginia Law Review*, 95 (2009), 785–824, suggesting that the SEC failed in its core mission to maintain investor confidence, particularly in the transparency of financial statements issued by financial institutions with large derivative positions.

[55] Generally, S. Schwarcz, "Protecting Financial Markets: Lessons from the Subprime Mortgage Meltdown," *Minnesota Law Review*, 93 (2008), 373–406 and S. Schwarcz, "Regulating Complexity in Financial Markets," *Washington University Law Review*, 87 (2009), 211–68; and, with respect to failures concerning the regulation of loan-level information on assets assigned to securitization pools, H. Jackson, "Loan-Level Disclosure in Securitization Transactions: A Problem with Three Dimensions," Harvard Public Law Working Paper No. 10–40 (July 2010, online: http://ssrn.com/abstract=1649651).

which drove the reliance on disclosure mechanisms were already under siege from the empirical findings of behavioral finance and cognate disciplines.[56] Efficiency and rationality assumptions have come under greater pressure since the crisis.[57] The *Turner Review* usefully summarized the prevailing views as suggesting that: market efficiency does not imply market rationality; individual rationality does not ensure collective rationality; individual behavior is not entirely rational; allocative efficiency benefits have limits; and large-scale herd effects and market over-shoots occur.[58] It drew the conclusion that market discipline, strongly associated with disclosure techniques, can be an inadequate means for constraining risk.[59] In the EU, Internal Market Commissioner Barnier, responsible for financial services regulation, has similarly suggested that the assumptions which prevailed pre-crisis, including that markets act rationally and that a "laissez-faire" approach would best stimulate growth, were wrong.[60]

Market regulation also failed to build on lessons from its earlier defining crisis. The Enron era underlined the risks which flawed incentives can pose to market efficiency.[61] The array of reforms worldwide, and particularly in the US, which addressed inter alia, investment analyst and auditor risk, did not sharpen the focus on incentive risks elsewhere in the financial markets. Similarly, the Enron-era focus on internal governance structures did not prompt wider consideration of the risks generated by flawed governance structures in systemically important financial institutions. But even had deeper lessons been learned, while incentive risks were a feature of the crisis,[62] they were not defining

[56] e.g., the articles examining the Efficient Capital Markets Hypothesis on the 20th anniversary of Gilson and Kraakman's seminal analysis of the mechanisms of market efficiency in *Journal of Corporation Law*, 28 (2003) summer issue, and M.S. Barr, S. Mullainathan and E. Shafir, "The Case for Behaviorally Informed Regulation," in D. Moss and J. Cistrenino (eds.), *New Perspectives on Regulation* (Cambridge, MA: The Tobin Project, 2009), pp. 25–61.

[57] E. Avgouleas, "The Global Financial Crisis, Behavioural Finance and Financial Regulation in Search of a New Orthodoxy," *Journal of Corporate Law Studies*, 9 (2009), 23–59.

[58] Turner, *Turner Review*, pp. 40–1.

[59] Ibid., pp. 45–7.

[60] EU Internal Market Commissioner M. Barnier, "Forging a New Deal between Finance and Society: Restoring Trust in the Financial Sector" (speech, April 26, 2010, online: http://europa.eu/rapid/pressReleasesAction.do?reference=SPEECH/10/178&type=HTML).

[61] J.C. Coffee, "Understanding Enron: It's the Gatekeepers, Stupid," *The Business Lawyer*, 57 (2002), 1403–20.

[62] For a recent review, Joint Forum (IOSCO, Basel Committee, IAS), *Report on Asset Securitization Incentives* (2011).

features.[63] Market regulators had little experience with the major risks related to pro-cyclicality and system inter-connectedness. Thus, despite the long-standing focus of market regulation on liquidity, market regulators failed to understand how changing risk profiles and systemic risks could lead to a catastrophic drying-up of liquidity and were unable to ensure that instruments remained tradable.[64]

Hamstrung by a long tradition of disclosure-based intervention, and by allowing discrete sectors to operate outside the regulatory net, regulators with a market regulation mandate struggled over the financial crisis to contain the build-up of risk. The first major initiative associated with market regulators was the autumn 2008 series of prohibitions on short selling internationally, which have since been associated with the need to be "seen to act"[65] and, with hindsight, have been of questionable value in supporting market stability by enhancing liquidity.[66] The International Organization of Securities Commissions (IOSCO) has suggested that the traditional conduct of business and disclosure tools used by market regulators were not specifically designed to address systemic risk reduction and were particularly problematic where rules were insufficient, inapplicable or inadequately applied;[67] overall, market regulators misunderstood risk and did not apply the tools at their disposal to limit undesirable or improperly priced risk-taking.[68] The US Securities and Exchange Commission (SEC), perhaps the paradigmatic example of the market regulator, has been widely criticized for its

[63] e.g., querying the limited impact of reforms to internal bank governance structures, P.O. Mülbert and R. Citlau, "The Uncertain Role of Banks' Corporate Governance in Systemic Risk Management," ECGI Law Working Paper No. 179/2011 (July 2011, online: http://ssrn.com/abstract=1885866).

[64] P. McCoy, A. Pavlov and S. Wachter, "System Risk through Securitization: The Result of Deregulation and Regulatory Failure," *Connecticut Law Review*, 41 (2009), 1327–75.

[65] L. Enriques, "Regulators' Response to the Current Crisis and the Upcoming Reregulation of Financial Markets: One Reluctant Regulator's View," *University of Pennsylvania Journal of International Law*, 30 (2009), 1147–55.

[66] For a review of the empirical evidence, see E. Avgouleas, "A New Framework for the Global Regulation of Short Sales: Why Prohibition is Inefficient and Disclosure Insufficient," *Stanford Journal of Law, Business and Finance*, 16 (2010), 376–425. See further Part III below.

[67] Particularly with respect to non-bank institutions, monitoring the interconnectedness of the global marketplace, product complexity and innovation, conflict of interest, OTC market risks, and the cyclicality of financial markets: IOSCO, *Mitigating Systemic Risk*.

[68] Ibid. ESMA Chairman Maijoor has similarly noted that pre-crisis, securities regulators were focused on transparency and investor protection and that stability was not a "topical topic": speech, May 26, 2011, online: www.esma.europa.eu/documents/overview/10.

failure to address the risk-regulation element of market regulation and for its limited response to the crisis;[69] this failure has been associated with the lack of a long-standing commitment to capital adequacy or other risk-reduction, stability-related mechanisms.[70] Particular attention has focused on its failure to appreciate the impact of lighter capital rules, adopted in response to the third country regime established under the EU's Financial Conglomerates Directive, on the trading activities of major investment banks under the Consolidated Supervised Entities Program.[71]

An expansion of the scope of market regulation to address systemic risk has since emerged as a major theme of the international reform movement, reflecting the G20 recommendation that appropriate bodies review the scope of financial regulation,[72] and the related Joint Forum's review of the differentiated nature and scope of financial regulation.[73] Similarly, in its 2010 revised Objectives and Principles of Securities Regulation, IOSCO added the new principle that the regulator have contributed or contribute to a process to review the perimeter of regulation generally.[74] Accordingly, a series of changes to the scope of market regulation in the EU are closely linked to systemic risk management and the international financial stability agenda, and reflect the reality that market regulation must address the cross-sector nature of risk as well as the risk build-up in unregulated sectors which the crisis exposed. In particular, lightly or unregulated market sectors, notably the hedge fund sector, the Over the Counter (OTC) derivative markets and credit rating agencies (CRAs), have been drawn further into the regulatory net under the 2011 Alternative Investment Fund Managers Directive (AIFMD),[75] the European Markets Infrastructure Regulation on OTC derivatives (EMIR),[76] and the Credit Rating Agency Regulations I (2009), II (2011) and III (Commission Proposal, 2011).[77]

[69] e.g., N. Poser, "Why the SEC Failed: Regulators Against Regulation," *Brooklyn Journal of Corporate Finance and Commercial Law*, 3 (2009), 289–324 and J. Seligman, "The SEC in a Time of Discontinuity," *Virginia Law Review*, 95 (2009), 667–83.

[70] Langevoort, "Global Securities Regulation."

[71] Fisch, "Top Cop."

[72] G20, *Declaration* (Washington DC: G20, November 2009).

[73] Joint Forum (IOSCO, Basel Committee and International Association of Insurance Supervisors), *Review of the Differentiated Nature and Scope of Financial Regulation. Key Issues and Recommendations* (2010).

[74] IOSCO, *Objectives and Principles of Securities Regulation* (Madrid: IOSCO, 2010), Principle 7.

[75] Directive 2011/61/EU, [2011] OJ L174/1.

[76] Regulation (EU) No. 648/2012, [2012] OJ L201/1.

[77] Respectively, Regulation (EC) No. 1060/2009, [2009] OJ L302/1, Regulation (EU) No. 513/2011, [2011], OJ L145/30, and European Commission Proposal COM (2011) 747/2.

The Short Selling Regulation[78] also forms part of this movement. Regulatory innovation has therefore taken the form of an expansion of the policy goals of market regulation to include the regulation of the systemic risks generated by markets.

The EU's attempts to grapple with the re-orientation of market regulation to address risk regulation have been well documented, and will not be revisited here.[79] They have led to some messy, if ultimately reasonably workable results, reflecting, as discussed in Chapter 1 of this book, the institutional, political and market interests at stake, with the AIFMD and the Short Selling Regulation perhaps the totemic examples of how political dynamics can complicate and prejudice regulatory design, and how regulatory innovation can generate risks.

But the major legacy effects of the crisis are likely to be considerably more far-reaching, and potentially more troubling, given the evidence, discussed in the following Parts, of a wider re-setting of the goals and policy concerns of market regulation and consumer protection. The traditional coverage and goals of market regulation and of consumer protection regulation are now coming under scrutiny, with regulatory innovation increasingly taking the form of a wider consideration of the essential utility of markets and of how regulation might, potentially, dampen market intensity and innovation.

II: The legacy effects for market and consumer protection regulation

Financial market intensity and innovation

The intermediation function of financial market structures and actors has long been recognized as efficient in addressing the frictions which information and transaction costs generate for efficient capital allocation.[80] Similarly, the financial innovation associated with intermediation

[78] Regulation (EU) No. 236/2012, [2012] OJ L86/1.

[79] e.g., on the AIFMD, see J. Payne, "Private Equity and its Regulation in Europe," *European Business Organization Law Review*, 12 (2012), 559–85; E. Ferran, "After the Crisis: The Regulation of Hedge Funds and Private Equity in the EU," *European Business Organization Law Review*, 12 (2012), 379–414; and D. Awrey, "The Limits of EU Hedge Fund Regulation," *Law and Financial Markets Review*, 5 (2011), 119–28.

[80] e.g., R. Levine, "Financial Development and Economic Growth: Views and Agenda," *Journal of Economic Literature*, 35 (1997), 688–726, examining market hedging and risk diversification, resource allocation, monitoring, savings mobilization and exchange support functions which support financial market growth.

and with financial market growth has been characterized as the catalyst for welfare-enhancing growth in the capitalist system.[81] Even allowing for different varieties of capitalism, discussed in Chapter 1 of this book, international regulatory policy pre-crisis tended to support the benefits of greater financial activity or "intensity" and "complete markets,"[82] by means of, for example, reliance on facilitative "new governance" techniques (noted below) and efforts to maintain international market competitiveness.[83] FSA Chairman Turner has suggested that greater financial intensity was generally regarded as beneficial pre-crisis as it completed more markets and increased financial stability.[84] Institutional support came internationally from, for example, the International Monetary Fund (IMF), which assumed that greater financial intensity would increase allocative efficiency by increasing liquidity, and would increase financial stability by dispersing risk more effectively.[85] Post-crisis, however, and reflecting the driving concern with financial stability,

[81] Notably under the Schumpeterian growth model. For a review of the literature, see D. Awrey, "Complexity, Innovation and the Regulation of Modern Financial Markets," Oxford University Legal Research Papers Series 49/2011 (August 2011, online http://ssrn.com/abstract=1916649).

[82] A theoretically complete market is one in which individuals can hedge against all contingencies: P. Spencer, *The Structure and Regulation of Financial Markets* (Oxford University Press, 2000), pp. 2–3. e.g., on the benefits (and risks) of collateralized debt obligations (CDOs) in "completing" fixed income securities markets by providing investment opportunities which would not otherwise be available, see F. Partnoy and D. Skeel, "The Promise and Perils of Credit Derivatives," *University of Cincinnati Law Review*, 75 (2007), 1019–51.

[83] Clear from efforts such as the accelerated adoption in the UK of the Investment Exchanges and Clearing Houses Act 2006. This very short Act gives the FSA a veto over any regulation proposed by a UK exchange or clearing house which is "excessive," and is designed to allow the FSA to reject any rule changes proposed by a foreign-owned UK exchange which are promoted or required by a foreign regulator and which might hinder the competitiveness of the UK market. Pre-crisis, high-level attention was also given to capital market competitiveness in the US, best exemplified in the initial report of the Committee on Capital Markets Competitiveness (Committee on Capital Market Regulation, *Interim Report* (2006), online: www.capmktsreg.org), which was followed by quarterly reviews and which has generated significant comment (e.g. L. Zingales, "Is the US Capital Market Losing its Competitive Edge?," ECGI Finance Working Paper No. 192/2007 (November 2007, online: http://ssrn.com/abstract=1028701)).

[84] FSA Chairman Adair Turner, "How Should the Crisis Affect our Views about Financial Intermediation?," (speech, March 7, 2011, online: www.fsa.gov.uk/pages/Library/Communication/Speeches/2011/0314_at.shtml).

[85] e.g., IMF, *Global Financial Stability Report* (Washington DC: IMF, April 2006), ch. 1, highlighting the importance of the dispersion of credit risks away from banks in de-risking banks and in increasing the "shock-absorbing" capacity of the financial system, although noting the related risks.

third-level regulatory innovation is increasingly taking the form of a policy questioning of the essential utility of markets.

The extent to which markets should be completed, and whether financial market intensity or "financialization," and related financial innovation, should be promoted, tolerated or dampened is a feature of pre-crisis financial market scholarship. Financialization, typically associated with more complete financial markets and a growth in finance,[86] prompted a vigorous debate on the extent to which capital allocation should be a function of government or market forces. One leading analysis has linked financialization to political support for, and belief in, the superior efficiency of allocation through competitive markets rather than through governmental intervention, the growth of market finance, financial deregulation, financial innovation and intermediation, and "financial markets becom[ing] the pace-setters of all markets."[87] The long-standing debate on varieties of capitalism, discussed in Chapter 1 of this book, engages with the drivers for, impact of, and appropriateness of different levels of market completion. Financial economists have similarly long queried whether "excessive" market liquidity can drive short-termism and lead to instability.[88]

The notion of the appropriate level of financial intensity is also a feature of consumer market scholarship pre-crisis, which addresses the appropriateness of the state's withdrawal from welfare provision and the related financialization of consumers who may be ill-equipped, but required, to take on risk-bearing burdens.[89] The related "responsibilization" literature queries the extent to which consumers should be drawn

86 See generally, S. Deakin, "The Rise of Finance: What is it, What is Driving it, What might Stop it?," *Comparative Labour Law & Policy Journal*, 30 (2008), 67–76. On the increase in financialization since 2005, in terms of the sharp increase in the global stock of financial assets, see M. Wolf, *Fixing Global Finance: How to Curb Financial Crises in the 21st Century* (New Haven, CT: Yale University Press, 2009), pp. 11–12.

87 R. Dole, *Stock Market Capitalism: Welfare Capitalism. Japan and Germany versus the Anglo-Saxons* (Oxford University Press, 2000), pp. 3–5.

88 e.g., M. O'Hara, "Liquidity and Financial Market Stability," National Bank of Belgium Working Paper No. 55 (May 2004, online: http://ssrn.com/abstract=1691574), highlighting the debate on the "dark side of liquidity" and its leading proponents, including Keynes in the 1930s and Tobin in the 1970s.

89 e.g., P. Ireland, "Shareholder Primacy and the Distribution of Wealth," *Modern Law Review*, 68 (2005), 49–81, I. Ertürk, J. Froud, S. Johal, A. Leaver and K. Williams, "The Democratization of Finance? Promises, Outcomes and Conditions," *Review of International Political Economy*, 14 (2007), 553–75, and D. Kingsford Smith, "Regulating Investment Risk: Individuals and the Global Financial Crisis," *University of New South Wales Law Journal*, 32 (2009), 514–46.

into the regulatory net as "risk regulators" and the appropriateness of regulatory and policy initiatives to build capable, independent and informed financial actors who can take on responsibility for welfare provision.[90]

Less directly, a major strand of law and finance scholarship focuses on the relationship between financial sector development, wider economic development and law.[91] But while it is related to and has further extended a cognate lively scholarship on the relative efficiency of bank and market finance,[92] it typically does not address whether there is an optimum level of financial market development or of financial intensity.[93]

The social utility of the intermediation function of markets is now, however, coming under more general scrutiny in the scholarly debate on the crisis,[94] as is the extent to which regulation and policy can be used as levers to limit or control levels of financial market development.[95] This movement reflects a wider focus on the deep-seated behavioral dynamics in the financial markets which can generate instability and which are very difficult to address through regulation. A massive canon of pre-crisis scholarship had already addressed the impact of behavioral drivers on market efficiency and the related challenges this posed to disclosure-based regulation in particular.[96] Since the crisis, this analysis has been applied to the difficulties the markets experienced in managing risk and

[90] T. Williams, "Empowerment of Whom and for What? Financial Literacy Education and the New Regulation of Consumer Financial Services," *Law & Policy*, 29 (2007), 226–56 and I. Ramsay, "Consumer Law, Regulatory Capitalism and New Learning in Regulation," *Sydney Law Review*, 28 (2006), 9–35.

[91] Spearheaded by the work of financial economists La Porta, Lopez de Silanes, Shleifer and Vishny ("LLSV") (e.g., R. La Porta, F. Lopez de Silanes, A. Shleifer and R. Vishny, "Law and Finance," *Journal of Political Economy*, 106 (1998), 1113–55.

[92] e.g., B. Black and R. Gilson, "Venture Capital and the Structure of Capital Markets: Banks or Stock Markets," *Journal of Financial Economics*, 47 (1998), 243–77.

[93] Although for a provocative and thoughtful assessment of the validity of stock market capitalization as an indicator of economic development, see R. Aguilera and C. Williams, "'Law and Finance': Inaccurate, Incomplete and Important," *Brigham Young University Law Review*, 6 (2009), 1413–34. Similarly, L. Mitchell, "Towards a New Law and Economics: The Case of the Stock Market" (February 2010, online: http://ssrn.com/abstract=1557730).

[94] From a growing scholarship see, e.g., Whitehead, "Reframing Financial Regulation," suggesting that while intermediation can smooth the allocation of capital, the related agency costs can be significant.

[95] e.g., C. Arup, "The Global Financial Crisis: Learning from Regulatory and Governance Studies," *Law & Policy*, 32 (2010), 363–81.

[96] e.g., references at n. 56 above.

to the destabilizing impact of incentives.[97] These difficulties have led Robert Shiller to call for finance to be "humanized,"[98] and Andrew Haldane to call for more attention to be paid to the "patience gene" and to suggest that "the fidgeting fingers of the invisible hand may need a steadying arm."[99] Close attention is also focusing on the nature of financial innovation[100] and on the ability of markets to manage innovation productively.[101]

From a policy perspective, the intensity and innovation debate is reflected in a wider political and populist concern in some EU Member States to address "speculation," which has taken the form of often hostile attacks on, variously, private equity, hedge funds and credit default swap (CDS) trading in Member States' sovereign debt.[102] But there is also evidence of cooler assessments of the extent to which markets should be completed and innovation supported, and of how policy levers can be deployed in this regard. An allied concern to support "fundamental investors," who operate on the basis of the fundamental value of securities rather than on speculative grounds, can also be discerned in the policy debate.[103]

97 e.g., D.C. Langevoort, "Chasing the Greased Pig Down Wall Street: A Gatekeeper's Guide to the Psychology, Culture and Ethics of Financial Risk," *Cornell Law Review*, 96 (2008), 1209–47.

98 R.J. Shiller, "Democratizing and Humanizing Finance," in Kroszner and Shiller, *Reforming US Financial Markets*, pp. 1–49.

99 A. Haldane (Bank of England), "Patience and Finance" (speech, September 2, 2010, online: www.bankofengland.co.uk/publications/speeches).

100 For an extensive review of the literature and a proposed research agenda, see J. Lerner and P. Tufano, "The Consequences of Financial Innovation: A Counterfactual Research Agenda," NBER Working Paper 16780 (February 2011, online: www.nber.org/papers/w16780).

101 e.g., E. Posner and E. Glen Weyl, "A Proposal for Limiting Speculation on Derivatives: An FDA for Financial Innovation," University of Chicago Institute for Law and Economics Olin Research Paper No. 594 (January 2012, online: http://ssrn.com/abstract=1995077), on testing new products for social utility, M. Blair, "Financial Innovation, Leverage, Bubbles and the Distribution of Income," *Review of Banking and Finance Law*, 30 (2010–11), 225–311, addressing innovations which allowed financial institutions to use excessive levels of leverage and N. Gennaioli, A. Shliefer and R. Vishny, "Financial Innovation and Financial Fragility," FEEM Working Paper (October 2010, online: http://faculty.chicagobooth.edu), modeling how financial innovation generates financial risks, and considering previous periods of risk-generating innovation.

102 e.g., European Parliament ECON Chair S. Bowles, "Market Abuse" (speech, 2 July, 2010), suggesting that "there has been too much uninformed speculation about speculation."

103 IOSCO, *Regulatory Issues Raised by the Impact of Technological Changes on Market Integrity and Efficiency. Consultation Report* (Madrid: IOSCO, 2011), p. 12.

Internationally, the OECD has signalled some cooling of policy enthusiasm for market completion and ever-increasing financial market intensity. In a 2011 paper on the systemic risks posed by the scale of derivative trading by G-SIFIs, it drew a distinction between "primary instruments" associated with consumption, saving and fixed capital formation and used to create wealth (loans and equity and debt securities), and "other instruments" used to hedge risk, arbitrage prices, gamble and reduce tax and regulatory/agency costs, and associated with wealth transfer. The market for the former financed productivity and enhanced innovation and investment. The market for the latter comprised the vast global derivatives market, was responsible for increasing system risk, and in many cases was used for "less socially useful" activities, including regulatory and tax arbitrage and gambling.[104]

In the UK, the FSA's 2009 *Turner Review* laid down a challenge to pre-crisis financial market orthodoxy. It highlighted the relative growth of the banking sector to that of the "end-services" sector,[105] and queried the efficiency of the financial sector, suggesting that "beyond a certain degree of liquidity and market completion, the additional allocative efficiency benefits of further liquidity and market completion" might be relatively slight and outweighed by additional instability risks. It called for regulatory policy to balance the benefits of market completion and market liquidity and the drawbacks of inherent instability in liquid markets.[106] A more radical agenda has since been aired by FSA Chairman Turner in recent speeches on the social utility of markets and on increasing financialization. In a widely reported November 2009 speech, Chairman Turner called for the assumption that all financial innovation is useful to be challenged, and for consideration to be given to the optimal size of the wholesale financial services industry and in particular of trading activities.[107] In a major February 2011 speech,[108] he questioned whether reforms should address the relative size of the financial industry, and queried the driving focus on the "too big to fail" question and

[104] OECD, *Bank Competition and Financial Stability* (Paris: OECD, 2011), pp. 36–9.

[105] Turner, *Turner Review*, pp. 16–18 and suggesting that "this development increased the potential impact of financial instability on the real economy" (at p. 18).

[106] At pp. 41–2. In a similar vein, Andrew Haldane of the Bank of England has suggested that liquidity may "unlock the impatience gene": "Patience and Finance."

[107] "Responding to the Financial Crisis: Challenging Past Assumptions" (speech, November 30, 2009, online: www.fsa.gov.uk/pages/Library/Communication/Speeches/2009/1130_at.shtml).

[108] "Reforming Finance."

incentive-related problems, suggesting that markets can remain deeply unstable, given deep-rooted behavioral problems, and noting that during the period of post-war "financial repression" (1935–75) economic growth was rapid and steady.[109] Chairman Turner also queried the benefits of ever-increasing financialization, noting inbuilt inefficiencies such as super profits, rent extraction through tax management and "valueless trading."[110] He has similarly queried the value of financial intermediation and asked "how much" financial intermediation is optimal.[111] A related concern can be identified in the UK's 2011–12 *Kay Review* of the UK equity markets; Chairman Kay has emphasized the "final goals" of markets with respect to capital allocation and the support of savings, by way of contrast with the "intermediate objectives" of markets concerning liquidity, transparency and price discovery. He has suggested that while the latter three may be good things, "they are not unambiguously [so]" and may have diminishing returns and entail costs.[112] The concern of the *Kay Review* with long-term investment horizons is reflected in a widening policy debate on equity market investment horizons in the UK.[113] Similarly, while the 2011 Independent Commission on Banking proposals for a limited ring-fence between (very broadly) retail/corporate and investment banking engages a multiplicity of reform drivers, it can, at least, be associated with a concern to ensure productive investment for

[109] Similarly, the contrast between the static, or at best "mildly positive" contribution of equity market growth to economic growth and a massive increase in trading volume has been noted: A. Haldane (Bank of England), "The Race to Zero" (speech, 8 July, 2011, online: www.bankofengland.co.uk/publications/news/2011/068.htm).

[110] See further Part III on high frequency trading.

[111] A. Turner, "How Should the Crisis Affect our Views about Financial Intermediation?" (speech, March 7, 2011, online: www.fsa.gov.uk/pages/Library/Communication/Speeches/2011/0314_at.shtml) and "The Future of Finance" (speech, July 14, 2010, online: www.fsa.gov.uk/pages/Library/Communication/Speeches/2010/0714_at.shtml).

[112] J. Kay, "Speech" (September 15, 2011, online: www.bis.gov.uk/kayreview). The February 2012 Interim Report of the Review adopted a similar approach, suggesting that: "Equity markets are a principal means by which savers can contribute to, and share in, the success of British business. . .While the growth of financial intermediation has many positive aspects, intermediation is not an end in itself": The Kay Review, *The Kay Review of UK Equity Markets and Long-Term Decision Making. Interim Report* (London: Kay Review, 2012), p. 2. A similar approach was adopted in the *Final Report*, published in July 2012, which extensively examined the risks of the "explosion in intermediation" in equity markets (p. 4).

[113] e.g., A. Haldane and R. Davies (Bank of England), "The Short Long" (speech, May 11, 2011, online: www.bankofengland.co.uk/publications/speeches), making an empirical case for short-termism in the pricing of equities in the US and UK and suggesting remedial policy measures.

business is supported[114] and thus, perhaps, "simpler" financing. Its concern is with protecting "vital banking services on which households and small and medium-sized enterprises (SMEs) depend."[115] It certainly assumes that investment-banking activities should not be supported by the implicit subsidy associated with government guarantee support, and tends to associate the risk-taking which market intensification through investment banking typically engages with "excessive" risk and with a need for curbing incentives.[116] The 2012 Financial Services Bill also carries the imprint of this move to acknowledge the limits of markets: as originally drafted, the Bill charged the new FCA with an underpinning strategic objective to "protect and enhance confidence in the UK financial system." This generated significant stakeholder concern that the objective was flawed given, in particular, the failures to which markets are vulnerable and the dangers were the new FCA to find itself promoting confidence in conditions where this was not appropriate given the risk of consumer detriment.[117] The 2012 Bill, accordingly, has replaced this objective with the strategic objective of ensuring that the relevant markets function well;[118] however elusive this objective may turn out to be, the change in tone is significant.

This concern is not limited to the UK in the EU, although its espousal within the UK, which is more traditionally associated with the financialization movement, is striking. French Autorité des Marchés Financiers (AMF) Chairman Jouyet, for example, has recently queried the "social utility" of high frequency trading,[119] while the current French policy priority appears to be to address what it regards as socially inefficient market speculation and to adopt a "back to basics" approach with respect to market transparency and fairness.[120]

A similar uneasiness concerning the speed and depth of market development can be charted in the more recent EU policy pronouncements.

[114] J. Kay, "Without Ringfencing it will Soon be a Case of 'Here We Go Again'," *Financial Times*, September 14, 2011, 15.

[115] ICB, *Final Report*, p. 25. [116] Ibid., ch. 2.

[117] Joint Committee, *Report: Draft Financial Services Bill*, pp. 26–8 and Treasury Select Committee, *26th Report, The Financial Conduct Authority*, January 2012, pp. 29–34. Treasury Select Committee Chair Andrew Tyrie warned that at times enhancing confidence in the financial system could be misplaced: B. Masters, "Watchdog Must Stay Wary," *Financial Times*, January 13, 2011, 3,

[118] Financial Services Bill, clause 1B(2).

[119] AMF Chairman J.P. Jouyet, "Keynote Speech to ICMA General Meeting and Conference" (May 27, 2011, online: www.amf-france.org/documents/general/9993_1.pdf).

[120] AMF, *What are the Priorities for Financial Markets?* (Paris: AMF, 2011).

In April 2010, Commissioner Barnier suggested that a "regulatory rethink" was required and called for a financial sector that supported job creation and sustainable growth.[121] Notwithstanding the long history of the universal banking model in continental Europe – as examined in Chapter 1 of this book – Commissioner Barnier has also suggested that the UK's ring-fencing model might be considered for the EU.[122] Although concerns to placate the European Parliament, which has called for this model, are at play here, it nonetheless underlines the extent to which uneasiness at intensification is coloring the policy debate. The EU Parliament's concern to address perceived over-intensification might also be associated with its recent calls for the overall volume of derivative trading to be reduced through regulatory intervention[123] and its concern to bring the OTC markets within the scope of trading market regulation under the ongoing MiFID Review.[124]

Some froth can, of course, be detected in this movement. The political context, national interests in responding to popular anger post-crisis, particularly as fiscal reforms bite, and opportunism cannot be ignored, particularly given tensions arising from the perceived association between the crisis and "Anglo-American" capitalism.[125] Nonetheless, a persistent concern with intensification can be observed in the current EU and Member State policy environment.

In tandem with what might be termed this nascent "de-intensification," or perhaps simplification movement, attention is also focusing on the nature of financial market innovation. Although the productive nature of financial market innovation has been repeatedly emphasized in crisis-era policy rhetoric,[126] the crisis has also prompted a policy and popular focus on perceived "bad" financial innovation. This is most strongly associated with stability risks and with the originate-to-distribute securitization

[121] Barnier, "Restoring Trust."

[122] S. Pignal and A. Barker, "Barnier Panel to Study break up of EU Banks," *Financial Times*, November 22, 2011. At the time of writing, the "Lii Kanen High Level Group" on the structure of the EU banking sector was expected to report in late summer 2012.

[123] European Parliament, *Report on Derivatives Markets: Future Policy Actions* (2010) (A7–0187/2010), para. 9.

[124] Part III below.

[125] Well-exemplified by President Sarkozy's remarks on the night of the UK's exercise of the veto over Treaty change to the effect that concessions to the UK on financial regulation were not acceptable, given the financial crisis. See further E. Ferran, Chapter 1 above.

[126] Including in the initial 2008 G20 *Washington Declaration*, which contained a commitment to ensuring that regulation would be efficient and not stifle innovation: G20, *Declaration* (Washington DC: G20, November 2009).

model and the exponential growth in related structured credit products and CDSs.[127] In the UK, former government minister Lord Mandelson, in a widely reported 2009 speech, called for "less financial engineering and a lot more real engineering."[128] The *Turner Review* linked financial market innovation to the development of the financial crisis.[129] More recently, and reflecting prominent criticism of financial innovation in the US,[130] speeches by senior FSA officials suggest considerable skepticism as to the sustainability and social utility of untramelled innovation.[131] Policy consequences have followed this movement in the UK; the new PRA and FCA have expressly not been charged with promoting innovation.[132] In the EU, although the seminal review of the crisis, the 2009 *De Larosière Report*, initially cautioned against regulation which might slow down financial innovation and undermine economic growth,[133] Commissioner Barnier has recently queried whether financial innovation is always useful and profitable.[134] The Commission has similarly identified a positive relationship between financial innovation and overall welfare as an indicator of progress on the reform agenda.[135] Internationally, IOSCO has identified a changed approach to innovation, with regulators now paying greater

[127] e.g., Blair, "Financial Innovation" and N. Jenkinson, A. Penlaver and N. Vause, "Financial Innovation: What have we Learnt?," *Bank of England Quarterly Bulletin*, 48 (2008), Quarter 3, 330–8.

[128] Lord Mandelson, Speech to Labour Party Conference, September 28, 2009.

[129] Turner, *Turner Review*, pp. 14–16. Similarly, from a policy perspective, N. Pain and O. Röhn, *Policy Frameworks in the Post-Crisis Environment*, OECD Economics Department Working Papers No. 857 (Paris: OECD, 2011), para. 11.

[130] e.g., by economist Paul Krugman, suggesting that it was hard to think of any major recent financial innovations that had aided society: "Money for Nothing," *New York Times*, April 27, 2009, A23.

[131] e.g., T. Huertas, Director, Banking Sector FSA, "Responsibility and Regulation: Where does the Balance lie with respect to Financial Innovation?" (speech, March 11, 2011, online: www.fsa.gov.uk/pages/Library/Communication/Speeches/2011/0311_th.shtml), in the context of derivatives and securitizations, and A. Turner, "Securitization, Shadow Banking and the Value of Innovation" (speech, April 19, 2012, online: www.fsa.gov.uk/static/pubs/speeches/0419-at.pdf).

[132] The government argued that "a more nuanced approach to innovation in financial services is required" and stated that "it did not consider it appropriate for either regulator to have to have regard to the desirability of facilitating innovation": HM Treasury, *A New Approach – Building*, p. 48.

[133] The High Level Group on Financial Supervision in the EU, *Report* (Brussels: March, 2009), p. 14 (the *De Larosière Report*).

[134] Barnier, "Restoring Trust."

[135] European Commission, *European Financial Stability and Integration Report* (2011) (SEC (2011) 489), p. 51.

attention to risks, and called for securities regulators to adopt an approach to financial innovation that seeks to better understand the potential risks and to find the right balance between unrestrained innovation and over-regulation; it has similarly suggested that a lack of transparency and product complexity should be of "great concern" to market regulators.[136] The Financial Stability Board (FSB) is monitoring financial innovation generally,[137] while the OECD has similarly focused on how innovation risks might be captured.[138] Speeches from the Bank for International Settlements (BIS) also form part of the growing policy association between innovation and risk-taking and enhanced regulation.[139] The monitoring of innovation is also beginning to appear in regulatory mandates. The SEC has established a division for monitoring financial innovation,[140] the first new SEC division to be established in thirty years.[141] In the EU, the new European Securities and Markets Authority (ESMA) has been charged with establishing a "financial innovation committee" which would support a coordinated approach across the EU's regulators to "new and innovative activities" and advise the EU legislators accordingly.[142] The default assumption that innovation generates risks which require intervention seems clear.

The implications

The debate as to whether markets are inherently inefficient, and whether and how "de-financialization" should proceed and innovation be curbed, is complex and multifaceted,[143] and is not the concern of this

[136] IOSCO, *Mitigating Systemic Risk.*

[137] FSB, *Progress in the Implementation of the G20 Recommendations for Strengthening Financial Stability* (Basel: FSB, 2011), pp. 11–12.

[138] S. Lumpkin, "Consumer Protection and Financial Innovation: A Few Basic Propositions," *OECD Financial Market Trends,* (2010), 1–23.

[139] BIS General Manager Caruana, "Welfare Effects of Financial Innovation" (speech, November 11, 2011, online: www.bis/org/speeches).

[140] Division of Risk, Strategy and Financial Innovation, established in 2009.

[141] Lerner and Tufano, "Consequences of Financial Innovation," p. 21.

[142] ESMA Regulation (EU) No. 1095/2010, [2010] OJ L33/84, art. 9(4). A related standing committee has since been established. This requirement applies to all three European Supervisory Authorities (ESMA, the European Banking Authority (EBA) and the European Insurance and Occupational Pensions Authority (EIOPA)). Early indications suggest the authorities are taking this mandate seriously. The EBA Financial Innovation Standing Committee produced a report in early 2012 which identified potentially harmful innovations, including collateralized commercial paper and convertible bonds, which were in need of further examination: EBA, *Financial Innovation and Consumer Protection* (2012).

[143] e.g., R. Bootle, *The Trouble with Markets: Saving Capitalism from Itself* (London, Boston: Nicholas Brealey, 2nd edn., 2011).

discussion. But from a regulatory design perspective, the optimum level of financial market development, and the optimum degree of financial innovation, even if they were measurable, are unlikely to be achievable by wielding the tools at regulators' disposal.

Financial innovation, for example, has long been associated with the financial markets,[144] but its nature is contested and research is limited.[145] It has been strongly associated with product complexity over the financial crisis.[146] But financial innovation can be characterized more generally in terms of the ongoing and dynamic process through which the institutional structures of finance change and, in particular, in terms of the movement of intermediation from banks to markets, which involves significant product innovation as bilaterally negotiated products are standardized and traded on platforms.[147] The financial crisis provides a paradigmatic example of this process with the transfer of loan credit risk into traded securitization products.[148] Similarly, financial innovation has been associated with the introduction of new products and services which can change the essential functions provided by institutions.[149] It is very doubtful that regulation should seek to control this process, which is hard-wired into the dynamic nature of financial markets. Neither is it clear what drives financial innovation, making a pre-emptive regulatory response all the more difficult. It has been associated with, for example, the discovery of more efficient means of performing the basic functions provided by the financial system,[150] with reaction to regulatory change and regulatory arbitrage,[151] with reducing

[144] For an early analysis of the derivatives market, see H. Hu, "Swaps, The Modern Process of Financial Innovation and Vulnerability of a Regulatory Paradigm," *University of Pennsylvania Law Review*, 138 (1989), 333–435.

[145] The "paucity of research" in this area has been noted: Lerner and Tufano, "Consequences of Financial Innovation," p. 3.

[146] e.g., from a finance perspective, and examining the risks which arise where innovative and higher risk products are regarded as substitutes for traditional securities, Gennaiolo *et al.*, "Financial Innovation."

[147] R. Merton, "A Functional Perspective of Financial Intermediation," *Financial Management*, 24 (1995), 23–41.

[148] Z. Gubler, "The Financial Innovation Process: Theory and Application," *Delaware Journal of Corporate Law*, 36 (2011), 55–119.

[149] Leading to the development of the shadow banking system: A. Mullineux, "Financial Innovation and Social Welfare," *Journal of Financial Regulation and Compliance*, 18 (2010), 243–56.

[150] Merton, "Functional Perspective."

[151] M. Miller, "Financial Innovation, The Last Twenty Years and the Next," *Journal of Financial and Quantitative Analysis*, 21 (1986), 459–71 and Mullineux, "Financial Innovation."

the costs of market imperfections and constraints (whether regulatory, market, or internal) on business,[152] with investor demand for particular cash flows[153] and with the particular incentives of intermediaries to produce financial innovation.[154] The financial crisis underlines the range of macroeconomic, political and regulatory factors which, for example, drove the "originate to distribute" model. Neither, of course, is it the case that all financial innovation is problematic.[155] Financial innovation, particularly when associated with the well-documented strengths of market intermediation in normal conditions, has been described as the engine driving the financial system to greater economic efficiency, supporting the completion of markets, the lowering of transaction costs and the reduction of agency costs.[156] It is when this process goes wrong, and when markets are not equipped to cope with new intermediation functions, that risks, and the potential need for intervention, arise.[157]

But identifying the action point is very difficult. One analysis has distinguished between innovation which is designed to circumvent regulation and innovation which is designed to reduce transaction costs and better manage risk.[158] But the pre-crisis development of the structured credit market could be, and was at the time, easily associated with the latter. What is most likely is that perceived "over" intensity and "bad" innovation become useful justifications for regulation. Regulators face considerable risk from emerging market sectors, actors and activities. The easier response is to impose regulation on these fields, particularly given public choice effects; the more difficult one is to

[152] W. Silber, "The Process of Financial Innovation," *American Economic Review*, 73 (1983), 89–95.

[153] The "canonical" driver, according to Lerner and Tufano, "Consequences of Financial Innovation," p. 10.

[154] Awrey, "Complexity."

[155] e.g., Lumpkin, "Consumer Protection," in the context of retail market product design. Similarly, a dominant view in the literature is, unsurprisingly, that innovation is neither all bad nor good: Lerner and Tufano, "Consequences of Financial Innovation," p. 4.

[156] Merton, "Functional Perspective."

[157] e.g., Gubler, "Financial Innovation Process". Similarly, Jenkinson *et al.*, "Financial Innovation," outlining the market frictions (such as poor transparency, illiquidity risks and weak market infrastructure) which can make innovation less productive, and F. Partnoy, "Historical Perspectives on the Financial Crisis: Ivan Krauger, the Credit-Rating Agencies and Two Theories about the Function and Dysfunction of Markets," *Yale Journal on Regulation*, 26 (2009), 431–43, on how innovation can lead to disclosure failures.

[158] Mullineux, "Financial Innovation."

assess whether nuanced supervision of pre-existing rules will suffice, and to judge the appropriate mix of intervention. As discussed in Parts III and IV below, the emerging intensity and innovation agenda, which seems to be taking the form of a de-intensification and simplification movement which is resetting the nature of market and consumer protection regulation, may prove problematic for the second-generation reforms to market regulation and consumer protection regulation.

Policy innovation and rule innovation

This emerging "third level" innovation poses further difficulties given the parallel, second-level form of regulatory innovation post-crisis with respect to the nature of rules. Pre-crisis, "new governance" techniques[159] for intervention were in the ascendant internationally. These techniques reflected a governing view of financial regulation as arising from an iterative process between private parties and regulators, developed in a series of regulatory dialogues, and resulting in a "de-centered" regulatory environment in which a range of public and private disciplining tools were relied on.[160] The regulator in effect acted as a "ringmaster," using a range of disciplining techniques beyond regulation and engaging multiple non-state actors, of domestic, regional and international character, and with industry and public sector roots. Reflecting the wider "regulation-skeptical" zeitgeist,[161] the tools of new governance in the financial markets included risk-based regulation,[162] principles-based

[159] An extensive social sciences literature considers the nature of new governance. For an early and leading discussion, see I. Ayres and J. Braithwaite, *Responsive Regulation. Transcending the Deregulation Debate* (Oxford University Press, 1992).

[160] J. Black, "Mapping the Contours of Contemporary Financial Services Regulation," *Journal of Corporate Law Studies*, 2 (2002), 253–88.

[161] The pre-crisis regulatory era was not a deregulatory era. But the governing assumption was that, in weighing the costs and benefits of intervention and of market discipline, market discipline would prove more effective. e.g., Langevoort, "Global Securities Regulation" and, from a policy perspective, Turner, "Reforming Finance."

[162] Risk-based regulation has been defined in terms of a systematized framework of inspection or supervision, primarily designed to manage regulatory or institutional risk and to prioritize action. Risk in this context is typically cast in terms of the risk of the supervisor not achieving its objectives. e.g., J. Black, *Risk-based Regulation. Choices, Practices and Lessons Being Learned* (Paris: OECD, 2008, OECD Report (SG/GRP (2008)) and R. Baldwin and J. Black, "Really Responsive Regulation," *Modern Law Review*, 71 (2008), 59–94.

regulation[163] and systems-and-controls/model-based regulation,[164] all of which, to different degrees, allowed the regulator to withdraw from direct monitoring and disciplining, or to pick and choose the nature of intervention.[165] This period also saw related strenuous efforts to "enroll" non-regulatory actors, including consumers,[166] into the regulatory process as market and risk monitors.[167] These tools, combined with the ever-increasing complexity of markets – which generated a degree of "capture by complexity"[168] – and prevailing support for more complete markets produced a regulatory system within which oversight of ever-larger sectors of the financial markets fell outside the main public regulatory perimeter,[169] and in which ever-greater pressure was placed on consumer decision-making.[170]

In the EU, "new governance" had more limited impact, as EU intervention over the markets was primarily a function of single market construction and accordingly associated with rules-based harmonization. The regulatory regime tended to track political, institutional and market support for liberalization in a particular market sector, and its substantive content was typically a function of institutional compromise. The traditional control of Member States over operational supervision,

[163] Principles-based regulation typically involves: the articulation of regulatory objectives and outcomes through high-level principles which are supported, where necessary, by rules, but also by guidance; a commitment to paring back unnecessary or ambiguous rules; a focus on the achievement of outcomes; and better engagement by industry and senior management with the delivery of outcomes. See, e.g., J. Black, M. Hopper and C. Band, "Making a Success of Principles-Based Regulation," *Law and Financial Markets Review*, 1 (2007), 191–206 and C. Ford, "New Governance, Compliance, and Principles-Based Securities Regulation," *American Business Law Journal*, 45 (2008), 1–60.

[164] e.g., E. Gerding, "Code, Crash and Open Source: the Outsourcing of Financial Regulation to Risk Models and the Global Financial Crisis," *Washington Law Review*, 84 (2009), 127–98, examining the over-reliance on proprietary computer models.

[165] See generally, J. Black, "The Rise (and Fall?) of Principles Based Regulation," in K. Alexander and N. Moloney (eds.), *Law Reform and Financial Markets* (Cheltenham: Elgar, 2011), pp. 3–34.

[166] Williams, "Empowerment."

[167] J. Black, "Enrolling Actors in Regulatory Processes: Examples from UK Financial Services Regulation," [2003] *Public Law*, 63–91.

[168] Suggesting that the SEC's initial failed attempts to regulate hedge funds reflected the extent to which regulators had become "daunted by complexity": Gerding, "Code, Crash," p. 134.

[169] e.g., B. Quinn, "The Failure of Private Ordering and Financial Crisis of 2008," *New York University Journal of Law and Business*, 5 (2009), 549–615.

[170] N. Moloney, *How to Protect Investors: Lessons from the EC and the UK* (Cambridge University Press, 2010), pp. 47–67.

combined with complex institutional dynamics which can lead to rules becoming an instrument of institutional power, also generated few incentives for new governance approaches. Nonetheless, the imprints of the new governance model can be seen in MiFID's reliance on a principles-based model for investment firm regulation and its incorporation of systems- and control-based rules;[171] in the prevailing willingness to leave large market sectors outside the EU's regulatory control (including hedge funds, rating agencies and clearing and settlement structures);[172] and in the Commission's wider support for a "regulatory pause" once the Financial Services Action Plan (FSAP) was completed in 2005.[173]

The nature of intervention is now changing. Traditional, rules-based "command and control" regulation is replacing the variants of self-regulation which dominated in certain market sectors pre-crisis. A retreat into hierarchical regulation is underway[174] and the new governance model is being withdrawn, or at least shrunk. Principles-based regulation, in particular, has become associated with a lax approach to regulation which increased systemic risk (in the UK, where the FSA was a standard-bearer for principles-based regulation, it has been replaced with "outcomes-based" regulation and coupled with an "Intensive Supervision" model), although the reality of its failure and demise is more complex,[175] not least given the persistent reliance on principles in key international standards.[176] The enrolment of market actors is being reassessed, with greater appreciation of the incentive risks which can limit the ability of private actors to monitor effectively, well exemplified by the regulatory treatment of rating agencies, hedge funds and the OTC derivatives markets under the G20 international reform agenda. Risk-based regulation alone appears relatively unscathed, although this also reflects the post-crisis heightened awareness of the reality that regulators cannot deliver a risk-free system.[177] Command

[171] Moloney, *EC Securities Regulation*, pp. 594–5.

[172] N. Moloney, "Innovation and Risk in EC Financial Market Regulation After the Financial Services Action Plan: New Instruments of Financial Market Intervention and the Committee of European Securities Regulators," *European Law Review*, 32 (2007), 627–63.

[173] European Commission, *White Paper on Financial Services Policy 2005–2010* (COM (2005) 629).

[174] Black, "Restructuring Global and EU Financial Regulation."

[175] e.g., C. Ford, "New Governance in the Teeth of Human Frailty: Lessons from Financial Regulation," *Wisconsin Law Review*, 101 (2010), 441–87.

[176] Black, "Restructuring Global and EU Financial Regulation."

[177] Risk-based supervision has been described as the engine room of the new FCA in the UK: FCA, *Approach to Regulation* (London: FCA, 2011), p. 30.

and control intervention is being further entrenched by the central steering internationally by the G20 agenda, and by the FSB's monitoring of domestic implementation of key international standards and targets.[178] This reaction is not unexpected. New governance techniques provided a relatively straightforward target for blame and reform, and more intensive intervention creates the impression of a regulator more in control of the markets.[179]

In the EU, reflecting this movement, harmonized regulation is intensifying. The drivers for this development are, as Chapter 1 examines, many and varied. From an early stage in the reform process, the notion of a "single rule-book" has been a driving concern of the reform program.[180] The rule-book objective is partly a function of the particular pathologies of the EU's single market and is designed to ensure that host Member States do not carry fiscal risks from failures of home State actors in their local markets.[181] The new institutional apparatus for law-making provides incentives for more intensive rule-making; ESMA is empowered to propose technical standards for adoption by the Commission and is more securely based than its precursor CESR (the Committee of European Securities Regulators) to adopt guidance and to advise the EU's legislative institutions on law-making.[182] Institutional dynamics, particularly those linked to a rejuvenated and generally pro-intervention European Parliament, are intensifying regulation, as are the international dynamics which, while unclear, can at least be associated with some EU concern to shape the international rulebook through third-country access techniques. This movement also reflects a policy suspicion of new governance techniques generally. Commissioner Barnier, for example, has suggested that "self-regulation has failed" and that "regulatory gaps are always exploited."[183] After early support for

[178] e.g., with respect to specific practices and standards, FSB, *Thematic Review on Risk Disclosure Practices* (Basel: FSB, 2011). More generally, the FSB is also engaging in a review of FSB member compliance with the recommendations of regular IMF "Financial Sector Assessment Programmes" (FSAPs), under its *Framework for Strengthening Adherence to International Standards* (Basel: FSB, 2010).

[179] E.J. Pan, "Understanding Financial Regulation," Cardozo Legal Studies Research Paper No. 329 (April 2011, online: http://ssrn.com/abstract=1805018).

[180] See further, N. Moloney, "EU Financial Market Regulation after the Financial Crisis: 'More Europe' or More Risks?," *Common Market Law Review*, 47 (2010), 1317–83.

[181] Ibid. [182] Moloney, "ESMA Part I".

[183] EU Commissioner M. Barnier, "Financial Regulation in Europe – Where Next?" (speech, March 31, 2010, online: http://europa.eu/rapid/pressReleasesAction.do?reference=SPEECH/10/141&format=HTML&aged=0&language=EN&guiLanguage=en).

principles-based regulation,[184] the European Parliament has been in the vanguard of the regulatory movement.

This development poses difficulties for regulation generally, given the complexity risks which rapidly evolving markets generate.[185] New governance may be in retreat at the very moment at which a brave, nuanced and battle-hardened application of its tools is required.[186] The risks of regulatory over-reaction in the wake of crisis have been well documented[187] and are considered further by John C. Coffee, Jr. in Chapter 4. The difficulties of international groupthink, the competition to control the international rulebook and poor governance in international institutions can all be added to the dangers of the current reform movement, given the influence of the G20 agenda and international standard-setters.[188] So, too, can the disabling of market mechanisms, including trust and reputation.[189] In the EU, concerns as to over-harmonization, the removal of Member State discretion and experimentation, and prejudice to regulatory competition and learning can be added.[190] It is not, of course, the case that command and control regulation is taking all the weight. Much greater attention is being given to ex-ante information-gathering, supervision and enforcement, regulatory learning and coordination, and to system-wide oversight, internationally and in

[184] In an autumn 2008 resolution on private equity and hedge funds, the Parliament highlighted the importance of principles-based regulation as a response to fast-moving markets: *Resolution on Hedge Funds and Private Equity* (P6_TA-PROV(2008)0425).

[185] On market complexity and regulation, see, e.g., A. Haldane (Bank of England), "Rethinking the Financial Network" (speech, April 28, 2009, online: www.bankofengland.co.uk/publications/speeches/2009/speech386.pdf) and A.W. Lo, "Regulatory Reform in the Wake of the Financial Crisis of 2007–2008," *Journal of Financial Economic Policy*, 1 (2009), 4–43.

[186] Similarly, suggesting that new governance techniques, allied to "real diversity and internal contestation" within regulators, may prove one of the few practical means for dealing with acute complexity: Ford, "New Governance."

[187] e.g., in the Enron-era context, R. Romano, "The Sarbanes-Oxley Act and the Making of Quack Corporate Governance," *Yale Law Journal*, 114 (2005), 1521–611 and L. Ribstein, "Bubble Laws," *Houston Law Review*, 40 (2003), 77–97. In the context of the global financial crisis, e.g., L. Cunningham and D.T. Zaring, "The Three or Four Approaches to Financial Regulation: A Cautionary Analysis," *George Washington Law Review*, 78 (2009–10), 39–113 and Enriques, "Reluctant Regulator."

[188] e.g., C.J. Brummer, "How International Financial Law Works (and How it Doesn't)," *Georgetown Law Journal*, 99 (2011), 257–327 and R. Romano, "Against Financial Regulation Harmonization: A Comment," Yale Law & Economics Research Paper No. 414 (November 2010, online: http://ssrn.com/abstract=1697348).

[189] e.g., J. Macey, "The Demise of the Reputational Model in Capital Markets: The Problem of the 'Last Period Parasites'," *Syracuse Law Review*, 60 (2009–10), 427–48.

[190] Moloney, "EU Financial Market Regulation after the Financial Crisis."

the EU.[191] The new EU rulebook is not monolithic, despite its scale. Calibration is a recurring feature, and flexibility and proportionality are recurring concerns.[192] But overall, more reliance is being placed on traditional rules. This raises difficulties for the second-generation market regulation and consumer protection regulation regimes, particularly as the de-intensification and simplification agenda may be leading to a default presumption in favor of some form of intervention.

De-intensification and simplification in the EU

Parts III and IV below explore how the emerging de-intensification and simplification movement may be shaping market and consumer protection regulation. But there are two horizontal aspects to this movement which may impact both regimes and which warrant consideration; first, with respect to the governing internal market construction objective, and second, with respect to the cooling of financial market development by means of a financial transaction tax.

As Chapter 1 of this book considers in detail, the construction of the internal market and the related liberalization program have long been the driving influences on EU financial market regulation. Pre-crisis, the 1999–2004 FSAP era led to an unprecedented widening and deepening of EU intervention in support of regulatory "passports" for EU actors. The headlong liberalization of recent years is now tempered by awareness of the need for the financial stability tools which have dominated the reform agenda; recent institutional reviews of EU financial market integration highlight the importance of financial stability mechanisms.[193] But has the internal market priority been changed more deeply by the nascent de-intensification movement, which is associated with some skepticism towards financial market integration internationally[194] – and what are the potential effects on regulatory design?

[191] Black, "Restructuring Global and EU Financial Regulation."

[192] The delegated rules being developed under the AIFMD, e.g., reflect concerns that the rules should reflect the different risks posed by different types of alternative investment fund, and take proportionality as a governing principle. ESMA, *Consultation Paper* (ESMA/2011/209) and *Final Advice* (ESMA/2011/379).

[193] ECB, *Financial Integration in Europe* (2011), European Commission, *European Financial Stability and Integration Report* (2011) (SEC (2011) 489), European Commission, *European Financial Stability and Integration Report* (2012) (SWD (2012) 103) and ECB, *Financial Integration in Europe* (2012).

[194] J. Ackerman, "The Global Financial System and the Challenges Ahead," *Fletcher Forum of World Affairs*, 35 (2011), 127–35.

It was always likely that the internal market priority would not change. The internal market must remain a governing priority, given the Treaty imperative and the related dependence of EU regulatory competence on the treaty powers concerning internal market construction and functioning. Market dynamics will also continually deepen the single market; after the initial retrenchment, the underlying trend is towards a deepening of financial market integration.[195] From a policy and political perspective, a "more Europe" approach (extensive EU regulation and supervision in support of cross-border activity) rather than the "less Europe" approach which was canvassed in the early stages of the crisis (a return to host state control of cross-border activity)[196] has followed. Integration policy also appears to be undergoing a re-orientation from the crisis-driven focus on the pathology of the internal financial market and its correction, and is re-engaging with active single market promotion. From an early stage in the crisis, the Commission identified the single market as a "lever for recovery" and warned against protectionism.[197] Its major 2011 policy document on the reform program,[198] however, represents the Commission's first significant post-crisis salvo in support of the single financial market. While it highlights the well-documented failures of the regulatory and supervisory system to keep pace with integration, it also calls for "deepening the single market" to form part of the post-crisis agenda and warns against a "retrenchment" of financial institutions within national borders, suggesting that a less integrated market post-crisis could hinder EU growth. The Commission's 2011 European Financial Stability and Integration Report similarly highlights financial integration as a "major policy objective" of the EU, underlines the benefits in terms of cost reduction, instruments which meet investor and issue needs, better risk diversification and easier access to finance, and warns against the dangers of the current standstill in the integration of the credit, money and sovereign debt markets[199]. The European Central Bank (ECB) has likewise suggested that euro-area capital markets will continue to increase and that the crisis should not endanger a long-term trend towards

[195] ECB, *Financial Integration in Europe* (2011), p. 7.

[196] Moloney, "EU Financial Market Regulation after the Financial Crisis."

[197] e.g., European Commission, *Driving European Recovery* (2009) (COM (2009) 114), pp. 10–11.

[198] European Commission, *Regulating Financial Services for Sustainable Growth – A Progress Report – February 2011* (2011).

[199] European Commission, *European Financial Stability and Integration Report (2011)*, p. 5. The 2012 *Report* adopts a similar approach, highlighting that financial integration is not an obstacle to financial stability (at pp. 13–14).

integration[200] and called for the removal of legal and regulatory impediment to cross-border activity while ensuring that financial stability safeguards are in place.[201] The Economic and Financial Affairs Council of Ministers (ECOFIN) has adopted a similar approach, suggesting that the "balanced development" of the EU financial system required regulatory reform, but also greater financial integration.[202] This reflects the EU's wider 2011 "Single Market Act" project, which is designed to combat "integration fatigue" post-crisis.[203] The Commission's 2011 Single Market Act (SMA) is an agenda to support the single market in achieving its full potential, based on twelve key action points.[204] Internal Market Commissioner Barnier has been vocal in support of the single market project as "our main asset to ensure financial stability, sustainable growth and job creation" and "our main safeguard against populism and protectionism and disintegration."[205] But amidst the seemingly irrepressible dynamism of the internal market movement, there is evidence recently of a more measured approach, which may reflect the wider caution on intensity and innovation. The 2011 European Financial Stability and Integration Report, for example, calls for integration to deepen at "more sustainable pace" and relates the "rapid convergence" pre-crisis to the credit boom and misperceptions as to credit risk.[206]

The impact of a more subdued internal market agenda, if such is developing, on market and consumer protection regulation is not yet clear. The AIFMD is the poster child for how a single market agenda – the conferral of a cross-border regulatory passport for alternative investment funds and their managers – can lead to regulatory over-reach and to a highly complex regulatory regime.[207] On the other hand, the emerging venture capital

[200] ECB, *Financial Integration in Europe* (2011), p. 7. Its 2012 *Financial Integration in Europe* Report highlighted the benefits of the single financial market (pp. 31–48).

[201] Ibid., ch. III. [202] ECOFIN, 2990th Meeting, January 19, 2010.

[203] ECB, *Annual Report* (2010), p. 158.

[204] European Commission, *The Single Market Act – Twelve Steps to Boost Growth and Strengthen Confidence* (2011) (COM (2011) 206). The SMA was supported by the Council in its competitiveness formation (3057th Meeting of the Competitiveness Council, December 10, 2010) and followed inter-institutional and public consultation designed to refocus attention on core single market priorities.

[205] EU Commissioner M. Barnier, "Time for delivery: Making the Reforms of the Financial System in Europe and in the United States a Reality" (speech, June 3, 2011, online: http://europa.eu/rapid/pressReleasesAction.do?reference=SPEECH/11/410&type=HTML).

[206] European Commission, *European Financial Stability and Integration Report* (2011), p. 8.

[207] The intricacies and sensitivities of the interaction between the AIFMD passport structure and third country fund and manager access to EU markets almost derailed the Directive, given the potential losses the fund management industry would have sustained from proposed restrictions on investments in third county funds, and difficulties with third country access: Ferran, "After the Crisis."

regime is showing better awareness of the limitations of law in driving a single market and is experimenting with potentially exciting opt-in mechanisms.[208] It is at least clear that the next phase of the single market movement will focus more closely on end-users; up until now, the supply side has been the dominant concern of liberalization.[209] Whether this will lead to productive regulatory innovation is less clear, given the direction of travel in consumer protection regulation (Part IV below).

It is, however, clear that the single market agenda is being partly re-characterized as a "fortress Europe" agenda, under which the EU, while reluctant to lead the international regulatory debate, as discussed further in Chapter 1 of this book, seems to be seeking to impose its regulatory policies by means of indirect equivalence techniques. This agenda can also be associated with de-intensification in that, along with a degree of regulatory imperialism, it implies suspicion of global liberalization.[210] The third country difficulties posed by the AIFMD negotiations and by the CRA Regulation I equivalence regime,[211] have not deterred the Commission from suggesting that a harmonized equivalence regime apply to third country actor access to the EU under MiFID with respect to investment services, and that the current flexible, Member State-driven regime be replaced with a "strict equivalence" system under the MiFID II proposals.[212] A more defensive approach can also be identified

[208] The regime proposed by the Commission in 2011 is voluntary and allows venture capital funds to opt for a "European registration" with their local authority as a European Venture Capital Fund, which would support passporting: COM (2011) 860/2.

[209] European Commission, *European Financial Stability and Integration Report* (2011), p. 40.

[210] The MiFID Review, e.g., links the standardization of third country equivalence assessments of investment firm regulation, previously made by Member States with limited EU intervention, to the effects of financial turmoil, malpractice and negligence internationally on the EU: European Commission, *Public Consultation on Review of the Markets in Financial Instruments Directive* (*MiFID Review*), p. 79.

[211] The 2009 CRA Regulation I attempts to export the EU model through equivalence techniques; the ratings of non-EU rating agencies may be used only on compliance with a certification/endorsement regime, based on equivalence techniques. This has proved controversial. ESMA's 2011 assessment of equivalence (ESMA, *Endorsement Guidance*, ESMA/2011/139), which links the "as stringent as" equivalence assessment to equivalent law and regulations, and which disregards related self-regulatory practices, has led to concerns that US securitization ratings in particular would face difficulties and market disruption would follow: N. Tait, "SEC and EU in Talks to Resolve Rating Impasse," *Financial Times*, April 24, 2011, 10, reporting tensions between the EU and SEC on the "as stringent as" model. ESMA has, however, stood firm.

[212] MiFID Directive Proposal (COM (2011) 656/4) (MiFID Directive Proposal), arts. 41–6. The proposed regime is based on a preliminary equivalence assessment by the Commission and significantly reduces the role of the Member States in equivalence determinations.

in the proposal for all retail investment services delivered by third country actors to be delivered by means of a branch, rather than through cross-border service provision.[213] Notably, where a more liberal approach applies, for example under the Short Selling Regulation which contains an exemption for shares the principal market for which is outside the EU, the competition implications for the EU are more obvious.[214] But this defensive trend does not augur well for regulatory design; equivalence determinations are complex and politically sensitive. They are likely to soak up considerable Commission and ESMA (typically empowered to advise the Commission on equivalence determinations) resources and to place significant demands on international political capital, already thinned out by the ongoing sovereign debt crisis.

In terms of more direct policy levers, the Financial Transaction Tax (FTT), which has received an international airing in the wake of the crisis,[215] appears the most likely vehicle for those seeking a more repressive approach to the financial markets. The roots of the FTT, in common use in different forms internationally,[216] go back to the 1970s and the oft-discussed Tobin Tax, which was designed to tax foreign exchange transactions and address excessive exchange rate fluctuation and speculation in currency flows. Over the crisis, FTT-style taxes and bank levies were canvassed as financial stability mechanisms, with the Pittsburgh September 2009 G20 meeting calling on the IMF to explore how the financial sector might contribute to the cost of financial system repair. Bank levies to recover the cost of government rescues and to provide resolution funds are now common across the EU, with a number of Member States imposing some form of bank levy.[217] Coordination and arbitrage risks are leading the EU institutions to consider the appropriateness of a pan-EU bank levy.[218] But an FTT is associated

[213] MiFID Directive Proposal, art. 41(2).

[214] Short Selling Regulation, art. 16. The Proposal noted the risk that issuers might be discouraged from having their shares traded on EU venues (COM (2010) 482, p. 8).

[215] e.g., 3030th ECOFIN Meeting, September 7, 2010, noting the international re-energizing of the FTT debate.

[216] Typically in the form of an *ad valorem* tax on share trades (10–50 basis points): *IMF Working Paper 111/54, Taxing Financial Transactions: Issues and Evidence* (Washington DC: IMF, 2011), prepared by Thornton Matheson, p. 4.

[217] Including, in late 2011, Belgium, which adopted a financial stability bank levy on December 28.

[218] European Commission, *Consultation on Financial Sector Taxation* (2011).

with much heavier policy lifting. An FTT is a means of yielding revenue from the financial market sector and for addressing the costs of recent interventions.[219] It is also associated with the curbing of activities which are perceived to be risky, of markets which are perceived to be excessively large, and of profits which are regarded as economic rents.[220] Design and implementation risks are considerable, with FTTs linked with, inter alia, a reduction in trading volume and liquidity, an increase in spreads, and increases in issuer cost of capital, as well as competitive distortions.[221] The IMF's response to the Pittsburgh G20 meeting did not endorse FTTs, although it suggested that a profit/wage-related Financial Activities Tax might be used to raise revenue.[222] In the EU,[223] the FTT question has become entwined with wider political tensions on the nature of financial market intervention. Institutionally, the European Council has expressed cautious support for an FTT to be explored, but this has typically been in the context of the EU "leading the global debate," and reflects the complex dynamics of international engagement.[224] ECOFIN has been similarly careful, being predominantly concerned with the coordination risks were Member States to adopt unilateral positions.[225] In September 2011 the Commission published a Proposal for an EU FTT to be adopted in 2014.[226] Although France and Germany supported the FTT from an early

[219] IMF, *FTT Report.*

[220] HM Treasury, *Risk, Reward and Responsibility: The Financial Sector and Society* (London: HM Treasury, 2009).

[221] IMF, *FTT Report*, HM Treasury, *Risk, Reward and Responsibility*, P. Honohan and S. Yoder, "Financial Transaction Taxes: Panacea, Threat or Damp Squib," World Bank Policy Research Working Paper No. 5230 (March 2009, online: http://ssrn.com/abstract=1505954) and A. Miller, *A Financial Transaction Tax – Review of Impact Assessments* (London: City of London Economic Development, 2012).

[222] IMF, *A Fair and Substantial Contribution: A Framework for Taxation and Resolution to Improve Financial Stability. Draft Response to G20* (Washington DC: IMF, 2010).

[223] Generally, B. Cortez and T. Vogel, "A Financial Transaction Tax for Europe," *EC Tax Review*, 20 (2011), 16–29.

[224] European Council Conclusions, March 24/25, 2011 and June 17, 2010.

[225] e.g., 2030th ECOFIN Meeting, September 7, 2010.

[226] COM (2011) 594. The Proposal provides for a tax on all transactions in financial instruments, whether carried out OTC or on a regulated venue, where at least one party is a financial institution, to be levied on financial institutions (widely defined) where one party to the transaction is established in a Member State. The rate, however, would be set by the Member States, subject to a minimum of 0.1 percent.

stage,[227] its prospects are not clear, particularly in the wake of the December 2011 summit. The proposed Treaty Financial Services Protocol, which the UK had called for, contained a proposed commitment that any "user charge" be subject to a Member State veto, reflecting UK concern that the FTT, in principle subject to a Member State veto as a matter of taxation policy, could not be recharacterized as a "user charge" and be subject to a qualified majority vote.[228] France and Germany, however, have called for the Eurozone to intensify cooperation in the financial services sphere, including by means of an FTT,[229] while Commissioner Barnier is also supportive.[230] Strong stakeholder disagreement,[231] combined with political tensions (Ireland and Sweden are also opposed to the FTT), the implementation complexities,[232] and competitiveness risks (particularly given the failure of the November 2011 Cannes G20 summit to support a global FTT), suggest that the FTT is unlikely, in the short term at least, to be a major policy lever with respect to financial intensity. This is all the more the case as the June 2012 ECOFIN meeting saw the Council fail to agree on the FTT but saw support from a number of Member States for an FTT to be adopted by a small number of Member States, using "enhanced co-operation" mechanisms under the Treaties.[233] The European Parliament appears to be the most vocal institutional supporter of an FTT, but its pan–EU realization will demand

[227] In June 2011 France's Assemblée Nationale adopted a Resolution calling for an EU FTT covering all transactions on organized markets and OTC. In September 2011, the finance ministers of France and Germany wrote to the Commission in support of a broadly-based FTT, while acknowledging the difficulties which international agreement as well as implementation would pose: V. Heaney, "Europe Takes a Step Closer to a Tax on Financial Transactions," *Financial Times Fund Management Supplement*, September 19, 2011, 12.

[228] A. Barber and G. Parker, "Cameron's Demands over Financial Regulation Spark French Resistance," *Financial Times*, December 9, 2011, 6.

[229] A. Barber and G. Parker, "'Bulldog' Cameron Risks having Bluff Called," *Financial Times*, December 8, 2011, 7.

[230] EU Commissioner M. Barnier, "Financial Regulation – A Review of 2011 and a Forward Look to 2012" (speech, January 23, 2012, online: http://europa.eu/rapid/pressReleasesAction.do?reference=SPEECH/12/23&type=HTML).

[231] Clear from reaction to the Commission's earlier consultation which it described as "strongly polarized": European Commission, *Results and Survey Report on Consultation COM (2010) 549* (2011).

[232] Particularly with respect to the cascade effect of an FTT as it moves from the original vendor and broker through clearing structures and on to ultimate investors, levying taxes and increasing costs along the chain: Clifford Chance, *Financial Transaction Tax: Update* (London: Clifford Chance, October 2011), p. 2.

[233] 3178th ECOFIN Meeting, June 22, 2012.

significantly greater institutional and political support. Therefore, de-intensification is likely to be a function of regulation, and not of direct policy levers.

III: The legacy impact of the crisis on market regulation

A re-orientation of the reform program?

The 2008 G20 Washington Declaration contained a commitment to promote integrity in financial markets, including by bolstering investor protection. But outside the risk-regulation/financial stability sphere, the regulation of financial markets did not form part of the initial global reform agenda.[234] After a period of intense focus on the risk-related pathologies of the financial markets, the international reform agenda is now turning to the traditional efficiency, transparency, liquidity and integrity concerns of market regulation. Allied to this, the international policy debate appears to be focusing on the importance of efficient financial markets to economic growth more generally.[235]

Over the crisis period, IOSCO's standard-setting activities moved decisively towards the risk regulation agenda, in support of the G20 agenda.[236] The Seoul Action Plan adopted at the November 2010 Seoul G20 meeting, and in response to a French initiative,[237] however, added

[234] e.g., I. MacNeil, "The Trajectory of Regulatory Reform in the UK in the Wake of the Financial Crisis," *European Business Organization Law Review*, 11 (2010), 483–526, noting that market failures were not at the top of the international reform agenda, which focused on regulatory capital and credit markets.

[235] e.g., IOSCO, *Mitigating Systemic Risk*, emphasizing the role of market regulators in ensuring that financial markets work efficiently and contribute positively to the real economy. Similarly, Pain and Röhn, *Policy Frameworks*.

[236] Major initiatives include: regulating and monitoring market participants (including 2009 high-level principles for regulating hedge funds); monitoring trading practices with respect to short selling; promoting transparency and soundness in the OTC derivatives markets and with respect to the securitization and CDS markets; improving cooperation between regulators; and preventing regulatory arbitrage: IOSCO, *Mitigating Systemic Risk*, pp. 59–60. See generally, R. Karmel, "IOSCO's Response to the Financial Crisis," Brooklyn Law School, Legal Studies Paper No. 268 (March 2012, online: http://ssrn.com/abstract=2025115).

[237] AMF, *Priorities* and AMF, *Risk and Trend Mapping No. 10* (Paris: AMF, 2011), p. 3, suggesting that the AMF's concerns related to markets which are "increasingly fast-paced, opaque and fragmented" had been added to the G20 agenda. Similarly, Jouyet, "ICMA Speech."

measures to improve market efficiency and integrity to the G20 agenda. IOSCO was charged with developing and reporting to the FSB on recommendations to support market integrity and efficiency; the mandate was not open-ended, but was linked to initiatives to mitigate the risks posed to the financial system by technological developments.[238] IOSCO's subsequent 2011 Principles for Dark Liquidity respond to the G20 agenda, as does its 2011 Consultation and subsequent Report on Regulatory Issues raised by the Impact of Technological Changes on Market Integrity and Efficiency. The G20 has retained its new focus on market issues, with the November 2011 Cannes G20 meeting highlighting the importance of markets for the efficient allocation of investment and savings, supporting IOSCO's initiatives and calling for IOSCO to examine the CDS markets.[239]

IOSCO has long been active in adopting best practices for market regulation. But it has struggled in embedding its standards internationally, beyond the disclosure standards for cross-border issuers which have enjoyed relatively wide support.[240] It has been relatively straightforward to reach international agreement on international disclosure standards given the benefits which they bring for issuers internationally, particularly with respect to access to the US capital market. Agreement becomes more elusive where standards have implications for international competitiveness, address areas where considerable disagreement exists with respect to regulatory treatment, or apply to markets with very different structures and contexts. IOSCO's initial 2004 Standards for Credit Rating Agencies, for example, which were based on an industry "comply or explain" mechanism, did not enjoy full compliance, particularly with respect to the most interventionist standards concerning conflict of interest management.[241] The objectives of the revised 2008 Standards, according to IOSCO, have now been embedded in different regulatory

[238] G20, *Leaders' Declaration* (Seoul: G20, November 2010), paras. 11 and 41. Similarly, and calling on IOSCO to take action, Communiqué, Meeting of Finance Ministers and Central Bank Governors, Paris, February 2011.

[239] G20, *Final Declaration* (Cannes: G20, November 2011), para. 31.

[240] On IOSCO's effectiveness as a standard setter pre-crisis, see G. Underhill and X. Zhang, "Setting the Rules: Private Power, Political Underpinnings and Legitimacy in Global Monetary and Financial Governance," *International Affairs*, 84 (2008), 535–54, G. Underhill and X. Zhang, *Global Financial Governance under Stress. Global Structures versus National Imperatives* (Cambridge University Press, 2003), and D.T. Zaring, "International Law by Other Means: the Twilight Existence of International Financial Regulatory Organizations," *Texas International Law Journal*, 33 (1998), 281–330.

[241] IOSCO, *A Review of the Implementation of the IOSCO Code of Conduct Fundamentals for CRAs* (Madrid: IOSCO, 2009).

programs worldwide and in 2008 were fully implemented by the three major global rating agencies.[242] But this reflects the inclusion of rating agencies on the G20 agenda, FSB monitoring of rating agency reforms, as well as a wider international consensus that rating agencies be regulated in some way. The G20 engagement with a market agenda, linked to FSB oversight, accordingly represents a potentially significant strengthening of international standards with respect to market regulation.

The international reform agenda is, however, relatively limited in scope. Trading market regulation, the main concern of the new G20 agenda, is deeply rooted in local market structures; the EU's equity market trading system, for example, reflects the competitive market model adopted by the EU, while the US equity market trading system is based on a central planning model adopted under Regulation National Market System (NMS).[243] This reality is reflected in the general and high-level nature of the 2011 IOSCO standards for markets noted above. The international market agenda may not therefore acquire much traction. This is not to suggest that IOSCO will not be influential. It seems clear that IOSCO standards and guidance are exerting a soft influence on the development of EU standards and rules, given the useful templates they can provide for regulators struggling with an avalanche of reforms.[244] But this form of soft influence is of a different nature to the more direct influence by the G20/FSB financial stability agenda on risk regulation.

The EU market regulation agenda

The EU's new market regulation agenda, the main proposals for which were adopted over autumn 2011, by contrast, is extensive. At its heart are the measures which form the proposed MiFID II regime, which were preceded by the 2010 MiFID Review consultation,[245] and which address trading market and investment services regulation: the 2011 MiFID II Proposal (a proposal for a Directive to reform MiFID) and the 2011

[242] IOSCO, *Regulatory Implications of the Statement of Principles Regarding Activities of CRAs* (Madrid: IOSCO, 2011) and IOSCO, *A Review of the Implementation of the IOSCO Code of Conduct Fundamentals for CRAs.*

[243] e.g., S. Gadinis, "Market Structure for Institutional Investors: Comparing the US and EU Regimes," *Virginia Law & Business Review*, 3 (2008), 311–56.

[244] ESMA has drawn on, e.g., IOSCO standards and guidance concerning private equity conflicts of interests, hedge fund valuation, and redemption restrictions in collective investment schemes in the development of the AIFMD delegated rules regime.

[245] Commission, *MiFID Review.*

MiFIR Proposal (a proposal for a Regulation to reform MiFID).[246] These are accompanied by the two measures which will reform the Market Abuse Directive: the 2011 Market Abuse Directive Proposal and the 2011 Market Abuse Regulation Proposal.[247] The pivotal disclosure-based Transparency Directive, which addresses issuer disclosure in the secondary markets, is also being reformed by the 2011 Transparency Directive Proposal.[248]

Two recurring themes arise from this agenda. The first is the extending reach of EU market regulation over a wider range of trading venues and a wider set of asset classes, particularly fixed income securities and derivatives.

The perimeter for most EU financial market regulation, in the primary and secondary markets, with respect to issuers and intermediaries and across all market segments, equity and non-equity, is a function of the bilateral distinction which splits organized trading markets in the EU between "regulated markets" and "multi-lateral trading facilities" (MTFs), defined in each case under MiFID. The regulated market concept is a proxy for large, heavily regulated organized markets.[249] Trading platforms opt in to regulated market status, which brings with it increased regulation (with respect to issuer disclosure and secondary market trading), but also strong branding effects. All "financial instruments" admitted to regulated markets are typically subject to the market abuse regime. A smaller subset of "securities" admitted to regulated markets are subject to the issuer initial/public offer disclosure and ongoing disclosure requirements under the Prospectus (primary markets) and Transparency (secondary markets)

[246] Respectively, COM (2011) 656/4 (addressing investment firm and trading market regulation) (MiFID Directive Proposal) and COM (2011) 652/4 (MiFIR Proposal) (addressing the detail of trading market transparency). At the time of writing, over 1,300 revisions had been presented by the European Parliament and ECOFIN had produced a June 2012 update on the negotiations (ECOFIN 11536/12) which are expected to continue into 2013.

[247] Respectively, COM (2011) 651 (proposing a new Directive-based regime for criminal sanctions) and COM (2011) 654 (reforming the Market Abuse Directive more generally by extending its scope through a Regulation) (Market Abuse Regulation Proposal).

[248] COM (2011) 683 (Transparency Directive Proposal).

[249] A regulated market is a multilateral facility operated and/or managed by a market operator, which brings together or facilitates the bringing together of multiple third-party buying and selling interests in financial instruments – in the system and in accordance with its non-discretionary rules – in a way that results in a contract, in respect of the financial instruments admitted to trading under its rules and/or systems, and which is authorized and functions regularly and in accordance with the regulated market provisions under MiFID (art. 4(1)(14)).

Directives (the prospectus rules also apply to publicly offered securities generally). Although the definitions of "financial instruments" and "securities" are not consistent across the major directives, both categories broadly cover equities, bonds and derivatives related to transferable securities, currencies, interest rates or yields, commodities, or other indices or measures. All other organized markets are designated as MTFs[250] and are subject, very broadly, to self regulation. The regulated market/MTF perimeter also governs the EU's regime for trading market regulation under MiFID. The most intense rules for trading markets, in terms of authorization and operating controls, apply to regulated markets, although the MTF regime is very similar. OTC venues are largely unregulated, save, under MiFID, for post-trade transparency requirements in the equity markets.

Within this perimeter, regulated markets for equity trading have long been the main target of financial market regulation. This reflects a policy preoccupation with promoting market finance, a concern to promote an EU equity culture, and the strong association between equity market regulation, the public markets, and the retail markets;[251] fixed income markets and the OTC derivative markets, by contrast, have largely been regarded as a function of market forces.[252] The Commission has recently acknowledged that the cornerstone MiFID creates a "regulatory framework centred on shares and regulated markets."[253] Bonds admitted to trading on a regulated market are subject to issuer-facing prospectus requirements under the Prospectus Directive and ongoing disclosure requirements under the Transparency Directive; but they benefit from lighter rules.[254] Organized bond trading platforms (both regulated markets and MTFs) are more lightly regulated than equivalent equity venues; in particular, they are not subject to the trading transparency rules

[250] An MTF is a multilateral facility operated by an investment firm or market operator, which brings together multiple third-party buying and selling interests in financial instruments – in the system and in accordance with its non-discretionary rules – in a way that results in a contract and in accordance with the rules which apply to investment firms under MiFID (art. 4(1)(15)).

[251] See Moloney, *EC Securities Regulation*, ch. 2.

[252] Well illustrated by the Commission's 2008 decision not to impose MiFID-style trading transparency requirements on fixed income markets: Commission, *Report on Non-equities Market Transparency pursuant to Article 65(1) of Directive 2004/39/EC on Markets in Financial Instruments* (2008).

[253] European Commission, *MiFID Review*, p. 6.

[254] Including exemption from the requirement to provide a retail market summary to the prospectus (Prospectus Directive, art. 5(2)) and from the ongoing issuer disclosure requirements related to the annual and half-yearly reports and interim management statements under the Transparency Directive (art. 8).

which apply to equity trading under MiFID. Like bonds, the issuance and trading of derivatives traded on a regulated market comes within the Market Abuse Directive, and within the Prospectus Directive's primary market disclosure regime, but is otherwise subject to self regulation.

As discussed below, this regime is now undergoing significant expansion and exposing related regulatory innovation. The innovations relate to first-level technical rule innovations as well as to second-level changes to the nature of intervention, particularly with respect to the decreasing reliance on self regulation. While the measures have different drivers, the overall impact, and certainly the relative lack of concern as to potential risks to liquidity, innovation and market efficiency, can be related to the wider third-level regulatory innovation with respect to financial intensity and innovation (Part II). The commitment to expanding the regulatory perimeter brings the particular difficulties discussed below in this Part. But it also brings a more general process risk. It suggests something of a state of permanent revolution in market regulation, as also seems to be supported by IOSCO; in its 2010 revision of its Objectives and Principles of Securities Regulation, IOSCO recommended that regulators have, or contribute to a process to review the perimeter of regulation regularly. This default presumption that intervention may be appropriate represents a decisive change from pre-crisis orthodoxy. In the risk regulation sphere, it is clear that regulation needed to be retooled to reflect better the nature of risk transmission and address regulatory gaps. But even in the risk regulation sector, it is not clear that optimal decisions have been made with respect to new targets of regulation, and the intensity with which they are being regulated, particularly with respect to the crisis "poster children" (including CRAs, hedge funds and executive pay structures). The risks are all the greater in the market regulation sphere. The discipline which can come from international standard-setting is much more limited. Regulators are more familiar with the tools of market regulation and likely to be more confident in extending their use. Unhelpful momentum effects may be injected into market regulation. The definitional issues, and related arbitrage risks are considerable. The EU regime is struggling with how to capture different asset classes previously largely outside the regulatory perimeter; the definition of sovereign debt and the nature of a covered or uncovered short sale, for example, proved troublesome over the Short Selling Regulation negotiations.[255] When allied to the

[255] e.g., the ECB's opinion of the Commission's original definition of sovereign debt, raising concerns as to potential gaps: [2011] OJ C91/1.

institutional and political dynamics discussed in Chapter 1 of this book, the design risks may be all the greater.

The second recurring theme is the troublesome interaction between these reforms and long-standing objectives of market regulation. In particular, market regulation has long been associated with the support of liquidity, in the interests of reducing the cost of capital by lowering transaction costs and supporting efficient resource allocation.[256] Although liquidity-constraining techniques were in use pre-crisis, typically short-selling curbs and, in some jurisdictions, transactions taxes, liquidity is generally promoted by regulators through, for example, disclosure techniques, insider-trading prohibitions and trading market rules.[257] Support of trading market liquidity has long been a concern in the EU. Recently, the MiFID II reforms to trading market regulation have become a battleground for competing positions on the extent to which liquidity would be damaged were venues which provide proprietary capital for trading services to be regulated in a similar manner to neutral multilateral platforms; this territory was previously the subject of the precursor febrile negotiations which led to MiFID's adoption in 2004 and to the earlier Investment Services Directive's adoption in 1993.[258] The financial crisis has also led to a sharper focus on liquidity across prudential regulation generally, given the instability generated by a loss of tradability in assets.[259] Chief among the related reforms are the Basel III agreement rules for liquidity risk management (to be implemented in the EU via the Capital Requirement Directive IV set of reforms).[260] Liquidity risk management is also a feature of the risk regulation reforms to market regulation. The AIFMD, for example, contains extensive

[256] e.g., Levine, "Financial Development" and Y. Amihud and H. Mendelson, "Asset Pricing and the Bid Ask Spread," *Journal of Financial Economics*, 17 (1986), 223–49.

[257] e.g., O'Hara, "Liquidity and Financial Market Stability."

[258] G. Ferrarini and N. Moloney, "Equity Trading and the MiFID Review," (November 2011, online: http://ssrn.com/abstract=1989041).

[259] The *Turner Review*, e.g., addressed the measurement and management of bank liquidity risk, underlining that while it was as important as capital and solvency risk management, it had not received sufficient attention pre-crisis: pp. 68–70.

[260] COM (2011) 453, setting out the proposal for a Directive (which can be implemented with some degree of flexibility by the Member States and covering bank risk governance, capital buffers and supervisory review), and COM (2011) 442, setting out the proposal for a Regulation, which will apply automatically within the Member States and may not be deviated from, and covering capital liquidity, the leverage ratio and counterparty credit risk. See, e.g., ECB, *Annual Report* (2010), pp. 142–3 on the likely impact of the CRD IV liquidity standards in the EU.

liquidity risk management principles for fund managers. The Short Selling Regulation contains exemptions for market makers in order to support liquidity[261] and limits disclosure of sovereign debt positions to competent authority reporting to ensure any liquidity risks are not exacerbated.[262]

But the emerging treatment of liquidity risk is not consistent. There are some indications that, reflecting the earlier and long-standing debate on the link between "excessive liquidity" and over-financialization,[263] "excessive" liquidity is being linked to financial instability and becoming associated with the de-intensification movement.[264] In particular, the Short Selling Regulation, which includes disclosure requirements with respect to short sovereign debt and uncovered CDS positions, restrictions on uncovered short sales of sovereign debt and uncovered CDS transactions, and extensive related intervention powers for national supervisors and ESMA, including national supervisor powers to prohibit short sales and CDS transactions in identified circumstances, may generate liquidity risks in the sovereign debt markets.[265] Reflecting significant political concern, some care has been taken to exclude sovereign debt and related CDS transactions from ESMA's prohibition powers and to address potential liquidity risks in the sovereign debt markets.[266] But even allowing for these calibrations, a relatively sanguine approach can be identified with respect to the cumulative risks the Regulation may pose to sovereign debt and CDS market liquidity. This is remarkable, given the stark contrast between the weight of evidence on the impact of short selling in the equity markets arising from the series of autumn

261 Short Selling Regulation, art. 17. 262 Ibid., art. 7.

263 O'Hara, "Liquidity and Financial Market Stability."

264 e.g., BIS, Committee on the Global Financial System Paper No. 45, *Global Liquidity – Concept, Measurement and Policy Implications* (Basel: BIS, 2011), relating excessive private sector liquidity, and cross-border portfolio movements, to financial stability risks.

265 ECOFIN discussions exposed considerable Member State concern on the fiscal implications of the sovereign debt rules, as well as the Regulation's poor empirical base: House of Commons, European Scrutiny Committee, *20th Report*, March 10, 2011. The UK government in particular was opposed to any regulation of the sovereign debt market: House of Commons, EU Committee, *20th Report of Sessions 2010–2012, The EU Financial Supervisory Framework: An Update*. There was also some (although less) European Parliament concern: Bowles, "Market Abuse," raising concern as to the implications of a ban on naked CDS trades. Industry concern as to liquidity risks was also significant. e.g., AFME, ISLA and ISDA, *Summary of the AFME, ISLA and ISDA Position on Short Selling* (May 2011), expressing the concerns of three major investment banking trade associations. See also Chapter 1 of this book.

266 The restrictions which the Regulation places on uncovered short sales of sovereign debt and on uncovered CDS transactions in sovereign debt can be lifted in exceptional circumstances where liquidity is restricted.

2008 prohibitions on equity short sales[267] and the limited evidence on short selling prohibitions in the sovereign debt and CDS markets.[268] The new generation of market regulation reforms may generate similar risks, as discussed below. It may be that a troublesome distinction is emerging between asset classes in which liquidity is protected and those in which, reflecting the de-intensification agenda, less care is taken.

Reshaping market regulation

Reshaping trading venue regulation

Regulators have long outsourced elements of market regulation to major trading venues.[269] They have accordingly grappled with the related choices which arise concerning the extent to which venues should be subject to regulatory oversight, given the risk of incentive mis-alignment between venue and investor interests and the wider systemic implications if competition fails to deliver appropriate discipline.[270] Trading venues were traditionally afforded significant discretion and flexibility in running their trading activities when they took the form of traditional stock exchanges. But the grip of regulation on major trading venues was tightening pre-crisis following the de-mutualization movement and the arrival of competition between stock exchanges and other execution venues, particularly alternative trading systems.[271]

A more ambitious agenda is now developing. This agenda relies on trading venues as devices for managing the gaps which arise when

[267] e.g., S. Gruenewald, A. Wagner and R. Weber, "Short Selling Regulation after the Financial Crisis – First Principles Revisited," *International Journal of Disclosure and Regulation*, 7 (2010), 108–35; A. Beber and M. Pagano, "Short Selling Bans around the World: Crisis after 2007–09" (August 2011, online: http://ssrn.com/abstract=1502184) and Avgouleas, "New Framework."

[268] R. Stulz, "Credit Default Swaps and the Credit Crisis," *Journal of Economic Perspectives*, 24 (2010), 73–92. Notably, the European Commission's Impact Assessment for the delegated rules adopted in summer 2012 which, inter alia, set the threshold for notifying short sovereign debt positions, notes the lack of empirical evidence: SWD (2012) 198, p. 33.

[269] This section uses the term "venue," given the array of trading platforms beyond traditional stock exchanges on which organized trading can take place and which can come within the regulatory net: J. Macey and M. O'Hara, "From Markets to Venues: Securities Regulation in an Evolving World," *Stanford Law Review*, 58 (2005), 563–99.

[270] P. Mahoney, "The Exchange as Regulator," *Virginia Law Review*, 83 (1997), 1453–500; R. Aggarwal, A. Ferrell and J. Katz, "US Securities Regulation in a World of Global Exchanges," ECGI Finance Working Paper No. 146/2007 (December 2006, online: www.ssrn.com/abstract=950530); A. Fleckner, "Stock Exchanges at the Crossroads," *Fordham Law Review*, 74 (2006), 2541–620; and C.J. Brummer, "Stock Exchanges and the New Markets for Securities Law," *University of Chicago Law Review*, 75 (2008), 1435–91.

[271] E. Ferran, *Building an EU Securities Market* (Cambridge University Press, 2004), pp. 239–54.

financial innovation moves ahead of market infrastructure, particularly in the derivatives field.[272] Internationally, efforts are being made to repatriate the OTC derivatives trading markets on to trading venues; the G20 has recommended that trading of standardized OTC derivatives move to "exchanges" or "electronic trading platforms."[273] The G20 recommendation is being implemented in the EU under the MiFID II reforms.[274] But the EU's agenda is more extensive. While it reflects the concern to close the gap between private and public trading markets implicit in the international OTC derivatives agenda, it is more ambitious in reach. It has two strands: first, a tightening of the regulation of OTC markets generally; and second, an intensification of the regulation of trading venues which are currently regulated and a related reduction in the ability of regulated trading venues to employ self-regulation.

Efforts to capture the diverse functionalities which different trading venues, organized and OTC, represent, and to identify which venues can act as proxies for regulatory intervention and/or which should be subject to regulation, have preoccupied market regulation since the growth of off-exchange trading and alternative trading venues.[275] As the OTC derivatives trading debate underlines,[276] questions as to characterization and classification are fundamental. The EU's attempt to capture different trading venue functionalities is currently set out in the tripartite regulated market, MTF and OTC distinction established under MiFID, as noted above. This regulatory model reflects difficult political and institutional negotiations and sharp conflicts between the incumbent exchange and the emergent investment firm/OTC lobbies during the development of MiFID's equity market transparency regime.[277] But it

[272] Merton, "Functional Perspective."

[273] G20, *Leaders' Statement* (Pittsburgh: G20, September 2009).

[274] MiFIR Proposal, arts. 24–7, which require trading in eligible derivatives (as determined by the Commission and ESMA) to take place on regulated platforms, in line with the G20 agreement: MiFIR Proposal, p. 11.

[275] See, e.g., the work of Ruben Lee, including R. Lee, *What is an Exchange? The Automation, Management and Regulation of Financial Markets* (Oxford University Press, 1998) and R. Lee, *Running the World's Markets. The Governance of Financial Infrastructure* (Princeton University Press, 2011).

[276] e.g., IOSCO, *Report on Trading of OTC Derivatives* (Madrid: IOSCO, 2011) and FSB, *Implementing OTC Derivatives Market Reform* (Basel; FSB, 2010), pp. 39–43.

[277] G. Ferrarini and F. Recine, "The MiFID and Internalisation," in G. Ferrarini and E. Wymeersch (eds.), *Investor Protection in Europe: Corporate Law Making, the MiFID and Beyond* (Oxford University Press, 2006), pp. 235–70.

also reflects a policy concern to accommodate different venue functionalities and to allow the OTC space to operate with limited regulation.[278]

This liberal model is now being reshaped under the MiFID II reforms. At the core of the proposals is a concern to extend the regulatory perimeter to encompass a wider range of venues, and to apply the same set of rules to this wider set of venues.[279] As noted above, two consequences follow: a tightening of the loosely-regulated OTC space and a limiting of the freedom of regulated venues to self regulate.

With respect to the tightening of the OTC space, the MiFID II Proposals propose that a new regulatory classification – the Organized Trading Facility (OTF) – additional to the current regulated market/MTF and OTC classifications, be created. This would have the effect of reducing the OTC space. OTF operators would become subject to broadly the same MiFID regulatory regime, including organization, market surveillance and trading transparency rules, as applies to regulated markets and MTFs. Instruments traded on OTFs would also become subject to the new market abuse regime, which currently applies only to regulated market traded securities.[280] This new venue classification is designed to capture all ex-regulated market/MTF trading on organized venues, save bilateral trading on an ad hoc basis between counterparties and not carried out under any organized system. OTC venues which would remain outside the new OTF classification are also being drawn into the regulatory net through other mechanisms. The new market abuse regime is likely to extend to the OTC markets by covering market manipulation by means of OTC derivatives which can influence instruments admitted to regulated markets or MTFs.[281] It is also extending to the wholesale markets for emission allowances, electricity, gas, and related products.[282] The Short Selling Regulation applies to short positions which are created outside the "trading venues" (regulated markets and MTFs) covered by the Regulation.[283] The reach of the

[278] Ferrarini and Moloney, "Equity Trading."

[279] MiFIR Proposal, p. 7.

[280] Market Abuse Regulation Proposal, art. 2.

[281] Ibid., art. 2.

[282] Ibid. (emission trading). The market abuse regime has also been extended to the wholesale energy markets: Regulation (EU) No. 1227/2011/EU, [2011] OJ L326/1.

[283] The Regulation applies to financial instruments admitted to trading on an in-scope trading venue, but also to related trades where the instrument is traded outside an in-scope venue and to related derivatives, including when traded outside an in-scope venue: art. 1. Short positions created by trading outside the trading venues which are in-scope are also covered: recital 10.

trading transparency regime over the OTC markets is also increasing. Equity trades in the OTC markets are already subject to post-trade transparency requirements under MiFID.[284] But, as noted below, post-trade transparency requirements are likely to apply to new classes of OTC trades.

The second effect of the new approach to venue regulation is an intensification of the regulation of currently in-scope trading venues. Under MiFID, regulated markets and MTFs are subject to high-level rules governing the authorization of platform operators and access, organizational and risk management procedures, reporting requirements, and transparency rules. But the MiFID rules have been generally high-level in nature; the regime was designed to be flexible, principles-based and to allow venues to design their own trading rules and operate different market segments. MTFs, in particular, have few restrictions on their access rules, and have been allowed to develop different market segments largely free of regulatory constraints. Regulated markets are subject to a more intensive regime, particularly with respect to admission requirements, but these are high level and have allowed regulated markets to develop competing products. Similarly, while the Prospectus, Transparency and Market Abuse Directives impose requirements for issuer disclosure on regulated markets, MTFs have more freedom to compete and to develop different segments.

This is now changing in a number of respects. The differentiation between MTFs and regulated markets is being dismantled. As noted below in this Part, the issuer disclosure regime is being expanded from regulated markets to include securities admitted to MTFs. The Market Abuse Directive's scope will be expanded from activity related to securities admitted to trading on regulated markets, to cover activity related to securities admitted to trading on MTFs (as well as trading on OTFs and OTC trading).[285] This reform is designed in particular to capture MTF markets for commodity and emission derivatives, as well as those MTFs likely to capture derivatives trading as derivative trading is moved on to organized platforms. A new generation of rules also looks set to apply to regulated markets and to MTFs under MiFID II. Proposals for a new "SME growth" market, for example, if adopted, may significantly limit the ability of regulated markets and MTFs to compete with respect to second-tier markets (discussed below). With respect to risk

[284] MiFID, art. 28. [285] Market Abuse Regulation Proposal, art. 2.

management, detailed rules governing high frequency trading look to be in the offing for regulated markets and MTFs (discussed below), as are rules on position limits. Equity trading transparency rules are also intensifying. Greater restrictions are likely to be placed on the waiver regime which currently applies to the equity trading transparency regime for regulated markets and MTFs. MiFID's equity transparency regime will also be extended to a range of equity-like instruments, including depositary receipts, exchange-traded funds and certificates and shares of issuers admitted only to MTFs. Most significantly, pre- and post-trade transparency rules will be extended beyond equities to bonds, structured finance products, emission allowances and derivatives admitted to trading on a regulated market, MTF, or OTF.[286] No differentiation is made concerning the nature of the trading platform – all regulated venues will be subject to transparency rules; the differentiation will apply at the level of the asset class in question. This last reform represents a major shift in regulatory design. In 2008, the Commission reviewed whether MiFID's equity market transparency rules should be extended to the bond markets and found that the markets were operating effectively.[287] Derivative market transparency did not feature in EU trading market regulation policy pre-crisis. Following a series of difficulties in the bond markets over the financial crisis, including a contraction of liquidity, a widening of spreads, valuation difficulties and a lack of post-trade information, CESR (now ESMA) re-opened the transparency debate,[288] and called for an enhanced post-trade transparency regime for corporate bonds, structured finance products and credit derivatives.[289] The MiFID II reform proposals follow CESR's approach.[290] This change underlines the scale of the EU's withdrawal from market discipline in the trading venue sphere, given the previous

[286] The new transparency regime will apply to bonds and structured finance products admitted to trading on a regulated market, or for which a prospectus has been published, emission allowances and derivatives admitted to trading: MIFIR Proposal, arts. 7–10.

[287] European Commission, *Report on Non-equities Markets Transparency*. It found "no convincing case of a market failure in the European wholesale bond markets has been made out" (at p. 10). Its response was based on an extensive CESR fact-find (CESR/07–284b) which warned, however, of poor levels of evidence on bond market activity.

[288] CESR/08–1014.

[289] CESR/09–348. While it did not consider that a lack of transparency was a key driver for the crisis-related difficulties in the bond markets, it related increased transparency to an improvement in market conditions.

[290] As set out in its formal advice to the Commission on the MiFID Review, which covers pre- and post-trade transparency, as well as the derivatives markets (CESR/10–799).

importance of market mechanisms, including the credit derivatives market, for disseminating trading information on non-equity asset classes.[291]

This package of reforms, which is changing the hitherto liberal nature of EU venue regulation, can be associated with a concern to limit market innovation and restrict market development. The new OTF classification is formally designed to deal with the regulatory challenges posed by new trading venues, to address the transparency and arbitrage difficulties posed by non-regulated venues, and to provide a dynamic framework which captures future developments.[292] But the Commission has also argued that the new OTF regime "should decrease the weight of OTC trading in equities and non-equities."[293] Similarly, the new cross-asset transparency regime can be related to policy suspicion of non-regulated sectors. The reform process has, notably, acknowledged that transparency-related weaknesses were not key to the difficulties the bond and derivative markets experienced over the crisis.[294] More general claims are made for the extension of transparency regulation, including that additional transparency should strengthen bond and derivatives markets, enhance the price formation process and improve market efficiency and resilience;[295] CESR similarly suggested that the MiFID Review presented an "ideal opportunity" to introduce far-reaching transparency measures across non-equity asset classes.[296]

These developments may, however, be problematic. The resilience of market structures is a key determinant of productive innovation generally[297] and more intense regulation may strengthen EU trading venues. But the rapid and simultaneous intensification and extension of EU venue regulation calls, at least, for careful post-implementation review, particularly given the greater pressure being placed on rule design and the related move away from self regulation. This is all the more necessary given the potential risks to liquidity which arise from extending regulatory models developed for the organized equity markets to a wider set of venues and asset classes. Trading transparency requirements, in particular, are highly sensitive to market microstructure; in dealer-based markets, often associated with the non-equity markets, disclosure of

291 e.g., FSA, *Feedback Statement 06/04, Trading Transparency in the UK Secondary Bond Markets* (London: FSA, 2006).

292 European Commission, *MiFID Proposals Impact Assessment, Impact Assessment* (SEC (2011) 1226), pp. 34–5.

293 Ibid., pp. 35–6.

294 e.g., CESR/09–348.

295 European Commission, *MiFID Review*, p. 27.

296 CESR/10–799.

297 Merton, "Functional Perspective."

pre- and post-trade positions can expose the dealer to position risks to its proprietary capital and lead to a withdrawal of liquidity.[298] The liquidity implications of the new regime are under consideration, with the Commission committing to calibrating the new generation of rules carefully by asset class and type, by trading venue, and with respect to pre- and post-trade rules.[299] The related MiFID Impact Assessment, however, made only limited efforts to quantify the likely impact on liquidity. It simply asserted that greater transparency would lead to stronger price formation and competition, greater investor certainty and reduced transaction costs, noting that much would depend on the nature of the technical rules which would follow.[300] This is a somewhat cavalier approach to the massive new cross-asset transparency regime, particularly as its development will place considerable pressure on the ability of the EU's law-making apparatus, and particularly ESMA, to make the necessary fine-tuning to adopt an equity-focused regulatory regime to one suitable for the risks generated by different asset classes.

Reshaping the regulation of trading practices

The EU's regime for trading practices is currently uneven. It is largely directed towards intermediating financial institutions. The Market Abuse Directive addresses abusive trading practices and imposes particular rules on sensitive trading techniques, notably stabilization activities. MiFID-scope investment firms are subject to reporting requirements related to trading transactions in financial instruments. MiFID's generic organizational and risk management rules apply to in-scope firms' trading activities, while discrete order execution and order handling rules apply to agency activities. But proprietary traders are exempt from MiFID, although they remain subject to the Market Abuse Directive.

The regulatory grip on trading practices, however, is tightening. The first-generation risk regulation-related reforms include the new capital

[298] e.g., with respect to the bond markets, Centre for Economic Policy Research (B. Biais, F. Declerck, J. Dow, R. Portes and E.L. von Thadden, *European Corporate Bond Markets: Transparency, Liquidity and Efficiency* (2006)).

[299] MiFIR Proposal, pp. 8–9. The new regime will be calibrated with respect to market model, characteristics of trading activity, liquidity and type of order (MiFIR Proposal, arts. 8 and 10).

[300] European Commission, *MiFID Proposals Impact Assessment*, pp. 12, 41, and 66–7.

requirements which will apply to the trading activities of financial institutions,[301] and the controls on short selling under the Short Selling Regulation, which apply to proprietary trading, although exemptions apply for market makers who support liquidity. Both of these reforms are related to the financial stability agenda. The more recent MiFID II reforms (reflecting a 2011 G20 commitment to tighter control over commodity derivative markets)[302] subject commodity derivatives trading to more extensive regulation, requiring, inter alia, regulated markets, MTFs and OTFs to impose position limits on traders and empowering ESMA with respect to these limits.[303] The inclusion of high frequency trading practices in the new generation of market regulation reforms, however, provides one of the clearest examples of regulatory innovation in the form of a suspicion of innovation and a concern to address perceived over-intensification.

High frequency trading (HFT) has its origins in the recent growth in electronic trading, competition between trading venues, and the related fragmentation of execution markets and generation of arbitrage opportunities, which are driving innovative trading technologies.[304] It is a form of algorithmic trading or automated trading based on sophisticated computer technology which dictates trading decisions and which takes advantage of arbitrage opportunities. HFT is latency (or speed of execution) sensitive. It is driven by computer programs which interpret market signals and execute related trading strategies, based on high frequency orders which are open often for less than a few seconds and are typically market neutral in effect, in order to take advantage of very short duration arbitrage opportunities. HFT is growing rapidly in the EU.[305] It can bring significant benefits to markets in the form of deeper liquidity, reduced spreads, stronger price discovery and better price

301 Based on revisions to the Basel II market risk framework. Basel Committee on Banking Supervision, *Consultative Document, Fundamental Review of the Trading Book* (Geneva: BIS, 2012).

302 G20, *Leaders' Declaration* (Cannes), para. 32.

303 MiFID Directive Proposal, art. 59 and MiFIR Proposal, art. 35.

304 e.g., A. Justham (FSA), "Evolving Market Structures and the Focus on Speed – How Regulators Should – Try to Keep Pace" (speech, November 25, 2010, online: www.fsa.gov.uk/pages/Library/Communication/Speeches/2010/1125_aj.shtml).

305 It is estimated to account for in the region of 30–50 percent of trading: FSA, *The FSA's Markets Regulatory Agenda* (London: FSA, 2010), p. 18; ESMA has reported that HFT firms accounted for some 40–70 percent of total equity trading volume in quarter 4 2010 in the EU equity market: ESMA, *HFT Consultation* (ESMA/2011/224), p. 49.

alignment across venues;[306] the liquidity benefits have led trading venues to create incentives in the form of liquidity-sensitive trading fees.[307] But risks can be generated, particularly where HFT traders withdraw in volatile market conditions and contribute to a contraction of liquidity.[308] Operational failures with respect to HFT can also threaten orderly trading, as suggested by the "Flash Crash" on US exchanges on May 6, 2010.[309] Related concerns have arisen as to whether trading venues have appropriately robust risk management structures to deal with very high volumes of HFT. Doubts have also been raised as to whether real liquidity benefits are created, in that HFT tends to lead to a decrease in trade order size rather than to new liquidity,[310] can lead to other liquidity providers leaving the market and can result in poor quality liquidity, volatility and churning.[311] HFT has also been associated with the growth of dark OTC equity trading which is proving controversial in the EU; the liquidity risks associated with HFT trading are associated with increased demand for dark OTC trading as a protection against market impact.[312]

306 T. Hendershott, C. Jones and A. Menkveld, "Does Algorithmic Trading Improve Liquidity?," *Journal of Finance*, 66 (2011), 1–33 (in the New York Stock Exchange context) and B. Jovanovic and A. Menkveld, "Middlemen in Limit Order Markets" (October 2011, online: http://ssrn.com/abstract=1624329) (examining the Belgian and Dutch markets). The UK FSA has reported that HFT has helped to reduce bid offer spreads and improved price consistency and price formation across trading venues: Justham "Evolving Market Structures."

307 CESR, *Impact of MiFID on Equity Market Functioning* (2009) (CESR/09–355), p. 18.

308 e.g., S. Grob, "The Fragmentation of the European Equity Markets," in V. Lazzari (ed.), *Trends in the European Securities Industry* (Milan: egea, 2011), pp. 127–70.

309 During the "Flash Crash", major US equity indices lost 5–6 percent of their value over a very short period. During a 20-minute period starting at 2:40 p.m., over 20,000 trades, across more than 300 securities, were executed at prices which were some 60 percent away from the 2:40 p.m. prices. While the subsequent SEC/CFTC Report identified a series of causes, it highlighted the impact of an automated "Sell Algorithm" which executed trades in some 75,000 derivative contracts: SEC and CFTC, *Findings Regarding the Market Events of May 6 2010* (2010).

310 The average trade size on the London Stock Exchange in 2009 was €11,608, down from €22,266 in 2006: CESR, *Consultation on Technical Advice to the European Commission in the Context of the MiFID Review, Equity Markets* (2010) (CESR/10–394), pp. 8–9.

311 G. Hertig, "MiFID and the Return to Concentration Rules," in S. Grundmann, B. Haar, H. Merkt, P.O. Mülbert and M. Wellenhofer (eds.), *Festschrift für Klaus Hopt zum 70. Geburtstag am 24 August 2010* (Berlin: De Gruyter, 2010), pp. 1989–2000.

312 London Economics, *Understanding the Impact of MiFID in the Context of Global and National Regulatory Innovation* (2010) and FSA, *Markets Regulatory Agenda*, p. 4.

The reform momentum is building, with the UK FSA and the French AFM among the EU regulators who have called for action,[313] the US SEC examining issues related to HFT,[314] and IOSCO, in response to a G20 mandate, addressing automated trading generally.[315] In late 2011, ESMA, based on earlier own-initiative work by CESR,[316] produced guidance for highly automated trading environments.[317]

The empirical evidence on the risks and benefits of HFT is contested,[318] but a reasonable case can be made for closer regulatory attention,[319] even if only to assess whether relevant generic risk management and market integrity rules are correctly applied to traders and venues, and appropriately supervised. But the reform movement is acquiring some momentum given its association with the de-intensification/simplification movement, and HFT has become a major flashpoint for the debate on the social utility of markets. *Andrew Haldane* of the Bank of England, for example, noting that the "sky is the limit" with respect to trading speeds, has suggested that trading practices may have increased abnormalities in the distribution of risk and return, and systemic risk.[320]

Thus far, the EU's approach has been relatively restrained, reflecting the limited enthusiasm among the EU's regulators for direct restrictions.[321] But it is nonetheless problematic. The MiFID II Directive Proposal has

313 FSA, *Markets Regulatory Agenda* and Jouyet, "ICMA Speech."

314 SEC, Concept Release 34–61358, *Concept Release on Equity Market Structure* (Washington DC: SEC, 2010). Regulatory action has followed.

315 IOSCO, *Regulatory Issues Raised by the Impact of Technological Changes on Market Integrity and Efficiency. Consultation Report* (Madrid: IOSCO, 2011) and earlier, IOSCO, *Principles for Direct Electronic Access* (Madrid: IOSCO, 2010).

316 Including CESR's examination of microstructural issues in European equity markets (CESR, *Microstructural Issues of the European Equity Markets* (CESR/10–142)).

317 ESMA, *Guidance on Systems and Controls in an Automated Trading Environment for Trading Platforms, Investment Firms and Competent Authorities* (2011) (ESMA/2011/456).

318 For a short summary, see IOSCO, *Technological Changes on Market Integrity and Efficiency*, pp. 24–6. A major UK government project is currently underway to assess HFT: Government Office for Science, Foresight Project on the Future of Computer Trading in Financial Markets.

319 e.g., J. Angel, L. Harris and C. Spatt, "Equity Trading in the 21st Century," Marshall School of Business Working Paper No. FBE 09–10 (February 2010, online: http://ssrn.com/abstract=1584026).

320 Haldane, "The Race to Zero."

321 FSA, *Markets Regulatory Agenda*, pp. 18–19, suggesting that the FSA's role was not to regulate technology but to engage in risk control. Similarly, Dutch AFM Board Member R. Matmann, "High Frequency Trading" (speech, October 7, 2010, online: www.afm.nl/layouts/afm/default.aspx~/media/files/lezingen/2010/speech-maatman-high-frequency-trading.ashx), suggesting that the burden of proof was on the HFT industry to explain that

proposed that algorithmic trading generally be defined and that MiFID-scope firms engaging in this form of trading be subject to discrete organizational requirements, including with respect to risk controls and competent authority notification of the algorithms used and their design, purpose and function.[322] Operators of regulated markets, MTFs and OTFs would also be required to impose additional risk control requirements, including circuit breakers, liquidity-supply obligations and minimum tick sizes for transactions.[323] The regulatory focus has extended beyond MiFID, with the Market Abuse Regulation Proposal including examples of when algorithmic trading and HFT would amount to market manipulation.[324]

The Commission's proposed regime for algorithmic trading does not directly curtail HFT, and there is much to commend in the proposals, particularly with respect to supporting the detection of market abuse. But there is a danger that an overly intrusive, static and complex regime, which will demand significant regulatory resources, will develop. The definitional difficulties will be significant given the range of venues, actors and strategies engaged. The impact on liquidity is unclear, as the MiFID Impact Assessment noted.[325] The more general lesson from the HFT problem, however, may be that problematic innovation can be a product of regulatory change. MiFID-induced competition between trading venues has been strongly associated with the growth of HFT.[326] The nascent innovation and intensification agenda should, therefore, be alert to the regulatory changes being employed to address perceived over-intensification and innovation and which may have unexpected effects. These effects may be all the greater, given the likelihood of arbitrage and gaming effects.

Reshaping financial market disclosure

Enhanced disclosure has been a frequent theme of the crisis-era reform agenda internationally.[327] The G20's 2008 Washington Declaration called for financial market transparency to be strengthened, particularly with respect to complex financial products, and made a related

it did not pose a threat to market confidence, and disclaiming any AFM interest in regulating technology.

322 MiFID Proposal, art. 17. 323 Ibid., arts. 19, 20, and 51.

324 Market Abuse Regulation Proposal, art. 8.

325 European Commission, *MiFID Impact Assessment*, p. 38.

326 Ferrarini and Moloney, "Equity Trading."

327 e.g., IOSCO, *Mitigating Systemic Risk*, underlining the importance of market transparency in managing risk and calling for enhanced access to trading information, and better surveillance systems.

commitment to close information gaps.[328] Specific initiatives include the FSB's agenda concerning financial institution reporting of exposures to structured credit products.[329] In the EU, the new risk regulation component of market regulation includes extensive new disclosures related to: capital levels under the series of reforms to the Capital Requirements Directive; credit rating agency policies and methodologies (CRA Regulations I–III); net short positions (Short Selling Regulation); alternative investment fund leverage (AIFMD); and OTC derivative transactions reported to trade repositories (EMIR). But traditional market disclosure is also being reshaped. The driving influence is the concern to address unregulated markets and sectors. A concern with intensity and innovation can also be identified as an influence on the tightening grip of regulation.

The issuer-facing disclosures in the market disclosure data-set have typically applied to securities admitted to trading on a regulated market, and have focused on equities. This is changing. The Market Abuse Directive's ongoing issuer-disclosure obligations concerning disclosure of inside information and selective disclosures are likely to extend from issuers of regulated-market-admitted instruments, to issuers of financial instruments admitted to MTFs and OTFs, albeit with some calibration for small and medium-sized issuers admitted to the new SME Growth Market (proposed under MiFID II).[330] More extensive investor-facing disclosures will also be required. Investors are not typically required to disclose trading positions, given the risk that they may become reluctant to commit capital. An exception applies to larger shareholdings, the acquisition or disposition of which must be notified to the market (and to regulators) when certain thresholds are reached under the Transparency Directive, given the implications for corporate control. These obligations are likely to be extended under the Transparency Directive Proposal to include economically-equivalent holdings in cash-settled derivatives, particularly contracts for difference (CfDs) which can generate control-related effects.[331] Investors will also be required to make the short-selling disclosures concerning net short positions in shares and sovereign debt required under the Short Selling

[328] FSB and IMF, *Financial Crisis and Information Gaps* (2009), addressing, inter alia, financial soundness indicators for financial institutions and disclosure on the CDS markets, linkages between SIFIs, and the vulnerability of domestic economies.

[329] e.g., FSB, *Thematic Review on Risk Disclosure Practices: Peer Review* (Basel: FSB, 2011).

[330] Market Abuse Regulation Proposal, art. 12. See further below on the SME Growth Market.

[331] Transparency Directive Proposal, art. 13.

Regulation. As noted above, a much wider data-set on trading transparency will also be made available to the market.

These reforms cannot be easily bundled together. They respond to different market efficiency as well as financial stability concerns and have varying political drivers.[332] Nonetheless, taken as a whole, these reforms amount to a material expansion in the volume of market disclosure. Additional disclosure may counter the more febrile hostility to perceived speculation and previously unregulated sectors.[333] The translation of the regulated market/equity disclosure model to other asset classes and venues may reap dividends in time; overall, more information is usually better than less.[334] But it remains the case that the new regime will be costly operationally[335] and may have unintended costs. Arbitrage risks may be significant.[336] And as noted above with respect to trading transparency, liquidity may be prejudiced.

Clearer evidence of productive innovation comes from the reforms to disclosures to competent authorities (rather than market disclosures) which temper the prevailing assumption, which persists despite the evidence from the crisis, that markets effectively decode disclosure. In the secondary markets, the MiFID Article 25 transaction reporting requirement, under which competent authorities must be informed of all transactions in financial instruments admitted to a regulated market made by MiFID-scope actors, is currently at the heart of the reporting system which allows EU regulators to monitor market abuse and market

[332] CfD disclosure requirements respond to concerns related to "empty voting" and are typically associated with long CfD positions, where the CfD counterparty acquires the related shares as a hedge, potentially allowing the CfD holder to exercise significant influence without disclosure to the market of stake building, but also reflect political interests with respect to take-over markets. While short-selling disclosure can have a market stability function, the political drivers of the short-selling regime are significant and are discussed in E. Ferran, Chapter 1 above. The new trading transparency disclosures are in part a function of a concern to address market fragmentation, efficiency and liquidity in the EU's liberalized order execution market, but are also a function of a political concern, led by France, to move trading on to "lit" organized platforms and to limit "dark" trading: Ferrarini and Moloney, "Equity Trading."

[333] Bowles, "Market Abuse."

[334] Lo, "Regulatory Reform," in the context of the crisis-driven "mark to market" accounting reforms.

[335] The costs of the Short Selling Regulation disclosure regime in the UK, with respect to sovereign debt alone, are estimated at £47 million initially, over £5 million annually: House of Commons, European Scrutiny Committee, *20th Report*, March 10, 2011.

[336] The ECB has highlighted its concerns as the need for consistency in the new regime which will apply to "varying types of assets and reporting entities": *Opinion on the Short Selling Proposal* [2011] OJ C91/1.

activity.[337] Competent authority-facing disclosures are now becoming more extensive, addressing a wider set of asset classes and markets, particularly derivative markets, and being linked directly to potential regulatory action. The risk regulation-driven market regulation reforms initially expanded the competent authority facing disclosures. The AIFMD contains extensive disclosure requirements, directed towards fund investors and the market, including annual reporting requirements and disclosures with respect to investment policy, liquidity, risk profile, stress testing and leverage.[338] But it also uses disclosure as a stepping stone to consequent action by supervisors. The Article 24 disclosures on leverage limits and levels are the starting point of a process which may lead to a competent authority imposing leverage limits in the interests of systemic stability (Article 25). The Short Selling Regulation is similar. It extends the reach of the market disclosure regime by requiring public disclosure of net short positions in equities. Competent authorities, however, must be informed of short positions in equity at a lower notification threshold, and of short positions in sovereign debt and uncovered CDS.[339] They will also be empowered to impose disclosure obligations on short positions in any financial instrument where financial stability is threatened.[340] These disclosures ultimately feed into the extensive powers competent authorities enjoy to prohibit or impose conditions on short sales under the Regulation.

This approach has been applied to the new generation of market regulation reforms. The MiFID II reforms are likely to lead to the Article 25 transaction reporting regime to be significantly extended in scope,[341] and to the imposition of reporting requirements on venues with respect to aggregate positions held by commodity derivative traders.[342] The Market Abuse Directive's "suspicious transaction reporting" regime, which relates to securities admitted to regulated markets, is also likely to be extended to require in-scope market actors to report suspicious orders and suspicious OTC, OTF and MTF transactions.[343]

[337] D. Lawton (FSA), "Strengthening Transparency in the Markets Transaction Chain" (speech, May 19, 2011, online: www.fsa.gov.uk/pages/Library/Communication/Speeches/2011/0519_dl.shtml).

[338] Arts. 22 and 24.

[339] Art. 6 (public disclosure of short positions in shares at 0.5 percent of issued share capital and each 0.1 thereafter), Art. 5 (competent authority notification of short share positions at 0.2 percent and each 0.1 percent thereafter) and Arts. 7–8 sovereign debt and uncovered CDS position notification.

[340] Short Selling Regulation, art. 18.

[341] MiFIR Proposal, arts. 21–3.

[342] MiFID Proposal, art. 60.

[343] Market Abuse Regulation Proposal, art. 11.

The expanded regulator-facing data-set should lead to better supervision. But there comes a point where the volume of regulator disclosures reaches a tipping point in terms of effectiveness. It is clear that regulators did not have clear information flows on unregulated sectors pre-crisis. But the volume of regulated disclosures can be problematic; considerable concerns have already been raised by the volume of often irrelevant information produced through the Market Abuse Directive's "suspicious transaction reports." Competent authorities across the EU are enjoying increased resource allocation and addressing the effectiveness of their information-gathering and assessment procedures.[344] ESMA may also provide a useful mechanism for supporting supervisory best practices with respect to the avalanche of regulated information. But the extent to which effective analysis of this new data-set is carried out will reveal whether the disclosure reforms have been productive for market regulation.

The equity markets

As discussed above, one of the defining features of second-generation EU market regulation is its extension beyond the organized public equity markets. But there is also some evidence of what might be termed a return to basics, and a concern to ensure that the public equity markets are working effectively.

Pre-crisis, little EU policy attention was directed to the relative efficiency of the public equity markets. This is notwithstanding the growth in private equity-based funding, the growing scale of private placement-led funding, and the intensification of risk management techniques which allowed issuers to diversify risk, all of which led to some concern that public equity markets were being eclipsed.[345] Private equity funding, for example, grew significantly in the lead-up to the financial crisis, raising some concern that the efficiency and transparency of the public equity markets might be compromised.[346] Even allowing for the

[344] e.g., AMF, *Better Regulation: Initial Assessment and 2008/2009 Work Agenda* (Paris: AMF, 2008).

[345] R. Gilson and C. Whitehead, "Deconstructing Equity: Public Ownership, Agency Costs and Complete Capital Markets," *Columbia Law Review*, 108 (2008), 231–64 and, more generally, M. Henderson and R. Epstein, "The Going Private Phenomenon: Causes and Implications," *University of Chicago Law Review*, 76 (2009), 1–6.

[346] Notably M.J. Roe, "The Eclipse of the Public Corporation," *Harvard Business Review*, 67 (1989), 61–74 (revised in 1997, online: http://ssrn.com/abstract=146149) and, more skeptically, B. Cheffins and J. Armour, "The Eclipse of Private Equity," ECGI Law Working Paper No. 82/2007 (April 2007, online: http://ssrn.com/abstract=982114). Similarly, from a policy

reality that most private equity funding in the EU was based in the UK,[347] the EU policy response was sanguine. Internal Market Commissioner McCreevy was supportive of the private equity funding model,[348] despite considerable opposition from the Parliament's Socialist grouping.[349] This is not to claim that the private equity funding model called for regulatory intervention, or that the EU public equity markets were inefficient, but simply to highlight the relative lack of attention given to the efficiency and quality of the public equity markets once the supporting passport regime for pan-EU public equity offers was in place under the Prospectus Directive.

Post-crisis, more attention is focusing internationally on the comparative advantages of the public equity markets.[350] Calls are being made (particularly in the US, reflecting the size and importance of the US equity markets) for the public securities – and particularly equity – markets to be supported as a major vehicle for finance raising, risk management and mobilizing long-term public savings.[351] The US Committee on Capital Market Regulation has continued to raise concern as to the relative competitiveness of the US public equity markets, reporting in its Quarter 7 2012 report that the markets continued to be uncompetitive, despite an improvement in that quarter.[352] In the UK, the *Kay Review* has identified problems in the UK equity market related to short termism and a lack of trust and confidence and proposed a series of reforms.[353] The UK Listing Authority's listing

perspective, FSA, *Discussion Paper 06/6, Private Equity: A Discussion of Risk and Regulatory Engagement* (London: FSA, 2006), noting the shrinkage in the UK equity market in 2006 at the height of the private equity boom.

[347] E. Ferran, "Regulation of Private Equity-Backed Leveraged Buyout Activity in Europe," ECGI Law Working Paper No. 084/2007 (May 2007, online: http://ssrn.com/abstract=989748).

[348] e.g., "Private Equity: Getting it Right" (speech, London, March 22, 2007, online: http://europa.eu/rapid/pressReleasesAction.do?reference=SPEECH/07/171&format).

[349] e.g., PES, *Hedge and Private Equity Funds* (2007). The clashes between Commissioner McCreevy and the Socialist grouping on his reluctance to regulate hedge funds and private equity were well reported. The more muted Resolution finally adopted by the Parliament on private equity (and hedge funds) in the teeth of the crisis in September 2008 adopted a measured approach: *Resolution on Hedge Funds and Private Equity* (P6_TA-PROV(2008)0425).

[350] Gerding, "Code, Crash" and Langevoort, "Global Securities Regulation."

[351] e.g., L. Zingales, "The Future of Securities Regulation," *Journal of Accounting Research*, 47 (2009), 391–426, R. Thomson, "The SEC after the Financial Meltdown: Social Control over Finance," *University of Pittsburgh Law Review*, 71 (2009–10), 567–83 and McCoy *et al.*, "Systemic Risk through Securitization."

[352] Committee on Capital Markets Regulation, *Quarter 1 2012 Report*, June 4, 2012, online: www.capmktsreg.org/competitiveness/index.html.

[353] The Kay Review of UK Equity Markets and Long-Term Decision Making, *Final Report* (London: May Review, 2012).

review, which completed over the crisis period and which has led to a re-organizing and re-branding of the UK listing regime,[354] underlines the continuing commitment of the UK regulatory authorities to equity market efficiency. France's AMF Chairman Jouyet has similarly recently suggested that the only indicator of the effectiveness of the international reform program will be the return of investors to the markets, and particularly the equity markets.[355]

From a regulatory perspective, and leaving aside the wider efficiency issues related to equity finance, a renewed focus on the equity markets is not unexpected given its attractiveness to the beleaguered regulator. Although equity markets experienced significant losses of value over the crisis,[356] they did not experience particular difficulties and the equity trading market infrastructure proved resilient.[357] The crisis did not expose systemic governance problems in traded companies generally, although risk management in systemically-significant financial institutions came under scrutiny.[358] Although, as noted below, conditions are now changing, in early to mid-2011 equity markets were regarded as recovering internationally,[359] with 2010 also seeing strong issuance activity.[360] With respect to EU market integration, while integration in the bond and money market instruments markets had, pre-crisis,

[354] e.g., FSA, *Discussion Paper 08/1, A Review of the Structure of the Listing Regime* (London: FSA, 2008) and *Policy Statement 10/2, The Listing Regime Review* (London: FSA, 2010).

[355] Jouyet, "ICMA Speech."

[356] e.g., S. Bartram and G. Bodner, "No Place to Hide: The Global Crisis in Equity Markets," *Journal of International Money and Finance*, 28 (2009), 1246–92, noting that major world indices fell 30–40 percent between September and October 2008. Similarly, J. Graham and C. Harvey, "The Equity Risk Premium amid a Global Financial Crisis" (May 2009, online: http://ssrn.com/abstract=1405459), charting the increase in the equity risk premium over the financial crisis.

[357] FSA, *Markets Regulatory Agenda*, pp. 4 and 19, noting that trading platforms were able to cope with the related market volatility and SEC, *Release No 34–61358, Concept Release on Equity Market Structure* (Washington DC: SEC, 2010), p. 64. Similarly, Angel *et al.*, "Equity Trading in the 21st Century."

[358] B. Cheffins, "Did Corporate Governance 'Fail' During the 2008 Stock Market Meltdown? The Case of the S & P 500" (May 2009, ECGI Law Working Paper No. 124/2009, online: http://ssrn.com/abstractid=1396126), p. 37.

[359] IMF, *Global Stability Report – Market Update January 2011* (Washington DC: IMF, 2011), p. 1, noting a global rise in equity markets. Similarly, ESMA *Annual Report* (2012), pp. 15–16, noting a rise in Initial Public Offer activity in the first half of 2011.

[360] Ackerman, "The Global Financial System," noting the 2010 Petrobas $70 billion offering. Similarly, FSA, *Financial Risk Outlook* (London: FSA, 2010), p. 11, noting strong recovery in equity market secondary issuance, and in the corporate bond market.

proceeded considerably faster than in the equity markets, it proved to be a shallow form of integration, fed by a credit boom and the mispricing of risks, and the crisis led to rapid retrenchment.[361] EU equity markets, however, performed reasonably well over the crisis and integration, while weakened, has not sustained significant damage.[362] A 2011 ECB study similarly reported that the global contagion in equity markets was relatively limited, with most contagion effects over the crisis associated with domestic equity markets.[363] The regulatory problems are also fewer and more tractable and the risks of capture by complexity considerably lower. The equity markets likewise have the advantage of a long-standing and well-tested regulatory model.

In a move which can be associated with the de-intensification/simplification movement, the EU's second-generation market regulation agenda is now addressing the efficiency of the public equity markets. This refocusing may be timely, given the recent evidence that world equity markets may be becoming less efficient in channeling resources to productive sources and in supporting savers. Overall, 2011 witnessed a marked slowdown in the global initial public offering (IPO) market[364] and there are growing concerns as to equity market efficiency generally.[365]

The new EU equity market agenda is focusing in particular on the poor ability of equity markets to support SMEs. This reflects a wider international concern with SME finance. The 2010 Seoul G20 Action Plan includes an SME finance framework.[366] The US SEC has recently

361 ECB, *Financial Integration in Europe* (2011), p. 7 and European Commission, *European Financial Stability and Integration Report* (2011) (SEC (2011) 489).

362 ECB, *Financial Integration in Europe* (2011), pp. 7 and 22 and European Commission, *European Financial Stability and Integration Report* (2011). The respective 2012 Reports took a similar view.

363 G. Bekaert, M. Ehrmann, M. Fratzcher and A. Mehl, "Global Crises and Equity Market Contagion," ECB Working Paper No. 1381/2011 (May 2011, online: http://ssrn.com/abstract=1856881).

364 As at November 2011, 34 percent of announced IPOs were postponed in the US and 45 percent in Europe, the Middle East and Africa: K. Burgess, J. Grant and T. Demos, "A Market Less Efficient," *Financial Times*, November 14, 2011, 11.

365 On the weaknesses in the UK equity market, see Kay Review, *Final Report*. In the EU high volatility in the sovereign debt market has had an impact on the ability of companies to raise capital: European Commission, *European Financial Stability and Integration Report (2012)*, pp. 31–2.

366 G20, *Leaders' Declaration* (Seoul), para. 9. For an early review of international efforts on SME financing, see OECD, *Impact of the Global Crisis on SME and Entrepreneurship Financing and Policy Measures* (Paris: OECD, 2009).

engaged in a review of small business capital formation,[367] while the 2012 Joss Act is designed to ease the equity offering process for emerging growth companies. In the EU, SME finance, while long a policy target of the Commission,[368] has not been the beneficiary of specific regulatory reform in the market regulation sphere. This is now changing. The Commission highlighted the SME sector at an early stage of the crisis reform program[369] and has since included SME financing as one of the 12 elements of the 2011 Single Market Act. The SME agenda is designed to ensure SMEs (estimated in the region of 21 million across the EU)[370] have sufficient access to equity finance,[371] given the difficulties they have faced over and since the crisis. In the wake of the financial crisis, venture capital funding, for example, has fallen from €6–7 billion annually pre-crisis to €3–4 billion in 2009 and 2010. Given equity market difficulties, the exit opportunities available to venture capital funds are still limited and have led to "relatively subdued" levels of finance in the EU and globally.[372] The proportion of small bank loans as a proportion of total lending has also dropped in the EU – from 30 percent in 2004 to 20 percent in 2008[373] – further increasing pressure on equity funding. There is also evidence of SMEs' de-listing from major public equity markets[374] and growing concern that the regulatory costs of regulated market admission do not generate the traditional benefits, such as visibility and

[367] SEC Chairman Schapiro, "Testimony on the Future of Capital Formation, House of Representatives" (speech, May 10, 2011, online: www.sec.gov.

[368] The initial policy agenda, which included support for strong pan-EU stock exchanges, was set out in European Commission, *Risk Capital: A Key to Job Creation in the EU* (1998) (SEC (1998) 552).

[369] European Commission, *Driving European Recovery* (2009) (COM (2009) 114), pp. 10–12.

[370] Single Market Act, para. 2.1.

[371] e.g., European Commission, *A New European Regime for Venture Capital. Consultation Document* (2011); *Communication on Review of the "Small Business Act" for Europe* (COM (2011) 78); *Communication on the Single Market Act* (COM (2011) 206) and *An Action Plan to Improve Access to Finance* (COM (2011) 8701).

[372] BVCA, *Private Equity and Venture Capital Report on Investment Activity* (2010) and BVCA, *2011 Global Trends in Venture Capital* (2011), both online: www.bvca.co.uk/home.

[373] European Commission, *European Financial Stability and Integration Report* (2011), p. 24.

[374] European Commission, *Transparency Directive Impact Assessment* (SEC (2011) 1279), pp. 22–3.

analyst coverage, for SMEs.[375] The regulatory ambition is considerable; the Commission is seeking to "tip the balance" between traditional bank-based finance and those sources which can sustain the more volatile patterns of SME growth and earnings.[376] This re-tooling of equity market regulation to reflect SME needs may, however, be injecting considerable uncertainty into well-settled equity market regulation principles.

For example, SME interests were reflected in the 2010 reforms to the 2003 Prospectus Directive. The Prospectus Directive requires that its disclosure rules take into account the various activities and size of issuers, including SMEs (Article 7). This injunction was not followed in the detailed rules which apply to particular issuers and securities under the related Prospectus Regulation.[377] This omission relates in part to lack of support for the key distinguishing requirement that 2 rather than 3 years' financial information be required for smaller issuers.[378] The 2010 reforms, however, focus more closely on the SME sector.[379] The 2010 Directive increases the threshold at which offers are exempted from the Directive, from total offer consideration of €2.5 million to €5 million. It also reinforces the need for a proportionate disclosure regime for SMEs and companies with a "reduced market capitalization."[380] The Commission also activated the related delegation for SME-specific rules, requesting advice from ESMA in 2011. But the new proportionate disclosure regime represents a muddled regulatory response to SME financing difficulties. Diluting the prospectus disclosure regime which applies to public offers and securities admitted to regulated markets cuts against the regulatory philosophy of the Directive, which is designed, for the most part, to support the public pan-EU retail equity markets. A lighter regime does not take account of the reality that SME issuers tend to be higher risk. It also risks damage to the branding effects associated with regulated markets. Trading markets can opt not to be

375 e.g., European Commission, *MiFID Proposals Impact Assessment*, charting the thin liquidity in SME stocks and the relative costs of admission to regulated markets as compared to the low amounts of capital raised: p. 97.

376 European Commission, *A New European Regime for Venture Capital*.

377 European Commission Delegated Regulation (EU) No. 809/2004/EC, [2004] OJ L149/1.

378 Ferran, *Building an EU Securities Market*, p. 181.

379 Directive 2010/73/EU, [2010] OJ L327/1.

380 Art. 7(2)(e). A proportionate regime is also to apply to credit institutions issuing debt securities and rights issues.

designated as regulated markets and to operate as MTFs (some 20 MTFs operate second-tier SME market segments),[381] in which case the issuer disclosure rules of the Prospectus Directive do not apply. A number of the EU's second-tier markets have followed this route and become MTFs in order to offer distinct listing products to smaller issuers and to signal to investors that they provide a platform for higher risk securities which are subject to a calibrated level of regulation.[382] The Prospectus Directive reform cuts against this classification, and injects uncertainty into regulated market brand. The new SME regime provides early evidence, however, that ESMA may act as a counterforce to potential regulatory error by the EU institutions; it was charged with providing advice on the regime to the Commission and advised against a differentiated regime, given the risks to investor protection and to regulatory consistency, and proposed, were the regime to be pursued, that any such differentiation not apply to initial public offers or to first admissions to trading on a regulated market. The Commission did not, however, follow this advice, placing weight on the potential for reducing SME costs.[383]

Related difficulties follow from the MiFID II Proposals. The MiFID II Directive Proposal proposes a new "SME Growth Market" classification as a subset of the MTF classification.[384] MiFID currently applies only minimal admission rules to MTF issuers. The MiFID II Proposal, however, would require that MTFs registered as SME Growth Markets ensure that the majority of admitted issuers were SMEs, appropriate criteria applied to the admission of these issuers, and that sufficient disclosure was available concerning the issuer to allow investors to make an informed judgment. Appropriate ongoing period reporting obligations would also be required. The Market Abuse Directive Proposal dovetails with this regime, providing that a lighter ad hoc issuer disclosure regime apply to Growth Market issuers.[385] The purpose of this regime is not clear. It is difficult to see how a new regulated segment would enhance the current second-tier, MTF-based regime. It may significantly increase costs by imposing regulatory determinations as to how second-tier markets should work. After some initial difficulties,

381 European Commission, *MiFID Proposals Impact Assessment*, p. 98.

382 See, e.g., S. Arcot, J. Black and G. Owen, *From Local to Global; The Rise of AIM as a Stock Market for Growing Companies* (London: LSE, 2007) and PriceWaterhouseCoopers, *IPO Watch Europe: A Survey* (2006).

383 ESMA's Advice is at ESMA, *Final Advice* (ESMA 2011/323). The Commission's reasoning is at European Commission, *Impact Assessment* (SWD (2012) 77).

384 MiFID Directive Proposal, art. 35.

385 Market Abuse Regulation Proposal, p. 10.

associated with the enforcement of market abuse prohibitions and in particular with Germany's Neuer Markt, market-based discipline appears to be operating well in the EU's second-tier markets.[386] A new SME regime, within the MTF regime, may bring uncertainties and costs, and will atomize the regulatory regime still further. Investor confusion may be considerable, particularly as the new regime is discretionary.

Similar issues have arisen with the Transparency Directive review of the ongoing issuer disclosure obligations imposed on issuers admitted to regulated markets.[387] In its 2010 Consultation, the Commission focused on enhancing the attractiveness of the regime for smaller issuers and queried whether a differentiated ongoing disclosure regime for "small listed companies" on regulated markets would ease regulatory burdens. Stakeholder reaction was hostile, with concern raised that the regulated market brand could be damaged by a change to the scope of the Directive.[388] Member States also showed limited enthusiasm.[389] The 2011 Transparency Directive Proposal, however, has adopted a compromise model. Highlighting the regulatory costs faced by regulated-market-admitted SMEs from ongoing issuer disclosure obligations, and the visibility problems which arise from the bottleneck of regulated disclosures which reduce analyst and investor capacity to follow SMEs at certain points of the year, the Proposal is designed to support the SME sector by abolishing the Directive's requirement for quarterly management reporting. The abolition of quarterly reporting in the EU (Member States will not be permitted to retain quarterly reporting obligations) which was introduced by the Transparency Directive in 2004, is potentially radical. There is only limited evidence, however, that the quarterly regime has been effective, it has been associated with prejudicial short-termism[390] and the original introduction of the obligation was controversial.[391] But the salient point for this discussion is that the Directive adopts a more

386 FSA, *Discussion Paper 08/1, A Review of the Listing Regime* (London: FSA, 2008), p. 16, noting the decline in companies listed on the UK's main regulated market (the London Stock Exchange main market) and the growth of AIM (a second-tier stock exchange market).

387 European Commission, *Consultation on Modernization of the Transparency Directive* (2010) and Transparency Directive Proposal.

388 European Commission, *Feedback Statement to Transparency Directive Proposal* (2010).

389 Concerns have been repeatedly raised at the Member States' European Securities Committee meetings (e.g., 72nd Meeting, November 9, 2010 and 71st Meeting, June 21, 2010).

390 European Commission, *Transparency Directive Proposal Impact Assessment.*

391 Moloney, *EC Securities Regulation*, pp. 177–82.

nuanced approach to SME support. The quarterly reporting requirement is removed for all companies and thus does not lead to uneven levels of investor protection in SME investments. Unlike the Prospectus Directive reforms, the regulated market brand is not disturbed.

The new focus on equity market regulation and SME finance can be associated with a concern to support more "fundamental" forms of financing and with the capital allocation, rather than intermediation function, of financial markets. It has much to commend it given the difficulties SMEs face. But dangers arise where related technical regulatory reform becomes a convenient proxy for the intervention necessary to address a problem which engages significantly wider issues, including with respect to taxation and enterprise policy. The dangers are all the greater where reforms have spill-over effects on settled regulatory regimes.

IV: The legacy effects of the crisis on consumer protection regulation

Refocusing on the consumer markets

In the EU, the consumer (or retail) investment markets were largely overlooked in the initial stages of the reform program. Notwithstanding the scale of the losses sustained by households[392] and the pressure which the financial crisis placed on the dominant EU regulatory model – the empowerment of retail investors and the financialization of households through disclosure and distribution-related regulation – there was little evidence of productive regulatory innovation, or even of policy focus, on the retail markets.[393] By contrast with the US reform agenda, for example, where consumer-related issues were an early target of reforms,[394] particularly with respect to the Consumer Financial Protection Bureau,[395] the EU retail investor did not feature to any material degree in the initial reform agenda. And unlike the Australian model, the recent reforms to which are discussed by Jennifer G. Hill in Chapter 3 below, and which reforms reflect

[392] On which, see Moloney, "Regulating the Retail Markets." [393] Ibid.

[394] One of the earliest initiatives in the US reform program related to investment advice. The investment advice process has, for example, been to the fore in the Dodd-Frank Act 2010 and the subject of a recent and wide-ranging SEC report, required under the Act (SEC, *Study on Investment Advisers and Broker Dealers* (2011)).

[395] See, generally, A. Wilmarth, "The Dodd-Frank Act's Expansion of State Authority to Protect Consumers of Financial Services," *Journal of Corporation Law*, 36 (2011), 893–954.

the importance of personal pension provision in Australia, the roots of EU retail investor protection law do not run deep.[396] But the "retail crisis" in the EU forms part of the wider financial crisis.

In particular, the period before and over the crisis was strongly associated with the "retailization" of complex structured products initially developed for the wholesale markets but subsequently sold in the retail markets. The crisis exposed their mis-selling in many Member States,[397] and enforcement action followed in, for example, the UK, [398] Spain and Germany.[399] Regulatory weakness is closely implicated in these failures. MiFID introduced a comprehensive EU regime for the regulation of product distribution, including marketing, disclosure and suitability/know-your-client rules. But the EU product distribution market remains subject to deep market failures. These derive from: the dominance of complex packaged products as household investments; persistent conflict of interest risk arising from the "financial supermarket" business model which is based on the distribution of proprietary products (dominant in Continental Europe), or arising from the commission-based adviser business model (dominant in the UK); a proliferation of complex products; and limited investor ability to decode complex product and conflict of interest-related disclosures.[400] In this environment, MiFID's process-based suitability rules are frequently unable to engage in the heavy lifting required of them. Significant regulatory arbitrage risks also arise, as MiFID's rules do not apply to unit-linked insurance products or deposit-based investment products. A recent examination of the EU product distribution sector has underlined the persistent and severe difficulties.[401] So, too, does the UK experience. Repeated cycles of mis-selling in the UK, and persistent failures to comply with suitability rules,[402] have led the FSA to engage in a re-engineering of the retail distribution market under the Retail

396 Moloney, *How to Protect Investors.*

397 See further, Moloney, "Regulating the Retail Markets."

398 e.g., FSA, *Quality of Advice on Structured Investment Products* (London: FSA, 2009).

399 Herbert Smith, *A Changing Landscape. Regulatory Developments in the Distribution of Retail Investment Products* (London: Herbert Smith, 2010), p. 1 and CESR, *The Lehman Brothers Default: An Assessment of the Market Impact* (2009) (CESR/09–255), p. 3.

400 Generally, Moloney, *How to Protect Investors.*

401 Synovate, *Consumer Market Study on Advice* (2011) (for the European Commission). The headline finding of the extensive field testing was that advice was unsuitable in 50 percent of cases.

402 e.g., FSA, *Guidance Consultation. Assessing Suitability* (London, FSA: 2011), outlining failures with respect to assessing the risks which consumers are prepared to sustain.

Distribution Review.[403] Three industry-changing reforms will be implemented: a prohibition on commission payments from product providers for all forms of investment advice; an obligation to label advice as either "independent" (when based on a fair and comprehensive review of the relevant (and widely cast) market) or "restricted" (when based on a restricted range of products – typically where proprietary products are advised on); and enhanced adviser qualification requirements. They are due to come into effect in early 2013 and look set to significantly restructure the investment distribution industry in the UK.

Although the financial stability agenda remains a drag on EU retail market reform,[404] the retail markets are now being pulled into the EU's reform agenda.[405] It is not entirely clear why. The wider momentum of the reform movement has no doubt played a role, as have particular retail market failures. Retail stakeholders are becoming more organized and vocal.[406] The political risks associated with the retail markets are considerable, and all the more so after the publicly-funded bailouts of the EU banking industry;[407] the Commission's *Eurobarometers* of public opinion unsurprisingly suggest significant hostility towards the financial sector.[408] The fiscal crisis cannot be discounted, given the need to

[403] Generally, FSA, *Policy Statement 10/6, Distribution of Retail Investments – Delivering the RDR* (London: FSA, 2010).

[404] The persistent delays to the package of reforms designed to address equivalent packaged retail investment products (PRIPs) by extending the MiFID regime, finally adopted in July 2012, have been related to the reality that regulators may be more concerned with ensuring that banks can repair their balance sheets, including by means of the income generated from structured retail instruments, and with allowing lighter regulatory regimes for these products: P. Skypala, "Unhealthy Truth behind Robust AUM," *Financial Times Fund Management Supplement*, June 27, 2011, 6.

[405] The FCA's proposed launch document, e.g., makes repeated references to the "strong consumer protection agenda" in the EU post-crisis: FCA, *Approach to Regulation.*

[406] Notably, Euroinvestors (now EuroFinuse), established in 2009, which has become an active participant in EU policy debates.

[407] e.g., S. Nicoll (FSA), "The FSA's Approach to Consumer Protection" (speech, June 24, 2010, online: www.fsa.gov.uk/pages/Library/Communication/Speeches/2010/0624_sn.shtml), noting the evolution of society's expectations of what the regulator must deliver. The *Financial Times* has similarly noted that "Regulators in Europe are practically falling over themselves to demonstrate their commitment to protecting the humble retail investor," P. Davis, "Protecting Investors Proves Tricky," *Financial Times Fund Management Supplement*, March 21, 2011, 11.

[408] Evidenced, e.g., by the significant pan-EU support for a tax on bank profits (81 percent of respondents), the regulation of bankers' bonuses (80 percent) and a tax on financial transactions (61 percent): European Commission, *Eurobarometer 74, Autumn 2010, Europeans, the EU and the Crisis* (2010).

monetize EU household savings as part of the response to the sovereign debt crisis and the related socialization of private and sovereign debt. The institutional restructuring of EU regulators is also playing a role. As outlined below, the establishment of ESMA, which has a specific retail market mandate, is bringing an influential new influence to bear. The retail agenda is also gaining ground domestically, and regulators are taking this agenda to the EU. France's AMF, for example, has adopted a new retail market agenda which it is pursuing at EU level.[409]

The international context has been less influential, reflecting the strong influence of local market context and culture on retail market practices and regulation. Nonetheless, and in a change which is likely to be of more optical than substantive significance, the international agenda has recently turned to the retail markets. The November 2010 Seoul G20 Declaration called on the FSB to work with the OECD and other organizations on consumer finance protection.[410] Common principles on consumer protection followed for the November 2011 Cannes G20 Meeting. The impact of this internationalization of retail regulation remains to be seen. The G20 agenda focuses on consumer finance generally[411] and on well-trodden elements of consumer policy. It does not engage with the difficult choices which the retail investment markets generate with respect to the levels of risk which individuals can be expected to sustain. The high-level and generic principles[412] which were endorsed by the November 2011 Cannes G20 Summit[413] are unlikely to

[409] Outlined in AMF, *The AMF's New Strategy Proposals* (Paris: AMF, 2010).

[410] G20, *Leaders' Declaration* (Seoul), para. 41.

[411] The related FSB-led work agenda addressed the financial stability aspects of consumer credit (including residential mortgages, credit cards and personal loans and policy options with respect to financial literacy and education, disclosure and transparency; product regulation; protection from fraud, abuse and errors; and mechanisms to resolve disputes). The OECD led the work-stream on common consumer protection principles: FSB, *Progress in the Implementation of the G20 Recommendations for Strengthening Financial Stability* (Basel: FSB, 2011).

[412] OECD, *G20 High Level Principles on Financial Consumer Protection* (Paris: OECD, 2011). They address in general terms 10 principles governing: the integral nature of consumer protection in regulation; the role of oversight bodies; equitable and fair treatment of consumers; disclosure and transparency; financial education and awareness; responsible business conduct; protection of consumer assets; data protection and privacy; complaints and redress; and competition. The FSB review examined the financial stability aspects of consumer finance protection with respect to consumer credit (including mortgages): FSB, *Consumer Finance Protection, With a Particular Focus on Credit* (Basel: FSB, 2011).

[413] G20, *Final Declaration* (Cannes), para. 33.

advance retail market regulatory design, given the long experience in many regulatory systems internationally with intractable retail market problems. The 2011 FSB Report on Consumer Finance Protection,[414] in particular, issued by a body concerned with financial stability, sits uneasily with the current recognition of the limits of consumer empowerment and responsibilization in financial services regulation[415] by emphasizing that consumer rights come with responsibilities, consumer protection is not designed to protect consumers from "bad decisions," and suggesting that consumer protection frameworks proved resilient over the crisis.

The rejuvenated EU retail market agenda incorporates the traditional disclosure[416] and distribution[417] elements which have long dominated the EU retail regime. There is also, however, strong evidence of first- and second-level regulatory innovation in the form of the emergence of product intervention as a retail market regulatory mechanism, at Member State and at EU levels. This development usefully exposes the impact of the associated third-level regulatory innovation with respect to policy suspicion of financial market intensity and innovation.

The rise of product intervention

Product intervention, the most interventionist form of retail market regulation, has not been entirely overlooked by EU retail market regulation. But it is primarily a function of the portfolio-shaping and risk management rules which apply to the Undertakings for Collective Inveatment in Transferable Securities (UCITS) mutual fund.[418] The UCITS regime, however, is more a function of liberalization and the extension of the UCITS market than of retail investor protection policy. This is

[414] FSB, *Consumer Finance Protection.*

[415] e.g., Kingsford Smith, "Regulating Investment Risk."

[416] The 2010 reforms to the Prospectus Directive, e.g., have led to significant reforms to the Directive's failed Retail Summary under Commission Delegated Regulation (EU) No. 486/2012, [2012] OJ L150/1. The summer 2012 proposal for a harmonized summary disclosure regime for PRIPs should also significantly enhance retail disclosures (COM (2012) 352/3).

[417] The MiFID Review proposes a host of potentially radical reforms to the regulation of investment product distribution, most notably the proposed prohibition on commissions, the requirement for the basis of investment advice to be made clear, and the labeling of investment advice as "independent" or "restricted": MiFID Directive Proposal, art. 24.

[418] UCITS Directive IV 2009/6/5EC, [2009] OJ L302/32.

clear from the extension of the UCITS product. Following the liberalization-driven UCITS III reforms, the UCITS product umbrella now includes complex and often hedge fund-like structured products. The related stretching of the UCITS label, which signals the UCITS to be a "gold standard" retail product, and the troublesome fit of some UCITS within MiFID's execution-only regime, which permits all UCITS products to be sold execution-only, raises significant retail market risks, as noted below. Prior to the crisis, there were some tentative moves towards product-related intervention at Member State level, including the UK FSA's "Treating Customers Fairly" supervisory initiative, which applied to the product life cycle and to the respective responsibilities of product providers and distributors.[419] But pre-crisis harmonized EU regulation and Member State rules largely avoided product intervention in favor of disclosure and distribution rules. This reflects the significant risks associated with product intervention,[420] certainly in the investment markets.[421] These include arbitrage, damage to innovation and investor choice – and related reputational and resource risk to the regulator – and moral hazard. The association between product intervention and "over-regulation" is also considerable, as the lively US debate on the appropriateness of product intervention underlines.[422]

Major change is now underway. The extent to which Member State regulators are now turning to product-related techniques in the retail markets, typically in the form of product prohibition and more general product oversight techniques, is striking. In August 2011 the Italian regulator, CONSOB, presented proposals to encourage credit institutions to raise finance through euro-denominated "simple bonds," which would guarantee repayment, be highly liquid, not rely on derivatives, provide simple and accessible disclosures and be easy to understand; incentives

419 FSA, *Policy Statement 7/11, The Responsibilities of Providers and Distributors for the Fair Treatment of Customers* (London: FSA, 2007).

420 R.S. Karmel, "Mutual Funds, Pension Funds and Stock Market Volatility – What Regulation by the Securities and Exchange Commission is Appropriate?," *Notre Dame Law Review*, 80 (2005), 909–49, 918.

421 Stronger arguments can be made in relation to the consumer finance markets given the ubiquity and necessity of basic banking and credit products. For a leading analysis, see E. Warren, "Product Safety Regulation as a Model for Financial Services Regulation," *Journal of Consumer Affairs*, 42 (2008), 452–60.

422 Illustrating the clash between the neo-classical economics view and a more behaviorally-oriented view, see R. Epstein, "The Neoclassical Economics of Consumer Contracts," *Minnesota Law Review*, 92 (2008), 803–58 and O. Bar Gill, "The Behavioral Economics of Consumer Contracts," ibid., 749–802.

were provided in the form of a streamlined approval process.[423] In June 2011, the Belgian regulator (the FSMA) called for the voluntary suspension by the industry of retail distribution of structured products which it deemed to be "needlessly complex."[424] In France, the AMF has targeted the distribution of "complex" products (mainly structured products and complex debt securities) to retail investors. In an October 2010 "position,"[425] the AMF in effect prohibited the marketing of complex[426] structured products to investors. Some industry anxiety concerning the current direction of travel can be read in the 2011 re-release of the principles which the industry Joint Association Committee adopted in 2008 concerning the distribution/investor relationship and provider/distributor relationship with respect to structured products.[427]

Horizontal product intervention measures have also been developed. In January 2011 the UK FSA launched a "new and more intrusive approach" to the retail markets in the form of a new "product intervention" regime.[428] It reflected the FSA's post-crisis adoption of a more intrusive, outcomes-based and pre-emptive approach to conduct regulation generally,[429] and the adoption over 2010–11 of a more interventionist approach to consumer detriment in order to engage with the

[423] Summary available online: www.consob.it.

[424] A product is needlessly complex where: the valuation of the underlying assets is not easily accessible; the investment strategy is too complicated (because of leverage, conditionality, lack of upward and downward symmetry, or initial temporary higher yields); the yield calculation formula is based on more than three components; or there is a lack of transparency about costs or risks: Allen & Overy, "Belgian FSMA launches voluntary moratorium on the distribution of complex retail structured products" (July 2010, online: http://www.allenovery.comarchive/Documents).

[425] AMF Position No. 2010–05. While non-binding, the position can be relied on in court proceedings, and has been followed by the industry: R. Jory, "New Regulations leave Retail Structured Products on Shaky Ground in France," *Financial Risk Management News and Analysis*, April 21, 2011.

[426] Four criteria determine a product's complexity: poor disclosure of the product's risk and payout profile; lack of familiarity with the product linked to the underlying assets used; the dependence of a payout on the simultaneous occurrence of several conditions across two or more asset classes; the number of mechanisms in the payout formula.

[427] Joint Associations Committee, *Combined Principles for Retail Structured Products* (2011).

[428] FSA, *Discussion Paper 11/1, Product Intervention* (2011) (London: FSA, 2011), p. 3. It was widely reported in the financial press as a major change. e.g., B. Masters, A. Ross and T. Powley, "Scandals Prompted Shift to New Rules," *Financial Times*, June 25, 2011, 3.

[429] Set out in a key speech by then FSA Chief Executive H. Sants, "UK Financial Regulation: After the Crisis" (March 12, 2010, online: www.fsa.gov.uk/pages/Library/Communication/Speeches/2010/0312_hs.shtml).

UK's experience of repeated cycles of mis-selling and of ex-post reform and redress.[430] The product intervention strategy was designed to use rules and regulatory oversight to intervene early in the product "value chain." It signalled a "decisive shift in [the FSA's] tolerance for the amount of actual harm or detriment we are prepared to allow happen."[431] The new model did not propose general ex-ante licensing of retail market products, but was "pitched between a strategy that relies on point-of-sale interventions and one that relies on product pre-approval."[432] "Product governance" forms one part of the strategy, and involves regulatory oversight of the product design process. The second strand is more intrusive, and comprises a range of product intervention techniques culminating, as a last resort, in pre-approval and prohibition techniques for specific products. This double-headed strategy has been adopted by the incoming FCA.[433] Its chief executive designate has taken a robust and ambitious approach, suggesting in early 2012 that product intervention could follow where a product was "inherently flawed" and contained disadvantageous features, where widespread selling to inappropriately targeted consumers took place and where strong incentives for mis-selling existed.[434] The related primary legislation proposals, contained in the 2012 Financial Services Bill, reflect this new "early and proactive" approach to the retail markets and the related "fundamental shift in approach"[435] and provide for new product intervention powers, including product prohibition powers.[436] The FCA will be permitted to prohibit products, or to impose requirements on products, where "necessary and expedient," to advance its consumer protection or competition objectives. Although the UK government has been careful to emphasize that the new regime does not imply a move towards product pre-approval generally, citing risks in terms of resources, costs and limitations on choice,[437] and has underlined that the product intervention powers are not to be used routinely,[438] a decisive

[430] e.g., FSA, *Annual Report 2010/2011* (London: FSA, 2011), p. 67.

[431] FSA, *Product Intervention*, p. 20.

[432] Ibid., p. 21.

[433] FCA, *Approach to Regulation.*

[434] M. Wheatley, "My Vision for the FCA" (speech, January 25, 2012, online: www.fsa.gov.uk/library/communication/speeches).

[435] Noted in the precursor HM Treasury, *A New Approach – Building a Stronger System*, p. 60.

[436] Financial Services Bill, clause 137C.

[437] HM Treasury, *A New Approach – Building*, p. 71.

[438] HM Treasury, *A New Approach – Securing Stability*, p. 31.

shift towards product-related intervention is underway. There seems to be some support for the governance/oversight strand of the UK reform, in particular, across the EU's regulators.[439] June 2011 saw the Dutch government announce proposals for the Dutch regulator to supervise the development of new financial products through design-oversight techniques.[440]

EU retail policy is following this direction. A product governance/oversight model, similar to the UK and Dutch models, was proposed in December 2010 under the MiFID Review. The review suggested that the general organizational and risk management requirements which apply to MiFID-scope product providers be enhanced and extended to capture the particular risks raised by product design. This was adopted in the MiFID Directive Proposal.[441] Product prohibition powers are also being proposed. The MiFID Regulation Proposal has suggested that national regulators be given the power to prohibit or restrict the marketing or sale of financial instruments where significant investor protection concerns arise, or a serious threat is posed to the orderly functioning and integrity of financial markets or to the stability of part or the whole of the financial system. Conditions apply in that existing EU rules must not sufficiently address the risk, and the risk cannot be addressed by improvements in supervision or enforcement. The action must also be proportionate to the risks identified, the level of sophistication of investors or market participants, and the likely effect of the action on investors and market participants. Regulators must also consult with other Member State authorities who may be significantly affected and the action must not have a discriminatory effect on services or activities provided from another Member State.[442] The MiFID Regulation Proposal also empowers ESMA to intervene in national markets by temporarily prohibiting the marketing or sale of financial instruments in similar circumstances[443] and also confers coordination powers on ESMA with respect to national authority prohibition powers.[444] This radical new ESMA power, which represents a significant ratcheting upwards of the

[439] The FSA has reported interest in its approach from other EU regulators: *Feedback Statement 11/3, Product Intervention. Feedback* (2011) (London: FSA, 2011), p. 20.

[440] The AFM would monitor whether new products are cost-efficient, what well-grounded purpose they would serve, whether they would function as intended, and whether they were intelligible for the intended investor.

[441] MiFID Proposal, art. 9. [442] MiFIR Proposal, art. 32.

[443] Ibid., art. 31. [444] Ibid., art. 33.

new authority's powers over national markets,[445] relates to the general enabling clause in the foundation ESMA Regulation, which empowers ESMA temporarily to prohibit or restrict certain financial activities, as specified in relevant EU legislation (ESMA Regulation, Article 9) – although this power, notably, is linked to financial stability risks, and not to the investor protection concerns to which the proposed MiFID Regulation Proposal is directed. ESMA appears ready to embrace these new powers; the initial, agenda-setting statements by ESMA's newly-appointed chairman in early 2011 suggested that Article 9 was a priority power for ESMA and that it would be willing to take action against high commission products where negative outcomes were likely for investors.[446]

Horizontal measures under MiFID aside, more specific product intervention initiatives are underway with respect to two classes of retail market product: structured UCITS funds and exchange-traded funds (ETFs). Structured UCITS funds form part of the wider universe of structured products in that the pay-off to investors is linked to the performance of underlying assets.[447] The new summary disclosure regime for UCITS (the "Key Investor Information Document" (KIID)) which came into force in 2010, contains distinct requirements for "structured UCITS."[448] Structured UCITS are also addressed by ESMA's proposed 2012 Guidance on UCITS and Exchange-Traded Funds, which

[445] See E. Ferran, "Understanding the New Institutional Architecture of EU Financial Market Supervision," in E. Wymeersch, K. J. Hopt and G. Ferrarini, *Financial Regulation and Supervision: A Post-Crisis Analysis* (Oxford University Press, 2012), and N. Moloney, "The European Securities and Markets Authority and Institutional Design for the EU Financial Market – A Tale of Two Competences: Part (2) Rules in Action," *European Business Organization Law Review*, 12 (2011), 177–225.

[446] N. Tait, "ESMA Watchdog prepared to Clash with Brussels," March 2, 2011, online: www.FT.com, and R. Froynovich, "ESMA to be Strongly Independent," March 2, 2011 (quoting Chairman Maijoor as stating that "we need to have an eye, and it needs to improve, on serving the interest of the financial consumer and retail investor"), online: http://WSJ.com. Similarly, ESMA Executive Director Verena Ross has welcomed the proposed powers as a "major leap forward": V. Ross, "Strengthening Investor Protection" (speech, December 5, 2011, online: www.esma.europa.eu/system/files/2012–77.pdf).

[447] Structured UCITS are defined under the UCITS regime as UCITS which provide investors, at certain predetermined dates, with algorithmic-based payoffs that are linked to the performance, or to the realization of price changes or other conditions, of financial assets, indices, or reference portfolios or UCITS with similar features: KII Regulation, Commission Regulation (EU) No. 583/2010, [2010] L176/1, art. 36.

[448] Ibid. In particular, the KIID must include explanations of the payout formula and different performance scenarios.

highlights the need for such funds to comply with the diversification and risk management rules which apply to UCITS generally.[449] But more interventionist measures look set to follow. MiFID's execution-only regime, which requires that only "non-complex" products can be sold without a suitability assessment, currently includes all UCITS as eligible non-complex investments. The 2010 MiFID Review originally queried whether the execution-only regime should be abolished, or whether it should be retained but with the exclusion of particular UCITS which employ more complex portfolio management techniques.[450] The 2011 MiFID Directive Proposal has taken a more limited approach, excluding only structured UCITS from the execution-only regime.[451] The issues raised by any change to the designation of UCITS as "non-complex" are many and complex. The risk of detriment to the consumer sector, following the stretching of the UCITS brand to include funds with complex and high-risk portfolio management techniques, in particular hedge fund-like products,[452] and the use by banks of complex UCITS products to generate balance-sheet-repairing revenues,[453] is potentially significant. There is support for the exclusion of structured UCITS from the execution-only regime from leading regulators[454] and consumer stakeholders.[455] But industry opposition is fierce, given the potential damage to the UCITS brand globally.[456] The wider consequential impact

[449] ESMA, *Consultation on Guidance on ETFs and other UCITS Issues* (ESMA/2012/220).

[450] European Commission, *MiFID Review*, pp. 54–6.

[451] MiFID Proposal, art. 25.

[452] This development has been extensively reported, e.g., E. Kelleher, "Listed Funds of Hedge Funds lose out to UCITS III," *Financial Times Fund Management Supplement*, April 18, 2011, 8. The leverage capacity of one UCITS fund, which holds a total return swap on a proprietary index that can be leveraged up to 35 times, while permissible, has been described by some industry figures as "horrid" and "extraordinary": S. Johnson, "Swaps Tactic threatens UCITS Brand," *Financial Times Fund Supplement*, November 14, 2011, 1.

[453] P. Skypala, "What will the Banks think of Next?" *Financial Times Fund Management Supplement*, November 14, 2011, 6.

[454] France's AMF has supported the treatment of structured UCITS as "complex" investments falling outside the execution-only regime (AMF, *Response to MiFID Review*, online: http://ec.europa.eu/internal_market/consultations/2010/mifid_en.htm.), and there is some support across the Member States: European Securities Committee, Minutes, April 2011.

[455] e.g., the responses by BEUC (the major EU consumer association) and Euroinvestors, in their responses to MiFID Review: Responses, online: http://ec.europa.eu/internal_market/consultations/2010/mifid_en.htm.

[456] e.g., the responses by the Association of British Insurers and the European Fund and Asset Managers Associator to the MiFID Review, online: http://ec.europa.eu/internal_market/consultations/2010/mifid_en.htm.

on UCITS regulation generally, which assumes that the UCITS product is a gold-standard retail market product, is considerable, as reflected in CESR's extreme nervousness in addressing this question.[457] ESMA, however, appears ready to take up the gauntlet.[458] The MiFID II proposal to remove structured UCITS from the execution-only regime accordingly highlights the adoption of a significantly more robust approach to the retail product market.

The emerging EU agenda for ETFs also illustrates the growing importance of product-related intervention. ETFs are open-ended UCITS funds which track an index or benchmark. When they were originally designed in the 1990s, they followed a relatively simple structure and were designed to track equity and bond indices. The ETF sector has experienced very strong growth globally (on average 40 percent annual growth over the last 10 years) and has become considerably more complex.[459] ETFs now address a wide range of sectors and assets, use physical or synthetic (derivative-based) techniques[460] to replicate indices, can rely heavily on leverage, and are increasingly engaging in securities-lending activities.[461] In a clear example of the closer focus on the potential of innovative products to generate risks, and notwithstanding the relatively small size of the EU ETF market and its predominantly institutional base,[462] closer EU regulatory attention has followed in the wake of the crisis, particularly with respect to retail market risk. Internationally, the FSB and IMF have highlighted the potential stability risks arising from ETF exposure to counterparty risk and from market illiquidity and called for careful monitoring.[463] But in the EU, ETF innovation and complexity is also being associated with retail market risks. At Member State level, the FSA and the Dutch regulator have highlighted the increased retailization of these products and the complexity risks which

457 e.g., CESR, *Advice on the MiFID Review* (2010) (CESR/10–859), declining to give the Commission formal technical advice on this question, given the complexities involved.

458 O. Lodge, "EU Financial Regulator tries to mend UCITS III," *Financial Times Fund Management Supplement*, August 8, 2011, 11.

459 IMF, *Global Financial Stability Report, April 2011* (Washington DC: IMF, 2011), p. 68.

460 Some 45 percent of EU ETFs are synthetic, with the index tracking being provided by an OTC derivative provided by a counterparty; the derivative is typically supported by collateral: FSB, *Potential Financial Stability Issues arising from Recent Trends in ETFs* (Basel: FSB, 2011), p. 2.

461 FSB, *Recent Trends in ETFs* and IMF, *Global Financial Stability Report, April 2011*, pp. 68–72.

462 N. Amenc, F. Ducoulombier, F. Goltz and L. Tang, *What are the Risks of European ETFs?* (Nice: EDHEC-Risk Institute, 2012).

463 n. 461 above.

they pose.[464] At EU level, intervention is planned. In 2012, ESMA produced guidance on ETFs.[465] Although ESMA's guidance is based on the disclosure model predominant pre-crisis, indications of a more robust approach which may come are evident in the identification of ETFs as a product in need of closer attention, and in the warning that ESMA may require product prohibition powers in this field.[466] Certainly the adoption by ESMA of a disclosure-based approach, which came as a relief to the industry,[467] might be related to its concern to wait for parallel work on the MiFID Review to complete[468] rather than to a wider lack of enthusiasm for product-related intervention. The trend towards pre-emptive intervention is all the more revealing as ETFs currently represent only a small part of the wider fund market.[469]

Has distrust of innovation led to a productive consumer market reform?

The array of new product intervention techniques, from the variety of Member State product prohibition and governance initiatives to the EU's product prohibition and execution-only reforms, to the product-specific initiatives with respect to ETFs and structured UCITS, all share a common concern with complexity and with innovative products. They can be associated with distrust of financial engineering and of innovation, and with an alignment between the complexity which innovation can generate, and potential detriment in the retail markets. Whether this distrust of innovation will lead to positive retail market outcomes is not yet clear.

The consumer or retail markets pose intractable problems to the regulator. Regulators are hobbled by an unhelpful retail cohort with limited ability to monitor risk and carry risk-monitoring responsibilities, limited (although increasing) information on retail investor behavior, high political risks and blunt distribution and disclosure-based regulatory tools which, as repeated failures make clear, struggle to address the

[464] FSA, *Retail Conduct Risk Outlook 2011*, pp. 69–71 and AMF, *2011 Risk and Trend Mapping for Financial Markets and Savings* (Paris: AMF, 2011), p. 6.

[465] ESMA, *Consultation on Guidance on ETFs and other UCITS Issues* (ESMA/2012/220). The *Guidance* reflected an earlier *Discussion Paper* (ESMA/2011/220). The EBA has also highlighted the potential retail markets risks from ETFs: EBA, *Financial Innovation and Consumer Protection*, Annex 2.

[466] Noted in the earlier ESMA, *Discussion Paper* (ESMA/2011/220), p. 6.

[467] e.g., Flood, "Regulator goes easy on ETFs," *Financial Times Fund Management Supplement*, January 30, 2012, 1.

[468] ESMA, *Consultation on ETF Guidance*, p. 7.

[469] EBA, *Financial Innovation and Consumer Protection*, Annex 2, para. 3.4 and n. 462 above.

significant market failures in the retail investment product market.[470] Behavioral risks are severe and significant, as a now massive canon of literature and a rapidly growing empirical data-set makes clear.[471] Incentive risks remain considerable in the retail markets, particularly given the strong commercial incentives for banks to design investment products, and provide related asset management services, given the revenue-generation and balance sheet-repairing benefits.[472] At first glance, the range of tools associated with product intervention, from governance/design oversight tools to outright prohibition powers, looks promising, particularly as there are few indications that the EU or its Member States are moving to a full-scale ex-ante product licensing regime with its attendant risks.[473] It is also the case that investment advice/product distribution poses complex problems for the regulator given the range of issues engaged, from industry structure and incentive issues (particularly with respect to commission payments), to access difficulties, to the ability and/or willingness of households to engage with investment advice.[474] Product

[470] The FSA's historical reliance (in common with other EU regulators) on disclosure and sales regulation has been described as "inadequate to meet the expectations of society with respect to protecting consumers in financial matters": then FSA Chief Executive Sants, "Creating the FCA" (speech, March 2, 2011, online: www.fsa.gov.uk/pages/Library/Communication/Speeches/2011/0302_hs.shtml).

[471] In the crisis-era context, see Kingsford Smith, *Regulating Investment Risk* and pre-crisis, e.g., J. Campbell, "Household Finance," *Journal of Finance*, 61 (2006), 1553–604 and S. M. Bainbridge, "Whither Securities Regulation? Some Behavioural Observations Regarding Proposals for its Future," *Duke Law Journal*, 51 (2002), 1397–511.

[472] The FSA has highlighted the related risks to consumers: FSA, *Retail Conduct Risk Outlook 2011* (London: FSA, 2011), pp. 75–6, while the European Systemic Risk Board (ESRB) has highlighted the systemic risks linked to banks' incentives to market complex products to retail investors: O. Burkart and A. Bouveret, *Systemic Risk due to Retailization* (Frankfort: ESRB, 2012).

[473] The MiFID Proposals' Impact Assessment expressly ruled out ex-ante licensing as an EU obligation, given moral hazard, innovation and opportunity cost risks: European Commission, *MiFID Proposals Impact Assessment*, p. 135.

[474] Two recent examples highlight the difficulties which can arise, particularly with respect to the current efforts to address unbiased, independent investment advice.

A recent large-scale study of the supply of independent investment advice in Germany to circa 8,000 clients of a retail brokerage has suggested that those retail investors who need investment advice are the least likely to obtain it, while those who do obtain it hardly ever follow the advice: U. Bhattacharya, A. Hackenthal, S. Kaesler, B. Loos and S. Meyer, "Is Unbiased Financial Advice to Retail Investors Sufficient? Answers from a Large Field Study" (September 2011, online: http://ssrn.com/abstract=1669015).

In the UK context, the large-scale restructuring of investment advice under the Retail Distribution Review by the removal of commission payments, and by a requirement that all advice be fee-based, has generated concerns that an "advice gap" will accordingly open up, given investor reluctance to pay for advice (and their inability to understand the rationale of a fee) which may prejudice the most vulnerable segment of the retail

regulation may, accordingly, provide a means of ensuring better outcomes for those investors who do not access advice. But product intervention is an unwieldy and untested tool and may have unexpected effects.

It may be that the new products agenda comes to engage and energize the EU's domestic retail market regulators, ESMA and the EU's law-making institutions; the June 2011 launch document for the UK's new FCA, even allowing for the need for the FCA to make an early impression, is striking in its apparent determination for a new approach to the retail markets, a large element of which is associated with the new products agenda. But product intervention, whether governance/design oversight-based or prohibition-based, implies that the regulator can second-guess weaknesses in the retail product market. Expectations may accordingly be unrealistically high. In the UK, the new FCA appears alert to this risk, warning that it will need to communicate that it cannot guarantee a return on a product deemed suitable,[475] the UK government has warned that the FCA will not be a "zero failure" regulator,[476] and the FCA chief executive designate has similarly underlined that product intervention does not absolve retail investors of responsibility or ensure a "zero failure regime."[477] But the nuances of product intervention may be lost on retail investors, particularly given the prominence which the new strategy is receiving and which might, indeed, be regarded as representing a degree of "product marketing" by the new FCA with respect to the potential of its new toolkit.

The very newness of product intervention may lead to an overly ambitious and heavy-handed approach; the new FCA's proposed focus on "inherently flawed" products certainly suggests a regulator with considerable ambitions in this field, and which might outrun the realities of what is achievable. This is all the more likely as product-related intervention, of whatever type, may prove to be more politically tractable than structural distribution-related reforms. Acute political and industry interests are at stake with the current wave of distribution-related reforms. At Member State level, the FSA's Retail Distribution Review faced significant industry opposition, with the FSA placed under significant political pressure, reflecting vigorous lobbying from the advice industry, to postpone implementation until 2014.[478] While the FSA successfully resisted this pressure, the

investor community: Treasury Select Committee, *15th Report, The Retail Distribution Review* (2011).

[475] FCA, *Approach to Regulation*, p. 21.

[476] HM Treasury, *A New Approach – Building*, p. 69. [477] Wheatley, "FCA."

[478] House of Commons, Treasury Committee, *Report. Retail Distribution Review* (2011).

political hostility towards it was considerable. At EU level, the MiFID Directive Proposal's proposition to abolish adviser commissions with respect to independent investment advice has generated sharp conflicts between the Member States, notably the Netherlands (in favour of a ban) and France (concerned as to the impact on its asset management industry).[479] While the new product powers are typically subject to stringent (if somewhat open-ended) conditions, as the MiFID Regulation Proposal's product prohibition powers underline, the new generation of powers may prove attractive to regulators seeking "quick wins" in the retail markets. But the incentive risks associated with product design are significant, particularly in the current climate as banks turn to product design to support revenues, and are likely to be no easier to resolve than incentive risks in the distribution process.[480] The risks to supervisory effectiveness will be all the greater if the new regime enmeshes the regulator in complex, detailed and resource incentive oversight of industry product development processes, with the attendant moral hazard and resource risk to the regulator.

Retail investor outcomes will also not be enhanced if regulators overlook long-standing distribution problems in their rush to deploy the new product intervention tools. The MiFID Directive Proposal does little to address directly the structural conflict of interest risks which continue to trouble the "financial supermarket" product distribution model which dominates in the EU, and which is based on proprietary product sales. It focuses instead on the "independent advice" model,[481] which dominates only in the UK market (which accounts for 60 percent of all independent investment advisers)[482] where the Retail Distribution Review is already bringing major industry change.[483] While there are many drivers of the new MiFID regime, it is not unreasonable to suggest

[479] R. Sullivan, "European States at Odds over Commission," *Financial Times Fund Management Supplement*, July 18, 2011, 3. ECOFIN's June 2012 Progress Report on the MiFID II negotiations noted little progress on this matter (ECOFIN 11536/12).

[480] FSA, *Retail Product Development and Governance. Structured Product Review* (London: FSA, 2011), reporting on persistent difficulties in the structured product design process and, overall, that firms were emphasizing their commercial position at the expense of consumer outcomes.

[481] The MiFID Proposal introduces requirements that investment advisers declare whether their advice is "independent" or "restricted" and also, as noted above, prohibits the payment of commissions when "independent advice" is delivered: art. 24.

[482] Commission, *MiFID Proposals Impact Assessment*, Annex.

[483] Retail stakeholder disquiet as to the failure to address proprietary product distribution has been significant: J. Woolfe, "Widespread Belief MiFID II set to Fail Retail Investors," *Financial Times Fund Management Supplement*, January 30, 2012, 8.

that the new focus on product design has led to less attention being directed to the long-standing difficulties posed by product distribution.

Product intervention can also be associated with a more intrusive approach to retail investor risk-taking. The placing of restrictions on the distribution of products to the public is a common feature of retail marketing regimes, but the perimeter for retail marketing is usually drawn very widely. The most high-profile example in the EU relates to the restrictions which apply in most Member States to hedge fund-related investments and which have been preserved by the AIFMD.[484] The new generation of intervention powers, however, imply that a wider group of products might face restrictions on retail distribution. Making a determination as to whether a product is not suitable for retail distribution, whether through governance/design oversight powers or prohibition powers, demands of the regulator that choices are made as to the optimum levels of risk and choice in the retail market. The new UK regime provides a useful example. The FCA's proposed statutory regime requires that it secure "an appropriate degree of protection" for consumers, and have regard to "the general principle that consumers should take responsibility for their decisions."[485] The government has similarly emphasized consumer responsibility and that the regulator should not take responsibility for consumer decisions.[486] But it is clear nonetheless that UK retail market protection is being reoriented from its previous empowerment-driven model[487] to a more protective model, and that a reconsideration of the levels of risk which retail investors should carry is underway. The new products regime is based on a political determination that regulatory tolerance of retail market risk and of mis-selling must reduce.[488] But it generates difficult questions as to where the balance should lie between product intervention and supporting innovation and choice.[489] The new FCA has similarly warned that the new approach will require judgment-led trade-offs between supporting the investor protection needs of some investors and reducing the investor choice needs of others.[490] In a similar vein, FSA Chairman Turner has warned that the more a regulator

[484] AIFMD, art. 31. [485] Financial Services Bill, clause 1C(2).

[486] HM Treasury, *A New Approach – Building*, pp. 60 and 62.

[487] e.g., J. Gray and J. Hamilton, *Implementing Financial Regulation* (Chichester: Wiley, 2006), pp. 188–225.

[488] HM Treasury, *A New Approach – The Blueprint*, p. 12.

[489] FSA, *Product Intervention*, p. 20. The FSA has acknowledged that there are "no easy answers": FSA, *Product Intervention Feedback*, p. 23.

[490] FCA, *Approach to Regulation*, p. 7.

intervenes in defence of the consumer interest, using more intrusive powers, the more the regulator makes crucial trade-off choices on behalf of society which are judgmental and political.[491] Then FSA Chief Executive Sants likewise warned that forward-looking judgments can, with hindsight, be questioned, and called for acceptance of this new reality by society and government.[492] However, the inherent difficulty and visibility of these choices at EU and Member State levels as the new powers are tested may bring a welcome prominence to retail market regulation.

Difficult regulatory design choices also arise. Governing concepts can be difficult to capture. Complexity risk is emerging as a key theme of the wave of EU and Member State product-related reforms, with complexity becoming a proxy for "excessive" retail market risk.[493] But complexity is difficult to capture. The UK has struggled for years with how to use regulatory and market mechanisms to deliver "simple" investment products which can be price-capped and sold through a simplified advice process; appropriate targeting of these products can be difficult, price caps diminish industry interest, accompanying and diluted regulatory regimes have proved problematic in terms of cost and legal risks, and levels of consumer interest, given limited industry incentives to market, can be low.[494] The US reform process, and hostility to the new Consumer Financial Protection Bureau,[495] underlines the significant difficulties attendant on regulator approval of a suite of "plain vanilla" or simple consumer finance products. The French AMF's 2010 prohibition of the distribution of complex structured products

[491] A. Turner, "Chairman's speech" (June 23, 2011, online: www.fsa.gov.uk/pages/Library/Communication/Speeches/2011/0623_at.shtml).

[492] Sants, "Twin Peaks."

[493] The FSA's product intervention model assumes that product complexity can be an indicator of problematic product features, although it acknowledges that complexity may be necessary to obtain benefits for the consumer: FSA, *Product Intervention*, p. 30. The Member State initiatives noted above similarly associate complexity with risk or promote simplicity.

[494] J. Devlin, *A Report for HM Treasury, Literature Review on Lessons Learned from Previous "Simple Products" Initiatives* (2010). Recently, renewed effort has been made to address the "simple products" conundrum: Sergeant Review of Simple Products, *Interim Report* (London: 2012).

[495] e.g., M. Jacoby, "Dodd-Frank, Regulatory Innovation, and the Safety of Consumer Financial Products," *North Carolina Banking Institute Journal*, 15 (2011), 99–110. Political hostility has been considerable, particularly from congressional Republicans. President Obama's appointment of Consumer Financial Protection Bureau chief Richard Cordray was made while Congress was in recess in January 2012 in order to defeat a veto by Senate Republicans: *New York Times*, "Editorial," January 4, 2011, online: www.nytimes.com.

has been criticized for relying on subjective criteria.[496] And some degree of complexity in the markets is good for investors and can deliver results. Innovation which, however complex, allows investors to achieve higher returns and better risk management, should not be obstructed. Robert Shiller has suggested that the necessary democratization of finance post-crisis calls for a focus on "creatively extending the capitalist principles of risk management so that they really work for everyone...[i]t means an adventure in financial innovation."[497] Synthetic ETFs, for example, can reduce the transaction costs and tracking errors associated with ETFs which physically track indices, while ETFs generally can support diversification and risk management by facilitating investor access to a wider range of assets and geographic sectors.[498] In the EU context, care is all the more important in associating complexity with investor detriment given the parallel movement to support fee-based investment advice by prohibition of commission, as this may lead to enhancements in the quality of investment advice and so soften complexity risks. Important determinants of investor outcomes also arise beyond complexity. The extent to which market risks were borne by households over the crisis suggests that close attention should be paid to diversification. The extent to which conflict of interest risk can lead to mis-selling also suggests that how commission and costs are embedded into a product's return should be addressed.

And how far can intervention, whether with respect to product governance/design oversight or product prohibition, be taken? To take the FCA example, when is a product "inherently flawed?" Is intervention appropriate where there is "too much" choice in the market and thus a risk of confusion? Might distrust of innovation and related financial intensification lead to judgments that products which do not appear to enhance investor choice and serve "only" profit-generation functions, but which are not inherently dangerous to retail investors, be restricted in the interests of addressing investor confusion? The implications for productive innovation, as well as for regulatory power and accountability, may be significant. The proposed new UK product regime is hedged about with references to "appropriate and proportionate" action, to consumer responsibility, and with reassurances that the new regime will not replace distribution regulation.[499] The proposed MiFID Regulation Proposal prohibition power is

[496] Jory, "New Regulations." [497] Shiller, *Democratizing*, p. 43.

[498] IMF, *Global Financial Stability Report, April 2011*, p. 68.

[499] The latter in legislation and the former in the policy discussion: HM Treasury, *A New Approach – The Blueprint*, p. 31 and HM Treasury, *A New Approach – Securing Stability*, p. 31.

similarly constrained. But any new power is likely to generate significant momentum. Execution risk is significant unless considerable regulatory resources are devoted to consideration of when products are likely to be problematic, and carefully designed safeguards apply.[500]

The leakage risks may also be considerable. It may be that the product agenda is beginning to influence the treatment of issuer disclosure, with some hints of a resurgence of merit-style disclosure regulation which hitherto has not had traction in the EU. The 2010 reforms to the Prospectus Directive address the "base prospectus" which is used by repeat issuers of program-based securities and facilitates rapid issuance of securities on the basis of a short-form "final terms" disclosure document when market conditions are appropriate. The reforms provide for delegated rules to address the relationship between base prospectus disclosures and those disclosures which can be included in the final terms document, which is not reviewed by a competent authority, and those disclosures which must be made in a base prospectus supplement, which is. The market favors a light touch regime which allows issuers flexibility. ESMA, however, has advised that more disclosures should be in the base prospectus and subject to review and that complex disclosures (including algebraic formulae related to products) be reviewed for comprehensibility, consistency and completeness.[501] ESMA has underlined that the Prospectus Directive does not empower competent authorities to make an economic assessment of a product in reviewing prospectus disclosures. But it may be difficult to draw a line between assessing the clarity and comprehensibility of product disclosure, and assessing whether the complexity of a product is such that it is not suitable for a public offering.

The difficulties should not detract from the merits of the new approach. Given repeated failures in the EU retail markets, the airing of a new strategy can only be a good thing. But the potential reach of the new generation of product intervention powers, combined with distrust of intensity and innovation, may lead to over-reaction. Careful testing and challenge of these new tools will be required.

V: Conclusion

The financial crisis has led to a significant reform of EU financial system regulation. The nature of this reform has been well charted with respect

[500] Industry respondents to the UK government's consultation on the new product intervention powers revealed concerns related to legal certainty, proportionality, choice, competitiveness and innovation: HM Treasury, *A New Approach – The Blueprint*.

[501] ESMA, *Final Prospectus Advice*, paras. 142–145.

to the first-generation suite of financial-stability reforms. This chapter, however, charts how the crisis era has led to a subsequent suite of second-generation reforms to market regulation and to consumer protection regulation, and assesses the nature of the regulatory innovation which has followed.

While some refreshing of cognate regulatory fields would have been expected as a result of the crisis, this chapter reveals the extent of the spillover effects of the financial stability phase on EU financial system regulation. In particular, it charts how transformative regulatory innovation, in the form of a third-level resetting of the underpinning objectives of market regulation and of consumer protection regulation to reflect a policy suspicion of market intensity and financial innovation, is underway and is influencing associated technical first- and second-level regulatory changes.

As Part II considers, the second-generation reforms can be located within a policy framework in which financial market intensity and innovation are under close scrutiny. This fundamental regulatory innovation has led to different technical regulatory innovations. In the market regulation sphere, it has led to a significant expansion of the regulatory perimeter. In the consumer protection sphere, it has led to the adoption of a new suite of retail market regulatory tools related to product intervention.

As with financial innovation and market intensity, these regulatory innovations are neither wholly good nor wholly bad. In the market regulation sphere, while the rapid and simultaneous imposition of new rules on a new range of trading venues and asset classes carries a series of risks, notably to liquidity, it may improve supervisory effectiveness, while the new focus on the equity markets may lead to enhancements. Similarly in the consumer protection field, new regulatory thinking has been long overdue. The dangers of an overly repressive approach to product intervention may be balanced by the emergence, in time, of a more imaginative approach to the consumer investment markets. The risks are, however, real. Identification, therefore, of the scale of the second-generation reforms, and of the connection which they have to a wider distrust of innovation and intensity, may prove useful in identifying the risks which the new regime poses as it matures and in designing the review of the crisis-era suite of measures to which the EU has committed itself.

3

Why did Australia fare so well in the global financial crisis?

JENNIFER G. HILL*

I: Introduction

The history of corporate governance is also a history of crises and scandals.

Klaus J. Hopt[1]

Australia provides an intriguing case study in relation to the global financial crisis. At first sight, at least, Australia appears to have withstood the crisis remarkably well, living up to its famous description as "the lucky country."[2] This has been the source of numerous laudatory statements by government officials and others throughout the global financial crisis. In 2008, the Governor of Reserve Bank of Australia commented, for example, that "there would be very few countries, if any, which would not envy Australia's fiscal position."[3]

Although the impact of the financial crisis has been less severe in Australia than in many other jurisdictions, including common law jurisdictions such as the United Kingdom and the United States, it cannot be said that Australia escaped the crisis unscathed. There were, for example, a

* I would like to thank a number of people for helpful suggestions, references and comments in relation to this project. Particular thanks go to Joanna Bird, Ron Masulis, John Stumbles and John Trowbridge, and also to Merilyn Alt, Ross Clare, John Keeves, Greg O'Mahoney, Warren Scott and Richard Vann. I am also grateful to Nikki Chong, Alice Grey and Chelsea Tabart for their excellent research and editorial assistance.

1 K. J. Hopt, "Comparative corporate governance: the state of the art and international regulation," *American Journal of Comparative Law*, 59 (2011), 1–72, at 4–5.

2 D. Horne, *The Lucky Country* (Melbourne: Penguin Books, 1964).

3 G. Stevens, "The Australian economy: then and now," address by Glenn Stevens, the Governor of the Reserve Bank of Australia, to the Inaugural Faculty of Economics and Business Alumni Dinner, the University of Sydney, May 15, 2008, p. 7, available at www.rba.gov.au/speeches/2008/sp-gov-150508.html.

number of high-profile corporate collapses.[4] Also, more recently, messages concerning the state of the Australian economy have become decidedly mixed.[5] There is a growing perception that economic performance is uneven,[6] and that there exists a widening "two speed"[7] or "multi-speed"[8] economy, where "not everybody. . . is in the fast lane."[9] This refers to the fact that, in contrast to Australia's booming resources sector, large segments of the economy have experienced weak consumer spending in recent times.

Just over a decade ago, the influential "law matters" hypothesis appeared on the corporate governance horizon. Its central claim was that there is a direct link between the structure of capital markets and a country's corporate governance regime.[10] The hypothesis provided strong support for a theory of regulatory convergence.[11] It also predicted that convergence would proceed inevitably in the direction of common law legal systems, on the basis that they offered superior legal protection to investors than civil law systems.[12]

Since the time of the "law matters" study, two major crises, the collapse of Enron in 2001 and the global financial crisis, commencing in the US subprime market in 2007, have complicated the international

[4] See generally Parliamentary Joint Committee on Corporations and Financial Services (Australia), *Inquiry into Financial Products and Services in Australia* (Canberra: Commonwealth of Australia, 2009).

[5] *Cf.* A. Critchlow, "The view from Sydney: the upbeat outlook fades down under," *Wall Street Journal*, July 18, 2011, p. C7; and P. Smith, "Australia growth exceeds expectations," *Financial Times*, September 8, 2011, p. 10.

[6] See G. Stevens, "Still interesting times," address by Glenn Stevens, the Governor of the Reserve Bank of Australia, to the Chamber of Commerce and Industry (Western Australia) and the Chamber of Minerals and Energy (Western Australia) Corporate Breakfast, Perth, September 7, 2011, available at www.rba.gov.au/speeches/2011/sp-gov-070911.html.

[7] See S. Murdoch, "Stevens delivers a wake-up call on rates – Quarterly economic outlook," *The Australian*, June 16, 2011, p. 32.

[8] RBA, "Minutes of the monetary policy meeting of the Reserve Bank Board," July 5, 2011, p. 3, available at www.rba.gov.au/monetary-policy/rba-board-minutes/2011/05072011.html, stating that recent economic data, including economic and housing data, clearly demonstrated the "multi-speed nature of the Australian economy."

[9] W. Swan, "Transcript," press conference by Deputy Prime Minister and Treasurer Wayne Swan, Sydney, August 2, 2011, 1, available at www.treasurer.gov.au/DisplayDocs.aspx?doc=transcripts/2011/113.htm&pageID=004&min=wms&Year=&DocType=.

[10] See R. La Porta, F. Lopez-de-Silanes, A. Shleifer and R. Vishny, "Law and finance," *Journal of Political Economy*, 106 (1998), 1113–55; R. La Porta, F. Lopez-de-Silanes and A. Shleifer, "Corporate ownership around the world," *Journal of Finance*, 54 (1999), 471–517. Specifically, the "law matters" hypothesis argued that jurisdictions with a high level of minority investor protection would develop dispersed ownership structures, such as those existing in the United States and the United Kingdom. Ibid.

[11] See D. A. Skeel Jnr., "Corporate anatomy lessons," *Yale Law Journal*, 113 (2004), 1519–77, at 1544–5.

[12] See ibid.

regulatory picture. There is a close correlation between corporate crises and regulation and this is by no means new.[13] Indeed, it has been suggested that corporate crashes were the primary impetus for securities market reform in the United Kingdom and the United States for over three hundred years.[14] The development of Australia's corporate and financial market laws reflects the same phenomenon.[15]

Whereas the "law matters" hypothesis envisaged an orderly and predictable trend towards convergence, the current international regulatory scene is far more complex, involving a clear tension between convergent and divergent factors. First, events, such as the global financial crisis, can have a significant effect on law reform and enforcement, which in turn can create new divergence in laws.[16] The impact of the crisis may be different across jurisdictions. Also, the architecture of the regulatory responses may vary significantly depending upon the impact, background political pressures[17] and differing interpretations of the cause of the crisis. These path-dependent factors can drive reform experiments at a national level. This makes comparison between jurisdictions, such as the United Kingdom, United States and Australia, which have a similar common law heritage, interesting and fruitful.[18]

Second, regulation involves considerable unpredictability.[19] Even where similar reforms are introduced, they may operate differently across jurisdictions, due to variations in judicial interpretation, compliance levels and enforcement intensity.[20] Also, given the dynamic

[13] See, for example, Hopt, "Comparative corporate governance," 4–5.

[14] See S. Banner, "What causes new securities regulation? 300 years of evidence," *Washington University Law Quarterly*, 75 (1997), 849–55, at 850, arguing that populist mistrust of securities trading and speculation recedes in boom times, but resurfaces during market crises. Ibid., 850–1.

[15] See B. Bora and M. K. Lewis, "The Australian financial system: evolution, regulation and globalization," *Law & Policy in International Business*, 28 (1997), 787–811, at 798–9; J. G. Hill, "Regulatory responses to global corporate scandals," *Wisconsin International Law Journal*, 23 (2005), 367–416.

[16] This is hardly surprising. As has recently been noted, "a crisis is a terrible thing to waste" (K. Lannoo, "A crisis is a terrible thing to waste," Centre for European Policy Studies (CEPS) Commentaries, May 27, 2009).

[17] See D. C. Langevoort, "The social construction of Sarbanes-Oxley," *Michigan Law Review*, 105 (2007), 1817–55, at 1821; R. Romano, "The Sarbanes-Oxley Act and the making of quack corporate governance," *Yale Law Journal*, 114 (2005), 1521–611, at 1544*ff*.

[18] See L. C. B. Gower, "Some contrasts between British and American corporation law," *Harvard Law Review*, 69 (1956), 1369–402, at 1370, who stated: "[I]f there are sufficient basic similarities to make a comparison possible, there are, equally, sufficient differences to make it fruitful."

[19] See generally, Langevoort, "Social construction of Sarbanes-Oxley."

[20] See, for example, J. C. Coffee Jnr., "Law and the market: the impact of enforcement," *University of Pennsylvania Law Review*, 156 (2007), 229–311; H. E. Jackson, "Variation in

operation of regulation, the strategic responses of regulated parties, or commercial pushback, may also affect the operation of legal rules.[21]

Third, supranational regulation has become increasingly important. UK law, for example, has been significantly affected by European Union (EU) integration, and the EU's outpouring of directives in response to the global financial crisis.[22] Transgovernmental networks of financial regulators, such as the Financial Stability Board, have also been particularly influential during the crisis. In contrast to the "law matters" paradigm of regulatory imitation, transgovernmental regulation operates on the basis of global promulgation/national implementation of legal rules. Bilateral mutual recognition arrangements are also on the rise. Although these developments might suggest a shift towards greater convergence, there is still much scope for national differences to persist,[23] especially in terms of enforcement.[24]

Given Australia's relatively good economic performance during the global financial crisis, its regulatory response might have been muted. This has not, however, been the case. Rather, the crisis, and resultant loss of public confidence, provided a "mandate for regulatory change"[25] and the opportunity to reassess Australia's system of financial market regulation. In the United Kingdom, the *Turner Review* considered that the crisis challenged a central assumption concerning the market's efficiency, rationality and ability to self-regulate that had underpinned prior financial law.[26] This was equally true

the intensity of financial regulation: preliminary evidence and potential implications," *Yale Journal on Regulation*, 24 (2007), 253–90.

[21] See D. A. Skeel, "Governance in the ruin," *Harvard Law Review*, 122 (2008), 696–743, at 697; C. J. Milhaupt and K. Pistor, *Law and Capitalism: What Corporate Crises reveal about Legal Systems and Economic Development around the World* (University of Chicago Press, 2008).

[22] See E. Ferran, "Crisis-driven regulatory reform: where in the world is the EU going?", Chapter 1 above; N. Moloney, "The legacy effects of the financial crisis on regulatory design in the EU: regulatory innovation or regulatory over-reach," Chapter 2 above.

[23] See, for example, C. Brummer, "Post-American securities regulation," *California Law Review*, 98 (2010), 327–84; P. Verdier, "Mutual recognition in international finance," *Harvard International Law Journal*, 52 (2011), 55–108, at 65.

[24] Coffee Jnr., "Law and the market"; Jackson, "Variation in the intensity of financial regulation."

[25] T. D'Aloisio, "Regulatory response to the financial crisis," speech by Australian Securities and Investments Commission Chairman, Tony D'Aloisio, to the Asia Securities Forum, Sydney, October 12, 2009, p. 7.

[26] Financial Services Authority (UK), *The Turner Review: A Regulatory Response to the Global Banking Crisis* (London: FSA, 2009), p. 39*ff*.

in Australia,[27] with the crisis highlighting the fact that there may be "costs to under-regulation."[28]

This chapter explores Australia's experience of, and response to, the global financial crisis. It is a very different story to that which unfolded in many other jurisdictions, such as the United Kingdom and the United States, but is an interesting story, nonetheless, particularly from a comparative perspective. The chapter is structured as follows. Part II provides an overview of Australia's economy and financial market regulation, including important historical background. It also examines the impact of the global financial crisis on Australia, and considers whether the perception that Australia fared well in the crisis is justified. Part III considers the role of regulatory structure in the crisis and examines Australia's "twin peaks" regulatory model from a comparative perspective. Part IV discusses the role of transgovernmental, multilateral and bilateral regulatory models in an era of financial market integration, paying particular attention to the US–Australian mutual recognition arrangement. Part V examines several prominent Australian regulatory responses to the global financial crisis, raising questions concerning the extent to which these reforms addressed international or national problems. Regulatory responses discussed in Part V include reforms and initiatives relating to: Australia's economic stimulus package; the deposit and wholesale funding guarantees; covered bonds; short selling; executive remuneration; and retail investment protection. Part VI returns to the theme of Australia's relatively strong economic performance during the crisis, and asks what might account for this. A common assumption is that Australia's economic stability was a direct result of the resources boom, coupled with the rise of China. This section of the chapter considers a range of other potentially relevant, but under-appreciated factors, which may have explanatory power in this regard. Part VII provides a brief conclusion.

[27] See D'Aloisio, "Regulatory response," pp. 11–12.

[28] J. C. Coffee Jnr., "Financial crises 101: what can we learn from scandals and meltdowns – from Enron to subprime?" in R. P. Austin (ed.), *The Credit Crunch and the Law* (Sydney: Ross Parsons Centre of Commercial, Corporate and Taxation Law, 2008), pp. 37–56, at p. 37. *Cf.*, however, T. A. Paredes, "The proper limits of shareholder proxy access," Posting to the Harvard Law School Forum on Corporate Governance and Financial Regulation, June 30, 2009, available at blogs.law.harvard.edu/corpgov/2009/06/30/the-proper-limits-of-shareholder-proxy-access/, who states "we cannot overlook the risk of overregulating."

II: The Australian economy and the impact of the global financial crisis on Australia's financial markets

Australia has actively and irreversibly embraced globalization.

The Wallis Report[29]

One of the key revelations of the financial crisis was the level of global "interconnectedness."[30] Australia's interconnectedness with global markets through cross-border financial flows has increased dramatically over the last twenty-five years or so.[31] This development can be traced to a major deregulatory reform program in the decade from the mid-1980s, which was based on recommendations of the Campbell Committee of Inquiry into the Australian Financial System.[32]

This period has been described as "perhaps the most eventful" in Australia's financial history.[33] It has been said that these deregulatory reforms converted Australia into a virtually deregulated system[34] and transformed its banking sector from one of the most, to one of the least, controlled in the world.[35] The reforms during this time included market liberalization;[36] the floating of the Australian dollar and abolition of exchange control;[37]

[29] Financial System Inquiry, *Final Report of the Financial System Inquiry* ("Wallis Report") (Canberra: Commonwealth of Australia, 1997), Overview, "The financial system: towards 2010," p. 6.

[30] World Economic Forum, *The Financial Development Report 2009* (Geneva and New York: World Economic Forum, 2009), p. xi.

[31] See K. Henry, "Mutual recognition of financial services regulation: opportunities and challenges for Australia," address to the Australian Securities and Investments Commission (ASIC) Summer School *Our Financial Markets: The Big Issues*, Melbourne, February 19, 2008.

[32] Committee of Inquiry into the Australian Financial System ("Campbell Committee"), *Australian Financial System – Interim Report* (Canberra: *Australian Government Publishing Service*, 1980).

[33] See Bora and Lewis, "The Australian financial system," 787.

[34] See Reserve Bank of Australia, "A brief history," at www.rba.gov.au/about-rba/history/.

[35] See Bora and Lewis, "The Australian financial system," 792 (citing J. O. N. Perkins, *The Deregulation of the Australian Financial System: The Experience of the 1980s* (Melbourne University Press, 1989)).

[36] The opening of Australian markets to international trade occurred from the mid-1980s onwards and was effected by tariff reform and other market liberalization policies. See Stevens, "The Australian economy," p. 2.

[37] The Australian exchange rate was floated on December 12, 1983. See G. Stevens, "Capital flows and monetary policy," remarks to Investor Insights: ANZ Asia Pacific 2006 Seminar, Singapore, September 17, 2006, describing the decision to float the Australian dollar as "one of the most important ever taken by an Australian Government in the field of economic policy." See also Reserve Bank of Australia, "Why does Australia have a floating exchange rate?" in RBA, "The exchange rate and the Reserve Bank's role in the foreign exchange

the opening of the Australian banking system to foreign banks;[38] and the introduction of a mandatory system of superannuation in Australia.[39]

This rapid deregulation program represented a kind of Antipodean "shock therapy."[40] It contributed to a significant shift in the Australian economy away from manufacturing and towards the financial services sector, a trend which has continued exponentially since that time.[41] The most striking growth has occurred in retirement funding through Australia's retirement funding, or superannuation, industry.[42] The superannuation funds industry represents 45 percent of the finance and insurance industry, well ahead of finance and insurance, which constitute 29 percent and 20 percent, respectively.[43]

The onset of the financial crisis in 2007 emphasized the fact that Australia was now connected with the rest of the world for better or for worse in terms of global market risk. As the crisis showed, high risk home loans in the United States could affect markets around the world, including Australia.[44] Of the total investment in the US subprime market of US$7.5 trillion, US$2.5 trillion was located offshore.[45]

market," at www.rba.gov.au/mkt-operations/foreign-exchg-mkt.html#two, noting the ability of a floating exchange rate to provide a buffer to external shocks.

38 See generally, G. K. Goddard, "Bank mergers policy and competition law enforcement: a comparison of recent experience in Australia and Canada," *Banking and Finance Law Review*, 15 [1999–2000], 181–248.

39 See generally, J. G. Hill, "Institutional investors and corporate governance in Australia" in T. Baums, R. M. Buxbaum and K. J. Hopt (eds.), *Institutional Investors and Corporate Governance* (Berlin, New York: Walter de Gruyter, 1994), pp. 583–607, at pp. 583, 588–9.

40 See J. Lloyd, "The Russian devolution," *New York Times*, August 15, 1999, p. 34, describing the policy tensions between "shock therapy" and gradualism in Russia's disastrous privatization process in the early 1990s. A comparison between Australia and Eastern Europe is not as fanciful as might first appear. See Bora and Lewis, "The Australian financial system," 789, claiming that a number of similarities existed between Australia's pre-deregulation financial system and those of some Eastern Europe countries prior to their economic liberalization.

41 See Stevens, "The Australian economy," p. 7; Bora and Lewis, "The Australian financial system," 791*ff*.

42 See Allen Consulting Group, *Enhancing Financial Stability and Economic Growth: The Contribution of Superannuation*, Report to the Association of Superannuation Funds of Australia (ASFA) (Melbourne: Allen Consulting Group, 2011), p. 7.

43 Ibid. (citing IBISWorld, *Finance and Insurance in Australia*, Industry Report (2008)).

44 Stevens, "The Australian economy," p. 8. See also P. Smith, "Lehman faces legal threat over CDO deals," *Financial Times*, December 17, 2007, 1; H. Grennan, "Subprime stoush head to court," *Sydney Morning Herald*, January 15, 2008, p. 22.

45 D'Aloisio, "Regulatory response," p. 13.

In spite of these intricate global financial linkages, it appears that the impact of the global financial crisis was considerably less severe in Australia than in many other parts of the world, including the United Kingdom and United States.[46] The economies worst hit by the crisis were those which expanded rapidly in the 2000s, and Australia constitutes an exception to this general trend.[47] Australia is certainly not alone in this regard. China, with which Australia has increasingly close economic ties, provides another exception.[48] So, too, does Canada, a country which has many interesting parallels with Australia in terms of economic regulatory history and banking structure.[49] Also, neither the Australian nor the Canadian government was required to bail out major financial institutions during the crisis,[50] in contrast to their UK[51] and US[52] counterparts.

Data across a range of indices supports the view that Australia weathered the global financial crisis remarkably well. In its 2010 *Economic Survey of Australia*, the Organisation for Economic Co-operation and Development (OECD) provides a very positive assessment of the performance of the Australian economy, concluding that it has been "one of the most resilient in the OECD during the global

[46] See E. Ferran, "The break-up of the Financial Services Authority," *Oxford Journal of Legal Studies*, 31 (2011) 455–80, at 463.

[47] United Nations Development Program (UNDP), *The Real Wealth of Nations: Pathways to Human Development*, Human Development Report 2010, 20th anniversary edition (New York: Palgrave Macmillan, 2010), p. 79.

[48] Ibid.

[49] See, for example, C. C. Nicholls, "The regulation of financial institutions: a reflective but selective retrospective," *Canadian Business Law Journal*, 50 (2011), 129–55; M. D. Bordo, A. Redish, and H. Rockoff, "Why didn't Canada have a banking crisis in 2008 (or in 1930, or 1907 or...)?" NBER Working Paper no. w17312, August (2011), available at papers.ssrn.com/sol3/papers.cfm?abstract_id=1918642.

[50] See W. Swan, "Emerging from the crisis: the G20 and the Asia-Pacific," address no. 020 by Deputy Prime Minister and Treasurer (Australia), Wayne Swan, to Canada 2020 and the Canadian Australian Chamber of Commerce, Toronto, Canada, June 27, 2010. Canada was the only country in the G-8 where a government bank bailout did not occur. Nicholls, "The regulation of financial institutions," 129.

[51] The Walker Review noted that under the UK bailout arrangement, the taxpayer had provided UK banks with nearly £1.3 trillion in funding. See D. Walker, *Walker Review: A Review of Corporate Governance in UK Banks and other Financial Industry Entities* (London: Walker Review Secretariat, 2009), [7.1].

[52] It has been estimated that beyond the US$700 billion bailout under the Troubled Asset Relief Program (TARP), the United States spent $2.5 trillion and made further commitments of $12.2 trillion up to April 30, 2011. See Business Day, "Adding up the government's total bailout tab," *New York Times*, July 24, 2011.

economic and financial crisis."[53] In 2009, at the height of the crisis, Australia was one of very few developed economies to escape recession.[54]

Australia's capital markets proved particularly resilient. Between 2002 and 2009, the number of listed corporations on the Australian Securities Exchange (ASX) rose by 47 percent to almost 2,000 companies,[55] although market capitalization is heavily concentrated in the ASX top 100 companies.[56] During the financial crisis larger corporations were still able to raise capital.[57] Throughout 2008 and 2009, there was a significant increase in Australian equity issuance,[58] and in the first three quarters of 2009, Australia was ranked third in the world in capital raisings.[59] Australian banks were especially active in capital raising during this period, boosting their capital adequacy to around 12 percent.[60] In the bond market, Australia saw relatively few ratings downgrades or bond defaults.[61]

Australia also fared well from an employment perspective compared with many countries, including the United Kingdom and the United

[53] Organisation for Economic Co-operation and Development (OECD), "OECD Economic Surveys: Australia, November 2010 – Overview," 2010, p. 2. See also *OECD Economic Surveys: Australia 2010* (OECD Publishing, 2010).

[54] See International Monetary Fund (IMF), *Australia: 2010 Article IV Consultation – Staff Report; and Public Information Notice on the Executive Board Discussion*, IMF Country Report no. 10/331 (Washington D.C.: IMF, 2010), p. 3. For an interesting comparative overview of Australia's performance across a range of areas, see data presented by M. Durand, "How does Australia compare in the global economy?" presentation by OECD Chief Statistician Martine Durand at the NatStats 2010 Conference, Sydney, September 15–17, 2010.

[55] See Australian Government Productivity Commission, *Executive Remuneration in Australia*, Report No. 49, Final Inquiry Report (Melbourne: Productivity Commission, 2009), p. 34. By January 2011, the number of ASX listed companies had risen to approximately 2,300. Australian Securities Exchange, "Listed companies," at www.asx.com.au/asx/research/listedCompanies.do.

[56] As at June 2009, total ASX market capitalization was over A$1 trillion, with the ASX top 100 accounting for 70 percent of that amount. Productivity Commission, *Executive Remuneration* (Report No. 49), pp. 34–5.

[57] Australian Financial Centre Forum, *Australia as a Financial Centre: Building on our Strengths* ("Johnson Report") (Canberra: Commonwealth of Australia, 2009), pp. 35–6. Data provided to Australian Financial Centre Forum by UBS Australia showed that between March 2008 and September 2009, capital raising occurred at 38 of the top ASX 50 listed companies. Ibid., p. 35.

[58] This increase was in both absolute terms and percentage of global issuance. Ibid.

[59] The United States was ranked first and the United Kingdom was ranked second. Ibid.

[60] International Monetary Fund, *Australia: 2010 Article IV Consultation*, p. 3.

[61] See S. Black, A. Brassil and M. Hack, "The impact of the financial crisis on the bond market," *Reserve Bank of Australia Bulletin*, June (2010), 55–62.

States. The average OECD unemployment rate, which was 5.7 percent in the pre-crisis period, peaked at 8.8 percent in late 2009, and by the second quarter of 2011 fell to 8.2 percent. In contrast, Australia's unemployment rate, which stood at 4.2 percent in the pre-crisis period, increased to a high of 5.7 percent during the crisis, and fell to 4.9 percent by the second quarter of 2011.[62] Long-term unemployment was also considerably lower in Australia than the OECD as a whole in 2011.[63] Australia's relatively low unemployment figures partly reflect the fact that, in responding to the crisis, many employers reduced working hours rather than retrenching staff.[64] The average reduction in hours worked as a result of the crisis was around 3.5 per cent.[65] This "internal adjustment" approach parallels that taken in Germany, where the labor market demonstrated greater resilience than other OECD countries.[66]

The unemployment rate in the United Kingdom during the crisis was generally consistent with the OECD average,[67] however, the US rate was far worse. Although the US pre-crisis unemployment rate was only 4.4 percent, it more than doubled by 2009 to 10 percent, before easing to 9.1 percent in 2011.[68] Also, the proportion of US unemployment which could be considered long term climbed steeply, from a mere 17 percent at the beginning of the crisis to 43 percent by August 2011.[69]

[62] The level of Australian unemployment rose slightly to 5.3 percent in August 2011. See Organisation for Economic Co-operation and Development (OECD), "Employment outlook 2011 – how does Australia compare?" September 15, 2011, p. 1.

[63] In 2011, 20 percent of unemployed Australians had been without work for 12 months or more, compared with over one-third for the OECD as a whole. Ibid.

[64] International Monetary Fund, *Australia: 2010 Article IV Consultation*, p. 7.

[65] Senate Economics Reference Committee, *Government's Economic Stimulus Initiatives* (Canberra: Commonwealth of Australia, 2009), government senators' minority report, pp. 60–1.

[66] See S. Cazes and S. Verick, "What has happened to Okun's law in the US and Europe? Insights from the Great Recession and longer term trends," presentation at International Labour Organization (ILO) Research Conference on *Key lessons from the crisis and way forward*, Geneva, February 16, 2011, p. 3.

[67] UK unemployment rate rose from a pre-crisis level of 5.1 percent to a high of 7.9 percent during the crisis, and was 7.7 percent in the first quarter of 2011. See Organisation for Economic Co-operation and Development (OECD), "Employment outlook 2011 – how does the United Kingdom compare?" September 15, 2011, p. 1.

[68] See Organisation for Economic Development (OECD), "Employment outlook 2011 – how does the United States compare?" September 15, 2011, p. 1.

[69] Ibid., p. 2, classifying long-term unemployment as comprising unemployed persons who have been out of work for more than 6 months.

A major casualty of the financial crisis was the residential property market, particularly in the United States.[70] In 2009, for example, it was estimated that approximately one-third of all mortgaged homes in the United States were in negative equity, with the value of the loan exceeding that of the property.[71] This was much higher than comparable figures for the United Kingdom (7–11 percent)[72] and Australia, where the incidence of negative equity was assessed at 1 percent or less.[73] The ratio of non-performing bank housing loans in Australia was also extremely low by international standards.[74] This trend was replicated in the Australian housing securitization market.[75]

In spite of this array of positive data, Australia was certainly not immune from the consequences of the crisis. By 2009, for example, Australia's stock market capitalization had fallen by over A$771 billion, constituting 65 per cent of Australia's 2008 gross domestic product (GDP)[76] and the household sector had experienced a steep decline in net worth.[77] Australia has a high level of share ownership, with approximately 43 per cent of the adult population owning shares either directly or indirectly.[78] This decline in net worth was mainly associated with a drop in the value of share portfolios, due to stock market falls.[79] By 2009, for example, the ASX price index was still

[70] See, for example, E. S. Browning, "Retiring boomers find 401(k) plans fall short," *Wall Street Journal Online*, February 19, 2011, p. A1, citing a report by the Rand Corporation's Center for the Study of Aging, which found that since the onset of the global financial crisis, 39 percent of all Americans had experienced mortgage foreclosure, negative equity, mortgage arrears or unemployment.

[71] See Reserve Bank of Australia, *Financial Stability Review – September 2009* (RBA, 2009), pp. 13–14.

[72] Ibid., p. 14. [73] Ibid., p. 47.

[74] Non-performing loan ratios in Australia rose to approximately 0.62 percent in 2009, compared to 5.7 percent in the United States and 2.4 percent in the United Kingdom. See ibid., pp. 20–1. For the definition of "non-performing" loans, see ibid., p. 56. See also G. Debelle, "The state of play in the Australian securitisation market," address by the Assistant Governor (Financial Markets) Guy Debelle to the Australian Securitisation Conference 2010, Sydney, November 30, 2010, pp. 6–7, graph 8.

[75] Arrears in securitization loans peaked at 1 percent in early 2009, which was substantially lower than the United States and United Kingdom. See Australian Trade Commission, *Securitisation: Australian Residential Mortgage Backed Securities*, January 2011, pp. 4, 7.

[76] See Australian Securities and Investments Commission, *ASIC Annual Report 08–09: A Year of Consolidation* (Melbourne: ASIC, 2009), p. 6.

[77] See Reserve Bank of Australia, *Financial Stability Review – September 2009*, p. 43.

[78] See Australian Securities Exchange, *2010 Australian Share Ownership Study* (Sydney: ASX, 2011), pp. 2–3.

[79] See C. Brown and K. Davis, "The sub-prime crisis Down Under," *Journal of Applied Finance*, 18 (2008), 16–28, noting that, although during this period the Australian economy proved resilient to the global financial crisis, the stock market did not.

30 percent lower than its November 2007 peak.[80] There is a strong perception that economic growth continues to be uneven,[81] and that a "two speed" economy exists.[82] A range of factors have contributed to this perception, including the impact of natural disasters, such as the 2010–11 Queensland floods[83] and the high Australian dollar.[84]

There were many high-profile Australian business collapses during the crisis. They included several managed investment scheme failures, particularly in the agribusiness sector.[85] These failures highlighted structural defects, especially in the insolvency context, in the design of managed investment schemes, which were heavily geared tax-driven investment vehicles.[86] Between 2007 and 2009, there were also collapses, totalling A$66 billion, of a number of highly leveraged organizations, including ABC Learning, Allco Finance and Babcock & Brown.[87] Finally, another

[80] See Reserve Bank of Australia, *Financial Stability Review – September 2009*, p. 43.

[81] According to the Governor of the Reserve Bank of Australia, "[e]conomic growth has been uneven and patchy, and financial concerns keep recurring, with waves of positive and negative sentiment sweeping global markets. Australians feel the effects of those swings in sentiment," Reserve Bank of Australia, Stevens, "Still interesting times."

[82] See S. Murdoch, "RBA governor Glenn Stevens defends case for raising interest rates," *The Australian*, June 15, 2011.

[83] These included the Queensland floods from December 2010 to early January 2011. The Australian federal government estimated that the economic cost of the floods was over A$9 billion. The disaster affected global markets, since Queensland supplies approximately two-thirds of the world's premium steelmaking coal and is a major exporter of sugar and cotton. See D. Fickling, "Floods hit Australia economy," *Wall Street Journal*, May 10, 2011, p. A9.

[84] See Swan, "Transcript," pp. 2–3; P. Garnham and P. Smith, "Aussie dollar gains as rate cut hopes dashed," *Financial Times (FT.com)*, July 27, 2011, p. 23.

[85] See P. F. Hanrahan, "ASIC and managed investments," *Company and Securities Law Journal*, 29 (2011), 287–312, at 306–7. These failures included the collapse of Timbercorp Securities Ltd and Great Southern Managers Australia Ltd. See generally Parliamentary Joint Committee on Corporations and Financial Services, *Inquiry into Aspects of Agribusiness Managed Investment Schemes* (Canberra: Commonwealth of Australia, 2009), pp. 14–16.

[86] Ibid., p. 32*ff.* See also Corporations and Markets Advisory Committee (Australia), *Managed Investment Schemes – Discussion Paper* (Sydney: CAMAC, 2011), p. 31*ff*, proposing a number of reforms to address problems relating to managed investment schemes.

[87] See Australian Securities and Investments Commission, *ASIC Annual Report 07–08: A Year of Change* (Melbourne: ASIC, 2008), p. 12; T. D'Aloisio, "The new regulatory landscape: opening and welcome address," in Australian Securities and Investments Commission, *The New Regulatory Landscape – Report*, ASIC Summer School, February 21–3, 2011 (ASIC, 2011), p. 6. See also H. Low, "Heat on banks after $500 million ABC payout," *Australian Financial Review*, June 6, 2011, p. 8; D. John, "Allco hearings reveal failure at every level," *Sydney Morning Herald*, March 29, 2010, p. 6; I. Verrender, "Those behind Babcock unscathed in the ruins," *Sydney Morning Herald*, September 1, 2011, p. 8.

string of collapses, including those of the Westpoint Group and Opes Prime Stockbroking Ltd (Opes Prime), resulted in massive retail investor losses.[88] The consequences of these collapses are now playing out both in the regulatory and judicial realms.

The global financial crisis also had a major impact on the residential mortgage-backed securities/securitization industry in Australia. The virtual collapse of this industry during the crisis resulted in a significant increase in bank mergers and the departure of some non-bank lenders,[89] which contributed to greater concentration in the banking sector as a whole.[90]

III: Regulatory structure and the global financial crisis

> Australia did not escape the GFC unscathed, but it did not experience the system-wide failures of its regulatory regime, as we saw in other markets...
>
> Tony D'Aloisio[91]

Increased financial market integration has led to a growing interest in regulatory and supervisory structures in recent years.[92] This interest intensified during the global financial crisis, where regulatory failures appeared to lie particularly close to the surface.[93]

A snapshot of Australia's corporate and financial services regulatory structure

Australia's corporate and financial services regulatory regime shares many features with other common law jurisdictions.[94] Nonetheless,

[88] See generally Parliamentary Joint Committee on Corporations and Financial Services, *Inquiry into Financial Products and Services.*

[89] See J. Murphy, "Bank competition in the post-crisis environment," address to the Citi Australia Investment Conference, Sydney, October 26, 2010, in The Treasury (Australia), *Economic Roundup*, Issue 4 (2010), pp. 43–51, at pp. 47–8.

[90] Senate Economics References Committee, *Competition within the Australian Banking Sector* (Canberra: Commonwealth of Australia, 2011), p. 1.

[91] D'Aloisio, "The new regulatory landscape," p. 6.

[92] E. Wymeersch, "The structure of financial supervision in Europe: about single financial supervisors, twin peaks and multiple financial supervisors," *European Business Organization Law Review*, 8 (2007), 237–306, at 241.

[93] D'Aloisio, "Regulatory response," p. 7.

[94] For a detailed discussion of Australia's regulatory structure and key regulatory bodies, see G. Pearson, *Financial Services Law and Compliance in Australia* (New York: Cambridge University Press, 2009), Chapter 2.

there are also interesting structural differences between Australia's regulatory framework and the systems that were operating in the United Kingdom and the United States prior to the global financial crisis. In both these jurisdictions, the crisis has prompted reconsideration of the basic structure of financial market regulation; however, this has not occurred in Australia.[95]

Like the United States and Canada, Australia technically has a state-based system of corporate law. However, a distinctive characteristic of the Australian system is a strong tendency towards centralized federal power with national regulators. The Corporations Act 2001 (Cth), for example, effectively operates as a "federal" law as a result of a constitutional referral by each State of its corporate law powers to the Australian Commonwealth government.[96] The most recent example of this phenomenon is in the area of personal property security law, where, as a result of this referral power, a single piece of national legislation will replace over 70 state and federal Acts in 2012.[97] The "federalization" of corporate law in Australia has been far less controversial than in the United States, where many commentators have condemned federal statutes, such as the Sarbanes-Oxley Act 2002[98] and the Dodd-Frank Act 2010,[99] for their encroachment on traditional US state-based corporate law.[100] Australia's "federalization" of corporate law, which paved the way for national, in lieu of state-based, regulators, also provides an interesting contrast with Canada, which

[95] See, for example, Senate Economics References Committee, *Competition within the Australian Banking Sector*, p. xxxiv.

[96] See Commonwealth of Australia Constitution Act, s. 51(xxxvii). The broad referral of powers by the states to the federal government was prompted by the decisions in *Re Wakim: Ex parte McNally* (1999) 198 CLR 511 (Australia) and *R* v. *Hughes* (2000) 202 CLR 535 (Australia), which identified constitutional problems in the structure of the previous corporations law scheme in this regard.

[97] See J. Stumbles, "Personal property security law in Australia and Canada: a comparison," *Canadian Business Law Journal*, 51 (2011), 425–46, at 425–6. The Australian Personal Property Securities Act 2009 (Cth) was passed in December 2009, commencing operation in 2012. Ibid.

[98] Sarbanes-Oxley Act, Pub. L. No. 107–204, 116 Stat. 745 (2002).

[99] The Dodd-Frank Wall Street Reform and Consumer Protection Act of 2010.

[100] See, for example, S. M. Bainbridge, "Dodd-Frank: quack federal corporate governance round II," *Minnesota Law Review*, 95 (2011), 1779–821; Paredes, "Proper limits of shareholder proxy access"; E. N. Veasey, "What would Madison think? The irony of the twists and turns of federalism," *Delaware Journal of Corporate Law*, 34 (2009), 35–56.

has thirteen provincial and territorial securities regulatory agencies. In December 2011, the Supreme Court of Canada unanimously held that a proposal to create a Canadian national securities regulator was unconstitutional.[101] Although Ontario, where the influential Ontario Securities Commission and the Toronto Stock Exchange are based, was in favor of a single national regulator, several other states, including Quebec, were strongly opposed.[102]

Australia operates under a "twin peaks" model of financial regulation.[103] Under this model, one regulator, the Australian Prudential Regulation Authority (APRA) is responsible for prudential regulation of financial institutions. It supervises deposit-taking, general insurance, life insurance and superannuation institutions.[104] Another agency, the Australian Securities and Investments Commission (ASIC) has responsibility for business conduct and consumer protection.[105] The responsibilities of APRA and ASIC are clearly defined, but intersect to some degree in the financial services area.[106]

A number of other organizations play a role in Australia's financial market regulatory system.[107] The Reserve Bank of Australia (RBA), which essentially constitutes a third peak in the regime,[108] controls

[101] See *Re Securities Act*, 2011 SCC 66.

[102] See A. Mayeda and S. B. Pasternak, "Canadian court says single regulator unconstitutional," *Bloomberg Businessweek*, December 23, 2011.

[103] See J. Trowbridge, "The regulatory environment: a brief tour," Australian Prudential Regulation Authority paper presented at the National Insurance Brokers Association (NIBA) Conference, Sydney, Australia, September 22, 2009, available at www.apra.gov.au/Speeches/Pages/niba-conference-speech_jt.aspx.

[104] Institutions over which APRA has supervisory responsibility currently hold approximately $3.7 trillion in assets on behalf of 22 million Australians. See Australian Prudential Regulation Authority, "About APRA," at www.apra.gov.au/AboutAPRA/Pages/Default.aspx.

[105] Although APRA has responsibility for prudential supervision of financial services entities, these entities will, in other respects, be subject to regulation by ASIC. See Corporations and Markets Advisory Committee (Australia), *Guidance for Directors – Report* (Sydney: CAMAC, 2010), p. 25.

[106] See ibid.; HIH Royal Commission, *The Failure of HIH Insurance: A Corporate Collapse and its Lessons*, 3 vols. (Canberra: Commonwealth of Australia, 2003), vol. I, [8.3], available at www.hihroyalcom.gov.au/finalreport/index.htm.

[107] Other relevant agencies include the Australian Competition and Consumer Commission (ACCC) and the Australian Takeovers Panel, which has operated as the primary forum for resolution of takeover disputes in Australia since 2000, when its powers were greatly expanded and takeover dispute resolution shifted from the courts to the Panel.

[108] See Financial System Inquiry, *Wallis Report*, p. 26.

monetary policy, systemic stability and payments systems.[109] The Council of Financial Regulators sits at the top of the regulatory totem pole and acts as the coordinating body for these key financial regulatory agencies and the Australian government.[110]

Australia's twin peaks regulatory configuration was introduced in 1998 in accordance with recommendations made a year earlier by the influential Wallis Committee's Financial System Inquiry ("Wallis Report").[111] Prior to adoption of the twin peaks model, Australia's regulatory system was complex, segmented and institutionally based.[112] It included several federal and state regulators with overlapping functions,[113] and reflected traditional specialized lines of business and products, which had increasingly blurred boundaries as a result of financial

[109] See Reserve Bank of Australia, *Reserve Bank of Australia Annual Report 2011* (Sydney: RBA, 2011), p. 3. For background information on the establishment of the RBA, see Reserve Bank of Australia, "Brief history." The functions of the RBA, as described in s. 10(2) of the Reserve Bank Act 1959, are as follows:

> It is the duty of the Reserve Bank Board, within the limits of its powers, to ensure that the monetary and banking policy of the Bank is directed to the greatest advantage of the people of Australia and that the powers of the Bank... are exercised in such a manner as, in the opinion of the Reserve Bank Board, will best contribute to:
>
> (a) the stability of the currency of Australia;
> (b) the maintenance of full employment in Australia; and
> (c) the economic prosperity and welfare of the people of Australia.

[110] Members of the Council of Financial Regulators are the RBA, which is chair of the Council, APRA, ASIC and the Australian Treasury. See Council of Financial Regulators, *The Council of Financial Regulators' Charter*, adopted January 13, 2004.

[111] See Financial System Inquiry, *Wallis Report*; I. R. Harper, "The Wallis Report: an overview," *Australian Economic Review*, 30 (1997), 288–300. The *Wallis Report* followed a succession of earlier reports on the Australian financial system, including: Royal Commission into the Monetary and Banking Systems in Australia, *Report* (Canberra: Commonwealth Govt. Printer, 1937); Committee of Inquiry into the Australian Financial System ("Campbell Committee"), *Australian Financial System: Final Report of the Committee of Inquiry* (Canberra: Australian Government Publishing Service, 1981); Australian Financial System Review Group ("Vic Martin Review"), *Report* (Canberra: Australian Government Publishing Service, 1984); and House of Representatives Standing Committee on Finance and Public Administration ("Stephen Martin Committee"), *Report – A Pocketful of Change: Banking and Deregulation* (Canberra: Commonwealth of Australia, 1991). For an overview of these inquiries and reports, see Senate Economics References Committee, *Competition within the Australian Banking Sector*, Chapter 3, "Past reviews and a call for a new review."

[112] For a depiction of the pre-Wallis Report prudential regulatory framework, see Financial System Inquiry, *Wallis Report*, p. 303.

[113] See Bora and Lewis, "The Australian financial system," 802, 803.

integration.[114] The two central themes emerging in the Wallis Report were financial stability and competitive neutrality between institutions offering analogous products and services.[115]

The timing of the Wallis Committee's Financial System Inquiry is noteworthy. It occurred halfway between the start of Australia's market liberalization program in the mid-1980s[116] and the onset of the global financial crisis in 2007. The Wallis Report's underlying philosophy of financial regulation reflects both points on this continuum. On the one hand, the report strongly advocated free and competitive markets,[117] while noting the increasing levels of global market integration.[118] Yet, it also stressed the important role of government in maintaining the integrity of a financial system,[119] and the value of financial safety regulation in preventing market failure, due to information asymmetry and systemic risk.[120]

A central plank of the Wallis Report's recommendations was that prudential oversight should be combined in a single agency, to allow for flexibility in the intensity of regulation.[121] The report noted that its recommendation in this regard was at odds with the regulatory structure adopted in many other jurisdictions, where specialized regulatory agencies had been established to deal with the increasing complexity of financial products.[122] Nonetheless, the Wallis Report warned against a specialized regulatory agency approach, on the basis that it was

[114] Financial System Inquiry, *Wallis Report*, p. 297.

[115] See C. Doan, V. Glanville, A. Russell and D. White, "Greater international links in banking – challenges for banking regulation" in The Treasury (Australia), *Economic Round-Up – Spring 2006* (Canberra: Commonwealth of Australia, 2006), pp. 117–30, at pp. 119–20.

[116] The Financial System Inquiry commenced soon after John Howard's Liberal-National Party coalition took office in 1996, and the Committee's brief was to assess the consequences of financial deregulation. See Senate Economics References Committee, *Competition within the Australian Banking Sector*, Chapter 3, "Past reviews and a call for a new review," [3.48]; Financial System Inquiry, *Wallis Report*, Overview, "The financial system: towards 2010," p. 1.

[117] The Wallis Report stated that "[f]ree and competitive markets can produce an efficient allocation of resources and provide a strong foundation for economic growth and development." See Financial System Inquiry, *Wallis Report*, p. 177.

[118] Ibid., p. 6.

[119] The Wallis Report stated that "[g]overnments. . .play a vital role in maintaining a healthy economic and social environment in which enterprises and their customers can interact with confidence." See ibid., p. 177.

[120] Ibid., p. 20. [121] Ibid., pp. 21–4. [122] Ibid., p. 18.

inconsistent with emerging market structure and could result in regulatory gaps and inefficiencies.[123]

APRA was established in July 1998. As recommended by the Wallis Report, APRA assumed prudential supervisory powers, which previously had been exercised by the RBA, the Australian Financial Institutions Commission (AFIC), and the Insurance and Superannuation Commission (ISC),[124] to achieve a cohesive system of prudential regulation of major classes of financial intermediaries under Commonwealth jurisdiction.[125] In particular, the report considered that the prudential regulatory authority should be separate from the central bank for efficiency reasons[126] and emphasized the fact that there is no implied government backing of financial institutions in the event of insolvency and failure.[127]

Nonetheless, APRA suffered a major set-back in its new role as prudential regulator as a result of the failure of HIH Insurance (HIH) in 2001. HIH was Australia's second-largest general insurer, and its failure coincided with the Enron and WorldCom scandals in the United States.[128] The HIH collapse, which was the largest in Australian corporate history, prompted a A$40 million investigative Royal Commission.[129] In a broad-ranging discussion of corporate governance,[130] the

123 Ibid. See also Wymeersch, "The structure of financial supervision in Europe," 253–4, arguing that such a supervisory model can result in unfair treatment if functionally equivalent products are regulated differently according to sector classification.

124 See Bora and Lewis, "The Australian financial system," 804.

125 Financial System Inquiry, *Wallis Report*, p. 21.

126 The Wallis Report expressed doubt as to whether a central bank, whose "operational skills and culture" were focused on banking, could effectively undertake the combination of deposit taking, insurance and superannuation. See ibid., p. 22. The RBA took a contrary view, however. See G. J. Thompson, "The Wallis Inquiry: perspectives from the Reserve Bank," *Reserve Bank of Australia Bulletin*, September (1996), 35–42.

127 Financial System Inquiry, *Wallis Report*, p. 22.

128 See generally Hill, "Regulatory responses," 369–75; C. Jay, "The day of reckoning" in John D. Adams (ed.), *Collapse Incorporated: Tales, Safeguards and Responsibilities of Corporate Australia* (North Ryde, NSW: CCH, 2001), pp. 9–40, at p. 10.

129 HIH Royal Commission, *The Failure of HIH Insurance*, vol. I. The HIH Royal Commission investigation lasted for 18 months. See F. Buffini, A. Hepworth and M. Priest, "Business hits back over HIH reforms," *Australian Financial Review*, April 22, 2003, p. 1.

130 See generally Corporations and Markets Advisory Committee, *Guidance for Directors*, pp. 32–4. In spite of the importance of the HIH Royal Commission for corporate governance, the Commissioner, Justice Neville Owen, expressed disquiet about the term, stating, "I am becoming less and less comfortable with the phrase 'corporate governance' – not because of its content but because it has been so widely used that it may become meaningless." HIH Royal Commission, *The Failure of HIH Insurance*, vol. I, p. xxxiii.

Royal Commission considered the role played by various regulators in the collapse.[131] APRA came in for close scrutiny, and the Royal Commission was critical of the quality of APRA's supervision in relation to HIH.[132] This resulted in major changes to APRA's regulatory approach, which are discussed later in this chapter.

The Australian "twin peaks" model compared to US and UK regulatory structures prior to the global financial crisis

Australia's "twin peaks" model provides an interesting contrast to the regulatory systems which operated in the United States and the United Kingdom at the time of the global financial crisis.[133]

Financial market regulation in the United States is a byzantine affair. As was acknowledged in a 2008 US Department of Treasury report, *Blueprint for a Modernized Financial Regulatory Structure* ("Blueprint Report"), it has a complex and fragmented structure, reflecting path dependence, rather than coherent regulatory design.[134] It is estimated, for example, that approximately 115 federal and state agencies are involved in some aspect of US financial services regulation.[135] The 2008 Blueprint Report recommended a radical overhaul of the system and proposed a "twin peaks" model, similar to the systems operating in Australia and the Netherlands, to try to eliminate regulatory segmentation and duplication.[136]

US regulatory complexity also came under the microscope in attempts to unravel the causes of the financial crisis. The 2011 majority report of the US Financial Crisis Inquiry Commission, for example, noted the existence of widespread failures in financial market

[131] For all findings, see: ibid., vol. III, [24.1.1]–[24.1.13], available at www.hihroyalcom.gov.au/finalreport/index.htm.

[132] See ibid., vol. I, p. lii.

[133] See generally E. F. Brown, "A comparison of the handling of the financial crisis in the United States, the United Kingdom, and Australia," *Villanova Law Review*, 55 (2010), 509–75.

[134] Department of the Treasury (US), *Blueprint for a Modernized Financial Regulatory Structure* (Washington D.C.: Department of the Treasury, 2008), pp. 32, 127.

[135] See E. F. Brown, "The new laws and regulations for financial conglomerates: will they better manage the risks than the previous ones?" *American University Law Review*, 60 (2011), 1339–415, at 1342.

[136] Department of the Treasury, *Blueprint for a Modernized Financial Regulatory Structure*, pp. 13–14, 142–3.

supervision as a factor which permitted regulatory arbitrage to flourish in a "race for the weakest supervisor."[137]

Yet, the issue of regulatory structure received only cursory attention in the most prominent US response to the financial crisis, the Dodd-Frank Act 2010, which provided a filleted version of earlier reform proposals.[138] Although, in response to the crisis, the US Department of Treasury had proposed consolidating supervision of all federally chartered banks into a single prudential regulator,[139] the Dodd-Frank Act retreated from such root and branch restructuring. It merely abolished one agency, the Office of Thrift Supervision (OTS), which had regulated American International Group, Inc. (AIG),[140] and redistributed regulatory powers among the remaining authorities.[141] It remains to be seen whether this relatively minor structural adjustment will eliminate the risk of regulatory arbitrage.[142]

In the United Kingdom, the regulatory structure of the financial sector prior to the global financial crisis offered a contrast with both the Australian and US models. Although the United Kingdom technically had a "tripartite" regulatory system,[143] power was concentrated in a single super-regulator, the Financial Services Authority (FSA).

Unlike Australia's post-Wallis regulatory structure, which split prudential oversight and business conduct regulatory functions between

137 Financial Crisis Inquiry Commission (US), *The Financial Crisis Inquiry Report: Final Report of the National Commission on the Causes of the Financial and Economic Crisis in the United States* (Washington D.C.: Financial Crisis Inquiry Commission, 2011), p. xviii.

138 Reform cutbacks also occurred in the area of corporate governance, leading one commentator to describe the Dodd-Frank Act 2010 as a "triumph of business lobbying." See J. Plender, "Rules of engagement," *Financial Times*, July 12, 2010, p. 7.

139 See T. Braithwaite, B. Masters and S. O'Connor, "Tolerance of patchwork rules poses big hurdle," *Financial Times*, November 11, 2009, p. 8; Davis Polk & Wardwell LLP, "Summary of the Dodd-Frank Wall Street Reform and Consumer Protection Act, enacted into law on July 21, 2010," July 21, 2010, p. 89, available at www.davispolk.com/files/Publication/7084f9fe-6580–413b-b870-b7c025ed2ecf/Presentation/PublicationAttachment/1d4495c7–0be0–4e9a-ba77-f786fb90464a/070910_Financial_Reform_Summary.pdf.

140 Brown, "The new laws," 1342, 1351–2.

141 See ibid., 1389–90; Davis Polk & Wardwell, "Summary of the Dodd-Frank Act," pp. 89–90.

142 *Cf.* Brown, "The new laws," 1389–90; M. Warner, "America needs a single bank regulator," *Financial Times*, August 6, 2009, p. 11.

143 The tripartite system comprised three authorities – the Bank of England, the Financial Services Authority and the Treasury. HM Treasury (UK), *A New Approach to Financial Regulation: Judgement, Focus and Stability* (London: HM Treasury, 2010), p. 3.

APRA and ASIC respectively, under the UK model, both these roles were performed by the FSA. In the post-Enron period, while APRA was receiving harsh criticism from the HIH Royal Commission for the standard of its prudential oversight in relation to HIH, the FSA was being fêted internationally for its light-touch, principles-based style of regulation. London was also challenging New York as a major global financial center,[144] and there was much concern in the United States that the stringency of the Sarbanes-Oxley Act 2002 had reduced the competitiveness of US markets.[145]

The FSA, however, suffered its own share of public censure following the liquidity crisis at Northern Rock plc in 2007.[146] This crisis damaged the reputation of both the FSA and its light-touch regulatory style.[147] It revealed that the FSA had been more successful as a business conduct regulator than in its other prudential supervision role.[148] It has been argued, for example, that it was unreasonable to place responsibility for financial supervision, both prudential and business conduct, "in the hands of a single, monolithic financial regulator."[149] Flaws in the FSA's prudential regulatory style during this period, particularly in regard to liquidity, also emerged in the recent Royal Bank of Scotland post-mortem.[150]

The FSA's regulatory status was significantly downgraded in mid-2010, when the UK government announced its intention to restructure the UK

[144] J. Black, "The rise, fall and fate of principles based regulation," LSE Legal Studies Working Paper no. 17/2010, London School of Economics, November 21 (2010), pp. 3, 12, available at papers.ssrn.com/sol3/papers.cfm?abstract_id=1712862; A. C. Pritchard, "London as Delaware?" *Regulation*, 32 (2009), 22–8, at 24*ff.*

[145] See generally, Committee on Capital Markets Regulation (US), *Interim Report of the Committee on Capital Markets Regulation* (Cambridge, MA: Committee on Capital Markets Regulation, 2006); McKinsey & Company, *Sustaining New York's and the U.S.' Global Financial Services Leadership*, Report to M. R. Bloomberg and C. E. Schumer (McKinsey & Co., 2007). *Cf.* C. Furse, "Comment: SOX is not to blame – London is just better as a market," *Financial Times*, September 18, 2006, p. 19.

[146] Financial Services Authority (UK), *The Supervision of Northern Rock: A Lessons Learned Review* (London: FSA Internal Audit, 2008).

[147] B. Masters, "Northern Rock woes take toll on city's reputation," *Financial Times*, August 27, 2008, p. 3; Ferran, "The break-up of the Financial Services Authority," p. 456*ff.*

[148] In a *mea culpa* report concerning the supervision of Northern Rock, the FSA identified a range of deficiencies in its own standards of regulatory oversight. See Financial Services Authority, *Supervision of Northern Rock*, pp. 2–9.

[149] HM Treasury, *A New Approach to Financial Regulation: Judgement*, p. 3.

[150] Financial Services Authority Board Report, *The Failure of the Royal Bank of Scotland* (London: FSA, 2011). According to this report, the FSA was applying "deficient rules" and had "explicitly accorded a relatively low priority to liquidity, which should be at the core of good prudential supervision." Ibid., p. 23.

financial market regulatory system.[151] Under this reconfiguration, the FSA would be split up in 2013, with overall control of prudential regulation of financial markets shifting to a subsidiary of the Bank of England.[152]

The UK regulatory overhaul got underway in June 2011, with the government's release of a draft Financial Services Bill and a White Paper on financial services regulation.[153] The Financial Secretary to the Treasury described the bill as an important step in developing a new financial regulation system "which will address the flaws in the 'tripartite' model that contributed to the financial crisis."[154]

The proposed UK scheme provides an interesting comparison with Australia's regulatory system. The proposed UK scheme will introduce its own version of a "twin peaks" regulatory model to replace the previous "tripartite" system.[155] However, the pivotal position of the Bank of England is very different from the Australian system, and the Wallis Report considered that prudential regulation should be clearly separated from the central bank for efficiency reasons.[156] A December 2011 report on the draft Financial Services Bill noted that the reforms will give the Bank of England "unprecedented new powers."[157] This echoes concerns that the proposed

[151] See Ferran, "The break-up of the Financial Services Authority," p. 456, describing this restructure as a "dramatic fall from grace" for the FSA.

[152] For an outline of the new regulatory scheme, see HM Treasury (UK), *A New Approach to Financial Regulation: The Blueprint for Reform*, Cm 8083 (London: HM Treasury 2011), pp. 3, 8. New "centres of regulatory excellence" under the scheme are the Financial Policy Committee (FPC) (macroprudential responsibility); Prudential Regulation Authority (PRA) (microprudential supervisor); and Financial Conduct Authority (FCA) (conduct of business and consumer protection regulator). Ibid.

[153] See HM Treasury, *A New Approach to Financial Regulation: The Blueprint.*

[154] See HM Treasury (UK), "Government publishes financial regulation White Paper and draft Bill," press notice 59/11, June 16, 2011. See also HM Treasury, *A New Approach to Financial Regulation: The Blueprint*, p. 3.

[155] See Draft Financial Services Bill Joint Committee (UK), *First Report: Draft Financial Services Bill*, December 19, 2011, "Executive Summary," available at www.publications.parliament.uk/pa/jt201012/jtselect/jtdraftfin/236/23602.htm.

[156] See Financial System Inquiry, *Wallis Report*, p. 22.

[157] Draft Financial Services Bill Joint Committee, *First Report*, "Executive Summary." In the light of the Bank of England's expanded powers, the report called for changes to modernize the bank, alter its governance structure, and make the bank more accountable to Parliament. The report also advocated clearer allocation of responsibilities between the FPC, PRA and FCA. See Draft Financial Services Bill Joint Committee (UK), "Financial Services Bill needs significant amendments if it is to help prevent a future crisis," Media Release, December 19, 2011, available at www.parliament.uk/business/committees/committees-a-z/joint-select/draft-financial-services-bill/news/report-published-today/.

UK regulatory reforms may simply replace "one super-regulator" with another.[158] The government published the Financial Services Bill on January 27, 2012.[159]

IV: Regulatory cooperation in the era of financial market integration and the US–Australian mutual recognition arrangement

> Borders that have blurred for most market participants are proving as sharp as ever where market regulation is concerned.
>
> Ethiopis Tafara and Robert J. Peterson[160]

International regulatory cooperation has become an increasingly familiar and important financial market integration technique in response to globalization. Such cooperation can occur through transgovernmental networks of financial regulators; complex multilateral arrangements; and bilateral mutual recognition agreements. Other familiar treaty-based organizations, such as the International Monetary Fund (IMF), World Bank and World Trade Organization (WTO) provide a backdrop to this complex international financial regulatory framework, but play only a marginal role in relation to supervision of financial markets.[161]

Transgovernmental networks of financial regulators, which came to the forefront during the global financial crisis, exemplify the phenomenon of "regulation beyond the state."[162] Although they have been criticized for regulatory limitations in failing to prevent the crisis,[163] these international networks have been highly visible in their regulatory

158 See BBC, "Mervyn King Questioned on Financial Regulation Reform," *BBC News* (online), November 3, 2011, Democracy Live, news.bbc.co.uk/democracylive/hi/house_of_commons/newsid_9628000/9628524.stm.

159 See HM Treasury (UK), "Government publishes Financial Services Bill," Press Notice 08/12, January 27, 2012.

160 E. Tafara and R. J. Peterson, "A blueprint for cross-border access to U.S. investors: a new international framework," *Harvard International Law Journal*, 48 (2007), 31–68, at 32.

161 See E. J. Pan, "Challenge of international cooperation and institutional design in financial supervision: beyond transgovernmental networks," *Chicago Journal of International Law*, 11 (2010), 243–84, at 251, who argues that the reason the IMF, World Bank and WTO play only a limited role in this respect is because they lack the legal powers and/or expertise, which are prerequisites to the ability to function as a financial regulator.

162 J. Black, "Empirical legal studies in financial markets: what have we learned?" LSE Law, Society and Economy Working Papers 4/2010, London School of Economics and Political Science (2010), p. 28, available at www.lse.ac.uk/collections/law/wps/WPS2010–04_Black.pdf.

163 Verdier, "Mutual recognition," 56.

responses to it. The networks include the Financial Stability Board (FSB), the Basel Committee on Banking Supervision (Basel Committee), International Organization of Securities Commissions (IOSCO), the Organization of Economic Cooperation and Development (OECD) and the International Association of Insurance Supervisors (IAIS).[164] Under the transgovernmental network paradigm, legal principles are promulgated at a global level, but implemented at a national or regional level. The transgovernmental networks themselves receive the backing of multi-state contact groups, such as the Group of Twenty (G20) and Group of Eight (G8).

One of the perceived benefits of this type of cross-border regulatory harmonization is a reduction in the risk of regulatory arbitrage.[165] Yet there are significant challenges to the effective implementation of globally coordinated regulation,[166] including the possibility of regulatory overlap across agencies that have different focal points or underlying philosophies. For example, it has been noted that, in relation to issues such as executive compensation and securitization, the FSB's main focus on stability could lead to different regulatory outcomes to those reached by another organization, such as IOSCO.[167] Therefore, the kind of regulatory fragmentation and overlap, which the Wallis Report attempted to eliminate from financial market regulation at a national level, may reappear at an international level. Also, different interpretations of international standards can create legal variations across jurisdictions or regions.[168]

Australia has a strong presence on international networks of financial regulators and financial standards bodies.[169] For example, ASIC's chairman[170] represents Australia on several committees of IOSCO, the peak

[164] Pan, "Challenge of international cooperation," 249–58.

[165] See, for example, G20 Working Group 1, *Enhancing Sound Regulation and Strengthening Transparency – Final Report* (2009), p. vi; Joint Forum of the Basel Committee on Banking Supervision, International Organization of Securities Commissions and the International Association of Insurance Supervisors, *Review of the Differentiated Nature and Scope of Financial Regulation: Key Issues and Recommendations* (Basel, Switzerland: Bank for International Settlements, 2010), p. 4.

[166] C. Brummer, "How international financial law works (and how it doesn't)," *Georgetown Law Journal*, 99 (2011), 257–327, at 290–5.

[167] See D'Aloisio, "Regulatory response," pp. 8, 10,

[168] See G. A. Ferrarini and M. C. Ungureanu, "Lost in implementation: the rise and value of the FSB principles for sound compensation practices at financial institutions," *Revue Trimestrielle de Droit Financier*, No. 1–2 (2011), 60–5.

[169] D'Aloisio, "Regulatory response," p. 8. [170] Mr Greg Medcraft.

international regulatory body for securities and investments regulators.[171] ASIC is also a member of IOSCO's Asia-Pacific Regional Committee (APRC). From 2010 to 2011, the former chairman of ASIC[172] chaired the Joint Forum, which is a cross-sector group established by the Basel Committee, IOSCO and the IAIS. APRA and ASIC are both representative members of the Joint Forum. The RBA and the Australian government's Treasury Department sit as member institutions on the FSB. APRA is a member of the Basel Committee,[173] and in 2011 a former executive general manager at APRA[174] was appointed Secretary-General of the Basel Committee.[175] Finally, there is also Australian representation on a number of international standard-setting agencies, including the International Accounting Standards Board (IASB);[176] various advisory and working groups of the International Financial Reporting Standards (IFRS) Foundation;[177] and on the International Auditing and Assurance Standards Board (IAASB).

Multi-state contact groups and transgovernmental networks of financial regulators have played an influential background role in relation to a number of Australian regulatory responses to the global financial crisis. For example, in 2009 APRA released enhanced guidelines on executive remuneration.[178] These prudential guidelines for Australian financial institutions were based upon the FSB's *Principles for Sound Compensation Practices*[179] and implementation standards,[180] which were

[171] Australia is represented on the President's Committee, the Executive Committee and the Technical Committee of IOSCO.

[172] Mr Tony D'Aloisio.

[173] See Australian Trade Commission, "APRA joins Basel Committee on Banking Supervision," Investor Updates, March 23, 2009, at www.austrade.gov.au/Invest/Investor-Updates/APRA-Basel-090323/default.aspx.

[174] Mr Wayne Byres.

[175] See Australian Prudential Regulation Authority, "Wayne Byres appointed Secretary General of Basel Committee," Media Release 11.22, October 13, 2011, available at www.apra.gov.au/MediaReleases/Pages/11_22.aspx.

[176] The IASB, which is the standard-setting body of the International Financial Reporting Standards (IFRS) Foundation.

[177] There is Australian membership on the IFRS Advisory Council; the Insurance Working Group; the Joint International Group on Financial Statement Presentation; and the Financial Instruments Working Group.

[178] See Australian Prudential Regulation Authority, *PPG 511 – Remuneration*, Prudential Practice Guide, November 30, 2009.

[179] See Financial Stability Forum, *FSF Principles for Sound Compensation Practices* (2009).

[180] Financial Stability Board, *FSB Principles for Sound Compensation Practices: Implementation Standards* (2009). See Australian Prudential Regulation Authority, *PPG 511 – Remuneration*, p. 3.

themselves supported at the G20 level.[181] In late 2011 APRA released capital requirement reform proposals[182] and liquidity reform proposals,[183] and the RBA announced related details of a committed liquidity facility.[184] This suite of proposed Australian reforms will translate and implement the Basel Committee's global regulatory standards on bank capital adequacy and liquidity, which were announced in December 2010 and are designed to strengthen the global banking system.[185]

A second type of cooperative regulatory model to achieve financial market integration, which to date has had less relevance for Australia, is a multilateral framework. The most prominent example of this paradigm is Europe's framework, which has been described as a complex "regulatory juggernaut."[186] The European version of this model is characterized by strong supranational institutions, which have extensive delegated powers in relation to rule-making, monitoring and enforcement.[187] It necessarily relies on high levels of intervention in member states' regulatory regimes.[188]

A third type of financial market integration technique is the bilateral mutual recognition model. The essence of mutual recognition is the

181 G20 Working Group 1, *Enhancing Sound Regulation*, pp. 32–5.

182 Australian Prudential Regulation Authority, "Implementing Basel III capital reforms in Australia," Discussion Paper, September 6, 2011.

183 See Australian Prudential Regulation Authority, "Implementing Basel III liquidity reforms in Australia," Discussion Paper, November 16, 2011; Australian Prudential Regulation Authority, "Draft Prudential Standard APS 210: Liquidity," November 2011.

184 See Reserve Bank of Australia, "The RBA committed liquidity facility," Media Release 2011–25, November 16, 2011, available at www.rba.gov.au/media-releases/2011/mr-11-25.html; G. Rogow, "Australia's APRA releases Basel III consultation reforms," *Wall Street Journal*, November 15, 2011.

185 See Basel Committee on Banking Supervision, *Basel III: A Global Regulatory Framework for More Resilient Banks and Banking Systems*, December 2010 (revised June 2011); J. F. Laker, "APRA's Basel III implementation: introductory remarks," speech given by the Chairman of the Australian Prudential Regulation Authority at the APRA Finsia Workshop, Sydney, November 23, 2011.

186 N. Moloney, "Financial market regulation in the post-financial services action plan era," *International and Comparative Law Quarterly*, 55 (2006), 982–92, at 992.

187 See generally Verdier, "Mutual recognition." See N. Moloney, "The European Securities and Markets Authority and institutional design for the EU financial market – a tale of two competences: Part (2) rules in action," *European Business Organization Law Review*, 12 (2011), 177–225, discussing the operation of the European Securities and Markets Authority (ESMA), which was established in January 2011. ESMA has responsibility for monitoring systemic risk, in conjunction with two other supranational bodies, the European Banking Authority (EBA) and the European Systemic Risk Board (ESRB). Ibid., 179.

188 Moloney, "Financial market regulation," 982, 986.

concept of bilateral "substituted compliance" with the regulatory regime of another jurisdiction.[189] This regulatory technique provides interesting contrasts to both the transgovernmental networks paradigm and the multilateral arrangements paradigm. Whereas transgovernmental networks operate as a form of meta-regulation,[190] bilateral mutual recognition preserves national regulatory autonomy.[191] Also, unlike the multilateral arrangements, bilateral mutual recognition agreements do not depend upon powerful supranational institutions for their enforcement. They also lack the substantial intrusion into national regulatory autonomy, which is a hallmark of the European multilateral arrangement. It has been argued that the bilateral mutual recognition model is therefore more likely to preserve national legal variance and regulatory competition than other techniques of financial market integration.[192]

The bilateral mutual recognition model is of particular relevance to Australia due to a decision in 2008 by the US Securities and Exchange Commission (SEC) to enter into a trial mutual recognition agreement with Australia.[193] Although the SEC also held preliminary mutual recognition discussions with regulators in Canada and the EU, ultimately Australia was the only country with which the United States concluded a mutual recognition agreement.[194] This appears to be at least partly

[189] Tafara and Peterson, "Blueprint for cross-border access to U.S. investors," 55; Verdier, "Mutual recognition," 57, 82.

[190] Black, "Empirical legal studies," p. 28. [191] Verdier, "Mutual recognition," 57, 81.

[192] Ibid., 65, who states that this potentially allows "individual states to serve as laboratories of regulatory innovation." This reference is reminiscent of a deeply entrenched idea under traditional US corporate law, under which each US state is viewed as a "laboratory" for corporate law reform. See W. L. Cary, "Federalism and corporate law: reflections upon Delaware," *Yale Law Journal*, 83 (1974), 663–705, at 696. Over time, however, these state laboratories have generated increasingly homogenous products. See W. J. Carney, "The production of corporate law," *Southern California Law Review*, 71 (1998), 715–77, at 755; J. G. Hill, "Regulatory show and tell: lessons from international statutory regimes," *Delaware Journal of Corporate Law*, 33 (2008), 819–43, at 841.

[193] See Securities and Exchange Commission (US), *Mutual recognition arrangement between the United States Securities and Exchange Commission and the Australian Securities and Investments Commission, together with the Australian Minister for Superannuation and Corporate Law*, August 25, 2008, available at www.sec.gov/about/offices/oia/oia_mutual_recognition/australia/framework_arrangement.pdf; Securities and Exchange Commission (US) and Australian Securities and Investment Commission (ASIC), *Memorandum of understanding concerning consultation, cooperation and the exchange of information related to the enforcement of securities laws*, August 25, 2008, available at www.sec.gov/about/offices/oia/oia_mutual_recognition/australia/enhanced_enforcement_mou.pdf.

[194] See Pan, "Challenge of international cooperation," 259–61.

attributable to the federalized nature of Australia's financial market regulatory structure. The cessation of US–Canadian talks,[195] for example, has been attributed to difficulties posed by the existence of provincial regulators under the Canadian state-based system.[196]

The framework for mutual recognition arrangements generally,[197] and the US–Australian agreement in particular, arose as a response not only to globalization, but also to technological improvements in capital markets,[198] and to Enron's collapse, which highlighted the importance of effective international supervision.[199] These developments posed particular challenges for the SEC, which had historically operated within the relatively insulated and protected confines of US capital markets.[200]

The US–Australian mutual recognition agreement was based upon a "comparability assessment" of each country's regulatory system to ensure equivalence of supervisory regimes.[201] The underpinning memorandum of understanding (MOU) provided for ongoing supervisory and enforcement cooperation and information sharing between the SEC and its Australian counterpart, ASIC.[202] The MOU provided, for example, that "[t]he Authorities recognize the importance of close communication and intend to consult regularly regarding developments and issues related to

195 See Securities and Exchange Commission (US), "Schedule announced for completion of U.S.-Canadian mutual recognition process agreement," Press Release 2008–98, May 29, 2008.

196 See Verdier, "Mutual recognition," 85.

197 See Tafara and Peterson, "Blueprint for cross-border access to U.S. investors," mapping out the contours of such a framework. As the authors note, the framework was based on "substituted compliance with SEC regulation" (ibid., 32). Thus, foreign stock exchanges and broker-dealers would be entitled to apply for exemption from SEC registration on the basis of regulation under a foreign regulatory system, which the SEC determines to be "substantively comparable" to that of the United States. Ibid.

198 For a skeptical view of the rhetoric underpinning certain deregulatory SEC actions, such as the mutual recognition program, see S. M. Davidoff, "Rhetoric and reality: a historical perspective on the regulation of foreign private issuers," *University of Cincinnati Law Review*, 79 (2010), 619–49.

199 Tafara and Peterson, "Blueprint for cross-border access to U.S. investors," 33.

200 See J. D. Cox, "Coping in a global marketplace: survival strategies for a 75-year-old SEC," *Virginia Law Review*, 95 (2009), 941–87, at 941, 943–6. See also Brummer, "Post-American securities regulation," discussing the challenges of international securities regulation for the SEC at a time when its reputation and regulatory power have declined.

201 See Securities and Exchange Commission (US), "SEC Chairman Cox, Prime Minister Rudd meet amid U.S.-Australia mutual recognition talks," Press Release 2008–52, March 29, 2008, available at www.sec.gov/news/press/2008/2008–52.htm; Moloney, "The European Securities and Markets Authority," 217.

202 See Pan, "Challenge of international cooperation," 260–1.

the operation of this Arrangement."[203] Nonetheless, implementation of the US–Australian agreement subsequently stalled at the US end, apparently as a result of the deepening global financial crisis and political issues involving the SEC.[204]

In spite of the deferral of implementation of this agreement with the United States, Australia now has mutual recognition arrangements with New Zealand[205] and Hong Kong.[206] Such arrangements have been viewed in a positive light as providing a range of benefits to Australia, including an increase in cross-border capital flows.[207] The Australian Financial Centre Forum has recommended that bilateral mutual recognition agreements should form the basis for a more ambitious multilateral scheme in the Asia-Pacific Region.[208] It has proposed a two-step approach for developing a multilateral scheme, the Asian Region Funds Passport. Under this proposal, ASIC would first enter into bilateral mutual recognition agreements with key Asian jurisdictions. This would be followed by cooperation between agencies and governments in the region to introduce a multilateral scheme to permit cross-border marketing of funds across participating jurisdictions.[209]

203 See Securities and Exchange Commission, *Mutual Recognition Arrangement*, [21].

204 For a description of the political background to this hiatus, see N. Mehta, "SEC's mutual recognition pause," *Traders Magazine Online News*, February 15, 2008; Verdier, "Mutual recognition," 87–8.

205 Agreement between the Government of Australia and the Government of New Zealand in relation to Mutual Recognition of Securities Offerings, signed February 22, 2006. This trans-Tasman mutual recognition regime came into force on June 13, 2008. See generally Australian Securities and Investments Commission, *Effects of the Australia-New Zealand Mutual Recognition Regime for Securities Offerings – Report 174* (ASIC, 2009); Australian Securities and Investments Commission, "Significant benefits from mutual recognition of securities offerings," Media Release 09–205AD, October 23, 2009.

206 Australian Securities and Investments Commission and Hong Kong Securities and Futures Commission, "Declaration on mutual recognition of cross-border offering of collective investment schemes," signed by ASIC and the Hong Kong Securities and Futures Commission (SFC), July 7, 2008. This was the first mutual recognition agreement that the SFC had reached with an international regulator. See Australian Securities and Investments Commission, "Australia and Hong Kong sign deal to allow cross-border marketing of retail funds," Media Release 08–152, July 7, 2008.

207 See Henry, "Mutual recognition of financial services regulation," pp. 12–13.

208 See Australian Financial Centre Forum, "*Australia as a Financial Centre*," pp. 84–8, 149–57; N. Sherry and C. Bowen, "Government responds to Australia as a financial services centre report," Joint Media Release no. 087 of the Australian Treasury by the Assistant Treasurer Nick Sherry and the Minister for Financial Services, Superannuation and Corporate Law Chris Bowen, May 11, 2010, Recommendation 4.3 "The Asia Region Funds Passport."

209 Australian Financial Centre Forum, "*Australia as a Financial Centre*," pp. 149–51.

V: Some Australian financial policy and regulatory responses to the global financial crisis

> The increasing interconnectedness of global markets means that the Australian regulatory framework must keep pace with developments offshore.
>
> The Council of Financial Regulators[210]

The global financial crisis caused a dramatic surge in financial market reforms around the world.[211] Given that the impact of the crisis was less severe in Australia than in many other jurisdictions, one might have expected that Australian reforms would have been subdued and limited. This was not the case, however, and the crisis became an important reference point for reassessing Australia's system of financial market regulation. A wide array of reforms was introduced in Australia in response to the crisis, and there has been an even larger number of inquiries, reviews and reports by government and regulatory authorities.[212] The scope of these reforms and reform proposals reflect the perceived political importance of ensuring that Australia's regulatory system is capable of withstanding future global market dislocation.[213]

The following Australian responses to the crisis are discussed below: the government's economic stimulus program; certain reforms designed to maintain and increase market liquidity, such as the deposit and

[210] The Council of Financial Regulators, *Review of Financial Market Infrastructure Regulation: Consultation Paper* (Canberra: Commonwealth of Australia, 2011), p. 3.

[211] For a broad overview of regulatory responses, see K. Davis, "Regulatory responses to the financial sector crisis," *Griffith Law Review*, 19 (2010), 117–37.

[212] These include, to name just a few, House of Representatives Standing Committee on Economics, *Competition in the Banking and Non-banking Sectors* (Canberra: Commonwealth of Australia, November 2008); Australian Securities and Investments Commission, "Short selling to hedge risk from market making activities," Consultation Paper 106, April 30, 2009; Corporations and Markets Advisory Committee (Australia), *Aspects of Market Integrity – Report* (Sydney: CAMAC, 2009); Australian Securities and Investments Commission, "Margin lending: financial requirements," Consultation Paper 109, July 13, 2009; Senate Economics References Committee, *Report on Bank Mergers* (Canberra: Commonwealth of Australia, 2009); Parliamentary Joint Committee on Corporations and Financial Services, *Inquiry into Financial Products and Services*; Productivity Commission, *Executive Remuneration* (Report No. 49); Super System Review ("Cooper Review"), *Final Report – Part One: Overview and Recommendations* (Canberra: Commonwealth of Australia, 2010); Corporations and Markets Advisory Committee (Australia), *Executive Remuneration: Report* (Sydney: CAMAC, 2011); Corporations and Markets Advisory Committee (Australia), *Derivatives: Report* (Sydney: CAMAC, 2011).

[213] Council of Financial Regulators, *Review of Financial Market Infrastructure*, p. 3.

wholesale funding guarantee; ASIC's temporary ban on short selling; executive remuneration reforms; and, finally, the Future of Financial Advice Reforms, targeting retail investor protection. These responses, although necessarily selective, cover a number of key reform initiatives in Australia during the crisis and reflect a variety of regulatory themes.

Some financial policy-related reforms, such as the deposit and wholesale funding guarantee, were emergency-style regulatory responses to market turmoil after Lehman Brothers Holdings Inc. (Lehman Brothers) filed for bankruptcy on September 15, 2008.[214] These responses were designed to ensure continued liquidity in Australian markets and were largely driven by the actions of other governments. Reforms, such as the Future of Financial Advice reforms, on the other hand, responded to distinctive local problems created as the crisis unfolded in Australia. Some reforms discussed were temporary only, whereas others represent potential long-term shifts in the direction and design of Australia's system of financial market regulation. Some of the reforms, such as the "two strikes" reform to executive remuneration, were nationally driven, whereas others, such as APRA's prudential guidelines on executive remuneration, derive from the international cooperative regulatory agenda of the FSB and G20. Many of the post-crisis regulatory developments involve a shift in the prior equilibrium between the twin policy goals of efficiency and investor protection in Australian financial regulation.[215] They also reflect a growing awareness that disclosure may be a flawed regulatory technique in the face of increased complexity of financial products.[216]

The Australian government's economic stimulus program

> If we are going to be Keynesians in the downturn, we have to be Keynesians on the way up again.
>
> Wayne Swan[217]

There are two techniques, at opposite ends of a broad spectrum, by which governments can respond to financial crises. The first involves fiscal austerity.[218] This type of approach was common during the East

[214] See C. Mollenkamp, S. Craig, S. Ng and A. Lucchetti, "Lehman files for bankruptcy, Merrill sold, AIG seeks cash," *Wall Street Journal*, September 16, 2008.

[215] See D'Aloisio, "Regulatory response," pp. 1, 10*ff.*

[216] Ibid., p. 13.

[217] W. Swan, "Keynesians in the recovery," *Australian Fabian News*, 51 (2011), 15–22.

[218] See "There could be trouble ahead," *The Economist*, December 10, 2011, p. 401.

Asian crisis of the 1990s,[219] and is currently making a strong reappearance in the euro zone. The other response involves increased social expenditure.[220] During the global financial crisis Australia introduced a major taxpayer-funded economic stimulus program, which clearly falls within the second category of response.

Between October 2008 and February 2009, the Australian government announced a raft of fiscal stimulus packages providing direct payments to certain groups, together with broad-based community and infrastructure funding.[221] The first of these packages was the Economic Security Strategy (ESS). The ESS, which had a combined funding level of A$10.4 billion, included cash transfers to low- and middle-income workers and a First Home Owners grant.[222] In November 2008, the Council of Australian Governments (COAG) announced a A$15.2 billion funding package for housing, hospitals and education,[223] and in December 2008, the government announced the A$4.7 billion Nation Building Package, which provided for investment in road, rail and education infrastructure.[224]

However, by far the largest of Australia's fiscal stimulus programs, was the A$42 billion Nation Building and Jobs Plan, which the government announced in February 2009 as the centerpiece of its stimulus response to the financial crisis.[225] This massive stimulus package included five key

[219] See UNDP, *The Real Wealth of Nations*, p. 79.

[220] See "There could be trouble ahead," p. 401.

[221] See generally, Senate Economics References Committee, *Government's Economic Stimulus Initiatives*, pp. 3–6. See also D. Uren and L. Taylor, "How Rudd bet the house," *The Australian*, June 19, 2010, p. 1.

[222] Key measures in the ESS were: A$4.8 billion for long-term pension reform; A$3.9 billion for payments to low- and middle-income families; A$1.5 billion to provide financial assistance to first home buyers; and A$187 million to create new training positions in 2008–9. See K. Rudd, "Economic security strategy," joint press conference by the Prime Minister of Australia Kevin Rudd, Main Committee Room, Parliament House, October 14, 2008. See also W. Swan, "Economic security strategy payments start today," joint Media Release no. 139 by the Treasurer (Australia) Wayne Swan, December 8, 2008.

[223] Senate Economics References Committee, *Government's Economic Stimulus Initiatives*, p. 3.

[224] See K. Rudd, "$4.7 billion nation building package," Media Release AA194/2008 by the Prime Minister of Australia Kevin Rudd, December 12, 2008. Key measures included in this Nation Building Package were: the injection of A$1.2 billion into the Australian Rail Track Corporation; acceleration of A$711 million in road spending; investment of A$1.6 billion in university and Technical and Further Education (TAFE). The package also included two temporary tax changes to encourage capital investment by businesses and to support small business. Ibid.

[225] K. Rudd, "$42 billion nation building and jobs plan," Joint Media Release no. 009 by the Prime Minister of Australia Kevin Rudd, February 3, 2009.

elements: (i) the "Building the Education Revolution" program to provide A$14.7 billion for building and rebuilding school infrastructure over a four-year period;[226] (ii) the Energy Efficient Homes program;[227] (iii) a program supporting the construction of new social dwellings for the homeless and low-income renters, and new defence homes;[228] (iv) a temporary A$2.7 billion business tax break;[229] and (v) a program targeting improvements to regional roads and community infrastructure.[230] The Nation Building and Jobs Plan announcement also included one-off cash bonuses of A$950 to eligible low- to middle-income individuals.[231] The combined effect of the series of economic stimulus measures was to commit the Australian government to almost A$90 billion of discretionary spending over a four-year period.[232]

[226] See K. Rudd, "Building the education revolution: new and upgraded buildings in every Australian school," Joint Media Release by the Prime Minister of Australia Kevin Rudd, February 3, 2009. Although the level of funding for the "Building the Education Revolution" was originally announced as A$14.7 billion, it appears that A$16.2 billion was actually spent on this program. See Nation Building Economic Stimulus Plan, "Education," at www.economicstimulusplan.gov.au/education/pages/default.aspx.

[227] This proposal included an ill-fated plan to install free ceiling insulation in around 2.7 million Australian homes. See K. Rudd, "Energy efficient homes – ceiling insulation in 2.7 million homes," Media Release by the Prime Minister of Australia Kevin Rudd, February 3, 2008.

[228] This package involved a plan to to build 20,000 new social housing dwellings and 802 new defence homes. See K. Rudd, "20,000 social and defence homes – nation building investment," Joint Media Release by the Prime Minister of Australia Kevin Rudd, February 3, 2009. As of June 30, 2011, this plan had provided a total of approximately A$5.6 billion for social housing, and A$245.58 million for defence housing. See Nation Building Economic Stimulus Plan, "Social housing," at www.economicstimulusplan.gov.au/housing/pages/default.aspx; and Nation Building Economic Stimulus Plan, "Defence housing," at www.economicstimulusplan.gov.au/housing_defence/pages/default.aspx.

[229] See K. Rudd, "Small business and general business tax break," Joint Media Release by the Prime Minister of Australia Kevin Rudd, February 3, 2009.

[230] See K. Rudd, "Black spots, boom gates, regional roads and community infrastructure," Joint Media Release AA011/2009 by the Prime Minister of Australia Kevin Rudd, February 3, 2009. As at June 30, 2011, A$800 million had been provided to the Regional and Local Community Infrastructure Program under this initiative. See Nation Building Economic Stimulus Plan, "Community infrastructure," at www.economicstimulusplan.gov.au/community_infrastructure/pages/default.aspx.

[231] Five cash bonuses of A$950 were included in the Nation Building and Jobs Plan announcement. These were a "Tax Bonus for Working Australians"; a "Single Income Family Bonus"; a "Farmers' Hardship Bonus"; a "Back to School Bonus"; and a "Training and Learning Bonus." See, generally, K. Rudd, "$950 one-off cash bonus to support jobs," Joint Media Release by the Prime Minister of Australia Kevin Rudd, February 3, 2009.

[232] Senate Economics References Committee, *Government's Economic Stimulus Initiatives*, pp. 3–4, Table 2.1.

Australia was not alone in its use of stimulus spending.[233] Fiscal measures of this kind to support national economies were used by almost all OECD countries during the crisis.[234] Nonetheless, Australia has been described as noticeably more fervent in its embrace of Keynes' philosophy regarding discretionary government spending than most other countries at that time.[235] Australia's approach also ran counter to the tendency in most countries to give priority to tax cuts over increased spending.[236]

There was wide variation in the size of stimulus packages introduced in OECD countries, and Australia's fiscal package was one of the largest compared to GDP.[237] Typical stimulus packages in OECD countries amounted to around 2.5 percent of GDP over the period 2008–10.[238] Australia was one of only five OECD countries to adopt a fiscal stimulus package that constituted more than 4 percent of 2008 GDP.[239] The US stimulus package was the largest of these at 5.5 percent of 2008 GDP, while Australia's package was slightly behind the United States and Korea, at just under 5 percent of 2008 GDP.[240]

The US fiscal package, which was signed into law in February 2009 as the American Recovery and Reinvestment Act 2009,[241] amounted to US$787 billion.[242] In contrast, the UK's main fiscal package in

233 UNDP, *The Real Wealth of Nations*, p. 79.

234 Organisation for Economic Co-operation and Development (OECD), *OECD Interim Economic Outlook – March 2009* (Paris: OECD, 2009), Chapter 3, "The effectiveness and scope of fiscal stimulus," pp. 105–50, at p. 108.

235 A. Robson, "Rudd the profligate; Australia's Prime Minister is making an expensive bet on Keynes," *Wall Street Journal Online*, April 23, 2009.

236 OECD, *Interim Economic Outlook – March 2009*, p. 107. Other countries which, like Australia, constituted exceptions in this regard, were Japan, France, Denmark and Mexico. Ibid., pp. 111–12. See also Senate Economics References Committee, *Government's Economic Stimulus Initiatives*, Government senators' minority report, pp. 55–6.

237 OECD, *Interim Economic Outlook – March 2009*, Chapter 3: "The effectiveness and scope of fiscal stimulus," pp. 107–9.

238 Ibid., p. 109.

239 These countries were Australia, Canada, Korea, New Zealand and the United States. Ibid.

240 Ibid., p. 109, Figure 3.2. See also J. Glynn and E. Curran, "Australia's fast recovery spurs fears it overdid stimulus," *Wall Street Journal*, October 13, 2009, p. A15, which show US 2008–10 stimulus spending at 5.6 percent of GDP and Australia's stimulus spending during the same period as 4.6 percent of GDP.

241 See generally Recovery.gov (US), "The Recovery Act," at www.recovery.gov/About/Pages/The_Act.aspx.

242 See L. Meckler, "Obama signs stimulus into law," *Wall Street Journal*, February 18, 2009. See also Recovery.gov (US), "Tracking the money," at www.recovery.gov/Pages/default.aspx, which details, on an ongoing basis, how much of this stimulus amount has been paid out to date.

November 2008, which was worth approximately £20 billion,[243] fell below the OECD median for government stimulus spending.[244] However, this amount was in addition to the UK government's huge bank rescue package announced in October 2008,[245] and it has been suggested that this may have constrained the UK's ability to adopt a more substantial stimulus package.[246] In a broader sense it might, of course, be argued that government-sponsored bank bailouts, of which there were more than fifty around the globe during the crisis,[247] though not in Australia, can themselves be viewed as forms of fiscal stimulus.

The composition of fiscal packages also varied across jurisdictions, displaying different policy focal points.[248] Support for children and pensioners, which is evident in parts of the Australian stimulus package, was replicated in measures adopted in Germany and Canada.[249] Australia's use of its fiscal package to address long-term policy issues in health and education was somewhat unusual. The IMF cites only Australia, China and Saudi Arabia as adopting this kind of long-term stimulus measure.[250]

Another interesting aspect of the Australian stimulus package was the high level of direct cash payments to individuals. The basis for this strategy appears to have been a perception that pure infrastructure spending had been too slow in bolstering consumer confidence during the recession that followed the East Asian crisis in the 1990s. Against this

[243] See J. Chisholm, "Darling unveils £20bn fiscal stimulus," *Financial Times*, November 24, 2008.

[244] OECD, *Interim Economic Outlook – March 2009*, p. 109, Figure 3.2. See also Glynn and Curran, "Australia's fast recovery," p. A15, which provides data showing that the UK stimulus package 2008–10 constituted only 1.4 percent of GDP.

[245] HM Treasury (UK), "Statement by the Chancellor on Financial Stability," Statement by the Chancellor of the Exchequer to the House of Commons, Parliament (UK), October 8, 2009.

[246] See BBC, "'Job not done', Darling tells G20," *BBC News* (online), September 3, 2009, news.bbc.co.uk/2/hi/business/8234497.stm, where BBC Economics reporter, Steve Schifferes, argued in 2009 that "... the UK ... has one of the smallest economic stimulus packages among G20 countries, having been forced to spend heavily on propping up the banking sector."

[247] See Senate Economics References Committee, *Government's Economic Stimulus Initiatives*, p. 50.

[248] OECD, *Interim Economic Outlook – March 2009*, pp. 111–12.

[249] See International Monetary Fund, Note by staff of the International Monetary Fund, *Group of Twenty – Meeting of the Deputies, January 31–February 1, 2009*, London, United Kingdom (Washington D.C.: IMF, 2009), p. 18.

[250] Ibid., p. 19.

backdrop, it has been reported that the Australian Secretary of the Treasury advised the government, in its design of the stimulus program, to "go hard, go early, go households."[251]

Emergency-style reforms – the Deposit and Wholesale Funding Guarantee Scheme and the RMBS Initiative

> There was a lot of feedback coming in from the RBA, the private sector and just generally that if we didn't act quickly...confidence in the financial system might collapse.
>
> Anonymous Australian government source[252]

Emergency-style, or panic, regulation has attracted much criticism in the United States since the legislature's hasty adoption of the Sarbanes-Oxley Act 2002 after the collapses of Enron and WorldCom,[253] and similar criticisms are now being levied against the Dodd-Frank Act 2010.[254]

Some of Australia's initiatives during the global financial crisis were of the emergency variety, responding to critical international developments at the time. A notable example of this phenomenon was the announcement on October 12, 2008 made by then Prime Minister, Kevin Rudd, that the Australian government would immediately introduce a deposit and wholesale funding guarantee scheme, and provide support in relation to residential mortgage-backed securities.[255] This announcement, designed to sustain public confidence and liquidity, was made less than a month after Lehman Brothers filed for bankruptcy.[256] It also came only days after the UK government disclosed that it would partly nationalize the country's largest banks under a £400 billion taxpayer-funded

[251] See Uren and Taylor, "How Rudd bet the house," p. 1.

[252] Cited by K. Jimenez, "How APRA handled the crisis," *The Australian*, April 27, 2010, p. 18.

[253] See, for example, Romano, "Sarbanes-Oxley Act," 1528, describing the Sarbanes-Oxley Act of 2002 as "emergency legislation" and "quack corporate governance." See also L. E. Ribstein, "Bubble laws," *Houston Law Review*, 40 (2003), 77–97, who criticizes panic regulation following market crashes, on the basis that it generally reduces entrepreneurialism. Ibid., 97.

[254] For criticism of the Dodd-Frank Act 2010, see Bainbridge, "Dodd-Frank: quack corporate governance." *Cf.* J. C. Coffee Jnr., "The political economy of Dodd-Frank: why financial reform tends to be frustrated and systemic risk perpetuated", Chapter 4 below.

[255] K. Rudd, "Global financial crisis," Media Release by the Department of the Prime Minister and Cabinet (Australia), October 12, 2008.

[256] Lehman Brothers filed for Chapter 11 bankruptcy on September 15, 2008. See Mollenkamp, Craig, Ng and Lucchetti, "Lehman files for bankruptcy."

bailout[257] and the G7 called for "urgent and exceptional action" to restore credit flow and to stabilize financial markets, which were in free fall.[258]

Australia and the Asia-Pacific region were by no means insulated from the global market turmoil during this period. One week before the government's announcement, the Australian dollar fell 16 per cent against the US dollar, which was the largest weekly drop in value since its float in 1983.[259] Two days before the announcement, the Australian stock market fell by 8.3 percent, a loss of A$73 billion, in the worst day in trading history since the 1987 stock market collapse.[260] Australian financial services, resources and property stocks were particularly affected.[261] The general decline in share prices was mirrored across Asian markets.[262]

It also appears that an acute home-grown threat placed pressure on the Australian government to respond to the crisis. A rumor was in circulation that on Monday, October 13, 2008, there could be a run on one of Australia's mid-tier banks, commensurate with the UK's Northern Rock experience.[263] There is anecdotal evidence suggesting that the Australian government viewed this as a genuine risk, and one which was only narrowly averted by the introduction of the government's guarantee scheme, one day before the bank run was rumored to occur.[264]

257 See HM Treasury, "Statement by the Chancellor"; P. T. Larsen, "Amid tumult, intervention is a capital idea," *Financial Times*, October 7, 2011, p. 2; G. Parker, P. T. Larsen and C. Giles, "UK banks to be part-nationalised," *Financial Times*, October 8, 2011, p. 1; P. T. Larsen, "Government's move to resuscitate failing system," *Financial Times*, October 9, 2011, p. 2.

258 G7/8 Finance Ministers Meeting, "G7 Finance Ministers and central bank governors plan of action," Washington D.C., October 10, 2008.

259 Senate Economics References Committee, *Government's Economic Stimulus Initiatives*, Government senators' minority report, p. 51.

260 See J. Saulwick and M. O'Sullivan, "Fears set investors panicking to grab cash," *Sydney Morning Herald*, October 11, 2008, p. 39; Senate Economics References Committee, *Government's Economic Stimulus Initiatives*, p. 51.

261 Saulwick and O'Sullivan, "Fears set investors panicking," p. 39.

262 Japanese shares, for example, fell by 9.4 percent and Hong Kong's Hang Seng dropped by 8.2 percent. See A. Wood and J. Aglionby, "Bourses in steep decline across the region," *Financial Times*, October 9, 2008, p. 28.

263 See Jimenez, "How APRA handled the crisis," p. 18.

264 Katherine Jimenez cites an anonymous senior Australian government source as stating; "There was a lot of feedback coming in from the RBA, the private sector and just generally that if we didn't act quickly, by Monday afternoon we might have to put a guarantee on but that might be after there had been a run on a bank and confidence in the financial system might collapse. It could have been any of the mid-tier banks on that Monday. Whether it was St George, Suncorp, Bendigo, Adelaide, you name it, people were taking money out. We think it [the threat] was real. We think that if we hadn't put the guarantee on, it would have happened. I don't think most people realise just how close we came." Ibid.

Prior to the global financial crisis, the Wallis Report's philosophy, which underpinned Australia's financial system, was that any bank could fail, and that it was not the role of government to "provide an absolute guarantee in any area of the financial system."[265] Nonetheless, the global financial crisis in effect forced the Australian government to come to the rescue of the banking system as a whole.

It is important to note, however, that the introduction of the deposit and wholesale funding guarantee scheme did not constitute a bank bailout. Against the background of massive US and UK government bailouts, the Australian Bankers' Association (ABA) expressed concern that the Australian government's actions in this regard might be misinterpreted as a bailout of the Australian financial sector.[266] The ABA stressed that this was incorrect since, contrary to the position in the United States and United Kingdom, no taxpayer funds had been allocated to support Australian banks, which, according to the ABA, were strongly capitalized and had high-quality asset holdings.[267]

The deposit guarantee

The first element of Mr Rudd's October 12, 2008 announcement related to the immediate introduction of a deposit guarantee for banks and other authorized deposit taking institutions (ADIs).[268] The announcement stated that the federal government would temporarily guarantee all deposits of Australian banks, building societies and credit unions, and locally incorporated subsidiaries of foreign-owned banks.[269] According to this initial announcement, the deposit guarantee would operate without any cap for a three-year period, after which time it would be

[265] See Financial System Inquiry, *Wallis Report*, p. 191. See also, J. F. Laker, "Risk management in banking – a prudential perspective," speech given by the Chairman of the Australian Prudential Regulation Authority to the 59th International Banking Summer School, Melbourne, September 6, 2006, p. 2, stating that "bank failure should be rare, but certainly not impossible."

[266] See Australian Bankers' Association Inc. (ABA), "No bail out of Australian banks," Media Release, October 14, 2008.

[267] Ibid. An IMF Working Paper shared this upbeat assessment of Australian banks. See E. Takáts and P. Tumbarello, "Australian bank and corporate sector vulnerabilities – an international perspective," IMF Working Paper WP/09/223, International Monetary Fund, October (2009), p. 6.

[268] The concept of "authorized deposit taking institutions" is broader than that of banks, and is used to refer to banks, building societies, credit unions and friendly societies. See generally Pearson, *Financial Services Law and Compliance*, pp. 38–9.

[269] Rudd, "Global financial crisis."

reassessed.[270] This "no cap" element was similar to measures taken by Ireland, Germany, Denmark and Iceland around that time.[271] It contrasted with jurisdictions, such as the United States, United Kingdom and the EU, which provided depositors with a capped guarantee only.[272]

Legislation supporting the deposit guarantee[273] received Royal Assent on October 17, 2008. The deposit guarantee was administered by APRA under the aegis of the Financial Claims Scheme (FCS),[274] which had been announced in June 2008, partly in response to the Northern Rock crisis.[275] The new legislation also provided APRA with stronger powers to intervene in the affairs of failing financial institutions.[276]

Nonetheless, political and industry pressure quickly led to some urgent adjustments to the structure of the deposit guarantee.[277] It appears that the RBA had warned of the unintended consequences of a "no cap" deposit guarantee, in terms of possible distortion to other financial sectors.[278] In the week following the announcement of the "no cap" deposit guarantee, that risk became a reality. During this period, more than A$2.5 billion flowed into the major Australian banks, as investors shifted funds from sections of the money market, which did not receive

270 Ibid.

271 Ibid. For a comparison of deposit insurance coverage limits in mid-September and early December 2008, see S. Schich, "Financial crisis: deposit insurance and related financial safety net aspects," *OECD Journal: Financial Market Trends*, Issue 2 (2008), 73–111, at 90, Figure 3.

272 These jurisdictions had, however, significantly increased the level of their deposit cap. In the United States, for example, the Federal Deposit Insurance Corporation (FDIC) raised the cap from US$100,000 to US$250,000 per depositor; the United Kingdom raised its cap from £35,000 to £50,000 and the EU increased it deposit insurance limit from €20,000 to €50,000. Ibid.

273 See Legislation Amendment (Financial Claims Scheme and Other Measures) Act 2008.

274 See W. Swan, "New protections for depositors and policyholders," Media Release no. 061 by Treasurer (Australia) Wayne Swan, June 2, 2008. Establishment of the FCS derived from recommendations of the HIH Royal Commission, the Council of Financial Regulators and, at an international level, the Financial Stability Forum. Ibid.

275 See M. Stutchbury, "Rudd needs to straighten out the details of bank guarantees," *The Australian*, October 17, 2008, p. 28.

276 See Australian Prudential Regulation Authority, *Annual Report 2009* (Commonwealth of Australia, 2009), p. 26.

277 See T. Wing Kee, "Guarantees turn into political beasts," *Australian Banking and Finance*, vol. 17 no. 19, November 30, 2008, pp. 1, 10–11, at p. 1; J. Durie, "Tweaks coming for deposit guarantee," *The Australian*, October 18, 2008, p. 37; D. Crowe, M. Ludlow and T. Sutherland, "Swan's deposit fix to calm investors," *Australian Financial Review*, October 25, 2008, p. 3.

278 See J. Hewett, "RBA warns on bank guarantee as Reserve and Treasury at loggerheads," *The Australian*, October 21, 2008.

the benefit of government backing, into ADI deposits that did.[279] The Commonwealth Bank of Australia, for example, which had A$110.7 billion in deposit holdings in August 2008, attracted an additional A$1 billion in deposits.[280] Although the main aim of the "no cap" deposit guarantee was to reassure small retail depositors, large institutional investors had quickly taken advantage of this form of selective governmental protection.[281]

On October 24, 2008, the Australian Treasurer, Wayne Swan, announced that on the advice of the Council of Financial Regulators the original unlimited deposit guarantee would be replaced with a new deposit threshold of A$1 million, above which a fee would be charged to access the guarantee.[282] The aim of this modification was to create a level playing field between ADI deposits and wholesale debt securities. In particular, the amendment sought to ensure that the deposit guarantee did not deter investment in short-term money markets.[283]

The introduction of a deposit guarantee during the global financial crisis constituted a significant change in regulatory direction for Australia. Unlike most other jurisdictions,[284] including the United States,[285] United Kingdom[286] and Japan,[287] Australia did not previously have any

[279] See A. Wood, "Message from Hayek to Rudd with love," *The Australian*, October 24, 2008, p. 12; Durie, "Tweaks coming," p. 37.

[280] Wing Kee, "Guarantees turn into political beasts," pp. 1, 10.

[281] Hewett, "RBA warns on bank guarantee."

[282] See W. Swan, "Government announces details of deposit and wholesale funding guarantees," Media Release no. 117 by Treasurer (Australia) Wayne Swan, October 24, 2008; W. Swan, "Guarantee scheme for large deposits and wholesale funding of deposit-taking institutions," Media Release no. 132 by Treasurer (Australia) Wayne Swan, November 28, 2008.

[283] Swan, "Government announces details."

[284] G. Pearson, "Safety in savings – a virtuous circle? – New laws for deposit guarantees, covered bonds and superannuation," (2011) (draft paper on file with the author).

[285] Federal deposit insurance in the United States dates back to the Depression era and is administered by the Federal Deposit Insurance Corporation (FDIC). See E. L. Symons Jnr., "The United States banking system," *Brooklyn Journal of International Law*, 19 (1993), 1–46.

[286] UK deposit insurance for banks and building societies dates back to the 1980s. See Pearson, "Safety in savings," p. 5; M. J. B. Hall, "Incentive compatibility and the optimal design of deposit protection: an assessment of UK arrangements," *Journal of Financial Regulation and Compliance*, 10 (2002), 115–34.

[287] Japan's deposit insurance system was introduced in 1971 and is administered by Deposit Insurance Corporation (DIC). See, generally, C. J. Milhaupt, "Japan's experience with deposit insurance and failing banks: implications for financial regulatory design?" *Washington University Law Quarterly*, 77 (1999), 399–431, at 408–13, noting, however, that this formal protective scheme had traditionally been less important than public confidence in the implicit protection of the Japanese Ministry of Finance and the Bank of Japan. Ibid., 410.

form of governmental deposit insurance protection.[288] As at September 2008, Australia was one of only two countries represented on the OECD's Committee on Financial Markets (CFM) that did not have some type of deposit insurance coverage.[289] Depositor protection in Australia had traditionally taken the form of domestic preference rules, by which depositors of ADIs have claim priority over all other liabilities.[290] Although the absence of a deposit insurance scheme in Australia was unusual by world standards, in fact, no depositor had ever lost funds in an authorized bank since the introduction of modern banking legislation in 1945.[291] It also appears that, prior to the global financial crisis at least, a large proportion of the Australian public believed either that the government had provided a guarantee or would bail out depositors of failed ADIs.[292]

The Australian deposit guarantee was not without its share of controversy and criticism. It has been argued, for example, that taxpayer-funded guarantees, such as the deposit guarantee, undermine the philosophy of the Wallis Report[293] that any bank can fail, and constitute recognition that Australia's four major banks are, indeed, too big to fail.[294] Complaints have also been leveled against the way in which the

[288] See Schich, "Financial crisis," p. 109, Annex, Table A.1.

[289] The other country without governmental deposit insurance was New Zealand. Ibid. The Australian and New Zealand banking markets are highly integrated due to the high proportion of New Zealand bank assets which are Australian owned. See Doan, Glanville, Russel and White, "Greater international links," p. 123, noting that as at 2006, 85 per cent of New Zealand bank assets were Australian owned, which constituted 15 per cent of total Australian bank assets.

[290] This priority was set out under s. 13A(3) of the Banking Act 1959. See Pearson, *Financial Services Law and Compliance*, p. 277; Doan, Glanville, Russel and White, "Greater international links," p. 119; Swan, "New protections for depositors."

[291] See Pearson, *Financial Services Law and Compliance*, p. 276; Australian Prudential Regulation Authority, "Core principles for effective banking supervision: self-assessment for Australia," Information Paper, April (2011), p. 3.

[292] See Pearson, *Financial Services Law and Compliance*, pp. 275–6; Reserve Bank of Australia, *Financial Stability Review – September 2009*, pp. 45–6, Table 14, noting that 60 percent of respondents believed there was a guarantee or that the government would step in if there were a bank failure.

[293] The Wallis Report had considered, but rejected, the need for a deposit guarantee. See Financial System Inquiry, *Wallis Report*, Overview, "The financial system: towards 2010." The Wallis Report advocated retention of the traditional depositor preference rules, on the basis that a deposit insurance scheme would not provide substantially greater protection. Ibid., pp. 297, 355, 356.

[294] See J. Hockey, "Banks need more competition, not more regulation," *The Australian*, December 6, 2010, p. 14.

deposit guarantee was introduced, on the basis that it was an emergency-style response to the global financial crisis, rather than part of a coherent and coordinated banking reform program.[295] Finally, there were concerns that the deposit guarantee unfairly discriminated between ADIs that received protection under the scheme, and other unprotected income investment funds, such as mortgage funds and cash management trusts, which were thereby placed at a competitive disadvantage.[296]

Following reassessment of the FCS,[297] in September 2011 the Treasurer announced several changes to the scheme. These included the introduction of a new permanent guarantee cap of A$250,000 on ADI deposits from February 2012.[298]

The wholesale funding guarantee

The second liquidity-related emergency reform announced by Mr Rudd on October 12, 2008 was the introduction of a temporary wholesale funding guarantee.[299] Under this scheme, the government agreed, on application and for a fee, to guarantee wholesale debt securities issued by Australian banks and other ADIs, and locally incorporated subsidiaries of foreign-owned banks.[300]

This reform was a direct response to the dramatic slowdown in global bond issuances after the Lehman Brothers collapse.[301] A distinctive feature of the Australian banking system is heavy reliance on wholesale funding, particularly offshore, compared to a relatively low proportion of domestic retail deposit funding.[302] Wholesale funding represents

[295] Ibid.

[296] See Wing Kee, "Guarantees turn into political beasts," pp. 1, 10; Senate Economic References Committee, *Government Measures to Address Confidence Concerns in the Financial Sector – The Financial Claims Scheme and the Guarantee Scheme for Large Deposits and Wholesale Funding* (Canberra: Commonwealth of Australia, 2009), p. vii.

[297] See The Treasury (Australia), *Post-implementation Review and Regulation Impact Statement: Financial Claims Scheme* (Commonwealth of Australia, 2011), pp. 1–9, 78.

[298] The guarantee cap is $250,000 per person per ADI. See W. Swan, "New permanent financial claims scheme cap to protect 99 per cent of Australian deposit accounts in full," Media Release no. 109 by Deputy Prime Minister and Treasurer (Australia) Wayne Swan, September 11, 2011.

[299] Rudd, "Global financial crisis."

[300] See C. Schwartz, "The Australian Government Guarantee Scheme," *Reserve Bank of Australia Bulletin*, March (2010), 19–26, at 20.

[301] See S. Black, A. Brassil and M. Hack, "Recent trends in Australian banks' bond issuance," *Reserve Bank of Australia Bulletin*, March (2010), 27–33, at 28.

[302] See Brown and Davis, "Sub-prime crisis," 18.

approximately 50 percent of Australian banks' total funding, and around 60 percent of that amount is from international markets.[303]

As the credit crisis deepened in late 2008, global demand for unguaranteed financial institution debt evaporated. The Australian government was effectively forced to follow the lead of several European governments, including the United Kingdom and Ireland, which had already introduced wholesale funding guarantee schemes to prop up their banking systems.[304] The danger for Australian banks in this new international environment was that, although they were strongly capitalized and had high-quality assets, their AA ratings would be trumped by other countries' banks, which had received the backing of AAA government guarantees.[305] The Australian government's wholesale funding guarantee, therefore, reacted to the possibility of serious competitive disadvantage for Australian banks seeking to access offshore wholesale funding.[306]

The Australian scheme, while tracking the broad contours of arrangements announced in other jurisdictions, was nonetheless more flexible in some key respects. For example, unlike most other countries, including the United Kingdom and the United States, Australia did not set a fixed date for termination of the wholesale funding guarantee scheme.[307] Rather, it was explicitly stated that the guarantee was temporary only and would be withdrawn once market conditions had "normalized."[308] Australia permitted guaranteed debt with a rolling maturity date of five years, in contrast to most other jurisdictions, which favored fixed and

[303] See Takáts and Tumbarello, "Australian bank and corporate sector vulnerabilities," p. 6.

[304] Other jurisdictions, which had already introduced wholesale funding guarantee schemes, included: Ireland (September 30, 2008); Denmark (October 6, 2008); Germany (October 6, 2008); United Kingdom (October 8, 2008); Belgium (October 9, 2008); and Spain (October 10, 2008). The United States followed suit on October 14, 2011. See Schwartz, "Australian Government Guarantee Scheme," 21.

[305] See Stutchbury, "Rudd needs to straighten out the details," p. 28.

[306] Australian Government Guarantee Scheme for Large Deposits and Wholesale Funding, "About the scheme," at www.guaranteescheme.gov.au; Black, Brassil and Hack, "Recent trends," 28; Schwartz, "Australian Government Guarantee Scheme," 19; Durie, "Tweaks coming," p. 37.

[307] Other countries which adopted specific finishing dates for the wholesale funding guarantee included Ireland, Denmark, Germany, Belgium, Spain, France, South Korea, Sweden, the Netherlands, Finland and Canada. New Zealand opted, like Australia, to have an unspecified finishing date. Schwartz, "Australian Government Guarantee Scheme," 20.

[308] Rudd, "Global financial crisis."

shorter maturity dates.[309] Finally, the fee introduced for access to the Australian wholesale funding guarantee was relatively low compared to other international schemes.[310]

There was pushback from global investment banks, such as JP Morgan, UBS, Deutsche Bank, Société Générale and BNP Paribas, which operated in Australia through branches rather than local subsidiaries, and were therefore excluded from both the deposit guarantee and the wholesale funding guarantee schemes as originally framed.[311] These banks successfully lobbied the government to amend the scope of the guarantees to cover their Australian operations, arguing that otherwise their lending capacity would be seriously affected, which in turn could damage the Australian economy.[312] In response to this pressure, the Treasurer announced on October 24, 2008 that foreign bank branches would have access to the government guarantee for short-term wholesale funding raised from Australian residents on the same basis as other ADIs, and that they could also access the deposit guarantee for deposits held by Australian residents, though without the benefit of any fee threshold exemption.[313]

The wholesale funding guarantee arrangements were implemented under the federal government's Guarantee Scheme for Large Deposits and Wholesale Funding, which commenced operation on November 28, 2008.[314] During its operation, the scheme provided wholesale funding protection to approximately 150 Australian ADIs, including regional banks, building societies and credit unions.[315] This guarantee scheme, which came at a commercial cost for banks and other ADIs that drew

[309] Schwartz, "Australian Government Guarantee Scheme," 20.

[310] Ibid., noting, however, that the gap between the fee payable by institutions with different credit ratings under the Australian funding guarantee was relatively large compared to other jurisdictions.

[311] Wing Kee, "Guarantees turn into political beasts," pp. 1, 10.

[312] See Hewett, "RBA warns on bank guarantee," p. 21.

[313] Swan, "Government announces details."

[314] Royal Assent was given to the Guarantee Scheme for Large Deposits and Wholesale Funding Appropriation Bill 2008. See also Australian Government, *Deed: Deed of Guarantee in respect of the Australian Government Guarantee Scheme for Large Deposits and Wholesale Funding*, November 28, 2008, available at www.guaranteescheme.gov.au/deed/pdf/deed-of-guarantee.pdf; Australian Government, *Australian Government Guarantee Scheme for Large Deposits and Wholesale Funding Rules*, November 20, 2008, available at www.guaranteescheme.gov.au/rules/pdf/scheme-rules-20042011.pdf; Swan, "Guarantee scheme."

[315] W. Swan, "Government withdraws bank funding guarantee and state guarantee," Media Release no. 13 by Treasurer (Australia) Wayne Swan, February 7, 2010.

upon it, closed to new borrowing on March 31, 2010.[316] The Council of Financial Regulators advised the government to withdraw the guarantee on the basis that bank funding circumstances had improved considerably.[317] In 2009, Australian banks had issued a record A$228 billion in bonds, compared to only A$61 billion in 2007.[318] Also, a number of other G20 countries, including the United States and the United Kingdom,[319] had now removed their guarantees.[320]

The residential mortgage-backed securities (RMBS) initiative

The third element of Mr Rudd's October 12, 2008 announcement related to providing support to Australia's mortgage lending market.[321] During the period following the collapse of Lehman Brothers, liquidity was greatly reduced in the Australian residential mortgage-backed securities (RMBS) market. Accordingly, Mr Rudd announced that he had directed the Australian Office of Financial Management (AOFM) to invest an additional A$4 billion in Australian RMBS.[322] The aim of this RMBS initiative was to enable small lenders to provide credit for residential mortgages. The financial market dislocation particularly affected these small lenders since, unlike their larger competitors, they were unable to raise funds from equity and debt markets.[323]

The RMBS initiative had been flagged by the Treasurer in an earlier media release on September 26, 2008, announcing that the AOFM would make an initial investment in AAA-rated RMBS in two tranches of A$2 billion each.[324] The Treasurer asserted that this was "an investment, not an expenditure," contrasting the Australian government's actions with

316 Ibid.; Schwartz, "Australian Government Guarantee Scheme," 25–6; J. J. Spigelman, "The global financial crisis and Australian courts," address by the Chief Justice of New South Wales, the Honourable J. J. Spigelman AC, at the Inter-Pacific Bar Association Conference, Singapore, May 4, 2010, p. 3.

317 Swan, "Government withdraws bank funding guarantee."

318 See Black, Brassil and Hack, "Recent trends," 29.

319 The announced closure dates for analogous guarantee schemes in the United States and United Kingdom were October 31, 2009 and February 28, 2010, respectively. Schwartz, "Australian Government Guarantee Scheme," 25.

320 Swan, "Government withdraws bank funding guarantee."

321 Rudd, "Global financial crisis." 322 Ibid.

323 See Murphy, "Bank competition," pp. 45–6.

324 See W. Swan, "Government initiative to support competition in mortgage market," Media Release no. 105 by Treasurer Wayne Swan, September 26, 2008; Mallesons Stephen Jaques, "Government to invest in Australian RMBS," September 29, 2008, at www.mallesons.com/publications/marketAlerts/2008/Documents/9632339w.htm.

those proposed by the US Treasury to support the ailing US subprime market. He stressed that the Australian banking system as a whole was profitable with limited exposure to troubled mortgage-related assets, and that the prime AAA-rated RMBS would be required to meet strict quality standards.[325] In October 2008, the Treasurer directed the AOFM to invest in up to A$8 billion in eligible RMBS.[326] Half of this amount was to be invested in securities offered by non-ADI institutions, which were not entitled to the benefit of the government's deposit and wholesale funding guarantee.[327]

The background to the government's RMBS initiative lay in important developments in the Australian mortgage market from the period of financial deregulation onwards. Over that time, the RMBS sector provided a significant source of funding for smaller non-bank originators in the mortgage lending sector, allowing them to compete against and undercut the banks and other ADIs.[328]

Australia's mortgage-backed securities market originated in some small private placement securitizations in the mid-1980s.[329] At that time, Australia also experimented with a government-sponsored program, FANMAC,[330] paralleling the US mortgage agency, Fannie Mae;[331] however FANMAC was wound down in the early 1990s, and private sector mortgage-backed securities filled this void.[332] Although securitization was originally limited to domestic issues, this changed in 1997,

325 Swan, "Government initiative."

326 See Treasurer of the Commonwealth of Australia, "Direction on investment in residential mortgage-backed securities 2008," October 3, 2008; Treasurer of the Commonwealth of Australia, "Direction on investment in residential mortgage-backed securities 2008 (No. 2)," October 16, 2008.

327 See Australian Office of Financial Management, *Annual Report 2008–2009* (Canberra: Commonwealth of Australia, 2009), Part 2, "Operations and Performance."

328 See ibid.; A. Liaw and G. Eastwood, "The Australian securitisation market," APRA Working Paper 6, Australian Prudential Regulation Authority, October (2000), p. 1; Debelle, "State of play," p. 2.

329 See G. Rajendra and I. Påhlson-Möller, "Australian residential mortgage-backed securities update" in Deutsche Bank, *Global Securitisation and Structured Finance 2008* (London: Globe White Page, 2008), pp. 76–84, at p. 76.

330 First Australian National Mortgage Acceptance Corporation (FANMAC) was a New South Wales government agency. In 1986, FANMAC made an issue of A$50 million, based on residential mortgages of cooperative housing societies. See P. J. Rajapakse, "Issuance of residential mortgage-backed securities in Australia – legal and regulatory aspects," *University of New South Wales Law Journal*, 29 (2006), 173–206.

331 Rajendra and Påhlson-Möller, "Australian residential mortgage-backed securities," p. 76.

332 Ibid.; Liaw and Eastwood, "Australian securitisation market," p. 10.

as a result of tax reforms enabling Australian mortgage lenders to have access to offshore markets.[333]

Securitization growth in Australia was modest until the mid-1990s, when it began to expand rapidly in terms of volume and asset diversity.[334] Between 1995[335] and 2007,[336] the Australian securitization market grew from an estimated A$10 billion to around A$270 billion, 78 percent of which comprised RMBS.[337] In 2007, Australia was ranked as the second-largest issuer of asset-backed securities after the United States.[338] Between the mid-1990s and 2008, the proportion of Australian home lending financed by securitization rose from less than 5 percent to a peak of more than 20 percent in 2008.[339] Over this time, offshore issuances also grew strongly, constituting more than 50 percent of outstanding Australian RMBS immediately prior to the global financial crisis.[340] Expansion of securitization in Australia occurred in a period marked by strong economic growth in Australia and low interest rates. Yet, as an APRA Working Paper noted with some prescience in 2000, Australia's securitization industry had yet to encounter a difficult economic climate.[341] When such testing economic times finally arrived in the guise of the global financial crisis, the Australian RMBS market was hard hit, in spite of its overall good performance.[342] In 2010, new RMBS issuance stood at around A$18 billion compared to more than A$50 billion pre-crisis.[343]

In announcing the 2008 RMBS initiative, the Australian Treasurer stressed that it was a temporary action only, responding to "highly unusual conditions in international capital markets" which had adversely affected the Australian mortgage lending market.[344] Nonetheless, governmental support for the RMBS sector continued over a

[333] Rajendra and Påhlson-Möller, "Australian residential mortgage-backed securities," p. 76.
[334] Liaw and Eastwood, "Australian securitisation market," pp. 8–9. See Debelle, "State of play," p. 2, attributing the rapid growth of securitization to changes in technology and a fall in nominal interest rates.
[335] See Liaw and Eastwood, "Australian securitisation market," p. 8.
[336] See Brown and Davis, "Sub-prime crisis," 17. [337] Ibid.
[338] Ibid. Brown and Davis list a range of factors, which they suggested would make Australian markets particularly susceptible to destabilization in the US sub-prime market. Ibid., 17–18.
[339] See Debelle, "State of play," pp. 1–2, Graph 1. [340] Ibid., p. 2, Graph 2.
[341] Liaw and Eastwood, "Australian securitisation market," p. 10.
[342] See Debelle, "State of play," p. 3.
[343] Almost all of the 2010 issuance was domestic. Ibid., pp. 3–4, Graph 4.
[344] Swan, "Government initiative."

number of years.[345] Between October 2008 and April 2011, the government's total investment under the RMBS initiative was A$20 billion.[346]

The Australian banking sector became far more concentrated during the global financial crisis, as a result of an increased number of bank mergers and the departure of some non-bank lenders.[347] The collapse of the securitization/RMBS market has been identified as a major contributor to this trend.[348] There were takeovers of many second-tier banks and non-bank lenders by the major banks.[349] High-profile non-bank financial lenders, such as RAMS, Wizard and Aussie Home Loans, which had operated in the RMBS market,[350] became "virtually extinct."[351] Those non-bank lenders that survived lost a substantial portion of their market share.[352]

Over the course of the global financial crisis, the proportion of the mortgage market held by the big four banks rose from 57 percent to 84 percent.[353] By May 2011, this figure had escalated further to 90 percent.[354] According to Allan Fels, Australia's former competition regulator, "in a few short months, we saw the biggest reversal in banking competition since the Depression."[355]

In 2010, the Australian government announced that it would introduce additional reforms to help small lenders compete with the major

345 See The Treasury (Australia), *Competitive and Sustainable Banking System* (Canberra: Commonwealth of Australia, 2010), pp. 19–20.

346 Deputy Prime Minister and Treasurer Wayne W. Swan, "More support for a competitive lending market," Media Release no. 031 by Deputy Prime Minister and Treasurer (Australia) Wayne Swan, April 8, 2011; see Treasurer of the Commonwealth of Australia, "Direction on investment in residential mortgage-backed securities 2011," April 5, 2011.

347 See Murphy, "Bank competition," pp. 47–8; Senate Economics Reference Committee, *Competition within the Australian Banking Sector*, p. 1.

348 See C. Yeates, "Level playing field would open doors for small lenders," *Sydney Morning Herald*, October 30, 2010, p. 6.

349 For example, Westpac Banking Corporation took over St George Bank and RAMS, and the Commonwealth Bank of Australia took over BankWest. See B. Drury, "Own your own bank and prosper," *Sydney Morning Herald*, July 21, 2010, p. 4.

350 See I. Verrender, "Dedicated little guys can give bankers a run for their money," *Sydney Morning Herald*, November 6, 2010, p. 7.

351 Drury, "Own your own bank," p. 4.

352 See, for example, M. Wayde, "Banks grab lion's share of all new home loans," *Sydney Morning Herald*, September 26, 2011, p. 5.

353 A. Ferguson and E. Johnston, "Back to the bad old days," *Sydney Morning Herald*, December 4, 2010, p. 8.

354 See G. Liondis, "Big four tighten grip on home loans," *Australian Financial Review*, July 13, 2011, p. 51, citing Australian Bureau of Statistics (ABS) data.

355 Quoted in Ferguson and Johnston, "Bad old days," p. 8.

banks under the 2010 Competitive and Sustainable Banking System reform package,[356] which includes, for example, a ban on mortgage exit fees for new home loans.[357] It remains to be seen whether these reforms will address the banking competition issues engendered in Australia by the global financial crisis.

Covered bonds

> We have already seen banks from Canada and Norway coming to Australia to issue covered bonds and take our savings home with them. It defies logic that our own banks cannot issue the same covered bonds themselves to our local superannuation funds for Australian investors.
>
> Wayne Swan[358]

A more recent Australian regulatory development, which is closely linked to the 2008 government deposit and wholesale funding guarantee, is the decision to permit Australian banks to issue covered bonds. Like the earlier wholesale funding guarantee, this reform responds to competitive pressures for Australian banks in offshore wholesale funding markets.

Covered bonds are dual recourse secured debt instruments, providing investors with enhanced protection. Investors have recourse against a cover pool of assets, such as mortgages, and also against the issuer if the cover pool is inadequate to satisfy the claim.[359] Although there is considerable international variation in the structure of covered bond schemes, according to the European Covered Bond Council, their core features are: (i) issuance by, and recourse against, a regulated credit institution; (ii) a preferential claim by bondholders against a pool of assets over unsecured creditors; (iii) a continuing obligation on the credit institution to maintain sufficient assets in the cover pool to satisfy bondholder claims; (iv) supervision by a public or independent body of the credit institution's obligations concerning the cover pool.[360]

[356] See Treasury (Australia), *Competitive and Sustainable Banking System*, pp. 7, 16–21.

[357] The prohibition on mortgage exit fees for new home loans became operative from July 1, 2011. Ibid., p. 7.

[358] Comments made in Parliament, quoted in C. Yeates, "Covered bonds another string in banks' bow," *Sydney Morning Herald*, September 16, 2011, p. 7.

[359] See The Parliament of the Commonwealth of Australia, House of Representatives, Banking Amendment (Covered Bonds) Bill 2011, *Explanatory Memorandum* (2011), [1.2].

[360] European Covered Bond Council, "ECBC essential features of covered bonds," available at http://ecbc.hypo.org/Content/default.asp?PageID=503.

Covered bonds are distinguishable from other asset-backed securities, such as RMBS, in that they place ultimate risk with the issuer, rather than the bondholder.[361] Covered bonds potentially offer advantages to both issuers and investors by, for example, enabling issuers to obtain lower-cost finance, and by providing investors with greater protection via access to the cover pool of collateral.[362]

Covered bonds are a familiar feature of European financial markets,[363] originating in eighteenth-century Prussia.[364] They have become an increasingly important form of bank funding in international markets since the global financial crisis. They are perceived to have been more resilient to financial market stress than many other securities,[365] and have become increasingly attractive amid growing concern about sovereign debt, and the dangers of providing unsecured loans to European banks.[366] Europe's early dominance in this market continues today. In 2010, banks issued a record US$365 billion globally in covered bonds, with Europe accounting for more than 80 percent of this amount.[367] As at October 2011, covered bonds constituted 43 percent of global bank debt, compared to only 25 percent in 2007 prior to the financial crisis.[368] In contrast to the European position, covered bonds were traditionally rare in the United States[369] and non-existent in Australia, and there was no legislative framework supporting them in either jurisdiction. In spite

[361] Banking Amendment (Covered Bonds) Bill 2011, *Explanatory Memorandum*, [1.3]. For a description of the core features of covered bonds, see European Covered Bond Council, "Essential features of covered bonds."

[362] "Understanding the key elements of covered bonds legislation," Address by J. Lonsdale, the General Manager of the Financial System Division, Markets Group, of the Australian Treasury at the INSTO Covered Bond Congress, August 15, 2011, pp. 10–12.

[363] See Australian Prudential Regulation Authority, *Annual Report 2008* (Commonwealth of Australia, 2008), p. 13.

[364] S. Mishkin and J. Hughes, "Australia dips its toe into covered bonds," *Financial Times*, November 18, 2011, p. 22.

[365] Lonsdale, "Key elements of covered bonds legislation," p. 12.

[366] See J. Hughes, "Support rises in US for covered bonds law," *Financial Times*, March 16, 2011; M. Maiden, "Covered bonds will help bank funding but aren't a game-changer," *Sydney Morning Herald*, November 17, 2011, p. 7; Mishkin and Hughes, "Australia dips its toe," p. 22.

[367] Hughes, "Support rises." [368] Maiden, "Covered bonds will help," p. 7.

[369] See generally S. Winkler, "United States" in European Covered Bond Council, *2010 ECBC European Covered Bond*, 5th edition (2010), pp. 341–4, at p. 341, noting that only two banks, Washington Mutual Bank and Bank of America, had made covered bond issues in the United States.

of this, however, covered bonds have recently become a regulatory focal point in both the United States and Australia.

In the United States, covered bonds have been viewed as a potential panacea to weaknesses in the property market since the global financial crisis,[370] and there have been several attempts to provide a legislative basis for their issue.[371] The Federal Deposit Insurance Corporation (FDIC), which guarantees US bank deposits, has resisted this development, citing concerns that covered bonds could dilute its Deposit Insurance Fund (DIF).[372] The United States, nonetheless, moved closer towards providing a legislative framework for covered bonds in November 2011, when a group of Republican and Democrat Senators introduced the Covered Bond Bill of 2011 into the US Senate.[373]

Prior to the global financial crisis, Australia also lacked a legal framework for covered bonds, in spite of the fact that APRA and the ADI industry had been consulting on the issue for several years.[374] In 2008, APRA expressed the view that covered bonds were prohibited, since they ran counter to Australia's long-standing principle of depositor preference under the Banking Act 1959.[375] APRA also raised certain in-principle objections based on the fact that covered bond structures privilege bondholder interests, by subordinating ADI depositor interests.[376]

In more recent times, however, the Australian regulation on this issue has done a U-turn. In December 2010, the government announced, as part of its broader Competitive and Sustainable Banking System reform package,[377] that Australian banks, credit unions and building societies would be permitted to issue covered bonds.[378] The government stated

[370] T. Alloway, "Plan for US covered bonds," *Financial Times*, November 10, 2011.

[371] See generally Winkler, "United States," p. 342*ff*.

[372] See Alloway, "US covered bonds"; M. H. Krimminger, Testimony of Deputy to the Chairman of the Federal Deposit Insurance Corporation, Michael H. Krimminger, at the U.S. Senate Committee on Banking, Housing, and Urban Affairs hearing, "Covered bonds: potential uses and regulatory issues," September 15, 2010.

[373] See J. Prior, "Covered bond legislation introduced in Senate," *Housing Wire*, November 9, 2011.

[374] See Australian Prudential Regulation Authority, *Annual Report 2008*, p. 13.

[375] See Australian Prudential Regulation Authority, *APS 120 – Securitisation*, Prudential Standard, January, 2008, [7].

[376] Australian Prudential Regulation Authority, *Annual Report 2008*, pp. 13–14.

[377] Australia's Competitive and Sustainable Banking System reform package was announced on December 12, 2010. See Treasury (Australia), *Competitive and Sustainable Banking System*, p. 23.

[378] See W. Swan, "A competitive and sustainable banking system," Media Release no. 091 by the Deputy Prime Minister and Treasurer (Australia) Wayne Swan, December 12, 2010.

that the initiative, which operates against the backdrop of the government deposit guarantee under the FCS, was designed to allow ADIs to "broaden access to cheaper, more stable and longer-term funding" and to harness national superannuation savings.[379]

In October 2011, the government passed the Banking Amendment (Covered Bonds) Act 2011[380] permitting Australian ADIs to issue covered bonds for the first time.[381] The new regime for covered bonds addresses depositor protection in several ways. First, depositors, who are subordinated to covered bondholders, will still receive the security offered by the government's deposit guarantee under the FCS. Second, the Banking Amendment (Covered Bonds) Act 2011 imposes a legislative cap. The Act prohibits the issue of a covered bond by an ADI if the combined value of cover pool assets exceeds 8 percent of the ADI's assets in Australia.[382] Finally, covered bonds will be subject to prudential regulation by APRA.[383] Some commentators have suggested that the impact of the new Australian scheme will be minimal as a result of the 8 percent asset cap,[384] which is far less than the European norm.[385] Nonetheless, with a combined Australian ADI asset base of almost A$2 trillion, the Australian covered bond market could theoretically reach A$160 billion.[386]

379 Ibid. As part of the Competitive and Sustainable Banking System initiative, the government also announced its intention to launch trading of Commonwealth Government Securities on a securities exchange to develop a deep corporate bond market and reduce reliance on international wholesale funding markets. Ibid.; Treasury (Australia), *Competitive and Sustainable Banking System*, p. 24.

380 The Banking Amendment (Covered Bonds) Act 2011 amended the Banking Act 1959 to introduce these changes.

381 A number of amendments were made between the release of the initial exposure draft of the proposed legislation in March 2011 and the final Banking Amendment (Covered Bonds) Act 2011, which became effective on October 17, 2011. See Mallesons Stephen Jaques, "Australian ADIs can now issue covered bonds," October 17, 2011, at www.mallesons.com/publications/marketAlerts/2011/Regulator_Nov_11/Pages/Australian-ADIs-can-now-issue-covered-bonds.aspx.

382 See Banking Amendment (Covered Bonds) Act 2011, Division 3A.

383 See Australian Prudential Regulation Authority, "APRA releases discussion paper on covered bonds and securitisation," Media Release 11.25, November 8, 2011; Australian Prudential Regulation Authority, "Covered bonds and securitisation matters," Discussion Paper, November 8, 2011; Australian Prudential Regulation Authority, "Draft Prudential Standard APS 121: Covered bonds," November 2011.

384 See, for example, Yeates, "Covered bonds," p. 7.

385 Indeed, it has been said that such a high proportion of European bank assets have now been used as bond collateral that "the covered bond well is dry." Maiden, "Covered bonds will help," p. 7.

386 Ibid. See also W. Swan, "First Australian covered bond issue," Media Release no. 139 by the Deputy Prime Minister and Treasurer Wayne Swan, November 16, 2011.

The 8 percent asset cap could, however, skew the use of covered bonds in offshore versus domestic markets. Given the growing popularity of covered bonds in international markets, Australian banks are under increasing competitive pressure to offer a cover pool when raising debt offshore. Yet, in spite of the Australian government's specific reference to harnessing national superannuation savings through use of covered bonds,[387] Australian banks are still able to borrow on an unsecured basis in the domestic market. The existence of the 8 percent asset cap may therefore deter banks from using covered bonds in the domestic context, effectively confining their use to offshore issuances.[388]

Australian banks initially embraced covered bonds with enthusiasm in the offshore context. Immediately after the Banking Amendment (Covered Bonds) Act 2011 was passed, Westpac Banking Corporation (Westpac) and Australian and New Zealand Banking Group (ANZ) sold US$1 billion and US$1.25 billion of five-year covered bonds in the United States.[389] However, the European debt crisis in late 2011 affected the burgeoning Australian covered bond market. Investor demand for the two US bond issues was weak, forcing Westpac and ANZ to pay a much higher price than anticipated.[390] Soon afterwards, the Commonwealth Bank of Australia announced that it had put a planned euro-denominated covered bond issue on hold.[391]

The danger to Australian banks of global market dislocation and rising financing costs may to some degree be alleviated by the RBA's commitment to provide emergency funding through its Committed Liquidity Facility under the Basel III liquidity reforms.[392] The Committed Liquidity Facility is intended to help Australian banks comply with new liquidity requirements which, at a global level, are aimed at ensuring that banks hold more liquid assets in the form of sovereign debt.

[387] See Swan, "Competitive and sustainable banking system."

[388] I am grateful to my colleague, John Stumbles, for drawing my attention to this possible outcome.

[389] See Mishkin and Hughes, "Australia dips its toe," p. 22; J. Shapiro, "Crisis delays CBA bond issue," *Australian Financial Review*, November 21, 2011, p. 46.

[390] See J. Shapiro, J. Kehoe and G. Liondis, "Euro crisis hits local banks," *Australian Financial Review*, November 26, 2011, p. 1.

[391] C. Yeates, "Europe turmoil forces CBA to delay covered bond issue," *Sydney Morning Herald*, November 22, 2011, p. 3; Shapiro, "Crisis delays CBA bond issue," p. 46.

[392] See Reserve Bank of Australia, "The RBA committed liquidity facility"; Australian Prudential Regulation Authority, "Implementing Basel III liquidity reforms"; Australian Prudential Regulation Authority, "Draft Prudential Standard APS 210."

This requirement has, however, provided difficulties in the Australian context, due to the extremely low level of government debt, which the RBA's Committed Liquidity Facility is designed to offset.[393]

ASIC's ban on short selling

> As long as securities have been traded, Anglo-American popular culture has contained a few strands of thought suspicious of trading and hostile to speculators.
>
> Stuart Banner[394]

Corporate crises elicit ambivalence about the role and incentives of shareholders.[395] They raise questions concerning whether shareholders are investors, traders or predators,[396] and the rise of hedge funds has only intensified this debate.[397] Financial crises also unmask tensions between short sellers and regulators, which may be concealed at other times.[398] Although regulators often acknowledge the presumed benefits of short selling in terms of market liquidity and accurate price discovery,[399] crises can narrow the divide between legitimate short selling and market manipulation by, for example, pushing the stock price

393 "Australia's APRA releases Basel III consultation reforms."

394 Banner, "What causes new securities regulation?" 850.

395 Nowhere is this more clearly revealed than in the continuing US shareholder empowerment debate. See, generally, J. G. Hill, "The rising tension between shareholder and director power in the common law world," *Corporate Governance: An International Review*, (18) 2010, 344–59.

396 See L. Mitchell, "Protect industry from predatory speculators," *Financial Times*, July 8, 2009, p. 9. In 2008, for example, Takao Kitabata, a Vice Minister of Japan's Ministry of Economy, Trade and Industry (METI), described shareholders as "fickle, irresponsible and greedy." See M. Nakamoto, "One-way street? As its companies expand abroad, Japan erects new barriers at home," *Financial Times*, March 3, 2008, p. 7.

397 In Germany, for example, short-term shareholders, such as hedge funds, were compared to "swarms of locusts" following the 2005 ouster of Werner G. Seifert from his position as Chief Executive of the German Stock Exchange. See M. Lander and H. Timmons, "Poison ink aimed at 'locusts'," *New York Times*, March 31, 2006, p. C8.

398 See G. O'Mahoney, "Recent legal developments on market manipulation and insider trading" in R. P. Austin and I. L. von Kowalski, *New Trends in Sharemarket Regulation* (Ross Parsons Centre of Commercial, Corporate and Taxation Law, 2011), pp. 59–73, at p. 67.

399 See ibid., citing Securities and Exchange Commission (US), "Statement of Securities and Exchange Commission concerning short selling and issuer stock repurchases," Press Release 2008–235, October 1, 2008.

downwards.[400] Indeed, according to one commentator, since the seventeenth century there has been a tendency to view short selling as "immoral."[401]

A falling stock market is fertile terrain for short selling,[402] and the period following the collapse of Lehman Brothers was one of "unprecedented market volatility."[403] As in earlier market downturns, short selling came to the regulatory forefront.[404] There was reported short-selling activity in the stock of several highly leveraged Australian companies, such as ABC Learning and Allco Finance, which subsequently failed during the global financial crisis.[405] There was particular concern about the conjunction of short selling and "rumourtrage,"[406] with ASIC declaring that "rumours. . .undermine confidence in the integrity of markets."[407] This was a sentiment echoed by numerous international regulators during this period.[408]

From mid-September 2008, there was a wave of responses to short selling by regulators around the world.[409] Several different regulatory

400 See O'Mahoney, "Recent legal developments," pp. 68–9.

401 P. Ali, "Short selling and securities lending in the midst of falling and volatile markets," *Journal of International Banking Law and Regulation*, 24 (2009), 1–12.

402 This is because the short seller can profit by a fall in share price. Ibid., 1, 3.

403 See Australian Securities and Investments Commission, "Naked short selling not permitted and covered short selling to be disclosed," Media Release no. 08–204, September 19, 2008.

404 See Ali, "Short selling and securities lending," noting that historically market downturns have routinely been followed by calls to ban short selling.

405 See K. Sheehan, "Principled regulatory action? The case of short selling," Working Paper, March 12 (2009), available at papers.ssrn.com/sol3/papers.cfm?abstract_id=1368531, p. 13.

406 See A. Black, "Insider trading and market misconduct," *Company and Securities Law Journal*, 29 (2011), 313–26, at 323; Allens Arthur Robinson, "Rumourtrage and a rising tide of market regulation," *Capital Markets*, March 31, 2009.

407 See Australian Securities and Investments Commission, "Responsible handling of rumours," Consultation Paper 118, September 15, 2009. See also Corporations and Markets Advisory Committee, *Aspects of Market Integrity*, p. 95*ff*.

408 The SEC, for example, asserted that "[f]alse rumors can lead to a loss of confidence in our markets." See Securities and Exchange Commission, "Emergency order pursuant to section 12(k)(2) of the Securities Exchange Act of 1934 taking temporary action to respond to market developments," United States of America before the Securities and Exchange Commission, Release no. 58166, July 15, 2008. In Europe, ESMA also stated that "[w]hile short selling can be a valid trading strategy, when used in combination with spreading false market rumours, this is clearly abusive." See ESMA, "ESMA promotes harmonised regulatory action on short selling in the EU," Public Statement, August 11, 2008.

409 See A. Beber and M. Pagano, "Short-selling bans around the world: evidence from the 2007–09 crisis," August (2011) (draft paper available on American Finance Association website, forthcoming, *Journal of Finance*), p. 11.

blueprints emerged, particularly in regard to the scope of the relevant bans. In most jurisdictions, including the United States, United Kingdom, Canada and Germany, short selling bans applied only to securities issued by designated financial institutions. In some other jurisdictions, however, such as Australia, Japan and South Korea, the restrictions applied to all listed stock.[410] Also, some regulatory responses distinguished between covered short selling and the practice of "naked" short selling, which involves short sales without a securities lending arrangement in place at the time of the sale.[411]

Historically, Australia, the United Kingdom and the United States displayed divergent attitudes to short selling, particularly naked short selling.[412] Across a regulatory spectrum, the UK approach was the most liberal and the US approach the least.[413] Although all three jurisdictions responded during the global financial crisis to the apparent threat posed by short selling to "fair and orderly markets,"[414] their regulatory starting points were vastly different.[415] On July 15, 2008, the SEC issued an emergency order, the effect of which was to prohibit temporarily naked short selling of shares in nineteen financial institutions, including Freddie Mac and Fannie Mae.[416] The SEC cited concerns about false rumors, such as those which had affected Bear Stearns, as justification for its actions.[417] On September 18, 2008, the FSA, acting in conjunction with the SEC, issued a temporary ban on all short sales, both naked and covered, in shares issued by thirty-two UK banks and insurance

[410] See O'Mahoney, "Recent legal developments," p. 69; Beber and Pagano, "Short-selling bans," p. 11.

[411] See Australian Securities and Investments Commission, "Short selling," Regulatory Guide 196, April 7, 2011, RG 196.4–RG 196.6; Black, "Insider trading," 323.

[412] See generally Sheehan, "Principled regulatory action?"

[413] See Ali, "Short selling and securities lending," 3–4, stating that traditionally naked short selling was essentially unregulated in the United Kingdom unless it infringed manipulative trading rules, in contrast to the United States, where naked short selling was viewed as "inherently abusive." In Australia prior to the global financial crisis, naked short selling was conditionally permitted with ASX approval to ensure adequate liquidity. The ASX had given approval for such short selling in relation to the shares of more than 400 issuers. Ibid., 4.

[414] See Securities and Exchange Commission, "Emergency order (Release no. 58166)." For a detailed discussion of the regulatory responses to short selling in Australia, the United Kingdom and the United States, see Sheehan, "Principled regulatory action?"

[415] Ibid., p. 40.

[416] Securities and Exchange Commission, "Emergency order (Release no. 58166)."

[417] Ibid.

companies.[418] At the same time, the SEC also introduced a revised set of temporary restrictions on short selling, which were far broader than those originally announced.[419] The new restrictions involved a ban on both naked and covered short selling of the stock of almost 800 US financial institutions.[420]

On September 19, 2008, Australia entered the international regulatory fray.[421] ASIC, in conjunction with the ASX,[422] announced controversial temporary restrictions on short selling, to commence on September 22, 2008.[423] ASIC's original announcement imposed an effective ban on naked short selling,[424] but this was expanded two days later to include covered short selling as well.[425] The Australian restrictions were much broader than the US and UK rules. Whereas the US and UK rules applied only to shares in designated financial institutions, the Australian restrictions applied to "all listed stocks."[426] ASIC subsequently relaxed the ban with respect to non-financial securities on November 19, 2008,[427]

[418] See Ali, "Short selling and securities lending," 3–4; White & Case, "SEC and FSA take action against abusive short selling," *Securities – Client Alert*, September 2008; Linklaters, "FSA update rules on short selling of financial stocks," September 2008.

[419] Securities and Exchange Commission, Emergency order pursuant to section 12(k)(2) of the Securities Exchange Act of 1934 taking temporary action to respond to market developments," Release no. 34–58572, September 17, 2008; Securities and Exchange Commission, "Emergency order pursuant to section 12(k)(2) of the Securities Exchange Act of 1934 taking temporary action to respond to market developments," United States of America before the Securities and Exchange Commission, Release no. 34–58592, September 18, 2008; White & Case, "SEC and FSA take action."

[420] See Ali, "Short selling and securities lending," 5; White & Case, "SEC and FSA take action."

[421] See generally Sheehan, "Principled regulatory action?" pp. 23–9.

[422] See Australian Securities and Investments Commission, "Naked short selling," removing shares from its previous list of shares in relation to which naked short selling was permissible. See also Ali, "Short selling and securities lending," 4, noting that before ASIC's November 19, 2008 announcement the shares of over 400 issuers had received ASX approval for naked short selling, on the basis of sufficient liquidity. Ibid.

[423] See Australian Securities and Investments Commission, "Naked short selling"; P. Durkin, A. Cornell and D. Crowe, "ASIC crackdown on short selling," *Australian Financial Review*, September 20, 2008, p. 12.

[424] Australian Securities and Investments Commission, "Naked short selling."

[425] Australian Securities and Investments Commission, "Covered short selling not permitted," Media Release no. 08–205, September 21, 2008.

[426] Ibid.; D. Hamson, M. Wanzare, G. Smith and P. Gardner, "Has the short-selling ban reduced liquidity in the Australian stock market?," 4 (2008), *Finsia Journal of Applied Finance*, 14–20, at 15.

[427] See Australian Securities and Investments Commission, "ASIC lifts ban on covered short selling for non-financial securities," Media Release no. AD08–65, November 13, 2008.

however, a ban on covered short sales of financial stock continued until May 25, 2009.[428] In the meantime, a legislative ban on all naked short selling of all listed stocks was introduced under the Corporations Amendment (Short Selling) Act 2008 (Cth), which became law in December 2008.[429] ASIC and the ASX have imposed fines and banning orders for short selling on a number of occasions.[430]

Australia's emergency response to short selling has been criticized on a number of grounds. One commentator has argued that it is difficult to discern any principled approach to the application and scope of the restrictions, and there is no evidence as to whether they were effective in restraining market manipulation.[431] Others have suggested that the scope of the short-selling prohibition in Australia was unnecessarily broad and amounted to regulatory overreaction.[432] There was also a significant amount of confusion and uncertainty surrounding the relevant rules.[433]

The Australian ban on covered short selling of financial stocks stayed in place far longer than in many other jurisdictions. Although it was anticipated that the ban would end in January 2009,[434] a number of Australian banks put pressure on ASIC to retain the ban following the

428 Australian Securities and Investments Commission, "ASIC lifts ban on covered short selling of financial securities," Media Release no. 09–94, May 25, 2009. See L. Battersby and R. Williams, "Bank stocks hit as ASIC lifts ban on short-selling," *Sydney Morning Herald*, May 26, 2009, p. 15.

429 There were three key measures contained in the Corporations Amendment (Short Selling) Act 2008 (Cth): (i) the ban on naked short selling; (ii) disclosure rules for permitted covered short selling; (iii) clarification of ASIC's powers. See J. Boynton, "New Australian short selling regime – 16 December 2008," Mallesons Stephen Jaques, December 12, 2008, at www.mallesons.com/publications/marketAlerts/2008/Documents/9733438w.htm.

430 Allens Arthur Robinson, "Rumourtrage." For example, ASIC prosecuted a Victorian share trader in November 2008 for violating the short selling ban. See Australian Securities and Investments Commission, "Victorian share trader to face ASIC short selling charges," Media Release no. AD08–53, November 6, 2008.

431 O'Mahoney, "Recent legal developments," p. 69. See also Sheehan, "Principled regulatory action?" p. 47, who analyzes the short selling regulatory responses in Australia, the United Kingdom and the United States, concluding that none of them amounted to principled regulatory action.

432 See, for example, V. O'Shaughnessy and R. Williams, "Heat on ASIC over short-selling ban," *The Age*, September 24, 2008, p. 1; Hamson, Wanzare, Smith and Gardner, "Short-selling ban reduced liquidity?"

433 See, for example, O'Shaughnessy and Williams, "Heat on ASIC," p. 1; A. Main, "A long way for short selling rules," *The Australian*, May 11, 2009, p. 22.

434 See A. Main, "ASIC's decision can help stability," *The Australian*, January 22, 2009, p. 25.

near-collapse of Royal Bank of Scotland,[435] and it ultimately stayed in place until May 25, 2009.[436] The lifting of the ban on short selling of financial stocks in Australia came much later than in a number of other major countries, including Canada (October 8, 2008), United States (October 8, 2008) and United Kingdom (January 16, 2009).[437] The SEC considered that its relatively short-lived ban had caused significant market distortion,[438] and it has been suggested that ASIC's short selling ban adversely affected liquidity in Australia's listed equity market.[439] Supporting such a claim is a recent empirical evidence study of global equity markets, which finds that Australia experienced one of the most serious declines in liquidity of any of the countries which introduced a short selling ban at that time.[440]

The short selling initiatives taken by ASIC, the FSA and the SEC during the global financial crisis demonstrated differences in their legal starting points and their regulatory scope.[441] The actions of the FSA and SEC were directed towards addressing a major crisis in their respective banking systems,[442] which was arguably a less severe problem in Australia. Although ASIC ostensibly followed the lead of the FSA and SEC in imposing restrictions on short selling, the Australian bans were broader, longer-lasting and possibly more detrimental to liquidity than the UK and US restraints. The short-selling regulatory responses provide an interesting example of national dynamics which can create new legal divergence in responding to corporate crises, in spite of harmonization efforts at a global level.

[435] See S. Murdoch, "Keep short ban, banks plead," *The Australian*, January 21, 2009, p. 19.

[436] Australian Securities and Investments Commission, "Ban on covered short selling of financial securities." See Battersby and Williams, "Bank stocks hit," p. 15.

[437] See Beber and Pagano, "Short-selling bans," p. 34, Table 1 (Figure 5); P. Durkin, "ASIC urged to lift short-sell ban," *Australian Financial Review*, January 7, 2009, p. 36; A. Ferguson, "Financial shorts ban divides market," *The Australian*, March 6, 2009, p. 17.

[438] See R. Williams and L. Battersby, "Ban stays as world view is sold short," *The Age*, March 7, 2009, p. 1, citing SEC Commissioner, Kathleen Casey.

[439] O'Mahoney, "Recent legal developments," p. 70; Hamson, Wanzare, Smith and Gardner, "Short-selling ban reduced liquidity?"

[440] According to this study, Italy suffered the worst deterioration in liquidity, followed by Denmark, Australia and Norway. See Beber and Pagano, "Short-selling bans," pp. 24, 47 (Figure 5).

[441] See Sheehan, "Principled regulatory action?"

[442] Ibid., p. 47.

Executive remuneration reforms

> [C]orporate excesses are reported by some as mainly a foreign phenomenon.
>
> Australian Government Productivity Commission[443]

Although Australia traditionally permitted market mechanisms to operate on executive pay with relatively little legislative intervention,[444] an array of regulatory constraints were introduced in the post-Enron period and during the global financial crisis.[445] Questions arise, however, as to whether the suite of reforms relating to executive remuneration, which were introduced in Australia during the global financial crisis, responded to problems at an international or a local level.

Executive remuneration came under the regulatory spotlight in Australia following the Enron scandal, although it was a much less significant theme in contemporaneous US reforms.[446] The focus on executive pay in Australia was partly attributable to the HIH Royal Commission, which highlighted directors' remuneration as a critical area for reform.[447] Australian legislative rhetoric at the time stressed the need for stronger shareholder participation rights,[448] and the most prominent of the post-Enron reforms was the introduction in 2004 of an annual non-binding shareholder vote on executive pay.[449] Stronger disclosure requirements were also implemented to

[443] Australian Government Productivity Commission, "Regulation of director and executive remuneration in Australia," Issues Paper, April 2009, p. 4 (on file with the author).

[444] See, generally, K. Sheehan, "The regulatory framework for executive remuneration in Australia," *Sydney Law Review*, 31 (2009), 273–308.

[445] Ibid.

[446] Only two provisions of the Sarbanes-Oxley Act 2002, ss. 304 and 402, related to executive pay. See, generally, J. G. Hill, R. W. Masulis and R. S. Thomas, "Comparing CEO employment contract provisions: differences between Australia and the United States," *Vanderbilt Law Review*, 64 (2011), 559–611, at 573–4.

[447] See HIH Royal Commission, *The Failure of HIH Insurance*, vol. I, Part 3 – "Directions for the future," Recommendation 1, p. 116.

[448] See The Parliament of the Commonwealth of Australia, House of Representatives, Corporate Law Economic Reform Program (Audit Reform and Corporate Disclosure) Bill 2003, *Explanatory Memorandum*, [4.271]–[4.280].

[449] Section 250R(2) of the Corporations Act 2001 (Cth) requires shareholders of an Australian listed company to pass a non-binding advisory vote at its annual general meeting, indicating whether they adopt the directors' remuneration report. This reform was introduced by the Corporate Law Economic Reform Program (Audit Reform and Corporate Disclosure) Act 2004 (CLERP 9 Act). See generally L. Chapple and B. Christensen, "The non-binding vote on executive pay: a review of the CLERP 9 reform," *Australian Journal of Corporate Law*, 18 (2005), 263–87. For a discussion of other post-Enron executive remuneration reforms in Australia, see, generally, J. G. Hill, "Regulatory responses to global corporate scandals," *Wisconsin International Law Journal*, 23 (2005), 367–416.

address concern that executive pay in Australian listed corporations was insufficiently linked to performance.[450]

From an international perspective, the global financial crisis had a far greater impact on the regulation of executive pay than the Enron scandal. Many commentators have argued that compensation practices, particularly in the banking sphere, directly contributed to the financial crisis by rewarding short-term profit that encouraged excessive risk-taking,[451] although not everyone accepts this diagnosis.[452]

At a meta-regulatory level, there has also been an unprecedented level of attention accorded to the issue of executive pay during the global financial crisis.[453] The G20, for example, stressed the need for greater global coordination in monitoring systemic risk[454] and implementing financial market reforms, such as those relating to executive remuneration.[455] The FSB[456] undertook the challenge of cross-border regulatory harmonization in this regard, formulating its *Principles for Sound Compensation Practices.*[457]

[450] See Corporate Law Economic Reform Program (Audit Reform and Corporate Disclosure) Bill 2003, *Explanatory Memorandum*, Schedule 5.

[451] See, for example, E. Avgouleas, "The global financial crisis, behavioural finance and financial regulation: in search of a new orthodoxy," *Journal of Corporate Law Studies*, 9 (2009), 23–59, at 42–5; L. Bebchuk and H. Spamann, "Regulating bankers' pay," *Georgetown Law Journal*, 98 (2010), 247–87, at 255–68; J. Crotty, "Structural causes of the global financial crisis: a critical assessment of the 'new financial architecture'," *Cambridge Journal of Economics*, 33 (2009), 563–80, at 565.

[452] Commentators who question the view that unsound remuneration practices contributed to the crisis include J. E. Core and W. R. Guay, "Is there a case for regulating executive pay in the financial services industry?" Working Paper, January 25 (2010), available at papers.ssrn.com/sol3/papers.cfm?abstract_id=1544104; R. Fahlenbrach and R. M. Stulz, "Bank CEO incentives and the credit crisis," Charles A. Dice Center Working Paper No. 2009–13, August 12 (2010), available at papers.ssrn.com/sol3/papers.cfm?abstract_id=1439859; G. Ferrarini and M. C. Ungureanu, "Economics, politics and the international principles for sound compensation practices: an analysis of executive pay at European banks," *Vanderbilt Law Review*, 62 (2011), 431–502.

[453] See, generally, J. G. Hill, "Regulating executive remuneration after the global financial crisis: common law perspectives" in R. S. Thomas and J. G. Hill (eds.), *Research Handbook on Executive Pay* (Cheltenham: Edward Elgar, 2012), pp. 219–40.

[454] G20 Working Group 1, *Enhancing Sound Regulation*, pp. xi–xii. This report also noted the need to avoid regulatory arbitrage, by ensuring greater cross-border regulatory consistency. Ibid., p. vi.

[455] Ibid., pp. 32–5.

[456] The FSB was originally named the Financial Stability Forum (FSF). For background on the FSB, see E. R. Carrasco, "The global financial crisis and the financial stability forum: the awakening and transformation of an international body," *Transnational Law & Contemporary Problems*, 19 (2010), 203–20.

[457] See Financial Stability Forum, *FSF Principles*; G20 Working Group 1, *Enhancing Sound Regulation*, pp. 32–3.

The FSB principles provide the basis for national prudential standards relating to remuneration in financial institutions, yet clearly the devil will lie in the detail as to how these principles are translated, interpreted and enforced in national regulatory schemes.[458]

Public concern about executive pay resurfaced in Australia during the global financial crisis. The tone came from the top in this regard. In October 2008, then Prime Minister, Mr Rudd, described the crisis as a consequence of the "twin evils" of fear and greed.[459] He stated that since, only a few days earlier, the Australian government had tackled the issue of fear through its initial stimulus package and emergency liquidity reforms, it would now turn its regulatory attention to the "greed which. . .caused the fear."[460]

The Australian government adopted a multifaceted approach to the perceived problem of executive pay.[461] Initiatives included heightened prudential regulation for banks and other ADIs,[462] the release of several discussion papers and reports,[463] and the introduction of new legislation dealing with executive pay.[464] Two developments, which are discussed in greater detail below are: (i) APRA's regulatory guidelines on executive pay; and (ii) a report on executive remuneration by the Australian Government Productivity Commission (Productivity Commission).

In 2009, APRA adopted new governance standards and guidance on remuneration for banks and other ADIs[465] in order to implement the FSB's *Principles for Sound Compensation Practices* in

[458] Ferrarini and Ungureanu, "Lost in implementation."

[459] See L. Bartlett, "Global crisis 'failure of extreme capitalism': Australian PM," *Agence France Presse*, October 15, 2008.

[460] Ibid.

[461] See, generally, Hill, "Regulating executive remuneration."

[462] See, for example, Australian Prudential Regulation Authority, *PPG 511 – Remuneration.*

[463] See, for example, Productivity Commission, *Executive Remuneration* (Report No. 49); Australian Government, "The clawback of executive remuneration where financial statements are materially misstated," Discussion Paper, December 2010; Corporations and Markets Advisory Committee, *Executive Remuneration.*

[464] Corporations Amendment (Improving Accountability on Termination Payments) Act 2009; Corporations Amendment (Improving Accountability on Director and Executive Remuneration) Act 2011.

[465] See Australian Prudential Regulation Authority, *PPG 511 – Remuneration*, which supports compliance with APRA's governance standards, contained in *Prudential Standard APS 510 – Governance*, September 2007; *Prudential Standard GPS 510 – Governance*, November 2009; and *Prudential Standard LPS 510 Governance*, July 2010.

Australia.[466] The APRA guidelines are principles-based, and constitute a more intense form of monitoring of executive pay than previously applied in Australia.[467] They reflect a strong risk management philosophy. The stated aim of APRA's *Prudential Practice Guide 511 – Remuneration* (PPG 511) is to assist regulated institutions "in considering and prudently managing the risks that may arise from their remuneration arrangements."[468] Another important theme in APRA's guidelines is avoiding conflicts of interest. PPG 511 states, for example, that "the Board would be expected to ensure that executive directors are not placed in a position of actual or perceived conflict of interest."[469]

These guidelines significantly expanded APRA's former prudential standards to impose a range of additional requirements on boards of financial institutions with respect to remuneration.[470] They require regulated institutions to develop a remuneration policy that accords with the detailed guidance provided by APRA, and to submit a risk management declaration concerning the remuneration policy to APRA on an annual basis.[471] The guidelines adopt a clear principle of board centrality, under which the board of directors retains ultimate responsibility for remuneration and represents the appropriate conduit for all regulatory dealings between APRA and the regulated institution.[472]

In contrast to APRA's industry-specific focus, the Productivity Commission undertook a broad general review of Australia's legal framework for remuneration of directors and executives. The Commission's final report, *Executive Remuneration in Australia*, was released in December

466 See Financial Stability Forum, *FSF Principles*; Financial Stability Board, *FSB Principles: Implementation Standards*. For a chronology of Australian and international regulatory developments concerning executive pay during 2008–9, see J. Trowbridge, "Executive remuneration: the regulatory debate," Speech by Executive Member John Trowbridge of the Australian Prudential Regulation Authority to the 2009 Remuneration Forum, CGI Glass Lewis and Guerdon Associates, Sydney, March 16, 2009, p. 3.

467 See, generally, Sheehan, "Regulatory framework."

468 Australian Prudential Regulation Authority, *PPG 511 – Remuneration*, p. 3.

469 Ibid., p. 5.

470 See Australian Prudential Regulation Authority, "APRA Outlines Approach on Executive Remuneration," Media Release no. 08–32, December 9, 2008; Australian Prudential Regulation Authority, "Remuneration: proposed extensions to governance requirements for APRA-regulated institutions," Discussion Paper, May 28, 2009.

471 For details of requirements under APRA's remuneration standards and guide, see Corporations and Markets Advisory Committee (Australia), *Executive Remuneration – Information Paper*, July (CAMAC, 2010).

472 Australian Prudential Regulation Authority, *PPG 511 – Remuneration*, p. 5.

2009 and made seventeen recommendations for reform.[473] These recommendations received strong government support,[474] and most were later enacted in the Corporations Amendment (Improving Accountability on Director and Executive Remuneration) Act 2011.

The most controversial aspect of the Productivity Commission's report related to shareholders' "say on pay." Since the introduction in 2004 of a provision granting shareholders an annual non-binding vote on remuneration,[475] large shareholder protest votes tended to be far more common in Australia than in the United Kingdom, at least until the global financial crisis.[476] The Productivity Commission considered that Australia's "say on pay" provision was generally an effective regulatory tool, which had contributed to improved dialogue between boards and shareholders.[477] The Commission was, however, concerned that some boards were non-responsive to shareholder views, and sought to strengthen the consequences of a significant "no" vote by means of a so-called "two strikes" proposal.[478]

Under the "two strikes" proposal, two shareholder "no" votes of 25 percent or more at consecutive annual shareholder meetings would activate a separate "board spill" resolution, which, if approved by simple majority, would then require all elected directors who signed the remuneration report to submit to re-election within 90 days.[479] The two strikes proposal was incorporated into the Corporations Amendment (Improving Accountability on Director and Executive Remuneration) Act 2011, and became law in Australia as of July 1, 2011.

[473] Productivity Commission, *Executive Remuneration* (Report No. 49), pp. xxxvii–xli. These recommendations mainly related to ensuring procedural integrity of the pay-setting process and to shareholder approval, together with increased disclosure and reporting requirements. G. Banks, "Executive pay: economic issues from the Commission's report," speech by Chairman of the Australian Government Productivity Commission, Gary Banks, to the Economics Society of Australia, Canberra Branch Annual Dinner, Barton, ACT, October 14, 2009.

[474] See C. Bowen, "Government responds to the Productivity Commission report on executive remuneration," Joint Media Release no. 033 by the Minister for Human Services, Financial Services, Superannuation and Corporate Law, Chris Bowen, April 16, 2010.

[475] See s. 250R(2) of the Corporations Act 2001 (Cth); Chapple and Christensen, "Non-binding vote on executive pay."

[476] See Hill, "Regulatory show and tell," 829–37; K. Burgess and M. Steen, "Shell's executive pay plan voted down in shareholder rebellion," *Financial Times*, May 20, 2009, p. 15.

[477] See Productivity Commission, *Executive Remuneration* (Report No. 49), p. 293. For a general discussion of the operation of the non-binding shareholder vote in Australia since its introduction, see p. 281*ff*.

[478] See ibid., pp. xxxi–xxxiii, p. 294*ff*.

[479] Ibid.

In the first series of annual shareholder meetings held in Australia after the "two strikes" rule commenced operation, a total of 108 corporations received shareholder "no" votes of 25 per cent or more on their remuneration reports.[480] The majority of these fell outside the top 300 companies; however, five companies in the top 100 and fourteen companies in the top 200 received a "first strike" under the new rule.[481] Institutional investors reported greater engagement by boards prior to annual shareholder meetings to avert high negative shareholder votes.[482]

Australia's two strikes rule on executive pay is considerably more demanding than an analogous "say on pay" provision which was introduced into US law in 2010 under s. 951 of the Dodd-Frank Act.[483] On the other hand, it appears that the United Kingdom will introduce legislation granting shareholders even stronger powers than under the Australian model. In January 2012, the UK Business Secretary, Vince Cable, announced that shareholders would be granted a binding vote on executive pay,[484] an option which was considered, but ultimately rejected, by the Productivity Commission in Australia.[485]

In the light of the intense focus on executive pay reform in Australia during the global financial crisis, an interesting question arises as to whether excessive remuneration was a genuine national problem, or

[480] See P. Durkin, "515 directors face shareholder axe," *Australian Financial Review*, February 4, 2012, p. 3.

[481] The total number of "first strikes" potentially affected around 500 Australian directors. Ibid.

[482] See J. Wiggins, "Companies learn the art of communication," *Australian Financial Review*, November 23, 2011.

[483] For example, s. 951 of the Dodd-Frank Act does not require an annual advisory shareholder vote on executive pay. Rather, shareholders may determine that the vote occur every one, two or three years, and must have the opportunity to cast a vote on this frequency issue at least once every six years. See, generally, Hill, "Regulating executive remuneration."

[484] See K. Burgess, "Measures 'send a powerful message to future chiefs'; plaudits for reforms," *Financial Times*, January 24, 2012, p. 3; K. Burgess, "Excessive executive pay faces UK curb," *Financial Times*, January 24, 2012, p. 4. Another development, which has strengthened the position of shareholders vis-à-vis the board in the United Kingdom is the recent adoption of a provision in the Corporate Governance Code, which states that all directors of FTSE 350 companies should be submitted for re-election annually. See Financial Reporting Council, *The UK Corporate Governance Code*, June 2010, Code provision B.7.1.

[485] See Productivity Commission, *Executive Remuneration* (Report No. 49), pp. 286–7.

whether these varied regulatory initiatives addressed an issue that was essentially a "foreign," particularly a US, problem.[486]

Although the policy justification for APRA's remuneration guidelines is to ensure that organizational risks associated with remuneration are prudently managed,[487] the Productivity Commission has suggested that the problem of excessive risk-taking was far less pervasive in Australia's financial industry than in many other countries.[488] The chairman of APRA has echoed this sentiment.[489] Nonetheless, the problem of remuneration incentives for excessive risk-taking is certainly not unknown in Australia. In 2004, perverse incentives in the performance bonuses of several foreign exchange traders led to a scandal at the National Australia Bank Ltd (NAB)[490] involving a loss of A$360 million.[491] The episode had major governance ramifications for NAB,[492] and ultimately led to an overhaul of the bank's risk management systems, remuneration structures[493] and corporate culture.[494]

In relation to executive compensation, there are interesting differences between chief executive officer (CEO) pay in Australia and the United States,

486 Productivity Commission, "Director and executive remuneration," p. 4. See generally Hill, "Regulating executive remuneration."

487 Australian Prudential Regulation Authority, *PPG 511 – Remuneration*, p. 3.

488 Productivity Commission, *Executive Remuneration* (Report No. 49), p. xxv.

489 John Laker, the Chairman of APRA, has stated: "I find the argument about the four pillars policy quite a persuasive one... and it's backed up by the sense that in executive remuneration arrangements in Australia in the regulated sector in particular, we didn't see the excesses that have been given so much publicity offshore." Comments delivered during the Panel discussion to I. Macfarlane, "The crisis: causes, consequences and lessons for the future: the Australian perspective," in ASIC, *Global Crisis: The Big Issues for Our Financial Markets*, ASIC Summer School 2009, March 2–3, 2009 (ASIC, 2009), 41–59, at 48–9. See also G. Winestock, "Meet the man we're all banking on," *Australian Financial Review*, March 14, 2009, p. 26.

490 See National Australia Bank, "Announcement of irregular trading losses," ASX announcement, January 13, 2004.

491 See, for example, A. Cornell and M. Drummond, "Culture allowed rogue traders to flourish," *Australian Financial Review*, May 29, 2006, p. 61.

492 See, generally, Hill, "The rising tension."

493 It was reported that after the scandal, NAB introduced a broader range of performance measures, rather than simply relying on financial measures, such as meeting profit targets. The bank also shifted towards group, rather than individual, assessment in relation to bonuses. Finally, managerial discretion in relation to sharing of the bonus pool was curbed. See A. Hepworth, "The dangers of the unearned bonus," *Australian Financial Review*, April 23, 2004, p. 45; J. Beveridge, "NAB eases back into forex," *Herald-Sun*, April 19, 2005, p. 29.

494 See, for example, S. Oldfield, "Stewart pledges strict new risk controls," *Australian Financial Review*, March 15, 2004, p. 53.

in terms of both quantum and structure.[495] There was a steep escalation in CEO pay in Australia over the last decade,[496] which has been attributed to a range of factors, including globalization and market liberalization.[497] Empirical studies show that CEO pay is strongly correlated with market capitalization increases,[498] and this is relevant to a number of Australian corporations, particularly in the mining sector. The market capitalization of BHP Billiton, for example, stood at A$16 billion in 1989 shortly after the Wallis Report, but is now over A$200 billion.[499] In 2011, BHP Billiton and three of Australia's major banks were ranked in the top 100 global corporations in terms of market capitalization,[500] and this is reflected in Australian CEO pay statistics.[501]

In spite of this rise in Australian CEO pay, US executives have traditionally received far higher pay than their counterparts in other jurisdictions, including Australia, although the US–UK gap narrowed over the last decade.[502] Data from 2008 suggested that Australian executive compensation was much closer to the European average than to US pay levels.[503] Income

[495] See, generally, Hill, Masulis and Thomas, "CEO employment contract provisions."

[496] For example, the average CEO pay in the top 100 listed Australian companies rose from A$3.77 million in 2005 to A$5.53 million in 2007. See Australian Council of Super Investors (ACSI), "Top 100 CEO pay research released," Media Release, October 27, 2008. See, generally, Hill, "Regulating executive remuneration."

[497] See Productivity Commission, *Executive Remuneration* (Report No. 49), pp. xviii–xix.

[498] See C. Frydman and R. E. Saks, "Executive compensation: a new view from a long-term perspective, 1936–2005," NBER Working Paper no. w14145, June (2008), available at papers.ssrn.com/sol3/papers.cfm?abstract_id=1152686; X. Gabaix and A. Landier, "Why has CEO pay increased so much?" *The Quarterly Journal of Economics*, 123 (2008), 49–100.

[499] See Productivity Commission, *Executive Remuneration* (Report No. 49), p. xviii.

[500] BHP Billiton was ranked 17 in the world on market capitalization on the FT Global 500 Index as at December 2011. Australian bank rankings were: Commonwealth Bank of Australia (62); Westpac Banking (88); ANZ Banking (99); National Bank of Australia (111). See FT Global 500 Index December 2011.

[501] For example, in 2010, the CEOs of the Commonwealth Bank of Australia and BHP Billiton were ranked first and fourth respectively on the list of highest paid executives in Australia's top 100 listed companies. Ralph Norris, CEO of the Commonwealth Bank of Australia, received total disclosed pay of A$16,157,746 and Marius Kloppers, CEO of BHP Billiton, received A$12,849,046. Australian Council of Super Investors (ACSI), *CEO Pay in the Top 100 Companies: 2010*, Research Paper (2011), p. 19.

[502] R. S. Thomas, "Explaining the international CEO pay gap: board capture or market driven?" *Vanderbilt Law Review*, 57 (2004), 1171–267, at 1173–5; Department for Business Innovation & Skills (BIS), *Executive Remuneration*, Discussion Paper (BIS, 2011), p. 8*ff*; Department for Business Innovation & Skills (BIS), *A Long-term Focus for Corporate Britain: A Call for Evidence* (BIS, 2010), p. 27; M. J. Conyon, J. E. Core and W. R. Guay, "Are U.S. CEOs paid more than U.K. CEOs? Inferences from risk-adjusted pay," *Review of Financial Studies*, 24 (2011), 402–38.

[503] See Productivity Commission, *Executive Remuneration* (Report No. 49), pp. xix–xx.

disparity between CEOs and average workers is also far less pronounced in Australia than in the United States.[504] Finally, in spite of some commonalities between US and Australian executive contracts, there are also intriguing structural differences.[505] For example, Australian executive contracts tend to be shorter than US contracts, and performance-based vesting conditions for restricted stock and options have traditionally been rare in the United States, but very common in Australia.[506]

These factors provide some support for the view that, in spite of the intense focus on the issue in Australia during the global financial crisis, excessive executive remuneration was in fact a much greater problem in some other jurisdictions, particularly in the United States.[507]

Retail investor protection and the Future of Financial Advice reforms

> [During the global financial crisis], we saw clients without the necessary investment experience exposed to complex financial products on the wholesale market.
>
> Bill Shorten[508]

A recent Australian regulatory change, which clearly tracks local, rather than international, developments, is the Future of Financial Advice (FoFA) program. The FoFA reforms involve enhanced retail investor protection, which became a more important regulatory theme in Australia than in many other jurisdictions,[509] due to some major domestic retail investor losses during the global financial crisis.

The basic blueprint for the regulation of financial products and services in Australia was established by the Wallis Report in 1997. ASIC, which has primary responsibility for oversight and enforcement of the

[504] In 2007, for example, the average executive manager in the largest fifteen US firms earned around 500 times more than an average employee. See International Institute for Labour Studies, *World of Work Report 2008: Income Inequalities in the Age of Financial Globalization*, Executive summary: preprint edition (IILS, 2008), p. 3. In Australia, the 2008 annual reports of the top fifteen companies showed that, excluding share-based compensation, the CEOs earned approximately 135 times more than the average Australian employee. D. Tarrant, "Payday paralysis," *Intheblack*, 79 (2009), 28–31.

[505] See, generally, Hill, Masulis and Thomas, "CEO employment contract provisions."

[506] See, generally, ibid., 593*ff.*

[507] See Winestock, "Meet the man," p. 26.

[508] B. Shorten, "Government releases options paper on investor protection threshold," Media Release no. 018 by Assistant Treasurer and Minister for Financial Services & Superannuation (Australia) Bill Shorten, January 24, 2011.

[509] I am grateful to my colleague, Joanna Bird, for drawing my attention to the regulatory divergence in this regard.

scheme, has stated that the financial services regime was firmly based on the efficient market hypothesis.[510] The regulatory linchpin of the scheme is certification,[511] whereby holders of an Australian Financial Services Licence (AFSL) are subject to conduct and disclosure regulation under the Corporations Act 2001 (Cth).[512]

Consumer protection became a prominent issue in Australia during the global financial crisis, due to a string of corporate collapses involving financial product and services providers, which resulted in large retail investor losses. ASIC launched investigations, or brought compensation actions, in relation to many of these collapses, including the Westpoint Group,[513] Opes Prime,[514] Fincorp[515] and Storm Financial Ltd (Storm).[516] In addition, civil

[510] See Parliamentary Joint Committee on Corporations and Financial Services, *Inquiry into Financial Products and Services*, p. 7.

[511] Ibid., pp. 8–10. ASIC has stated, however, that its powers to deny a licensing application are restricted. Ibid., p. 9.

[512] Ibid., pp. 11–14.

[513] The Westpoint property development companies collapsed in January 2006. Retail losses in relation to the group's financial products totaled approximately A$310 million, affecting approximately 3,000 investors. See Australian Securities and Investments Commission, *Working for Australia: Consumers, Investors, Business and Markets*, ASIC Annual Report 2005–06 (ASIC, 2006), p. 5; Australian Securities and Investments Commission, Westpoint Investors website, https://westpoint.asic.gov.au/wstpoint/wstpoint.nsf/byheadline/home?opendocument.

[514] Opes Prime collapsed in March 2008. ASIC became involved in mediation proceedings to recover compensation for investors without recourse to litigation. Schemes of arrangement giving effect to the resultant settlement were approved by the Federal Court of Australia in 2009. It was estimated that approximately A$253 million, constituting a payment of 37 cents in the dollar, would be available to creditors as a result of the settlement. See Australian Securities and Investments Commission, "Opes Prime: proposed settlement and ANZ enforceable undertaking," Media Release 09–37, March 6, 2009; Australian Securities and Investments Commission, "Opes Prime schemes of arrangement approved," Media Release AD 09–135, August 4, 2009. For background to the Opes Prime collapse, see Parliamentary Joint Committee on Corporations and Financial Services, *Inquiry into Financial Products and Services*, pp. 51–67.

[515] Fincorp was a property and investment company, which collapsed in March 2007 owing a total of A$200 million to approximately 8,000 investors. See A. Klan, "Savings at risk after Fincorp collapse," *The Australian*, March 26, 2007, p. 3.

[516] Storm was placed in liquidation in March 2009. For background to the Storm collapse, see Parliamentary Joint Committee on Corporations and Financial Services, *Inquiry into Financial Products and Services*, pp. 19–50. In November 2010, ASIC announced that it intended to bring legal proceedings against several parties, including the Commonwealth Bank of Australia Ltd, the Bank of Queensland and Macquarie Bank Ltd, which had loaned money to Storm's investors. See Australian Securities and Investments Commission, "ASIC announces intention to commence legal action," Media Release 10–250MR, November 26, 2010.

or criminal proceedings were brought against the directors of several of these corporations.[517] A central aspect of these retail losses involved the blurring of the boundary between wholesale and retail investors in relation to certain complex financial products.[518] Opes Prime and Storm were emblematic of this problem. Although Opes Prime portrayed its client base as consisting of sophisticated and high net wealth individuals, those affected were often small retail investors saving for retirement.[519] Storm, a financial advice firm located in Townsville, Queensland, had approximately 14,000 clients. A significant proportion of Storm's clients were retired, or close to retirement, and had been encouraged to borrow money for investment against the equity of their family homes.[520] Many of these double-geared clients suffered "catastrophic" losses when they were subsequently unable to satisfy margin calls, fell into negative equity, and exited their portfolios at the nadir of the market.[521]

In February 2009, the Parliamentary Joint Committee on Corporations and Financial Services (PJC) announced that it would conduct an inquiry into issues surrounding these events. The PJC Inquiry, which issued its report in November 2009,[522] identified many troubling aspects to the collapses. The PJC considered, for example, that Opes Prime had inappropriately supplied a product, designed for the sophisticated wholesale market, to unsophisticated retail clients.[523] In the case of Storm, the PJC found that some investors had limited understanding of the complex structure of the financial arrangements, which combined high leverage with margin loans,[524] and, in particular, were unaware that they ran a substantial risk of losing their homes.[525]

517 For example, two directors of Opes Prime received jail sentences. See Australian Securities and Investments Commission, "Opes Prime directors jailed," Media Release 11–150MR, July 27, 2011.

518 Parliamentary Joint Committee on Corporations and Financial Services, *Inquiry into Financial Products and Services*, pp. 65–6.

519 Ibid., pp. 19, 21, 51.

520 Approximately 3,000 of Storm's clients fell within this category of leveraged investment clients. Ibid., p. 21.

521 Ibid., p. 19.

522 Parliamentary Joint Committee on Corporations and Financial Services, *Inquiry into Financial Products and Services.*

523 Ibid., p. 65.

524 Although margin loan products did not fall within the financial services regulatory regime prior to the global financial crisis, legislation reversing this position was passed in October 2009. See Corporations Legislation Amendment (Financial Services Modernisation) Act 2009. See Parliamentary Joint Committee on Corporations and Financial Services, *Inquiry into Financial Products and Services*, pp. 14–15, 149–50.

525 Ibid., pp. 28–30.

The PJC made a number of recommendations for reform in the financial advice sector.[526] Although recognizing the dangers of regulating in response to particular corporate collapses, the committee believed that sufficient consistent evidence had emerged from the inquiry to justify reforms aimed at increasing consumer protection.[527] However, the PJC rejected calls for additional regulation to ensure that products are always "safe" for investors.[528] It refused to adopt such an approach, which it said would interfere with the financial products market by prohibiting the sale of certain products to retail investors.[529] Rather, it favored a regulatory technique that focused on improving the quality and availability of financial advice itself.[530]

The FoFA reforms constitute a direct response to these domestic corporate collapses and to the recommendations of the PJC Inquiry.[531] The reforms were announced in 2010,[532] revised in 2011,[533] and will commence in 2012–13.[534] The reforms, which seek to enhance consumer trust and confidence and improve the quality of financial advice, reflect two basic principles, namely the need to ensure: (i) that financial advice is in the client's best interests and (ii) that such advice is available to consumers who would benefit from it.[535]

The FoFA reforms radically alter the legal landscape concerning financial advice and product distribution in Australia. First, they target perverse incentives in the remuneration structure of financial advisers. This aspect of the reforms is particularly prescriptive, imposing bans on a range of payments which are perceived to create conflicts of interest that could potentially affect the financial advice provided to retail

526 Ibid., pp. 149–51. 527 Ibid., p. 149. 528 Ibid., p. 140.
529 Ibid., p. 65. 530 Ibid., p. 140.
531 See ibid., pp. 149–51. For a comparison of the PJC Inquiry's recommendations and the Government's response, see C. Bowen, "The future of financial advice," Information Pack, Office of the Hon. Chris Bowen MP, Minister for Human Services, Financial Services, Superannuation and Corporate Law, Canberra, April 26, 2010 ("Bowen, 2010 Information Pack"), pp. 9–12.
532 See Bowen, 2010 Information Pack.
533 See B. Shorten, "The future of financial advice," Information Pack, Office of the Hon. Bill Shorten MP, Minister for Financial Services and Superannuation, Canberra, April 28, 2011 ("Shorten, 2011 Information Pack"), pp. 5–6.
534 The majority of the FoFA reforms come into force on July 1, 2012, and the balance will apply from July 1, 2013. See Bowen, 2010 Information Pack, p. 2; Shorten, 2011 Information Pack, pp. 5–6.
535 Bowen, 2010 Information Pack, p. 2.

investors.[536] Prohibited payments include commissions by product providers to financial advisers and certain payments relating to volume or sales targets.[537] There is also a ban on charging retail investors an "assets under management" fee on geared sums. This prohibition addresses the problem posed by incentives to engage in aggressive leveraging, as exemplified by the financial arrangements at Storm.[538] The 2011 FoFA revisions contain a number of additional payment bans.[539] The scope of the prohibitions is broad, covering all financial products, including managed investment scheme, superannuation and margin loans.[540]

Second, the FoFA reforms establish a new charging regime in relation to financial advice provided to retail investors. This includes stronger consumer protection through more detailed, periodic disclosure.[541] Third, in keeping with the principle that financial advice should be in the client's best interests, the reforms impose a statutory fiduciary duty on AFSL holders and their representatives.[542] Finally, the reforms strengthen ASIC's powers in relation to licensing and banning financial advisers.[543]

Many of the issues considered by the PJC Inquiry concerning complexity of financial products re-emerged recently in a judicial context. The *Wingecarribee Shire Council* litigation (*Wingecarribee* litigation) involved a class action in the Federal Court of Australia. The action, which commenced in 2011, was brought by 74 class action group members, including local councils, such as Wingecarribee, and various charities and churches, which had purchased complex financial products between 2003 and 2008.[544]

536 The contours of the prohibitions of the bans on payments that could create conflicts of interest altered somewhat in the 2011 FoFA revisions. See, generally, Shorten, 2011 Information Pack, pp. 5–6; J. Boynton and R. Cush, "Future of financial advice – second round of legislation released," Mallesons Stephen Jaques, Market Alert, September 29, 2009.

537 Bowen, 2010 Information Pack, p. 4.

538 Ibid.

539 See Shorten, 2011 Information Pack, pp. 5–6.

540 The reforms do not cover risk insurance outside superannuation. See Bowen, 2010 Information Pack, p. 4; Shorten, 2011 Information Pack, p. 7.

541 Bowen, 2010 Information Pack, p. 5.

542 Ibid.

543 Ibid., p. 6. In December 2011, ASIC announced its plans for publishing guidance on the FoFA reforms, including the reforms related to its own expanded powers. See Australian Securities and Investments Commission, "ASIC's plans for FoFA reforms," Media Release 11–294AD, December 13, 2011.

544 For procedural background to the *Wingecarribee* class action, see PPB Advisory, *Lehman Brothers Australia Ltd (In Liquidation) – Report to Creditors*, January 19, 2011, pp. 18–19.

The *Wingecarribee* litigation was inextricably linked to the global financial crisis. The class action related to 39 issues of risky and complex synthetic collateralized debt obligations (CDOs). These CDOs were issued by the investment advice firm, Grange Securities (Grange), which, following its acquisition in March 2007,[545] became Lehman Brothers Australia Ltd (Lehman Brothers).[546] One of these financial products, titled Federation notes, consisted of credit default swaps, which were ultimately linked to the US sub-prime mortgage market. In January 2008, during the US subprime market turmoil, Wingecarribee Shire Council sold its Federation notes for A$450,000, which constituted an 85 percent write-down on its original investment. Not all councils that invested in Federation notes issue suffered such significant losses. Some councils, which retained the notes, ultimately received full repayment, due to a contractual clause which was triggered by Lehman Brothers' bankruptcy filing in September 2008.[547]

The plaintiffs' action was based on claims of negligence, misleading and deceptive conduct and breach of fiduciary duty. The plaintiffs argued that they had been unaware of the high risks, in terms of price volatility and liquidity, attached to the securities. Lehman Brothers, on the other hand, countered that the financial information about the products contained adequate disclosure of the relevant risks.[548] An interesting question is why these local councils, which had previously pursued extremely low-risk investment policies, purchased the CDOs. The answer appears to lie partly in the fact that the investments were permitted by an order published by the Minister for Local Government in 2000.[549] The list of approved investments under the minister's order, which was revoked after the global financial crisis, permitted council investment in any securities receiving a minimum credit rating of A by Standard & Poor's or A2 by Moody's.[550] Yet, in 2007, the Governor of the

[545] See L. Egan, "Lehman Brothers buys Grange Securities," *Money Management*, January 19, 2007.

[546] See, generally, E. Sexton, "Devil in the detail for complex case," *Sydney Morning Herald*, June 17, 2011, p. 1.

[547] See E. Sexton, "Dante notes led to a financial inferno," *Sydney Morning Herald*, February 23, 2011. See J. Barrett, "Lehman's back...in $70m cash grab," *Australian Financial Review*, November 11, 2011, p. 13.

[548] Sexton, "Devil in the detail," p. 1.

[549] Department of Local Government Circular to Councils, "Forms of investment – Minister's order," Circular No. 00/71, November 29, 2000.

[550] See ibid.; Sexton, "Devil in the detail," p. 1.

RBA issued a warning about the investment behavior of some local government authorities, voicing concern that they might not understand the risk implications of the financial products they were buying.[551]

The Federal Court decision in the *Wingecarribee* litigation is pending. Like the Opes Prime and Storm collapses, the case highlights the blurred boundary between wholesale and retail investors in relation to certain complex financial products. In January 2011, the Australian government released an options paper reviewing the distinction between retail and wholesale clients, for the purposes of determining appropriate levels of investor protection.[552] As the government noted, there is a real question as to whether bodies such as local councils, which can be classified as wholesale investors, in fact need greater regulatory protection.[553] The *Wingecarribee* litigation also highlights the potential limits of disclosure as a regulatory technique in the face of increased complexity of financial products.[554] Finally, the case will test the PJC's view that improvements in the provision of financial advice are more effective than attempting to ensure, through regulation, that products are "safe" for investors.[555]

VI: Why did Australia fare so well during the global financial crisis?

When Donald Horne first coined the phrase "the lucky country" to describe Australia in the 1960s, it was hardly a flattering epithet. Horne stated that "Australia is a lucky country, run by second-rate people who share its luck."[556]

The concept of luck, which is possibly undeserved, re-emerged strongly in the context of Australia's economic performance during the global financial crisis. For many the stock answer as to why Australia fared so well during the crisis is that it was "lucky," in that its economy was buoyed by China's growing demand for resources.[557] Although strong trade links with China undoubtedly constitute part of the puzzle of why Australia fared so well, as the following discussion demonstrates,

[551] See "Australia's Stevens warns on CDOs," *Central Banking*, July 24, 2007.

[552] Shorten, "Options paper on investor protection threshold." [553] Ibid.

[554] See D'Aloisio, "Regulatory response," pp. 1, 10*ff.*

[555] Parliamentary Joint Committee on Corporations and Financial Services, *Inquiry into Financial Products and Services*, p. 140.

[556] Horne, *The Lucky Country.*

[557] See P. Cleary, *Too Much Luck: The Mining Boom and Australia's Future* (Black Inc., 2011).

there are also a number of other relevant, but under-appreciated, factors which have contributed to Australia's resilience during the crisis.

China and Australia's resources boom

> If we didn't have mining, Australia would be like Portugal, Spain, maybe Greece and Ireland.
>
> Michael Byrne[558]

It is impossible to overlook the effect of the current resources boom on Australia's recent economic performance. The Governor of the RBA has described it as one of the most significant, and expansionary, economic events in Australia's history.[559] The boom is the fifth since European settlement a little more than two centuries ago.[560] It is, however, the first to occur since the floating of the Australian dollar in 1983,[561] and has led to a sharp increase in the exchange rate, coupled with a reduction in inflationary pressure.[562]

The size of the resources boom, and its impact on Australia, is considerable.[563] There has been a 50 percent increase in global coal consumption over the last decade and an 80 percent increase in iron ore consumption since 2003, with China and India accounting for much of this rise in demand.[564] In 2010, Australia's two-way trade amounted to A$552.4 billion, with resource commodities, including iron ore and coal, comprising 47.5 percent of all Australian exports.[565] This represented a

558 Quoted in P. Smith, "Australia's mining boom masks crisis in economy," *Financial Times*, August 5, 2011, p. 4.

559 G. Stevens, "The resources boom," remarks by the Governor of the Reserve Bank of Australia Glenn Stevens at the Victoria University Public Conference on *The Resources Boom: Understanding National and Regional Implications*, Melbourne, February 23, 2011; G. Stevens, "The challenge of prosperity," address by the Governor of the Reserve Bank of Australia Glenn Stevens to the Committee for Economic Development of Australia (CEDA) Annual Dinner, Melbourne, November 29, 2010.

560 Earlier major mining booms in Australia were: (i) the 1850s goldrush; (ii) late nineteenth-century mining boom; (iii) 1960s–early 1970s mineral and resources boom; (iv) late 1970s–early 1980s energy boom. R. Battellino, "Mining booms and the Australian economy," address by the Deputy Governor of the Reserve Bank of Australia to The Sydney Institute, Sydney, February 23, 2010, pp. 1–5.

561 Reserve Bank of Australia, "Why does Australia have a floating exchange rate?" p. 2.

562 This contrasts with earlier booms, which were generally associated with a rise in inflation. See Battellino, "Mining booms," pp. 6, 7; Stevens, "The resources boom," p. 2.

563 Brown, "Comparison of the handling of the financial crisis," 572–3.

564 See Stevens, "The resources boom," p. 3.

565 See Department of Foreign Affairs and Trade (Australia), *Trade at a Glance 2011* (ACT: DFAT, 2011), p. 2.

A$16.8 billion trade surplus in 2010, following a A$4 billion trade deficit in 2009.[566] In 2010, Australia's total trade with China, which replaced Japan as Australia's largest trading partner one year earlier,[567] was A$105 billion. This was an increase of almost 24 percent on the 2009 level, and represented the first time that Australia's two-way trade with a single nation had exceeded A$100 billion.[568] A total of 22.6 percent of all Australian exports in 2010 went to China,[569] compared to 13.2 percent in 2008.[570]

One recent incident highlights the growing wealth and power of the Australian resources sector. In May 2010, the Australian government announced its intention to introduce a 40 percent resource super profits tax,[571] based on recommendations of the *Australia's Future Tax System Review* (Henry Tax Review).[572] The stated goals of the resource super profits tax were to ensure that "Australians get a fair share from. . .valuable non-renewable resources" and to address concerns about Australia's "two speed" economy.[573] The proposed tax became the subject of a bitter conflict between the government, led by Kevin Rudd, and Australia's large mining companies.[574] This battle ended with Mr Rudd's replacement as Prime Minister of Australia by Julia Gillard, who then entered into a compromise with the resources sector, by reducing the level of the proposed tax.[575] Shortly after Mr Rudd was deposed as Prime Minister,

[566] Ibid., p. 3.

[567] See Brown, "Comparison of the handling of the financial crisis," 572–3.

[568] Department of Foreign Affairs and Trade, *Trade at a Glance 2011*, Minister for Trade's Foreword 2011, p. 2.

[569] This compared to 16 percent for Japan, 5.1 percent for the United States and 4.4 percent for the United Kingdom. See Department of Foreign Affairs and Trade, *Trade at a Glance 2011*, p. 7.

[570] Ibid., p. 10.

[571] See W. Swan, "Release of 'Stronger, fairer, simpler – a tax plan for our future'," Joint Press Conference by the Treasurer (Australia) Wayne Swan, Media Release 028, May 2, 2010.

[572] The Treasury (Australia), *Australia's Future Tax System Review – Report to the Treasurer* (ACT: Commonwealth of Australia, 2009), Part One: Overview, Chapter 6: "Land and Resource Taxes."

[573] See Swan, "Release of 'Stronger, fairer, simpler'."

[574] See generally Cleary, *Too Much Luck*, pp. 73–96.

[575] This compromise was announced on July 1, 2010. See E. Fry, "Australian PM waters down mining tax," *Financial Times*, July 1, 2010. The mineral resources rent tax (MRRT) will apply to coal and iron ore producers at an effective rate of 22.5 percent, rather than the 40 percent rate originally proposed by Mr Rudd, from July 1, 2012. There have been some recent proposals to extend the tax to other high performing sectors of the Australian economy, such as the banks. See K. Walsh, "Call to take slice of bank profits," *Australian Financial Review*, September 28, 2011, p. 10.

the CEO of Rio Tinto, a major Australian resource company,[576] held up the political events in Australia as a lesson to policymakers around the world, who might be considering the imposition of an analogous tax.[577]

All of Australia's previous mining booms have been of limited duration,[578] and the most recent resources boom is contingent on China's continuing economic growth.[579] Although the resources boom clearly played a role in Australia's economic resilience during the global financial crisis,[580] the boom is of relatively recent origin. Commencing around 2005,[581] it has escalated dramatically since that time. Nonetheless, a single-minded focus on the resources boom can obscure the fact that, irrespective of this event, Australia's economic position was very strong prior to the global financial crisis in comparison with many other major countries around the world.

The period from the early 1990s to 2007 was one of sustained economic growth in Australia, with real gross domestic income rising by 68.4 percent between 1995 and 2007.[582] According to the OECD, 2008 was Australia's seventeenth consecutive year of economic growth.[583] This growth was matched by increases in total government spending,

576 Rio Tinto comprises Rio Tinto plc and Rio Tinto Ltd, which are listed respectively in the United Kingdom and in Australia. The two corporations operate as a combined economic entity, the Rio Tinto Group, by virtue of a dual listed companies (DLC) merger, which was effected in December 1995. See Rio Tinto, *Rio Tinto 2010 Annual Report: Striving for Global Sector Leadership*, p. 162.

577 See T. Albanese, "Mining issues, a global view," address by the CEO of Rio Tinto at the Melbourne Mining Club, London, July 8, 2010, at http://www.riotinto.com/media/18435_presentations_19361.asp; P. Wilson, "Rio chief uses Rudd case as a warning – mining tax battle," *The Australian*, July 10, 2010, p. 28.

578 See Battellino, "Mining booms," p. 6, stating that most previous booms have ended after about 15 years, after developments such as resource depletion or an economic slowdown.

579 For a discussion of China's economic performance during the global financial crisis, see G. Stevens, "The economic situation," address by the Governor of the Reserve Bank of Australia to the CEDA Annual Dinner, Melbourne, November 19, 2008, *Reserve Bank of Australia Bulletin*, December (2008), 13–17, at 13, 16; T. McDonald and S. Morling, "The Australian economy and the global downturn – Part 1: Reasons for resilience" in The Treasury (Australia), *Economic Roundup*, Issue 2 (2011), pp. 1–31, at pp. 22–4.

580 See, for example, Organisation for Economic Co-operation and Development (OECD), "Economic Survey of Australia, 2008," *Policy Brief*, October 2008, p. 3, noting the role of China and India in creating strong demand for Australian resources.

581 Battellino, "Mining booms," p. 6.

582 See, generally, J. Stone, "Growth, jobs and prosperity: economic progress under the Howard government," *Quadrant* (Sydney), 53 (1–2) (2009), 14–20.

583 See OECD, "Economic survey of Australia, 2008," p. 3.

particularly since 2004–5.[584] The contrast between Australia's economy and that of many other major jurisdictions in the decade before the global financial crisis is striking. Australia had significant budget surpluses throughout virtually this whole period,[585] compared to other OECD countries, which were generally in deficit.[586] The United Kingdom and the United States, for example, had budget deficits from 2002 onwards.[587]

Australia also had remarkably low levels of government debt compared to many other nations. Government responses to the global financial crisis around the world led to much higher levels of national debt. Australia's net debt position went from a low of minus 3.8 percent of GDP in 2007–8 to a projected high of 6 percent in 2012–13. In contrast, the average for G7 nations[588] spanned a low of 53 percent in 2007 to a projected high of 94.2 percent in 2015.[589] UK and US net debt is estimated to be around 85 percent by 2015,[590] and Japan's net debt is projected to reach 154.7 percent.[591]

Therefore, although the current resources boom in Australia is certainly a relevant factor in assessing Australia's strong economic performance during the global financial crisis, it is by no means the whole story.

[584] K. Laurie and J. McDonald, "A perspective on trends in Australian Government spending," in The Treasury (Australia), *Economic Roundup*, Summer 2008, pp. 27–49, at p. 44.

[585] Australia had budget surpluses in ten out of the eleven years between 1998 and 2008. See Brown, "Comparison of the handling of the financial crisis," 573.

[586] See Senate Economics References Committee, *Government's Economic Stimulus Initiatives*, pp. 22–3, Chart 4.2.

[587] Brown, "Comparison of the handling of the financial crisis," 573–4, Figure 27.

[588] G7 countries comprise Canada, France, Germany, Italy, Japan, United Kingdom and the United States.

[589] See Guy Woods, "International Comparisons of National Debt," Parliamentary Briefing Book, Parliament of Australia, Parliamentary Library (2010), citing data from International Monetary Fund, *Navigating the Fiscal Challenges Ahead*, Fiscal Monitor, May 14, 2010, available at www.imf.org/external/pubs/ft/fm/2010/fm1001.pdf, regarding the change in Australia's net debt position over the course of the global financial crisis in comparison to other countries. See also Senate Economics References Committee, *Government's Economic Stimulus Initiatives*, Government senators' minority report, pp. 64–5.

[590] Estimated UK net debt by 2015 is 83.9 percent and estimated US net debt is 85.5 percent. Woods, "International comparisons of national debt," citing data from International Monetary Fund, *Fiscal Challenges Ahead*.

[591] Ibid.

The Reserve Bank's monetary policy and the economic stimulus program

> Even though many countries moved quickly to enact large fiscal stimulus packages, these packages generally have not had a strong effect in cushioning the initial decline in employment caused by the crisis, although Australia is a notable exception.
>
> OECD[592]

There has been recent recognition of the potential benefits of increased spending and the dangers of fiscal tightening during economic downturns.[593] Australia's expansionary approach in responding to the global financial crisis is interesting from this perspective.

Australia's strong economic position provided it with much flexibility in terms of ability to address the global financial crisis through monetary policy and increased spending.[594] The OECD considered it to be one of several countries, including Germany and Canada,[595] with the most scope for such fiscal maneuvering.[596] Two particular aspects of Australia's response to the crisis, which are relevant to the issue of why it fared so well, are discussed in this section. These are, first, the RBA's monetary policy response and second, Australia's taxpayer-funded economic stimulus program.

The OECD singled out Australia's central bank, the RBA, for praise over its rapid, hands-on monetary policy response to the global financial crisis.[597] On September 2, 2008, only two weeks before Lehman Brothers filed for bankruptcy, the RBA eased monetary policy through an announced cut in its official interest rate from 7.25 percent to 7 percent.[598] This rate cut addressed concern that monetary policy was too restrictive in the face of the burgeoning economic slowdown.[599] The RBA had much

592 OECD, *OECD Employment Outlook 2009: Tackling the Jobs Crisis* (Paris: OECD, 2009), p. 31.

593 See "There could be trouble ahead," p. 401.

594 See Stevens, "Economic situation," pp. 13, 16.

595 Other countries included by the OECD in this group were the Netherlands, Switzerland, Korea and some Nordic countries. See OECD, *Interim Economic Outlook – March 2009*, Chapter 3: "The effectiveness and scope of fiscal stimulus," pp. 106, 108, 123.

596 Ibid.

597 See OECD, "Economic surveys: Australia, November 2010 – Overview," pp. 2, 4–5.

598 Reserve Bank of Australia, "Statement by Glenn Stevens, Governor: Monetary Policy," Media Release no. 2008–14, September 2, 2008, noting the likelihood that household demand and economic growth generally would remain subdued in the immediate future.

599 See R. Guy and D. Kitney, "RBA cut to boost economy," *Australian Financial Review*, September 1, 2008, p. 1; P. Smith, "Australia makes first rate cut in seven years," *Financial Times*, September 3, 2008, p. 4; see Stevens, "Economic situation," pp. 13, 17.

more flexibility in relation to monetary policy than its counterparts in many other jurisdictions over this period.[600] In the United States, for example, the Federal Reserve cut the discount rate by 50 basis points to a mere 1 percent on October 29, 2008.[601] The RBA's September 2, 2008 rate reduction was the first official interest rate cut in Australia in almost seven years.[602] It was followed by a rapid succession of further rate cuts over the next few months, and by April 2009 the official interest rate stood at just 3 percent.[603] In October 2009, Australia became the first of the G20 nations to raise interest rates, signaling that the RBA considered that the risk of a serious economic downturn for Australia had passed.[604]

The RBA's official interest rate cuts during this critical period of international market turmoil have been described as the most "aggressive easing cycle" since the recession of the early 1990s.[605] The OECD commended the speed with which the RBA reacted and the fact that it did not wait for hard data to support its actions, which would necessarily have involved delay.[606] Yet, information has subsequently emerged suggesting that the Australian government favored even more extreme up-front rate cuts, and disagreed strongly with the RBA's decision to stagger the rate reductions across a period of several months.[607] If this is correct, it is testament to the political independence of Australia's central bank.

600 See P. Hartcher, "Fortress Australia," *Sydney Morning Herald*, October 1, 2008, p. 1; Uren and Taylor, "How Rudd bet the house," p. 1.

601 See Board of Governors of the Federal Reserve, Press Release, October 29, 2008.

602 The RBA's September 2, 2008 rate reduction came after a series of twelve consecutive rate rises, from May 8, 2002 onwards. See Reserve Bank of Australia, "Cash Rate Target," at www.rba.gov.au/statistics/cash-rate.html; Guy and Kitney, "RBA cut," p. 1.

603 Reserve Bank of Australia, "Statement by Glenn Stevens, Governor: Monetary Policy," Media Release No. 2009–06, April 7, 2009.

604 Reserve Bank of Australia, "Statement by Glenn Stevens, Governor: Monetary Policy," Media Release no. 2009–23, October 6, 2009 (noting that Australia's economic performance had been stronger than expected and announcing an increase in the cash rate to 3.25 percent); A. Frangos and J. Hilsenrath, "Australia rate rise poses a global policy challenge," *Wall Street Journal*, October 7, 2009, p. A14; T. Lauricella, "Recovery hopes stir markets – Australian rate rise spurs stock, commodity rallies; gold hits record high as dollar falls," *Wall Street Journal*, October 7, 2009, p. A1. The RBA announced further official interest rate increases in November 2009 and December 2009. In March 2010, the RBA again raised the interest rate to 4 percent.

605 See P. Smith, "Rates cut as Rudd warns on growth," *Financial Times*, December 3, 2008, p. 3, quoting Michael Blythe, Chief Economist of the Commonwealth Bank of Australia.

606 OECD, "Economic surveys: Australia, November 2010 – Overview," pp. 4–5.

607 The information was contained in a US embassy cable released by WikiLeaks. See S. Ryan, "Labor, RBA in post-GFC split: WikiLeaks," *The Australian*, August 31, 2011, p. 1; S. Ryan, "Turnbull 'vindicated' in opposition to stimulus," *The Australian*, September 1, 2011, p. 2.

Another significant factor in Australia's economic performance during the global financial crisis was the government's stimulus program. As previously noted, the Australian stimulus program, with the A$42 billion Nation Building and Jobs Plan as its centerpiece,[608] was one of the largest fiscal packages compared to GDP among OECD countries.[609] Australia was one of only five OECD countries, together with Canada, Korea, New Zealand and the United States, to adopt a program that constituted more than 4 percent of 2008 GDP,[610] compared to an OECD average of 2.5 percent from 2008 to 2010. Australia's stimulus program was also distinctive in a number of ways. First, it showed a strong preference for increased spending over tax cuts, which were given priority in many other jurisdictions.[611] Second, the focus on long-term policy issues, such as education and health, was fairly atypical.[612] For example, the Australian stimulus program included extensive construction work in schools around the country. It has been estimated that this aspect of the stimulus package delivered around 10,000 new school buildings, thereby generating widespread economic activity across different communities.[613] Finally, the Australian program was unusual in terms of the high level of direct cash payments to individuals, under the mantra, "go hard, go early, go households."[614]

Australia's large stimulus program was directly attributable to the country's history of budgetary surpluses, and the ability of the government to deplete the surplus as the economy slowed.[615] Opinion has been sharply divided on the stimulus program. A number of commentators have criticized the magnitude and time frame of the stimulus package, and have questioned whether, in fact, it provided any protection to the Australian economy during the crisis, noting that some other countries with large

608 See Rudd, "$42 billion nation building package."

609 OECD, *Interim Economic Outlook – March 2009*, Chapter 3: "The effectiveness and scope of fiscal stimulus," pp. 107–9.

610 Ibid., p. 109.

611 Ibid., p. 107. Other countries which, like Australia, constituted exceptions in this regard, were Japan, France, Denmark and Mexico. Ibid., pp. 111–12. See also Senate Economics References Committee, *Government's Economic Stimulus Initiatives*, Government senators' minority report, pp. 55–6.

612 See International Monetary Fund, *Group of Twenty – Meeting of Deputies*, p. 19.

613 R. Robertson, Economist, Macquarie Bank, Opening Statement to the Senate Economic Committee Inquiry, *Proof Committee Hansard*, October 28, 2009, p. 43.

614 See Uren and Taylor, "How Rudd bet the house," p. 1.

615 See OECD, "Economic surveys: Australia, November 2010 – Overview," p. 5; Brown, "Comparison of the handling of the financial crisis," 573–4; Hartcher, "Fortress Australia," p. 1.

stimulus packages, such as the United States, fared anything but well during the crisis.[616] Malcolm Turnbull, who was Leader of the Opposition at the time, encapsulated such criticism in his complaint that the government had engaged in reckless borrowing and spending which would "impose higher costs on future generations of Australians."[617] Also, when Australia became the first of the G20 nations to raise interest rates in October 2009 after the lowest point of the crisis had passed,[618] some concerns were voiced internationally that Australia may have "overdone" its stimulus.[619]

On the other hand, there is much positive commentary, which views the stimulus package as timely, well-targeted and effective. According to the Minority Report of a 2009 Senate Inquiry, for example, the stimulus program prevented Australia from going into recession.[620] The OECD has also stated that Australia's stimulus package was more effective in providing a buffer to declining employment than discretionary spending measures in many other jurisdictions,[621] and that the government's policy response was a key factor in Australia's resilience during the crisis.[622] It appears that the impact of Australia's discretionary spending was significantly greater than most other G20 countries as a share of GDP.[623] Finally, Nobel Laureate, Joseph Stiglitz, has weighed into the debate, describing Australia's economic stimulus package as "probably, the best designed stimulus package of any of the. . .advanced industrial countries, both in size and in design, timing and how it was spent."[624]

616 See, generally, McDonald and Morling, "The Australian economy and the global downturn – Part 1," pp. 1, 12–13; Ryan, "Turnbull 'vindicated'," p. 2.

617 M. Turnbull, "Address to the 2009 Economic and Social Outlook Conference," speech delivered at the Economic and Social Outlook Conference, University of Melbourne, November 2009.

618 Reserve Bank of Australia, "Statement by Glenn Stevens, Governor: Monetary Policy," Media Release no. 2009–23, October 6, 2009.

619 See Glynn and Curran, "Australia's fast recovery," p. A15.

620 Senate Economics References Committee, *Government's Economic Stimulus Initiatives*, Government senators' minority report, p. 52*ff.*

621 OECD, *Employment Outlook 2009: Tackling the Jobs Crisis*, p. 31.

622 OECD, "Economic surveys: Australia, November 2010 – Overview," p. 3.

623 OECD, *Interim Economic Outlook – March 2009*, Chapter 3: "The effectiveness and scope of fiscal stimulus," p. 109.

624 See L. Metherell, "Stimulus 'served Australia well' despite waste," *ABC News (online)*, August 6, 2010. Professor Stiglitz has also stated: "Kevin Rudd, who was prime minister when the crisis struck, put in place one of the best-designed Keynesian stimulus packages of any country. . .Rudd's stimulus worked: Australia had the shortest and shallowest of recessions of the advanced industrial countries." See J. Stiglitz, "In praise of stimulus," *The Age*, August 9, 2010, p. 8.

Australia's regulatory structure, APRA and the HIH Royal Commission

APRA does not have a mortgage on conservatism.

John F. Laker[625]

Australia's "twin peaks" regulatory structure provided a clear contrast to both the US and UK models, which operated during the global financial crisis. As discussed earlier, there is a clear and well-understood delineation of responsibility between APRA, as prudential supervisor for a range of financial institutions, and ASIC, which has responsibility for business conduct and consumer protection.

As the UK Turner Committee has noted, it is far too simplistic to attribute the relative success of some jurisdictions in withstanding the impact of the global financial crisis to either regulatory structure or supervisory style.[626] Nonetheless, the "twin peaks" paradigm did offer certain advantages compared to some other models. For example, it avoided the danger of regulatory arbitrage, which appears to have been a problem under the segmented US model. It also avoided possible conflicts of interest that may arise when prudential oversight and business conduct regulatory functions are concentrated in a single regulator, such as the FSA.[627]

The "twin peaks" model also offered advantages over its pre-Wallis Report forerunner, which was a complex and institutionally based scheme[628] that included both federal and state regulators.[629] The kind of active collaboration which occurred between the government, APRA, ASIC and the RBA during the global financial crisis would have been far more difficult under the pre-Wallis Report financial market regulatory structure.[630] Yet, obviously financial market regulatory structure per se is no guarantee of success. Regulatory culture and enforcement matter greatly.[631] Australia's prudential regulator, APRA, occupied a front-line role in Australia's experience of the global financial crisis, and the development of APRA's regulatory culture is important in this regard.

[625] Laker, "APRA's Basel III implementation," p. 2.

[626] Financial Services Authority, *Turner Review*, p. 91.

[627] See ibid., pp. 574–5.

[628] See Financial System Inquiry, *Wallis Report*, p. 303.

[629] See Bora and Lewis, "The Australian financial system," 802, 803.

[630] See, for example, Jimenez, "How APRA handled the crisis," p. 18.

[631] See, for example, Draft Financial Services Bill Joint Committee, *First Report: Draft Financial Services Bill*, Executive Summary, positing the need for "a new regulatory philosophy and culture" in the United Kingdom, which will be based on "judgment-led" supervision.

As noted earlier in this chapter, soon after its creation in July 1998, APRA experienced its own personal crisis in the form of the HIH collapse. In its 2003 report, the HIH Royal Commission closely examined the role of APRA in this event. Although concluding that APRA did not contribute directly to the collapse,[632] the Royal Commission Report nonetheless characterized APRA's supervision of HIH as "not good," and as failing to meet a standard that the public was entitled to expect.[633] It considered APRA had overlooked many warning signs, been slow to act and made numerous errors of judgement.[634] According to the HIH Royal Commission Report, these supervisory deficiencies were only partly explained by obstacles to effective regulation arising from the transition to the post-Wallis Report "twin peaks" regulatory model.[635] The report also suggested that APRA's board had underestimated the challenges inherent in an integrated regulatory model.[636]

To re-establish public confidence, the HIH Royal Commission Report recommended major changes to APRA's operational structures and basic approach to prudential supervision,[637] and, in some cases, reversed aspects of the Wallis Report.[638] Recommendation 18, for example, proposed governance changes, including replacement of APRA's non-executive board with a full-time executive group comprising a CEO and 2–3 commissioners.[639] Recommendation 20 suggested discontinuing any

[632] The HIH Royal Commission stated that "APRA did not cause or contribute to the collapse of HIH; nor could it have taken steps to prevent the failure of the company. A regulator cannot be expected to provide a guarantee that no company under its supervision will ever fail." See HIH Royal Commission, *The Failure of HIH Insurance*, vol. I, p. *lii*.

[633] Ibid. [634] Ibid.

[635] Ibid. The Royal Commission considered that a range of logistical matters associated with the implementation of the post-*Wallis* regime had interfered with APRA's ability to supervise HIH effectively. These matters included: APRA's relocation from Canberra to Sydney and high levels of staff attrition resulting in a dearth of specialist insurance skills. Ibid.

[636] Ibid., p. 210. [637] Ibid., p. *liv*.

[638] The Royal Commission made 61 recommendations in total. Of these, many applied specifically to APRA (see, for example, Recommendations 15–31). See, generally, P. Costello, "Government's response to the recommendations of the HIH Royal Commission," Press Release by the Commonwealth Treasurer, September 12, 2003.

[639] The Royal Commission considered that APRA's non-executive board structure reflected a "governance board," rather than an "advisory board," as envisaged by the Wallis Report. A specific problem concerning APRA's "governance board" identified by the Royal Commission was that its insertion between the chief executive and Treasury could potentially blur lines of accountability. Recommendation 19 provided that the chief executive should have power to establish an advisory board. See HIH Royal Commission, *The Failure of HIH Insurance*, vol. I, pp. 208–9. For the Wallis Report's approach to the governance structure of regulatory agencies, such as APRA, see Financial System Inquiry, *Wallis Report*, pp. 535–7.

direct involvement by representatives of ASIC or the RBA in APRA's governance, on the basis that it could hinder, rather than enhance, regulatory coordination.[640] The HIH Royal Commission considered that the Council of Financial Regulators was a more appropriate forum for collaboration and exchange of information between regulators.[641] Finally, Recommendation 21 proposed an urgent review of APRA's organizational structure, to ensure effective supervision.[642]

Three of the HIH Royal Commission Report's recommendations, Recommendations 26 to 28,[643] were particularly important in terms of regulatory culture. The report recommended, for example, that APRA develop "a more sceptical, questioning and, where necessary, aggressive" approach to its prudential supervision,[644] together with systems that encouraged employees continually to question assumptions about the solvency and viability of regulated entities.[645] The Australian government subsequently introduced legislation implementing the HIH Royal Commission's recommendations,[646] including the reconfiguration of APRA's board.[647] Also, the liquidator of HIH ultimately abandoned threatened legal action against APRA for negligence.[648]

The HIH Royal Commission Report had a profound and enduring effect on APRA's regulatory culture and style. HIH was an insurance company, but since APRA was a multi-regulator, the lessons learned in the HIH collapse could be transmitted into the banking realm. Between 2003 and 2005, APRA created a new regulatory framework, which was focused on close supervision, effective risk management, governance, and strong, well-enforced, capital adequacy rules.[649] A central feature of this regime is that the board of directors of financial institutions is the appropriate channel for all regulatory dealings with APRA.

[640] HIH Royal Commission, *The Failure of HIH Insurance*, vol. I, p. 209.

[641] Ibid., pp. 209–10. [642] Ibid., pp. 210–11. [643] Ibid., pp. 220–1.

[644] See Recommendation 26, ibid., p. 220. [645] See Recommendation 28, ibid., p. 221.

[646] The Treasurer, Peter Costello, introduced the Australian Prudential Regulation Authority Amendment Bill 2003 (Cth) on June 5, 2003, and the Bill received assent on June 24, 2003. See generally The Parliament of the Commonwealth of Australia, House of Representatives, Australian Prudential Regulation Authority Amendment Bill 2003 (Cth) ("APRA Amendment Bill 2003"), *Explanatory Memorandum* (2003); Costello, "Government's response."

[647] See T. Boreham, "Costello moves to sack APRA board," *The Australian*, June 6, 2003, p. 18.

[648] D. Elias, "Damages for HIH bust may top $1bn," *The Age*, July 15, 2003, p. 1.

[649] See, generally, Laker, "Risk management in banking."

APRA has displayed its post-HIH regulatory style of close supervision in its oversight of some of Australia's major banks. In 2004, for example, APRA responded to NAB's A$360 million foreign exchange trading scandal, which occurred on its watch.[650] It required NAB to undertake a broad range of remedial actions.[651] APRA's report on the scandal explicitly stated that NAB was to remain under APRA's close supervision until all actions were implemented.[652] In addition, APRA required a 10 percent increase in NAB's internal capital adequacy ratio until it was satisfied that the bank had rectified material weaknesses.[653] In April 2005, NAB's CEO confirmed that the bank had submitted 72 of 81 remedial actions required by APRA.[654] It has been said that a team of regulatory staff virtually lived in NAB's offices for two years following the foreign exchange trading scandal.[655]

As a result of this regulatory history, APRA has adopted a conservative approach to banking, particularly in relation to capital adequacy requirements. In late 2008, for example, APRA put pressure on Australia's largest bank, the Commonwealth Bank of Australia (CBA), to raise its Tier 1 capital beyond its then level of 7.5 percent, as a cushion against loss.[656] Although CBA initially resisted, disagreeing with APRA's risk-based assessment concerning a hedging agreement,[657] the following month the bank raised A$750 million to satisfy APRA's requirements.[658] Conservatism is the new byword in international banking regulation in the post-global financial crisis era. APRA has indicated that it intends to maintain its approach to capital adequacy, which is in some respects more demanding than the Basel III minimum capital adequacy requirements.[659]

[650] See Winestock, "Meet the man," p. 26.

[651] Australian Prudential Regulation Authority, "Report into irregular currency options trading at the National Australia Bank," March 23, 2004, pp. 7–8.

[652] Ibid., p. 8. [653] Ibid.

[654] See Beveridge, "NAB eases back into forex," p. 29.

[655] Winestock, "Meet the man," p. 26. [656] Ibid.

[657] See "CBA says loan losses will increase," *AAP Bulletins*, November 13, 2008.

[658] Winestock, "Meet the man," p. 26. See Commonwealth Bank of Australia, *Annual Report 2009*, p. 3.

[659] See Laker, "APRA's Basel III implementation," p. 2; Australian Prudential Regulation Authority, "Implementing Basel III capital reforms," p. 7. See also Fitch Ratings, "Australian and Canadian major banks: structural features favourable, but funding remains a key issue for Australian banks," Special Report, January 30, 2012, p. 8.

The Australian banking system

> Hands up all those who think Australian banks escaped the meltdown so far because of dumb luck?
>
> Tony D'Aloisio[660]

The Australian banking industry, or parts of it at least, withstood the global financial crisis remarkably well. The hallmarks of Australia's banking industry are stability and market concentration. In this respect, there are strong parallels with the Canadian banking sector, which also remained sound during the crisis.[661] Neither jurisdiction experienced any bank failure or the need for government-sponsored bank bailouts. The Australian banking system's relative stability[662] is reflected in the fact that no depositor has lost funds in an authorized bank since the introduction of modern banking legislation in 1945.[663] The sector covers a range of institutions, including domestic banks, foreign banks, investment banks, credit unions, building societies and friendly societies.[664]

The banking sector is, nonetheless, extremely concentrated. It is dominated by four major banks: Australia and New Zealand Bank (ANZ); CBA; NAB; and Westpac, which constitute "the four pillars" of the banking system and provide retail and commercial lending in the Australian economy.[665] Australia's four leading banks also dominate the New Zealand banking market, holding almost 90 percent of New Zealand banking assets.[666] The level of banking concentration in Australia grew markedly during the global financial crisis, due to the exit of some non-bank lenders,[667] and the decline of the securitization/RMBS

660 This comment was made by Tony D'Aloisio, then Commissioner of ASIC at the 2009 Annual ASIC Summer School (quoted in A. Kohler, "Saved by dumb luck," *Business Spectator*, March 2, 2008).

661 See Bordo, Redish and Rockoff, "Why didn't Canada have a banking crisis?"

662 See generally Australian Bankers' Association Inc. (ABA), "A strong banking system," Fact Sheet, June 2004.

663 See Pearson, *Financial Services Law and Compliance*, p. 276; Australian Prudential Regulation Authority, "Core principles for effective banking supervision," p. 3.

664 See L. McCoach and D. Landy, "Australia" in J. Putnis (ed.), *The Banking Regulation Review* (London: Law Business Research Ltd, 2010), Chapter 3, p. 28. For a breakdown of APRA-regulated institutions as at June 30, 2011, see Australian Prudential Regulation Authority, *Annual Report 2011* (Commonwealth of Australia, 2011), Chapter 3.

665 See Australian Trade Commission, *Australia's Banking Industry*, May 2011, p. 5.

666 See ibid.

667 See Murphy, "Bank competition," pp. 47–8; Senate Economics Reference Committee, *Competition within the Australian Banking Sector*, p. 1.

market.[668] There were also a number of bank mergers and takeovers.[669] For example, Westpac acquired St George Bank, and the CBA took over BankWest.[670] St George Bank and the foreign-owned BankWest were ranked fifth and eighth respectively in terms of size in Australia's banking hierarchy at the time they were acquired.[671]

The four major banks are very large – indeed, in the context of the Australian market, so large that they are arguably "too big to fail."[672] They are also, apparently, too big to merge. The controversial "four pillars" policy prevents a merger between any of the four major Australian banks.[673] CBA, NAB and Westpac are all ranked in the top 100 global corporations in terms of market capitalization,[674] and in the top 50 banks.[675] The four big Australian banks are also among the most profitable worldwide,[676] and have reported annual profits continuously since a recession in the early 1990s.[677]

In 2011, Australia was ranked fifth, and Canada sixth, in the World Economic Forum's Financial Development Index.[678] As at December 2010, Australian financial institutions held approximately A$4.6 trillion in total assets, constituting almost 3.5 percent of nominal GDP.[679] ADI assets represent 60 percent of this amount,[680] and banks accounted for 97 percent of those ADI assets.[681] Australia's four major banks represent

[668] See C. Yeates, "Level playing field would open doors for small lenders," *Sydney Morning Herald*, October 30, 2010, p. 6.

[669] See Senate Economics References Committee, *Competition within the Australian Banking Sector*, pp. 9–10.

[670] See Drury, "Own your own bank," p. 4.

[671] B. Donovan and A. Gorajek, "Developments in the structure of the Australian financial system," *Reserve Bank of Australia Bulletin*, June Quarter (2011), 29–40, at 30.

[672] I am grateful to my colleague, John Stumbles, for this insight.

[673] See Senate Economics References Committee, *Report on Bank Mergers*, pp. 54–6.

[674] Australian bank rankings on the FT Global 500 Index as at December 2011 were: Commonwealth Bank of Australia (62); Westpac Banking (88); ANZ Banking (99); National Bank of Australia (111). See FT Global 500 Index December 2011.

[675] See BankersAlmanac, "Top banks in the world," at www.bankersalmanac.com/addcon/infobank/bank-rankings.aspx. All four banks also appeared in a 2011 ranking of the world's 50 safest banks. See Global Finance, "World's 50 safest banks 2011," *Global Finance Magazine*, August 18, 2011 (ratings as of August 11, 2011).

[676] See Fitch Ratings, "Australian and Canadian major banks," p. 1.

[677] Ibid., p. 15.

[678] See World Economic Forum, *The Financial Development Report 2011*, Insight Report (World Economic Forum, 2011), p. xiii, Table 1.

[679] See Donovan and Gorajek, "Structure of the Australian financial system," 29.

[680] ADI assets increased from 50 percent of Australian financial system assets in 2005 to almost 60 percent in 2010. Ibid., 30.

[681] Ibid., 29–30.

approximately 75 percent of all banking assets. There is analogous concentration in the Canadian banking sector, where the top six banks account for 90 percent of all banking assets.[682]

One significant difference between Australian and Canadian banks is their funding profiles. In contrast to their Canadian counterparts, Australian banks have a relatively low proportion of deposit funding to assets and instead rely heavily on wholesale funding, particularly from overseas markets.[683] For example, whereas deposits account for 68–88 percent of Canadian bank funding, they represent only 54–65 percent of Australian bank funding.[684] In recent times, this heavy reliance on offshore wholesale funding placed pressure on the AA ratings that Australia's major banks enjoyed during the global financial crisis, due to the perceived risks associated with this source of funding.[685]

Australian banks have, however, traditionally adopted a very cautious approach in relation to lending. They have had a much stronger focus on domestic home lending than banks in many other jurisdictions.[686] During the financial crisis, the proportion of the Australian mortgage market held by the big four banks rose steeply as banking concentration increased.[687] However, the ratio of non-performing bank housing loans in Australia was extremely low by international standards.[688]

Australian banks had no history of subprime lending, and no government policy supporting it. It has often been asserted that there were fewer examples of excessive risk-taking in the Australian finance industry than internationally,[689] and that Australian banks were not involved in risky lending.[690] Australian banks also had minimal exposure to high-risk securities, such as credit default swaps.[691] Nonetheless, the specter of high-risk lending and exotic securities is not wholly absent from the Australian banking sector. For example, unlike most of the

[682] See Fitch Ratings, "Australian and Canadian major banks," p. 9.

[683] See Brown and Davis, "Sub-prime crisis," 18. See Shapiro, Kehoe and Liondis, "Euro crisis hits local banks," p. 1, stating that the four major banks rely on offshore funding for approximately 25 percent of their total borrowings.

[684] See Fitch Ratings, "Australian and Canadian major banks," pp. 11–14; A. Bell, "Banks face ratings downgrade on funding," *AAP Financial News Wire*, January 30, 2012.

[685] Ibid. [686] See Fitch Ratings, "Australian and Canadian major banks," p. 9.

[687] Ferguson and Johnston, "Bad old days," p. 8.

[688] See Reserve Bank of Australia, *Financial Stability Review – September 2009*, pp. 20–1; Debelle, "State of play," pp. 6–7.

[689] See Productivity Commission, *Executive Remuneration* (Report No. 49), p. xxv.

[690] See, for example, Swan, "Government withdraws bank funding guarantee."

[691] See Winestock, "Meet the man," p. 26.

Australian banks, NAB incurred losses associated with a A$1.8 billion portfolio of synthetic CDOs during the financial crisis.[692] Also, in March 2011 the RBA warned that risky lending practices could "re-emerge," in the context of growing competition in the home lending market and limited scope for domestic growth.[693]

There are several possible explanations as to why the major Australian banks escaped the worst of the financial crisis. A prevalent story is again one of undeserved, or "dumb," luck.[694] Nonetheless, there are competing explanations that can illustrate the cautious behavior and resilience of the Australian banks. One of these relates to history and banking cycles. In spite of its relative stability, Australian banking has experienced some turbulence. In the late 1980s and early 1990s, following deregulation, the State Bank of South Australia and the State Bank of Victoria collapsed and the Pyramid Building Society went into insolvency.[695] However, perhaps the most cautionary tale in Australia's banking history was a "near death experience" for one of the big four Australian banks in 1992, when Westpac almost failed as a result of poor quality loans.[696]

Just over a decade after the Westpac episode, however, the RBA, in a 2004 Stability Review, gave Australian banks a clean bill of health, in terms of profitability and minimal levels of bad debt.[697] According to the RBA, the banks were in a particularly strong position, not only because of the long period of economic expansion, but also due to "improvements in banks' systems for managing credit risks following problems in the early 1990s."[698]

An alternative explanation for the good performance of the Australian banking system during the global financial crisis argues that, as a result of the four pillars policy and a virtual oligopoly of the four major Australian banks, there was no market for corporate control among them, which had the effect of preventing excessive risk-taking in boom times.[699]

[692] See M. Drummond, "Bad debts mar NAB's $2 bn profit," *Australian Financial Review*, April 29, 2009, p. 1.

[693] See A. Rollins and A. White, "Lenders countenance new era of low credit growth," *Australian Financial Review*, March 25, 2011, p. 47.

[694] See Kohler, "Saved by dumb luck."

[695] See The Treasury (Australia), *Study of Financial System Guarantees* ("Davis Report") (Commonwealth of Australia, 2004), Chapter 2. The Victorian government was required to undertake a A$900 billion bailout of the Pyramid Building Society.

[696] See A. Cornell, "Once bitten: how Australia's banks dodged the crisis," *Australian Financial Review*, December 21, 2009, p. 1.

[697] See Reserve Bank of Australia, *Financial Stability Review*, 2004, p. 2 [698] Ibid.

[699] See C. Yeates, "Four Pillars policy saved us: Macfarlane," *Sydney Morning Herald*, March 3, 2009.

Yet another explanation focuses on APRA's conservative regulatory style. It has been suggested, for example, that one of the reasons why Australian banks had very low levels of non-conforming, or low-doc loans, was that APRA would have required higher capital adequacy levels in these circumstances.[700] A recent report on Australian and Canadian banks confirms that both APRA and the Canadian Office of the Superintendent of Financial Institutions (OSFI) are widely regarded as conservative in terms of capital requirements for banks.[701] The RBA has also noted that lending standards were not relaxed in Australia to the same extent as elsewhere in the lead-up to the financial crisis.[702]

There were also some critical differences in the Australian mortgage market compared, for example, to the US mortgage market. Subprime, or non-conforming, mortgages accounted for a very small portion of the Australian mortgage market compared to the United States.[703] In 2007, non-conforming loans accounted for only 1 percent of outstanding loans in Australia, compared to 13 percent in the US market. This was partly due to the fact that subprime loans were available from a wide variety of financial institutions in the United States, but were available from only a few small, specialized, non-deposit taking lenders in Australia.[704] Certain features of the Australian mortgage market also made it much safer for lenders. For example, interest rates did not reach such low levels as to encourage borrowing by those with limited ability to repay the loan.[705]

Another important difference is that all Australian mortgages are "full recourse" loans, granting the lender recourse to all the borrower's assets.[706] In contrast, "non-recourse" loans operate in a number of US states.[707] Homeowners with mortgage debt exceeding the value

[700] Brown, "Comparison of the handling of the financial crisis," 539; Winestock, "Meet the man," p. 26.

[701] Fitch Ratings, "Australian and Canadian major banks," p. 8.

[702] Reserve Bank of Australia's *Financial Stability Review*, September 2009, p. 21.

[703] See G. Debelle, "A comparison of the US and Australia housing markets," address by the Assistant Governor of the Reserve Bank of Australia to the Sub-prime Mortgage Meltdown Symposium, Adelaide, May 16, 2008.

[704] Ibid.

[705] Reserve Bank of Australia, *Financial Stability Review – September 2009*, p. 21.

[706] See P. Tumbarello, "Australian, New Zealand banks remain sound during global crisis," *IMF Survey Magazine: Countries & Regions*, January 22, 2010; H. Dale, "Australian dwelling prices," HIA Economics Group, August 10, 2011.

[707] See A. C. Ghent and M. Kudlyak, "Recourse and residential mortgage default: theory and evidence from U.S. States," Federal Reserve Bank of Richmond Working Paper No. 09–10, July 7, 2009, p. 5, available at www.fhfa.gov/webfiles/15051/website_ghent.pdf.

of their homes have far greater incentives to default on the loan under a "non-recourse" system.[708]

Finally, there are possible corporate governance constraints, which may contribute to more cautious lender conduct in Australia. In contrast to the United States, where directors, particularly non-executive directors, are effectively insulated from liability for breach of the duty of care,[709] Australian directors are not. In recent times, ASIC has launched a string of high-profile enforcement actions against both executive and non-executive directors under Australia's civil penalty regime.[710] A recent example of this risk to Australian directors was a successful action by ASIC against several executive and non-executive directors of the Centro Property Group, on the basis that the directors had breached their duties to the company in approving final accounts which wrongly classified more than A$2 billion of debt.[711]

Australia's insolvent trading laws also arguably contribute to conservative behavior by directors. The Chief Justice of Western Australia, for example, has stated that "[t]he laws of Australia which expose directors to personal liability in the event that a company trades while insolvent are arguably the strictest in the world."[712] Furthermore, financiers may be subject to risk under the insolvency laws if they participate in restructuring arrangements, and their intervention is sufficient to render them "shadow directors."[713]

In spite of the widespread perception that Australia's banks escaped the full brunt of the crisis as a result of good fortune, there were a

[708] See M. Feldstein, "How to help people whose home values are underwater; the economic spiral will get worse unless we do something about negative equity," *Wall Street Journal*, November 18, 2008, p. A21.

[709] B. Black, B. Cheffins and M. Klausner, "Outside director liability," *Stanford Law Review*, 58 (2006), 1055–159, at 1090–5.

[710] See, generally, J. G. Hill, "The architecture of corporate governance in Australia," Australian National Report on Corporate Governance, International Academy of Comparative Law, 18th International Congress of Comparative Law, Washington, July 25–August 1, 2010, Sydney Law School Research Paper no. 10/75, August 2010, p. 44*ff*, available at papers.ssrn.com/sol3/papers.cfm?abstract_id=1657810.

[711] See *ASIC* v. *Healey* [2011] FCA 717. See also D. A. Katz, "For directors, a wake-up call from down under", Posting to the Harvard Law School Forum on Corporate Governance and Financial Regulation, October 4, 2011, available at blogs.law.harvard.edu/corpgov/2011/10/04/for-directors-a-wake-up-call-from-down-under/.

[712] W. Martin, "Official opening address," speech delivered by the Chief Justice of Western Australia at the Insolvency Practitioners' Association of Australia 16th National Conference, Perth, May 28, 2009.

[713] See Spigelman, "Global financial crisis and Australian courts," pp. 13–14.

number of features within the banking system which provided the incentives for prudent conduct and which also provided the banks with strong protection, through, for example, "full recourse" loans.

Australia's superannuation system

> [Superannuation] has turned into the financial equivalent of the Swiss army knife, with a multiplicity of benefits. . .Aussies are now a nation of capitalists.
>
> *The Economist*[714]

Another factor contributing to Australia's strong economic performance during the global financial crisis is its distinctive system of retirement, or superannuation, funding.[715]

Although superannuation as a form of retirement savings has existed in Australia for more than a century,[716] its scope was traditionally quite limited.[717] In 1992, however, a radical change in the picture of Australian superannuation occurred, with the introduction of superannuation guarantee legislation.[718] Under this scheme, employers became legally obliged to make tax-deductible superannuation contributions on behalf of their workers. Designed to create a near-universal retirement savings system, the scheme straddles public policy and private markets.[719] At the time of its introduction, it was described as "perhaps unique by world standards. . .a curious combination of compulsory but private sector located funding."[720]

714 "Super-duper supers: In Australia's superannuation scheme, everyone's a winner," *The Economist*, May 28, 2011, p. 6.

715 Cooper Review, *Final Report – Part One*, Appendix B, pp. 69–71. For a history of retirement income in Australia 1900–2010, see L. Nielson and B. Harris, "Chronology of superannuation and retirement income in Australia," Parliamentary Library Background Note, Parliament of Australia, updated June 1, 2010.

716 See generally Hill, "Institutional investors," p. 586.

717 See Australian Prudential Regulation Authority, "A recent history of superannuation in Australia," *APRA Insight*, 2 (2007), 3–10.

718 Superannuation Guarantee (Administration) Act 1992 (Cth). For a brief overview of superannuation developments since the introduction of the superannuation guarantee, see Allen Consulting Group, *Enhancing Financial Stability*, pp. 5–6.

719 M. Scott Donald, "What's in a name? Examining the consequences of inter-legality in Australia's superannuation system," *Sydney Law Review*, 33 (2011), 295–318, at 295, 317.

720 Hill, "Institutional investors," p. 589 (citing Evidence of Association of Superannuation Funds of Australia representative, Senate Select Committee on Superannuation, 643).

Employer contributions under the superannuation guarantee rose gradually over time from an initial rate of 3 percent of salary in 1993, to 9 percent a decade later,[721] and in late 2011, the government introduced a Bill further lifting the contribution rate to 12 percent.[722] This increase addresses concern that some workers may have insufficient savings for retirement.[723] The global financial crisis has exposed this as a problem in the United States in relation to 401(k) retirement plans.[724]

Since the introduction of compulsory employer-funded contributions, superannuation has risen dramatically in Australia to become the largest source of long-term savings.[725] Aggregate assets of superannuation now stand at more than A$1.3 trillion.[726] Superannuation assets constitute "a pool of capital...that might not otherwise have existed,"[727] and are predicted to reach A$6.1 trillion by 2035.[728]

Australia's superannuation industry has a strong presence across a broad range of investment assets. The proportion of Australian equities held by superannuation funds grew from 8.5 percent in 1998 to 29 percent of the total market capitalization of the ASX in 2009/10.[729] Superannuation funds are the major contributor to managed funds,[730] and also comprise 60 percent of funds directed toward venture capital and later stage private equity projects.[731] A total of 93 percent of funds allocated to such projects originate in Australia.[732] Finally, 22 percent of all assets invested by the superannuation industry, equaling A$295 billion, is invested in Australia's financial sector, in the form of ADI deposits or as ADI equity.[733]

Australian superannuation schemes are predominantly defined contribution schemes, under which members, rather than employers, bear the investment risk.[734] Members of defined contribution superannuation

[721] Australian Prudential Regulation Authority, "A recent history of superannuation," 4.

[722] See Superannuation Guarantee (Administration) Amendment Bill 2011 (Cth); The Parliament of the Commonwealth of Australia, Superannuation Guarantee (Administration) Amendment Bill 2011 (Cth), *Explanatory Memorandum* (2011), p. 3. See also Allen Consulting Group, *Enhancing Financial Stability*, p. 17.

[723] Ibid., pp. v–vi. [724] See Browning, "Retiring boomers," p. A1.

[725] The Treasury (Australia), *Stronger Super – Government Response* (Canberra: Commonwealth of Australia, 2010), p. 3.

[726] As at March 2011. Allen Consulting Group, *Enhancing Financial Stability*, p. 7.

[727] "Super-duper supers," p. 6. [728] Cooper Review, *Final Report – Part One*, p. 5.

[729] Allen Consulting Group, *Enhancing Financial Stability*, p. 9.

[730] Ibid. [731] Ibid., p. 10. [732] Ibid. [733] Ibid.

[734] Prior to 1986, however, most Australian superannuation schemes were defined benefit schemes, in which the employer bore the investment risk. See Australian Prudential Regulation Authority, "A recent history of superannuation," pp. 5–6.

schemes are particularly vulnerable to market volatility of the kind that occurred during the global financial crisis.[735]

In 2010, the Cooper Review undertook a comprehensive review of Australia's superannuation system to ensure that there was adequate protection for retirement savings. The review stressed the non-voluntary aspect of the system, noting that "Australians have contributions made to their super funds whether they like it or not."[736] This comment reflects the fact that, increasingly, we live in an age of "forced capitalism."[737] Australia's superannuation scheme effectively places it within the realm of Robert Clark's fourth stage of capitalism, where the government itself appropriates the savings-decision function.[738] In recognition of the compulsory nature of Australia's super system, the Cooper Review recommended a range of reforms to provide greater protection for superannuation funds,[739] which have now been included in the Australian government's *Stronger Super* reform program.[740]

An interesting question is the extent to which the superannuation system contributed to Australia's economic stability in the global financial crisis. A 2011 report prepared for the Association of Superannuation Funds of Australia (ASFA) suggests that superannuation played a key protective role during the crisis.[741]

Two specific financial events, which are relevant in this regard occurred immediately prior to the financial crisis. The first of these was a massive one-off injection of funds into superannuation, as a result of an initiative announced by the Howard government in its 2006–7

[735] See H. Ergas, "Super chance to reform system," *The Australian*, April 27, 2011, p. 1; Browning, "Retiring boomers," p. A1.

[736] Cooper Review, *Final Report – Part One*, p. 1.

[737] L. E. Strine Jnr., "Toward common sense and common ground? Reflections on the shared interests of managers and labor in a more rational system of corporate governance," *Journal of Corporate Law*, 33 (2007), 1–20, at 6. According to Chancellor Strine, most US employees in the private sector with 401(k) retirement plans "have little choice but to invest in the market." *Cf.* L. A. Stout, "The mythical benefits of shareholder control," *Virginia Law Review*, 93 (2007), 789–809, at 801, who adopts a more traditional "voluntary investment" paradigm, stating "investors are not forced to purchase shares in public corporations at gunpoint."

[738] R. C. Clark, "The four stages of capitalism: reflections on investment management treatises," *Harvard Law Review*, 94 (1981), 561–82, at 565–6.

[739] For a pithy summary of the findings of the Cooper Review, see Boujos, "Cooper Review."

[740] See Treasury (Australia), *Stronger Super – Government Response*, pp. 3–4.

[741] Allen Consulting Group, *Enhancing Financial Stability*, pp. v, 7–16.

budget.[742] The government created a narrow window in which members of the public could voluntarily inject up to A$1 million into their individual superannuation funds on a tax-free basis.[743] This made superannuation a particularly attractive form of investment,[744] and produced a large wealth transfer from property into superannuation.[745]

The second financial event was the creation in 2006 of the Future Fund.[746] The Future Fund is a sovereign wealth fund,[747] analogous to pension funds operating in Norway and New Zealand.[748] Its objective was to strengthen the Australian government's long-term financial position,[749] in particular by offsetting the government's unfunded superannuation liabilities under defined benefit schemes.[750] By 2007, the government's original seed funding of A$18 billion had been increased to A$52 billion.[751] This constituted the largest investment pool in Australia, representing around 5 percent of all superannuation assets.[752] This funding derived exclusively from the government's budget surpluses

742 See P. Costello, "Budget speech 2006–07," delivered May 9, 2006, on the Second Reading of the Appropriation Bill (No. 1) 2006–07 by the Honourable Peter Costello MP, Treasurer of the Commonwealth of Australia, pp. 5–6 available at www.budget.gov.au/2006–07/speech/html/Speech.htm.

743 The cut-off date was June 30, 2007. See J. Barrett, "Making good use of that spare magic $1 million," *Australian Financial Review*, February 7, 2007, p. 29.

744 M. Taylor, "The million dollar question," *Money Management*, April 5, 2007, p. 32.

745 The changes, which removed the tax on superannuation exit, particularly targeted people close to retirement with significant wealth outside the superannuation system. See ibid.; S. G. Venkatramani, "Increase in the flow of money," Presentation by the Australian Prudential Regulation Authority to the Financial Services Institute of Australasia (FINSIA), February 22, 2007, p. 1.

746 The fund was established under the Future Fund Act 2006 (Cth), which commenced operation on April 3, 2006. See Australian Government Future Fund, *Future Fund Annual Report 2005–06* (Commonwealth of Australia, 2006), p. 8; B. Toohey, "Solving a problem that's already fixed," *Australian Financial Review*, September 13, 2004, p. 8.

747 See Australian Government Future Fund, *Future Fund: Australia's Sovereign Wealth Fund – Annual Report 2010–2011* (Future Fund Board of Guardians, 2011), p. 3.

748 These are Norway's Government Pension Fund Global and the NZ Superannuation Fund, respectively. The Norwegian fund, comprising profits from the country's petroleum industry, is one of the world's largest pension funds. See Norge Bank Investment Management (NBIM), *Government Pension Fund Global Annual Report 2010*, p. 4.

749 See Australian Government Future Fund, *Annual Report 2010–2011*, p. 3; A. Mitchell, "Future Fund shouldn't be shackled," *Australian Financial Review*, June 18, 2005, p. 45.

750 The federal government's unfunded superannuation liabilities have been estimated to be in the vicinity of A$90 billion. See P. Baker and M. Skulley, "Piggy bank for super bills welcomed," *Australian Financial Review*, September 13, 2004, p. 22; B. Dunstan, "The biggest bucket of money, unspent," *Australian Financial Review*, January 20, 2007, p. 24.

751 Australian Government Future Fund, *Annual Report 2005–06*, p. 8.

752 Dunstan, "Biggest bucket of money," p. 24.

and the proceeds of its T3 privatisation of Telstra, Australia's primary telecommunications service.[753]

The Future Fund commenced its investment strategy in 2007.[754] Unlike Norway's equivalent pension fund,[755] which is invested entirely outside Norway, there are strong tax incentives, which encourage the Future Fund to overweight its investment in Australian equities.[756] As at June 30, 2007, the Future Fund's exposure to domestic equities[757] was A $1.85 billion, compared to A$2 billion in international equities.[758]

Some commentators have expressed concern that superannuation and the Future Fund could distort Australian financial markets, given their enormous level of funds.[759] However, it appears that superannuation may have provided a valuable buffer to Australian companies faced with growing illiquidity in international debt markets during the global financial crisis.[760] For example, superannuation insulated Australian corporations by facilitating capital raisings, and Australian banks, in particular, took advantage of this alternative source of funding.[761]

VII: Conclusion

> There is enormous inertia – a tyranny of the status quo – in private and especially governmental arrangements. Only a crisis – actual or perceived – produces real change.
>
> Milton Friedman[762]

753 See Australian Government Future Fund, *Annual Report 2006–07* (Future Fund Board of Guardians, 2007), p. 8; A. Mitchell, "Future Fund shouldn't be shackled," p. 45, who states that a potential problem arising from the Future Fund's reliance on budgetary surpluses is that governments might be able to exercise "enormous invisible influence over private sector decisions."

754 See Australian Government Future Fund, *Annual Report 2006–07*, p. 8.

755 Norge Bank Investment Management, *Government Pension Fund Global: Annual Report 2010*, p. 3.

756 The Future Fund receives full credit for company tax on dividends. See Australian Government Future Fund, *Annual Report 2006–07*, p. 21; S. Murdoch, "Big shot," *The Australian*, February 7, 2007, p. 24. For other benefits to investment in Australian equities, see Australian Government Future Fund, *Annual Report 2010–2011*, p. 19.

757 Excluding the Future Fund's holding in Telstra. Australian Government Future Fund, *Annual Report 2006–07*, pp. 8, 21.

758 Ibid. For details of the Future Fund's 2011 asset allocation, see Australian Government Future Fund, *Annual Report 2010–2011*, p. 4.

759 See C. Wright, "Surcharge savings to give super boost to funds," *Australian Financial Review*, May 25, 2005, p. 44.

760 Allen Consulting Group, *Enhancing Financial Stability*, p. v.

761 Ibid.

762 M. Friedman (with the assistance of R. D. Friedman), *Capitalism and Freedom* (1962), Preface (1982 edition), p. ix.

The global financial crisis had an extraordinary impact on countries around the world. It overcame the tyranny of the status quo, and led to an outpouring of regulatory responses. Yet, although most major nations responded forcefully to the crisis, its effects were by no means identical across different jurisdictions.

This chapter has explored why Australia fared relatively well. Although there is a general perception that Australia's economy was sustained by trade with China, the chapter argues that there are a number of other important factors which contributed to Australia's resilience. Initial economic conditions were quite varied across jurisdictions before the crisis, and these different starting points seem to have been significant in terms of the impact of the crisis. Australia's solid economic starting point was a clear advantage. However, a range of other factors also contributed to Australia's strong performance, including monetary and fiscal policy; legal structures and reform; regulatory history; banking history; and corporate governance. Australia's experience of the global financial crisis is a reminder that financial markets do not operate in a vacuum, but rather, form part of a complex economic, legal and regulatory ecosystem.[763]

[763] See K. Moore and D. Lewis, *Foundations of Corporate Empire: Is History Repeating Itself?* (Financial Times Prentice Hall, 2000), stating that "[t]he lesson of history. . .is that while markets have always been there, they have always operated in the context of geography, religion, language, folkways, families, armies, and governments, never in a vacuum" (at p. 291).

4

The political economy of Dodd-Frank: Why financial reform tends to be frustrated and systemic risk perpetuated

JOHN C. COFFEE, JR.*

The following chapter is reprinted in its entirely from its original publication as an article in the Cornell Law Review, 97 Cornell L. Rev. __ (forthcoming 2012)

I: Introduction

A good crisis should never go to waste. In the world of financial regulation, experience has shown – since at least the time of the South Sea Bubble three hundred years ago – that only after a catastrophic market collapse can legislators and regulators overcome the resistance of the financial community and adopt comprehensive "reform" legislation.[1] US financial history both confirms and conforms to this broader generalization. The Securities Act of 1933 and the Securities Exchange Act of 1934 were the product of the 1929 stock-market crash and the Great Depression, and their enactment had to await the inauguration of President Franklin Roosevelt in 1933. The decisive event fueling public indignation and shaping these statutes was the Pecora Hearings before the Senate Banking and Currency Committee, which continued from

* Adolf A. Berle Professor of Law, Columbia University Law School. The author wishes to thank his colleague Professor Robert Jackson for assistance and also acknowledge helpful comments from Lucian Bebchuk and the participants at the Cornell Law Review and Clarke Business Law Institute Symposium: *Financial Regulatory Reform in the wake of the Dodd-Frank Act.*

1 For the view that securities regulation, over the last 300 years, has depended on market crashes to fuel it, see S. Banner "What Causes New Securities Regulation? 300 Years of Evidence," *Washington University Law Quarterly*, 75 (1997), 849, 849–51.

1932 to 1934.[2] The Sarbanes-Oxley Act ("SOX")[3] was enacted, possibly in some haste, in 2002, following the collapse of Enron in late 2001 and WorldCom in 2002 and an accelerating crescendo of financial statement restatements by other public corporations.[4] Finally, the Dodd-Frank Act, enacted in 2010,[5] followed an even greater financial collapse, one that threatened financial institutions on a global scale and brought the problem of systemic risk to the attention of a public already infuriated at financial institutions (and their highly compensated investment bankers) being bailed out at taxpayer expense. In each of these episodes, abundant evidence of financial chicanery and fraud was uncovered, and the public was outraged and revulsed.[6] Not surprisingly, in each of these cases, the comprehensive reform legislation that followed in the wake of the market collapse showed hints of the public's desire for retribution.[7] All that is different this time is that the crisis may be wasted – as hereinafter explained.

Why is it that securities and financial reform legislation seems only to be passed after a crash or similar crisis? The most plausible answer involves a basic and foundational theory of political science. Numerous as investors and shareholders are in the United States, they are dispersed, disorganized, and their potential political power is diffused. Easily distracted by other important issues, their attention span is also short. In contrast, the financial services industry is well organized, can keep

[2] See J. Seligman, *The Transformation of Wall Street: A History of the Securities and Exchange Commission and Modern Corporate Finance* (Wilmington, Massachusetts: Houghton Mifflin, 1982), pp. 1–2, 39–40.

[3] Pub. L. No. 107–204, 116 Stat. 745 (codified as amended in scattered sections of Titles 11, 15, 18, 28, and 29 of the United States Code).

[4] For a description of the increasing rate of financial irregularity and accounting restatements in this era leading up to the enactment of SOX, see J. C. Coffee, Jr., "What Caused Enron? A Capsule Social and Economic History of the 1990s," *Cornell Law Review*, 89 (2004), 269, 281–6.

[5] The full title of this statute is the Dodd-Frank Wall Street Reform and Consumer Protection Act, Pub. L. No. 111–203, 124 Stat. 1376 (2010). It will be called the Dodd-Frank Act herein.

[6] See, e.g., J. Zeleny, "As the Public Simmers, Obama Lets Off Steam," *New York Times*, March 21, 2009, A10 (describing "the searing outrage over bonuses paid by companies being kept afloat" with public funds); G. Strauss, "How Did Business Get So Darn Dirty?," *USA Today*, June 12, 2002, IB, online: www.usatoday.com/money/covers/2002–06–12-dirty-business.htm (noting public anger at the financial crises of 2001–2).

[7] In the case of SOX, this is clearest in the new criminal penalties and enhanced penalties in Sections 902 to 906 of SOX. In the case of Dodd-Frank, Section 748 sets forth elaborate provisions to protect and subsidize "whistleblowers" who report misconduct to the SEC. Both provisions seek to detect and punish miscreants.

its focus on the issues that most affect it, and has an obvious incentive to maintain a powerful lobbying presence that will give them disproportionate influence. Hence, as any reader of Mancur Olson's classic book, *The Logic of Collective Action*,[8] will recognize, smaller, better-organized groups are likely to dominate larger, but more diffuse, groups with much greater memberships, in seeking to influence either legislation or regulatory policy.[9] Olson's prediction that smaller, but more cohesive, interest groups would predictably outperform larger citizen-based "latent" groups now seems obvious, but it implies that groups representing investors or shareholders are likely to be at a severe disadvantage in competing with well-funded business lobbies.

If so, how is it, then, that reform legislation ever passes? Later theorists, building on Olson's model, have focused on the role of "political entrepreneurs."[10] In crises, including market crashes, political

[8] M. Olson, Jr., *The Logic of Collective Action: Public Goods and the Theory of Groups*, 2nd edn. (Harvard Economic Studies, 1971).

[9] Ibid., pp. 33–6. For later and fuller statements of Olson's seminal "public choice" perspective, see R. Hardin, *Collective Action* (Baltimore, Maryland: The Johns Hopkins University Press, 1982), pp. 20–2 and T. Sandler, *Collective Action: Theory and Applications* (University of Michigan Press, 1992), pp. 3–7. For a specific application of Olson's ideas to the world of corporate governance, see R. A. Prentice and D. B. Spence, "Sarbanes-Oxley as Quack Corporate Governance: How Wise is the Received Wisdom?," *Georgetown Law Journal*, 95 (2007), 1843, 1847–9.

[10] The "political entrepreneur" or "public entrepreneur" is a creative actor, modeled after Joseph Schumpeter's economic entrepreneur, who solves the essential dilemma in Mancur Olson's theory of collective action: namely, that individuals would rationally prefer to free-ride on the efforts of others. See Olson, *The Logic of Collective Action*, pp. 33–5. See generally E. Ostrom, "Public Entrepreneurship: A Case Study in Ground Water Basin Management," unpublished Ph.D. thesis, University of California Los Angeles UCLA Press (1965, online: http://dlc.dlib.indiana.edu/dlc/bitstream/handle/10535/3581/eostr001.pdf) (introducing the concept of a "public entrepreneur"). Olson was extremely pessimistic about the ability of large groups to take meaningful action. See Olson, *The Logic of Collective Action*, pp. 33–6. Later theorists explain reform legislation as the product of "public entrepreneurs" seeking "political profit" in the form of votes or election to office. See R. E. Wagner, "Pressure Groups and Political Entrepreneurs: A Review Article," *Public Choice*, 1 (1966), 161, 163–5 (using the term "political profit" in a review of Olson's *The Logic of Collective Action*); S. Kuhnert, "An Evolutionary Theory of Collective Action: Schumpeterian Entrepreneurship for the Common Good," *Constitutional Political Economy*, 12 (2001), 13, 15 (defining "political profit" to mean "democratic votes, specifically a maximized share of votes"). By manipulating incentives and rewarding their coalition partners, these actors motivate otherwise passive "latent groups." See E. Ostrom, *Governing the Commons: The Evolution of Institutions for Collective Action* (Cambridge University Press, 1990), p. 41. To summarize, from the perspective of political science, the "public entrepreneur" is the dynamic actor who makes possible collective action in the common interest by bearing the transaction costs

entrepreneurs gain attention and electoral success, they argue, by exploiting the popular discontent.[11] Essentially, these entrepreneurs assume the transaction costs of organizing otherwise latent interest groups in order to secure election (or re-election) by assisting the public to overcome entrenched business interests.[12]

For many, this is precisely how republican government ought to function: leaders arise to aggregate the discontent and frustrations of citizens.[13] But to a vocal school of conservative critics of securities regulation, such democratic eruptions are dismaying, dangerous and need to be discouraged. The most outspoken and doctrinaire of these critics is undoubtedly Yale Law School Professor Roberta Romano. In a well-known article, she condemned SOX for imposing "quack corporate governance" on the United States.[14] Her thesis is, narrowly, that SOX's key provisions on corporate governance were not supported by the then available empirical academic literature and, more generally, that when Congress acts in the wake of a financial crisis, it will predictably

that group members will not bear. Some political figures do appear to have played such an entrepreneurial role after both the Enron/WorldCom scandals of 2001–2 and the 2008 financial crisis. The most obvious nominees for such a role, in this author's judgment, would be Eliot Spitzer and Andrew Cuomo, who each moved from New York Attorney General to New York Governor after achieving broad recognition for actively challenging misconduct and conflicts of interest on Wall Street. See, e.g., J. R. Macey, "Wall Street in Turmoil: State-Federal Relations Post-Eliot Spitzer," *Brooklyn Law Review*, 70 (2004), 117 (calling Spitzer a regulatory entrepreneur, who "achieve[d] fame and political support by aggressively entering the regulatory vacuum created by [the SEC's] failure vigorously to pursue the corporations implicated in the various scandals"). It is unclear whether any figure, since possibly SEC Chairman Arthur Levitt, has played a corresponding role in the national government.

[11] See Macey, "Wall Street in Turmoil."

[12] See Hardin, *Collective Action*, pp. 35–7 (explaining the role of political entrepreneurs who market ideas and aggregate support from latent groups). Anthony Downs argues persuasively that legislative inertia and interest group veto power can be overcome and reform legislation passed only during periods of intense public pressure for change. See A. Downs, "Up and Down with Ecology – The 'Issue-Attention Cycle'," *Public Interest*, 28 (1972), 38, 39–41. The passage of environmental laws has followed this same cycle in the view of several commentators. See C. H. Schroeder, "Rational Choice Versus Republican Moment – Explanations for Environmental Laws, 1969–73," *Duke Environmental Law & Policy Forum*, 9 (1998), 29, 33–56.

[13] See, e.g., M. S. Kang, "Race and Democratic Contestation," *Yale Law Journal*, 117 (2008), 734, 755 (noting that political leaders "help the mass public overcome the usual collective action problems that beset mass coordination").

[14] See R. Romano, "The Sarbanes-Oxley Act and the Making of Quack Corporate Governance," *Yale Law Journal*, 114 (2005), 1521, 1526–7.

adopt hasty, ill-conceived legislation.[15] Thus, she proposes, among other restrictions, that all Congressional legislation regulating the securities markets or corporate governance come with a mandatory sunset provision under which the legislation would expire within a relatively brief period thereafter, unless it was re-adopted by a subsequent Congress.[16]

Any such reform, of course, would ignore Mancur Olson's critical insight: the majority will likely be dominated over the longer term by smaller, but better-motivated, interest groups.[17] Thus, crisis breeds an opportunity to overcome legislative inertia. From this starting point, it follows that the consequence of a mandatory sunset rule is to protect the hegemony of well-financed and better-organized interest groups from majoritarian attack. After the financial crisis passes and some semblance of "normalcy" returns, potential political entrepreneurs will be less willing to take on a coalition of well-financed, tightly organized business interest groups, because they would know that the dispersed investor community could not maintain its zeal for long. Financial industry lobbyists could then easily organize to prevent the re-enactment of the original legislation, once it reached its moment of sunset. As a result, passage of significant legislation would mark only the midpoint of the political battle, which would become more protracted and costly,

[15] See ibid. 1526–7, 1591–4 (asserting that existing empirical studies were "unnoticed or . . . ignored" by legislators who formulated SOX, and making the larger point that "congressional lawmaking in times of perceived emergency offers windows of opportunity to well-positioned policy entrepreneurs . . . when there is little time for reflective deliberation").

[16] See ibid., 1600–2. Professor Romano is also highly critical of the role of "policy entrepreneurs" in the passage of SOX. See ibid., 1568–9. However, she does not use this term in any defined or theoretical sense, but simply levies *ad hoc* criticisms at a variety of officials (some elected and some administrative officials), most notably Senator Sarbanes. See ibid., 1584 (singling out without defining the committee chairman's "critical entrepreneurial role" in SOX's passage). Indeed, the "policy entrepreneurs" she most frequently criticizes are SEC Chairman Arthur Levitt and SEC chief accountant Lynn Turner. See ibid., 1549–50. Neither were politicians who held (or had sought) elective office, and hence they did not stand to gain from political activism. Thus, they would not satisfy the definition of public entrepreneurs used in much of the political science literature as one seeking political profit. See above n. 10. Rather, these persons come closer to being technocrats (although on the highest level). Thus, Professor Romano's critique of the individuals most involved in the enactment of SOX never integrates with any broader theory, and she never discusses Mancur Olson or other political science theorists. Her article seems generally unaware of the political science literature and focuses exclusively on empirical economics.

[17] See Olson, *The Logic of Collective Action*, pp. 33–6.

extending to the end of the sunset period and potentially chilling aggressive administrative implementation during the interim.

Under the original Romano proposal, reform legislation would automatically lapse unless (1) the impact of these provisions were first studied and approved by the Securities Exchange Commission (SEC), and (2) Congress then re-enacted these provisions, based on the SEC's endorsement, within a few years thereafter.[18] More recently, she has refined her procedures, but still insisted on a mandatory sunset after five to six years, not just for securities laws, but for all "foundational financial legislation."[19] Thus, under her approach, not only the Securities Act of 1933 and the Securities Exchange Act of 1934 would have expired by the end of the 1930s, but similarly the Glass-Steagall Act or legislation regulating the capital adequacy and risk management policies of banks and other financial institutions would also self-destruct, unless spared by Congress. Such an outcome seems sensible only if one believes (as she may) that markets need little regulation (and thus that regulatory interventions should be short-lived, disappearing like snowflakes in the sun).

Nonetheless, Professor Romano has her loyal allies.[20] Together, they comprise what might be called the "Tea Party Caucus" of corporate and

[18] See Romano, "The Sarbanes-Oxley Act," 1601. Even with SEC endorsement, she contemplates that Congress would still have to re-enact the statute. See ibid.

[19] See R. Romano, "Regulating in the Dark," Yale Law School Working Paper, (Dec. 18, 2011, online: http://ssrn.com/abstract=1974148), 1. Under her revised proposal, the sunset would take effect in five to six years. Ibid., 15.

[20] See S. M. Bainbridge, *The Complete Guide to Sarbanes-Oxley: Understanding How Sarbanes-Oxley Affects Your Business* (Avon, MA: Adams Media, 2007), p. 20; H. N. Butler and L. E. Ribstein, *The Sarbanes-Oxley Debacle: What We've Learned; How to Fix it* (Washington DC: AEI Press, 2006), pp. 16–18; S. M. Bainbridge, "Sarbanes-Oxley: Legislating in Haste, Repenting in Leisure," *Corporate Governance Law Review*, 2 (2006), 69, 70; L. E. Ribstein, "Sarbox: The Road to Nirvana," *Michigan State Law Review*, (2004), 279, 293–4; L. E. Ribstein, "Bubble Laws," *Houston Law Review*, 40 (2003), 77, 79–82, 87–90; L. E. Ribstein, "International Implications of Sarbanes-Oxley: Raising the Rent on US Law," *Journal of Corporate Law Studies*, 3 (2003), 299, 301–5; L. E. Ribstein, "Market vs. Regulatory Responses to Corporate Fraud: A Critique of the Sarbanes-Oxley Act of 2002," *Journal of Corporation Law*, 28 (2002), 1, 57–61; L. E. Ribstein, "Sarbanes-Oxley After Three Years," *New Zealand Law Review* (2005), 365. Although these authors do not tire of criticizing SOX, they have not convinced others. Reviewing the same economic evidence, Professor John C. Coates finds it harder to balance the costs and benefits of SOX and generally takes a more balanced position. See J. C. Coates IV, "The Goals and Promise of the Sarbanes-Oxley Act," *Journal of Economic Perspectives*, 21 (2007), 91, 91–2. Viewing SOX in a less economic light, Professor Donald Langevoort sees it as reflecting a shift by Congress from an exclusively contractarian perspective to a more trust-based conception of the corporation. See D. C. Langevoort, "The Social Construction of Sarbanes-Oxley," *Michigan Law Review*, 105 (2007), 1817, 1828–33.

securities law professors,[21] and their key themes are: (1) Congress should not legislate after a market crash, because the result will be a "Bubble Law" that crudely overregulates;[22] (2) state laws are superior to federal law in regulating corporate governance, because the states are restrained by the competitive pressure of the market for corporate charters;[23] and (3) federal securities law should limit itself to disclosure (at most) and not attempt substantive regulation of corporate governance.[24] The underlying theory here comes very close to asserting that democracy is bad for corporate efficiency, and thus legislative inertia should be encouraged.

This chapter is not a response to Professor Romano's sunset proposal. That idea is unlikely to gain any serious traction outside of the small community of free market and libertarian theorists who believe financial

[21] While there is irony in this term, it is also intended to be accurate; the three occupy a polar position at one end of the continuum in terms of their unbroken skepticism and rejection of governmental regulation. At the same time, as I am happy to recognize, all three are original and creative legal scholars.

[22] Both Professors Bainbridge and Ribstein regularly use the term "Bubble Law" to refer to federal legislation adopted in the wake of a crash that tends to displace state corporate law. See Ribstein, "Bubble Laws," 97; S. M. Bainbridge, "Dodd-Frank: Quack Federal Corporate Governance Round II," *Minnesota Law Review*, 95 (2011), 1779, 1786–8.

[23] See Ribstein, "Market vs. Regulatory Responses to Corporate Fraud," 57–61.

[24] Professor Romano has argued that the federal securities laws had historically avoided substantive regulation of corporate behavior, staying safely "within a disclosure regime." See R. Romano, "Does the Sarbanes-Oxley Act Have a Future?," *Yale Journal on Regulation*, 26 (2009), 229, 231. The distinctive failure of SOX in her view "is its break with the historic federal regulatory approach of requiring disclosure and leaving substantive governance rules to the states' corporation codes," ibid., 232; see also Ribstein, "International Implications of Sarbanes-Oxley," 301–5. This is a dubious historical generalization. Although the Securities Act of 1933 and the Securities Exchange Act of 1934 do utilize disclosure as their preferred tool, the federal securities laws have frequently regulated substantive corporate conduct and governance. The most controversial federal securities statute of the 1930s was the Public Utility Holding Company Act of 1935, which imposed a "death sentence" on public utility pyramids and holding company structures – clearly an example of aggressive substantive regulation. See J. Seligman, *The Transformation of Wall Street*, pp. 122–3 (describing the Public Utility Holding Company Act as "the most radical reform measure of the Roosevelt administration"). Similarly, the Investment Company Act of 1940 regulates the board structure of investment companies; initially, it required a minimum 40% of each investment company's board be composed of disinterested directors, and also compelled them to hold a diversified portfolio and not sell securities "short" – again substantive regulation. See ibid., pp. 228–9. More recently, the Foreign Corrupt Practices Act requires stronger internal controls over financial reporting (as Professor Romano acknowledges). See Romano, "Does the Sarbanes-Oxley Act Have a Future?" 231. Thus, SOX was only a break with an imagined past in which the federal securities laws exclusively required disclosure.

markets are naturally self-regulating. But this chapter is a response to the worldview favored by these scholars and an attempt to focus attention on the critical implementation stage at which reform legislation is regularly frustrated. Here, it must be acknowledged that the Tea Party Caucus is having an impact, particularly as they shift their focus from SOX to the Dodd-Frank Act where the stakes are higher. With the same fervor that they once attacked SOX, they are now seeking the dismantling of the Dodd-Frank Act, which they also view as having imposed "quack corporate governance" on the financial markets.[25]

In response, this chapter will argue that their shared thesis is unsound for at least three reasons: (1) unhappy as they may be with democratic majorities, they have no coherent theory that explains why democratic majorities should be constrained in their ability to act after a crisis;[26] (2) they fail to understand the ease with which legislative mistakes or misjudgments can be corrected in the process of administrative implementation;[27] and (3) even if it is conceded that legislative misjudgments

[25] See Bainbridge, "Dodd-Frank," 1796–1819. Like Professor Romano, Professor Bainbridge is also suspicious of "suspect policy entrepreneurs" who were, in his view, seeking "to advance a long-standing political agenda." Ibid., 1815–16. For him, the "suspects" are activists within the "institutional investor community, especially union and state and local pension funds." Ibid., 1816. Citing Professor Romano, he speculates that these activists are seeking to "reap private benefits not shared with other investors." Ibid. Although this could conceivably be true in some instances, he provides little, if any, evidence and wholly ignores the even greater possibility that the business interests resisting "reform" are also seeking to gain (or protect) private benefits of their own. For example, corporate executives opposed to "say on pay" or other compensation reforms have a clearer self-interest and more evident desire for private benefits than do the public pension funds who favor "say on pay." Professor Romano has also made clear that she views the Dodd-Frank Act as being as defective as SOX. See Romano, "Regulating in the Dark," 9–11.

[26] Reasonable people can, of course, disagree about the costs and benefits of most statutes. But the claim made by Professor Romano and her allies is that post-crash legislation almost invariably fails. This is a heroic claim that must also factor into its calculus the costs of crashes in under-regulated markets. Professor Romano's distinctive claim is that "policy entrepreneurs" incorporate their preconceived policy agendas into hasty legislation. See Romano, "The Sarbanes-Oxley Act," 1568–9. Ultimately, everyone has preconceived ideas to which they turn in a crisis, and, as later discussed, the core ideas underlying SOX came from the administrative agency with the most information and experience in the field (i.e. the SEC), not from some idiosyncratic lone Congressman.

[27] See nn. 62–3 and accompanying text below (discussing exemptive authority possessed by the SEC under the federal securities laws). Professor Romano at no point discusses this authority, which permits the SEC to escape overly burdensome regulation without the need for legislative action. Perhaps she believes the SEC is "captured" by liberal "policy entrepreneurs," but her silence on this point is revealing.

are often made, their proposed reforms (most notably the mandatory sunset provision) are an unnecessary "fifth wheel," given the ease with which business interest groups can push back, repealing or downsizing legislation whenever they can make a colorable case that the legislation's costs exceed its benefits. Although Professor Romano argues that it would "take a Herculean effort to repeal [SOX's reforms] given the organization of government,"[28] one has to wear blinders to make this statement. The downsizing of SOX, as later detailed, began quickly after its passage in 2002 and continues to date. Legislative efforts to repeal or downsize much of the Dodd-Frank Act are already well advanced.[29] Professor Romano and her allies thus miss exactly what a Mancur Olson would have predicted: once the crisis subsides, more organized interest groups regain the upper hand and begin to extract concessions, exemptions or outright repeal.

Interestingly, the erosion of SOX has had almost nothing to do with the weaknesses diagnosed by Professor Romano – i.e. the haste surrounding its passage or the asserted lack of empirical evidence supporting its reforms.[30] Rather, what has most motivated the opposition to SOX was the high costs of the requirement in Section 404 for tighter internal controls on financial reporting.[31] Yet, these costs resulted not from the legislation itself, but from unanticipated, post-enactment administrative action.[32] Those costs have already been reduced by administrative and legislative action, but the business community remains unsatisfied and senses that complete victory is obtainable (and without any mandatory sunset legislation).[33] Given their relative success, this episode hardly evidences the need for sunset

[28] See Romano, "Regulating in the Dark," 6–7.

[29] See nn. 238–46 and accompanying text below.

[30] See Romano, "Regulating in the Dark," 6–7.

[31] See 15 U.S.C. § 7262. For a more detailed discussion of this provision, see nn. 74–94 and accompanying text below.

[32] As later discussed, the high costs of Section 404 came not from any provision of the statute, but from action taken by a self-regulatory body (the Public Company Accounting Oversight Board ["PCAOB"]), which required that the auditors conduct a full-scale audit before attesting under Section 404(b) to management's evaluation of its internal controls. See nn. 74–94 and accompanying text below. SOX's Section 404 imposed only the requirement that the auditor "attest to . . . the assessment made by the management." This is hardly evidence of legislative haste or of a populist eruption. A cynic might well attribute the high costs of a Section 404 audit either to a desire on the part of the accountants' self-regulator to benefit accountants with high fees, or to the limited competition within the highly concentrated accounting industry.

[33] See nn. 90–2, 238–46 and accompanying text below.

provisions, as the business community seems more than capable of protecting its own interests.

Similarly, as the opposition to the Dodd-Frank Act mounts, this counterreaction is being driven by attempts to protect executive compensation, high leverage, bank profitability and managerial discretion – each of which has powerful champions. In contrast, the goal of curbing systemic risk has no obvious political champion among the usual participants in the political process of financial regulation.[34] Given the resulting imbalance, Mancur Olson's model predicts the likely outcome: interest group politics will produce major revisions to the Dodd-Frank Act, both in the administrative and legislative processes.

Although SOX and the Dodd-Frank Act share many similarities, two major differences between them stand out and suggest that the Dodd-Frank Act is even more vulnerable: First, the Dodd-Frank Act has a much narrower focus than SOX and intends reforms that could prove much more costly to financial institutions than anything in SOX. Although the Dodd-Frank Act also makes some attempts to regulate corporate governance at public corporations, it concentrates to a much greater extent on the problem of systemic risk at large ("too big to fail") financial institutions.[35] Unfortunately, systemic risk is a complex and relatively opaque concept which the average citizen does not understand or easily identify with.[36] Second, the Dodd-Frank Act depends upon administrative implementation to a far greater degree than did SOX, because Congress simply could not specify in detail all the proper steps that needed to be taken with respect to capital adequacy, liquidity ratios, OTC derivatives and similar complex financial issues applicable mainly to large financial institutions. For both reasons, the Dodd-Frank Act is particularly exposed to what may happen in the post-euphoric period after the legislation passes when the public's attention turns elsewhere and business interest groups reestablish their usual dominance over the technical process of policy implementation.

If one believes that systemic risk is a serious problem that needs to be addressed rigorously, this vulnerability is disquieting because, as later described, SOX was effectively downsized in the period after its passage – by subsequent legislation, equivocal agency rule-making, judicial hostility and timid underenforcement by regulators.[37] That pattern

[34] See nn. 49–53 and accompanying text below.

[35] See Part IV below.

[36] See n. 163 and accompanying text below.

[37] See nn. 81–90 and accompanying text below.

may well repeat – with the result that adequate protections against systemic risk will not be implemented. This claim does not rest on any premise that regulatory agencies have actually been "captured" by the financial industry,[38] but that industry may gain influence at the administrative implementation stage and may force regulators to trim their sails. Not only does the administrative stage inherently have lower visibility and is at least as susceptible to lobbying pressure (because of the influence of the "revolving door" on bureaucratic staffers who expect eventually to return to the financial industry),[39] but industry efforts at this later, more pedestrian stage are less likely to attract challenges from political entrepreneurs who appear in crises to champion the cause of investors.

A roadmap of this chapter is now in order. Part II presents a model of how financial reform legislation is frustrated and downsized. This model does not depend on "capture" by the industry,[40] but rather applies the insights of Mancur Olson (and others) to the real world of lobbying and administrative implementation. Part II will also contrast this model with that offered by Professor Romano and her allies. Next, on the premise that what is past is prologue, Part III of this chapter will examine how SOX's provisions were weakened, abandoned, or downsized at the implementation stage. Such administrative softening (or even abandonment) of legislative enactments may be even more likely in the case of the Dodd-Frank Act, because (1) the prospective costs to the financial industry are higher; (2) the Dodd-Frank Act has no natural allies among the major political players who usually support "reform" legislation applicable to the financial markets;[41] and (3) the Dodd-Frank Act is even more dependent on administrative implementation and rule-making. Part IV will examine the policy premises underlying the Dodd-Frank Act. Rather than idealize this legislation, it will acknowledge that some of its reforms were flawed, or even inconsistent. But

[38] The term "capture" is inherently elusive and suggests that a permanent victory is won by the industry. In contrast, this chapter suggests that the opposing sides can each dominate at various points, but the forces championing public-regarding legislation are only advantaged after a major crisis.

[39] This topic is being increasingly debated in the press. See A. R. Sorkin, "The SEC's Revolving Door," *New York Times DealBook*, Aug. 2, 2011, 1.

[40] Professor Romano asserts that this author assumes that administrative agencies have been captured. See Romano, "Regulating in the Dark," 18–19. No such assumption is made, but some agencies are very resource constrained and may also be intimidated by a hostile Congress with control over their budget.

[41] See nn. 48–53 and accompanying text below.

legislation in the real world will always be imperfect; this is the necessary consequence of the logrolling and compromise needed to assemble a majority in a divided political environment. Part V will then turn to the implementation of Dodd-Frank and the associated attempts – legislative and judicial – to downsize it. The evidence to date suggests that a crisis is being wasted, and thus the danger of future systemic risk catastrophes remains clear and present. All this will set the stage for Part VI, a concluding section that will ask (and only partially answer) the ultimate question: what reforms could work?

II: The Regulatory Sine Curve and statutory correction

This chapter's fundamental premise is that a "Regulatory Sine Curve" governs the intensity of the oversight exercised by financial regulators. By this phrase is meant both that (1) regulatory intensity is never constant, but rather increases after a market crash, and then wanes as (and to the extent that) society and the market return to normalcy; and (2) the public's passion for reform is short-lived and the support it gives to political entrepreneurs who seek to oppose powerful interest groups on behalf of the public also wanes after a brief window of opportunity. This same pattern may characterize other forms of regulation (for example, environmental regulation may also wax and wane with highly publicized, vivid environmental disasters), but important differences exist. Financial regulation is inherently opaque, and the public lacks the same visceral identification with the key values in play. Few in the public care as passionately about systemic risk as they may care about the environment or civil rights. Thus, the public's attention span may be shorter, and the window of opportunity briefer within which reform legislation can be passed.

The key implication of the Regulatory Sine Curve is not that legislation is futile, but that erosion of the statute's commands will predictably begin shortly after its passage. Core provisions of the legislation will likely remain (just as the core provisions of the federal securities laws, including those of SOX, remain in place), and sometimes courts will fill in the gaps in legislation expansively.[42] Nonetheless, the greater the

[42] Certainly, the federal courts aggressively filled in the gaps in the federal securities laws in the 1960s by, among other things, implying private causes of action. See *J.I. Case Co.* v. *Borak*, 377 U.S. 426, 430–31 (1964) (implying a private cause of action to enforce federal securities laws). That period of liberal construction of the federal securities laws has now

legislation's reliance on administrative implementation, the greater the erosion that becomes likely, at least if the legislation conflicts with the industry's preferences. This perspective posits both that downsizing and correction is inevitable and that, to a degree, it may often even be desirable. But the likelihood of such erosion also justifies strong legislative action in the first instance (and possibly the framing of some key policies in prophylactic terms that prevent, or at least retard their erosion). This perspective fundamentally conflicts with that of Professor Romano and the Tea Party Caucus, who believe that reform legislation passed after a crash will always enact foolish "quack cures" and thus should be discouraged.[43] For both sides, a common starting point is the recognition that (i) legislation is often flawed and unrationalized and (ii) SOX and the Dodd-Frank Act have their own curious, overbroad and inconsistent elements. But this chapter responds that the likelihood of legislative errors and misjudgments hardly merits draconian measures (such as a sunset provision) because "correction" is both possible through a variety of less drastic and more feasible means, and probably inevitable in light of the Regulatory Sine Curve.

The standard cyclical progression along the Regulatory Sine Curve (from intense to lax enforcement) is driven by a basic asymmetry between the power, resources and organization of the latent group (i.e. investors) and the interest groups affected by the specific legislation. Cohesion among investors begins to break down once "normalcy" returns. Professor Romano has disputed this view of investors as a dispersed latent group,[44] chiefly for two reasons: (1) investors, she argues, are effectively represented in the typical legislative battles over financial regulation by powerful champions, most notably, in her view, "well-funded and politically influential labor unions, public pension funds, and the plaintiff's bar";[45] and (2) business is not "monolithic," but has often conflicting interests.[46]

Both claims are easily refuted. The claim that investors have powerful champions with equal political influence fails for at least three independent reasons. First, the contest for political influence basically pits the

ended, but courts may uphold or invalidate administrative rules implementing the Dodd-Frank Act to the extent they understand and accept the purpose of the legislation.

43 See, e.g., Romano, "The Sarbanes-Oxley Act," 1526–7.

44 She acknowledges that her work never discusses Mancur Olson and related theorists but asserts that "it would be a mistake to do so." See Romano, "Regulating in the Dark," 20, n. 11.

45 Ibid., 21. 46 Ibid.

financial services industry (and those corporate insiders who do not want executive compensation limited or shareholder power strengthened) against investors. This is an inherently one-sided battle, as most recent studies have found that business groups dominate the lobbying process.[47] To consider public pension funds a counterweight to major financial institutions is to mistake an ox for a bull. Pension funds, as fiduciaries for their beneficiaries, do not make political contributions and are thus relatively impotent as political actors. Labor unions can, of course, lobby and make political contributions, but their political power has steadily subsided for decades as the percentage of the US workforce that is unionized has declined.[48] The plaintiff's bar may be active in politics, but its financial resources are also dwarfed by those of the major financial institutions, and, as a practical matter, both unions and the plaintiff's bar largely limit their efforts to the Democratic side of the political aisle (while business groups contribute heavily to both sides).[49]

[47] Political scientists have assembled a great deal of evidence on this score. As one survey by them summarizes:

> Whether we measure it by organizations represented, by money spent, by issues acted on, or participation in rule-making, we see that businesses and trade associations consistently mobilize at roughly ten times the rate that those forces that might countervail them do.

See D. Apollonio, B. E. Cain and L. Drutman, "Access and Lobbying: Looking Beyond the Corruption Paradigm," *Hastings Constitutional Law Quarterly*, 36 (2008), 13, 47. This study further reports data on lobbying expenditures and finds that 71.7% of such expenditures are made by "Business," while only 4.2% are made by "Labor." Ibid., 50, Table 2. Examining spending on federal lobbying, they find that the "Finance/Insur/RealEst" sector is the single largest spender, while labor ranks only eighth. Ibid. at Table 3. Finally, focusing on past disparities in political and lobbying expenditures may overlook the growing prospective disparity, given the significance of the Supreme Court's decision in *Citizens United* v. *FEC*, 130 S. Ct. 876 (2010), which holds that the First Amendment protects the corporation's right to make certain political contributions. In the wake of this decision, new evidence shows that corporate political and lobbying expenditures have significantly increased. See J. C. Coates, IV, "Corporate Politics, Governance and Value Before and After Citizens United" (December 22, 2011, online: http://ssrn.com/abstract=1975421).

[48] Apollonio, Cain and Drutman report that in 2006 the "Finance/Insur/RealEst" lobby expended $258.9 million, while "Labor" expended $66.6 million – a roughly four-to-one ratio. Apollonio, Cain and Drutman, "Access and Lobbying," 50, Table 3. Of course, this understates the real disparity, because political contributions and lobbying by labor almost certainly does not concentrate on financial sector issues, but on traditional labor issues.

[49] Apollonio, Cain and Drutman report data showing that the "Finance/Insur/RealEst" lobby allocates its expenditures 54% to Republicans and 44% to Democrats, while the labor lobby allocates 12% to Republicans and 87% to Democrats. Ibid.

Second, even if institutional investors can be expected to make some effort at lobbying for protection against systemic risk, logically they will spend less than would rationally be expended by the class of public investors as a whole. Institutional investors represent just over half of all public investors,[50] and because they will receive roughly only half of the benefits from increased protection, they can be expected to spend only half of what all investors might pay.[51] But collective action problems impede any attempt to tax other investors, and thus a shortfall results. On the other side of the equation, corporate insiders may spend their shareholders' funds, even though the result of the insiders' lobbying expenditures is to reduce investor welfare. Simply put, this is a mismatch.

Third, the interest groups pointed to by Professor Romano – unions, public pension funds and the plaintiff's bar – may in fact have interests that conflict with those of other public investors and that compromise their asserted role as champions for investors generally. To the extent that closer regulation of banks and financial institutions would restrict their ability to increase lending or to underwrite subprime mortgages, such a policy is contrary to the natural interests of unions, who tend to favor easy credit and increased lending. Increased lending, after all, creates jobs, and job creation is a principal goal of both labor and some civil rights groups. In short, those seeking to reduce systemic risk have few natural political allies; it is a cause that unites largely the technocrats.

Professor Romano's other claim that business is not "monolithic" is, of course, correct to a degree.[52] Often, business interest groups do battle each other. But the interests of the financial services industry are remarkably well aligned in opposing increased regulation of their capital structure, leverage, executive compensation and risk management policies, and they have been both vocal and united in claiming that the Dodd-Frank Act places them at a competitive disadvantage in

[50] Institutional investors hold slightly over 50% of the equity in US public corporations. See M. Tonello and S. Rabinow, *The 2010 Institutional Investment Report: Trends in Asset Allocation and Portfolio Composition* (The Conference Board Research Report No. R-1468–10-RR [2010], online: http://ssrn.com/abstract=1707512), 22 tbl. 10.

[51] This point is well made in L. A. Bebchuk and Z. Neeman, "Investor Protection and Interest Group Politics," John M. Olin Center for Law, Economics and Business Discussion Paper No. 603 (November 2, 2007, online: http://ssrn.com/abstract=1030355), 3–4.

[52] See Romano, "Regulating in the Dark," 21.

an increasingly global marketplace.[53] At a minimum, the business community shares a common desire to resist the encroachment of regulatory power over their capital, leverage and compensation decision-making. It is entirely understandable that they resist, but such regulatory oversight is exactly what the goal of limiting systemic risk requires.

Professor Romano proceeds directly from her premise that reform legislation is always flawed to her conclusion that mandatory sunset legislation is necessary. Others have pointed out that the mandatory sunset remedy lacks any serious empirical support.[54] This seems a curious omission for someone whose primary objection to reform legislation is that Congress did not wait for empirical research to discover the optimal remedy.[55] Still, in the absence of such research, it is useful to ask two questions: (1) What would be the likely consequences of a sunset requirement? and (2) What are the less drastic alternatives to her proposed sunset rule?

With regard to the first question, the existing imbalance between the resources of the contending sides in legislative battles over financial regulation would be greatly compounded by any mandatory sunset remedy. The "reform" side would have to win twice, including after the crisis subsides. The necessary second legislative affirmation of

[53] Indeed, Professor Romano herself argues that much of the business community is united in opposition to the Dodd-Frank Act, believing it has "exacerbated the severe economic downturn that has followed the global financial crisis." See Romano, "Regulating in the Dark," 9. For a representative and revealing statement by the financial services industry that it considers both the Dodd-Frank Act and Basel III a threat to the US economy and international competitiveness, see "Rules Present a Grave Threat to the Economy," *Targeted News Service*, October 3, 2011 (summarizing press release issued by The Financial Services Roundtable, a major trade association for the financial services industry).

[54] See Prentice and Spence, "Sarbanes-Oxley as Quack Corporate Governance," 1855–6 (noting that Professor Romano "offers no evidence that laws enacted in a short time frame tend to have more problems than laws enacted over a longer period" and "no empirical evidence that sunshine provisions provide any benefits on balance"). It seems ironically inconsistent for Professor Romano to criticize Congress for enacting many of SOX's provisions without (in her view) adequate empirical support and then for her to propose a legislative remedy of her own (a mandatory sunset rule) that also has no empirical support.

[55] Although Professor Romano believes there is "long and well-established U.S. experience with sunset legislation," she concedes that "[t]here is . . . a dearth of research empirically analyzing sunset reviews," and the research that does exist is "mostly qualitative." See Romano, "Regulating in the Dark," 17 n. 9. In short, her own proposal does not have the empirical foundation that she insisted SOX and the Dodd-Frank Act should have.

the original victory might be denied because of a minority veto (for example, because of a blocking position on a key committee or a filibuster). It was exactly for this reason that Justice (then Professor) Breyer in a well-known book on reforming the administrative process decided that a mandatory sunset law was too draconian a remedy.[56] Further, to the extent that the recurring battle over financial regulation is between those who want more regulation and those who want less, a sunset remedy is inherently one-sided because it applies only to legislation that imposes new regulation, and not to legislation that repeals existing regulation. In truth, deregulation can equally be achieved in haste, with the consequence being ill-considered "reforms" that expose financial markets to catastrophe.[57] If her remedy were truly even-handed, it would apply to deregulatory provisions as well. Either way, the cost of such a remedy is continuing uncertainty and potential paralysis, as nothing could be assumed to be permanent.[58]

To disagree with Professor Romano's reforms, it is not necessary to take the opposite position to her on all issues. One need not claim that reform legislation is typically carefully written or well planned. Rather, this chapter starts from the view stated by Bismarck over a century ago, when he compared the framing of legislation to the making of sausage.[59] Political compromises are often unprincipled, odd and place together strange bedfellows. Haste (Professor Romano's obsession)

[56] See S. Breyer, *Regulation and Its Reform* (Harvard University Press, 1982), pp. 366–7.

[57] A good example of hasty deregulatory legislation would be the Commodity Futures Modernization Act of 2000 ("CFMA"), Pub. L. No. 106–554, 114 Stat. 2763, 2763A-365, which exempted over-the-counter derivatives, including swaps, from the jurisdiction of both the Commodities Future Trading Commission and the SEC. The Act's wholesale deregulation of swaps in 2000 set the stage for AIG's collapse in 2008 when it could not honor the enormous commitments that it had made by means of unregulated credit default swaps. See nn. 120–7 and accompanying text below.

[58] For example, if, pursuant to such an even-handed sunset, the CFMA had been subjected to an automatic termination if Congress did not reaffirm it within five years, the institutions writing credit defaults swaps over this interim might have faced considerable uncertainty that could have chilled their willingness to enter this field. Even more frightening (to all except the extreme right) is the idea that the Federal Reserve Board could similarly vanish, if a polarized Congress could not act within Professor Romano's proposed deadline.

[59] Otto von Bismarck (1815–98), the Chancellor of Imperial Germany, is reputed to have said: "Laws are like sausages, it is better not to see them being made." See www.brainyquote.com/quotes/o/ottovonbis161318.html.

contributes to this state of affairs,[60] but it is only one of many factors. Indeed, it is not clear that slow and piecemeal legislative reform is any less flawed.[61]

Even if haste does produce error (as seems logical), this risk does not imply that reformers should remain passive after a financial crisis. At worst, they will face an imperfect choice: act quickly and imperfectly, within a brief window of opportunity, or face the likelihood that the forces of legislative inertia will regain the upper hand and prevent any reform. In fact, however, the choice is usually less stark than this. The key lesson to be learned from reviewing the response to SOX is that the "correction" of reform legislation is virtually inevitable. In turn, this undercuts the case for legislative passivity or mandatory sunsets. Those whose oxen are gored will predictably organize to secure relief. As later described, SOX exemplifies this pattern.

Accordingly, what is the best, most feasible remedy for legislative error and misjudgment? In this chapter's view, it is the remedy that already exists under the federal securities laws and that Professor Romano never discusses. Under Section 36 of the Securities Exchange Act of 1934 (and similar sections in other federal securities laws), the SEC possesses "general exemptive authority" and can "conditionally or unconditionally exempt any person, security, or transaction, or any class or classes of persons, securities or transactions, from any provision or provisions of

[60] In fact, courts have noted that SOX was "hastily passed and 'poorly drafted.'" See *Newby* v. *Enron*, 2004 U.S. Dist. LEXIS 8158 at *46 (S.D. Tex. Feb. 25, 2004); *In re Adelphia Comm. Corp.*, 2005 U.S. Dist. LEXIS 10349 at *20 n. 8 (S.D.N.Y. May 31, 2005); *SEC* v. *WorldCom, Inc.*, No. 02 Civ. 4963 (S.D.N.Y. Aug. 26, 2003). On the other hand, other commentators have observed that drafting ambiguities arise in all major legislation and are eventually corrected or clarified. Thus, in *Restoring Trust: Report to Hon. Jed S. Rakoff, The United States District Court for the Southern District of New York, on Corporate Governance for the Future of MCI* (online: www.sec.gov/spotlight/worldcom/wcomreport0803.pdf), WorldCom corporate monitor and former SEC Chairman Richard C. Breeden wrote: "While Sarbanes-Oxley has been criticized in some quarters, there can be no doubt that it addresses some of the very problems presented by this Company's history . . . . As with other major legislation covering significant new territory, there are provisions of Sarbanes-Oxley that will benefit from either clarifying regulations or from exemptive actions." Ibid. at 38 and n. 43. This chapter agrees with Chairman Breeden: a corrective process naturally follows comprehensive legislation (whether it is adopted in haste or more deliberately).

[61] Congress passed the Glass-Steagall Act, Pub. L. No 73–66, 48 Stat. 162 (1933), separating investment banking from commercial banking in haste in 1932, then repealed it slowly over several decades, culminating with the Graham-Leach-Bliley Act of 1999, Pub. L. No. 106–102, 113 Stat. 1338 (1999). Reasonable persons can disagree over which statute was more flawed.

this chapter or of any rule or regulation thereunder, to the extent that such exemption is necessary or appropriate in the public interest, and is consistent with the protection of investors."[62] This is fairly sweeping language that gives broad authority to the administrative agency, which will have the benefit of greater information and post-enactment experience, to override Congress.

The advantages of such an administrative exemptive approach begin with the fact that, under it, delay, stalling tactics, or a minority veto could not overturn a prior Congressional enactment. Uncertainty is also reduced, as an administrative agency, with greater experience and objectivity, must be persuaded to act. The agency's actions are likely to be both more predictable and more incremental, thus avoiding the uncertain all-or-nothing choice inherent in sunset provisions. Only if one believes that the SEC has been "captured" by some interest group does this more tailored and precise remedy seem inferior to a gamble on a sunset provision.[63]

To sum up, the contrast between the Tea Party Caucus's perspective and that taken here is basic, but both share some common elements. Under the world as viewed by Professor Romano and her allies, reform legislation follows "a media clamor for action,"[64] and this "'media frenzy' ... compels legislators not only to respond, but to respond quickly, even though they ... cannot possibly determine what would be the best policy to adopt in the circumstances."[65] Typically, she argues, they adopt "recycled proposals fashioned to resolve quite unrelated problems, imagined or real, which policy entrepreneurs advance as ready-made solutions to immediate concerns, to a Congress in need of off-the-shelf proposals that can be enacted quickly."[66] Further, because Congress is risk averse and self-interested, it delegates great discretion to administrative agencies as "a means by which legislators can avoid responsibility for adverse policy consequences."[67]

The alternative view, here presented, agrees that crisis is a precipitant, allowing legislative inertia to be overcome. After a crisis, Congress tends

[62] See 15 U.S.C. § 78mm(a)(1). This provision was added in 1996 by Pub. L. 104–290. Similar exemptive provisions are set forth in Section 28 ("General exemptive authority") of the Securities Act of 1933, 15 U.S.C. § 77z-3, and Section 206A ("Exemptions") of the Investment Advisers Act of 1940, 15 U.S.C. § 80b-6a.

[63] Because Professor Romano never discusses the option of agency exemptive authority, one cannot know her criticisms of it (or even if she was aware of these provisions).

[64] See Romano, "Regulating in the Dark," 4. [65] Ibid., 5–6. [66] Ibid., 6.

[67] Ibid. at 8.

to adopt proposals that the relevant administrative agency has long favored, but that were frustrated by powerful lobbies. Only with a crisis can reformers (or "political entrepreneurs" in the political science vernacular) aggregate sufficient support to pass reform legislation. For example, in the years prior to the Enron and WorldCom crisis in 2001–2, SEC Chairman Arthur Levitt had sought to respond to a soaring number of financial statement restatements and had campaigned to restrict auditor conflicts of interest.[68] But he was rebuffed by the industry.[69] With the Enron and WorldCom insolvencies and the evidence of financial impropriety manifest to all, Levitt and others (most notably, Senator Paul Sarbanes) were able to convince Congress to replace auditor self-regulation with a new body: the Public Company Accounting Oversight Board ("PCAOB").[70] The PCAOB was the centerpiece of SOX, but it was hardly an "off-the-shelf" proposal. But for the crisis, auditor self-regulation would have persisted. Depending on which perspective is preferred, Arthur Levitt and Paul Sarbanes are either the heroes or villains of this story.[71]

But the story does not end there. "Correction" does follow, both in the form of administrative rules that soften some legislative commands and

[68] See Prentice and Spence, "Sarbanes-Oxley as Quack Corporate Governance," 1852 (reporting that Levitt "had been warning of conflicts of interest and other structural problems in the accounting industry"). Financial statement restatements at publicly traded companies appear to have risen from 49 in 1996 to an estimated 250 in 2002, or an increase of approximately 270% over the five years ending in 2002. See Coffee, "What Caused Enron?," 283.

[69] Even Professor Romano has recognized that "the provision of nonaudit services by auditors had been subject to persistent efforts at elimination by the SEC prior to SOX's prohibition." See Romano, "The Sarbanes-Oxley Act," 1534. Thus, the legislative provisions that she most objects to in SOX did not come from the liberal constituencies of which she is suspicious (unions, public pension funds, and the plaintiff's bar), but from the administrative agency with the most experience in the field. This does not fit her diagnosis that Congress turns in a crisis to the pet ideas of special interest groups or individual Congressmen, and adopts them without careful evaluation. Similarly, Professor Bainbridge claims that "suspect policy entrepreneurs" conspire to "hijack the legislative process to advance a long-standing political agenda." See Bainbridge, "Dodd-Frank," 1815–16. This simply did not happen in the case of SOX, where the principal administrative agency in the field had clearly detected a decline in the performance of a critical gatekeeper. See n. 68 above.

[70] The PCAOB is established, and its powers specified, in Title I of the Sarbanes-Oxley Act of 2002. See sections 101–110, 15 U.S.C. §§ 7211–7220.

[71] Professor Romano has made it very clear that she considers both to have been "policy entrepreneurs" who foisted flawed legislation on the country. See Romano, "The Sarbanes-Oxley Act," 1549–50, 1584.

in the form of legislation curbing the prior statute. The next part will describe this process in more detail, as it applied to SOX, and a later part will turn to the Dodd-Frank Act. Reasonable persons can disagree about whether this corrective process went too far (as this author tends to believe) or not far enough. But it is an inevitable part of the Regulatory Sine Curve, which is next examined in operation.

III: SOX revisited: the downsizing of reform

Professor Romano's article on "quack corporate governance" principally focused on four areas where, in her view, SOX's reforms were unsupported by the empirical academic literature: (1) independent audit committees; (2) the restrictions on auditors providing nonaudit services to audit clients; (3) executive loans; and (4) executive certification of financial statements.[72] Interestingly, the efforts to revise or downsize SOX have largely ignored the first three of these areas. In contrast, the fourth area (the prohibition on executive loans) has been quickly and quietly curtailed as a result of collective action taken by the private bar (and acquiesced in by the SEC).[73] The weight of academic empirical research appears not to have had much impact either on SOX's proponents or its critics. Instead, the business community focused primarily on softening the requirements imposed by SOX's Section 404, which required an annual independent review of a public company's internal controls that became more costly than most had anticipated.

This section will focus on those areas where SOX encountered the greatest resistance or has been the most abandoned: (1) Section 404; (2) executive loans; and (3) Section 307, which required lawyers representing the corporation to report securities (and similar) violations up the corporate ladder.

Section 404 and internal control reports

Although Section 404 of SOX became highly controversial in time, it was a "sleeper" provision that attracted comparatively little attention initially. As passed, it mandated only that the SEC adopt a new "internal

[72] See ibid., 1529–43. [73] See nn. 95–106 and accompanying text below.

control report" that had to be included in the issuers' annual report on Form 10-K.[74] In this report, management had to assess the effectiveness of its internal controls over financial reporting.[75] Then, Section 404(b) required the company's outside auditor to "attest to, and report on" management's assessment.[76] Such an attestation requirement was not inherently costly. What made this provision become costly and controversial was the subsequent decision of the PCAOB, made two years after SOX's passage, to require a full-scale audit of the issuer's internal controls before the auditor might so attest. Under its Auditing Standard No. 2, adopted in 2004, the PCAOB required the auditor to test and evaluate both the design and operating effectiveness of the issuer's internal controls before it could deem itself satisfied with management's own assessment requirement.[77] Effectively, this implied that the auditor must conduct two full audits: the first being the traditional audit of the issuer's financial statements, and the second being the audit of the issuer's internal controls.

This proved expensive and provoked a political reaction.[78] But the decision to require a full audit was not the product of SOX itself. The accounting profession largely welcomed this dual audit requirement,

[74] Section 404(a) of the Sarbanes-Oxley Act ("Management assessment of internal controls") required an annual "internal control report" that contained "an assessment, as of the end of the most recent fiscal year of the issuer, of the effectiveness of the internal control structure and procedures of the issuer for financial reporting." See 15 U.S.C. § 7262(a). As the caption to the section states, this Section 404(a) report was to be prepared by the issuer's management.

[75] Ibid.

[76] See 15 U.S.C. § 7262(b). The last sentence of Section 404(b) then added that this attestation "shall be made in accordance with standards for attestation engagements issued or adopted by the [Public Company Accounting Oversight Board]."

[77] See Order Approving Proposed Auditing Standard No. 2, Exchange Act Release No. 49,884, 69 Fed. Reg. 35,083, 35,083–84 (June 23, 2004). The PCAOB's authority to adopt this rule came from Section 404(b). See 15 U.S.C. § 7262(b).

[78] See generally Transcript of Discussion, 2005 Roundtable on Implementation of Internal Control Reporting Provisions, An Audit of Internal Control Over Financial Reporting Performed in Conjunction With an Audit of Financial Statements (April 13, 2005, online: www.sec.gov/spotlight/soxcomp/soxcomp-transcript.txt) (recording the concerns and reports of excessive expense of issuers attempting to apply Auditing Standard No. 2); P.S. Atkins (Commissioner, SEC), "Remarks Before the International Corporate Governance Network 11th Annual Conference" (July 6, 2006, online: www.sec.gov/news/speech/2006/spch070606psa.htm) (acknowledging the high cost of compliance with Section 404 "because of the excessive way in which accountants and management have implemented it").

which proved very lucrative for them.[79] Nonetheless, if auditors were happy with this rule, issuers were not. Almost immediately following the adoption of Auditing Standard No. 2 in 2004, issuers and others began to call for it to be downsized, particularly as applied to smaller public companies.[80] In 2006, an SEC Advisory Committee recommended that this internal controls audit be waived in the case of smaller companies, which it defined as those with a market capitalization under $125 million.[81] Foreign issuers, who began to delist from US exchanges in significant numbers in the period after 2000, often pointed to Section 404 as a leading cause of their decision to flee the US markets.[82] Both successfully delayed the application of Section 404 to them.[83]

Finally, in 2007, the PCAOB relaxed Auditing Standard No. 2 by replacing it with Auditing Standard No. 5, which softened a number of its requirements.[84] An announced intention of this revision was to reduce audit costs, particularly for smaller companies.[85] A follow-up SEC study of Section 404 found a significant decrease in audit costs as a result of the 2007 changes.[86]

Still, this marginal improvement did not satisfy Congress. The Dodd-Frank Act continued the downsizing of the internal controls audit by

[79] See K. Crandell (Arch Venture Partners), "Sarbanes Oxley Section 404: What is the Proper Balance Between Investor Protection and Capital Formation for Smaller Public Companies?" (hearing before the Comm. on Small Bus., 109th Cong. (2d Sess. 2006)) (claiming that auditors had shifted their focus to "lucrative 404 practices").

[80] See, e.g., Exposure Draft of Final Report of Advisory Committee on Smaller Public Companies, Securities Act Release No. 8666, Exchange Act Release No. 53,385, 71 Fed. Reg. 11,090, 11,098 n. 60 (Mar. 3, 2006).

[81] Ibid. at 11,092–93.

[82] See, e.g., Photowatt Technologies Inc., "Registration Statement" (Form F-1), 23 (Sept. 1, 2006) (complaining that Section 404 compliance is "expensive and time consuming" and carries serious risks of administration sanctions and related risks); Pernod Ricard SA, "Annual Report" (Form 20-F), 15 (Dec. 20, 2006) (reporting the company's desire to terminate its 1934 Act registration and thus cease to be a "reporting company" was motivated in part by a desire to escape SOX).

[83] See n. 80 above at 11,103.

[84] See Order Approving Auditing Standard No. 5, An Audit of Internal Control Over Financial Reporting that is Integrated with an Audit of Financial Statements, Securities Exchange Act Release No. 56,152, 72 Fed. Reg. 42,141, 42,141–42 (Aug. 1, 2007).

[85] The SEC emphasized this likely cost reduction in approving Auditing Standard No. 5. Ibid. at 42,145 (noting that most commentators on proposed Auditing Standard No. 5 believed it would reduce the costs of compliance with Section 404).

[86] See U.S. Sec. & Exch. Comm'n, "Study and Recommendations on Section 404(B) of the Sarbanes-Oxley Act of 2002 for Issuers with Public Float Between $75 and $250 Million 49 n.86" (April 2011, online: http://www.sec.gov/news/studies/2011/404bfloat-study.pdf).

exempting from Section 404(b) issuers that were neither "accelerated filers" nor "large accelerated filers."[87] Effectively, this meant that non-accelerated filers (i.e. filers with a market capitalization of $75 million or less) were still required to include management's evaluation of its internal controls in their Annual Report on Form 10-K, but they no longer had to include their auditor's attestation to that report (which would have required an audit under the PCAOB's rules).[88] The SEC further accommodated newer issuers by delaying Section 404's internal control attestations until a public company was required to file its second Form 10-K, thereby effectively giving a company two years after its initial public offering (IPO) before such a report was due.[89]

Even the Dodd-Frank Act's partial repeal of Section 404 has not ended the push for still greater downsizing. In late 2011, the President's Council on Jobs and Competitiveness, a White House-created advisory body, issued a report calling for the massive downsizing of SOX's requirements with respect to public companies having a market capitalization below $1 billion.[90] Section 404 seems to be the primary target (but hardly the exclusive one).[91] The proposed $1 billion market capitalization cutoff would exempt approximately two-thirds of the roughly 5,700 public companies listed on major US stock exchanges.[92] This proposal has already elicited a sharp editorial rebuke from the *New York Times*, but the proposal does appear to have bipartisan support.[93]

[87] See Section 989G of the Dodd-Frank Act (adding new Section 404(c) to the Sarbanes-Oxley Act of 2002).

[88] See Internal Control over Financial Reporting in Exchange Act Periodic Reports of Non-Accelerated Filers, Exchange Act Release No. 9142, 75 Fed. Reg. 57,385, 57,385 (Sept. 21, 2010) (adopting new rules in response to Section 989G of the Dodd-Frank Act).

[89] See 17 C.F.R. § 229.308 (2011). This provision permits newly public companies to delay until their second annual report on Form 10-K the filing of management's assessment (and the accompanying auditor's attestation) of internal controls over financial reporting.

[90] See President's Council on Jobs and Competitiveness, "Taking Action, Building Confidence: Five Common-Sense Initiatives to Boost Jobs and Competitiveness" (2011, online: http://files.jobs-council.com/jobscouncil/files/2011/10/JobsCouncil_InterimReport_Oct11.pdf), 19.

[91] D. Milstead, "A Desperate Obama Kicks Investor Protection to the Curb," *The Globe and Mail*, Oct. 18, 2011, at B19.

[92] Ibid.

[93] See Editorial, "Not Their Job," *New York Times*, Oct. 20, 2011, at A24. Pending legislation would exempt "emerging growth companies," which are defined as companies with less than $1 billion in gross revenues and $700 million in public float, from Section 404(b). See nn. 238–46 and accompanying text below.

Reasonable persons can debate the wisdom of the PCAOB's various actions (both in requiring an audit of internal controls and then in sparing from that audit smaller issuers, who are actually more likely to experience internal control problems).[94] But three conclusions seem justified: (1) "hasty" Congressional action did not cause the Section 404 crisis (rather more deliberate action by a politically neutral, self-regulatory organization did); (2) a corrective process curbed much of the perceived problem within a few years of SOX's passage (and may yet sweep away still more of SOX's provisions); and (3) even Section 404 will not be nullified, as the maximum proposed retrenchment would still leave the internal controls audit in place for larger companies with a market capitalization over $1 billion. Again, whether this corrective process went too far or not far enough can be debated, but it exemplifies the Regulatory Sine Curve in operation. Dodd-Frank is likely to receive similar treatment.

Executive loans and Section 402

Section 402 of SOX is distinctive. Unlike other provisions of SOX (or the Dodd-Frank Act) that authorize agency rule-making, Section 402 baldly prohibited public companies from arranging or extending credit to their executive officers or directors.[95] Adopted with little discussion and late in the process of drafting SOX,[96] it did not address such obvious issues as travel advances, relocation and retention loans, and broker-assisted cashless stock option exercises. Thus, Section 402 provides some support for the Romano critique that post-crash reform legislation can be overbroad and can disrupt legitimate business practices and objectives. What she ignores, however, is that it did not last long.

Despite Professor Romano's views that executive loans were a matter of "settled state law" and had not generated "scholarly

[94] For evidence in support of a strong internal controls audit requirement, see R. Prentice, "Sarbanes-Oxley: The Evidence Regarding the Impact of SOX 404," *Cardozo Law Review*, 29 (2007), 703, 711–25. This issue is not, however, the focus of this chapter.

[95] Section 402 has been codified as Section 13(k) of the Securities Exchange Act of 1934 ("Prohibition on Personal Loans to Executives"). See 15 U.S.C. § 78m(k). The language of Section 13(k) is broad, because it precludes the issuer not only "to extend or maintain credit," but also "to arrange for the extension of credit, or to renew an extension of credit." See ibid. at § 78m(k)(1).

[96] As Professor Romano notes, Section 402 "was introduced at the end of the legislative process in the Senate as a floor amendment substitute for a provision" that was initially drafted "as a disclosure measure." See Romano, "The Sarbanes-Oxley Act," 1538.

controversy,"[97] the empirical evidence actually seems to indicate that such loans resulted in stealth compensation and were associated with both higher rates of financial misstatement and lower industry-adjusted returns.[98] Further, although Professor Romano defends executive loans as leading to greater stock ownership and thus a better alignment of interests between corporate management and shareholders, several studies question this linkage (partly because the stock so acquired could be immediately sold) and in any event find that such loans may have induced managers to pursue high-risk corporate investment policies.[99]

Of course, what moved Congress in adopting SOX was not the empirical studies or the economic arguments, but the anecdotal evidence of extreme abuse: Bernie Ebbers, Chief Executive Officer (CEO) of WorldCom, borrowed $408 million from his company (and could ultimately repay none of it); Ken Lay, CEO of Enron, received $70 million in loans from it (as opposed to only $67 million in compensation); and Dennis Kozlowski, CEO of Tyco, borrowed approximately $270 million (which he largely used to purchase personal assets and real estate, rather than stock).[100] As of the time that Congress enacted SOX in 2002, the average cash loan disclosed by those public companies that disclosed loans to executives was $11 million, and the total insider indebtedness for such companies was $4.5 billion.[101] Worse yet, many of these executive loans were secured only by the stock itself; thus, if the stock price dropped, the board faced the choice of lending additional amounts to the executives or watching them sell their stock and drive down the company's stock price.[102]

97 Ibid.

98 See Prentice and Spence, "Sarbanes-Oxley as Quack Corporate Governance," 1894–5 (summarizing this evidence); see also K. M. Kahle and K. Shastri, "Executive Loans," *Journal of Financial & Quantitative Analysis*, 39 (2004), 791, 794–5; C. P. Cullinan *et al.*, "A Test of the Loan Prohibition of the Sarbanes-Oxley Act: Are Firms that Grant Loans to Executives More Likely to Misstate Their Financial Results?" *Journal of Accounting & Public Policy*, 25 (2006), 485, 485–6 (finding "significant association between executive loans and financial misstatements"); E. A. Gordon *et al.*, "Related Party Transactions: Associations with Corporate Governance and Firm Value" (EFA 2004 Maastricht Meeting, September 2004, Paper No. 4377, online: http://ssrn.com/abstract=558983), 5 (finding "strong negative relationship between industry-adjusted returns and loans" to executives).

99 See Prentice and Spence, "Sarbanes-Oxley as Quack Corporate Governance," 1893–4.

100 Ibid.

101 See L. Bebchuk and J. Fried, *Pay Without Performance: The Unfulfilled Promise of Executive Compensation* (Harvard University Press, 2004), pp. 113–14.

102 See Prentice and Spence, "Sarbanes-Oxley as Quack Corporate Governance," 1894.

The bottom line, then, is that Congress had legitimate justifications for seeking to curb executive loans, but arguably did so clumsily and in an overbroad fashion. What happened next? The real surprise in the aftermath to Section 402 is that the SEC did virtually nothing. Instead, a coalition of some twenty-five major law firms drafted and publicly released a memorandum explaining how they would interpret Section 402,[103] and the SEC quietly acquiesced.[104] Many of the positions taken in this memorandum were quite reasonable, while others were more questionable (and almost certainly would not have been proposed in an SEC release). More important than the particular positions taken is the fact that the bar simply replaced the SEC as the authoritative interpreter of the statute's meaning. This example shows the Regulatory Sine Curve on steroids.

Why did the SEC behave so passively? One reason may have been that the corporate power to make loans to executives is usually governed by state law, and the SEC may not have felt comfortable invading Delaware's territory. More likely, however, is a second explanation: the SEC is a lawyer-dominated agency that does not want to become involved in a confrontation with the elite law firms of the private bar. Once those firms had taken a collective position, the confrontation would have been personal and even bruising if the SEC had rejected their interpretation (on which advice their clients were presumably relying). Here, we need to take into account the much discussed "revolving door" phenomenon under which SEC staffers join the Commission for a brief tour of duty before returning to positions on Wall Street or in the private bar.[105] Given such career expectations, SEC staffers may be far more anxious about confronting the bar than any other interest group.

Still, the result was that the SEC allowed the bar to dictate the interpretation of a statutory provision in a manner that closely circumscribed what Congress had broadly, if clumsily, forbidden. The result was that a legislative "thou shall not" was converted into a much weaker administrative "thou generally should not . . ." Interestingly, in

103 See Alston & Bird LLP *et al.*, "Memorandum Re: Sarbanes-Oxley § 402 – Interpretations Issued By 25 Law Firms" (October 15, 2002, online: www.adrbnymellon.com/files/climail4.pdf), 1. The memorandum was jointly released by 25 law firms, and other firms joined in later. It is available on several websites, and the author is relying on the version posted by Sullivan & Cromwell.

104 See D. Solomon, "Sarbanes and Oxley Agree to Disagree," *Wall Street Journal*, Jul. 24, 2003, at C1.

105 See Sorkin, "The SEC's Revolving Door."

the time since the twenty-five law firm memorandum was adopted, the SEC – with one exception – has never brought an enforcement proceeding to contest an executive loan.[106] One suspects that the opportunities were there for enforcement actions if the SEC had been willing to pursue them.

Attorneys as whistle blowers and Section 307

Section 307 of SOX instructed the SEC to adopt minimum standards of professional conduct for attorneys appearing and practicing before the Commission in the representation of public companies. This provision was adopted with considerable fanfare by Senators, who noted that lawyers were always present "at the scene of the crime" when securities frauds occurred.[107] The Commission responded by adopting its "Standards of Professional Conduct for Attorneys Appearing and Practicing Before the Commission in the Representation of an Issuer" with even greater fanfare in 2003.[108] Under it, attorneys have an obligation to

[106] The lone exception to this generalization appears to be *Goodfellow and Molaris*, Exchange Act Release No. 52,865, 2005 WL 3240602 (Dec. 1, 2005). In this case, the CFO of a public corporation authorized an interest-free loan to the CEO, and two weeks later the CEO approved a similar interest-free loan to the CFO. Ibid. at *2. The approval of the board of directors was never sought; nor was disclosure made to the board. Ibid. This last fact (the absence of board approval) plus the fact that the officers acknowledged their awareness of SOX's prohibition on executive loans (but did not consult counsel) may explain why the SEC made an exception and sued in this case and not in others (at least to date).

[107] See 148 Cong. Rec. S6556 (daily edn., Jul. 10, 2002) (Statement of Sen. Corzine). The co-sponsors of Section 307 ("Rules of Professional Responsibility for Attorneys") were Senator Michael Enzi (R-Wyo.), the Senate's lone accountant and Senator John Corzine. Reviewing Enron, WorldCom and other recent scandals, Senator Enzi told the Senate: "One of the thoughts that occurred to me was that probably in almost every transaction there was a lawyer who drew up the documents involved in that procedure,"148 Cong. Rec. S6554 (daily edn., Jul. 10, 2002) (Statement of Sen. Enzi). For a fuller discussion of Section 307 and the debate over it, see generally, J. C. Coffee, Jr., "The Attorney As Gatekeeper: An Agenda for the SEC," *Columbia Law Review*, 103 (2003), 1293.

[108] See 17 C.F.R. § 205.1–205.7. See also Implementation of Standards of Professional Conduct for Attorneys, Securities Act Release No. 8185, Exchange Act Release No. 47,276, Investment Company Act Release No. 25,919, 68 Fed. Reg. 6296, 6296 (Feb. 6, 2003). Although the Commission adopted its "up the ladder" reporting requirement of evidence of material violations of law, under pressure from the American Bar Association, it abandoned its original proposal that the attorney resign and report to the SEC when the corporate client refuses to correct or rectify a material violation of law. See Implementation of Standards of Professional Conduct for Attorneys, Securities Act Release No. 8186, Exchange Act Release No. 47,282, 68 Fed. Reg. 6324. 6324 (Feb. 6, 2003).

report material violations of federal or state securities laws, or breaches of fiduciary duty, to the issuer's chief legal officer or to its CEO.[109] If the issuer still fails to take action, the lawyer may be required to report further to the company's audit committee.[110] Under some limited circumstances, the lawyer is even permitted (but not required) to disclose a material violation of law directly to the SEC.[111]

Aspirational as SEC Standards of Professional Conduct are, they have been followed by total silence on the enforcement front. Despite numerous instances in which lawyers were clearly aware of executive misconduct – and both the stock option backdating scandal and the mutual fund market timing scandal followed the adoption of these standards and presented instances in which attorneys were deeply implicated in misconduct involving violations of the federal securities laws – the SEC appears never to have charged an attorney representing a public corporation with violating this rule. To be sure, lawyers have been indicted for securities fraud and insider trading and civilly sued by the SEC, but these cases usually involve egregious self-dealing.[112] The lesser remedy of asserting a professional conduct violation has simply not been used by the SEC.

Why not? Sanctioning attorneys for failure to report violations up the ladder within the corporate structure would again place the SEC in a position of high conflict with the bar. In contrast to prosecutions of attorneys for insider trading or other scienter-based offenses, the SEC's enforcement of reporting rules would reach attorneys who acted only negligently and/or who declined to act (without in either case any clear element of self-dealing).

The SEC has long (and perhaps unwisely) resisted entering this zone, based on the overbroad rationale that to discipline attorneys for negligence or inaction would chill the attorney/client relationship and might dissuade clients from seeking legal advice.[113] A recent case exemplifies

[109] Rule 3 ("Issuer as Client") requires an attorney appearing and practicing before the Commission in the representation of an issuer (which terms are very broadly defined) who "becomes aware of evidence of a material violation by the issuer or by any officer, director, employee or agent of the issuer" to "report such evidence to the issuer's chief legal officer . . . forthwith." 17 C.F.R. § 205.3(b).

[110] See 17 C.F.R. § 205.3(b)(3)(i).

[111] See 17 C.F.R. § 205.3(d)(2).

[112] See, e.g., *SEC* v. *Starr*, Lit. Rel. No. 21541 (June 1, 2010, online: www.sec.gov/litigation/litreleases/2010/lr21541.htm) (suing a former Winston & Strawn partner for misappropriating approximately $7 million in client funds).

[113] For a brief period, the SEC had ruled that a securities attorney was obligated (under some circumstances) to advise the board if the attorney became aware that the corporation was acting in violation of the federal securities laws. This position still fell far short

the SEC's continuing reluctance to engage in non-scienter-based enforcement actions against attorneys. In *Monson*,[114] the SEC's staff brought a cease and desist proceeding against a general counsel of a publicly held broker-dealer, who had allegedly facilitated late trading by that broker-dealer on behalf of its clients in over 600 mutual funds in violation of a very explicit and well-known Investment Company Act rule.[115] The attorney had drafted an agreement pursuant to which the broker-dealer's clients were authorized to engage in "late trading," but the SEC's staff did not allege that the attorney either knew that late trading violated the securities laws or that late trading was occurring.[116] Noting that it had long avoided bringing cases against an attorney on the theory that the attorney "departed from professional standards of competence in rendering private legal advice to their clients,"[117] the Commission explained that such restraint was necessary to avoid "encroachment by the Commission on regulation of private attorney conduct historically performed by the states; interference with lawyers' ability to provide unbiased, independent legal advice regarding the securities laws; and chilled advocacy on behalf of clients in proceedings before the Commission."[118]

Arguably, these concerns are overblown when applied to an attorney who drafts an agreement expressly authorizing clearly unlawful conduct. Late trading is not a gray offense. More importantly, such an explanation – that the Commission will not normally proceed against professionals absent evidence of scienter – virtually implies that the

of a "whistle blowing" obligation and only recognized that the issuer was the client. See *Carter and Johnson*, 47 S.E.C. 471, 1981 WL 384414 at *28 (1981). Still, it did recognize a professional obligation for the attorney sometimes to go to the board. Later, however, the Commission retreated from even this position. See Disciplinary Proceedings Involving Professionals Appearing or Practicing Before the Commission, Securities Act Release No. 6783, 41 SEC Docket 388, 395 n. 31 (Jul. 7, 1988) (noting that "[s]ince *Carter and Johnson*, the Commission has not attempted to set professional standards of conduct in Rule 2(e) proceedings, but has relied on a showing of violations of the securities laws"). Ibid. Section 307 of the Dodd-Frank Act essentially imposed a *Carter and Johnson*-like standard on the SEC, which it has so far failed to enforce.

[114] Investment Company Act Release No. 28323, Admin. Proc. File No. 3–12429, 2008 SEC LEXIS 1503 (June 30, 2008).

[115] See 17 C.F.R. § 270.22c-1. [116] See *Monson*, at *2. [117] Ibid. at *7.

[118] Ibid. at 7–8 (internal footnotes omitted). The Commission affirmed the dismissal of the Enforcement Division's complaint on grounds unrelated to the above arguments about interfering with independent legal advice, citing insufficient evidence that the attorney had in fact acted negligently (ibid. at 8–10). Still, the decision stands (and has been read) as a signal that the Commission did not wish to go further into this area.

Commission will not seriously enforce Section 307. Thus, it should not be surprising that Section 307 seems to have been abandoned by the Commission. As with its refusal to enforce the executive loan prohibition, the Commission seems unwilling to enter areas where it might either infringe on state regulation or encounter resistance from the bar. The consequence is that clear Congressional pronouncements are watered down or abandoned, and the rationale is basically the same rationale advocated by critics such as Professors Romano and Bainbridge: namely, that federal agencies should not "encroach" upon areas traditionally relegated to state regulation.

Possibly, this explanation for equivocal SEC enforcement in the case of the financial industry is too narrow. Some federal courts have expressed concern that the SEC is too easily satisfied with symbolic, but hollow, victories and too apprehensive about the prospect of a litigation defeat in truly contested litigation to take on a major opponent. That was the thrust of Judge Rakoff's recent *Bank of America* decision.[119] For present purposes, it is not necessary to select the best explanation to reach the conclusion that equivocal enforcement by the SEC in cases involving major players in the financial industry has long been the pattern, and that pattern does not seem likely to change markedly in the near future.

An evaluation

The Tea Party critics of both SOX and the Dodd-Frank Act argue that, because "reform" legislation is rushed and hastily framed, the policy formulation is distorted by "suspect policy entrepreneurs" who "hijack the legislative process to advance a long-standing political agenda."[120] Brief as this review of SOX has been, it should make clear that "suspect policy entrepreneurs" did not play a major role in adopting or expanding SOX's most controversial provision, Section 404. Nor is the

[119] See *SEC* v. *Bank of America Corp.*, 653 F. Supp. 2d 507 (S.D.N.Y. 2009). The court did ultimately approve a revised settlement. See *SEC* v. *Bank of America Corp.*, Fed. Sec. L. Rep. P 95, 614, 2010 WL 624581 (S.D.N.Y., Feb. 22 2010). More recently, Judge Rakoff has questioned the SEC's long-standing policy of allowing defendants to neither admit nor deny its allegations and settle the case without their resolution. See *SEC* v. *Citigroup Global Markets Inc.*, 2011 U.S. Dist. LEXIS 135914 (S.D.N.Y. Nov. 28, 2011) (declining to approve proposed settlement). This decision is on appeal and the issues in the case are beyond the scope of this chapter.

[120] See Bainbridge, "Dodd-Frank," 1815–16 (describing the drafting of the Dodd-Frank Act).

meaning of "suspect policy entrepreneur" analytically clear or helpful. Many interest groups attempt to influence legislation and regulation (and business interest groups are particularly active). Why investor-oriented groups (such as public pension funds) are "suspect," while groups favoring the status quo (such as business interest groups) are not considered equally "suspect" has not been adequately explained by these critics.

As next explained, the same critique has been directed at the Dodd-Frank Act.[121] Once again, it has only limited explanatory power. Even if it were the case that investor-oriented groups (such as pension funds and unions) are more active politically in the period following a crash, it remains unclear why their activity is "suspect," while the far better funded political activity of business interest groups in seeking to repeal or curtail such legislation after normalcy returns is not.

IV: The Dodd-Frank Act: premises and policy options

In 2008, Congress saw the nation's largest financial institutions race like lemmings over the cliff and into insolvency. Why did they all become insolvent at once? Three credible scenarios have been offered by a variety of commentators. Each seems correct in part, and each motivated the legislative effort that produced the Dodd-Frank Act.

Three credible scenarios

Moral hazard: "Executive compensation caused the crash"

Because a rapid shift towards incentive-based compensation at financial institutions focused senior management on short-term results, longer-term risks were ignored or underweighed.[122] For example, if the executives in charge of asset-backed securitizations at a financial institution could make $100 million in bonuses in a single year if sufficient deals closed that year, such expected compensation could easily produce a "damn-the-torpedoes, full-speed-ahead" approach to risk taking.

[121] See ibid., 1815–20.

[122] For the fullest statement that executive compensation (and in particular incentive compensation) gave rise to a moral hazard problem, see L. A. Bebchuk and H. Spamann, "Regulating Bankers' Pay," *Georgetown Law Journal*, 98 (2010) 247, 255–74; L. A. Bebchuk *et al.*, "The Wages of Failure: Executive Compensation at Bear Stearns and Lehman 2000–2008," *Yale Journal on Regulation*, 27 (2010) 257, 273–6.

Indeed, why should such executives worry at all about the longer-term risks to their bank? Excessive compensation thus led to moral hazard. Inevitably, such a diagnosis leads to proposals to restrict executive compensation. But how, and by whom? Here, the devil is in the details. Once we descend into the details in the implementation process, the special interests and their lobbyists hold all the advantages.

Because Creditors Believed That "Too Big to Fail" ("TBTF") Banks Would Always Be Bailed Out, They Advanced Funds Too Cheaply and Allowed Banks to Become Overleveraged

Economists generally agree that an implicit governmental subsidy for TBTF banks arose because the market assumed that such institutions would be bailed out.[123] Such an implicit guarantee of their solvency leads investors to lend more cheaply to TBTF banks in comparison to smaller banks.[124] The larger the bank, the cheaper it could borrow, in part because all assumed that the government would not allow the bank to fail. Seeing this subsidy, the shareholders and managers of such financial institutions rationally exploited it by taking on excessive debt and leverage.[125] In effect, the banking system was encouraged to risk a solvency crisis because all market participants believed that the government would have to bail it out. From this perspective, the core evil is the implicit subsidy for TBTF banks through cheaper borrowing costs, and the obvious economic answer is to tax this externality and cancel this subsidy. But eliminating subsidies and taxing externalities means making banks less profitable, and any such program will predictably be fought by the industry at every possible level – usually with the counterargument that imposing higher costs on TBTF banks will mean reduced employment and lending.

Bounded Rationality: Cognitive Limitations, Conflicts of Interest, and a Lack of Transparency Induced Market Participants to Repress Recognition of the Problems Overtaking the Market

[123] For an aggressive statement of this view, see A. R. Admati *et al.*, "Fallacies, Irrelevant Facts, and Myths in the Discussion of Capital Regulation: Why Bank Equity Is *Not* Expensive," Rock Center for Corporate Governance at Stanford University. Working Paper No. 86, 2010, 1–7 (March 23, 2011, online: https://gsbapps.stanford.edu/researchpapers/library/RP2065R1&86.pdf).

[124] See J. C. Coffee, Jr., "Systemic Risk After Dodd-Frank: Contingent Capital and the Need for Regulatory Strategies Beyond Oversight," *Columbia Law Review*, 111 (2011), 795, 800–1.

[125] See ibid. at 798–9.

The American International Group (AIG) provides the paradigm of this problem.[126] By 2008, most major financial institutions had come to rely, directly or indirectly, on credit default swaps issued (or backstopped) by AIG to hedge these institutions' exposure to financial risks.[127] Had AIG's aggregate contingent liability on credit default swaps been publicly recognized, many would have recognized that AIG alone could not insure them against an exposure of this magnitude. Instead, even if the market's extraordinary dependence on AIG was dimly perceived, market participants were not forced to admit that the emperor had no clothes. Instead, the problem was collectively repressed, which occurred to a considerable degree because the credit default swap market was itself opaque. Often for self-interested reasons (again involving executive compensation), financial managers persisted in maintaining highly vulnerable portfolios and remaining exposed to enormous risk, relying on an illusory form of insurance.

So what is the appropriate answer to this recurring tendency? If a stubborn refusal to recognize inconvenient truths is the problem, the obvious policy reform is greater transparency: require over-the-counter (OTC) derivatives to be traded over exchanges and through clearing-houses, and it will be less possible for one actor to assume AIG's position as the counterparty for the entire market. As will be seen, the Dodd-Frank Act moves in this direction – equivocally and in a manner dependent on still pending implementation.

Responses

In response to all these perceived causes of the 2008 crisis, the Dodd-Frank Act pursued several strategies, broadly delegating authority to administrative agencies to fill in the details. First, in response to the

[126] For representative critiques from this perspective of bounded rationality, see C. M. Reinhart and K. S. Rogoff, *This Time is Different: Eight Centuries of Financial Folly* (Princeton University Press, 2009), pp. xxxix–xlv; D. C. Langevoort, "Chasing the Greased Pig Down Wall Street: A Gatekeeper's Guide to the Psychology, Culture, and Ethics of Financial Risk Taking," *Cornell Law Review*, 96 (2011), 1209, 1242; G. Gorton, "The Subprime Panic," 15 *European Financial Management*, 10 (2009), 36–7.

[127] By the end of 2007, AIG had sold credit default swaps with a notional amount of roughly $527 billion, of which $61.4 billion referenced CDOs holding mortgage-backed securities as collateral. See American International Group, Inc., Annual Report (Form 10-K), at 122 (February 28, 2008, online: www.ezodproxy.com/AIG/2008/AR2007/images/AIG_10K2007.pdf); M. Lewis, *The Big Short: Inside the Doomsday Machine* (London: Penguin Group, 2009), p. 197.

initial hypothesis that excessive compensation induced excessive risk-taking, the Dodd-Frank Act adopted two somewhat inconsistent strategies. On one hand, it sided with traditional corporate governance reformers, enacting much of their standard agenda: access to the proxy statement, "say on pay" advisory shareholder votes, and the elimination of broker votes.[128] On the other hand, the Dodd-Frank Act gave financial regulators a broad paternalistic power to restrict executive compensation.[129] As will be seen, with the return of "normalcy," courts have struck down some of the corporate governance reforms (and others are in jeopardy).[130] Meanwhile, regulators are quietly downsizing the restrictions authorized by the Dodd-Frank Act on executive compensation.[131]

With respect to the second diagnosis that the TBTF subsidy for banks induced the excessive leverage that underlay the 2008 crisis, the Dodd-Frank Act took elaborate steps to restrict federal lending to large financial institutions, except when they are being liquidated. The Dodd-Frank Act's goal was to signal that there would be no more bailouts, and hence creditors should not lend to TBTF banks on the same discounted terms. Yet, liquidity crises are endemic to banking, and whether the Dodd-Frank Act resolves or aggravates the "TBTF problem" is debatable. All that is clear is that, post-2008, the US banking industry has become even more consolidated (as the survivors acquired those institutions that failed), and the failure of a TBTF bank would be even more catastrophic. Perhaps, as many suspect, financial regulators can still outflank the Dodd-Frank Act's restrictions and find ways to bail out a failing bank. But, if so, the implicit subsidy has not been ended and the potential for another systemic risk crisis remains latent beneath the surface of reform.

Finally, looking at the AIG paradigm, Congress decided to shift the trading of OTC derivatives to exchanges and require the use of clearinghouses, but stopped short of deciding how far to push this reform and instead delegated the issue (subject to some substantial exemptions) to financial regulators.[132]

[128] See Dodd-Frank Act §§ 951, 957 and 971.

[129] See ibid. at § 956, and nn. 209–23 and accompanying text below.

[130] See *Business Roundtable* v. *S.E.C.*, 647 F.3d 1144, 1148–56 (D.C. Cir. 2011) (invalidating SEC's proxy access rule, which was adopted pursuant to Section 971 of the Dodd-Frank Act); nn. 202–7 and accompanying text below.

[131] See nn. 209–23 and accompanying text below.

[132] See Dodd-Frank Act, Pub. L. No. 111–203, tit. 7, pt. 2, 124 Stat. 1376, 1658–1754 (2010) ("Regulation of Swap Markets").

This chapter does not portray the Dodd-Frank Act as "perfect" legislation. Like much "reform" legislation, it is a potpourri of different provisions, some of which may be inconsistent or poorly conceived. That is inevitable in the real world when Congress must act under time pressure and faces the need to satisfy many constituencies. Thus, this chapter focuses more on the incompleteness of the Dodd-Frank Act, the continuing need for detailed implementation, and the erosive impact of the Regulatory Sine Curve on that process. It will focus primarily on three areas: (1) executive compensation; (2) the TBTF problem and proposed reforms to restrain risk-taking by TBTF banks; and (3) the OTC derivatives area (where the AIG bailout provided the motivating force for Congress). Although it will agree that the Dodd-Frank Act was in some respects imperfectly designed, the greater problem is that it relies on administrative implementation that can too easily be frustrated.

Executive compensation and shareholder pressure

The conventional story of the 2008 crisis – as best told by Professor Lucian Bebchuk and his coauthors – focuses on the perverse influences created by executive compensation formulas.[133] They argue not only that executive pay packages were excessively focused on short-term results, but that because senior executives' compensation packages were closely tied to highly levered bets on the value of the banks' assets, such executives shared in any shareholder gains, but were insulated from shareholder losses.[134] Hence, they could focus on the upside and ignore the downside of any risky strategy. The result, they argue, is a classic moral hazard problem.[135]

To corroborate their claim, Bebchuk and his coauthors have collected data showing that senior managers appeared to have profited handsomely even when shareholders lost virtually everything. Examining the failures of Bear Stearns and Lehman, they find that the top five executives at each firm cashed out extraordinary amounts of performance-based compensation during the 2000–8 period.[136] Specifically, they estimate that these top five management teams derived $1.4 billion and

[133] See generally Bebchuk and Spamann, "Regulating Bankers' Pay,"; Bebchuk *et al.*, "The Wages of Failure" (framing the crisis as a consequence of misaligned incentives and moral hazard).

[134] See Bebchuk and Spamann, "Regulating Bankers' Pay," 249–50.

[135] Ibid. at 257–64.

[136] See Bebchuk *et al.*, "The Wages of Failure," 257.

$1 billion, respectively, from cash bonuses and equity sales during this period.[137] These amounts substantially exceeded the same executives' stock holdings at the beginning of the period.[138] If managers win when shareholders lose, this finding would seem to confirm the moral hazard diagnosis of Bebchuk and his coauthors.

Their research has not, however, gone unchallenged. In particular, René Stulz has coauthored several papers that dispute this thesis that the executive compensation formulas for senior executives at financial institutions drove the 2008 crisis by creating an incentive to accept excessive risk.[139] In one paper, he and a coauthor find evidence that those banks with CEOs whose incentives were better aligned with their shareholders actually performed worse during the crisis.[140] They suggest that "CEOs with better incentives to maximize shareholder wealth took risks that other CEOs did not."[141] Nor do they find that bank CEOs reduced their stock holdings prior to 2008; hence, they suffered large wealth losses along with the shareholders.[142] In short, little evidence supports the claim that shareholders were being overreached by their CEOs.

In another study, Stulz and a coauthor find that banks with "shareholder-friendly" corporate governance performed worse during the 2008 crisis.[143] Indeed, banks that the market had favored in 2006 had especially poor returns during the crisis.[144] In other words, financial institutions that led the market in 2006 encountered disaster in 2008. In contrast, financial institutions that had seemed stodgy and unresponsive to shareholder desires in 2006 experienced the least losses in 2008.[145]

137 Ibid. at 271. 138 See ibid. at 271–2.

139 See A. Beltratti and R. M. Stulz, "Why Did Some Banks Perform Better During the Credit Crisis? A Cross-Country Study of the Impact of Governance and Regulation," European Corporate Governance Institute, Fisher College of Business Working Paper No. 2009–03–12, 2–4 (July 13, 2009, online: www.ssrn.com/abstract=1433502); R. Fahlenbrach and R. M. Stulz, "Bank CEO Incentives and the Credit Crisis," The Ohio State University, Fisher College of Business, Working Paper No. 2009–03–13, 1–5 (August 12, 2010, online: www.ssrn.com/abstract=1439859).

140 See Fahlenbrach and Stulz, "Bank CEO Incentives," 1–2 (arguing that the most plausible explanation for these findings is that CEOs "took actions that they believed the market would welcome," but "[e]x post, these actions were costly to their banks").

141 See ibid. at 26. 142 See ibid. at 2, 4.

143 See Beltratti and Stulz, "Why Did Some Banks Perform Better?," 3.

144 See ibid. at 2. Banks that performed in the worst quartile of performance during the 2008 crisis had average returns of −87.44% during the crisis, but an average return of +33.07% in 2006. Ibid. at 14.

145 The best performing banks during the crisis had average returns of −16.58% during the crisis, but only average returns of +7.80% in 2006. Ibid.

Such findings are at least consistent with the view that shareholder pressure led managers to take on higher leverage and accept greater risk in the boom years – with catastrophic consequences later in 2008. Shareholders in effect opted for a financial roller coaster, and the firms they controlled soared to record peaks and plunged to deep valleys in rapid succession.

Other studies by different teams of researchers have reached similar conclusions. Gropp and Köhler find that "owner-controlled" banks had higher profits in the years before the 2008 crisis in comparison to "manager-controlled" banks, but experienced larger losses and were more likely to require governmental assistance during the 2008 crisis.[146] Using a sample of 296 firms from thirty countries, Erkens, Hung and Matos show that firms with more independent boards and higher institutional ownership experienced worse stock returns during the 2007–8 crisis.[147] Specifically, they found that firms with higher institutional ownership took "greater risk in their investment policies before the onset of the crisis."[148] Such evidence suggests that even if managers would prefer to avoid high risk and leverage, their preferences can be overridden by shareholders, and that institutional investors in particular can compel firms to accept greater risk and thus cause them to suffer worse losses in a crisis.

The point here is not that Professor Bebchuk and his coauthors are wrong. They argue that the pay formulas used to compensate senior management at banks gave them an excessive incentive to accept risk.[149] But such an increased incentive could be exactly what shareholders wanted. Shareholders have long used executive compensation to align managerial preferences with their own, and institutional investors certainly understand that managers are undiversified and thus risk averse about corporate insolvency. Being diversified and having limited liability, shareholders do not suffer as much as managers from a bankruptcy. To "correct" the managerial tendency toward risk aversion, shareholders might have been willing to accept even imperfect compensation formulas to seduce managers into accepting increased risk. Thus, both sides in

[146] See R. Gropp and M. Köhler, "Bank Owners or Bank Managers: Who is Keen on Risk? Evidence from the Financial Crisis," 21 European Business School, Research Paper No. 10–02, 2010 (February 23, 2010, online: http://ssrn.com/abstract=1555663).

[147] See D. Erkens, M. Hung and P. Matos, "Corporate Governance in the 2007–2008 Financial Crisis: Evidence from Financial Institutions Worldwide," (2012) 18 *Journal of Corporate Finance*, 389.

[148] Ibid. at 2. [149] Bebchuk *et al.*, "The Wages of Failure," 264–5.

this debate could have valid points. Bebchuk and company appear correct in arguing that compensation formulas create excessive incentives for bank managers to engage in risky activities, and Stulz and others can legitimately interpret their own data to mean that shareholder-controlled firms accept higher risk and hence are more prone to failure in a crisis than firms in which managers are free to enjoy the quiet life (and so avoid risk). Rather than managers overreaching shareholders, instead it looks as if these compensation formulas crudely aligned managerial and shareholder interests, but created a socially excessive incentive for risk-taking. Under this synthesis, shareholders, as principals, simply found ways to contract with managers, as their agents, to accept greater risk through lucrative compensation formulas.

But that only brings us back to the centrality of shareholder pressure and the gap in bank governance between what is privately optimal and what is socially optimal. Arguably, shareholders of financial institutions were willing to accept high leverage and risk, not simply because they were diversified, but because they believed that (1) major banks were "too big to fail," and (2) the implicit reduction in interest expense charged to TBTF banks created an opportunity for "cheap" capital that could not be spurned. Based on these expectations, shareholders of major financial institutions could rationally pressure management to accept more risk than shareholders might consider advisable at industrial corporations.

At this point, it is necessary to disaggregate shareholders. Individual shareholders may sometimes also be risk averse and disinclined to pressure management toward greater risk and leverage, but they are a decreasing minority of all shareholders.[150] Yet, not only do institutional investors own a majority of the equity in US public corporations, but their level of ownership rises to 73 per cent when we focus on the top 1,000 US corporations (among which large financial institutions easily rank).[151]

[150] Recent estimates find retail (or individual) shareholders own only roughly 25% of the stock in publicly traded firms, with the balance being owned by institutional investors and foreign investors (who are also largely institutions). See A. R. Palmiter, "Staying Public: Institutional Investors in U.S. Capital Markets," *Brooklyn Journal of Corporate, Financial and Commercial Law*, 3 (2009), 245, 262 Table 1. Since 2001, institutional investors have held over 50% of the total outstanding equity in U.S. public corporations. See M. Tonello and S. Rabimov, "The 2010 Institutional Investment Report: Trends in Asset Allocation and Portfolio Composition," 22 (2010) (The Conference Board Research Report No. R-1468–10-RR [2010] online: http://ssrn.com/abstract=1707512) tbl.10.

[151] See Tonello and Rabimov, "The 2010 Institutional Investment Report," 27, chart 14 (showing this percentage to have been 76.4 in 2007 and 73 in 2009).

Mutual funds now represent the largest category of institutional owner (in terms of equity holdings).[152] Their rise is important because, in comparison to pension funds, mutual funds more actively compete for the investor's favor, and their recent investment returns are likely to heavily influence this competition. As a result, they tend to be more proactive investors.

Historically, pension funds were largely indexed investors, holding large portfolios that mimicked the broader market. Thus, they were disinclined to become involved in individual corporate governance disputes, because they could not profit significantly from them.[153] But this is changing. Increasingly, pension funds are investing their stock portfolios in hedge funds to obtain returns superior to simple indexing.[154] In turn, these hedge funds pursue proactive strategies, and one of their favorite targets is the underleveraged firm.[155]

The shareholders' preference for leverage is complemented (and to a degree made possible) by the creditors' continuing expectation that they will be protected in a federally-assisted rescue of a failing financial institution. When faced with a failing bank, the federal government has traditionally arranged shotgun marriages through mergers (with federal assumption of at least some of the failing firm's liabilities).[156]

152 Ibid. at 24, 25–6, Table 12 (showing mutual funds held 20.9% of the total equity US market in 2009, slightly more than pension funds in aggregate).

153 For the standard observation that many institutional investors hold too large a portfolio to have much interest in firm-specific corporate governance, see, e.g., R. Cyran, "Beware: Activists Are on the Hunt," *New York Times*, March 4, 2010, at B2.

154 See Coffee, "Systemic Risk After Dodd-Frank," 812, n. 54; C. Williamson, "Big Public Funds Outperform Their Hedge Fund Yardsticks: Plans Studied by P&I Post Average Gain of 11% in the Portfolios," *Pensions & Investments*, (September 20, 2010), at 1, 42 (noting that the $205.5 billion California Public Employees' Retirement System ("CalPERS") began investing in hedge funds in 2002 and has "moved the majority of its portfolio into direct investments in single and multistrategy hedge funds"). A number of other state pension funds have followed CalPERS in this shift. See ibid.

155 Typically, the target of such an activist shareholder is an underperforming firm "with a pristine balance sheet." See Cyran, "Beware: Activists Are on the Hunt," B2. Often, the activist shareholder proposes the sale of assets and a special dividend of the proceeds, which also raises leverage. See ibid.

156 Confronted with an approaching bank failure, the FDIC's preferred strategy has long been to arrange a "purchase and assumption" transaction with another bank – in effect, a shotgun marriage aided by the FDIC assuming some of the failed bank's liabilities. See J. R. Macey and G. P. Miller, "Bank Failures, Risk Monitoring, and the Market for Bank Control," *Columbia Law Review*, 88 (1988), 1153, 1182–3. In the standard "purchase and assumption" transaction, "the deposits of the failed bank are assumed by another bank, which also purchases some of the failed bank's assets." See ibid. at 1182.

This was the strategy followed to rescue Bear Stearns, Merrill Lynch and Wachovia during the 2008 crisis.[157] Under this standard pattern, even if the shareholders of the failed bank were not protected, its creditors were. Thus, the implicit subsidy in interest rates remains and should logically continue to motivate shareholders to seek to exploit "cheap" financing at the cost of excessive leverage.

From this perspective, it seems ironically counter-productive that the Dodd-Frank Act actually sought to increase the ability of shareholders to pressure managers, because such shareholder pressure would predictably often seek to compel managers to increase leverage and accept greater risk. Yet, the Dodd-Frank Act authorized the SEC to adopt rules giving shareholders "access to the proxy statement," enabling dissidents to mount campaigns for minority seats on the board without having to undertake costly proxy fights.[158] The SEC responded to this invitation by quickly adopting new Rule 14a-11, which authorizes dissident shareholders to place their nominees on the corporate board at low cost.[159] Rule 14a-11 could be a desirable counterweight to entrenched managerial power in much of corporate America, but again financial institutions are a special case. Given the

[157] See, e.g., R. Sidel *et al.*, "J.P. Morgan Buys Bear in Fire Sale, as Fed Widens Credit to Avert Crisis," *Wall Street Journal*, March 17, 2008, at A1.

[158] Section 971 ("Proxy access") of the Dodd-Frank Act added a new § 14(a)(2) to the Securities Exchange Act of 1934 that authorizes the SEC to adopt rules under which dissident shareholders may nominate candidates for the board of directors of a public company and include their nominees in the issuer's own proxy statement (thereby permitting these insurgents to economize on the costs of conducting a proxy fight). See Dodd-Frank Act, Pub. L. No. 111–203, § 971, 124 Stat. 1376, 1915 (2010) (to be codified at 15 U.S.C. § 78n).

[159] See Facilitating Shareholder Director Nominations, Securities Act Release No. 9136, Exchange Act Release No. 62,764, Investment Company Act Release No. 29,384, 75 Fed. Reg. 56,668, 56,668 (September 16, 2010). Specifically, if certain conditions are satisfied, the new rule would permit shareholders holding 3% or more of the corporation's voting power for a three-year holding period to nominate candidates to fill up to the greater of (1) 25% of the director positions to be elected, or (2) one director. See ibid. at 56,674–75. These alternative candidates would run against those nominated by the Board's nominating committee. See ibid. at 56,761. Effectively, this procedure would have spared the insurgents much of the costs of a proxy contest. See ibid. (noting that shareholders may prefer to use the new rules instead of launching "a costly traditional proxy contest").

The business community challenged the SEC's new "proxy access" rule and invalidated it in court. See n. 130 above, *Business Roundtable* v. *S.E.C.*, at 1148–49 (invalidating Rule 14a-11 for failure to "adequately . . . assess the economic effects" of the rule). The impact of this case and the weapon it gives business interests to challenge "reform" legislation is assessed. See nn. 202–7 and accompanying text below.

natural tension between the social interest in prudent bank regulation and the shareholder interest in profit maximization through higher leverage, corporate governance reforms that enhance shareholder power may at the same time weaken regulatory control over financial institutions.

Still, if the drafters of the Dodd-Frank Act made a misjudgment in seeking to use shareholders to restrain corporate risk-taking, it was probably a minor error. Close students of the proxy rules doubt that the "proxy access" rule would have significantly altered the corporate governance landscape or that the most powerful activists (i.e. hedge funds) would have used it.[160]

In fairness to Congress, the Dodd-Frank Act did not rely exclusively on corporate governance reforms to restrict executive compensation. Rather than depending exclusively on the fox to guard the executive compensation henhouse, Congress also enacted a very paternalistic Section 956 of the Dodd-Frank Act, which authorized regulators to prohibit excessive incentive-based compensation at "covered financial institutions" that "could lead to material financial loss to the covered financial institution."[161] This was a more direct route to reform, but, as will be seen, financial regulators appear to be backing away from implementing Section 956 effectively.[162]

Systemic risk and the "too big to fail" problem

The overriding goal of the Dodd-Frank Act was to reduce systemic risk. But dealing with systemic risk requires that we first understand it. Although there is no universally accepted definition of the term,[163] most agree that it has three faces:

[160] See, e.g., M. Kahan and E. Rock, "The Insignificance of Proxy Access," *Virginia Law Review*, 97 (2011), 1347, 1352, 1426–31. Under Rule 14a-11, activists who wish to use the rule must disclaim any intent to seek control. See Securities Act Release No. 9136, n. 159 above. Hedge funds may often be unwilling to do this, as they wish to create at least the appearance of an impending control battle to boost the target's stock price. Also, the cost savings offered by the rule to them are insignificant where they would need to invest billions to acquire a significant position in a large financial institution.

[161] Section 956 also requires disclosure by the covered financial institution of "the structures of all incentive-based compensation" in order to enable the regulator to preclude excessive compensation.

[162] See nn. 208–15 and accompanying text below.

[163] For a fuller definition of the term, see S. L. Schwarcz, "Systemic Risk," *Georgetown Law Journal*, 97 (2008), 193, 204.

(1) A financial institution can simply be "too big to fail."[164] A Citigroup probably is, but Lehman was perceived not to be.
(2) An institution can be "too connected to fail," largely as the result of the increased use of OTC derivatives (including credit default swaps).[165] As a result, the failure of one can imply the eventual failure of its counterparties in a cascade of falling financial dominoes. This scenario explains the Government's bailout of AIG, upon whom all other major financial institutions had relied for protection.[166]
(3) Financial institutions can also be too risk correlated to fail, with the result that the failure of one implies intense stress for the others. Although uncorrelated risk can be managed through policies such as diversification, risks that are correlated cannot be similarly resolved or protected against.[167]

This last face of systemic risk – risk correlation – is probably the least understood and most dangerous. Because of market pressures (fueled again in part by shareholders willing to accept risk), large financial institutions are inclined to adopt similar investment and strategic policies (or face a stock market penalty for their refusal). Thus, in the late 1990s, large financial institutions began aggressively to develop their asset-backed securitization business, because it appeared to offer the highest return on their capital. Assume next that one such institution encounters a liquidity crisis (as Bear Stearns did in early 2008) and must sell illiquid assets (such as interests in asset-backed securitizations) into a thin market. Prices fall quickly throughout this market, and as a result other financial institutions are forced to write down their investments in similar assets. Moreover, short sellers and others realize that trouble at

[164] For more on financial institutions that are "Too Big to Fail" see generally M. Dabós, "Too Big To Fail in the Banking Industry: A Survey," in B. E. Gup (ed.), *Too Big To Fail: Policies and Practices in Government Bailouts* (Westport, CT: Greenwood Publishing Group, 2004), p. 141.

[165] See Schwarcz, "Systemic Risk," 202–4 (describing how interconnectedness leads to systemic risk).

[166] See W. K. Sjostrom, Jr., "The AIG Bailout," *Washington and Lee Law Review*, 66 (2009), 943, 979 (noting that "[b]ecause of AIG's size and interconnectedness . . . it was feared that AIG's failure would lead to the collapse of the entire financial system").

[167] See Schwarcz, "Systemic Risk," 200–1 (contrasting uncorrelated individual risk with correlated systemic risk that affects every market participant); Coffee, "Systemic Risk After Dodd-Frank," 816–17 (noting that financial institutions were exposed to increasingly correlated risk in the years prior to 2008).

one financial institution signals distress at other similar institutions and compound the market pressure. This crisis then feeds on itself, as all these banks begin to sell the same, now disfavored, investments into the same, even thinner market.

How can one design an intelligent policy that reduces systemic risk, given the likelihood that market and shareholder pressures will lead financial institutions to follow the herd and pursue similar investment policies? Among the obvious options are the following.

Higher equity capital requirements

Such a strategy makes sense, but precisely because it will reduce leverage and thus bank profitability, it will be quietly resisted by banks. A variant on this general technique is to employ "contingent capital" – namely, a debt security that automatically converts by its terms into an equity security when the institution encounters a defined level of economic stress.[168]

A private, industry-funded insurance system

Such an insurance system is essentially what the Federal Deposit Insurance Corporation ("FDIC") manages, and it has long been the preferred policy of the International Monetary Fund ("IMF").[169] Essentially, it replaces a public bailout with a private industry bail-out, and forces the banking industry to internalize the costs of higher leverage. Put differently, this approach taxes the externality by imposing a charge on the industry to prefund such an insurance fund; this offsets the externality that arises when TBTF banks are able to borrow funds too cheaply because of an expected governmental guarantee.[170]

168 This conversion could be piecemeal and progressive, as the stock price fell to various lower levels, or it could occur when certain accounting-based tests are triggered. The conversion could be to a common stock or to a preferred stock (possibly with special voting rights). Either way, the primary goal is to avert bankruptcy and financial contagion. For a fuller review of the potential designs for contingent capital, see Coffee,"Systemic Risk After Dodd-Frank," 828–33.

169 See L.Yueh, "IMF Gets Tough on Banks with 'FAT' Levy," *Guardian* (London), (April 21, 2010, online: www.guardian.co.uk/commentisfree/2010/apr/21/imf-levy-bank-fat-tax) (noting that the IMF has proposed a "financial stability contribution" toward a self-insurance fund equivalent to 4–5% of each country's GDP).

170 For the case for such a private, pre-funded fund, see J. N. Gordon and C. Muller, "Confronting Financial Crisis: Dodd-Frank's Dangers and the Case for a Systemic Emergency Insurance Fund," *Yale Journal on Regulation*, 28 (2011), 151, 157.

Reducing risk through prophylactic rules

A third approach is to reduce the risk level of TBTF banks by denying them authority to engage in certain higher risk activities. As discussed later, the "Volcker Rule," which Dodd-Frank partially adopted, intends such a result by prohibiting large banks from engaging in proprietary trading or running hedge funds. Similarly, the now repealed Glass-Steagall Act separated investment banking from commercial banking in order to protect the latter institutions.[171]

Dodd-Frank mandates only the last of these steps, through a provision popularly known as "the Volcker Rule."[172] It will be discussed shortly, but it is the primary exception to the generally accurate generalization that the Dodd-Frank Act did not mandate stricter standards on TBTF banks (but only authorized regulators to do so). For example, although Dodd-Frank authorizes the Federal Reserve to impose higher and more restrictive standards with regard to bank capital and leverage, it did not direct any specific such action and instead leaves these issues to the discretion of the Federal Reserve Board ("FRB") and a new body called the Financial Stability Oversight Council ("FSOC").[173] At earlier stages in the Dodd-Frank legislation, both the House and Senate versions of the Act did contain important provisions mandating a private industry insurance fund (modeled after the FDIC), but these provisions were ultimately deleted at the conference stage.[174] Why? Populist anger at the costly bailout of the banks (compounded by resentment over continued high executive compensation in the financial industry) made any "bailout" proposal politically unacceptable.[175] In addition, some feared that the existence of such a fund would perpetuate a moral hazard problem, as creditors would feel protected and continue to lend at a discount.[176]

Instead, Congress's attention in Dodd-Frank was chiefly directed at prohibiting future public bailouts by the Federal Reserve or the FDIC. To

171 See ibid. at 190.

172 See Section 619 of the Dodd-Frank Act. For a fuller review of the rule, see D. H. Carpenter and M. M. Murphy, "The 'Volcker Rule': Proposals to Limit 'Speculative' Proprietary Trading by Banks," Congressional Research Service (2010), 10–20.

173 See Section 111 of the Dodd-Frank Act (establishing the Financial Stability Oversight Council).

174 See Gordon and Muller, "Confronting Financial Crisis," 193.

175 See ibid. (noting that this proposal was "[a]ttacked as fostering 'bailouts'").

176 See ibid. at 207; Admati, "Fallacies, Irrelevant Facts, and Myths," iii (noting that such a fund "could create significant distortions, particularly excessive risk taking").

this end, regulators were stripped of their former authority to advance funds to major financial institutions facing a liquidity crisis.[177] Yet, it is still not clear that the market really believes that any future administration could truly tolerate a major bank failure, and many suspect that some means would be found to evade statutory obstacles in a major crisis. A future administration might also be unwilling to liquidate a failing financial institution if its liquidation would be read politically as a failure of oversight on its part. Even among experienced practitioners, uncertainty surrounds what will actually happen the next time a major liquidity crisis erupts and a significant financial institution nears insolvency.[178] Possibly, the FDIC could liquidate the bank, but still spare its creditors by forming a "bridge company" whose debts would be assumed

[177] Section 1101(a)(6) of the Dodd-Frank Act restricts the Federal Reserve Board's former authority under section 13(3) of the Federal Reserve Act to make emergency loans to a failing institution. Dodd-Frank Act, Pub. L. No. 111–203, § 1101(a)(6), 124 Stat. 1376, 2113–15 (2010) (to be codified at 12 U.S.C. § 343). Under section 1101(a)(6), the FRB can no longer lend to a single firm, but it can make emergency loans "for the purpose of providing liquidity to the financial system, and not to aid a failing financial company." Ibid. Such lending must be incident to a "program or facility with broad-based eligibility." Ibid. Further, section 1101(a)(6) provides that such loans must be fully and adequately collateralized in a manner that "is sufficient to protect taxpayers from losses." Ibid. Neither Lehman nor AIG could have satisfied this standard. Finally, section 1101(a)(6) specifically denies the FRB the power to make loans to a "single and specific company" under its emergency lending authority or to make loans "for the purpose of assisting a single and specific company avoid bankruptcy, resolution under title II of the Dodd-Frank" Act. In substance, this language means that the Federal Reserve's emergency lending authority cannot extend to a targeted bailout loan to a future Lehman, AIG or Bear Stearns. In the case of the FDIC, which is permitted to lend to a "covered financial company" in receivership under section 204(d) of the Dodd-Frank Act, section 212(a) ("No Other Funding") bars the provision of funds by the FDIC to such companies outside of a Title II receivership. Ibid. Sections 204(d), 212(a) (to be codified at 12 U.S.C. §§ 5384, 5392). Although the FDIC can guarantee the obligations of a firm that is being liquidated (and there is no ceiling on its authority in this regard), it can do nothing for an individual firm that remains solvent. See ibid. at section 212(a). Possibly, the FDIC will continue to arrange mergers or "purchases and assumptions."

[178] This view has been expressed to the author by several experienced banking and securities law practitioners, including at conferences and symposia. Many believe the Federal Reserve both could and would find ways to skirt statutory obstacles in a major crisis, but they also recognize that political considerations might deter the Federal Reserve in a lesser crisis. Also, few institutions (other than Congressmen) would have standing to challenge unauthorized lending by the Federal Reserve. Still, because the Federal Reserve has received intense criticism and "second guessing" from Congress since 2008, it has to fear that any defiance by it of Congress's intent could lead to loss of its autonomy. The bottom line is that it is hard to predict whether and how far the Federal Reserve might dare to go in bending the law.

or guaranteed by it.[179] As a result, the market may still consider the creditors of large banks to be protected from failure, and hence the TBTF subsidy may continue, even if to a reduced degree.

Rightly or wrongly, the Dodd-Frank Act seeks to cut off the possibility of central bank emergency funding for a bank in distress in order (in part) to end the idea that a bank can be "too big to fail." This reverses a policy followed by most central banks since at least the late eighteenth century, when Walter Bagehot defined the role of the central banker as that of serving as the lender of last resort.[180] Although a policy of ending emergency funding is at least a relevant response to the problem of the TBTF subsidy, it is a draconian policy that represents a huge gamble.

Put simply, the core problem is that banks are inherently fragile. They (and similar financial institutions) are subject to a fundamental mismatch between the short-term character of their liabilities and the longer-term character of their assets.[181] Depositors expect and receive high liquidity, while borrowers expect to repay their loans over a longer, multiyear period. In good times, banks profit from this "maturity transformation," realizing the spread between the lower rate paid depositors and the higher rate charged borrowers. But, in bad times, banks have been classically subject to "runs" when depositor confidence is shaken.[182]

This mismatch is compounded by the practical necessity for a financial institution of using leverage. Arguably, only banks that employ high leverage can realize the full economies of scale that are inherent to the banking business. The more that a bank borrows and lends, the more that it can profit on its fixed costs.

Although investment banks are different from commercial banks in that they do not have depositors, they are equally subject to the same mismatch of short-term liabilities and long-term assets, typically because

[179] Section 204(d) of the Dodd-Frank Act gives the FDIC this authority once it chooses to liquidate the financial institution. See n. 177 above.

[180] See W. Bagehot, *Lombard Street: A Description of the Money Market* (London: Henry King and Co, 1873), pp. 196–8 (outlining the duties of a central bank during a banking panic).

[181] For an overview, see R. A. Posner, *A Failure of Capitalism: The Crisis of '08 and the Descent Into Depression* (Harvard University Press, 2009), pp. 128–30.

[182] For standard accounts of this mismatch, see generally C. W. Calomiris and J. R. Mason, "Fundamentals, Panics, and Bank Distress During the Depression," *American Economic Review*, 93 (2003), 1615; D. W. Diamond and P. H. Dybvig, "Bank Runs, Deposit Insurance, and Liquidity," *Journal of Political Economy*, 91 (1983), 401. For a concise summary of this literature as it applies to the 2008 crisis, see Gordon and Muller, "Confronting Financial Crisis," 158–66.

they finance their operations with short-term, often overnight borrowings in the "repo" market.[183] Thus, when the market suspects that a financial institution is subject to a risk of insolvency, short-term creditors may stage their own bank "run" by refusing to renew short-term credit lines or vastly increasing the interest rate. This functional equivalent to a "run" by depositors appears to have happened not only at Bear Stearns and Lehman, but across the banking system in 2008.[184] Yale Economics Professor Gary Gorton has argued that the 2008 panic was different from most panics in the nineteenth and early twentieth centuries in that it was a "wholesale" panic, not a "retail" panic, because the market suddenly learned that the banking system as a whole had become insolvent.[185]

This point about the "wholesale" character of the crisis explains why reforms such as private, industry-funded bailout funds are unlikely to prove adequate by themselves. Insurance can work to avert a crisis when a small percentage of the industry may fail, but not when a plurality may all fail contemporaneously because of risk correlation. A private insurance fund might be sufficient to bail out a Lehman (at most), but not the aggregate of Lehman, Citigroup and Goldman Sachs. To the extent that a systemic risk crisis is provoked by risk correlation, multiple contemporaneous failures that could dwarf such a fund become more likely. In 2009, much of the financial industry was threatened and the banking system effectively froze.[186]

The Dodd-Frank Act's decision to withdraw traditional emergency lending authority from the FRB and the FDIC for solvent banks facing only liquidity crises and its failure to adopt any FDIC-like, prefunded private insurance bailout fund, in time may prove to have been right or

[183] The term "repo" refers to "security repurchase agreements," which usually involve highly liquid, investment grade securities that the borrower sells to the creditor at a slight discount but agrees to repurchase at the higher market price on a very short-term basis. If the borrower fails to repurchase, it suffers the loss of this discount. For discussion of the repo market and its destabilizing impact on the contemporary banking system, see generally G. Gorton and A. Metrick, "Regulating the Shadow Banking System," Brookings Papers on Economic Activity (Fall 2010) 261 (online://ssrn.com/abstract=1676947).

[184] See G. Gorton, "Slapped in the Face by the Invisible Hand: Banking and the Panic of 2007," unpublished working paper (May 9, 2009, Online: http://ssrn.com/abstract=1401882), at 4–5.

[185] See ibid. at 37–8.

[186] See V. Ivashina and D. Scharfstein, "Bank Lending During the Financial Crisis of 2008," unpublished working paper (July 2009, online: http://ssrn.com/abstract=1297337) at 7–8 (finding that new loans to large borrowers fell by 47% in the fourth quarter of 2008 in comparison to the prior quarter, as banks cut back lending).

wrong, but they were certainly not the product of the "policy entrepreneurs" and activist investors that Professors Romano and Bainbridge accuse of "highjacking" reform legislation. Moreover, because these decisions were essentially negative ones that took authority away from (or did not extend authority to) financial regulators, they underscore the importance of the two affirmative steps that the Dodd-Frank Act did take: (1) It sought to reduce systemic risk at large financial institutions by adopting the Volcker Rule; (2) It authorized the FRB to adopt higher capital, liquidity and related prudential standards.

Thus, at the end of the day, the Dodd-Frank Act largely left everything up to the financial regulators, delegating them discretion but mandating relatively little. Such a strategy depends on whether effective implementation is possible in the current political environment, and there are substantial reasons to doubt that it is.

The OTC derivatives market

The 2008 financial crisis crested when in rapid succession Lehman failed and AIG was bailed out. Lehman is the paradigm of the bank that arguably was "too big to fail," but AIG's story is more complex. It poses the problem of an opaque technology whose full impact was not clear. Potentially, AIG's failure could have sunk far more counterparties than Lehman ever conceivably threatened.

In response to the AIG episode, the Dodd-Frank Act sought to bring transparency to the OTC market by mandating the use of clearinghouses, exchange trading of OTC derivatives, and trade reporting. This effort was entirely rational and may yet be successful, but it is very much in doubt. Title VII of the Dodd-Frank Act establishes for the first time an integrated legal regime for the regulation of the derivatives market, assigning security-based swaps to the SEC and other swaps to the Commodities Futures Trading Commission ("CFTC").[187] Although this

[187] For overviews of regulation in these markets, see generally J. C. Kress, "Credit Default Swaps, Clearinghouses, and Systemic Risk: Why Centralized Counterparties Must Have Access to Central Bank Liquidity," *Harvard Journal on Legislation*, 48 (2011), 49; J. Urban, "Developments in Banking and Financial Law: 2009–2010: The Shadow Financial System, Regulation of Over-the-Counter Derivatives: The Ultimate Lesson of Regulatory Reform," *Review of Banking and Financial Law*, 29 (2010), 49; Further Definition of "Swap Dealer," "Security-Based Swap Dealer," "Major Swap Participant," "Major Security-Based Swap Participant" and "Eligible Contract Participant," Exchange Act Release No. 63,452, 75 Fed. Reg. 80174, 80174 (December 21, 2010) (proposing rules to be codified at 17 C.F.R. 240).

division perpetuates the US long-standing preference for a multi-peaked regulatory structure, the two agencies seem to be operating in unison – at least for the time being. Both agencies are seeking to increase the standardization of swap agreements in order to facilitate their trading through a central clearinghouse.[188] The key goal is to eliminate counterparty risk for dealers and investors by replacing the bilateral trading of OTC derivatives with trading through a centralized clearinghouse.[189]

Yet, inevitably, such a restructuring does not eliminate risk, but only shifts it. The new central clearinghouses will bear the counterparty risk, and the failure of any major clearinghouse could be an event that would trigger a major systemic risk crisis. Once again, systemic risk is being concentrated with the creation of another "TBTF" institution.

Because private mechanisms for dealing with counterparty risk clearly failed in 2008 (and indeed, many financial institutions did not require major dealers, including AIG, to post collateral to secure their trades until the advent of the crisis), the case for use of clearinghouses is strong, but not without problems.[190] Critics of the idea believe that clearinghouses are inherently exposed to failure. They argue that clearinghouses will be bureaucratic institutions less able or willing to assess risk positions in credit default swaps because they will not be as motivated by profit opportunities as individual dealers.[191] Others make a related argument: a meaningful reduction of counterparty risk in swap trading through multilateral netting of investment positions in a clearinghouse requires that the vast majority of the volume in swaps traded must clear through that clearinghouse.[192] In effect, to work, the clearinghouse must gain a near monopoly.

But here politics intervened. The Dodd-Frank Act contains an important exemption – known as the "end user exemption" – which exempts from its mandatory clearing requirement for swaps any counterparty who (1) is not a "financial entity," (2) uses the swap to hedge or mitigate commercial risk, and (3) notifies the appropriate regulatory agency (SEC or CFTC) as to how it generally meets its financial obligations associated with entering into such non-cleared swaps.[193] Politically, this was

[188] See Kress, "Credit Default Swaps, Clearinghouses, and Systemic Risk," 69–71.
[189] See ibid. at 65–9. [190] See ibid. at 72–6.
[191] See C. Pirrong, "The Clearinghouse Cure," *Regulation Magazine* (Winter 2008–9) 44, 47–8.
[192] See D. Duffie and H. Zhu, "Does a Central Clearing Counterparty Reduce Counterparty Risk?," *The Review of Asset Pricing Studies*, 1 (2011) 74, 76–7.
[193] See 7 U.S.C. § 2(h)(3) (2010).

necessary to exempt major swap users who might otherwise have been able to block the legislation: for example, major airlines seeking to hedge the future cost of aviation fuel. Such "end users" did not wish to be subjected to the minimum capital and margin requirements that the Dodd-Frank Act imposed on swap dealers.[194] The consequence is that much of the volume in swaps will not be cleared and will escape margin requirements.

The SEC and the CFTC have proposed a joint rule to distinguish the commercial "end user" from more speculative financial investors in swaps.[195] Under it, much of swap trading will escape the collateral and capital rules that are intended to mitigate systemic risk.[196] The two agencies cannot be faulted for obeying Congress, but politics has produced a strange hybrid that could either reduce or exacerbate systemic risk. This vulnerability is compounded by a second difficulty: non-standardized swap contracts cannot be easily cleared.[197] Worse yet, forcing complex derivatives into clearinghouses increases the operational risk for the clearinghouse, because it will be required to clear products that it cannot easily price (and thereby set appropriate margins).[198] To the extent that clearinghouse members have a better, more accurate understanding of these risks, they will possess asymmetric information and may be able to trade to their advantage and the clearinghouse's disadvantage.[199] Although swap dealers would have to share the costs of a clearinghouse failure, each has an incentive to trade against the clearinghouse in a way that in the aggregate increases the risk of systemic failure.[200]

V: The implementation of the Dodd-Frank Act

The foregoing section has argued that the Dodd-Frank Act is a skeletal structure that has few affirmative commands, but rather, is heavily dependent on administrative implementation. As noted earlier, the

194 See 15 U.S.C. § 8323(a) (2010).

195 See End-User Exception to Mandatory Clearing of Security-Based Swaps, Exchange Act Release No. 63,556, 75 Fed. Reg. 79992, 79992 (December 21, 2010).

196 See ibid.

197 See Pirrong, "The Clearinghouse Cure," 49 (noting that "the more complex the product . . . the greater the cost of sharing a risk through a [clearinghouse] relative to the cost of . . . the over-the-counter market").

198 See International Monetary Fund, Global Financial Stability Report: Meeting New Challenges to Stability and Building a Safer System, 91 (2010) (online: www.imf.org/external/pubs/ft/gfsr/2010/01/pdf/text.pdf).

199 See Pirrong, "The Clearinghouse Cure," 47–8.

200 See ibid.

financial industry's best opportunity to nullify costly regulation is often at the level of administrative implementation. Because (1) the administrative process is less visible and politically accountable, (2) some agencies (most notably the FRB) may be too closely aligned with the financial entities they are to regulate, or (3) the financial industry can both win concessions through negotiations and then challenge in court those regulations not otherwise watered down, the industry may win much at the implementation level that it could not achieve at the legislative level. In addition, the Regulatory Sine Curve concept discussed earlier suggests that regulatory ardor wanes once the sense of emergency is lost.

Against that backdrop, this chapter will next survey the progress of the Dodd-Frank Act's implementation in three critical areas: (1) the attempt to curb excessive executive compensation; (2) the effort to end the "TBTF problem" by restricting risky activities that may cause bank failure; and (3) the effort to move OTC trading out of the shadows and into the sunlight of greater transparency. It is still premature to evaluate implementation with respect to the last two objectives, but a fuller assessment is possible of the effort to curb executive compensation.

Curbing executive compensation: the road not taken

A major goal of the Dodd-Frank Act was to reduce the danger of moral hazard by better relating executive compensation to long-term performance. The Dodd-Frank Act approached this goal by two distinct means, both of which have now been largely frustrated. Each will be examined separately.

Proxy access and corporate governance

As already noted, the Dodd-Frank Act instructed the SEC to use the standard inventory of corporate governance reform – proxy access, "say on pay" and a restriction on broker voting – to make corporate managers more accountable to shareholders.[201] As discussed above, this may have been an ill-advised tactic (at least in the context of large financial institutions where excessive leverage needs to be discouraged). But vastly overshadowing the significance of the SEC's proxy access rule are the

[201] See Part IV above.

implications of the D.C. Circuit's decision in the *Business Roundtable* suit to invalidate that rule. The decision in *Business Roundtable* v. *SEC*[202] casts a substantial cloud over the SEC's ability to adopt other rules, even if not related to corporate governance, in implementing the Dodd-Frank Act.

In adopting Rule 14a-11 (the proxy access rule), the Commission relied on Section 971 of Dodd-Frank, which authorized, but did not mandate, the Commission to adopt such a rule giving shareholders an alternative means by which to nominate and elect directors.[203] Because the Commission had discretion, it was subject to Section 3(f) of the Securities Exchange Act of 1934, which requires the Commission, when it determines if a rule is in the public interest, to "also consider, in addition to the protection of investors, whether the action will promote efficiency, competition, and capital formation."[204] On its face, this language has a relatively "soft" sound, mandating only consideration of these impacts, not that the Commission must determine that the interests of investor protection outweigh those of efficiency, competition and capital formation. Nonetheless, the D.C. Circuit now has several times invalidated SEC rules under this provision, finding that the Commission has a "statutory obligation to determine as best it can the economic implications of the rule."[205]

In fact, the SEC did consider several economic studies on the likely impact of encouraging the election of dissident candidates and expressly noted the limitations of these studies. In their lawsuit, the Business Roundtable and the Chamber of Commerce asserted both that (1) "the Commission failed to appreciate the intensity with which issuers would oppose nominees and arbitrarily dismissed the probability that directors

[202] 647 F.3d 1144 (D.C. Cir. 2011).

[203] The Commission proposed the proxy access rule in December, 2009. See Facilitating Shareholder Director Nominations, Securities Act Release No. 9086, Investment Company Act Release No. 29,069, 74 Fed. Reg. 67,144 (proposed December 14, 2009). The Commission adopted it in September, 2011. See Facilitating Shareholder Director Nominations, Securities Act Release No. 9259, Investment Company Act Release No. 29,788, 76 Fed. Reg. 58100, 58100 (September 20, 2011) (to be codified at 17 C.F.R. pts. 200, 232, 240 and 249).

[204] See Securities Exchange Act of 1934 § 3(f), 15 U.S.C. § 78c(f). Similar language also appears in the Investment Company Act. See, e.g., 15 U.S.C. § 80a-2(c).

[205] See *Chamber of Commerce* v. *SEC*, 412 F.3d 133, 143 (D.C. Cir. 2005). See also, *Am. Equity Inv. Life Ins. Co.* v. *SEC*, 613 F.3d 166, 167–68, 178 (D.C. Cir. 2010).

would conclude their fiduciary duties required them to support their own nominees,"[206] and (2) the Commission arbitrarily failed "to estimate the costs of solicitation and campaigning that companies would incur to oppose candidates nominated by shareholders."[207] Thus, a rule basically intended to tilt the balance of advantage in corporate board elections in favor of dissident shareholders was invalidated because the Commission did not (or could not) estimate the costs of the hostile corporate reaction to such efforts. By analogy, this is equivalent to invalidating an Environmental Protection Agency ("EPA") rule mandating that toxic wastes not be dumped into rivers and waterways because the EPA had not adequately estimated the costs to companies of alternative means of disposal.

Still, the relevant issue for this chapter is the decision's impact on future SEC attempts to adopt rules under the Dodd-Frank Act. The critics of SEC attempts to "federalize" corporate law by mandating corporate governance practices will celebrate the *Business Roundtable* decision because it seems to require the Commission to consider the empirical studies that they feel were disregarded in the enactment of SOX. Presumably, the D.C. Circuit would not attempt to hold Congress to this same standard, but to the extent that Congress enacts legislation giving the SEC any discretion as to the means to be used, the SEC's exercise of that discretion could be closely reviewed by the D.C. Circuit under the Section 3(f) standard.

This problem is not limited to SEC rules addressing corporate governance. Eventually, when the SEC adopts rules implementing the "Volcker Rule" (Section 619 of the Dodd-Frank Act) or mandating the use of clearinghouses or exchanges for the trading of security-based swaps, some interest group or individual financial institutions will feel aggrieved and sue. The outcome of such litigation cannot be predicted today, but it is sufficiently threatening that an overworked and underfunded SEC may compromise its rules, watering them down, to avoid the risk of another humiliating decision from the D.C. Circuit. Although Congress could legislate its own standards without delegating the matter to administrative agencies, that would imply abandoning the contemporary administrative state and reliance on administrative expertise. Not since the New Deal has the prospect of judicial challenge to legislative supremacy loomed as large on the horizon. To be sure, Congress could

[206] 647 F.3d at 1149. [207] Ibid. at 1150.

curb the D.C. Circuit's activism, but in the current polarized political environment such an effort seems unlikely.

Section 956

Congress did not rely exclusively (or even primarily) on corporate governance reforms to curb excessive executive compensation. Section 956 of the Dodd-Frank Act broadly authorized financial regulators to limit excessive compensation, but financial regulators have been equivocal in using the powers it conferred on them.[208] Somewhat vaguely, Section 956 instructed a "covered financial institution" to disclose to its respective regulator "the structures of all incentive-based compensation" paid to officers, directors and employees in order to enable the regulator to prohibit excessive incentive-based compensation "that could lead to material financial loss to the covered financial institution."[209]

The issue was how broadly to construe this disclosure obligation. Although Section 956 made clear that it was not requiring the disclosure of the individual executive's compensation,[210] regulators could have insisted on quantitative data about the aggregate incentive compensation paid by the firm and its distribution among employees and executives. What could such disclosure reveal that might be of material interest to investors? The following chart, taken from a study conducted by then New York Attorney General, Andrew Cuomo, of the incentive compensation received in 2008 by employees of the original Troubled Asset Relief Program (TARP) recipient financial institutions, shows the disclosures that could have been mandated under Section 956 (but were not):[211]

[208] Section 956 of the Dodd-Frank Act has been codified at 12 U.S.C. § 564.

[209] Dodd-Frank does not require the disclosure of the actual compensation of any particular individual, but only the structure of incentive compensation. The term "covered financial institution" is broadly defined to include depositary institutions, broker-dealers and other financial institutions having more than $1 billion in assets. See § 956(e)(2).

[210] See § 956(a)(2) of the Dodd-Frank Act ("Nothing in this section shall be construed as requiring the reporting of the actual compensation of particular individuals").

[211] See A. M. Cuomo, "No Rhyme or Reason: The 'Heads I Win, Tails You Lose' Bank Bonus Culture," (2009), 5 (online: www.oag.state.ny.us/media_center/2009/july/pdfs/Bonus%20Report%20Final%207.30.09.pdf.)

Selected TARP recipients 2008 bonus compensation

Institution	Earnings/ (Losses)	Bonus pool	No. of Employees Receiving Bonus ≥ $3 million	No. of Employees Receiving Bonus ≥ $1 million
Bank of America	$4 billion	$3.3 billion	28	172
Citigroup, Inc.	$(27.7 billion)	$5.33 billion	124	738
Goldman Sachs Group	$2.322 billion	$4.823 billion	212	953
J.P. Morgan Chase & Co.	$5.6 billion	$8.693 billion	>200	1,626
Merrill Lynch	$(27.6 billion)	$3.6 billion	149	696
Morgan Stanley	$1.707 billion	$4.475 billion	101	428

As this chart makes clear, even when financial institutions lost billions, they still paid out bonuses totaling in the billions to hundreds of employees (see Citigroup and Merrill Lynch in the above chart). When the firm did profit, the bonus pool was often a multiple of earnings (see Goldman Sachs, J.P. Morgan and Morgan Stanley's in the above chart). Moreover, practices varied, thus making firm-specific disclosure more important. Reading the Cuomo data more closely, one finds the following number of employees receiving over $10 million in bonus compensation in 2008 at these firms: Merrill Lynch (14); Morgan Stanley (10); J.P. Morgan Chase & Co. (10); Goldman Sachs (6); Bank of America (4); Citigroup (3).[212] In sum, the Cuomo data underscores three conclusions: (1) the bonus culture persisted even in bad times; (2) bonus payments to executives often exceeded distributions to shareholders; and (3) some individuals received extraordinary incentive compensation that logically could cause a moral hazard problem.

Revealing as this information may be, disclosure pursuant to Section 956 will not yield anything remotely equivalent. This is because the major financial regulators have read Section 956 narrowly. The first

[212] See ibid. at 6–11.

interpretive problem posed by Section 956's broad language involved identifying those persons whose behavior could inflict "material financial loss" on their institutions. Only incentive compensation to such persons was subject to regulation.[213] Obviously, the bank's janitor cannot ordinarily inflict a "material financial loss," but the history of broker-dealer firms suggests that traders often can (as happened in recent memory at both Barings and Société Générale).[214]

The principal financial regulators responded in unison to this challenge in April, 2011 with a joint set of rules that each adopted.[215] In the case of "covered financial institutions" (meaning basically any financial institution with total consolidated assets of $1 billion or more), these rules require an annual report that "describes the structure of the covered financial institution's incentive-based compensation arrangements . . . that is sufficient to allow an assessment of whether the structure or features of those arrangements provide or are likely to provide covered persons with excessive compensation, fees, or benefits to covered persons or could lead to material financial loss to the covered financial institution."[216] This is rather general and abstract language, and no specific data was required. For example, regulators might have followed Andrew Cuomo's lead and required disclosure of the number of employees at a firm who received bonuses of over $1 million in the prior year (even if none were identified by name).[217] Instead, the new rules do not require disclosure of quantitative data, but only a generalized narrative description.[218] This seems likely to produce long-winded boilerplate from securities lawyers adept at covering the waterfront in opaque prose.

In the case of financial institutions with over $50 billion in total consolidated assets (i.e. the TBTF category), more was required by these regulations. Such institutions must provide a description of "incentive-based compensation policies and procedures" for two

[213] See Dodd-Frank Act § 956(a)(1).

[214] See, e.g., N. Thompson, "The World's Biggest Rogue Traders in Recent History," *CNN* (September 15, 2011, online: http://edition.cnn.com/2011/BUSINESS/09/15/unauthorized.trades/index.html).

[215] See Proposed Rules on Incentive-Based Compensation Arrangements, Exchange Act Release No. 64,140, 76 Fed. Reg. 21170, 21170 (April 14, 2011). Similar releases were contemporaneously proposed by the Treasury, the FRB, the FDIC and other agencies. See ibid.

[216] See Proposed § 248.204(a) of Regulation S-P (to be codified at 17 C.F.R. 248.204(a)).

[217] See Cuomo, "No Rhyme or Reason," 5. [218] See n. 209 above.

categories of persons: (1) executive officers, and (2) such "[o]ther covered persons who the board of directors, or a committee thereof, of the covered financial institution has identified and determined . . . individually have the ability to expose the covered financial institution to possible losses that are substantial in relation to the covered financial institution's size, capital, or overall risk tolerance."[219] Again, this stops well short of revealing the full depth of the bonus culture at a firm, because many (potentially hundreds of employees) could receive incentive compensation in the million dollar range and yet be exempted from disclosure because the board did not believe they could cause a "substantial loss" to the firm.

In short, only in the case of TBTF institutions do the rules require any specific disclosure or serious assessment of who could actually cause a substantial loss to the financial institution, but even in these cases, the regulations still delegate to each covered financial institution the determination of who (beyond its executive officers) could expose it to such a "substantial loss." This delegation is significant because only the covered persons so identified (and executive officers) become subject to additional substantive requirements. In the case of the executive officers of these TBTF institutions, the proposed rules require deferral of at least 50 percent of the annual incentive-based compensation awarded for a period of not less than three years.[220] That may or may not be adequate, but the real surprise in these regulations is that, in the case of those persons specifically identified by the TBTF institution's board as being capable of exposing the institution to "substantial loss," no deferral was required. Instead, all that was mandated was that the board or committee must approve the incentive-based compensation arrangements for such persons and further determine "that the arrangement . . . effectively balances the financial rewards to the covered person and the range and time horizon of risks associated with the covered person's activities, employing appropriate methods for ensuring risk sensitivity such as deferral of payments."[221] In short, the only requirement for even those persons identified by the firm as being capable of causing it "substantial losses" is that the board or committee think seriously about deferral or some other means of ensuring "risk sensitivity."

[219] Ibid. at § 248.204(c)(3).

[220] See § 248.205(b)(3) ("Prohibitions") (requiring a 50% deferral for "executive officers" (as defined) of "covered financial institutions" with assets in excess of $50 billion).

[221] See proposed § 248.205(b)(3)(ii)(c).

The proposed rules thus fall breathtakingly short of adequacy on two major grounds: (1) they wholly delegate to the firm the decision of who could cause it "substantial loss," and (2) even with respect to the persons so identified, the rules require only process and no minimum deferral.

Why have financial regulators, in common, pulled their punches by (1) requiring little specific data, (2) allowing the firms alone to decide who (besides executive officers) can cause them significant loss, and (3) not even requiring some deferral of bonuses by the persons so identified? The most plausible answer is that regulators knew that a more effective rule might provoke significant employee defections, as "star" traders (and others) moved from investment banks to less-regulated trading firms. Realistically, the non-executive officer most likely to be able to cause a substantial loss to a "covered financial institution" is a trader who is authorized to trade on a large position basis. Such traders in recent memory have caused staggering losses to some financial institutions (remember Nicholas Leeson at Barings and Jerome Kerviel at Société Générale).[222]

Although it is likely that most covered firms will report some employees who can cause it substantial losses, the number so reported will likely be far below the number that would be disclosed if more objective criteria were used. Underreporting the number of such persons has several attractions: (1) it makes the firm appear safer in general; (2) it spares the board (or committee) the obligation to engage in additional specific assessments of whether adequate risk sensitivity has been structured into each such person's incentive compensation; and (3) it ensures that the persons who otherwise would be identified as being capable of causing "substantial loss" to the firm will not be restricted in their compensation by the appropriate regulatory agency. That is, despite the board or committee's findings, the relevant regulator might still determine that there was inadequate risk sensitivity and thus that the compensation was excessive. However, if the "star" personnel are never so identified, this problem simply does not arise.

To summarize, the problem for the TBTF financial institution was that if highly compensated "stars" were subjected to the same deferral of incentive compensation as are executive officers, they might flee "covered financial institutions" to relocate at hedge funds, smaller banks,

[222] See Thompson, "The World's Biggest Rogue Traders." Nicholas Leeson's unauthorized trades caused the failure of Barings in 1995, and Jerome Kerviel racked up losses in excess of £5 billion at Société Générale in 2008. Ibid.

or go abroad to escape such controls. Fearing such migration, financial institutions probably lobbied for a weaker rule (and appear to have succeeded). Still, the irony is that few vice presidents at a financial institution can cause the same injury to it as can a star trader (such as celebrated rogue traders Jerome Kervais or Nicholas Leeson).[223] The choice for financial regulators was between an effective rule and some competitive injury to the TBTF banks. The latter consideration appears to have dominated, and that pattern may recur regularly as the implementation of the Dodd-Frank Act continues.

Executive compensation was the leading topic on which Congress (pushed by taxpayers) showed real anger. Still, once the negotiations moved from Congress to the regulatory agencies, that anger dissipated, or at least yielded to concerns about employee defections and competitive injury. That could happen even more easily in other areas where the public anger was less intense.

The TBTF problem

In the Dodd-Frank Act, Congress sought to address the TBTF bank in several ways: (1) providing for "resolution authority" to quickly liquidate a failed bank without the interminable process of a bankruptcy proceeding;[224] (2) reducing the risk level of banks, including by means of the Volcker Rule;[225] and (3) authorizing stricter prudential standards, including the use of a contingent capital standard.[226] As we have seen earlier with respect to SOX's prohibition of executive loans and, most recently, the Dodd-Frank Act's equivocal executive compensation rules, even clear Congressional statements can be enervated through administrative interpretation and underenforcement.[227] Yet, in the case of the Dodd-Frank Act's approach to TBTF institutions, the legislation never articulated clear standards to begin with, and equivocal implementation will likely weaken these standards further.

223 To illustrate this irony, the general counsel of a TBTF institution is typically an executive officer and thus subject to a 50% deferral. But the star trader who weekly bets billions of dollars in volatile markets is not subject to any similar deferral. This disparity cannot be easily justified.

224 See Dodd-Frank Act, Title II, §§ 201–217 (codified at 12 U.S.C. §§ 5381–5394) (conferring authority to commence "orderly liquidation").

225 See § 619 of the Dodd-Frank Act.

226 See §§ 112(a)(2), 115(b) and 165(b) of the Dodd-Frank Act (to be codified at 12 U.S.C. §§ 5322, 5325 and 5365, respectively).

227 See Parts III and IV above.

Resolution authority

The fact that financial regulators, acting in virtual unison, can liquidate a TBTF institution before it becomes legally insolvent does not mean that they will actually do so. Such action would imply a black eye for almost any administration, suggesting that it had been a poor financial watchdog. Regulators might also fear that such action would trigger a financial panic. The temptation for regulators is thus "to kick the can down the road," hoping for the best and seeing little advantage in early intervention. Moreover, as the financial industry has grown more concentrated in the wake of the 2008 failures and consequent mergers, the remaining TBTF banks are even larger. Thus, any failure of one of them would be more serious. For all of these reasons, the TBTF banks have increased incentives to maintain large lobbying cadres in Washington to protect their interests from adverse actions (which could never occur quickly in any event, because it would require high coordination and unanimity among regulators).

Still, suppose a TBTF bank does fail? At this point, the FDIC may be able to provide financing to a bridge company that acquires most of its assets. It could either decide to bail out the bondholders or to let them share in the pain in order to end the TBTF subsidy. The highly discretionary character of this choice suggests it, too, will invite heavy lobbying. In turn, the more that bondholders are in fact paid off from an FDIC fund (and the FDIC can borrow from the FRB for this purpose), the more that the TBTF subsidy survives. Ultimately, one cannot predict what will happen in any specific case, but the greater the fear of a financial panic, the more financial regulators are likely to want to cause bondholders to be paid in full to avert panic. Little may change, and the TBTF subsidy may persist.

The Volcker Rule

The Volcker Rule[228] is a coherent response to the TBTF problem: that is, if banks are too big to fail, they must be regulated so that their risk-taking is constrained in order that they do not fail. But the Volcker Rule faces political problems. First, there is almost no evidence that proprietary trading was responsible for the failure (or near failure) of any financial institution in the 2008 crisis. In contrast, firms like Lehman failed because of their principal investments: Lehman made disastrous

[228] See Dodd-Frank Act, § 619.

acquisitions of major real estate lenders and developers (including SunCal and Archstone), but those acquisitions, which made it undiversified and overleveraged, fell well outside the definition of proprietary trading in the Dodd-Frank Act.[229] In this respect, the Volcker Rule is seriously underinclusive, because it exempts principal investments from its ban, despite the Lehman experience.

Second, the Volcker Rule contains numerous loopholes and exceptions.[230] Chief among these are exceptions for hedging and market making by the covered financial institution.[231] The financial regulators have recently released their proposed draft of the Volcker Rule.[232] On a preliminary review, it seems potentially tougher and more restrictive than many had expected. Still, the start of the process is not the end of the process, and opposition to it is mounting.[233] Always opportunistic, the financial services industry has seized on the crisis in European sovereign debt to warn that the Volcker Rule's implementation will curtail the demand for European sovereign debt and aggravate that crisis.[234] The irony here is that precisely at the moment that the collapse of MF Global, based on its ill-fated bet on European sovereign debt, has shown that proprietary trading in sovereign debt is indeed risky, political

229 See, e.g., T. Pristin, "Risky Real Estate Deals Helped Doom Lehman," *New York Times*, September 17, 2008, at C6 (discussing Lehman's multi-billion dollar acquisition of Archstone-Smith).

230 See § 619(d)(1). These include: (1) underwriting and market-making-related activities; (2) risk-mitigating hedging activities; (3) investments driven by customer demand; (4) proprietary trading done outside the United States, and (5) such other activities as regulators determine by rule would promote safety and soundness of the banking system.

231 See § 619(d)(1)(B), (C).

232 On October 12, 2011, the SEC voted to propose a version of the Volcker Rule that was drafted in common with other financial regulators. (See online: www.sec.gov/news/press/2011/2011–204.htm.) A proposed release has not yet been issued, but a final rule must be adopted in 2012.

233 See J. B. Stewart, "Volcker Rule, Once Simple, Now Boggles," *New York Times*, October 22, 2011, at B-1; see also Editorial, "So Much for the Volcker Rule," *Wall Street Journal*, October 24, 2011, at A-14 (noting that the 298-page proposed rule contains some "1,347 queries" that must be considered before a final rule is adopted).

234 See B. Masters and D. Oakley, "Bankers in Eurozone Warning," *Financial Times*, November 22, 2011, at 15. Japan has expressed similar fears, asking that the Volcker Rule be relaxed. See S. Patterson and J. Trindle, "Japan Joins the Chorus of Volcker Rule Critics," *Wall Street Journal*, January 13, 2012, at C-3. See also n. 256 below (describing the prediction of two attorneys at Davis Polk that the proposed regulation implementing the Volcker Rule will be withdrawn).

pressure is mounting in Europe and elsewhere to insist that TBTF banks in the United States continue to support this market.[235] Once again, the experience with SOX predicts the fate of the Dodd-Frank Act, as the proposed rules on proprietary trading appear likely to be watered down.

Contingent capital

One of the most original ideas proposed to avert TBTF debacles is a requirement that some portion of the financial institution's debt securities in the original bond contract, be required to convert into an equity security if the financial institution begins to approach insolvency.[236] Although the original idea was to convert the debt to equity on the doorsteps of insolvency, much more can be done with this flexible idea. Uniquely, it provides an *ex ante* tool. As the stock price of the institution declines, debt could convert at several stages on an incremental basis into an equity security, thereby diluting the equity and punishing the stockholders for their pursuit of higher leverage and risk-taking. Used this way, the tool has a prospective deterrent power. This author has proposed conversion of the debt into a voting preferred stock, whose holders would have incentives naturally aligned with other debt holders and adverse to the common stockholders.[237] The goal is again to create a counterbalancing constituency that would resist shareholder pressure.

Other innovative designs are possible, but the likelihood is high that the Federal Reserve will ignore all these possibilities. Instead, it will likely propose that contingent capital be used only as a form of prepackaged bankruptcy. If insolvency has become inevitable, even the

[235] See A. R. Sorkin, "Volker Rule Stirs Up Opposition Overseas," *New York Times*, January 31, 2012, Section B, 1 (noting European governmental pressure to relax the Volcker Rule with regard to trading in sovereign debt, notwithstanding the failure of MF Global, which became insolvent based on such trading). For an overview of the causes of the demise of MF Global, a major dealer in the derivatives market, where some $1.2 billion in customer money disappeared in late 2011, see B. Protess and A. Ahmed, "Lax Oversight Is Blamed in Demise of MF Global," *New York Times*, February 3, 2012, at B-6.

[236] While this technique for averting bankruptcy can be traced back for a considerable period, the author most responsible for its consideration in the context of a TBTF institution is Professor Mark J. Flannery. See M. J. Flannery, "No Pain, No Gain? Effecting Market Discipline via Reverse Convertible Debentures" in Hal S. Scott (ed.), *Capital Adequacy Beyond Basel: Banking, Securities, and Insurance* (Oxford University Press, 2005), pp. 171, 171–5. See also Coffee, "Systemic Risk After Dodd-Frank," 828–33 (reviewing possible designs for the use of contingent capital).

[237] See ibid., 805–7, 828–34.

financial industry recognizes that it would be quicker and simpler to convert much of the debt into equity than utilize the cumbersome procedures of resolution authority. The banking community would probably also prefer such a modest use of contingent capital because it reduces the uncertainty incident to a liquidation and avoids the mandatory ouster of responsible management that is required under "resolution authority."

Still, such a minimal use of contingent capital is myopic. It surrenders the possibility of *ex ante* measures that could precede and avert insolvency. But if anything can be safely predicted, it is that the Federal Reserve is too closely imbedded within the banking community to propose any intrusive remedy that would be invoked well before a banking crisis has begun.

The legislative counterattack

As of early 2012, legislation is pending that would severely curtail many of the corporate governance provisions of the Dodd-Frank Act.[238] Essentially, the legislation would create a new category of issuer called an "emerging growth company," which would be exempt from many of the provisions of the proxy rules, including the Dodd-Frank Act's provisions such as "say on pay" and related compensation disclosures, as well as Section 404(b) of SOX.[239] The term "emerging growth company" is broadly defined to include any issuer that has annual gross revenues of less than $1 billion and a public float of less than

[238] The most relevant bill (and there are several) is the "Reopening American Capital Markets to Emerging Growth Companies Act of 2011." See H. R. 3606, 112th Cong. (2011) (House Bill); S. 1933, 112th Cong. (2011) (Senate Bill). For a brief description of this legislation, see M. Rosenberg, IPO "On-Ramp," *Mondaq Business Briefing*, December 27, 2011.

[239] Senate Bill 1933 and House Bill 3606 would each amend Section 2(a) of the Securities Act of 1933 and Section 3(a) of the Securities Exchange Act of 1934 to define the term "emerging growth company." See, e.g., House Bill 3606 § 2(a), (b). So long as currently private companies remained "emerging growth companies," these issuers would be exempt from Section 14A of the Securities Exchange Act of 1934 ("Shareholder Approval of Executive Compensation"), which mandates a shareholder advisory vote on executive compensation not less frequently than once every three years. See, e.g., Senate Bill 1933 § 3(a)(1). Disclosure of the median of the annual total compensation of all employees, which was mandated by Section 953(b)(1) of the Dodd-Frank Act, would also be waived for "emerging growth companies" (as would compliance with Section 404(b) of SOX). See, e.g., House Bill 3606 § 3(a)(3).

$700 million.[240] The rationale for this broad exemption is that it would spur job creation by encouraging smaller companies to conduct initial public offerings.[241] This rationale is doubtful, because the decline in IPOs, while real, dates back at least to the burst of the Internet IPO bubble in 2001 and thus could hardly have been caused by either the Dodd-Frank Act or SOX's Section 404.[242] Many other factors better explain the decline in IPOs than any increase in regulatory costs after 2001.[243]

Still, these deregulatory proposals chiefly demonstrate the continuing persistence of the Regulatory Sine Curve, even after a major crisis. In 2011, financial industry representatives formed an industry study group, which called itself the "IPO Task Force," and it quickly prepared a report attributing the decline in IPOs to regulatory and market structure

240 S. 1933 and H.R. 3606 require both that the issuer have less than $1 billion in gross revenues for its last fiscal year and that the issuer not have common stock held by non-affiliates with a market value of $700 million or more. See, e.g., Senate Bill 1933 § 2(a)(19). This market value standard, known as the "public float," was adopted by the SEC to define a "Well-Known Seasoned Issuer," which is entitled to use automatic shelf registration. See SEC Rule 405, 17 C.F.R. 230.405. Thus, companies with a relatively large public ownership would still qualify as "emerging growth companies" and escape the Dodd-Frank Act's corporate governance provisions.

241 See Senate Bill 193 (asserting the Bill's purpose is "[t]o increase American job creation and economic growth").

242 No dispute exists that the number of IPOs declined significantly after 2000. This number appears to have peaked at 791 in 1996 and then fallen to an average of 157 from 2001 to 2008, with a low of 45 in the financial crisis year of 2008. See IPO Task Force, "Rebuilding the IPO On-Ramp," presented to the U.S. Treasury (October 20, 2011) (hereinafter, "IPO Task Force Report").

243 Industry groups cite costly regulation, but the impact of SOX's Section 404(b) was not felt until 2004 when Accounting Standard No. 2 was adopted by the PCAOB (see n. 77 and accompanying text above), and the Dodd-Frank Act's rules have still not become effective. Thus, the legal environment of the 1990s, when IPOs peaked, was similar to that in the post-2000 decade, when they declined. Better explanations involve: (1) the loss of investor confidence in IPOs after the Internet bubble burst in 2000 and severe conflicts of interest involving securities analysts were exposed by Eliot Spitzer and others; (2) the "de-retailization of the market," as individual investors have left the market and institutional investors are less dependent on sell-side analysts; (3) the loss of interest by institutional investors in smaller IPOs, which cannot provide them with sufficient market depth to assure liquidity; and (4) the high fixed costs of smaller IPOs, which make it more cost efficient for smaller companies to raise capital in the private placement market. For a discussion of some of these explanations, see Examining Investor Risks in Capital Raising: Hearing Before the S. Subcomm. on Sec., Ins., and Inv., 112th Cong, 20–23 (2011) (Statement of John Coates, Professor of Law and Economics, Harvard Law School (hereinafter "Coates Hearing")).

changes.[244] Entirely ignored by this report was the likely loss in investor confidence following the burst of the Internet stock bubble in 2000 or the Enron and WorldCom insolvencies in 2001–2. The IPO Task Force proposed to remedy the decline in IPOs by dismantling many of the regulatory changes that were adopted following the 2001 market crash.[245]

Time and again, this is the key move: to blame economic stagnation and job loss, not on a crash or a bubble, but on the regulation that follows it. The legislation proposed by the IPO Task Force has broad bipartisan support and is one of several deregulatory proposals that seem likely to pass Congress as part of a job creation program.[246]

[244] See IPO Task Force Report, "Rebuilding the IPO On-Ramp." For a more affirmative discussion of this report by its chairman, see generally Reopening American Capital Markets to Emerging Growth Companies Act of 2011: Hearing Before the H. Subcomm. on Capital Mkts. and Gov't Sponsored Enters., 112th Cong. (2011) (Statement of Kate Mitchell, Managing Director at Scale Venture Partners). Her testimony does not focus on any of the provisions in the Dodd-Frank Act as a significant barrier to an IPO, but does identify SOX's Section 404(b) as the most costly barrier to becoming a public company. Ibid. at 8–9. Still, if so, this diagnosis hardly leads to a prescription for rolling back the Dodd-Frank Act.

[245] In particular, the IPO Task Force Report would override the existing rules of FINRA and permit securities analysts associated with an underwriter who is participating in the offering to issue reports on the issuer at the time of the offering. See IPO Task Force Report, "Rebuilding the IPO On-Ramp," 27–8. Today, FINRA Rule 2711 precludes a managing underwriter from distributing a research report about an issuer client until 40 days after the registration statement becomes effective (and other underwriters in the offering are similarly precluded for 25 days). See ibid. at 27, n. 3. This was a rule adopted by an industry self-regulatory body, not Congress, and these rules were adopted in response to the 2000–2 controversy involving Internet securities analysts, most notably Henry Blodget and Jack Grubman, who became iconic examples of conflicted securities analysts as a result of enforcement actions undertaken by then New York Attorney General Eliot Spitzer. See Jill I. Gross, "Securities Analysts' Undisclosed Conflicts of Interest: Unfair Dealing or Securities Fraud?" *Columbia Business Law Review*, 3 (2002), 631, 635–46. Nonetheless, the IPO Task Force displays a collective amnesia about these conflicts, and Congress appears unable to resist the seductive argument that deregulation means job creation.

[246] A number of bills that would enable smaller companies to avoid either or both of the registration requirements of the Securities Act of 1933 or the reporting requirements of the Securities Exchange Act of 1934 are pending and seem likely to pass in 2012. For detailed reviews of them, see generally Coates Hearing, n. 243 above; "Spurring Job Growth Through Capital Formation While Protecting Investors": Hearing Before the S. Comm. on Banking, Hous. and Urban Affairs, 112th Cong. (2011) (Statement of John C. Coffee, Jr., Adolf A. Berle Professor of Law, Columbia University Law School). It is not the contention of this chapter that these bills undermine the federal securities laws, but only that they show a recurrent pattern of thinking that considers only the costs of regulation and not the cost of crashes and bubbles. Absent restored investor confidence or major technological breakthroughs, there is little prospect of an upsurge in the number of IPOs.

Although it will likely accomplish little in terms of reversing the decline in initial public offerings, this legislation will ease constraints imposed on the financial services industry. Above all, this episode shows again that, once a crisis has passed, Congress can easily be persuaded to repeal legislation that it passed in response to the crisis. This does not prove that the original legislation was flawed, but only that Congress can be manipulated and, absent some countervailing force, has a limited attention span and will sometimes accept makeweight arguments. To be sure, in a national crisis, countervailing forces sometimes arise, but they do not remain organized and vigilant indefinitely – hence, the Regulatory Sine Curve persists.

VI: Conclusion

The key and recurring debate over financial reform is between those who distrust both legislation and regulation (a position that the Tea Party Caucus exemplifies) and those who believe strong regulation is necessary to restrain systemic risk. In this debate, the standard move of those who distrust regulation is to attribute economic stagnation and job loss to costly regulation, ignoring that the costs of market bubbles and crashes dwarf those of regulation. Their ability to do this (and with considerable success) is evidence of a collective social amnesia that appears to overtake Congress and others, as soon as the crisis fades from the headlines. This recurrent amnesia is in turn the product of what this chapter has termed the Regulatory Sine Curve – a cycle that is driven by the differential in resources, organization and lobbying capacity that favors those interests determined to resist further regulation.[247]

Without doubt, some regulation is foolish and overbroad, but the point emphasized by this chapter is that such overbroad regulation is usually repealed or curtailed relatively quickly (and without the need for mandatory sunsets). The greater danger is that the forces of inertia will veto or block all change. The pervasive underregulation of "shadow banking," which has continued for decades, appears to have been a

[247] This disparity will only grow in the wake of *Citizens United* v. *FEC*, 558 U.S. _, 130 S. Ct. 876 (2010) (holding that the First Amendment protects independent expenditures by corporations and unions in support of a political candidate from governmental regulation limiting such contributions). For the finding that corporate political and lobbying expenditures are increasing in the wake of this decision, see Coates, "Corporate Politics, Governance and Value".

leading cause of the 2008 financial debacle and the current economic stagnation.[248] Failing meaningful implementation of the Dodd-Frank Act, financial executives may once again race like lemmings over the financial cliffs by taking on leverage that they cannot sustain. One cannot pretend to predict when this will occur, but driving this process will be the same perverse incentives: basically, short-term executive compensation and market pressure for higher leverage and greater risk-taking. These root causes will again be aided and abetted by equivocal regulation and bounded rationality.

In short, history repeats itself, particularly when it is ignored. In truth, the Dodd-Frank Act potentially faces even greater downsizing than SOX has experienced. This is because its effective implementation requires greater regulatory encroachment into the core business decisions of financial institutions over their capital adequacy, leverage and compensation. Thus, the Dodd-Frank Act seems destined to be resisted even more aggressively than SOX was. If, however, it is similarly neutralized by a combination of equivocal rule-making and legal challenges, the consequences may be far more ominous. Systemic risk poses a far greater threat to both the United States' and the world's economy than did the corporate governance failures and accounting irregularities to which SOX responded.

It is not the contention of this chapter that sustained reform is impossible or that, in response to a crisis, regulatory agencies are only capable of "rearranging the deck chairs on the Titanic." That would overstate. Indeed, political entrepreneurs who unite and sustain a political coalition of investors and enable them to resist better-funded special interest groups would be the heroes of this story – if only such actors were more visible.[249] In the absence of such leaders, the first and reflexive response of many regulatory agencies after a crash is simply to move the deck chairs around in a sufficiently noisy fashion to show that they are on the job. Some evidence suggests that is again happening.[250] Beyond this lack of imagination and political nerve, the

[248] See Gorton and Metrick, "Regulating the Shadow Banking System," 1–5.

[249] As earlier suggested (see n. 10 above), Eliot Spitzer and Andrew Cuomo have at times played the "public entrepreneur" role, but the SEC has been far more cautious and bureaucratic.

[250] An excellent example is the SEC's latest release containing proposed rules for credit rating agencies. See Proposed Rules for Nationally Recognized Statistical Rating Organizations, Exchange Act Release No. 64,514, 76 Fed. Reg. 33420, 33420 (June 8, 2011). The release contains voluminous rules governing the training and supervision of credit

greater problem is that financial regulators are often so closely intertwined with those that they regulate that they respond in an equivocal and even timid fashion.[251] The recent and joint rules on executive compensation adopted by the principal federal financial regulators exemplify this problem, because the limited reach of these rules seems motivated more by a desire to protect the industry from competition than to control moral hazard.[252]

What could be done to compensate for the predictable tendency toward rapid erosion of reform legislation? One might advocate the use of stronger prophylactic rules in the original reform legislation with less delegation to administrative agencies.[253] Indeed, had Congress known the degree to which the D.C. Circuit would broadly employ its own cost/benefit analysis to reject proposed agency rules of which that Court disapproved, it might have delegated less to the SEC and attempted to resolve issues legislatively on incomplete knowledge. Such a proposal for more prophylactic legislative rules would be the polar opposite of Professor Romano's mandatory sunset rule. Justifiable as such a shift might be, this chapter still stops short of recommending any across-the-board shift towards greater legislative specificity, because it would entail undesirable rigidity. Still, legislative restrictions on judicial cost/benefit oversight of administrative agencies may be needed. Another second-best substitute may be to employ market-based reforms that use objective market tests and thus depend less on administrative implementation.[254] Although disclosure is always a useful remedy, it needs to be refocused. Hopefully, the financial press might be persuaded

rating agency employees, but never recognizes that the underlying problem was not their lack of competence, but conflicts of interest and the pressure on them. See J. C. Coffee, Jr., "Ratings Reform: The Good, the Bad, and the Ugly," *Harvard Business Law Review*, 1 (2011) 231, 236–44.

251 This may be because of the "revolving door" phenomenon, Sorkin, "The SEC's Revolving Door," 1, risk aversion about the political or reputational consequences of the agency suffering a litigation defeat, or budgetary constraints that limit the agency's ability to engage in aggressive enforcement. No attempt is made here to disentangle the various causes. Finally, fear of judicial rejection of proposed rules may also cause the regulator to trim its sails and propose only equivocal rules.

252 See nn. 215–18 and accompanying text above.

253 The Securities Exchange Act of 1934 does contain several such prophylactic rules. For example, Section 16(b) of that Act broadly prohibits "short swing" trading without any need to prove scienter or the possession of material information. See 15 U.S.C. § 78p. The Public Utility Company Act of 1935's infamous "death sentence" for holding companies would be another example. See n. 24 above.

254 For such a proposal, see Coffee, "Systemic Risk After Dodd-Frank," 822–3, 828–46.

to focus more on weak or equivocal administrative implementation. Some courts may also embarrass the SEC into stronger enforcement action.[255] It is premature, however, to evaluate these options until the implementation of the Dodd-Frank Act is further along.

"Capture" is an overused and underdefined term. This chapter does not assert that financial regulators have been captured, but does conclude that they are far better at prosecuting outliers and crooks than in controlling reckless ambition by those at the top of the corporate hierarchy. To be sure, some desirable reforms will emerge from the Dodd-Frank Act that will reduce the risk (marginally at least) of another systemic risk crisis for the immediate future. Predictably, capital adequacy standards will be raised and leverage ratios marginally restricted at TBTF institutions. But the pursuit of higher leverage has not yet been checked. The acid test for meaningful reform is likely to lie in the outcomes in three areas: (1) the implementation of the Volcker Rule,[256] (2) the fate of the Dodd-Frank Act's preference for trading OTC derivatives through exchanges and clearinghouses,[257] and (3) the strength of the capital adequacy rules for TBTF banks.[258] In each case, the exceptions may overwhelm the rule.

Across most financial regulatory agencies, the deep-seated preference is to depend upon bureaucratic oversight and case-by-case monitoring in preference to more prophylactic rules. But, as prior market crashes have shown, the same cognitive limitations that blind market participants also cloud the vision of regulators. More objective, market-based

[255] See n. 119 and accompanying text above (discussing Judge Rakoff's refusal to accept proposed SEC settlements).

[256] Two experienced attorneys at Davis Polk (one a former SEC Commissioner) have recently predicted that financial regulators will be forced to withdraw their 298-page proposal to implement the Volcker Rule and in effect start over by re-proposing it. See A. L. Nazareth and G. D. Rosenberg, Comment: "12 Regulatory Reform Predictions for '12," *Financial Times*, December 23, 2011, online: www.ft.com/intl/cms/s/0/e6fc8ce4–2d4a-11e1-b985–00144feabdc0.html#axzz1ksetdcgB. If this happens, a significantly weaker rule will likely follow. See also text and notes at nn. 233–6 above.

[257] The major industry counterattack here has been to demand that the Dodd-Frank Act's rules for the trading of swaps not apply extraterritorially. See "Banks Air Fears Over Scope of U.S. Swaps Rules," *Hedgeworld Daily News*, February 8, 2012 (noting that US and foreign banks are pressing the CFTC and the SEC not to impose these rules on US banks offshore, arguing as usual that it will destroy their international competitiveness).

[258] The Federal Reserve has announced relatively tough capital adequacy rules, but not more stringent than those that would be required by Basel III. The *New York Times* described the proposal as "a small victory for banks." See E. Wyatt, "Fed Unveils Plan to Limit Chance of a Banking Crisis," *New York Times*, December 21, 2011, at B-1.

tests are possible and desirable,[259] but they have no constituency supporting them. As a result, the same regulators who missed the Long-Term Capital Management crisis in 1998, the IPO Bubble in 2000, the Enron and WorldCom failures in 2001–2, the market timing scandal in mutual funds in 2004, Bernie Madoff in 2008 and the Lehman and AIG collapses in 2008 seem likely in time to do it again. Sadly, the inevitability of bounded rationality, compounded by the Regulatory Sine Curve, implies that eventually we will face another systemic risk crisis.

It is still too soon to say that the 2008 crisis was wasted, but it has not been exploited. Rather, the equivocal response to date implies that the Dodd-Frank Act's reforms will over time be trivialized.

[259] For a discussion of possible market-based tests to supplement regulatory oversight, see Coffee, "Systemic Risk After Dodd-Frank," 828–46.

INDEX